Frommer's®

Costa Rica 2010

BY ELIOT GREENSPAN

WILEY
Wiley Publishing, Inc.

Published by:
WILEY PUBLISHING, INC.
111 River St.
Hoboken, NJ 07030-5774

Copyright © 2010 Wiley Publishing, Inc., Hoboken, New Jersey. All rights reserved. No part of this publication may be reproduced, stored in a retrieval system or transmitted in any form or by any means, electronic, mechanical, photocopying, recording, scanning or otherwise, except as permitted under Sections 107 or 108 of the 1976 United States Copyright Act, without either the prior written permission of the Publisher, or authorization through payment of the appropriate per-copy fee to the Copyright Clearance Center, 222 Rosewood Drive, Danvers, MA 01923, 978/750-8400, fax 978/646-8600. Requests to the Publisher for permission should be addressed to the Permissions Department, John Wiley & Sons, Inc., 111 River Street, Hoboken, NJ 07030, 201/748-6011, fax 201/748-6008, or online at http://www.wiley.com/go/permissions.

Wiley and the Wiley Publishing logo are trademarks or registered trademarks of John Wiley & Sons, Inc. and/or its affiliates. Frommer's is a trademark or registered trademark of Arthur Frommer. Used under license. All other trademarks are the property of their respective owners. Wiley Publishing, Inc. is not associated with any product or vendor mentioned in this book.

ISBN 978-0-470-48217-9

Editor: Jennifer Reilly
Production Editor: Heather Wilcox
Cartographer: Andrew Murphy
Photo Editor: Cherie Cincilla, Richard Fox
Design and layout by Vertigo Design NYC
Graphics and prepress by Wiley Indianapolis Composition Services

Front cover photo: Costa Rica: The Red-eyed Tree Frog (Agalychnis callidryas) peering out from leaf © Dieter Herrmann/Mauritius/PhotoLibrary
Back cover photos, left to right: White Faced Capuchin monkey in tree waiting to steal food © Travelib Prime/Alamy Images; Tourists walking on suspension bridges in Monteverde Canopy, Monteverde, Santa Elena, Costa Rica © Jan Csernoch/Alamy Images; Profile of a couple and a young man running on the beach with surfboards © Masterfile; Resplendent Quetzal taking wild avocado to nest, San Gerardo de Dota Cloud Forest, Costa Rica © Keith and Rebecca Snell/DanitaDelimont.com/Alamy Images

For information on our other products and services or to obtain technical support, please contact our Customer Care Department within the U.S. at 800/762-2974, outside the U.S. at 317/572-3993 or fax 317/572-4002.

Wiley also publishes its books in a variety of electronic formats. Some content that appears in print may not be available in electronic formats.

Manufactured in the United States of America

5 4 3 2 1

CONTENTS

List of Maps vii

1 THE BEST OF COSTA RICA 1

The Best of Natural Costa Rica 2

The Best Beaches 7

The Best Adventures 8

The Best Day Hikes & Nature Walks 11

The Best Bird-Watching 13

The Best Destinations for Families 15

The Best Luxury Hotels & Resorts 17

The Best Moderately Priced Hotels 19

The Best Ecolodges & Wilderness Resorts 20

The Best Bed & Breakfasts & Small Inns 21

The Best Restaurants 22

The Best Views 24

The Best After-Dark Fun 25

The Best Websites About Costa Rica 27

2 COSTA RICA IN DEPTH 28

Costa Rica Today 29

Looking Back at Costa Rica 31

Art & Architecture 34

The Lay of the Land 36

Costa Rica in Popular Culture: Books, Film & Music 39

TICO ETIQUETTE & CUSTOMS 41

Eating & Drinking in Costa Rica 42

TIPS ON SHOPPING IN COSTA RICA 46

3 PLANNING YOUR TRIP TO COSTA RICA 48

When to Go 48

CALENDAR OF EVENTS 51

Entry Requirements 52

Getting There & Getting Around 54

PLANNING A COSTA RICAN WEDDING 59

Money & Costs 61

THE VALUE OF THE COLON VS. OTHER POPULAR CURRENCIES 61

WHAT THINGS COST IN COSTA RICA 62

Health 63

Safety 65

Specialized Travel Resources 66

Sustainable Tourism 68

SUSTAINABLE PROPERTIES IN COSTA RICA 68

RESOURCES FOR GREEN TRAVEL 70

Staying Connected 71

Tips on Accommodations 73

4 SUGGESTED ITINERARIES 75

Costa Rica Regions in Brief 76
Costa Rica in 1 Week 80
Costa Rica in 2 Weeks 83

Costa Rica for Families 85
A Week of Adventures in Costa Rica 88
San José & Environs in 3 Days 90

5 THE ACTIVE VACATION PLANNER 92

Organized Adventure Trips 93
Activities A to Z 95
WHERE TO SEE THE RESPLENDENT QUETZAL 98
IN SEARCH OF TURTLES 105

Costa Rica's Top National Parks & Bioreserves 107
Tips on Health, Safety & Etiquette in the Wilderness 111
Volunteer & Study Programs 112
MONKEY BUSINESS 113

6 SAN JOSE 116

Orientation 117
"I KNOW THERE'S GOT TO BE A NUMBER HERE SOMEWHERE . . ." 120
Getting Around 123
FAST FACTS: SAN JOSE 126
Where to Stay 129
IT'S IN THE BEANS 136
Where to Dine 147
DINING UNDER THE STARS 150

What to See & Do 155
Outdoor Activities & Spectator Sports 163
Shopping 166
JOE TO GO 167
San José After Dark 171
Side Trips from San José 177
HOLY SMOKE! CHOOSING THE VOLCANO TRIP THAT'S RIGHT FOR YOU 182

7 GUANACASTE: THE GOLD COAST 192

Liberia 194
La Cruz & Bahía Salinas 205
Playa Hermosa, Playa Panamá &
  Papagayo 209
Playa del Coco & Playa Ocotal 216

Playas Flamingo, Potrero, Brasilito
  & Conchal 222
Playa Tamarindo & Playa Grande
  231
Playa Junquillal 245

8 PUNTARENAS & THE NICOYA PENINSULA 248

Puntarenas 249
DIVING TRIPS TO ISLA DEL COCO
  (COCOS ISLAND) 254
Playa Tambor 256
Playa Montezuma 260

Malpaís & Santa Teresa 268
Playa Sámara 273
Playa Nosara 280

9 THE NORTHERN ZONE: MOUNTAIN LAKES, CLOUD FORESTS & A VOLCANO 287

Puerto Viejo de Sarapiquí 288
Arenal Volcano & La Fortuna 296
BOATS, HORSES & TAXIS 298
TAKING A SOOTHING SOAK IN HOT SPRINGS
  302

Along the Shores of Lake Arenal
  315
Monteverde 321

10 THE CENTRAL PACIFIC COAST: WHERE THE MOUNTAINS MEET THE SEA 338

Playa de Jacó, Playa Hermosa &
  Playa Herradura 339
Manuel Antonio National Park 359

Dominical 379
San Isidro de El General: A Base
  for Exploring Chirripó National
  Park 390

11 THE SOUTHERN ZONE 397

Drake Bay 398

THOSE MYSTERIOUS STONE SPHERES 404

Puerto Jiménez: Gateway to Corcovado National Park 409

Golfito: Gateway to the Golfo Dulce 421

Playa Zancudo 429

Playa Pavones: A Surfer's Mecca 433

12 THE CARIBBEAN COAST 436

Barra del Colorado 438

Tortuguero National Park 441

Limón: Gateway to Tortuguero National Park & Southern Coastal Beaches 451

Cahuita 454

Puerto Viejo 463

13 FAST FACTS: COSTA RICA 482

Airline, Hotel & Car-Rental Websites 486

14 SPANISH TERMS & PHRASES 488

Basic Words & Phrases 489

Some Typical Tico Words & Phrases 491

Menu Terms 492

Other Useful Terms 494

15 COSTA RICAN WILDLIFE 495

Fauna 496

Flora 505

Index 508

Accommodations Index 514

LIST OF MAPS

The Best of Costa Rica   4

Costa Rica Regions in Brief   77

Costa Rica in 1 Week   81

Costa Rica in 2 Weeks   85

Costa Rica for Families   87

A Week of Adventures in Costa Rica   89

San José in 3 Days   91

San José Orientation   121

San José   130

The Central Valley   179

Guanacaste   195

Santa Rosa National Park   207

Tamarindo   233

The Nicoya Peninsula   251

Montezuma   265

The Northern Zone   289

Along the Shores of Lake Arenal   317

Monteverde   323

The Central Pacific Coast   341

Playa Jacó   349

Manuel Antonio & Quepos   371

The Southern Zone   399

Drake Bay   401

Puerto Jiménez   411

Corcovado National Park   413

The Caribbean Coast   439

Puerto Viejo   465

ABOUT THE AUTHOR

Eliot Greenspan is a poet, journalist, musician, and travel writer who took his backpack and typewriter the length of Mesoamerica before settling in Costa Rica in 1992. Since then, he has worked steadily as a travel writer, freelance journalist, and translator, and continued his travels in the region. He is the author of *Frommer's Belize, Frommer's Ecuador, Frommer's Guatemala, Costa Rica For Dummies, Costa Rica Day By Day,* and *The Tico Times Restaurant Guide to Costa Rica,* as well as the chapter on Venezuela in *Frommer's South America.*

ACKNOWLEDGMENTS

I say this every year, but I continue to be eternally grateful to Anne Becher and Joe Richey, who were instrumental in getting me this gig—*muchas gracias.* I'd also like to thank my parents, Marilyn and Warren Greenspan, who showed unwavering love, support, and encouragement (well, one out of three ain't bad) when I chose words and world-wandering over becoming a lawyer or a doctor. Jody and Ted Ejnes (my sister and brother-in-law) deserve a mention; they risked life and limb—literally—leading to two important tips that may help you save yours. (I now believe Ted, and he may have actually almost stepped on a crocodile.) Mayling Charpentier did some excellent phone, fax, and fact-checking work on this edition. And a big tip of my hat to Jennifer Reilly for her editorial diligence and patience.

HOW TO CONTACT US

In researching this book, we discovered many wonderful places—hotels, restaurants, shops, and more. We're sure you'll find others. Please tell us about them, so we can share the information with your fellow travelers in upcoming editions. If you were disappointed with a recommendation, we'd love to know that, too. Please write to:
Frommer's Costa Rica 2010
Wiley Publishing, Inc. * 111 River St. * Hoboken, NJ 07030-5774

AN ADDITIONAL NOTE

Please be advised that travel information is subject to change at any time—and this is especially true of prices. We therefore suggest that you write or call ahead for confirmation when making your travel plans. The authors, editors, and publisher cannot be held responsible for the experiences of readers while traveling. Your safety is important to us, however, so we encourage you to stay alert and be aware of your surroundings. Keep a close eye on cameras, purses, and wallets, all favorite targets of thieves and pickpockets.

FROMMER'S STAR RATINGS, ICONS & ABBREVIATIONS

Every hotel, restaurant, and attraction listing in this guide has been ranked for quality, value, service, amenities, and special features using a star-rating system. In country, state, and regional guides, we also rate towns and regions to help you narrow down your choices and budget your time accordingly. Hotels and restaurants are rated on a scale of zero (recommended) to three stars (exceptional). Attractions, shopping, nightlife, towns, and regions are rated according to the following scale: zero stars (recommended), one star (highly recommended), two stars (very highly recommended), and three stars (must-see).

In addition to the star-rating system, we also use seven feature icons that point you to the great deals, in-the-know advice, and unique experiences that separate travelers from tourists. Throughout the book, look for:

special finds—those places only insiders know about

fun facts—details that make travelers more informed and their trips more fun

kids—best bets for kids and advice for the whole family

special moments—those experiences that memories are made of

overrated—places or experiences not worth your time or money

insider tips—great ways to save time and money

great values—where to get the best deals

The following abbreviations are used for credit cards:

AE	American Express	DISC	Discover	V	Visa
DC	Diners Club	MC	MasterCard		

TRAVEL RESOURCES AT FROMMERS.COM

Frommer's travel resources don't end with this guide. **Frommers.com** has travel information on more than 4,000 destinations. We update features regularly, giving you access to the most current trip-planning information and the best airfare, lodging, and car-rental bargains. You can also listen to podcasts, connect with other Frommers.com members through our active-reader forums, share your travel photos, read blogs from guidebook editors and fellow travelers, and much more.

THE BEST OF COSTA RICA

Frist coming to the attention of international travelers in the mid-1990s, Costa Rica is currently—and consistently—one of the hottest vacation and adventure-travel destinations in Latin America, with over two million visitors each year. Despite the boom in vacationers, Costa Rica remains a place rich in natural wonders and biodiversity, where you can still find yourself far from the maddening crowds. The country boasts a wealth of unsullied beaches that stretch for miles, small lodgings that haven't attracted hordes of tourists, jungle rivers for rafting and kayaking, and spectacular cloud- and rainforests with ample opportunities for bird-watching and hiking. In addition to the country's trademark eco- and adventure-tourism offerings, you will also find luxury resorts and golf courses, plush spas, and some truly spectacular boutique hotels and lodges.

Having lived in Costa Rica for more than 18 years, I continue to explore and discover new spots, adventures, restaurants, and lodgings—and my "best of" experiences keep on coming. In this chapter I've selected the very best of what this unique country has to offer. These places and experiences are covered in greater detail elsewhere in the book; this chapter is merely meant to give you an overview of the highlights so that you can start planning your own adventure.

THE best OF NATURAL COSTA RICA

o **Rincón de la Vieja National Park** (northeast of Liberia, in Guanacaste): This is an area of rugged beauty and high volcanic activity. The Rincón de la Vieja Volcano rises to 1,848m (6,061 ft.), but the thermal activity is spread out along its flanks, where numerous geysers, vents, and fumaroles let off its heat and steam. This is a great place to hire a guide and a horse for a day of rugged exploration. There are waterfalls and mud baths, hot springs, and cool jungle swimming holes. You'll pass through pastureland, scrub savanna, and moist secondary forest; the bird-watching is excellent. See p. 198

o **The Río Sarapiquí Region** (north of San José between Guanacaste in the west and the Caribbean coast in the east): This region is a prime place for an ecolodge experience. Protected tropical forests climb from the Caribbean coastal lowlands up into the central mountains, affording you a glimpse of a plethora of life zones and ecosystems. **Braulio Carrillo National Park** borders several other private reserves here, and a variety of ecolodges will suit any budget. See "Puerto Viejo de Sarapiquí" in chapter 9.

PREVIOUS PAGE: **Arenal Volcano.**

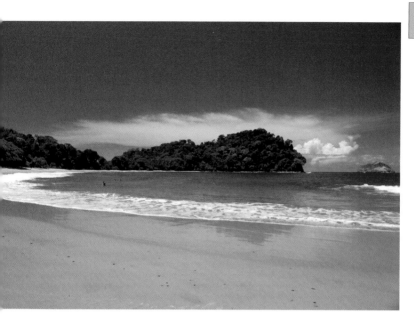

Manuel Antonio National Park.

○ **Arenal Volcano/Tabacón Hot Springs** (near La Fortuna, northwest of San José): When the skies are clear and the lava is flowing, Arenal Volcano offers a thrilling light show accompanied by an earthshaking rumble that defies description. You can even see the show while soaking in a natural hot spring and having a drink at the swim-up bar at **Tabacón Grand Spa Thermal Resort** (☎2519-1900; www.tabacon.com). If the rushing torrent of volcano-heated spring water isn't therapeutic enough, you can get an incredibly inexpensive massage here. See "Arenal Volcano & La Fortuna" in chapter 9.

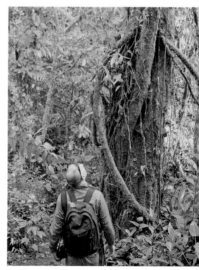

○ **Monteverde Biological Cloud Forest Reserve** (in the mountains northwest of San José): There's something both eerie and majestic about walking around in the early morning mist surrounded by bird calls and towering trees hung heavy in broad bromeliads, flowering orchids, and hanging moss and vines. The reserve has a well-maintained network of trails, and the community is truly involved in conservation. Not only that, but in and around Monteverde and Santa Elena, you'll find

Monteverde Biological Cloud Forest Reserve.

THE BEST OF NATURAL COSTA RICA

Arenal Volcano/Tabacón Hot Springs **5**
Braulio Carrillo National Park **18**
Manuel Antonio National Park **25**
Monteverde Biological
   Cloud Forest Reserve **6**
Osa Peninsula &
   Corcovado National Park **26**
Rincón de la Vieja National Park **2**
The Río Sarapiquí Region **14**
Tortuguero Village & Jungle Canals **15**

THE BEST BEACHES

The Beaches around Playa Sámara **9**
Malpaís **11**
Manuel Antonio **25**
Playa Montezuma **12**
Punta Uva & Manzanillo **21**
Santa Rosa National Park **1**

THE BEST ADVENTURES

Battling a Billfish off the Pacific Coast **24**
Diving off Isla del Coco **10**
Hiking Mount Chirripó **22**
Kayaking Around Golfo Dulce **27**
Rafting the Upper Reventazón River **16**
Surfing & Four-Wheeling Guanacaste **8**
Surfing Pavones **28**
Windsurfing Lake Arenal **4**

THE BEST BIRD-WATCHING

Aviarios del Caribe/Cahuita National Park **20**
Caño Negro Wildlife Refuge **3**
Carara National Park **13**
Cerro de la Muerte **23**
La Selva Biological Station **17**
Parque del Este **19**
Río Tempisque Basin **7**
Wilson Botanical Gardens **29**

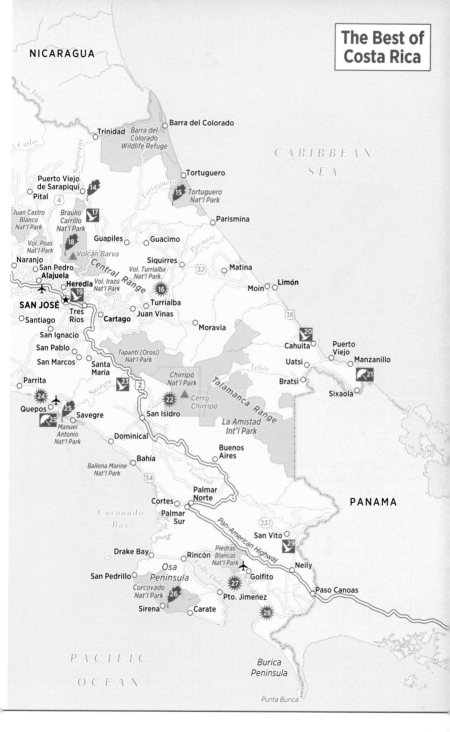

The Best of Costa Rica

NICARAGUA

CARIBBEAN SEA

Barra del Colorado
Trinidad
Barra del Colorado Wildlife Refuge

Tortuguero
Puerto Viejo de Sarapiquí
Pital
Tortuguero Nat'l Park

Juan Castro Blanco Nat'l Park
Braulio Carrillo Nat'l Park
Parismina
Vol. Poas Nat'l Park
Naranjo
San Pedro
Alajuela
Guapiles
Guacimo
Volcán Barva
Heredia
Central Range
Siquirres
Vol. Turrialba Nat'l Park
Matina
Limón
Moin
SAN JOSÉ
Vol. Irazú Nat'l Park
Santiago
Tres Rios
Cartago
Turrialba
Juan Vinas
Moravia
San Ignacio
San Pablo
Tapanti (Orosi) Nat'l Park
Cahuita
Puerto Viejo
San Marcos
Santa Maria
Chirripó Nat'l Park
Talamanca Range
Uatsi
Manzanillo
Parrita
Savegre
Cerro Chirripó
Bratsi
Sixaola
Quepos
Savegre
San Isidro
La Amistad Int'l Park
Manuel Antonio Nat'l Park
Dominical
Buenos Aires
Ballena Marine Nat'l Park
Bahía
PANAMA
Cortes
Palmar Norte
Coronado Bay
Palmar Sur
San Vito
Drake Bay
Rincón
Piedras Blancas Nat'l Park
Neily
San Pedrillo
Osa Peninsula
Golfito
Corcovado Nat'l Park
Pto. Jimenez
Paso Canoas
Sirena
Carate
PACIFIC OCEAN
Burica Peninsula
Punta Burica

a whole slew of related activities and attractions, including canopy tours that allow you to swing from treetop to treetop while hanging from a skinny cable. See p. 326.

o **Manuel Antonio** (near Quepos on the central Pacific coast): There's a reason this place is so popular and renowned: monkeys! The national park here is full of them, even the endangered squirrel monkeys. But you'll also find plenty to see and do outside the park. The road into Manuel Antonio has many lookouts that consistently offer postcard-perfect snapshots of steep jungle hills meeting the sea. Uninhabited islands lie just off the coast, and the beaches here are perfect crescents of soft, white sand. See "Manuel Antonio National Park" in chapter 10.

o **Osa Peninsula** (in southern Costa Rica): This is Costa Rica's most remote and biologically rich region. **Corcovado National Park,** the largest remaining patch of virgin lowland tropical rainforest in Central America, takes up much of the Osa Peninsula. Jaguars, crocodiles, and scarlet macaws all call this place home. Whether you stay in a luxury nature lodge in **Drake Bay** or outside of **Puerto Jiménez,** or camp in the park itself, you will be surrounded by some of the most lush and most intense jungle this country has to offer. See chapter 11.

o **Tortuguero Village & Jungle Canals** (on the Caribbean coast, north of Limón): Tortuguero Village is a small collection of rustic wooden shacks on a narrow spit of land between the Caribbean Sea and a dense maze of jungle canals. It's been called Costa Rica's Venice, but it actually has more in common with the South American Amazon. As you explore the narrow canals here, you'll see a wide variety of herons and other water birds, three types of monkeys, three-toed sloths, and caimans. If you come between June and October, you might be treated to the awe-inspiring spectacle of a green turtle nesting—the small stretch of Tortuguero beach is the last remaining major nesting site of this endangered animal. See "Tortuguero National Park" in chapter 12.

Leatherback turtle tracks heading to the sea.

THE best BEACHES

With more than 1,200km (750 miles) of shoreline on its Pacific and Caribbean coasts, Costa Rica offers beachgoers an embarrassment of riches.

o **Santa Rosa National Park:** If you really want to get away from it all, the beaches here in the northwest corner of Costa Rica are a good bet. You'll have to four-wheel-drive or hike 13km (8 miles) from the central ranger station to reach them. And once there, you'll find only the most basic of camping facilities: outhouse latrines and cold-water showers. But you'll probably have the place almost to yourself. In fact, the only time it gets crowded is in October, when thousands of olive ridley sea turtles nest in one of their yearly *arribadas* (arrivals). See p. 206.

o **Playa Tamarindo:** Although it can be argued that Tamarindo has become too overdeveloped, crowded, and chaotic, it still earns a place on this list. The beach here is long and broad, with sections calm enough for swimmers and others just right for surfers. Tamarindo also has lodgings to suit every budget, a host of tour and activity options to keep you busy, as well as excellent restaurants at almost every turn. Located about midway along the beaches of Guanacaste province, Tamarindo makes a good base for exploring other nearby stretches of sand, as well. See "Playa Tamarindo & Playa Grande" in chapter 7.

o **Playa Avellanas:** Just south of Tamarindo, this long, white-sand beach has long been a favorite haunt for surfers, locals, and those in-the-know. Playa Avellanas stretches on for miles, backed largely by protected mangrove forests. On the verge of "being discovered," there's still very little going on here—aside from the new, nearby JW Marriott resort and Lola's, perhaps my favorite beachfront restaurant in the country. See p. 244.

o **The Beaches Around Playa Sámara:** Playa Sámara itself is nice enough, but if you venture just slightly farther afield, you'll find some of the nicest and least developed beaches along the entire Guanacaste coast. **Playa Carrillo** is a long, almost always deserted crescent of palm-backed white sand located just south of Sámara, while **Playa Barrigona** and **Playa Buena Vista** are two hidden gems tucked down a couple of dirt roads to the north. The land all around Playa Barrigona was purchased by actor Mel Gibson, but the beach, like all beaches in Costa Rica, remains open to the public. See "Playa Sámara" in chapter 8.

o **Playa Montezuma:** This tiny beach town at the southern tip of the Nicoya Peninsula has weathered fame and infamy, but retains a funky sense of individuality. European backpackers, vegetarian yoga enthusiasts, and UFO seekers choose Montezuma's beach over any other in Costa Rica. The waterfalls are what set it apart from the competition, but the beach stretches for miles, with plenty of isolated spots to plop down your towel or mat. Nearby are the **Cabo Blanco** and **Curú** wildlife preserves. See "Playa Montezuma" in chapter 8.

Santa Teresa surfer.

Punta Uva.

○ **Malpaís:** While the secret is certainly out, there's still some time to visit Costa Rica's fastest growing hot spot before the throngs and large resorts arrive. With just a smattering of luxury lodges, surf camps, and assorted hotels and cabinas, Malpaís is the place to come if you're looking for miles of deserted beaches and great surf. If you find Malpaís is too crowded, head farther on down the road to Santa Teresa, Playa Hermosa, and Manzanillo. See "Malpaís & Santa Teresa" in chapter 8.

○ **Manuel Antonio:** The first beach destination to become popular in Costa Rica, Manuel Antonio retains its charms despite burgeoning crowds and mushrooming hotels. The beaches inside the national park are idyllic, and the views from the hills approaching the park are enchanting. This is one of the few remaining habitats for the endangered squirrel monkey. Rooms with views tend to be a bit expensive, but many a satisfied guest will tell you they're worth it. See "Manuel Antonio National Park" in chapter 10.

○ **Punta Uva & Manzanillo:** Below Puerto Viejo, the beaches of Costa Rica's eastern coast take on true Caribbean splendor, with turquoise waters, coral reefs, and palm-lined stretches of nearly deserted white-sand beach. Punta Uva and Manzanillo are the two most sparkling gems of this coastline. Tall coconut palms line the shore, providing shady respite for those who like to spend a full day on the sand, and the water is usually quite calm and good for swimming. See "Puerto Viejo" in chapter 12.

THE best ADVENTURES

○ **Mountain-Biking the Back Roads of Costa Rica:** The lack of infrastructure and paved roads here that most folks bemoan is a huge boon for mountain bikers. There are endless back roads and cattle paths to explore. Tours of differing lengths and all difficulty levels are available. Contact **Coast to Coast Adventures** (☎2280-8054; www.ctocadventures.com). See p. 184.

- **Swinging Through the Treetops on a Canopy Tour:** This unique adventure has become ubiquitous in Costa Rica. You'll find zip-line canopy tours all over the country. In most cases, after a strenuous climb using ascenders, you strap on a harness and zip from treetop to treetop while dangling from a cable. Check the various destination chapters to find a canopy tour operation near you.

- **Rafting the Upper Reventazón River** (near Turrialba): The Class V Guayabo section of this popular river is serious white water. Only experienced and gutsy river runners need apply. If you're not quite up to that, try a 2-day Pacuare River trip, which passes through primary and secondary forests and a beautiful steep gorge. Plans to build a dam here have thankfully been rejected, or at least stalled, for the time being. **Aventuras Naturales (☎800/321-8410** in the U.S., or 2225-3939 in Costa Rica; www.toenjoynature.com) can arrange these tours. See p. 106.

- **Surfing and Four-Wheeling Guanacaste Province:** This northwestern province has dozens of respectable beach and reef breaks, from Witch's Rock at Playa Naranjo near the Nicaraguan border to Playa Nosara more than 100km (62 miles) away. In addition to these two prime spots, try a turn at Playa Grande, Punta Langosta, and playas Negra, Avellanas, and Junquillal. Or find your own secret spot. Rent a four-by-four with a roof rack, pile on the boards, and explore. See chapter 7.

- **Battling a Billfish off the Pacific Coast:** Billfish are plentiful all along Costa Rica's Pacific coast, and boats operate from Playa del Coco to Playa Zancudo. Costa Rican anglers hold world records for both blue marlin and Pacific sailfish. Go to Quepos (just outside Manuel Antonio) for the best après-fish scene, or head down to Drake Bay, the Osa Peninsula, or Golfo Dulce if you want some isolation. **Costa Rica Outdoors (☎800/308-3394** or 2231-0306; www.costaricaoutdoors.com) can help you find a good charter skipper or specialized fishing lodge. See chapters 7, 8, 10, 11, and 12.

- **Trying the Adventure Sport of Canyoning:** While far from standardized, canyoning usually involves hiking along and through the rivers and creeks of steep mountain canyons, with periodic breaks to rappel down the face of a waterfall, jump off a rock into a jungle pool, or float down a small rapid. **Pure Trek Canyoning (☎866/569-5723** or 2479-1313; www.puretrekcostarica.com) and **Desafío Expeditions ★★ (☎2479-9464;** www.desafiocostarica.com) in La Fortuna, and **Psycho Tours (☎8353-8619;** www.psychotours.com) near Puerto Jiménez, are the prime operators. See chapters 9 and 11.

A canyoning tour.

Lake Arenal kitesurfing.

Hammerhead shark.

o **Windsurfing or Kitesurfing on Lake Arenal:** With steady gale-force winds (at certain times of the year) and stunning scenery, the northern end of Lake Arenal has become a major international windsurfing and kitesurfing hot spot. See chapter 9.

o **Diving off the Shores of Isla del Coco** (off the Pacific coast): Legendary among treasure seekers, pirate buffs, and scuba divers, this small island is consistently rated one of the 10 best dive sites in the world. A protected national park, Isla del Coco is surrounded by clear Pacific waters, and its reefs are teeming with life (divers regularly encounter large schools of hammerhead sharks, curious manta rays, and docile whale sharks). Because the island is so remote and has no overnight facilities for visitors, the most popular way to visit is on 10-day excursions on a live-aboard boat, where guests live, eat, and sleep onboard—with nights anchored in the harbor. See p. 254.

o **Hiking Mount Chirripó** (near San Isidro de El General on the central Pacific coast): The highest mountain in Costa Rica, Mount Chirripó is one of the few places in the world where (on a clear day) you can see both the Caribbean Sea and the Pacific Ocean at the same time. Hiking to Chirripó's 3,724m (12,215-ft.) summit takes you through a number of distinct bioregions, ranging from lowland pastures and a cloud forest to a high-altitude páramo, a tundralike landscape with stunted trees and morning frosts. See "San Isidro de El General: A Base for Exploring Chirripó National Park" in chapter 10.

o **Kayaking Around the Golfo Dulce:** Slipping through the waters of the Golfo Dulce by kayak gets you intimately in touch with the raw beauty of this underdeveloped region. Spend several days poking around in mangrove swamps, fishing in estuaries, and watching dolphins frolic in the bay. **Escondido Trex** (✆ 2735-5210; www.escondidotrex.com) provides multiday custom kayaking trips out of Puerto Jiménez on the Osa Peninsula. See "Puerto Jiménez: Gateway to Corcovado National Park" in chapter 11.

- **Surfing Pavones** (on the southern Pacific coast): Just 13km (8 miles) from the Panamanian border at the southern reaches of Costa Rica's Pacific coast, Pavones is reputed to have one of the longest rideable waves in the world. When this left-point break is working, surfers enjoy rides of almost a mile in length. Much more can be said about this experience, but if you're a surfer, you've heard it all before. Contact **Casa Siempre Domingo** (**☎8820-4709;** www.casa-domingo.com), the most comfortable hotel in town, for current wave reports and other local information. See "Playa Pavones: A Surfer's Mecca" in chapter 11.

THE best DAY HIKES & NATURE WALKS

- **Lankester Gardens:** If you want a really pleasant but not overly challenging day hike, consider a walk among the hundreds of distinct species of flora on display here. **Lankester Gardens** (**☎2552-3247;** www.jardinbotanicolankester.org) is just 27km (17 miles) from San José and makes a wonderful day's expedition. The trails meander from areas of well-tended open garden to shady natural forest. See p. 162.

- **Rincón de la Vieja National Park:** This park has a number of wonderful trails through a variety of ecosystems and natural wonders. My favorite hike is down to the Blue Lake and Cangrejo Falls. It's 5.1km (3¼ miles) each way, and you'll want to spend some time at the base of this amazing lake; plan on

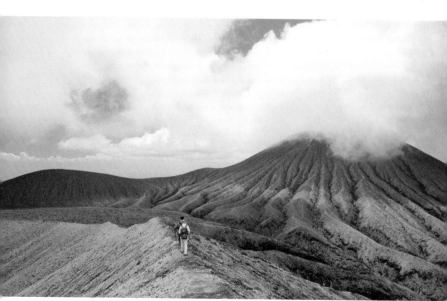

Rincón de la Vieja National Park.

La Selva Biological Station.

at least 5 hours for the outing, and bring along lunch and plenty of water. You can also hike up to two craters and a crater lake here, and the Las Pailas loop is ideal for those seeking a less strenuous hike. This remote volcanic national park is about an hour north of Liberia (it's only 25km/16 miles, but the road is quite rough), or about 5 hours from San José. See p. 198.

o **La Selva Biological Station:** This combination research facility and rustic nature lodge has an extensive and well-marked network of trails. You'll have to reserve in advance (☏2524-0607; www.threepaths.co.cr) and take the guided tour if you aren't a guest at the lodge. But the hikes are led by very informed naturalists, so you might not mind the company. The Biological Station is located north-northeast on the Caribbean slope of Costa Rica's central mountain range. It'll take you about 1½ hours to drive from San José via the Guápiles Highway. See p. 293.

o **Arenal National Park and Environs:** There's great hiking all around this area. The national park itself has several excellent trails that visit a variety of ecosystems, including rainforest, secondary forest, savanna, and, my favorite, old lava flows. Most of them are on the relatively flat flanks of the volcano, so there's not too much climbing involved. There's also great hiking on the trails at the Arenal Observatory Lodge, and the trail down to the base of the La Fortuna Waterfall is a fun scramble. It's about a 3½-hour drive from San José to La Fortuna and Arenal National Park. See "Arenal Volcano & La Fortuna" in chapter 9.

o **Monteverde Biological Cloud Forest Reserve:** In the morning rush of high season, when groups and tours line up to enter the reserve, you'd think the park was named "Crowd Forest." Still, the guides here are some of the most professional and knowledgeable in the country. Take a tour in the morning to familiarize yourself with the forest, and then spend the late morning or afternoon (your entrance ticket is good for the entire day) exploring the reserve. Off the main thoroughfares, Monteverde reveals its rich mysteries with stunning regularity. Walk through the gray mist and look up at the dense tangle of epiphytes and vines. The only noises are the rustlings of birds or monkeys and the occasional distant rumble of Arenal Volcano. The trails are well marked and regularly tended. It's about 3½ hours by bus or car to Monteverde from San José. See p. 326.

○ **Corcovado National Park:** This large swath of dense lowland rainforest is home to Costa Rica's second-largest population of scarlet macaws. The park has a well-designed network of trails, ranger stations, and camping facilities. Most of the lodges in Drake Bay and Puerto Jiménez offer day hikes through the park, but if you really want to experience it, you should hike in and stay at one or more of the campgrounds. This is strenuous hiking, and you will have to pack in some gear and food, but the reward is some of Costa Rica's most spectacular and unspoiled scenery. Because strict limits are placed on the number of visitors allowed into the park, you'll always be far from the crowds. See "Puerto Jiménez: Gateway to Corcovado National Park" in chapter 11.

○ **Cahuita National Park:** The trails here are flat, well-maintained paths through thick lowland forest. Most of the way they parallel the beach, which is usually no more than 90m (295 ft.) away, so you can hike out on the trail and back along the beach, or vice versa. White-faced and howler monkeys are common, as are brightly colored land crabs. See p. 456.

THE best BIRD-WATCHING

○ **Observing Oropendola and Blue-Crowned Motmot at Parque del Este:** A boon for city bird-watchers, this San José park rambles through a collection of lawns, planted gardens, and harvested forest, but it also includes second-growth scrub and dense woodland. Oropendola and blue-crowned motmot are common species here. See p. 163.

○ **Spotting Hundreds of Marsh and Stream Birds Along the Río Tempisque Basin:** Hike around the Palo Verde Biological Station, or take a boat trip down the Bebedero River with **Swiss Travel Services** (**℡2282-4898;** www.swisstravelcr.com) or **Safaris Corobicí** (**℡2669-6191;** www.nicoya.com). This area is an important breeding ground for gallinules, jacanas, and limpkins, and is a common habitat for numerous heron and kingfisher species. Palo Verde is about a 3½-hour drive from San José. See p. 200.

Boat-billed heron.

Red-lored parrot.

o **Looking for 300-plus Species of Birds in La Selva Biological Station:**
With an excellent trail system through a variety of habitats, from dense primary rainforest to open pasturelands and cacao plantations, this is one of the
finest places for bird-watching in Costa Rica. With such a variety of habitats,
the number of species spotted runs to well over 300. La Selva is located just
a few miles south of Puerto Viejo. See p. 293.

o **Sizing Up a Jabiru Stork at Caño Negro National Wildlife Refuge:** Caño
Negro Lake and the Río Frío that feeds it are incredibly rich in wildlife and
a major nesting and gathering site for aquatic bird species. These massive
birds are getting less common in Costa Rica, but this is still one of the best
places to spot one. **Caño Negro Natural Lodge** (℡**2265-3302;** www.
canonegrolodge.com) sits right on the edge of the refuge and makes a great
base for exploring this region to the north of La Fortuna. See p. 305.

o **Catching a Scarlet Macaw in Flight over Carara National Park:** Home to
Costa Rica's largest population of scarlet macaws, Carara Biological Reserve
is a special place for devoted bird-watchers and recent converts. Macaws are
noisy and colorful birds that spend their days in the park but choose to roost
in the evenings near the coast. They arrive like clockwork every morning and
then head for the coastal mangroves around dusk. These daily migrations give
birders a great chance to see these magnificent birds in flight. The reserve is
located about 2 hours from San José along the central Pacific coast. See p.
345.

o **Looking for a Resplendent Quetzal in the Cerro de la Muerte:** Don't let
the name (Mountain of Death) scare you away from the opportunity to see
this spectacular bird, revered by the ancient Aztecs and Mayas. Serious bird-
watchers won't want to leave Costa Rica without crossing this bird off their
lists, and neophytes might be hooked for life after seeing one of these iridescent
green wonders fly overhead, flashing its brilliant red breast and trailing 2-foot-
long tail feathers. **Trogon Lodge** (℡**2293-8181;** www.grupomawamba.com)

can almost guarantee a sighting. The Cerro de la Muerte is a high mountain pass along the way to San Isidro de El General about 1½ hours from San José. See "En Route to San José: Three Places to See Quetzals in the Wild" in chapter 10.

○ **Spotting Hundreds of Species at Wilson Botanical Gardens:** With more than 7,000 species of tropical plants and flowers, the well-tended trails and grounds of this beautiful research facility are fabulous for bird-watching. Hummingbirds and tanagers are particularly plentiful, but the bounty doesn't end there—more than 360 different species of birds have been recorded here. Wilson Gardens is located about an hour outside the town of Golfito. See "Golfito: Gateway to the Golfo Dulce" in chapter 11.

○ **Taking Advantage of the Caribbean's Best Birding at Aviarios del Caribe:** In just a few short years, Aviarios del Caribe (☎2750-0775; www. slothrescue.org) has established itself as the prime bird-watching resort on the Caribbean. If it flies along this coast, chances are good that you'll spot it here; more than 330 species of birds have been spotted so far. Located on the Caribbean coast, Aviarios del Caribe is about a 3-hour drive from San José. See p. 459.

THE best DESTINATIONS FOR FAMILIES

○ **San José:** If you're spending any time in San José, you'll probably want to be outside the rough-and-tumble downtown area. The best place to experience Costa Rica's capital city (and still get a decent night's sleep) is the **Doubletree Cariari By Hilton** (☎800/222-8733 or 2239-0022; www.cariarisanjose. doubletree.com). With facilities that include several large pools, a gym, a casino, shuttle service to a nearby spa and 18-hole golf course, and a game room (not to mention a babysitting service), there's something here for everyone.

If you're traveling with teens, they'll feel right at home at the nearby Mall Cariari, which has a multiplex theater, an indoor skating rink, and, of course, a food court. Just 15 minutes from downtown, it's well situated for exploring all of the city's sights and attractions. See p. 144.

○ **La Paz Waterfall Gardens** (☎2225-0643; www.waterfall gardens.com): This multifaceted attraction features paths and suspended walkways alongside a series of impressive jungle waterfalls. Kids

San José Children's Museum.

La Paz Waterfall Gardens.

love the variety and vibrancy of the various attractions, from the buzzing hummingbirds to the impressive power of the waterfalls. The rooms at the **Peace Lodge** here are some of the best in the country. See p. 162.

o **Playa Hermosa:** The protected waters of this Pacific beach make it a family favorite. However, just because the waters are calm doesn't mean it's boring here. I recommend staying at the beachfront **Hotel Playa Hermosa Bosque del Mar** (☎2672-0046; www.hotelplayahermosa.com) and checking in at **Aqua Sport** (☎2672-0050), where you can rent sea kayaks, sailboards, paddleboats, beach umbrellas, and bicycles. See "Playa Hermosa, Playa Panamá & Papagayo" in chapter 7.

o **Playa Tamarindo:** This lively surf town has a bit of something for everyone. This is a great spot for teens to learn how to surf or boogie-board, and there are a host of tours and activities to please the entire family. **Hotel Capitán Suizo** (☎2653-0353; www.hotelcapitansuizo.com; p. 238) has an excellent location on a calm section of beach, spacious rooms, and a great pool for kids and adults alike. See "Playa Tamarindo & Playa Grande" in chapter 7.

o **Monteverde:** Located about 160km (99 miles) northwest of San José, this area not only boasts the country's most famous cloud forest, but also sports a wide variety of related attractions and activities. After hiking through the reserve, you should be able to keep most kids happy and occupied riding horses; squirming at the local serpentarium; or visiting the butterfly farm, frog pond, bat jungle, and hummingbird gallery. More adventurous families can take a horseback ride or one of the local zip-line canopy tours. See "Monteverde" in chapter 9.

o **Playa de Jacó:** On the central Pacific coast, this is Costa Rica's liveliest and most developed beach town. The streets are lined with souvenir shops, ice-cream stands, and inexpensive eateries; there's even a miniature-golf course.

Older kids can rent a surf- or boogie board, although everyone should be careful with the rough surf. The **Club del Mar Condominiums & Resort** (☎866/978-5669 or 2643-3194; p. 349) is situated at the calm southern end of the beach. The hotel has a large free-form pool and some shady grounds, and is accommodating to families with small children. See "Playa de Jacó, Playa Hermosa & Playa Herradura" in chapter 10.

○ **Manuel Antonio:** Manuel Antonio has a little bit of everything: miles of gorgeous beaches, tons of wildlife (with almost guaranteed monkey sightings), and plenty of active-tour options. There's a load of lodging options, but **Hotel Sí Como No** (☎2777-0777; www.sicomono.com), with its large suites, two pools, water slide, and nightly movies, is probably your best bet. See "Manuel Antonio National Park" in chapter 10.

THE best LUXURY HOTELS & RESORTS

○ **Marriott Costa Rica Hotel** (San Antonio de Belén, San José area; ☎888/236-2427 or 2298-0844; www.marriott.com): Of all the contenders in the upscale urban market, the Marriott seems to be doing the best job. Maybe because it's the newest, but everything is in great shape, the service is bend-over-backward, the restaurants are excellent, and the hotel boasts all the facilities and amenities you could want. See p. 143.

○ **Peace Lodge** (north of Varablanca; ☎954/727-3997 in the U.S., or 2482-2720 in Costa Rica; www.waterfallgardens.com): While the bathrooms of the deluxe units are the most luxurious and unique in the country, everything else is done in grand style as well. Each room comes with at least one custom-tiled Jacuzzi on a private balcony. The hotel adjoins the popular La Paz Waterfall Gardens. See p. 143.

○ **Four Seasons Resort Costa Rica** (Papagayo Peninsula; ☎800/819-5053 or 2696-0000; www.fourseasons.com/costarica): This was the first large resort to cater to the high-end luxury market in Costa Rica, and it's still the best. Within its first month of operation Michael Jordan and Madonna were notable guests, and the stars keep coming. A beautiful setting, wonderful installations, a world-class golf course, and stellar service continue to make this the current king of the hill in the upscale market. See p. 212.

○ **Florblanca Resort** (Playa Santa Teresa; ☎2640-0232; www.florblanca.com): The individual villas at this intimate resort are some of the largest and most luxurious in the country. The service and food are outstanding, and the location is breathtaking, spread over a lushly planted hillside steps away from Playa Santa Teresa. See p. 270.

○ **Hotel Punta Islita** (on the Pacific coast in central Guanacaste; ☎866/446-4053 in the U.S. and Canada, or 2231-6122 in Costa Rica; www.hotelpuntaislita.com): This great getaway is perched on a high, flat bluff overlooking the Pacific Ocean. The rooms are large and comfortable, the food is excellent, and the setting is stunning. If you venture beyond your room and the hotel's inviting hillside pool, there's a long, almost always deserted beach for you to explore, as well as a wealth of activities for the more adventurous. See p. 279.

o **The Springs Resort & Spa** (near Arenal Volcano; ☎954/727-8333 in the U.S. and Canada, or 2461-1700 in Costa Rica; www.thespringscostarica. com): Opulent rooms with extravagant bathrooms, a series of sculpted hot spring pools, excellent restaurants, extensive facilities, and fabulous views make this the top luxury hotel near the Arenal Volcano. See p. 308.

o **Villa Caletas** (north of Jacó; ☎2630-3003; www.hotelvillacaletas.com): Spread out over a steep hillside high above the Pacific, these individual villas have a Mediterranean feel. The Greek Doric amphitheater follows the same motif. Carved into the hillside, the theater frequently features evening concerts of jazz or classical music. The "infinity pool" here was one of the first in Costa Rica and is still my favorite. Sitting in a lounge chair at the pool's edge, you'll swear that it joins the sea beyond. See p. 353.

o **Arenas del Mar** (Manuel Antonio; ☎/fax **2777-2777**; www.arenasdelmar. com): With large and ample rooms, excellent service and amenities, a beautiful little spa, and the best beach access and location in Manuel Antonio, this hotel has a lot to offer. See p. 370.

o **Hotel Sí Como No** (Manuel Antonio; ☎2777-0777; www.sicomono.com): Although there are fancier and more posh places in Costa Rica, the large modern suites and villas, spectacular views, attentive service, and first-rate facilities here earn this small resort a spot on this list. See p. 373.

Villa Caletas.

THE best MODERATELY PRICED HOTELS

- **Hotel Grano de Oro** (San José; ☎2255-3322; www.hotelgranodeoro.com): San José boasts dozens of old homes that have been converted into hotels, but few offer the luxurious accommodations or professional service found at the Grano de Oro. All the guest rooms have attractive hardwood furniture, including old-fashioned wardrobes in some rooms. When it's time to relax, you can soak in a hot tub or have a drink in the rooftop lounge while taking in San José's commanding view. See p. 137.

- **Hôtel Le Bergerac** (San José; ☎2234-7850; www.bergerachotel.com): This classy little hotel has been pleasing diplomats, dignitaries, and other discerning travelers for years. Ask for one of the garden rooms or get the old master bedroom with its small private balcony. See p. 139.

- **Villa del Sueño Hotel** (Playa Hermosa; ☎800/378-8599 or ☎/fax 2672-0026; www.villadelsueno.com): It's not right on the beach (you'll have to walk about 90m/295 ft.), but everything else here is right on the money: clean, comfortable rooms; a nice refreshing pool; and an excellent restaurant. You can't do better in Playa Hermosa. See p. 215.

- **Amor de Mar** (Montezuma; ☎/fax 2642-0262; www.amordemar.com): Clean, spacious, and comfortable rooms set on a sloping lawn that leads down to a rocky coastline, with a natural pool carved into the rocks, all add up to my idea of a tropical paradise. See p. 264.

- **Samara Tree House Inn** (Playa Samara; ☎2656-0733; www.samaratreehouse.com): The beachfront studio apartments, set on raised stilts, are just steps from the sand. The whole complex is centrally located and well-run, making this the best hotel option in Playa Sámara at any price. See p. 278.

- **Hotel Fonda Vela** (Monteverde; ☎2257-1413; www.fondavela.com): With plush, modern rooms and an excellent restaurant, the Fonda Vela, one of the original hotels here, is perennially a top choice in Monteverde. The hotel is located close enough to the Cloud Forest Reserve that you can even walk there. See p. 334.

- **Cabinas Sol y Mar** (Playa Zancudo; ☎2776-0014; www.zancudo.com): These beachfront rooms are a real bargain. In fact, they fall into our "inexpensive" category. No matter, they feel out of that price range with a prime location just steps from the surf, surrounded by lush gardens and shady palm trees. The bar and restaurant here are excellent, lively, and justifiably popular. See p. 432.

- **Cariblue Bungalows** (Playa Cocles; ☎2750-0035; www.cariblue.com): Try to get one of the private wooden bungalows here. If you do, you might be so happy and comfortable that you won't want to leave. Just 90m (295 ft.) or so away, however, are the warm waves of the Caribbean Sea. If this place is full, the neighboring **Azania Bungalows** (☎2750-0540; www.azania-costarica.com) is just about as good. See p. 476.

THE best ECOLODGES & WILDERNESS RESORTS

Ecolodge options in Costa Rica range from tent camps with no electricity, cold-water showers, and communal buffet-style meals to some of the most luxurious accommodations in the country. Generally, outstanding ecolodges and wilderness resorts are set apart by an ongoing commitment (financial or otherwise) to minimizing their effect on surrounding ecosystems and to supporting both conservation efforts and the residents of local communities. They should also be able to provide naturalist guides and plentiful information. All of the following do.

See "Sustainable Tourism" on p. 68 for more info on sustainable travel to Costa Rica.

- **La Selva Biological Station** (south of Puerto Viejo; **2524-0607;** www. threepaths.co.cr): Sure, this place is geared more toward researchers than tourists, but that (along with the surrounding rainforest and extensive trail system) is what makes this one of the best ecotourism spots in the country. See p. 293.

- **Arenal Observatory Lodge** (near La Fortuna; **2290-7011;** www.arenal observatorylodge.com): Originally a research facility, this lodge has upgraded over the years and features comfortable rooms with impressive views of Arenal Volcano. There are excellent trails to nearby lava flows and a nice waterfall. Toucans frequent the trees near the lodge, and howler monkeys provide the wake-up calls. See p. 310.

- **Monteverde Lodge & Gardens** (Monteverde; **2257-0766;** www.monte verdelodge.com): One of the original ecolodges in Monteverde, this place has only improved over the years, with great guides, updated rooms, and lush gardens. The operation is run by the very dependable and experienced Costa Rica Expeditions. See p. 334.

- **La Paloma Lodge** (Drake Bay; **2293-7502;** www.lapalomalodge.com): If your idea of the perfect nature lodge is one where your front porch provides some prime-time viewing of flora and fauna, this place is for you. If you decide to leave the comfort of your porch, the Osa Peninsula's lowland rainforests are just outside your door. See p. 407.

- **Bosque del Cabo Rainforest Lodge** (Osa Peninsula; /fax **2735-5206;** www.bosquedelcabo.com): Large, comfortable private cabins perched on the edge of a cliff overlooking the Pacific Ocean and surrounded by lush rainforest make this one of my favorite spots in the country. There's plenty to do, and there are always great guides here. See p. 420.

- **Playa Nicuesa Rainforest Lodge** (Golfo Dulce; **866/504-8116** or 2258-8250; www.nicuesalodge.com): This lodge is by far the best option on the Golfo Dulce. Set in deep forest, the individual bungalows here are a perfect blend of rusticity and luxury. See p. 428.

- **Tortuga Lodge** (Tortuguero; **800/886-2609** in the U.S. and Canada, or 2257-0766 in Costa Rica; www.tortugalodge.com): The canals of Tortuguero snake through a maze of lowland primary rainforest. The beaches here are major sea-turtle nesting sites. This is not only the most comfortable option

Tortuga Lodge.

in the area, but also another of the excellent ecolodges run by Costa Rica Expeditions. See p. 448.

o **Selva Bananito Lodge** (in the Talamanca Mountains south of Limón; ℂ2253-8118; www.selvabananito.com): This is one of the few lodges providing direct access to the southern Caribbean lowland rainforests. There's no electricity here, but that doesn't mean it's not plush. Hike along a riverbed, ride horses through the rainforest, climb 30m (100 ft.) up a ceiba tree, or rappel down a jungle waterfall. There's fabulous bird-watching in the area, and the Caribbean beaches are nearby. See p. 454.

THE best BED & BREAKFASTS & SMALL INNS

o **Finca Rosa Blanca Coffee Plantation & Inn** (Heredia; ℂ2269-9392; www. fincarosablanca.com): If the cookie-cutter rooms of international resorts leave you cold, then perhaps the unique rooms of this unusual inn will be more your style. Square corners seem to have been prohibited here in favor of turrets and curving walls of glass, arched windows, and a semicircular built-in couch. It's set into the lush hillsides just 20 minutes from San José. See p. 142.

o **Vista del Valle Plantation Inn** (near Grecia; ℂ2450-0800; www.vistadel valle.com): This is a great choice if you want something close to the airport but have no need for San José. The separate cabins are influenced by traditional Japanese architecture, with lots of polished woodwork and plenty of light. The gardens are meticulously tended, and the restaurant is excellent. A nice tile pool and Jacuzzi overlook a deep river canyon. See p. 145.

- **Sueño del Mar** (Playa Tamarindo; ☎/fax **2653-0284**; www.sueno-del-mar.com): You might think you're dreaming here. The rooms feature African dolls on the windowsills, Kokopeli candleholders, and open-air showers with sculpted angelfish, hand-painted tiles, and lush tropical plants. The fabrics are from Bali and Guatemala. Somehow all this works well together. Add in the requisite hammocks under shade trees right on the beach and a small pool, and you really have something. The lodge's breakfasts are earning local renown; yours is included in the price of your room. See p. 239.

- **Arco Iris Lodge** (Monteverde; ☎**2645-5067**; www.arcoirislodge.com): This small lodge is right in Santa Elena, and it's the best deal in the Monteverde area. The owners are extremely knowledgeable and helpful. See p. 333.

- **Cabinas Los Cocos** (Playa Zancudo; ☎/fax **2776-0012**; www.loscocos.com): If you've ever dreamed about chucking it all and setting up shop in a simple house right on the beach, give it a trial run here first. See p. 431.

- **Casa Verde Lodge** (Puerto Viejo; ☎**2750-0015**; www.cabinascasaverde.com): This is my favorite budget lodging along the Caribbean coast. The rooms are clean and airy and have comfortable beds with mosquito nets. The owners are friendly and always doing some work in the gardens or around the grounds. See p. 474.

- **Tree House Lodge** (Punta Uva; ☎**2750-0706**; www.costaricatreehouse.com): The collection of private houses at this small beachfront property are the most creative and luxurious accommodations to be found on the Caribbean coast. I like the namesake Tree House, although the Beach House Suite is quite spectacular as well. See p. 475.

THE best RESTAURANTS

- **Grano de Oro Restaurant** (San José; ☎**2255-3322**): This elegant little hotel has an elegant restaurant serving delicious Continental dishes and decadent desserts. The open-air seating in the lushly planted central courtyard is delightful, especially for lunch. See p. 150.

- **Bacchus** (Santa Ana; ☎**2282-5441**): Set in a wonderfully restored and updated ancient adobe home, this restaurant serves up arguably the best Italian fare in the San José metropolitan area. See p. 153.

- **Park Café** (San José; ☎**2290-6324**): A former Michelin two-star chef has set up shop in the interior patio garden of an old downtown mansion. The results are predictably fabulous. The regularly changing menu here is always varied, creative, and fairly priced. See p. 150.

- **Ginger** (Playa Hermosa; ☎**2672-0041**): Serving an eclectic mix of traditional and Pan Asian–influenced tapas, this sophisticated little joint is taking this part of Guanacaste by storm. They've got a list of creative cocktails to match the inventive dishes. See p. 215.

- **Mar y Sol** (Playa Flamingo; ☎**2654-4151**): In a beautiful room on a high hilltop with great views, the Catalan chef here serves top-notch international fare. See p. 229.

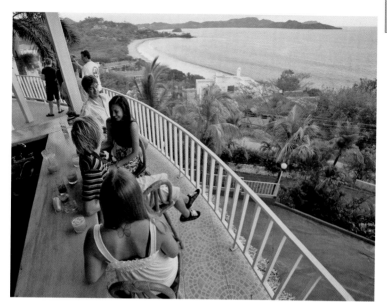

Mar y Sol.

- **Dragonfly Bar & Grill** (Tamarindo; ☎2653-1506): Southwestern American and Pacific Rim fusion cuisines are the primary culinary influences at this popular restaurant. Portions are large, service excellent, and prices fair. See p. 242.

- **Lola's** (Playa Avellanas; ☎2652-9097): With a perfect setting on the sand and excellent hearty fare, this is one of the best beachfront restaurants in the country. See p. 245.

- **Nectar** (at Florblanca Resort, Santa Teresa; ☎2640-0232): Guanacaste's best boutique resort also has one of its best restaurants. The menu changes nightly but always has a heavy Pan-Asian fusion flavor to it. The setting is romantic and subdued, in an open-air space just steps from the sand. See p. 272.

- **Playa de los Artistas** (Montezuma; ☎2642-0920): This place has the perfect blend of refined cuisine and beachside funkiness. There are only a few tables, so make sure you get here early. Fresh, grilled seafood is served in oversize ceramic bowls and on large wooden slabs lined with banana leaves. See p. 267.

- **El Lagarto** (Playa Sámara; ☎2656-0750): Witnessing the giant grill stations being fed with fresh coals from a raging fire overhead is worth the price of admission here, but the food and ambience are also fabulous. The menu is large, and the fresh seafood and massive steaks are all expertly prepared. See p. 279.

- **Sofia** (Monteverde; ☎2645-7017): Sofia serves excellent New Latin–fusion fare at a small space about halfway along the rough dirt road between Santa

Elena and the Monteverde Cloud Forest Preserve. Their sister restaurant, **Chimera** (☎2645-6081), which specializes in creative tapas, is also excellent. See p. 337.

o **El Galeón** (Playa Herradura; ☎2630-4555): If you're looking for fine dining with an inviting ambience in the Jacó and Playa Herradura area, it's hard to beat this fusion restaurant. I recommend one of the outdoor tables, with a view of the bay and marina. See p. 354.

o **El Patio Bistro Latino** (Quepos; ☎2777-4982): A casually elegant little place, El Patio Bistro Latino has made a name for itself in the Manuel Antonio area. The chef's creative concoctions take full advantage of fresh local ingredients. Its intimate setting is a welcome little oasis in Quepos. See p. 376.

o **La Pecora Nera** (Puerto Viejo; ☎2750-0490): I'm not sure that a tiny surfer town on the remote Caribbean coast deserves such fine Italian food, but it's got it. Your best bet here is to allow yourself to be taken on a culinary roller-coaster ride with a mixed feast of the chef's nightly specials and suggestions. See p. 480.

THE best VIEWS

o **The Summit of Irazú Volcano** (near San José): On a very clear day, you can see both the Pacific Ocean and the Caribbean Sea from this vantage point. Even if visibility is low and this experience eludes you, you can view the volcano's spectacular landscape, the Meseta Central, and the Orosi Valley. See p. 182.

o **Iguanazul Hotel** (Playa Junquillal; ☎2658-8123; www.iguanazul.com): On a high bluff above Playa Junquillal, this hotel has a wonderful view of the Pacific and the windswept coastline in either direction. It gets best around sunset and is better yet if you can commandeer one of the hammocks set in a little palapa on the hillside itself. See p. 247.

o **Tabacón Grand Spa Thermal Resort** (near Arenal Volcano; 877/277-8291 or 2460-2020; www.tabacon.com): Arenal Volcano seems so close, you'll swear you can reach out and touch it. Unlike Irazú Volcano (see above), when *this* volcano rumbles and spews, you may feel the urge to seek cover. Most rooms have spectacular views from sheltered private patios or balconies. See p. 308.

o **Villa Caletas** (Playa Hermosa de Jacó; ☎2630-3003): You'll have a view over the Golfo de Nicoya and the Pacific Ocean beyond. Sunsets at the hotel's outdoor amphitheater are legendary, but it's beautiful here during the day as well. See p. 353.

o **Hotel La Mariposa** (Quepos; ☎800/549-0157 or 2777-0355; www.lamariposa.com): This place has arguably the best view in Manuel Antonio, and that's saying a lot. Come for breakfast or a sunset drink because, unfortunately, I've had bad luck with dinner here. See p. 372.

Summit of Mount Chirripó.

- **The Summit of Mount Chirripó** (near San Isidro): What more can one say? At 3,724m (12,215 ft.), this is the highest spot in Costa Rica. On a clear day, you can see both the Pacific Ocean and the Caribbean Sea from here. Even if it isn't clear, you can catch some pretty amazing views and scenery. See "San Isidro de El General: A Base for Exploring Chirripó National Park" in chapter 10.

THE best AFTER-DARK FUN

- **Night Tours** (countrywide): Most Neotropical forest dwellers are nocturnal. Animal and insect calls fill the air, and the rustling on the ground all around takes on new meaning. Night tours are offered at most rain- and cloud-forest destinations throughout the country. Many use high-powered flashlights to catch glimpses of various animals. Some of the better spots for night tours are **Monteverde, Tortuguero,** and the **Osa Peninsula.** Volcano viewing in **Arenal** is another not-to-miss nighttime activity.

- **El Cuartel de la Boca del Monte** (San José; ☎2221-0327): From Wednesday to Saturday, San José's young, restless, and beautiful pack it in here. Originally a gay and bohemian hangout, it is now decidedly mixed and leaning toward yuppie. There's frequently live music. See p. 175.

- **San Pedro** (San José): This is San José's university district, and at night its streets are filled with students strolling among a variety of bars and cafes. If you'd like to join them, keep in mind that **Terra U** caters to the college crowd, **Mosaikos** is popular with young Tico rockers, **Omar Khayyam** is a great

San Pedro at night.

place to grab an outdoor table and watch the crowds walk by, and the **Jazz Café,** as its name indicates, is a hip live-music venue that often features local jazz and rock outfits. See "San José After Dark" in chapter 6.

o **Tamarindo** (Guanacaste): The most developed and popular destination on Guanacaste's Gold Coast, Tamarindo also boasts the area's best nightlife scene. **Bar 1** is my first choice. But I also like the open-mic nights at **Pasatiempo,** and the after-hours scene at **Rey Sol.** See "Tamarindo & Playa Grande" in chapter 7.

o **San Clemente Bar & Grill** (Dominical; **2787-0055**): This is a quintessential surfers' joint, but whether you hang ten or not, this is where you'll want to hang

San Clemente Bar & Grill.

out in Dominical at night. The fresh seafood and Tex-Mex specialties are hearty, tasty, and inexpensive. And there are pool, Ping-Pong, and foosball tables, as well as televised sporting events and surf videos. See "Dominical" in chapter 10.

o **Jacó** (Central Pacific coast): While some of the late-night scene here can be seedy—you'll find a few strip clubs and brothels—plenty of respectable places are around for those looking for after-hours fun. My top spot is the laid-back beach front **Ganesha Lounge.** I also like to shoot pool and toss down a few at **Tabacón.** See "Playa de Jacó After Dark" in chapter 10.

○ **Puerto Viejo:** This small beach town on the southern end of Costa Rica's Caribbean coast is one of the most active after-dark scenes in the country. **Johnny's Place** and **Stanford's** take turns as the major dance-and-party spot, but there are several other happening places, as well as a few after-hours beach bonfires and jam sessions, to be found. See "Puerto Viejo" in chapter 12.

THE best WEBSITES ABOUT COSTA RICA

○ **The *Tico Times*** (www.ticotimes.net): The English-language *Tico Times* makes it easy for *norteamericanos* (and other English speakers) to see what's happening in Costa Rica. It features the top story from its weekly print edition, as well as a daily update of news briefs, a business article, regional news, a fishing column, and travel reviews. There's also a link to current currency-exchange rates.

○ **Latin American Network Information Center** (http://lanic.utexas.edu/la/ca/cr): This site houses a vast collection of information about Costa Rica, and is hands-down the best one-stop shop for browsing, with helpful links to a diverse range of tourism and general information sites.

○ **Costa Rica Maps** (www.mapcr.com): In addition to offering up, for sale, a wonderful waterproof map to the country, this site features several excellent downloadable nationwide, regional, and city maps, and a host of other useful information.

○ **The U.S. Embassy in Costa Rica** (www.usembassy.or.cr): The official site of the U.S. Embassy in Costa Rica has a good base of information and regular updates of concern to U.S. citizens abroad, as well as about Costa Rica in general.

○ **CostaRicaLiving E-Board** (www.crl-eboard.info): This is an information clearing house site put together by the folks at Costa Rica Living newsgroup. This site is chock-full of useful information, suggestions, reviews, and tips. If you want more information, feel free to join the newsgroup. The active newsgroup deals with a wide range of issues, and its membership includes many longtime residents and bona fide experts.

○ **La Nación Digital** (www.nacion.com): If you can read Spanish, this is an excellent site to read regularly or simply browse. The entire content of the country's paper of record is placed online daily, and there's also an extensive searchable archive. It does maintain a small summary of major news items in English, although this section tends to run about a week behind current events.

2

COSTA RICA
IN DEPTH

P*ura Vida!* (Pure Life!) is Costa Rica's unofficial national slogan, and in many ways it defines the country. You'll hear it exclaimed, proclaimed, and simply stated by Ticos from all walks of life, from children to octogenarians. It can be used as a cheer after your favorite soccer team scores a goal, or as a descriptive response when someone asks you, "How are you?" *("¿Como estas?").* It is symbolic of the easygoing nature of this country's people, politics, and personality.

Costa Rica itself is a mostly rural country with vast areas of protected tropical forests. It is one of the biologically richest places on earth, with a wealth of flora and fauna that attracts and captivates biologists, photographers, ecotourists, and casual visitors alike.

Often called the "Switzerland of Central America," Costa Rica is, and historically has been, a sea of tranquillity in a region that has been troubled by turmoil for centuries. For over 100 years, it has enjoyed a stable democracy and a relatively high standard of living for Latin America. The literacy rate is high, as are medical standards and facilities. Perhaps most significant, at least for proud and peace-loving Costa Ricans, is that this country does not have an army.

COSTA RICA TODAY

Costa Rica has a population of just over four million, more than half of whom live in the Central Valley and are considered as urban. Some 94% of the population is of Spanish or otherwise European descent, and it is not at all unusual to see fair-skinned and blond Costa Ricans. This is largely because the indigenous population in place when the first Spaniards arrived was small and thereafter was quickly reduced to even more of a minority by wars and disease. There are still some remnant indigenous populations, primarily on reservations around the country; the principal tribes include the Bribri, Cabécar, Boruca, and Guayamí. In addition, on the Caribbean coast and in the big cities, there is a substantial population of English-speaking black Creoles who came over from the Antilles to work on building the railroad and on the banana plantations. Racial tension isn't palpable, but it exists, perhaps more out of standard ignorance and fear rather than an organized or articulated prejudice.

In general, Costa Ricans are a friendly and outgoing people. While interacting with visitors, Ticos are very open and helpful. Time has relative meaning to Ticos. Although most tour companies and other establishments operate efficiently, don't expect punctuality, in general.

In a region historically plagued by internal strife and civil wars, Costa Ricans are proud of their peaceful history, political stability, and relatively high level of development. However, this can also translate into arrogance and prejudice toward

FACING PAGE: **Resplendent quetzal.**

COSTA RICA IN DEPTH

Where There Is a Tico, There Is Freedom

In 1989, on a visit to Costa Rica, Uruguayan President Julio María Sanguinetti famously declared: *"Donde hay un costarricense, esté donde esté, hay libertad,"* which is roughly translated in the title above.

Personally, I get a kick out of the version co-opted by a local condiment company in their advertising campaign, which states, "Where there is a Tico, there is Salsa Lizano." I find it to be equally true.

immigrants from neighboring countries, particularly Nicaraguans, who make up a large percentage of the workforce on the banana and coffee plantations.

Roman Catholicism is the official religion of Costa Rica, although freedom to practice any religion is guaranteed by the country's constitution. More than 75% of the population identifies itself as Roman Catholic, while another 14% are part of a number of evangelical Christian congregations. There is a small but visible Jewish community as well. By and large, a large section of Ticos are religiously observant, if not fervent. Although it seems that just as many lead quite secular lives.

Costa Rica is the most technologically advanced and politically stable nation in Central America, and it has the largest middle class. Even the smallest towns have electricity, the water is mostly safe to drink, and the phone system is relatively good and very widespread. Still, the gap between rich and poor has been widening for years. Government, banking, and social institutions are regularly embroiled in scandal. The roads, hospitals, and school systems have been in a slow but steady state of decay for decades. And there are no immediate signs that these matters will improve. Several "Free Zones" and some high-tech investments and production facilities have dramatically changed the face of Costa Rica's economy. Intel, which opened two side-by-side assembly plants in Costa Rica, currently accounts for more than 20% of the country's exports, compared with traditional exports such as coffee (3%) and bananas (8%). Although Intel and other international companies often trumpet a growing gross domestic product, very little of the profits actually make their way into the Costa Rican economy.

Still, tourism is the nation's true principal source of income, surpassing cattle ranching, textiles, and exports of coffee, pineapples, bananas, and Intel microchips. Over two million tourists visit Costa Rica each year, and over half the working population is employed in the tourism and service industries. Ticos whose fathers and grandfathers were farmers and ranchers find themselves hotel owners, tour guides, and waiters. Although most have adapted gracefully and regard the industry as a source of new jobs and opportunities for economic advancement, restaurant and hotel staff can seem gruff and uninterested at times, especially in rural areas. And, unfortunately, an

Bananas at one of Costa Rica's many banana plantations.

increase in the number of visitors has led to an increase in crime, prostitution, and drug trafficking. Common sense and street savvy are required in San José and in many of the more popular tourist destinations.

The global economic crisis of 2008 to 2009 has been slow to hit Costa Rica. Because credit has historically been so tight, there was no major mortgage or banking crisis in the country. Still, early anecdotal reports show tourism down substantially in early 2009, and it's unclear how profound an impact on the economy this and other global factors will have.

LOOKING BACK AT COSTA RICA

EARLY HISTORY Little is known of Costa Rica's history before its colonization by Spanish settlers. The pre-Columbian Indians who made their home in this region of Central America never developed the large cities or advanced culture that flowered farther north in what would become Guatemala, Belize, and Mexico. However, ancient artifacts indicating a strong sense of aesthetics have been unearthed from scattered excavations around the country. Beautiful gold and jade jewelry, intricately carved grinding stones, and artistically painted terra-cotta objects point to a small but highly skilled population.

SPAIN SETTLES COSTA RICA In 1502, on his fourth and last voyage to the New World, Christopher Columbus anchored just offshore from present-day Limón. Whether he actually gave the country its name—"the rich coast"— is open to debate, but the Spaniards never did find much gold or minerals to exploit here.

The earliest Spanish settlers found that, unlike settlements to the north, the native population of Costa Rica was unwilling to submit to slavery. Despite their small numbers, scattered villages, and tribal differences, they fought back against the Spanish until they were overcome by superior firepower and European diseases. When the fighting ended, the European settlers in Costa Rica found that very few Indians were left to force into servitude. The settlers were thus forced to till their own lands, a situation unheard of in other parts of Central America. Few pioneers headed this way because they could settle in Guatemala, with its large native workforce. Costa Rica was nearly forgotten, as the Spanish crown looked elsewhere for riches to plunder and souls to convert.

It didn't take long for Costa Rica's few Spanish settlers to head for the hills, where they found rich volcanic soil and a climate that was less oppressive than in the lowlands. Cartago, the colony's first capital, was founded in 1563, but it was not until the 1700s that additional cities were established in this agriculturally rich region. In the late 18th century, the first coffee plants were introduced, and because these plants thrived in the highlands, Costa Rica began to develop its first cash crop. Unfortunately, it was a long and difficult journey transporting the

The Last Costa Rican Warrior

"Military victories, by themselves, are not worth much. It's what are built from them that matters."
—Jose "Pepe" Figueres

Cartago's Basilica.

coffee to the Caribbean coast and then onward to Europe, where the demand for coffee was growing.

FROM INDEPENDENCE TO THE PRESENT In 1821, Spain granted independence to its colonies in Central America. Costa Rica joined with its neighbors to form the Central American Federation; but in 1838, it withdrew to form a new nation and pursue its own interests. By the mid-1800s, coffee was the country's main export. Free land was given to anyone willing to plant coffee on it, and plantation owners soon grew wealthy and powerful, creating Costa Rica's first elite class. Coffee plantation owners were powerful enough to elect their own representatives to the presidency.

This was a stormy period in Costa Rican history. In 1856, the country was invaded by William Walker, a soldier of fortune from Tennessee who, with the backing of U.S. President James Buchanan, was attempting to fulfill his grandiose dreams of presiding over a slave state in Central America (before his invasion of Costa Rica, he had invaded Nicaragua and Baja, California). The people of Costa Rica, led by their own president, Juan Rafael Mora, marched against Walker and chased him back to Nicaragua. Walker eventually surrendered to a U.S. warship in 1857, but, in 1860, he attacked Honduras, claiming to be the president of that country. The Hondurans, who had had enough of Walker's shenanigans, promptly executed him.

Until 1890, coffee growers had to transport their coffee either by oxcart to the Pacific port of Puntarenas or by boat down the Río Sarapiquí to the Caribbean. In the 1870s, a progressive president proposed a railway from San José to the Caribbean coast to facilitate the transport of coffee to European markets. It took nearly 20 years for this plan to reach fruition, and more than 4,000 workers lost their

The Peace President

"Peace is the most honorable form of exhaustion, and the most exhausting form of honor."
—Oscar Arias

lives constructing the railway, which passed through dense jungles and rugged mountains on its journey from the Central Valley to the coast. Partway through the project, as funds were dwindling, the second chief engineer, Minor Keith, proposed an idea that not only enhanced his fortunes but also changed the course of Central American history. Banana plantations would be developed along the railway right of way (land on either side of the tracks). The export of this crop would help to finance the railway, and, in exchange, Keith would get a 99-year lease on 1,976,000 hectares (800,000 acres) of land with a 20-year tax deferment. The Costa Rican government gave its consent, and in 1878 the first bananas were shipped from the country. In 1899, Keith and a partner formed the United Fruit Company, a business that eventually became the largest landholder in Central America and caused political disputes and wars throughout the region.

In 1889, Costa Rica held what is considered the first free election in Central American history. The opposition candidate won the election, and the control of the government passed from the hands of one political party to those of another without bloodshed or hostilities. Thus, Costa Rica established itself as the region's only true democracy. In 1948, this democratic process was challenged by Rafael Angel Calderón, who had served as the country's president from 1940 to 1944. After losing by a narrow margin, Calderón, who had the backing of the communist labor unions and the Catholic Church, refused to concede the country's leadership to the rightfully elected president, Otillio Ulate, and a civil war ensued. Calderón was eventually defeated by José "Pepe" Figueres. In the wake of this crisis, a new constitution was drafted; among other changes, it abolished Costa Rica's army so that such a revolution could never happen again.

In 1994, history seemed to repeat itself—peacefully this time—when José María Figueres took the reins of government from the son of his father's adversary, Rafael Angel Calderón. In 2001, Otton Solís and his new Citizen's Action Party (PAC) forced the presidential elections into a second round, opening a crack in a two-party system that had become seemingly entrenched for good. Although Solis himself finished third and didn't make it to the runoff, his upstart Citizen's Action Party won quite a few deputy slots.

The battered traditional two-party system was further threatened in 2004, when major corruption scandals became public. Two former presidents are currently under house arrest (Miguel Angel Rodríguez and Rafael Angel Calderón), and another (José María Figueres) is in Switzerland refusing a legislative call to return

The Little Drummer Boy

Costa Rica's national hero is Juan Santamaría. The legend goes that young Juan enlisted as a drummer boy in the campaign against Walker. On April 11, 1865, when Costa Rican troops had a band of Walker's men cornered in a downtown hostel in Rivas, Nicaragua, Santamaría volunteered for a nearly certain suicide mission to set the building on fire. Although he was mortally wounded, Santamaría was successful in torching the building and driving Walker's men out, where they were swiftly routed. Today, April 11 is a national holiday.

and testify, as well as avoiding an Interpol warrant for his capture and arrest. All are implicated, as well as a long list of high-level government employees and deputies, in various financial scandals or bribery cases. While it's unclear how these various scandals and trials will play out in the courts, they have already had a profound effect on the country's political landscape.

In 2006, former president Oscar Arias Sánchez, a Nobel Peace Prize laureate who had presided over the country during the mid-1980s, was re-elected, defeating Otton Solís by an incredibly slim margin. The election was historic on two fronts. First, Arias needed to amend the national law prohibiting reelection in order to run—it still prohibits consecutive terms. More importantly, spurred on by all the scandals, the traditional two-party system fractured into a multitude of smaller parties; Solis's PAC emerged as the second political power in the country, behind Arias's PLN, with the traditional PUSC party almost disintegrating.

The most dramatic event during the early years of Arias's presidency was the October 2007 national referendum on whether or not to allow approval of a free trade agreement between Costa Rica and the United States and other Central American nations. That approval was passed by a very slim margin. Two years later, a series of legislative changes still need final approval before it can go into effect.

ART & ARCHITECTURE

Since it's a small and provincial country, you'll find Costa Rica's culture somewhat similarly limited in size and scope. That said, there are vibrant current scenes in all the major arts—music, literature, architecture, dance, and even film.

Architecture

Costa Rica lacks the large-scale pre-Columbian ceremonial ruins found throughout much of the rest of Mesoamerica. The only notable early archaeological site is **Guayabo** (p. 187). However, only the foundations of a few dwellings, a handful of carved petroglyphs, and some road and water infrastructure are still visible here.

Similarly, Costa Rica lacks the large and well-preserved colonial-era cities found throughout much of the rest of Latin America. The original capital of **Cartago** (p. 184) has some old ruins and a few colonial-era buildings, as well as the country's grandest church, **La Basílica de Nuestra Señora de los Angeles (Basilica of Our Lady of the Angels)** ★ (p. 185), which was built in honor of the country's patron saint, La Negrita, or the Virgin of Guadalupe.

In downtown San José, Barrio Amón and Barrio Otoya are two side-by-side upscale neighborhoods replete with a stately mix of

Colonial-Era Remnant or Crime Deterrent?

Most Costa Rican homes feature steel or iron grating over the doors and windows. I've heard more than one tour guide say this can be traced back to colonial-era architecture and design. However, I'm fairly convinced it is a relatively modern adaptation to the local crime scene.

architectural stylings, with everything from colonial-era residential mansions, to Art Deco apartment buildings, and modern high-rise skyscrapers. One of the standout buildings here is the **Metal School (Escuela Metalica),** which dates to the 1880s, and was shipped over piece-by-piece from France, and erected in place.

On much of the Caribbean coast, you will find mostly wooden houses, built on raised stilts to rise above the wet ground and occasional flooding. Some of these houses feature ornate gingerbread trim.

Much of the rest of the country's architecture is pretty plain. Most residential houses are simple concrete-block affairs, with zinc roofs. A few modern architects are creating names for themselves. **Ronald Zurcher,** who designed the Four Seasons Resort (p. 212) and several other large hotel projects, is one of the shining lights of contemporary Costa Rican architecture.

Art

Unlike Guatemala, Mexico, or even Nicaragua, Costa Rica does not have a strong tradition of local or indigenous arts and crafts. The strong suit of Costa Rican art is European and Western influenced, ranging from neoclassical to modern in style.

Early painters to look out for include **Max Jimenez, Francisco Amighetti, Manuel de la Cruz,** and **Teodorico Quiros.** Recently deceased and living legends of the art world include **Rafa Fernández, Lola Fernández,** and **Cesar Valverde.**

FROM TOP: Guayabo National Park; Wood artwork at Original Grand Gallery in La Fortuna.

Contemporary artists making waves and names for themselves include **Fernando Carballo, Rodolfo Stanley, Lionel Gonzalez, Manuel Zumbado,** and **Karla Solano.**

Sculpture is perhaps one of the strongest aspects of the Costa Rican art scene, with the large bronze works of **Francisco "Paco" Zuñiga** among the best of the genre. Meanwhile, the artists **José Sancho, Edgar Zuñiga,** and **Jiménez Deredia** are all producing internationally acclaimed pieces, many of monumental proportions. You can see examples by all of these sculptors around the country, as well as at San José's downtown **Museo de Arte Costarricense** (p. 156). I also enjoy the whimsical works of **Leda Astorga,** who sculpts and then paints a pantheon of plump and voluptuous figures in interesting, and at times, compromising, poses.

You'll find several excellent museums and galleries in San José (p. 155), as well as in some of the larger and more popular tourist destinations.

THE LAY OF THE LAND

Costa Rica occupies a central spot in the isthmus that joins North and South America. For millennia, this land bridge served as a migratory thoroughfare and mating ground for species native to the once-separate continents. It was also where the Mesoamerican and Andean pre-Columbian indigenous cultures met.

The country comprises only .01% of the earth's landmass, yet it is home to 5% of the planet's biodiversity. More than 10,000 identified species of plants, 880 species of birds, 9,000 species of butterflies and moths, and 500 species of mammals, reptiles, and amphibians are found here.

The key to this biological richness lies in the many distinct life zones and ecosystems found in Costa Rica. It might all seem like one big mass of green to the untrained eye, but the differences are profound.

For more information and details on Costa Rican flora and fauna, see "Costa Rican Wildlife." For information on sustainable issues in the country, see p. 68 in chapter 3.

Costa Rica's Ecosystems

Costa Rica's **lowland rainforests** are true tropical jungles. Some are deluged with more than 200 inches of rainfall per year, and their climate is hot and humid. Trees grow tall and fast, fighting for sunlight in the upper reaches. In fact, life and foliage on the forest floor are surprisingly sparse. The action is typically 30m (98 ft.) up, in the canopy, where long vines stream down, lianas climb up, and bromeliads grow on the branches and trunks of towering hardwood trees. You can find these lowland rainforests along the southern Pacific coast and Osa Peninsula, as well as along the Caribbean coast. **Corcovado, Cahuita,** and **Manuel Antonio** national parks, as well as the **Manzanillo-Gandoca Wildlife Refuge,** are fine examples of lowland rainforests.

At higher altitudes you'll find Costa Rica's famed **cloud forests.** Here the steady flow of moist air meets the mountains and creates a nearly constant mist. Epiphytes—resourceful plants that live cooperatively on the branches and trunks of other trees—grow abundantly in the cloud forests, where they must extract moisture and nutrients from the air. Because cloud forests are found in generally steep, mountainous terrain, the canopy here is lower and less uniform than in lowland rainforests, providing better chances for viewing elusive fauna. Costa Rica's most spectacular cloud forest is the **Monteverde Biological Cloud Forest Reserve** in Guanacaste province (see chapter 9).

At the highest reaches, the cloud forests give way to **elfin forests** and **páramos.** More commonly associated with the South American Andes, a páramo is characterized by a variety of tundralike shrubs and grasses, with a scattering of

Guaria Morada, the national flower.   Hot Lips flower.

twisted, windblown trees. Reptiles, rodents, and raptors are the most common residents here. **Mount Chirripó, Chirripó National Park,** and the **Cerro de la Muerte (Mountain of Death)** are the principal areas of páramo in Costa Rica.

In a few protected areas of Guanacaste, you will still find examples of the otherwise vanishing **tropical dry forest.** During the long and pronounced dry season (late Nov to late Apr), no rain relieves the unabated heat. In an effort to conserve much-needed water, the trees drop their leaves but bloom in a riot of color: Purple jacaranda, scarlet *poró,* and brilliant orange flame-of-the-forest are just a few examples. Then during the rainy season, this deciduous forest is transformed into a lush and verdant landscape. Because the foliage is not so dense, the dry forests are excellent places to view a variety of wildlife species, especially howler monkeys and *pizotes* (coati). Dry forests are found in **Santa Rosa** and **Guanacaste** national parks.

Along the coasts, primarily where river mouths meet the ocean, you will find extensive **mangrove forests** and **swamps.** Around these seemingly monotonous tangles of roots exists one of the most diverse and rich ecosystems in the country. All sorts of fish and crustaceans live in the brackish tidal waters. Caimans and crocodiles cruise the maze of rivers and unmarked canals, and hundreds of herons, ibises, egrets, and other marsh birds nest and feed along the silted banks. Mangrove swamps are often havens for water birds: cormorants, frigate birds, pelicans, and herons. The larger birds tend to nest up high in the canopy, while the smaller ones nestle in the underbrush. The **Gulf of Nicoya** is particularly popular among frigate birds and brown pelicans, as well as all manner of terns and seagulls.

This is also a land of high volcanic and seismic activity. There are three major **volcanic mountain ranges** in Costa Rica, and many of the volcanoes are still active, allowing visitors to experience the awe-inspiring sight of steaming fumaroles and intense lava flows during their stay. Two volcanoes near the capital—Poás and Irazú—are currently active, although relatively quiet. The best places to see volcanic activity are farther north in **Rincón de la Vieja National Park** and at **Arenal Volcano** (see chapters 7 and 9).

In any one spot in Costa Rica, temperatures remain relatively constant year-round. However, as seen above, they vary dramatically according to altitude, from tropically hot and steamy along the coasts to below freezing at the highest elevations.

Searching for Wildlife

Animals in the forests are predominantly nocturnal. When they are active in the daytime, they are usually elusive and on the watch for predators. Birds are easier to spot in clearings or secondary forests than they are in primary forests. Unless you have lots of experience in the Tropics, your best hope for enjoying a walk through the jungle lies in employing a trained and knowledgeable guide. (By the way, if it's been raining a lot and the trails are muddy, a good pair of rubber boots comes in handy. These are usually provided by the lodges or at the sites, where necessary.)

Here are a few helpful hints:

- **Listen.** Pay attention to rustling in the leaves; whether it's monkeys up above or *pizotes* on the ground, you're most likely to hear an animal before seeing one.

- **Keep quiet.** Noise will scare off animals and prevent you from hearing their movements and calls.

- **Don't try too hard.** Soften your focus and allow your peripheral vision to take over. This way you can catch glimpses of motion and then focus in on the prey.

- **Bring binoculars.** It's also a good idea to practice a little first to get the hang of them. It would be a shame to be fiddling around and staring into space while everyone else in your group oohs and aahs over a quetzal.

Jaguar.

- **Dress appropriately.** You'll have a hard time focusing your binoculars if you're busy swatting mosquitoes. Light, long pants and long-sleeved shirts are your best bet. Comfortable hiking boots are a real boon, except where heavy rubber boots are necessary. Avoid loud colors; the better you blend in with your surroundings, the better your chances are of spotting wildlife.

- **Be patient.** The jungle isn't on a schedule. However, your best shots at seeing forest fauna are in the very early morning and late afternoon hours.

- **Read up.** Familiarize yourself with what you're most likely to see. Most lodges and hotels have a copy of *A Guide to the Birds of Costa Rica* and other wildlife field guides, although it's always best to have your own. A good all-around book to use is Carrol Henderson's *The Field Guide to the Wildlife of Costa Rica.*

COSTA RICA IN POPULAR CULTURE: BOOKS, FILM & MUSIC

Books

Though Costa Rica's literary output is sparsely translated and little known outside of Costa Rica, there are some notable authors to look out for, especially if you can read in Spanish.

Some of the books mentioned below might be difficult to track down in U.S. bookstores, but you'll find them all in abundance in Costa Rica. A good place to check for most of these titles is **Seventh Street Books,** on Calle 7 between avenidas 1 and Central in San José (☎2256-8251).

GENERAL INTEREST For a straightforward, albeit somewhat dry, historical overview, there's *The History of Costa Rica,* by Ivan Molina and Steven Palmer. For a more readable look into Costa Rican society, pick up *The Ticos: Culture and Social Change* by Richard, Karen, and Mavis Biesanz, an examination of the country's politics and culture, by the authors of the out-of-print *The Costa Ricans.* Another work worth checking out is *The Costa Rica Reader: History, Culture, Politics,* a broad selection of stories, essays, and excerpts edited by Steven Palmer and Ivan Molina, the authors of the history book mentioned above.

To learn more about the life and culture of Costa Rica's Talamanca coast, an area populated by Afro-Caribbean people whose forebears emigrated from Caribbean islands in the early 19th century, look for *What Happen: A Folk-History of Costa Rica's Talamanca Coast* by Paula Palmer. This book is a collection of oral histories taken from a wide range of local characters.

FICTION & POETRY *Costa Rica: A Traveler's Literary Companion,* edited by Barbara Ras and with a foreword by Oscar Arias Sánchez, is a collection of short stories by Costa Rican writers, organized by region of the country. If you're lucky, you might find a copy of *Stories of Tatamundo,* by Fabian Dobles, or *Lo Peor/The Worst,* by Fernando Contreras.

Young adults will enjoy Kristin Joy Pratt's *A Walk in the Rainforest,* while younger children will like the beautifully illustrated *The Forest in the Clouds,* by Sneed Collard and Michael Rothman, and *The Umbrella.* **Pachanga Kids ★** (www.pachangakids.com) has published several illustrated bilingual children's books with delightful illustrations by Ruth Angulo, including *Mar Azucarada/Sugar Sea* by Roberto Boccanera and *El Coyote y la Luciernaga/The Coyote and the Firefly* by Yazmin Ross, which (full disclosure) I translated, and which includes a musical CD that features your humble author's singing. Another bilingual children's book worth checking out is *Zari & Marinita: Adventures in a Costa Rican Rainforest.*

One of the most important pieces in the Costa Rican canon, Carlos Luis Fallas's 1941 tome *Mamita Yunai* is a stark look at the impact of the large banana giant United Fruit on the country. More recently, Fernando Contreras takes up where his predecessor left off in *Unico Mirando al Mar,* which describes the conditions of the poor, predominantly children, who scavenge Costa Rica's garbage dumps.

In the field of poetry, **Eunice Odio, Juaquín Gutiérrez,** and **Jorge Debravo** are early poets who set the gold standard. Their more modern successors include **Alfonso Chase, Virginia Grutter, Laureano Alban, Ana Istaru, Osvaldo Sauma,** and **Luis Chavez.**

NATURAL HISTORY I think that everyone coming to Costa Rica should read *Tropical Nature* by Adrian Forsyth and Ken Miyata. My all-time favorite book on tropical biology, this is a wonderfully written and lively collection of tales and adventures by two Neotropical biologists who spent quite some time in the forests of Costa Rica.

Mario A. Boza's beautiful *Costa Rica National Parks* has been reissued in an elegant coffee-table edition. Other worthwhile coffee-table books include *Rainforests: Costa Rica and Beyond* ★ by Adrian Forsyth, with photographs by Michael and Patricia Fogden, and *Costa Rica: A Journey Through Nature* by Adrian Hepworth.

For an introduction to a wide range of Costa Rican fauna, there's *The Field Guide to the Wildlife of Costa Rica,* by Carrol Henderson, or *Costa Rica: Traveller's Wildlife Guides,* by Les Beletsky. Both pack a lot of useful information into a concise package and make great field guides for amateur naturalists and inquisitive tourists.

A Guide to the Birds of Costa Rica, by F. Gary Stiles and Alexander Skutch, is an invaluable guide to identifying the many birds you'll see during your stay. Most guides and nature lodges have a copy of this book on hand. This classic faces competition from the more recent *Birds of Costa Rica,* by Richard Garrigues and Robert Dean. Bird-watchers might also enjoy Dennis Rodgers's *Site Guides: Costa Rica & Panama,* which details each country's bird-watching bounty by site and region.

Other interesting natural-history books that will give you a look at the plants and animals of Costa Rica include *Costa Rica Natural History,* by Daniel Janzen; *A Guide to Tropical Plants of Costa Rica,* by Willow Zuchowsky; *The Natural History of Costa Rican Mammals,* by Mark Wainwright; *A Guide to the Amphibians and Reptiles of Costa Rica,* by Twan Leenders; and the classic *A Neotropical Companion,* by John C. Kricher, reissued in an expanded edition with color photos.

For a rather complete list of field guides, check out www.zonatropical.net.

Film

Costa Rica has a budding and promising young film industry. Local feature films like *Tropix, Caribe,* and *Passport* are all out on subtitled DVD. In 2008, *El Camino (The Path)* by Costa Rican filmmaker Ishtar Yasin Gutiérrez was screened at the Berlin Film Festival. Several other feature films are expected to be produced in 2009 and 2010, including *Del Amor y Otros Demonios,* based on a Gabriel García Márquez novel.

If you want to see Costa Rica used simply as a backdrop, the major motion picture productions of *1492,* by Ridley Scott and starring Gerard Depardieu and Sigourney Weaver; *Congo,* featuring Laura Linney and Ernie Hudson; and *The Blue Butterfly,* with William Hurt, all feature sets and scenery from around the country.

There's a small **Costa Rican Film and Video festival** (www.centro decine.go.cr) each November in San José.

Music

Several musical traditions and styles meet and mingle in Costa Rica. The northern Guanacaste region is a hotbed of folk music that is strongly influenced by the *marimba* (wooden xylophone) traditions of Guatemala and Nicaragua, while also featuring guitars, maracas, and the occasional harp. On the Caribbean coast you can hear traditional calypso sung by descendants of the original black workers

TICO etiquette & CUSTOMS

In general, Costa Ricans are easygoing, friendly, and informal. That said, Ticos tend to be conservative and try to treat everyone very respectfully. Moreover, in conversation, Ticos are relatively formal. When addressing someone, they use the formal *usted* in most instances, reserving the familiar *vos* for close friends, family, and children or teenagers.

Upon greeting or saying goodbye, both sexes shake hands, although across genders, a light kiss on one cheek is common.

Proud of their neutrality and lack of armed forces, everyday Costa Ricans are uncomfortable with confrontation. What may seem like playful banter or justified outrage to a foreign tourist may be taken very badly by a Tico.

In some cases, especially in the service industry, a Tico may tell you what he or she thinks you want to hear, just to avoid a confrontation—even if he or she knows there's little chance of follow-through or ultimate customer satisfaction. I've also had, on more than one occasion, a Tico give me wrong directions, instead of telling me they didn't know the way.

The two words mentioned at the start of this chapter—*pura vida*—will go a long way to endearing you to most Ticos. In conversation, *pura vida* is used as a greeting, exclamation, adjective, and general space filler. Feel free to sprinkle a *pura vida* or two into your conversations with locals. I'm sure it will be well received. For more tips on talking like a Tico, see "Some Typical Tico Words & Phrases" on p. 491.

Tico men dress conservatively. It is very rare to see Costa Rican men wear short pants except at the beach. In most towns and cities, while accepted, tourists will stand out when wearing short pants, sandals, and other typical beach, golf, or vacation wear. Costa Rican women, on the other hand, especially young women, do tend to show some skin in everyday, and even business, situations. Still, be respectful in your dress, especially if you plan on visiting churches, small towns, or local families.

Women, no matter how they dress, may find themselves on the receiving end of whistles, honks, hoots, hisses, and catcalls. For more information on this manifestation of Costa Rican machismo, see "Women Travelers" on p. 67.

Punctuality is not a Costa Rican strong suit. Ticos often show up anywhere from 15 minutes to an hour or more late to meetings and appointments—this is known as *la hora tica,* or "Tico time." That said, buses and local airlines, tour operators, movie theaters, and most businesses do tend to run on a relatively timely schedule.

brought over to build the railroads and tend the banana plantations. Roving bands play a mix of guitar, banjo, washtub bass, and percussion in the bars and restaurants of Cahuita and Puerto Viejo.

There's also a healthy contemporary music scene. The jazz-fusion trio **Editus** has won two Grammy awards for its work with Panamanian salsa giant (and movie star and Tourism minister) **Rubén Blades.** Meanwhile, **Malpaís,** the closest thing Costa Rica has to a super-group, is a pop-rock outfit that is tearing it up in Costa Rica and around Central America.

You should also seek out discs by **Cantoamérica,** which plays upbeat dance music ranging from salsa to calypso to merengue. Jazz pianist **Manuel Obregón** (a member of Malpaís) has several excellent solo albums out, including *Simbiosis,* on which he improvises along with the sounds of Costa Rica's wildlife, waterfalls, and weather; as well as his work with the *Papaya Orchestra,* a collaboration and gathering of musicians from around Central America.

Local label **Papaya Music ★** (www.papayamusic.com) has done an excellent job promoting and producing albums by Costa Rican musicians in a range of styles and genres. Their offerings range from the Guanacasteca folk songs of **Max Goldemberg,** to the boleros of **Ray Tico,** to the original calypso of **Walter "Gavitt" Ferguson.** You can find their discs at gift shops and record stores around the country, as well as at airport souvenir stores.

Classical music lovers will want to head to San José, where there's a symphony orchestra, youth symphony, opera company, and choir. The local symphony sometimes features the works of local composers like **Benjamin Guitiérrez** and **Eddie Mora.** On occasion, small-scale music festivals will bring classical offerings to some of the beach and inland tourist destinations around the country.

Bars and discos around the country spin salsa, merengue, and cumbia, as well as more modern grooves that include house, electronic, trip-hop, and reggaeton.

EATING & DRINKING IN COSTA RICA

Costa Rican food is not especially memorable. Perhaps that's why there's so much international food available here. San José remains the unquestioned gastronomic capital of the country, and here you can find many of the cuisines of the world served at moderate prices. At even the more expensive restaurants, it's

 Coconut, Straight Up

Throughout Costa Rica (particularly on the coastal road between Limón and Cahuita), keep your eye out for roadside stands selling fresh, green coconuts, or *pipas* in Spanish. Green coconuts have very little meat, but are filled with copious amounts of a slightly sweet, clear liquid that is amazingly refreshing. According to local legend, this liquid is pure enough to be used as plasma in an emergency situation. Armed with a machete, the *pipa* seller will cut out the top and stick in a straw. In the best of cases, the *pipa* will have been cooled over ice. The entire thing should cost $1 or less.

hard to spend more than $50 per person unless you really splurge on drinks and wine. It gets even cheaper outside the city. You can find several excellent French, Italian, and contemporary fusion restaurants around the San José area, as well as Peruvian, Japanese, Swiss, and Spanish establishments.

However, if you really want to save money, Costa Rican, or *típico*, food is always the cheapest nourishment available. It's primarily served in *sodas*, Costa Rica's equivalent of diners.

Outside the capital and major tourist destinations, your options get very limited very fast. In fact, many beach destinations are so remote that you have no choice but to eat in the hotel's dining room. Even on the more accessible beaches, the only choices aside from the hotel dining rooms are often cheap local places or overpriced tourist traps serving indifferent meals. At remote jungle lodges, the food is usually served buffet- or family-style and can range from bland to inspired, depending on who's doing the cooking, and turnover is high.

If you see a restaurant billing itself as a **mirador,** it means it has a view. If you are driving around the country, don't miss an opportunity to dine with a view at some little roadside restaurant. The food might not be fantastic, but the scenery will be.

I have separated restaurant listings throughout this book into three price categories, based on the average cost of a meal per person, including tax and service charge. The categories are **Expensive,** more than $25; **Moderate,** $10 to $25; and **Inexpensive,** less than $10. (Note, however, that individual items in the listings—entrees, for instance—do not include the sales or service taxes.) Keep in mind that there is an additional 13% sales tax, as well as a 10% service charge. Ticos rarely tip, but that doesn't mean that you shouldn't. If the service was particularly good and attentive, you should probably leave a little extra.

Meals & Dining Customs

Rice and beans are the bases of Costa Rican meals—all three of them. At breakfast, they're called *gallo pinto* and come with everything from eggs to steak to seafood. At lunch or dinner, rice and beans are an integral part of a *casado* (which translates as "married" and is the name for the local version of a blue-plate special). A *casado* usually consists of cabbage-and-tomato salad, fried plantains (a starchy, banana-like fruit), and a chicken, fish, or meat dish of some sort. On the Caribbean coast, rice and beans are called "rice 'n' beans," and are cooked in coconut milk.

Dining hours in Costa Rica are flexible but generally follow North American customs. Some downtown restaurants in San José are open 24 hours; however, expensive restaurants tend to be open for lunch between 11am and 3pm and for dinner between 6 and 11pm.

Dish of red snapper.

APPETIZERS Known as *bocas* in Costa Rica, appetizers are served with drinks in most bars. Often the *bocas* are free, but even if they aren't, they're very inexpensive. Popular *bocas* include *gallos* (tortillas piled with meat, chicken, cheese, or beans), *ceviche* (a marinated seafood salad), tamales (stuffed cornmeal patties wrapped and steamed inside banana leaves), *patacones* (fried green plantain chips), and fried yuca.

SANDWICHES & SNACKS Ticos love to snack, and there's a large variety of tasty little sandwiches and snacks available on the street, at snack bars, and in *sodas*. *Arreglados* are little meat-filled sandwiches, as are *tortas*, which are served on little rolls with a bit of salad tucked into them. Tacos, tamales, *gallos* (see above), and *empanadas* (turnovers) also are quite common.

MEAT Costa Rica is beef country, having converted much of its rainforest land to pastures for raising beef cattle. Consequently, beef is cheap and plentiful, although it might be a bit tougher—and cut and served thinner—than it is back home. One typical local dish is called *olla de carne*, a bowl of beef broth with large chunks of meat, local tubers, and corn. Spit-roasted chicken is also very popular here and is surprisingly tender.

SEAFOOD Costa Rica has two coasts, and, as you'd expect, plenty of seafood is available everywhere in the country. *Corvina* (sea bass) is the most commonly served fish and is prepared innumerable ways, including as *ceviche*. (**Be careful:** In many cheaper restaurants, particularly in San José, shark meat is often sold as corvina.) You should also come across *pargo* (red snapper), *dorado* (mahimahi), and tuna on some menus, especially along the coasts. Although Costa Rica is a major exporter of shrimp and lobster, both are relatively expensive and in short supply here.

VEGETABLES On the whole, you'll find vegetables surprisingly lacking in the meals you're served in Costa Rica—usually nothing more than a little pile of shredded cabbage topped with a slice or two of tomato. For a much more satisfying and filling salad, order *palmito* (hearts of palm salad). The heart

(actually the stalk or trunk of these small palms) is first boiled and then chopped into circular pieces and served with other fresh vegetables, with a salad dressing on top. If you want something more than this, you'll have to order a side dish such as *picadillo*, a stew or purée of vegetables with a bit of meat in it.

Though they are giant relatives of bananas and are technically considered a fruit, *plátanos* (plantains) are really more like vegetables and require cooking before they can be eaten. Green plantains have a very starchy flavor and consistency, but they become as sweet as candy as they ripen. Fried *plátanos* are one

A typical *casado*.

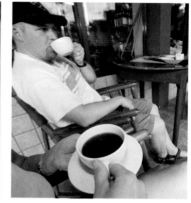

Tropical fruit.

Tourist sipping coffee.

of my favorite dishes. Yuca (manioc root or cassava in English) is another starchy staple root vegetable in Costa Rica.

One more vegetable worth mentioning is the *pejibaye,* a form of palm fruit that looks like a miniature orange coconut. Boiled *pejibayes* are frequently sold from carts on the streets of San José. When cut in half, a *pejibaye* reveals a large seed surrounded by soft, fibrous flesh. You can eat it plain, but it's usually topped with a dollop of mayonnaise.

FRUITS Costa Rica has a wealth of delicious tropical fruits. The most common are mangoes (the season begins in May), papayas, pineapples, melons, and bananas. Other fruits include *marañón,* which is the fruit of the cashew tree and has orange or yellow glossy skin; *granadilla* or *maracuyá* (passion fruit); *mamón chino,* which Asian travelers will immediately recognize as rambutan; and *carambola* (star fruit).

DESSERTS *Queque seco,* literally "dry cake," is the same as pound cake. *Tres leches* cake, on the other hand, is so moist that you almost need to eat it with a spoon. Flan is a typical custard dessert. It often comes as either *flan de caramelo* (caramel) or *flan de coco* (coconut). Numerous other sweets are available, many of which are made with condensed milk and raw sugar. *Cajetas* are popular handmade candies, made from sugar and various mixes of evaporated, condensed, and powdered milk. They are sold in differing-size bits and chunks at most *pulperías* (general stores) and streetside food stands.

Beverages

Frescos, refrescos, and *jugos naturales* are my favorite drinks in Costa Rica. They are usually made with fresh fruit and milk or water. Among the more common fruits used are mangoes, papayas, blackberries, and pineapples. You'll also come across *maracuyá* (passion fruit) and *carambola* (star fruit). Some of the more unusual frescos are *horchata* (made with rice flour and a lot of cinnamon) and *chan* (made with the seed of a plant found mostly in Guanacaste—definitely an acquired taste). The former is wonderful; the latter requires an open mind (it's reputed to be good for the digestive system). Order *un fresco con leche sin hielo* (a *fresco* with milk but without ice) if you're avoiding untreated water.

If you're a coffee drinker, you might be disappointed here. Most of the best coffee has traditionally been targeted for export, and Ticos tend to prefer theirs weak and sugary. Better hotels and restaurants are starting to cater to gringo and European tastes and are serving up superior blends. If you want black coffee, ask for *café negro*; if you want it with milk, order *café con leche.*

For something different for your morning beverage, ask for *agua dulce,* a warm drink made from melted sugar cane and served either with milk or lemon, or straight.

WATER Although water in most of Costa Rica is safe to drink, bottled water is readily available and is a good option if you're worried about an upset stomach. *Agua mineral,* or simply soda, is sparkling water in Costa Rica. If you like your water without bubbles, request *aqua mineral sin gas,* or *agua en botella.*

BEER, WINE & LIQUOR The German presence in Costa Rica over the years has produced several fine beers, which are fairly inexpensive. Most Costa Rican beers are light pilsners. The most popular brands are Bavaria, Imperial, and Pilsen. I personally can't tell much of a difference between any of them. Licensed local versions of Heineken and Rock Ice are also available.

TIPS ON shopping IN COSTA RICA

International laws prohibit trade in endangered wildlife, so don't buy any plants or animals, even if they're readily for sale. Do not buy any kind of sea-turtle products (including jewelry); wild birds; lizards, snakes, or cat skins; corals; or orchids (except those grown commercially). No matter how unique, beautiful, insignificant, or inexpensive it might seem, your purchase will directly contribute to the further hunting of these species.

Costa Rica is not known for its handicrafts. So scant are its offerings that most tourist shops sell Guatemalan clothing, Panamanian appliquéd textiles, El Salvadoran painted wood souvenirs, and Nicaraguan rocking chairs.

Still, Costa Rica does have a town, Sarchí, that's filled with handicraft shops. **Sarchí** is best known as the home of the colorfully painted Costa Rican **oxcart,** reproductions of which are manufactured in various scaled-down sizes. These make excellent gifts. (Larger oxcarts can be easily disassembled and shipped to your home.) There's also a lot of furniture made here.

The small town of **Guaitíl,** in central Guanacaste, is famous for its pottery.

You can find examples of this low-fired simple ceramic work in many gift shops.

There's quite a bit of Costa Rican woodcarving, but it is, for the most part, either tourist-souvenir wooden bowls, napkin holders, and the like, or elegant and expensive art pieces. One exception is the work of **Barry Biensanz,** whose excellent hardwood creations are sold at better gift shops around the country.

You might also run across **carved masks** made by the indigenous Boruca people of southern Costa Rica. These full-size balsa-wood masks come in a variety of styles, both painted and unpainted, and run anywhere from $20 to $150, depending on the quality of workmanship.

You can find imported wines at reasonable prices in the better restaurants throughout the country. You can usually save money by ordering a Chilean wine over a Californian or European one.

Costa Rica distills a wide variety of liquors, and you'll save money by ordering these over imported brands. The national liquor is *guaro,* a crude cane liquor that's often combined with a soft drink or tonic. When drinking it straight, it's customary to follow a shot with a bite into a fresh lime covered in salt. If you want to try *guaro,* stick to the Cacique brand.

Several brands and styles of coffee-based liqueurs are also produced in Costa Rica. **Café Rica** is similar to Kahlúa, and you can also find several types of coffee cream liqueurs. The folks at **Café Britt** produce their own line of coffee liqueurs which are quite good and available in most supermarkets, liquor stores, and tourist shops.

Costa Ricans also drink a lot of rum. The premier Costa Rican rum is **Centenario,** but I recommend that you opt for the Nicaraguan **Flor de Caña ★** or Cuban **Havana Club ★**, both of which are far superior rums. *Note:* Because of the trade embargo, it is illegal to bring Havana Club into the United States.

A few other items worth keeping an eye out for include reproductions of pre-**Columbian gold jewelry** and **carved-stone figurines.** The former are available as either solid gold, silver, or gold-plated. The latter, although interesting, are extremely heavy.

Across the country you'll find hammocks for sale. I personally find the Costa Rican **hammocks** a little crude and unstable. The same vendors usually have single-person hanging chairs, which are strung similarly to the full-size hammocks and are a better bet.

It's especially hard to capture the subtle shades and colors of the rainforests and cloud forests, and many a traveler has gone home thinking that his or her undeveloped film contained the full beauty of the jungle, only to return from the photo developer with 36 bright-green blurs. To avoid this heartache, you might want to pick up some **postcards** of the sights you want

to remember forever and send them to yourself.

Finally, one item that you'll see at gift shops around the country is **Cuban cigars.** Although these are illegal to bring into the United States, they are perfectly legal and readily available in Costa Rica.

See the "Joe to Go" box on p. 167 for tips on buying **coffee** in Costa Rica.

PLANNING YOUR TRIP TO COSTA RICA

Costa Rica is no longer news. It seems like almost everybody's already been, or knows someone who's been. As Costa Rica has matured as a tourist destination, things have gotten easier and easier for international travelers. There are more and more hotels, restaurants, and rental car agencies to choose from, and services have been expanding and improving across the board. That said, most travelers—even experienced travelers and repeat visitors—will want to do some serious pretrip planning.

Some basic questions need to be addressed right from the get-go. When is the best time to go to Costa Rica? Should you rent a car (or will you need 4WD), and what will it cost? What are the hotels like? How much should you budget for your trip? How can you save money? How does the local currency work, and should you use cash or credit cards? These are just a few of the important questions that this chapter answers so that you can be prepared when you arrive in Costa Rica.

The question of where to go is actually addressed elsewhere—in fact, throughout the book. For a start in narrowing down your choices, read the "Suggested Itineraries" and "The Active Vacation Planner" chapters 4 and 5, as well as my "Best Of" selections in chapter 1 and individual destination chapters, to see what most strikes your fancy.

For additional help in planning your trip and for more on-the-ground resources in Costa Rica, please turn to the "Fast Facts" on p. 482.

WHEN TO GO

Costa Rica's high season for tourism runs from late November to late April, which coincides almost perfectly with the chill of winter in the United States, Canada, and Great Britain, and includes Christmas, New Years, Easter, and most school spring breaks. The high season is also the dry season. If you want some unadulterated time on a tropical beach and a little less rain during your rainforest experience, this is the time to come. During this period (and especially around the Christmas holiday), the tourism industry operates at full tilt—prices are higher, attractions are more crowded, and reservations need to be made in advance.

Local tourism operators often call the tropical rainy season (May through mid-Nov) the "green season." The adjective is appropriate. At this time of year, even brown and barren Guanacaste province becomes lush and verdant. I personally love traveling around Costa Rica during the rainy season (but then again, I'm not trying to flee cold snaps in Canada). It's easy to find or at least negotiate

FACING PAGE: **Sunset over the Pacific Ocean.**

reduced rates, there are far fewer fellow travelers, and the rain is often limited to a few hours each afternoon (although you can occasionally get socked in for a week at a time). *A drawback:* Some of the country's rugged roads become downright impassable without four-wheel-drive during the rainy season.

Climate

Costa Rica is a tropical country and has distinct wet and dry seasons. However, some regions are rainy all year, and others are very dry and sunny for most of the year. Temperatures vary primarily with elevations, not with seasons: On the coasts it's hot all year; in the mountains it can be cool at night any time of year. Frost is common at the highest elevations (3,000–3,600m/9,840–11,808 ft.).

Average Daytime High Temperatures & Rainfall in San José

	JAN	FEB	MAR	APR	MAY	JUNE	JULY	AUG	SEPT	OCT	NOV	DEC
TEMP. ºF	75	76	79	79	80	79	77	78	79	77	77	75
TEMP. ºC	24	24	26	26	27	26	25	26	26	25	25	24
DAYS OF RAIN	1.3	1.5	2.2	4.2	11.5	14.5	13.7	14.5	18.1	17.9	8.6	2.3

Generally, the **rainy season** (or "green season") is from May to mid-November. Costa Ricans call this wet time of year their winter. The **dry season,** considered summer by Costa Ricans, is from mid-November to April. In Guanacaste, the dry northwestern province, the dry season lasts several weeks longer than in other places. Even in the rainy season, days often start sunny, with rain falling in the afternoon and evening. On the Caribbean coast, especially south of Limón, you can count on rain year-round, although this area gets less rain in September and October than the rest of the country.

In general, the best time of year to visit weather-wise is in December and January, when everything is still green from the rains, but the sky is clear.

Holidays

Because Costa Rica is a Roman Catholic country, most of its holidays are church-related. The biggies are Christmas, New Year's, and Easter, which are all celebrated for several days. Keep in mind that Holy Week (Easter week) is the biggest holiday time in Costa Rica, and many families head for the beach. (This is the last holiday before school starts.) Also, there is no public transportation on Holy Thursday or Good Friday. Government offices and banks are closed on official holidays, transportation services are reduced, and stores and markets might also close.

Official holidays in Costa Rica include **January 1** (New Year's Day), **March 19** (St. Joseph's Day), Thursday and Friday of Holy Week, **April 11** (Juan Santamaría's Day), **May 1** (Labor Day), **June 29** (St. Peter and St. Paul Day), **July 25** (annexation of the province of Guanacaste), **August 2** (Virgin of Los Angeles's Day), **August 15** (Mother's Day), **September 15** (Independence Day), **October 12** (Discovery of America/Día de la Raza), **December 8** (Immaculate Conception of the Virgin Mary), **December 24** and **25** (Christmas), and **December 31** (New Year's Eve).

Calendar of Events

Some of the events listed here might be considered more of a happening than an event—there's not, for instance, a Virgin of Los Angeles PR Committee that readily dispenses information. If I haven't listed a contact number, your best bet is to call the Costa Rican Tourist Board (ICT) at ☎866/COSTA RICA in the U.S. and Canada, or 2223-1733 in Costa Rica, or visit www.visitcostarica.com.

For an exhaustive list of events beyond those listed here, check http://events.frommers.com, where you'll find a searchable, up-to-the-minute roster of what's happening in cities all over the world.

JANUARY

Copa del Café (Coffee Cup), San José. Matches for this international event on the junior tennis tour are held at the Costa Rica Country Club (☎2228-9333). First week in January.

Fiesta of Palmares, Palmares. Perhaps the largest and best organized of the traditional *fiestas,* it includes bull-fights, a horseback parade *(tope),* and many concerts, carnival rides, and food booths. First 2 weeks in January.

Fiesta of Santa Cruz, Santa Cruz, Guanacaste. This religious celebration honors the Black Christ of Esquipulas (a famous Guatemalan statue), featuring folk dancing, marimba music, and bull-fights. Mid-January.

Fiesta of the Diablitos, Rey Curré village near San Isidro de El General. Boruca Indians wearing wooden devil and bull masks perform dances representative of the Spanish conquest of Central America; there are fireworks displays and an Indian handicrafts market. Late January.

MARCH

Día del Boyero (Oxcart Drivers' Day), San Antonio de Escazú. Colorfully painted oxcarts parade through this suburb of San José, and local priests bless the oxen. Second Sunday in March.

National Orchid Show, San José. Orchid growers throughout the world gather to show their wares, trade tales and secrets, and admire the hundreds of species on display. Contact the Costa Rican Tourist Board for location and dates in 2010. Mid-March.

APRIL

Holy Week. Religious processions are held in cities and towns throughout the country. Week before Easter.

Juan Santamaría Day, Alajuela. Costa Rica's national hero is honored with parades, concerts, and dances. April 11.

MAY

Carrera de San Juan. The country's biggest marathon runs through the mountains, from the outskirts of Cartago to the outskirts of San José. May 17.

JULY

Fiesta of the Virgin of the Sea, Puntarenas. A regatta of colorfully decorated boats carrying a statue of Puntarenas's patron saint marks this festival. A similar event is held at Playa de Coco. Saturday closest to July 16.

Annexation of Guanacaste Day, Liberia. Tico-style bullfights, folk dancing, horseback parades, rodeos, concerts, and other events celebrate the day when this region became part of Costa Rica. July 25.

AUGUST

Fiesta of the Virgin of Los Angeles, Cartago. This is the annual pilgrimage day of the patron saint of Costa Rica. Many people walk from San José 24km (15 miles) to the basilica in Cartago. August 2.

Día de San Ramón, San Ramón. More than two dozen statues of saints from various towns are brought to San Ramón, where they are paraded through the streets. August 31.

SEPTEMBER

Costa Rica's Independence Day, celebrated all over the country. One of the most distinctive aspects of this festival is the nighttime marching band parades of children in their school uniforms, who play the national anthem on steel xylophones. September 15.

International Beach Clean-Up Day. This is a good excuse to chip in and help clean up the beleaguered shoreline of your favorite beach. Third Saturday in September.

OCTOBER

Fiesta del Maíz, Upala. At this celebration of corn, local beauty queens wear outfits made from corn plants. October 12.

Limón Carnival/Día de la Raza, Limón. A smaller version of Mardi Gras, complete with floats and dancing in the streets, commemorates Columbus's discovery of Costa Rica. Week of October 12.

NOVEMBER

All Souls' Day/Día de los Muertos, celebrated countrywide. Although it is not as elaborate or ritualized as in Mexico, most Costa Ricans take some time this day to remember the dead with flowers and trips to cemeteries. November 2.

DECEMBER

Día de la Pólvora, San Antonio de Belén and Jesús María de San Mateo. Fireworks honor Our Lady of the Immaculate Conception. December 8.

Fiesta de los Negritos, Boruca. Boruca Indians celebrate the feast day of their patron saint, the Virgin of the Immaculate Conception, with costumed dances and traditional music. December 8.

Fiesta de la Yeguita, Nicoya. A statue of the Virgin of Guadalupe is paraded through the streets, accompanied by traditional music and dancing. December 12.

Las Posadas. Countrywide, children and carolers go door-to-door seeking lodging in a reenactment of Joseph and Mary's search for a place to stay. Begins December 15.

El Tope and Carnival, San José. The streets of downtown belong to horses and their riders in a proud recognition of the country's important agricultural heritage. The next day, those same streets are taken over by carnival floats, marching bands, and street dancers. December 26 and 27.

Festejos Populares, San José. Bullfights and a pretty respectable bunch of carnival rides, games of chance, and fast-food stands are set up at the fairgrounds in Zapote. Last week of December.

ENTRY REQUIREMENTS

Passports

Citizens of the United States, Canada, Great Britain, and most European nations may visit Costa Rica for a maximum of 90 days. No visa is necessary, but you must have a valid passport, which you should carry with you at all times while you're in Costa Rica. Citizens of Australia, Ireland, and New Zealand can enter the country without a visa and stay for 30 days, although once in the country, visitors can apply for an extension.

If you overstay your visa or original entry stamp, you will have to pay around $45 for an exit visa. If you need to get an exit visa, a travel agent in San José can usually obtain one for a small fee and save you the hassle of dealing with Immigration. If you want to stay longer than the validity of your entry stamp or visa, the easiest thing to do is cross the border into Panama or Nicaragua for 72 hours and then reenter Costa Rica on a new entry stamp or visa. However, be careful: Periodically the Costa Rican government has cracked down on "perpetual tourists"; if it notices a continued pattern of exits and entries designed simply to support an extended stay, it might deny you reentry.

If you need a visa or have other questions about Costa Rica, you can contact any of the following Costa Rican embassies or consulates: in the **United States,** 2114 S St. NW, Washington, DC 20008 (☎202/234-2945; www. costarica-embassy.org for consulate locations around the country); in **Canada,** 325 Dalhousie St., Ste. 407, Ottawa, Ontario K1N 5TA (☎613/562-2855); and in **Great Britain,** 14 Lancaster Gate, London, England W2 3LH (☎020/7706-8844). There are no Costa Rican embassies in Australia or New Zealand, but you could try contacting the honorary consul in Sydney, Australia, at Level 11, De La Sala House, 30 Clarence St., Sydney NSW 2000 (☎02/9261-1177).

Customs

Visitors to Costa Rica are permitted to bring in all manner of items for personal use, including cameras, video cameras and accessories, tape recorders, personal computers, and music players. Customs officials in Costa Rica seldom check tourists' luggage.

WHAT YOU CAN TAKE HOME FROM COSTA RICA

For information on what you're allowed to bring home, contact one of the following agencies:

U.S. CITIZENS: U.S. Customs & Border Protection (CBP), 1300 Pennsylvania Ave., NW, Washington, DC 20229 (☎877/287-8667; www.cbp.gov).

CANADIAN CITIZENS: Canada Border Services Agency (☎800/461-9999 in Canada, or 204/983-3500; www.cbsa-asfc.gc.ca).

U.K. CITIZENS: HM Customs & Excise (☎0845/010-9000, or 020/8929-0152 from outside the U.K.; www.hmce.gov.uk).

AUSTRALIAN CITIZENS: Australian Customs Service (☎1300/363-263; www. customs.gov.au).

NEW ZEALAND CITIZENS: New Zealand Customs, The Customhouse, 17–21 Whitmore St., Box 2218, Wellington (☎04/473-6099 or 0800/428-786; www.customs.govt.nz).

Medical Requirements

No shots or inoculations are required to enter Costa Rica. The exception to this is for those who have recently been traveling in a country or region known to have yellow fever. In this case, proof of a yellow fever vaccination is required.

For more on medical concerns and recommendations, see "Health," p. 63.

GETTING THERE & GETTING AROUND
Getting to Costa Rica

BY PLANE

It takes between 3 and 7 hours to fly to Costa Rica from most U.S. cities, from where most direct and connecting flights will depart. Most international flights still land in San José's **Juan Santamaría International Airport** (airport code SJO). However, more and more direct international flights are touching down in Liberia's **Daniel Oduber International Airport** (airport code LIR).

Liberia is the gateway to the beaches of the Guanacaste region and the Nicoya Peninsula, and a direct flight here eliminates the need for a separate commuter flight in a small aircraft or roughly 5 hours in a car or bus. If you are planning to spend all, or most, of your vacation time in the Guanacaste region, you'll want to fly in and out of Liberia. However, San José is a much more convenient gateway if you are planning to head to Manuel Antonio, the Central Pacific coast, the Caribbean coast, or the Southern zone.

Numerous airlines fly into Costa Rica. Be warned that the smaller Latin American carriers tend to make several stops (sometimes unscheduled) en route to San José, thus increasing flying time.

From North America, **Air Canada, American Airlines, Continental, Delta, Frontier, Grupo Taca, Jet Blue, Mexicana, Spirit Air,** and **US Airways** all have regular direct flights to Costa Rica.

From Europe, **Iberia** is the only airline with regular routes to San José, some direct and others with one connection. Alternately, you can fly to any major U.S. hub city and make connections to one of the airlines mentioned above.

For more info on which airlines travel to Costa Rica, please see "Airline, Hotel & Car-Rental Websites," p. 486.

BY CRUISE

Some 200 cruise ships stop each year in Costa Rica, calling at Limón on the Caribbean coast, and at Puerto Caldera and Puntarenas on the Pacific coast. Many are part of routes that cruise through the Panama Canal. Cruise lines that offer stops in Costa Rica include **Crystal Cruises** (☎888/722-0021; www.crystalcruises.com), **Celebrity Cruises** (☎800/760-0654; www.celebritycruises.com), **Holland America** (☎877/932-4259; www.hollandamerica.com), **Norwegian Cruise Line** (☎866/234-7650; www.ncl.com), **Royal Caribbean** (☎866/562-7625; www.rccl.com), **Radisson Seven Seas Cruises** (☎877/505-5370; www.rssc.com), and **Silver Sea Cruises** (☎800/722-9955; www.silversea.com).

It might pay off to book through a travel agency that specializes in cruises; these companies buy in bulk and stay on top of the latest specials and promotions. Try the **Cruise Company** (☎800/289-5505; www.thecruisecompany.com) or **World Wide Cruises** (☎800/882-9000; www.wwcruises.com).

BY CAR

It's possible to travel to Costa Rica by car, but it can be difficult. After leaving Mexico, the Interamerican Highway (Carretera Interamericana, also known as the Pan-American Hwy.) passes through Guatemala, El Salvador, Honduras, and Nicaragua before reaching Costa Rica. All of these countries can be problematic for travelers for a variety of reasons, including internal violence, crime, corrupt border crossings, and visa formalities. If you do decide to undertake this adventure, take the **Gulf Coast route** from the border crossing at Brownsville, Texas, because it involves traveling the fewest miles through Mexico. Those planning to travel this route should purchase a copy of *You Can Drive to Costa Rica in 8 Days!* by Dawn Rae Lessler, which is available from the major online bookstores. You might also try to find a copy of *Driving the Pan-Am Highway to Mexico and Central America,* by Audrey and Raymond Pritchard, which is harder to find. There is also a wealth of information online at **www.sanborns insurance.com** and **www.drivemeloco.com**.

CAR DOCUMENTS You will need a current driver's license, as well as your vehicle's registration and the original title (no photocopies), to enter the country.

CENTRAL AMERICAN AUTO INSURANCE Contact **Sanborn's Insurance Company** (☎**800/222-0158** or 956/686-0711; www.sanbornsinsurance. com), which has agents at various border towns in the United States. These folks have been servicing this niche for more than 50 years. They can supply you with trip insurance for Mexico and Central America (you won't be able to buy insurance after you've left the U.S.), driving tips, and an itinerary.

CAR SAFETY Be sure your car is in excellent working order. It's advisable not to drive at night because of the danger of being robbed by bandits, especially in Mexico, Guatemala, El Salvador, and Honduras.

For listings of the major car-rental agencies in Costa Rica, please see "Fast Facts: Costa Rica" (p. 482).

Getting Around

BY PLANE

Flying is one of the best ways to get around Costa Rica. Because the country is quite small, flights are short and not too expensive. The domestic airlines of Costa Rica are Sansa and Nature Air.

Sansa (☎**877/767-2672** in the U.S. and Canada, or 2290-4100 in Costa Rica; www.flysansa.com) operates from a separate terminal at San José's **Juan Santamaría International Airport,** and offers a free shuttle bus from its downtown San José office to the airport.

Nature Air (☎**800/235-9272** in the U.S. and Canada, or 2299-6000; www. natureair.com) operates from **Tobías Bolaños International Airport** (SYQ) in Pavas, 6.4km (4 miles) from San José. The ride from downtown to Pavas takes about 10 minutes, and a metered taxi fare should cost $10 to $20.

In the high season (late Nov to late Apr), be sure to book reservations well in advance. Both companies have online booking systems via their websites.

BY CAR

Renting a car in Costa Rica is no idle proposition. The roads are riddled with potholes, most rural intersections are unmarked, and, for some reason, sitting behind the wheel of a car seems to turn peaceful Ticos into homicidal maniacs. But unless you want to see the country from the window of a bus or pay exorbitant amounts for private transfers, renting a car might be your best option for independent exploring. (That said, if you don't want to put up with any stress on your vacation, it might be worthwhile springing for a driver.)

Be forewarned, however: Although rental cars no longer bear special license plates, they are still readily identifiable to thieves and are frequently targeted. (Nothing is ever safe in a car in Costa Rica, although parking in guarded parking lots helps.) Transit police also seem to target tourists; never pay money directly to a police officer who stops you for any traffic violation.

Before driving off with a rental car, be sure that you inspect the exterior and point out to the rental-company representative every tiny scratch, dent, tear, or any other damage. It's a common practice with many Costa Rican car-rental companies to claim that you owe payment for minor dings and dents that the company finds when you return the car. Also, if you get into an accident, be sure that the rental company doesn't try to bill you for a higher amount than the deductible on your rental contract.

These caveats aren't meant to scare you off from driving in Costa Rica. Thousands of tourists rent cars here every year, and the large majority of them encounter no problems. Just keep your wits about you and guard against car theft (see p. 58 for info) and you'll do fine. Also keep in mind that four-wheel-drives are particularly useful in the rainy season (May to mid-Nov) and for navigating the bumpy, poorly paved roads year-round.

Note: It's sometimes cheaper to reserve a car in your home country rather than book when you arrive in Costa Rica. If you know you'll be renting a car, it's always wise to reserve it well in advance for the high season because the rental fleet still can't match demand.

Among the major international agencies operating in Costa Rica are **Alamo, Avis, Budget, Hertz, National, Payless,** and **Thrifty.** For a complete list of car-rental agencies and their contact information, see "Fast Facts: Costa Rica," p. 482, as well as the "Getting Around" sections of major tourist destinations in this book.

GASOLINE Gasoline is sold as "regular" and "super." Both are unleaded; super is just higher octane. Diesel is available at almost every gas station as well. Most rental cars run on super, but always ask your rental agent what type of gas your car takes. When going off to remote places, try to leave with a full tank of gas because gas stations can be hard to find. If you need to gas up in a small town, you can sometimes get gasoline from enterprising families who sell it by the liter from their houses. Look for hand-lettered signs that say GASOLINA. At press time a liter of super cost 435 colones, or roughly $2.95 per gallon.

ROAD CONDITIONS The awful road conditions throughout Costa Rica are legendary, and deservedly so. Despite constant promises to fix the problem and sporadic repair attempts, the hot sun, hard rain, and rampant corruption outpace any progress made toward improving the condition of roads. Even paved roads are often badly potholed, so stay alert. Road conditions get especially tricky during the rainy season, when heavy rains and runoff can destroy a stretch of pavement in the blink of an eye.

Note: Estimated driving times are listed throughout this book, but bear in mind that it might take longer than estimated to reach your destination during the rainy season or if roads have deteriorated.

Route numbers are very rarely used on road signs in Costa Rica, although there are frequent signs listing the number of kilometers to various towns or cities. Your best bets for on-road directions are billboards and advertisements for hotels. It's always a good idea to know the names of a few hotels at your destination, just in case your specific hotel hasn't put up any billboards or signs.

RENTER'S INSURANCE Even if you hold **your own car-insurance policy** at home, coverage doesn't always extend abroad. Be sure to find out whether you'll be covered in Costa Rica, whether your policy extends to all persons who will be driving the rental car, how much liability is covered in case an outside party is injured in an accident, and whether the *type* of vehicle you are renting is included under your contract.

DRIVING RULES A current foreign driver's license is valid for the first 3 months you are in Costa Rica. Seat belts are required for the driver and front-seat passengers. Motorcyclists must wear helmets. Highway police use radar, so keep to the speed limit (usually 60–90kmph/37–56 mph) if you don't want to get pulled over. Speeding tickets can be charged to your credit card for up to a year after you leave the country if they are not paid before departure.

To reduce congestion and fuel consumption, a rotating ban on rush-hour traffic takes place in the central core of San José Monday through Friday from 7 to 8:30am and from 4 to 5:30pm. The ban affects cars with licenses ending in the digits 1 or 2 on Monday; 3 or 4 on Tuesday; 5 or 6 on Wednesday; 7 or 8 on Thursday; and 9 or 0 on Friday. If you are caught driving a car with the banned license plate during these hours on a specified day, you will be ticketed.

BREAKDOWNS Be warned that emergency services, both vehicular and medical, are extremely limited outside San José, and their availability is directly related to the remoteness of your location at the time of breakdown. You'll find service stations spread over the entire length of the Interamerican Highway, and most of these have tow trucks and mechanics. The major towns of Puntarenas, Liberia, Quepos, San Isidro, Palmar, and Golfito all have hospitals, and most other moderately sized cities and tourist destinations have some sort of clinic or health-services provider.

If you're involved in an accident, you should contact the **National Insurance Institute (INS)** at ☎800/800-8000. You should probably also call the **Transit Police** (☎2222-9330 or 2222-9245); if they have a unit close by, they'll send one. An official transit police report will greatly facilitate any insurance claim. If you can't get help from any of these, try to get written statements from any witnesses. Finally, you can also call ☎911, and they should be able to redirect your call to the appropriate agency.

If the police do show up, you've got a 50-50 chance of finding them helpful or downright antagonistic. Many officers are unsympathetic to the problems of what they perceive to be rich tourists running around in fancy cars with lots of expensive toys and trinkets. Success and happy endings run about equal with horror stories.

If you don't speak Spanish, expect added difficulty in any emergency or stressful situation. Don't expect that rural (or urban) police officers, hospital personnel, service-station personnel, or mechanics will speak English.

If your car breaks down and you're unable to get well off the road, check your trunk for reflecting triangles. If you find some, place them as a warning for approaching traffic, arranged in a wedge that starts at the shoulder about 30m

Toll Tips

In mid-2009, the first section of a long-awaited highway to Caldera was opened. This toll road will greatly reduce the travel time from San José to the Central Pacific coast. As part of the highway, it has already greatly improved the section between San José and the western suburbs of Escazú, Santa Ana, and Ciudad Colón. This improvement comes at a cost, specifically 310 colones (55¢) each way between San José and Escazú, and an additional 160 colones (28¢) between Escazú and Ciudad Colón. For those traveling between Caldera and Orotina, the toll is 470 colones (84¢). Between Ciudad Colón and Orotina, the highway is still a work in progress, and is expected to be finished in mid-2010—at which point tolls will be set.

(98 ft.) back and nudges gradually toward your car. If your car has no triangles, try to create a similar warning marker using a pile of leaves or branches.

Finally, although not endemic, there have been reports of folks being robbed by seemingly friendly Ticos who stop to give assistance. To add insult to injury, there have even been reports of organized gangs who puncture tires of rental cars at rest stops or busy intersections, only to follow them, offer assistance, and make off with belongings and valuables. If you find yourself with a flat tire, try to ride it to the nearest gas station. If that's not possible, try to pull over into a well-lit public spot. Keep the doors of the car locked and an eye on your belongings while changing the tire, by yourself.

BY BUS

This is by far the most economical way to get around Costa Rica. Buses are inexpensive and relatively well maintained, and they go nearly everywhere. There are two types: **Local buses** are the cheapest and slowest; they stop frequently and are generally a bit dilapidated. **Express buses** run between San José and most beach towns and major cities; these tend to be newer units and more comfortable, although very few are so new or modern as to have bathroom facilities, and they sometimes operate only on weekends and holidays.

Two companies run regular, fixed-schedule departures in passenger vans and small buses to most of the major tourist destinations in the country. **Gray Line** (☎ 2220-2126; www.graylinecostarica.com) is run by Fantasy Tours, and has about 10 departures leaving San José each morning and heading or connecting to Jacó, Manuel Antonio, Liberia, Playa Hermosa, La Fortuna, Tamarindo, and playas Conchal and Flamingo. There are return trips to San José every day from these destinations and a variety of interconnecting routes. A similar service, **Interbus** (☎ 2283-5573; www.interbusonline.com) has a slightly more extensive route map and more connections. Fares run between $27 and $45 depending upon the destination. **Beware:** Both of these companies offer pickup and drop-off at a wide range of hotels. This means that if you are the first picked up or last dropped off, you might have to sit through a long period of subsequent stops before finally hitting the road or reaching your destination. Moreover, I've heard

PLANNING A COSTA RICAN
wedding

Getting married in Costa Rica is simple and straightforward. In most cases, all you need are current passports. You'll have to provide some basic information, including a copy of each passport, your dates of birth, your occupations, your current address, and the names and addresses of your parents. Two witnesses are required to be present at the ceremony. If you're traveling alone, your hotel or wedding consultant will provide the required witnesses.

Things are slightly more complicated if one or more of the partners was previously married. In such a case, the previously married partner must provide an official copy of the divorce decree.

Most travelers who get married in Costa Rica do so in a civil ceremony officiated by a local lawyer. After the ceremony, the lawyer records the marriage with Costa Rica's National Registry, which issues an official marriage certificate. This process generally takes between 4 and 6 weeks. Most lawyers or wedding coordinators then have the document translated and certified by the Costa Rican Foreign Ministry and at the embassy or consulate of your home country within Costa Rica before mailing it to you. From here, it's a matter of bringing this document to your local civil or religious authorities, if necessary.

Because Costa Rica is more than 90% Roman Catholic, arranging for a church wedding is usually easy in all but the most isolated and remote locations. To a lesser extent, a variety of denominational Christian churches and priests are often available to perform or host the ceremony. If you're Jewish, Muslim, Buddhist, or a follower of some other religion, bringing your own officiant is a good idea.

Tip: Officially, the lawyer must read all or parts of the Costa Rican civil code on marriage during your ceremony. This is a rather uninspired and somewhat dated legal code that, at some weddings, can take as much as 20 minutes to slog through. Most lawyers and wedding coordinators are quite flexible and can work with you to design a ceremony and text that fits your needs and desires. Insist on this.

Most of the higher-end and romantic hotels in Costa Rica have ample experience in hosting weddings. Many have an in-house wedding planner. Narrowing the list is tough, but I'd say the top choices include Hotel Punta Islita (p. 279), Villa Caletas (p. 353), Makanda by the Sea (p. 373), Florblanca Resort (p. 270), and the Four Seasons Resort (p. 212). If you want a remote, yet luxurious, rainforest lodge to serve as host and backdrop, try La Paloma Lodge (p. 407), Bosque del Cabo Rainforest Lodge (p. 420), or Lapa Ríos (p. 421). Another interesting option is Punta Coral, a private reserve owned by Calypso Tours (☎800/887-1969; www.calypsotours.com).

If you're looking for service beyond what your hotel can offer, or if you want to do it yourself, check out www.weddings.co.cr, www.weddingscostarica.net, www.liquidweddings.com, or www.tropicaloccasions.com.

some horror stories about both lines, concerning missed or severely delayed connections and rude drivers. For details on how to get to various destinations from San José, see the "Getting There" sections in the chapters that follow.

BY TAXI

Taxis are readily available in San José and most popular tourist towns and destinations. In San José, your best bet is usually just to hail one down in the street. However, during rush hours and rain storms, and in more remote destinations, it is probably best to call a cab. Throughout the book, I've listed numbers for local taxi companies in the "Getting Around" sections. If no number is listed, ask at your hotel, or, if you're out and about, at the nearest restaurant or shop; someone will be more than happy to call you a cab.

All city taxis, and even some rural cabs, have meters (*marías*), although drivers sometimes refuse to use them, particularly with foreigners. If this is the case, be sure to negotiate the price up front. Always try to get drivers to use the meter first (say *"ponga la maría, por favor"*). The official rate at press time is around 80¢ for the first kilometer (½ mile) and around 60¢ for each additional kilometer. If you have a rough idea of how far it is to your destination, you can estimate how much it should cost from these figures, or you can ask at your hotel how much a specific ride should cost. After 10pm, taxis are legally allowed to add a 20% surcharge. Some of the meters are programmed to include the extra charge automatically, but be careful: Some drivers will use the evening setting during the daytime or (at night) to charge an extra 20% on top of the higher meter setting.

BY FERRY

Three different ferries operate across the Gulf of Nicoya. Two are car ferries: one from Puntarenas to Playa Naranjo, and one from Puntarenas to Paquera. The third is a passenger ferry that runs between Puntarenas and Paquera. There's also regular passenger ferry service between the southern cities of Golfito and Puerto Jiménez. See the destination chapters for details. ***Note:*** Be careful while waiting in line for the ferry and on board any ferry. Thieves prey on the hefty bounty carried in most tourist rental cars.

BY THUMB

Although buses serve most towns in Costa Rica, service can be infrequent in the remote regions, so local people often hitchhike to get to their destinations sooner. If you're driving a car, people will frequently ask you for a ride. In remote rural areas, a hitchhiker carrying a machete is not necessarily a great danger, but use your judgment. Hitchhiking is not recommended on major roadways or in urban areas. In rural areas it's usually pretty safe. (However, women should be extremely cautious about hitchhiking anywhere in Costa Rica.) If you choose to hitchhike, keep in mind that if a bus doesn't go to your destination, there probably aren't too many cars going there, either. Good luck.

BY TRAIN

See p. 125 in "San José" for info on the country's recently reopened commuter train line.

MONEY & COSTS
Currency

The Value of the Colón vs. Other Popular Currencies

Colón	US$	Can$	UK£	Euro (€)	Aus$	NZ$
560	$1	C$1.24	£0.69	0.73€	A$1.46	NZ$1.08

The unit of currency in Costa Rica is the **colón.** Frommer's lists exact prices in this book, in U.S. dollars, because the Costa Rican colón is in a constant state of devaluation and fluctuation. More importantly, almost every hotel in the country, as well as a fair number of restaurants in popular tourist destinations, advertise and list their prices in U.S. dollars. Finally, those hotels and restaurants that don't usually peg their prices to the dollar make periodic adjustments. Airport taxis will all accept U.S. dollars, as will virtually every hotel and many restaurants.

The currency conversions quoted above were correct at press time. However, rates fluctuate, so before departing consult a currency exchange website such as **www.oanda.com/convert/classic** to check up-to-the-minute rates.

The colón is divided into 100 **céntimos.** Currently, two types of coins are in circulation. The older and larger nickel-alloy coins come in denominations of 10, 25, and 50 céntimos and 1, 2, 5, 10, and 20 colones; however, because of their evaporating value, you will probably never see or have to handle céntimos, or anything lower than a 5-colón coin. In 1997 the government introduced gold-hued 5-, 10-, 25-, 50-, 100-, and 500-colón coins. They are smaller and heavier than the older coins, and while the plan was to have them eventually phase out the other currency, this hasn't happened yet.

There are paper notes in denominations of 1,000, 2,000, 5,000, and 10,000 colones. You might also encounter a special-issue 5-colón bill that is a popular gift and souvenir. It is valid currency, although it sells for much more than its face value. You might hear people refer to a *rojo* or *tucán,* which are slang terms for the 1,000- and 5,000-colón bills, respectively. One-hundred-colón denominations are called *tejas,* so *cinco tejas* is 500 colones. I've yet to encounter a slang equivalent for the 2,000 and 10,000 bills.

Forged bills are not entirely uncommon. When receiving change in colones, it's a good idea to check the larger-denomination bills, which should have protective bands or hidden images that appear when held up to the light.

You can change money at all banks in Costa Rica. The principal state banks are Banco Nacional and Banco de Costa Rica. However, be forewarned that service at state banks can be slow and tedious. You're almost always better off finding a private bank. Luckily, there are hosts of private banks around San José and in most major tourist destinations.

Since banks handle money exchanges, there are very, very few exchange houses in Costa Rica. One major exception to this is the **Global Exchange** office at the airport. However, be forewarned they exchange at more than 10% below the official exchange rate.

Hotels will often exchange money and cash traveler's checks as well; there usually isn't much of a line, but they might shave a few colones off the exchange rate. Be very careful about exchanging money on the streets; it's extremely risky. In addition to forged bills and short counts, street money-changers frequently work in teams that can leave you holding neither colones nor dollars. Also be very careful when leaving a bank. Criminals are often looking for foreigners who have just withdrawn or exchanged cash.

ATMs

The easiest and best way to get cash away from home is from an ATM (automated teller machine). Costa Rica has a modern and widespread network of ATMs. You should find ATM machines in all but the most remote tourist destinations and isolated nature lodges.

In 2009, in response to a rash of "express kidnappings" in San José, in which folks were taken at gun point to an ATM to clean out their bank accounts, both Banco Nacional and Banco de Costa Rica stopped ATM service between the hours of 10pm and 5am. Other networks still dispense money 24 hours a day.

It's probably a good idea to change your PIN to a four-digit PIN. While many ATMs in Costa Rica will accept five- and six-digit PINs, some will only accept four-digit PINs.

Credit Cards

MasterCard and Visa are the most widely accepted credit cards in Costa Rica, followed by American Express. Most hotels and restaurants accept all of these, especially in tourist destination areas. Discover and Diners Club are far less commonly accepted.

You can withdraw cash advances from your credit cards at banks or ATMs but high fees make credit card cash advances a pricey way to get cash. Keep in mind that you'll pay interest from the moment of your withdrawal, even if you pay your monthly bills on time. Also, note that many banks now assess a 1% to 3% "foreign transaction fee" on **all** charges you incur abroad (whether you're using the local currency or your native currency).

WHAT THINGS COST IN COSTA RICA	US$
Taxi from the airport to downtown San José	18.00
Double room, moderate	90.00
Double room, inexpensive	40.00
Three-course dinner for one without wine, moderate	15.00–25.00
Bottle of Imperial beer	1.00–1.50
Bottle of Coca-Cola	1.00
Cup of coffee	1.00–1.50
Gallon of premium gas	2.95
Admission to most museums	2.00–5.00
Admission to most national parks	10.00

HEALTH
Staying Healthy

Staying healthy on a trip to Costa Rica is predominantly a matter of being a little cautious about what you eat and drink, and using common sense. Know your physical limits, and don't overexert yourself in the ocean, on hikes, or in athletic activities. Respect the tropical sun and protect yourself from it. Limit your exposure to the sun, especially during the first few days of your trip and, thereafter, from 11am to 2pm. Use sunscreen with a high protection factor, and apply it liberally. Remember that children need more protection than adults. I recommend buying and drinking bottled water or soft drinks, but the water in San José and in most of the country's heavily visited spots is safe to drink.

GENERAL AVAILABILITY OF HEALTH CARE

In general, Costa Rica has a high level of medical care and services for a developing nation. The better private hospitals and doctors in San José are very good. In fact, given the relatively budget nature of care and treatment, a sizable number of Americans come to Costa Rica each year for elective surgery and other care.

Pharmacies are widely available, and generally well stocked. In most cases you will not need a doctor's script to fill or refill a prescription.

I list **additional emergency numbers** in the various destination chapters, as well as in the "Fast Facts," p. 482.

Common Ailments

TROPICAL ILLNESSES Your chance of contracting any serious tropical disease in Costa Rica is slim, especially if you stick to the beaches or traditional spots for visitors. However, malaria, dengue fever, and leptospirosis all exist in Costa Rica, so it's a good idea to know what they are.

Malaria is found in the lowlands on both coasts and in the northern zone. Although it's rarely found in urban areas, it's still a problem in remote wooded regions and along the Caribbean coast. Malaria prophylaxes are available, but several have side effects, and others are of questionable effectiveness. Consult your doctor regarding what is currently considered the best preventive treatment for malaria. Be sure to ask whether a recommended drug will cause you to be hypersensitive to the sun; it would be a shame to come down here for the beaches and then have to hide under an umbrella the whole time. Because malaria-carrying mosquitoes usually come out at night, you should do as much as possible to avoid being bitten after dark. If you are in a malaria-prone area, wear long pants and long sleeves, use insect repellent, and either sleep under a mosquito net or burn mosquito coils (similar to incense, but with a pesticide).

Of greater concern is **dengue fever,** which has had periodic outbreaks in Latin America since the mid-1990s. Dengue fever is similar to malaria and is spread by an aggressive daytime mosquito. This mosquito seems to be most common in lowland urban areas, and Puntarenas, Liberia, and Limón have been the worst-hit cities in Costa Rica. Dengue is also known as "bone-break fever" because it is usually accompanied by severe body aches. The first infection with dengue fever will make you very sick but should cause no serious damage. However, a second infection with a different strain of the dengue virus can lead to internal hemorrhaging and could be life threatening.

Many people are convinced that taking B-complex vitamins daily will help prevent mosquitoes from biting you. I don't think the American Medical Association has endorsed this idea yet, but I've run across it in enough places to think that there might be something to it.

One final tropical fever that I think you should know about (because I got it myself) is **leptospirosis.** There are more than 200 strains of leptospires, which are animal-borne bacteria transmitted to humans via contact with drinking, swimming, or bathing water. This bacterial infection is easily treated with antibiotics; however, it can quickly cause very high fever and chills, and should be treated promptly.

If you develop a high fever accompanied by severe body aches, nausea, diarrhea, or vomiting during or shortly after a visit to Costa Rica, consult a physician as soon as possible.

Costa Rica has been relatively free of the cholera epidemic that has spread through much of Latin America in recent years. This is largely due to an extensive public-awareness campaign that has promoted good hygiene and increased sanitation. Your chances of contracting cholera while you're here are very slight.

DIETARY RED FLAGS Even though the water in San José and most popular destinations in Costa Rica is generally safe, and even if you're careful to buy bottled water, order *frescos en leche* (fruit shakes made with milk rather than water), and drink your soft drink without ice cubes, you still might encounter some intestinal difficulties. Most of this is just due to tender stomachs coming into contact with slightly more aggressive Latin American intestinal flora. In extreme cases of diarrhea or intestinal discomfort, it's worth taking a stool sample to a lab for analysis. The results will usually pinpoint the amoebic or parasitic culprit, which can then be readily treated with available over-the-counter medicines.

Except in the most established and hygienic of restaurants, it's also advisable to avoid *ceviche*, a raw seafood salad, especially if it has any shellfish in it. It could be home to any number of bacterial critters.

BUGS, BITES & OTHER WILDLIFE CONCERNS Although Costa Rica has Africanized bees (the notorious "killer bees" of fact and fable) and several species of venomous snakes, your chances of being bitten are minimal, especially if you refrain from sticking your hands into hives or under rocks in the forest. If you know that you're allergic to bee stings, consult your doctor before traveling.

At the beaches, you'll probably be bitten by *pirujas* (sand fleas). These nearly invisible insects leave an irritating welt. Try not to scratch because this can lead to open sores and infections. *Pirujas* are most active at sunrise and sunset, so you might want to cover up or avoid the beaches at these times.

Snake sightings, much less snakebites, are very rare. Moreover, the majority of snakes in Costa Rica are nonpoisonous. If you do encounter a snake, stay calm, don't make any sudden movements, and do not try to handle it. As recommended above, avoid sticking your hands under rocks, branches, and fallen trees.

Scorpions, black widow spiders, tarantulas, bullet ants, and biting insects of many types can all be found in Costa Rica. In general, they are not nearly the danger or nuisance most visitors fear. Watch where you stick your hands; in addition, you might want to shake out your clothes and shoes before putting them on to avoid any unpleasant and painful surprises.

TROPICAL SUN Limit your exposure to the sun, especially during the first few days of your trip and, thereafter, from 11am to 2pm. Use a sunscreen with a high protection factor, and apply it liberally. Remember that children need more protection than adults.

RIPTIDES Many of Costa Rica's beaches have riptides: strong currents that can drag swimmers out to sea. A riptide occurs when water that has been dumped on the shore by strong waves forms a channel back out to open water. These channels have strong currents. If you get caught in a riptide, you can't escape the current by swimming toward shore; it's like trying to swim upstream in a river. To break free of the current, swim parallel to shore and use the energy of the waves to help you get back to the beach.

What to Do If You Get Sick Away from Home

Your hotel front desk should be your best source of information and assistance if you get sick while in Costa Rica. In addition, your local consulate in Costa Rica can provide a list of area doctors who speak English. The local English-language newspaper, the *Tico Times,* is another good resource. I've listed the best hospitals in San José in "Fast Facts: San José," in chapter 6; these have the most modern facilities in the country. Most state-run hospitals and walk-in clinics around the country have emergency rooms that can treat most conditions, although I highly recommend the private hospitals in San José if your condition is not life-threatening and can wait for treatment until you reach one of them.

I list **additional emergency numbers** in the various destination chapters, as well as in the "Fast Facts," p. 482.

SAFETY

Although most of Costa Rica is safe, petty crime and robberies committed against tourists are endemic. San José, in particular, is known for its pickpockets, so never carry a wallet in your back pocket. A woman should keep a tight grip on her purse (keep it tucked under your arm). Thieves also target gold chains, cameras and video cameras, prominent jewelry, and nice sunglasses. Be sure not to leave valuables unsecured in your hotel room, or unattended on the beach. Given the high rate of stolen passports in Costa Rica, mostly as collateral damage in a typical pickpocketing or room robbery, it is recommended that, whenever possible, you leave your passport in a hotel safe, and travel with a photocopy of the pertinent pages. Don't park a car on the street in Costa Rica, especially in San José; plenty of public parking lots are around the city.

Rental cars generally stick out and are easily spotted by thieves. Don't leave anything of value in a car parked on the street, not even for a moment. Be wary of solicitous strangers who stop to help you change a tire or take you to a service station. Although most are truly good Samaritans, there have been reports of thieves preying on roadside breakdowns. See p. 58 for more info.

Inter-city buses are also frequent targets of stealthy thieves. Try not to check your bags into the hold of a bus, if they will fit in the rack above your seat. If this can't be avoided, keep your eye on what leaves the hold. If you put your bags in an overhead rack, be sure you can see the bags at all times. Try not to fall asleep.

Single women should use common sense and take precaution, especially after dark. I don't recommend that single women walk alone anywhere at night, especially on seemingly deserted beaches, or dark uncrowded streets.

SPECIALIZED TRAVEL RESOURCES

In addition to the destination-specific resources listed below, please visit Frommers.com for additional specialized travel resources.

Gay & Lesbian Travelers

Costa Rica is a Catholic, conservative, macho country where public displays of same-sex affection are rare and considered somewhat shocking. Public figures, politicians, and religious leaders periodically denounce homosexuality. However, gay and lesbian tourism to Costa Rica is quite robust, and gay and lesbian travelers are generally treated with respect and should not experience any harassment.

For a general overview of the current situation, news of any special events or meetings, and up-to-date information, the website **www.gaycostarica.com** is your best bet, especially for gay men, and to a much lesser extent for lesbian women.

The **International Gay and Lesbian Travel Association** (**IGLTA;** ☎**800/ 448-8550** or 954/776-2626; www.iglta.org) is the trade association for the gay and lesbian travel industry, and offers an online directory of gay- and lesbian-friendly travel businesses and tour operators.

Travelers with Disabilities

Most disabilities shouldn't stop anyone from traveling. There are more options and resources out there than ever before.

Still, although Costa Rica does have a law mandating Equality of Opportunities for People with Disabilities, and facilities are beginning to be adapted, in general, there are relatively few buildings for travelers with disabilities in the country. In San José, sidewalks are particularly crowded and uneven, and they are nonexistent in most of the rest of the country. Few hotels offer wheelchair-accessible accommodations, and there are no public buses thus equipped. In short, it can be difficult for a person with disabilities to get around San José and Costa Rica.

However, one local agency specializes in tours for travelers with disabilities and restricted ability. **Vaya Con Silla de Ruedas** (☎/fax **2454-2810;** www.gowithwheelchairs.com) has a ramp- and elevator-equipped van and knowledgeable, bilingual guides. It charges very reasonable prices and can provide anything from simple airport transfers to complete multiday tours.

Family Travelers

To locate accommodations, restaurants, and attractions that are particularly kid-friendly, refer to the "Kids" icons throughout this guide.

Hotels in Costa Rica often give discounts for children 11 or 12 and under, and children under 3 or 4 are usually allowed to stay for free. Discounts for children and the cutoff ages vary according to the hotel, but in general, don't assume that your kids can stay in your room for free.

Some hotels, villas, and cabinas come equipped with kitchenettes or full kitchen facilities. These can be a real money-saver for those traveling with children, and I've listed many of these accommodations in the destination chapters in this book.

Hotels offering regular, dependable babysitting service are few and far between. If you will need babysitting, make sure that your hotel offers it, and be sure to ask whether the babysitters are bilingual. In many cases they are not. This is usually not a problem with infants and toddlers, but it can cause problems with older children.

Women Travelers

For lack of better phrasing, Costa Rica is a typically "macho" Latin American nation. Single women can expect catcalls, hisses, whistles, and car horns, especially in San José. In most cases, while annoying, this is harmless and intended by Tico men as a compliment. Nonetheless, women should be careful walking alone at night throughout the country.

Senior Travelers

Be sure to mention that you're a senior when you make your travel reservations. Although it's not common policy in Costa Rica to offer senior discounts, don't be shy about asking for one anyway. You never know. Always carry some kind of identification, such as a driver's license, that shows your date of birth, especially if you've kept your youthful glow.

Many reliable agencies and organizations target the 50-plus market. **Elderhostel** (℡800/454-5768; www.elderhostel.org) arranges Costa Rica study programs for those ages 55 and older, as well as intergenerational trips good for families. **ElderTreks** (℡800/741-7956 or 416/558-5000 outside North America; www.eldertreks.com) offers small-group tours to Costa Rica, restricted to travelers 50 and older.

Student Travelers

In Costa Rica, there is one travel agency specializing in student and youth travel: **OTEC** (℡2523-0500; www.otecviajes.com). These folks have three offices in San José, located in downtown, Escazú, and the university district of San Pedro, and another office across from the National University in Heredia. OTEC also has sister operations throughout Central America.

Although you won't find any discounts at the national parks, most museums and other attractions around Costa Rica do offer discounts for students. It always pays to ask.

SUSTAINABLE TOURISM

Costa Rica is one of the planet's prime ecotourism destinations. Many of the small hotels, isolated nature lodges, and tour operators around the country are pioneers and dedicated professionals in the sustainable tourism field. Many other hotels, lodges, and tour operators are honestly and earnestly jumping on the bandwagon and improving their practices, while still others are simply "greenwashing," using the terms "eco," "green," and "sustainable" in their promo materials, but doing little real good in their daily operations.

SUSTAINABLE properties IN COSTA RICA

Following is a selection of the **Certificate of Sustainable Tourism Program**'s **(CST)** top recommended sustainable properties in Costa Rica, as well as some that fit my own personal criteria for sustainability but that don't participate in the CST program. Throughout the book, I've also tried to highlight hotels, as well as restaurants and attractions, that pay more than mere lip service to sustainable practices.

San José & the Central Valley:
Finca Rosa Blanca (p. 142)
Hotel Bougainvillea (p. 146)
Hotel 1492 Jade y Oro (p. 139)
Xandari Resort & Spa (p. 144)

Guanacaste:
Four Seasons Resort (p. 212)
Hacienda Guachipelin (p. 203)
Hotel Las Tortugas (p. 241)
Hotel Playa Hermosa Bosque del Mar (p. 214)

Nicoya Peninsula:
Florblanca Resort (p. 270)
Hotel Punta Islita (p. 279)
The Harmony Hotel & Spa (p. 283)
Ylang Ylang Beach Resort (p. 263)

The Northern Zone:
Arenal Observatory Lodge (p. 310)
Caño Negro Natural Lodge (p. 313)
La Laguna del Lagarto Lodge (p. 314)
La Selva Biological Station (p. 293)
Monteverde Lodge & Gardens (p. 334)
Rara Avis (p. 294)
Selva Verde Lodge (p. 294)

Tabacón Grand Spa Thermal Resort (p. 308)
Villa Blanca Cloud Forest & Spa (p. 314)

The Central Pacific Coast:
Arenas del Mar (p. 370)
Gaia Hotel & Reserve (p. 372)
Hacienda Barú (p. 383)
Hotel Sí Como No (p. 373)
La Cusinga Lodge (p. 389)
Savegre Mountain Hotel (p. 396)

The Southern Zone:
Bosque del Cabo Rainforest Lodge (p. 420)
El Remanso (p. 420)
Golfo Dulce Lodge (p. 427)
La Paloma Lodge (p. 407)
Lapa Ríos (p. 421)
Luna Lodge (p. 420)
Playa Nicuesa Rainforest Lodge (p. 428)
Tiskita Jungle Lodge (p. 435)

The Caribbean Coast:
Almonds & Corals Hotel (p. 475)
Casa Marbella (p. 450)
Casa Verde Lodge (p. 474)
Selva Bananito Lodge (p. 454)
Tortuga Lodge (p. 448)

Despite its reputation, the substantial amounts of good work being done, and ongoing advances being made in the field, Costa Rica is by no means an ecological paradise free from environmental and social threats. Untreated sewage is dumped into rivers, bays, oceans, and watersheds at an alarming rate. Child labor and sexual exploitation are rampant, and certain sectors of the tourism trade only make these matters worse.

Over the last decade or so, Costa Rica has taken great strides toward protecting its rich biodiversity, however. Thirty years ago it was difficult to find a protected area anywhere, but now more than 11% of the country is protected within the national park system. Another 10% to 15% of the land enjoys moderately effective preservation as part of private and public reserves, Indian reserves, and wildlife refuges and corridors. Still, Costa Rica's precious tropical hardwoods continue to be harvested at an alarming rate, often illegally, while other primary forests are clear-cut for short-term agricultural gain. Many experts predict that Costa Rica's unprotected forests could be gone within the early part of this century.

Recycling is just beginning to gather momentum in Costa Rica. More and more you will see separate bins for plastics, glass, and paper on town and city streets, at national parks, and at the country's more sustainable hotels and restaurants. This is a nascent phenomenon, but I expect it to continue to grow and spread. Your hotel will be your best bet for finding a place to deposit recyclable waste, especially if you choose a hotel that has instituted sustainable practices.

While you can find hotels and tour operators using comprehensive sustainable practices all across Costa Rica—even in the San José metropolitan area—a few prime destinations are particular hot spots for ecotourism and sustainable tourism practices. Of note are the remote and wild Osa Peninsula and Golfo Dulce area of southern Costa Rica, the rural northern zone that includes both Monteverde and the Arenal Volcano and Lake Arenal attractions, and the underdeveloped Caribbean coast, with the rainforest canals of Tortuguero, Cahuita National Park, and the Manzanillo-Gandoca Wildlife Refuge.

In addition to focusing on wildlife viewing and adventure activities in the wild, ecolodges in these areas tend to be smaller, often lacking televisions, air-conditioning, and other typical luxury amenities. The more remote lodges usually depend largely or entirely on small solar and hydro plants for their power consumption. That said, some of these hotels and lodges provide levels of comfort and service that are quite luxurious.

In Costa Rica, the government-run tourism institute (ICT) provides a sustainability rating of a host of hotels and tour agencies under their **Certificate of Sustainable Tourism Program (CST).** You can look up the ratings at the website www.turismo-sostenible.co.cr.

Bear in mind that this program is relatively new and the list is far from comprehensive. Moreover, die-hard ecologists find some of these listings somewhat suspect. Still, this list and rating system is a good start, and is improving and evolving constantly.

A parallel program, **"The Blue Flag,"** is used to rate specific beaches and communities in terms of their environmental condition and practices. The Blue Flags are reviewed and handed out annually. Current listings of Blue Flag approved beaches and communities can be found at www.visitcostarica.com.

See above for a list of hotels and lodges that I consider leaders in sustainable tourism practices in Costa Rica. As I've said earlier, more and more hotels are continuing to adopt sustainable and ethical tourism practices. Please supplement my recommendations with your own research via the Web, and sites such as the CST site mentioned above.

While sustainable tourism options are widespread in Costa Rica, organic and sustainably grown fruits and vegetables (as well as coffee) are just beginning to become available. Very few restaurants feature organic produce, although hopefully that will change in the near future.

If you're not booking your hotel, tours, and transportation by yourself, you might want to consider using a tour agency that has earned high marks in

RESOURCES FOR green TRAVEL

In addition to the resources for Costa Rica listed above, the following websites provide valuable wide-ranging information on sustainable travel. For a list of even more sustainable resources, as well as tips and explanations on how to travel greener, visit www.frommers.com/planning.

- **Responsible Travel** (www. responsibletravel.com) is a great source of sustainable travel ideas; the site is run by a spokesperson for ethical tourism in the travel industry. **Sustainable Travel International** (www.sustainabletravelinternational.org) promotes ethical tourism practices, and manages an extensive directory of sustainable properties and tour operators around the world.

- In the U.K., **Tourism Concern** (www.tourismconcern.org.uk) works to reduce social and environmental problems connected to tourism. The **Association of Independent Tour Operators** (**AITO;** www.aito.co.uk) is a group of specialist operators leading the field in making holidays sustainable.

- **Carbonfund** (www.carbonfund.org), **TerraPass** (www.terrapass.org), and **Carbon Neutral** (www.carbonneutral.org) provide info on "carbon offsetting," or offsetting the greenhouse gas emitted during flights.

- **Greenhotels** (www.greenhotels.com) recommends green-rated member hotels around the world that fulfill the company's stringent environmental requirements. **Environmentally Friendly Hotels** (www.environmentallyfriendlyhotels.com) offers more green accommodation ratings.

- **Sustain Lane** (www.sustainlane.com) and **www.eatwellguide.org** offer tips on eating sustainably.

- For information on animal-friendly issues throughout the world, visit **Tread Lightly** (www.treadlightly.org). For information about the ethics of swimming with dolphins, visit the **Whale and Dolphin Conservation Society** (www.wdcs.org).

- **Volunteer International** (www.volunteerinternational.org) has a list of questions to help you determine the intentions and the nature of a volunteer program. For general info on volunteer travel, visit **www.volunteerabroad.org** and **www.idealist.org**.

this area. In Costa Rica, **Horizontes** ★★, Calle 32 between avenidas 3 and 5 (☎2222-2022; www.horizontes.com), has garnered particularly high marks from several rating agencies and organizations. Other exemplary operators include **Costa Rica Expeditions** ★★ (☎2257-0766; www.costaricaexpeditions.com), **Costa Rica Sun Tours** ★ (☎2296-7757; www.crsuntours.com), and **Swiss Travel Service** (☎2282-4898; www.swisstravelcr.com).

In addition to the agencies listed above, those looking for a taste of what many consider "the real" Costa Rica, should consider booking through **ACTUAR** ★ (☎877/922-8827 in the U.S. and Canada, or 2248-9470 in Costa Rica; www.actuarcostarica.com). This organization groups together a network of small, rural lodges and tour operators. In many cases, accommodations are quite rustic. Bunk beds and thin foam mattresses are common. However, all of the hotels, lodges, and tour operators are small-scale and local. In many cases, they are family operations. If you want a true taste of typical, rural Costa Rica, traveling with ACTUAR is a great way to go.

Finally, another great way to make your tourism experience more sustainable is to volunteer. For specific information on volunteer options in Costa Rica, see "Volunteer & Study Programs," in chapter 5, "The Active Vacation Planner."

Beyond the country's hotels, tour operators, and volunteer options, it's worth noting here that the local commuter airline **Nature Air** (☎800/235-9272 in the U.S. and Canada, or 2299-6000; www.natureair.com) has been a pioneer in the field. In 2004, Nature Air became the first certified carbon neutral airline on the planet, and they continue to supplement their own sustainable practices with contributions to reforestation and conservation programs.

See "The Lay of the Land" in chapter 2 for additional information on the various ecosystems and geographical highlights you'll find around the country. For information on Costa Rica's national parks and info about what to expect and how to take care of yourself in the Costa Rican rivers, forests, and seas, turn to chapter 5.

STAYING CONNECTED
Telephones

Costa Rica has an excellent and widespread phone system. A phone call within the country costs around 10 colones per minute. Pay phones take a calling card or 5-, 10-, or 20-colón coins. Calling cards are much more practical, and coin-operated phones are getting harder and harder to find. You can purchase calling cards in a host of gift shops and pharmacies. However, there are several competing calling-card companies, and certain cards work only with certain phones. **CHIP** calling cards work with a computer chip and just slide into specific phones, although these phones aren't widely available. Better bets are the **197** and **199** calling cards, which are sold in varying denominations. These have a scratch-off PIN and can be used from any phone in the country. Generally, the 197 cards are sold in smaller denominations and are used for local calling, while the 199 cards are deemed international and are easier to find in larger denominations. Either card can be used to make any call, however, provided that the card can cover the costs. Another perk of the 199 cards is the fact that you can get the instructions in English. For local calls, it is often easiest to call from your hotel, although you will likely be charged around 150 to 300 colones per call.

To call Costa Rica from abroad:

1. Dial the international access code: 011 from the U.S. and Canada; 00 from the U.K., Ireland, or New Zealand; or 0011 from Australia.

2. Dial the country code 506.

3. Dial the 8-digit number.

To make international calls: To make international calls from Costa Rica, first dial 00 and then the country code (U.S. or Canada 1, U.K. 44, Ireland 353, Australia 61, New Zealand 64). Next you dial the area code and number. For example, if you wanted to call the British Embassy in Washington, D.C., you would dial 00-1-202-588-7800.

For directory assistance: Dial 113 if you're looking for a number inside Costa Rica, and dial 124 for numbers to all other countries.

For operator assistance: If you need operator assistance in making a call, dial 116 if you're trying to make an international call and 0 if you want to call a number in Costa Rica.

Toll-free numbers: Numbers beginning with 0800 or 800 within Costa Rica are toll-free, but calling a 1-800 number in the States from Costa Rica is not toll-free. In fact, it costs the same as an overseas call.

Cellphones

Costa Rica primarily uses **GSM** (Global System for Mobile Communications) networks. If your cellphone is on a GSM system, and you have a world-capable multiband phone such as many Sony Ericsson, LG, Motorola, or Samsung models, you can make and receive calls across civilized areas around much of the globe. Just call your wireless operator and ask for "international roaming" to be activated on your account. Per-minute charges can be high, though—up to $5 in Costa Rica, depending upon your plan.

Unfortunately, those with unlocked tri- and quad-band GSM phones still cannot simply buy a local SIM card in Costa Rica. However, a free trade agreement with the United States and other Central American nations is expected to open up the state monopoly on telecommunications during 2010, and this should change.

Several local firms rent cellphones to visiting tourists and businessmen. However, none of the rental companies has a booth or office at the airport, so you'll have to contact them either beforehand or from your hotel. Most will deliver the phone to your hotel. **Cell Service** (✆2296-5553; www.cellservicecr.com), **Costa Rica Cellular Connection** (✆800/372-3183 in the U.S. and Canada, or 8876-1776 in Costa Rica; www.costaricacellularconnection.com), and **GSM Rent A Cell** (✆2231-5410; www.gsmrentacell.com) all rent cellphones. Rates run around $5 to $10 per day or $30 to $50 per week for the rental, with charges of 50¢ to $1.50 per minute for local calls and $1 to $3 per minute for international calls.

In addition to the above companies, most of the major car-rental agencies offer cellphone rentals, for rates similar to those listed above.

Internet & E-Mail

WITHOUT YOUR OWN COMPUTER

Cybercafes can be found all over Costa Rica, especially in the more popular tourist destinations. For help locating cybercafes and other establishments where you can go for Internet access, please see the destination chapters throughout this book.

WITH YOUR OWN COMPUTER

More and more hotels, resorts, cafes, and retailers around Costa Rica are offering high-speed Wi-Fi access, either free or for a small fee. Throughout the book, I list which hotels provide free, or for a fee, Wi-Fi and high-speed Ethernet access.

Costa Rica uses standard U.S.-style two- and three-prong electric outlets with 110-volt AC current, and standard U.S.-style phone jacks. Wherever you go, bring a **connection kit** with power and phone adapters, a spare phone cord, and a spare Ethernet network cable—or find out whether your hotel supplies them to guests.

TIPS ON ACCOMMODATIONS

When the Costa Rican tourist boom began in the late 1980s, hotels popped up like mushrooms after a heavy rain. By the 1990s the country's first true megaresorts opened, more followed, and still more are under construction or in the planning phase. Except during the few busiest weeks of the year, there's a relative glut of rooms in Costa Rica. That said, most hotels are small to midsize, and the best ones fill up fast most of the year. You'll generally have to reserve well in advance if you want to land a room at any of the hotels on my "Best of" lists in chapter 1. Still, in broader terms, the glut of rooms is good news for travelers and bargain hunters. Less popular hotels that want to survive are being forced to reduce their rates and provide better service.

Your best bet in Costa Rica is negotiating directly with the hotels themselves, especially the smaller hotels. Almost every hotel in Costa Rica has e-mail, if not its own website, and you'll find the contact information in this book. However, be aware that response times might be slower than you'd like, and many of the smaller hotels might have some trouble communicating back and forth in English.

Throughout this book, I separate hotel listings into several broad categories: **Very Expensive,** $200 and up; **Expensive,** $125 to $199; **Moderate,** $60 to $124; and **Inexpensive,** under $60 for a double. *Rates given in this book do not include the 13% room taxes, unless otherwise specified.* These taxes will add considerably to the cost of your room.

Throughout Costa Rica, rates generally fluctuate somewhat according to season and demand, with a majority of hotels offering lower rates in the off season, and charging higher rates during peak periods.

Hotel Options

There are hotels to suit every budget and travel style in Costa Rica. In addition to the Four Seasons and JW Marriott, the host of amazing boutique hotels around the country will satisfy the high-end and luxury traveler.

Still, the country's strong suit is its **moderately priced hotels.** In the $80-to-$125 price range, you'll find comfortable and sometimes outstanding accommodations almost anywhere in the country. However, room size and quality vary quite a bit within this price range, so don't expect the kind of uniformity that you may find at home.

If you're even more budget- or bohemian-minded, you can find quite a few good deals for less than $50 a double. ***But beware:*** Budget-oriented lodgings often

Skip the Motel

You'll want to avoid motels in Costa Rica. To a fault, these are cut-rate affairs geared toward lovers consummating their affairs— usually illicit. Most rent out rooms by the hour, and most have private garages with roll-down doors outside each room, so that snoopy spouses or ex-lovers can't check for cars or license plates.

feature shared bathrooms and either cold-water showers or showers heated by electrical heat-coil units mounted at the shower head, affectionately known as "suicide showers." If your hotel has one, do not adjust it while the water is running. Unless specifically noted, all rooms listed in this guide have a private bathroom.

Note: Air-conditioning is not necessarily a given in many mid-range hotels and even some upscale joints. In general, this is not a problem. Cooler nights and a well-placed ceiling fan are often more than enough to keep things pleasant, unless I mention otherwise in the hotel reviews.

Bed-and-breakfasts are also abundant. Although the majority are in the San José area, you'll also find B&Bs (often gringo-owned and operated) throughout the country. Another welcome hotel trend in the San José area is the renovation and conversion of old homes into **small hotels.** Most are in the Barrio Amón district of downtown San José, which means that you'll sometimes have to put up with noise and exhaust fumes, but these establishments have more character than any other hotels in the country. You'll find similar hotels in the Paseo Colón and Los Yoses districts.

Costa Rica is still riding the ecotourism wave, and you'll find small nature-oriented **ecolodges** throughout the country. These lodges offer opportunities to see wildlife (including sloths, monkeys, and hundreds of species of birds) and learn about tropical forests. They range from spartan facilities catering primarily to scientific researchers, to luxury accommodations that are among the finest in the country. Keep in mind that although the nightly room rates at these lodges are often quite moderate, prices start to climb when you throw in transportation (often on chartered planes), guided excursions, and meals. Also, just because you can book a reservation at most of these lodges doesn't mean that they're not remote. Be sure to find out how you get to and from the ecolodge, and what tours and services are included in your stay. Then think long and hard about whether you really want to put up with hot, humid weather (cool and wet in the cloud forests); biting insects; rugged transportation; and strenuous hikes to see wildlife. For a list of key ecolodges in the country, see p. 20.

A couple of uniquely Costa Rican accommodations types that you might encounter are the **apartotel** and the **cabina.** An apartotel is just what it sounds like: an apartment hotel where you'll get a full kitchen and one or two bedrooms, along with daily maid service. Cabinas are Costa Rica's version of cheap vacation lodging. They're very inexpensive and very basic—often just cinder-block buildings divided into small rooms. Occasionally, you'll find a cabina in which the units are actually cabins, but these are a rarity. Cabinas often have clothes-washing sinks (*pilas*), and some come with kitchenettes; they cater primarily to Tico families on vacation.

For tips on surfing for hotel deals online, visit Frommers.com.

4

SUGGESTED ITINERARIES

C osta Rica is a compact, yet varied, destination with numerous natural attractions and a broad selection of exciting sights, scenery, adventure activities, and ecosystems. On a trip to Costa Rica you can visit rainforests, cloud forests, and active volcanoes, and walk along miles of beautiful beaches on both the Pacific and Caribbean coasts. Adventure hounds will have their fill choosing from an exciting array of activities, and those looking for some rest and relaxation can grab a chaise longue and a good book. Costa Rica is also a relatively compact country, which makes visiting several destinations during a single vacation both easy and enjoyable.

The fastest and easiest way to get around the country is by small commuter aircraft. Most major destinations are serviced by regular commuter or charter airline companies. However, this does imply using San José or Liberia as periodic transfer hubs. If your connections don't line up, you may end up having to tack on nights in either of these cities in the middle of your trip. Luckily, there are sufficient flights and internal connections to make this an infrequent inconvenience.

Getting around Costa Rica by car is another excellent option. Most major destinations are between 3 and 5 hours from San José by car, and many can be linked together in a well-planned and convenient loop. For example, one popular loop links Arenal Volcano, Monteverde, and Manuel Antonio. However, be forewarned that the roads here are often in terrible shape, many major roads and intersections are unmarked, and Tico drivers can be reckless and rude. See "By Car" under "Getting Around Costa Rica," in chapter 3 for more information on driving in Costa Rica.

The following itineraries are specific blueprints for fabulous vacations, and you can follow them to the letter. You might also decide to use one or more of them as an outline and then fill in some blanks with other destinations, activities, and attractions that strike your fancy from the rest of this book.

COSTA RICA REGIONS IN BRIEF

Costa Rica rightfully should be called "Costas Ricas" because it has two coasts: one on the Pacific Ocean and one on the Caribbean Sea. These two coasts are as different from each other as are the Atlantic and Pacific coasts of North America.

Costa Rica's **Pacific coast** is the most extensive, and is characterized by a rugged (although mostly accessible) coastline where forested mountains often meet the sea. It can be divided into four distinct regions—Guanacaste, the Nicoya Peninsula, the Central Coast, and the Southern Coast. There are some spectacular stretches of coastline, and most of the country's top beaches are

PREVIOUS PAGE: **Capuchin monkey.**

Costa Rica Regions in Brief

here. This coast varies from the dry, sunny climate of the northwest to the hot, humid rainforests of the south.

The **Caribbean coast** can be divided into two roughly equal stretches. The remote northeast coastline is a vast flat plain laced with rivers and covered with rainforest; it is accessible only by boat or small plane. Farther south, along the stretch of coast accessible by car, there are uncrowded beaches and even a bit of coral reef.

Bordered by Nicaragua in the north and Panama in the southeast, Costa Rica is only slightly larger than Vermont and New Hampshire combined. Much of the country is mountainous, with three major ranges running northwest to southeast. Among these mountains are several volcanic peaks, some of which are still active. Between the mountain ranges are fertile valleys, the largest and most populated of which is the Central Valley. With the exception of the dry Guanacaste region, much of Costa Rica's coastal area is hot and humid and covered with dense rainforests.

See the map pictured directly above for a visual of the regions detailed below.

SAN JOSE & THE CENTRAL VALLEY The Central Valley is characterized by rolling green hills that rise to heights between 900 and 1,200m (2,952–3,936 ft.) above sea level. The climate here is mild and springlike year-round. It's Costa Rica's primary agricultural region, with coffee farms making up the majority of landholdings. The rich volcanic soil of this region makes it ideal for farming. The country's earliest settlements were in this area, and today the Central Valley (which includes San José) is densely populated, crisscrossed by decent roads, and dotted with small towns. Surrounding the Central Valley are high mountains, among which are four volcanic peaks. Two of these, **Poás** and **Irazú,** are still active and have caused extensive damage during cycles of activity in the past 2 centuries. Many of the mountainous regions to the north and to the south of the capital of San José have been declared national parks (Tapantí, Juan Castro, and Braulio Carrillo) to protect their virgin rainforests against logging.

GUANACASTE The northwestern corner of the country near the Nicaraguan border is the site of many of Costa Rica's sunniest and most popular **beaches,** including **Playa del Coco, Playa Hermosa, Playa Flamingo,** and **Tamarindo.** There are literally scores of beach destinations, towns, and resorts along this long string of coastline. Because many foreigners have chosen to build beach houses and retirement homes here, Guanacaste has experienced considerable development over the years. You won't find a glut of Cancún-style high-rise hotels, but condos, luxury resorts, and golf courses have sprung up all up and down the coastline here. Still, you won't be towel-to-towel with thousands of strangers. On the contrary, you can still find long stretches of deserted sands. However, more and more travelers are using Liberia as their gateway to Costa Rica, bypassing San José and the central and southern parts of the country entirely.

With about 65 inches of rain a year, this region is by far the driest in the country and has been likened to west Texas. Guanacaste province is named after the shady trees that still shelter the herds of cattle roaming the dusty savanna here. In addition to cattle ranches, Guanacaste boasts semiactive volcanoes, several lakes, and one of the last remnants of tropical dry forest left in Central America. (Dry forest once stretched all the way from Costa Rica up to the Mexican state of Chiapas.)

PUNTARENAS & THE NICOYA PENINSULA Just south of Guanacaste lies the Nicoya peninsula. Similar to Guanacaste in many ways, the Nicoya peninsula is nonetheless somewhat more inaccessible, and thus much less developed and crowded. However, this is already starting to change. The neighboring beaches of **Malpaís** and **Santa Teresa** are perhaps the fastest growing hot spots anywhere along the Costa Rican coast.

Tamarindo.

Corcovado National Park.

While similar in terms of geography, climate, and ecosystems, as you head south from Guanacaste, the region begins to get more humid and moist. The forests are taller and lusher than those found in Guanacaste. The Nicoya peninsula itself juts out to form the Golfo de Nicoya (Nicoya Gulf), a large, protected body of water. **Puntarenas,** a small fishing city, is the main port found inside this gulf, and one of the main commercial ports in all of Costa Rica. Puntarenas is also the departure point for the regular ferries that connect the Nicoya peninsula to San José and most of mainland Costa Rica.

THE NORTHERN ZONE This inland region lies to the north of San José and includes rainforests, cloud forests, hot springs, the country's two most active volcanoes (**Arenal** and **Rincón de la Vieja**), **Braulio Carrillo National Park,** and numerous remote lodges. Because this is one of the few regions of Costa Rica without any beaches, it primarily attracts people interested in nature and active sports. **Lake Arenal** boasts some of the best windsurfing and kitesurfing in the world, as well as several good mountain-biking trails along its shores. The **Monteverde Cloud Forest,** perhaps Costa Rica's most internationally recognized attraction, is another top draw in this region.

THE CENTRAL PACIFIC COAST Because it's the most easily accessible coastline in Costa Rica, the central Pacific coast boasts the greatest number of beach resorts and hotels. **Playa de Jacó,** a beach within a few hours drive of San José, attracts many Canadian and German charter groups and plenty of Tico tourists on weekends. It is also very popular with young surfers, and has a distinct party vibe to it. **Manuel Antonio,** one of the most emblematic destinations in Costa Rica, is built up around a popular coastal national park, and caters to people looking to blend beach time and fabulous panoramic views with some wildlife viewing and active adventures. This region is also home to the highest peak in Costa Rica—**Mount Chirripó**—a beautiful summit, where frost is common.

THE SOUTHERN ZONE This hot, humid region is one of Costa Rica's most remote and undeveloped. It is characterized by dense rainforests, large national parks and protected areas, and rugged coastlines. Much of the area is protected in **Corcovado** and **La Amistad** national parks. A number of wonderful nature lodges are spread around the shores of the **Golfo Dulce** and along the **Osa Peninsula.** There's a lot of solitude to be found here, due in no small part to the fact that it's hard to get here and hard to get around. But if you like your ecotourism authentic and challenging, you'll find the southern zone to your liking.

THE CARIBBEAN COAST Most of the Caribbean coast is a wide, steamy lowland laced with rivers and blanketed with rainforests and banana plantations. The culture here is predominantly Afro-Caribbean, with many residents speaking an English or Caribbean patois. The northern section of this coast is accessible only by boat or small plane and is the site of **Tortuguero National Park,** which is known for its nesting sea turtles and riverboat trips. The towns of **Cahuita, Puerto Viejo,** and **Manzanillo,** on the southern half of the Caribbean coast, are increasingly popular destinations. The coastline here boasts many beautiful beaches and, as yet, few large hotels. However, this area can be rainy, especially between December and April.

COSTA RICA IN 1 WEEK

The timing is tight, but this itinerary packs a lot into a weeklong vacation. This route takes you to a trifecta of Costa Rica's primary tourist attractions: Arenal Volcano, Monteverde, and Manuel Antonio. You can explore and enjoy tropical nature, take in some beach time, and experience a few high-adrenaline adventures to boot.

DAY 1: Arrive & Settle into San José

Arrive and get settled in **San José.** If your flight gets in early enough and you have time, head downtown and tour the **Museos del Banco Central de Costa Rica (Gold Museum) ★★** (p. 158).

☕ Fresh Fruit

As you walk around town, stop at one of the roadside stands or kiosks selling small bags of precut and prepared fruit. Depending on the season, you might find mango, pineapple, or papaya on offer. If you're lucky they'll have *mamon chino,* an odd-looking golf ball–size fruit you might also know as rambutan or litchi nut, if you've been to Asia.

Tabacón Grand Spa Thermal Resort.

NICARAGUA

Lake Nicaragua

Golfo de Papagayo

Lake Arenal

Tabacón Hot Springs

Arenal National Park

Monteverde
Monteverde Cloud Forest Reserve

SAN JOSÉ
★ Start & End Here

Nicoya Peninsula

Golfo de Nicoya

CARIBBEAN SEA

Manuel Antonio National Park

PACIFIC OCEAN

Coronado Bay

PANAMA

Osa Peninsula

0   40 mi
0   40 km

Head over to the Teatro Nacional (National Theater; p. 172). If anything is playing that night, buy tickets for the show. For an elegant and delicious dinner, I recommend Grano de Oro Restaurant ★★★ (p. 150), which is a chic restaurant with seating in and around an open-air central courtyard in a beautiful downtown hotel.

DAY 2: Hot Rocks ★★

Rent a car and head to the Arenal National Park to see **Arenal Volcano ★★**. Settle into your hotel and spend the afternoon at the **Tabacón Grand Spa Thermal Resort ★★★** (p. 308) working out the kinks from the road. In the evening either sign up for a volcano-watching tour or take one on your own by driving the road to **Arenal National Park** and finding a quiet spot to pull over and wait for the sparks to fly.

DAY 3: Adventures Around Arenal, Ending Up in Monteverde ★★

Spend the morning doing something adventurous around Arenal National Park. Your options range from white-water rafting to mountain biking to horseback riding and then hiking to the Río Fortuna Waterfall. My favorite is the **canyoning** adventure offered by **Pure Trek Canyoning ★★** (p. 301). Allow at least 4 hours of daylight to drive around **Lake Arenal** to **Monteverde.** Stop for a break at the **Lucky Bug Gallery ★★** (p. 317),

Canopy tour at Selvatura.

along the road between Tabacón and Nuevo Arenal, and an excellent place to shop for gifts, artwork, and souvenirs. Once you get to Monteverde, settle into your hotel and head for a drink and dinner at **Chimera ★★** (p. 335).

DAY 4: Monteverde Cloud Forest Reserve ★★★

Wake up early and take a guided tour of the **Monteverde Cloud Forest Reserve ★★★** (p. 322). Be sure to stop in at the **Hummingbird Gallery ★** (p. 332) next door to the entrance after your tour. There's great shopping, and the scores of brilliant hummingbirds buzzing around your head at this attraction are always fascinating. Spend the afternoon visiting several of the area's attractions, which might include any combination of the following: the **Butterfly Garden ★**, **Orchid Garden ★**, **Monteverde Serpentarium**, **Frog Pond of Monteverde ★**, the **Bat Jungle,** and the **World of Insects** (p. 330).

DAY 5: From the Treetops to the Coast ★★★

Use the morning to take one of the **zip-line canopy tours** here. I recommend **Selvatura Park ★★** (p. 328), which has a wonderful canopy tour, as well as other interesting exhibits. Be sure to schedule the tour early enough so that you can hit the road by noon for your drive to **Manuel Antonio National Park.** Settle into your hotel and head for a **sunset drink** at one of the several roadside restaurants with spectacular views over the rainforest to the sea. You can drop your car off at any point now and just rely on taxis and tours.

DAY 6: Manuel Antonio ★★

In the morning take a boat tour of the **Damas Island estuary** (p. 366) with Jorge Cruz, and then reward yourself for all the hard touring so far with an afternoon lazing on one of the beautiful beaches inside **Manuel Antonio National Park ★★** (p. 364). If you just can't lie still, be sure to hike the loop trail through the rainforest here and around **Cathedral Point ★★**. Make reservations at the **Sunspot Bar & Grill ★★** (p. 377) for an elegant and intimate final dinner in Costa Rica.

DAY 7: Saying Adiós

Fly back to **San José** in time to connect with your departing flight home. If you have extra time, feel free to head back into Manuel Antonio National Park, do some souvenir shopping, or simply laze around your hotel pool. You've earned it.

COSTA RICA IN 2 WEEKS

If you have 2 weeks, you'll be able to hit all the highlights mentioned above, as well as some others, and at a slightly more relaxed pace to boot. The first part of this itinerary is very similar to the 1-week itinerary laid out above. It's a real judgment call, but you might want to substitute a 2- to 3-day trip to Tortuguero for either the Guanacaste or the southern zone section listed below, or whittle down a day here or there along the way in order to squeeze in Tortuguero.

DAYS 1 & 2: San José

Follow the options listed under **DAYS 1 AND 2** in "Costa Rica in 1 Week," above. Another option for dinner on your second night is **Café Mundo ★** (p. 148), a lively restaurant and nightspot set in a wonderfully restored old colonial home in the heart of downtown.

DAY 3: Active in Arenal

Spend the morning doing something adventurous in **Arenal National Park,** as recommended in **DAY 3** in "Costa Rica in 1 Week," above. If you're really active, you can schedule a second adventure for the afternoon or take time to visit the town of **La Fortuna.** In the evening return to the **Tabacón Grand Spa Thermal Resort ★★★** (p. 308). If you were smart, you'll have already booked yourself a **spa treatment.**

DAY 4: Driving (& Shopping) Your Way Around the Lake to Monteverde

Give yourself at least 4 hours of daylight to drive around **Lake Arenal** to **Monteverde.** But you can take even longer. During your drive, be sure to stop at the **Lucky Bug Gallery ★★** (p. 317), where you can shop for gifts, artwork, and souvenirs. Once you're in Monteverde, settle into your hotel and head for a drink and dinner at **Chimera ★★** (p. 335).

DAY 5: Monteverde Cloud Forest Reserve

Spend **DAY 5** as described for **DAY 4** of "Costa Rica in 1 Week," above; however, head to **Sofia ★★** (p. 337) for dinner and grab a window table fronting its well-lighted and lush gardens.

DAY 6: More Monteverde

There's just no way you can hit all the local **Monteverde** attractions in a day. Use today to visit a few that you missed. Also be sure to stop in at several of the local **art galleries** and **crafts shops.** Monteverde has one of the country's most vibrant arts scenes, and there are several worthwhile galleries, including **Casa de Arte ★** (p. 332). In the evening, be sure to try **El Sapo Dorado ★** (p. 336) a long-standing and deservedly popular restaurant serving eclectic international fare.

Butterfly at Monteverde Butterfly Garden.   Relaxing in a Guanacaste hammock.

DAY 7: Monteverde to Manuel Antonio

Spend this day as in **DAY 5** of "Costa Rica in 1 Week," above. However, after your sunset drink, head down into the town of Quepos for dinner at **El Patio Bistro Latino ★★★** (p. 376), a cozy little spot serving some of the best food in the area.

DAY 8: Manuel Antonio ★★

Spend this day as in **DAY 6** of "Costa Rica in 1 Week," above.

DAYS 9, 10 & 11: Southern Costa Rica

Fly from Quepos and Manuel Antonio to **Drake Bay** and settle into a remote **ecolodge,** such as **La Paloma Lodge ★★★** (p. 407). You'll need 3 days to experience the many natural wonders of this southern zone. Aside from hiking in the rainforest, you'll be able to take scuba or snorkel outings, sportfishing trips, kayak adventures, and surfing lessons.

DAYS 12, 13 & 14: Guanacaste's Gold Coast

You've had enough nature and adventure; it's time to enjoy some pure R & R. From the southern zone, fly up to **Guanacaste** and spend your final days enjoying the pleasures of one of Costa Rica's **Gold Coast** beaches. If you can afford it and rooms are available, I recommend the **Four Seasons Resort ★★★** (p. 212). Alternatively, you might enjoy a smaller boutique hotel such as **Sueño del Mar ★** (p. 239).

    If just lying on the beach or poolside is too mellow, there are scores of tour and activity options. If you're not feeling that active or adventurous, simply break out that novel you've been too busy to open and enjoy. On your last day, fly home from **Liberia** or **San José.**

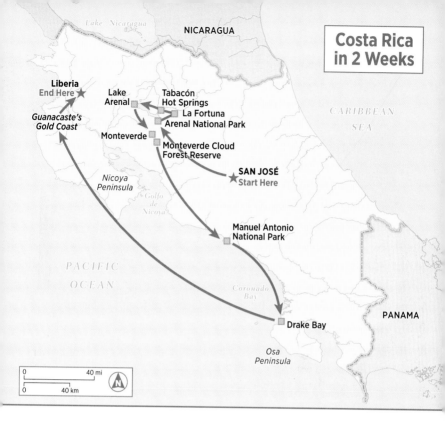

NICARAGUA

Lake Nicaragua

Liberia
End Here ★

Lake
Arenal

Tabacón
Hot Springs
La Fortuna
Arenal National Park

Guanacaste's
Gold Coast

Monteverde

Monteverde Cloud
Forest Reserve

SAN JOSÉ
★ **Start Here**

Nicoya
Peninsula

Golfo
de
Nicoya

CARIBBEAN
SEA

Manuel Antonio
National Park

PACIFIC
OCEAN

Coronado
Bay

Drake Bay

PANAMA

Osa
Peninsula

0   40 mi
0   40 km

COSTA RICA FOR FAMILIES

While Costa Rica is not a particularly kid-friendly destination, it isn't especially un-
friendly either. So far, there are few attractions or activities geared for the very young
and few resorts with well-developed children's programs. However, youngsters and
teens, especially those with strong adventurous and inquisitive traits, will do great
here. The biggest challenges to families traveling with children are travel distances
and the logistical challenges of moving around within the country, which is why I
recommend flying in and out of Liberia and basing yourself in Guanacaste.

DAY 1: Arrive in Guanacaste

Fly directly into **Liberia.** From here it's a drive of 30 to 45 minutes to any of
the area's many beach resorts, especially around the **Papagayo Peninsula.**
I recommend either the **Four Seasons Resort ★★★** (p. 212) or the **Hilton Papagayo Resort ★** (p. 213). Both have excellent children's programs
and tons of activity and tour options.

DAY 2: Get Your Bearings & Enjoy Your Resort

Get to know and enjoy the facilities and activities offered up at your hotel
or resort. Spend some time on the beach or at the pool. Enjoy the resort's

A sailboat cruise.

on-hand watersports equipment and activities. Check out the **children's program** and any scheduled **activities** or **tours** that particularly appeal to anyone in the family. Feel free to adapt the following days' suggestions accordingly.

DAY 3: Rafting on the Corobicí River

The whole family will enjoy a **rafting tour** on the gentle Corobicí River. **Safaris Corobicí** (p. 200) offers leisurely trips that are appropriate for all ages, except infants. In addition to the slow float and occasional mellow rapids, there'll be plenty of opportunities to watch birds and other wildlife along the way. If you're here between late September and late February, book a **turtle tour** (p. 236) at nearby **Playa Grande** for the evening. The whole family will be awe-struck by the amazing spectacle of a giant leather-back turtle digging a nest and laying its eggs.

DAY 4: Parent's Day Off

Drop the kids off with the children's program for at least 1 full day and treat yourselves to a **sailboat cruise.** You'll spend some time cruising the coast, take a break or two to snorkel, and probably stop for lunch at a deserted beach. If you really want to pamper yourself, also schedule in some **spa services.**

DAY 5: Hacienda Guachipelin ★

It's time to head for the hills, which are mostly volcanoes in this neck of the woods. Book a full-day outing to **Hacienda Guachipelin ★** (p. 203), near the Rincón de la Vieja National Park. Older and more adventurous children can sign up for a **horseback ride** or **canopy tour.** Younger children should get a kick out of visiting this working farm and cattle ranch.

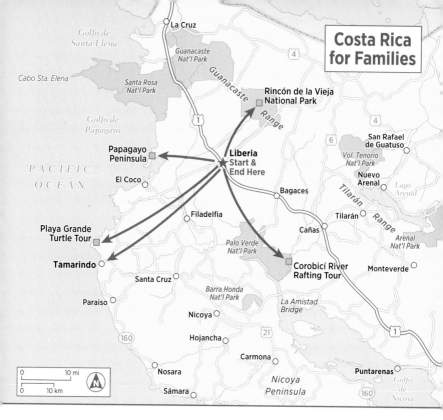

Costa Rica for Families

Golfo de Santa Elena

Cabo Sta. Elena

La Cruz

Guanacaste Nat'l Park

Santa Rosa Nat'l Park

Guanacaste Range

Rincón de la Vieja National Park

Golfo de Papagayo

San Rafael de Guatuso

PACIFIC OCEAN

Papagayo Peninsula

Liberia **Start & End Here**

El Coco

Vol. Tenorio Nat'l Park

Nuevo Arenal

Lago Arenal

Bagaces

Tilarán Range

Filadelfia

Tilarán

Playa Grande Turtle Tour

Cañas

Arenal Nat'l Park

Palo Verde Nat'l Park

Tamarindo

Corobicí River Rafting Tour

Monteverde

Santa Cruz

Barra Honda Nat'l Park

La Amistad Bridge

Paraiso

Nicoya

Hojancha

Carmona

Puntarenas

Golfo de Nicoya

Nosara

Nicoya Peninsula

Sámara

0   10 mi
0   10 km

DAY 6: Learn to Surf

Head to **Tamarindo ★** (p. 231) and arrange for the whole family to take **surf** or **boogie-board lessons**. Hopefully you will have already booked a class with **Tamarindo Surf School** or **Witch's Rock Surf Camp** (p. 237). Be sure to rent your boards for a full day, so that you can practice after the lesson is over.

DAY 7: Leaving Liberia

Use any spare time you have before your flight out of **Liberia** to buy last-minute souvenirs and gifts, or just laze on the beach or by the pool.

Your best bet for shopping is probably the **Kaltak Arts & Craft Market** (☏2667-0696), which is conveniently located on the way to the airport.

Learning to surf.

Pacuare River rafting.

Biking Costa Rica.

A WEEK OF ADVENTURES IN COSTA RICA

Costa Rica is a major adventure-tourism destination. The following basic itinerary packs a lot of adventure into a single week; if you want to do more mountain biking or kayaking, just schedule that time in. If you're into windsurfing or kiteboarding, you'll definitely want to visit Lake Arenal between December and March.

DAY 1: Arrive & Settle into San José

Arrive and get settled in **San José.** If your flight gets in early enough and you have time, head downtown and tour the **Museos del Banco Central de Costa Rica** ★★ (p. 158) and the **Teatro Nacional** (p. 172). Take a break for an afternoon coffee at the **Cafeteria 1930** (p. 148). Be sure to grab an outdoor table and enjoy some people-watching. For a delicious dinner with a spectacular view, head to **La Cava Grill** ★ (p. 154), which is located in the hills above Escazú.

DAYS 2 & 3: Get Wet & Wild

Take a 2-day white-water rafting expedition on the **Pacuare River** with **Exploradores Outdoors** ★ (p. 106). Camp out at their rustic tent camp on the river's edge. When you finish running the Pacuare, have them arrange for a transfer to **La Fortuna** at the end of your rafting trip. Settle into your hotel and head to the **Tabacón Grand Spa Thermal Resort** ★★★ (p. 308) to have a soothing soak and to watch the volcano.

DAY 4: Waterfalls Two Ways

Go canyoning with **Pure Trek Canyoning** ★★ (p. 99) in the morning, and then hop on a horse or a mountain bike in the afternoon and be sure to stop at the **Río Fortuna Waterfall** ★ (p. 304). Take the short hike down to the base of the falls and take a dip in one of the pools there. In the evening, check out the **Eco Termales** ★★ (p. 303) hot springs.

A Week of Adventures in Costa Rica

DAY 5: Getting There Is Part of the Fun & Adventure

Arrange a **taxi-to-boat-to-horse** transfer over to **Monteverde** with **Desafío Expeditions ★★** (p. 298). Settle in quickly at your hotel and take a zip-line **canopy tour** in the afternoon. I recommend the **Original Canopy Tour ★** (p. 99) in Monteverde. Finally, if you've got the energy, take a **night tour** through the Monteverde Cloud Forest Reserve.

DAY 6: Monteverde Cloud Forest Reserve ★★★

Wake up early and head back to take a daytime guided tour of the **Monteverde Cloud Forest Reserve ★★★**. Be sure to bring a packed lunch. After the guided tour, spend the next few hours continuing to explore the trails through the cloud forest here. See if you can spot a **quetzal** (p. 332) on your own. Then transfer back to San José.

DAY 7: Squeeze in a Soccer Game Before Splitting

Unfortunately, you'll most likely be on an early flight home from **San José.** If you have a few hours to kill, head for a **hike** or **jog** around Parque La Sabana or, better yet, try to join a **pickup soccer game** (p. 163) here.

SAN JOSE & ENVIRONS IN 3 DAYS

While most tourists seek to almost immediately get out of San José for greener pastures, there's still plenty to see and do in Costa Rica's vibrant capital. If you have even more days, take a white-water rafting trip on the Pacuare River, or head out to the Irazú Volcano, Orosi Valley, and Cartago area.

DAY 1: Getting to Know the City

Start your day on the **Plaza de la Cultura.** Visit the **Museos del Banco Central de Costa Rica ★★** (p. 158), and see if you can get tickets for a performance that night at the **Teatro Nacional** (p. 172). From the Plaza de la Cultura, stroll up Avenida Central to the **Museo Nacional de Costa Rica (National Museum) ★** (p. 157). After touring the museum, have lunch at one of the neighborhood restaurants. Then, head over to the neighboring **Centro Nacional de Arte y Cultura (National Center of Art and Culture) ★** (p. 156). After you're finished taking in all this culture, some shopping at the open-air stalls at the **Plaza de la Democracia** (p. 166) is in order.

☕ Cafe Mundo ★

Try dinner at the popular local hangout Café Mundo, at Calle 15 and Avenida 9, 200m (656 ft.) east and 100m (328 ft.) north of the INS building. See p. 148.

After dinner, head to the Teatro Nacional for the night's performance.

DAY 2: Enjoying Some Nearby Attractions

Get an early start for the **Poás Volcano ★★** (p. 182), before the clouds sock the main crater in. After visiting the volcano, head to the **La Paz Waterfall Gardens ★★** (p. 162). Take a walk on the waterfall trail, and also enjoy the immense butterfly garden and lively hummingbird garden. This is a good place to have lunch. On your way back to San José, you'll be making a loop through the hills of **Heredia,** with a stop at **INBio Park ★★** (p. 161). In addition to being a fascinating natural-history museum, INBio Park also has

San José street scene.

a wonderful collection of intriguing animal sculptures by Costa Rican artist José Sancho.

San José in 3 Days

1 Plaza de la Cultura
2 Museos del Banco Central de Costa Rica
3 Museo Nacional de Costa Rica
4 Centro Nacional de Arte y Cultura
5 Plaza de la Democracia
☕ Café Mundo

6 Teatro Nacional
7 Museo de Arte Costarricense
8 Parque La Sabana
9 Spirogyra Butterfly Garden
10 Mercado Central
☕ Restaurante Nuestra Tierra

DAY 3: More City Sights & Shopping

Spend your third day further exploring the capital. Start by heading out on Paseo Colón to the **Museo de Arte Costarricense (Costa Rican Art Museum) ★★** (p. 156) and **Parque La Sabana** (p. 163). Tour the museum and its growing sculpture garden, but also take a stroll around the beautiful and expansive downtown park. If you've brought kids along, you'll definitely want to visit the **Spirogyra Butterfly Garden** (p. 159). Intrepid travelers can also do some shopping at the **Mercado Central** (p. 166).

☕ Restaurante Nuestra Tierra
For a final taste of local culture, head for dinner at **Restaurante Nuestra Tierra,** located right downtown, across from the Plaza de la Democracia. See p. 149.

Museo Nacional de Costa Rica.

THE ACTIVE VACATION PLANNER

A ctive and adventure travelers will have their hands full in Costa Rica. While it's possible to stay clean and dry, most visitors want to spend at least some time getting their hair wet, their feet muddy, and their adrenaline pumping. Opportunities range from bird-watching to scuba diving to kiteboarding, and beyond.

There are myriad approaches to planning an active vacation in Costa Rica. This chapter lays out your options, from tour operators who run multiactivity package tours that often include stays at ecolodges, to the best places in Costa Rica to pursue active endeavors (with listings of tour operators, guides, and outfitters that specialize in each), to an overview of the country's national parks and bioreserves. I also list some educational and volunteer travel options for those of you with a little more time on your hands and a desire to actively contribute to the country's social welfare, or assist Costa Rica in the maintenance and preservation of its natural wonders.

ORGANIZED ADVENTURE TRIPS

Because many travelers have limited time and resources, organized ecotourism or adventure-travel packages, arranged by tour operators in either Costa Rica or the United States, are a popular way of combining several activities. Bird-watching, horseback riding, rafting, and hiking can be teamed with, say, visits to Monteverde Biological Cloud Forest Reserve and Manuel Antonio National Park.

Traveling with a group has several advantages over traveling independently: Your accommodations and transportation are arranged, and most (if not all) of your meals are included in the cost of a package. If your tour operator has a reasonable amount of experience and a decent track record, you should proceed to each of your destinations quickly without the snags and long delays that those traveling on their own can occasionally face. You'll also have the opportunity to meet like-minded souls who are interested in nature and active sports. Of course, you'll pay more for the convenience of having all your arrangements handled in advance.

In the best cases, group size is kept small (10–20 people), and tours are escorted by knowledgeable guides who are either naturalists or biologists. Be sure to ask about difficulty levels when you're choosing a tour. Most companies offer "soft adventure" packages that those in moderately good, but not phenomenal, shape can handle; others focus on more hard-core activities geared toward only seasoned athletes or adventure travelers.

Costa Rican Tour Agencies

Because many U.S.-based companies subcontract portions of their tours to established Costa Rican companies, some travelers like to cut out the middleman and set up their tours directly with these companies. That means that these

FACING PAGE: **Bungee jumping in Costa Rica.**

packages are often less expensive than those offered by U.S. companies, but it doesn't mean they are cheap. You're still paying for the convenience of having your arrangements handled for you.

Scores of agencies in San José offer a plethora of adventure options. These agencies can arrange everything from white-water rafting to sightseeing at one of the nearby volcanoes or a visit to a butterfly farm. Although it's generally quite easy to arrange a day trip at the last minute, other tours are offered only on set dates or when enough people are interested. It pays to contact a few of the companies before you leave home and find out what they might be doing when you arrive. These local operators tend to be a fair share less expensive than their international counterparts, with 10-day tours generally costing in the neighborhood of $1,500 to $3,000 per person, not including airfare to Costa Rica.

Coast to Coast Adventures ★ (℡2280-8054; www.ctocadventures.com) has a unique excursion involving no motor vehicles. The company's namesake 2-week trip spans the country, with participants traveling on horses and rafts, by mountain bike, and on foot. Custom-designed trips (with a minimum of motorized transport) of shorter duration are also available.

Costa Rica Expeditions ★★ (℡2257-0766; www.costaricaexpeditions. com) offers everything from 10-day tours covering the entire country to 3-day/2-night and 2-day/1-night tours of Monteverde Biological Cloud Forest Reserve and Tortuguero National Park, where they run their own lodges. It also offers 1- to 2-day white-water rafting trips and other excursions. All tours and excursions include transportation, meals, and lodging. Its tours are some of the most expensive in the country, but it is the most consistently reliable outfitter as well (and its customer service is excellent). If you want to go out on your own, Costa Rica Expeditions can supply you with just transportation from place to place.

Costa Rica Sun Tours ★ (℡2296-7757; www.crsuntours.com) offers a wide range of tours and adventures and specializes in multiday tours that include stays at small country lodges for travelers interested in experiencing nature.

Horizontes ★★ (℡2222-2022; www.horizontes.com) is not a specifically adventure-oriented operator, but it offers a wide range of individual, group, and package tours, including those geared toward active and adventure travelers. The company generally hires responsible and knowledgeable guides.

Serendipity Adventures ★ (℡877/507-1358 in the U.S. and Canada, or 2558-1000; www.serendipityadventures.com), an adventure-travel operator, offers everything from ballooning to mountain biking, and sea kayaking to canyoning, as well as most of the popular white-water rafting trips.

International Adventure Tour Operators

These agencies and operators specialize in well-organized and coordinated tours that cover your entire stay. Many travelers prefer to have everything arranged and confirmed before arriving in Costa Rica, and this is a good idea for first-timers and during the high season. **Be warned:** Most of these operators are not cheap, with 10-day tours generally costing in the neighborhood of $2,500 to $4,500 per person, not including airfare to Costa Rica.

Abercrombie & Kent ★★ (℡800/554-7016; www.abercrombiekent. com) is a luxury-tour company that offers upscale trips around the globe, and it has several tours of Costa Rica on its menu. It specializes in 9-day highlight tours hitting Monteverde, Arenal, and Tortuguero. Service is personalized and the guides are top-notch.

Butterfield & Robinson ★★ (☎866/551-9090; www.butterfield.com) is another company specializing in the very high-end market. One of its most interesting options is a trip designed for families with children over 8 years old. The trip provides a wealth of activities and adventures for parents and children to enjoy both together and apart.

Costa Rica Experts ★ (☎800/827-9046 or 773/935-1009; www.costa ricaexperts.com) offers a large menu of a la carte and scheduled departures, as well as day trips and adventure packages.

Nature Expeditions International ★ (☎800/869-0639; www.naturexp. com) specializes in educational and "low intensity adventure" trips tailored to independent travelers and small groups. These folks have a steady stream of pro-grammed departures or can customize a trip to your needs.

Overseas Adventure Travel ★★ (☎800/493-6824; www.oattravel.com) offers good-value natural-history and "soft adventure" itineraries with optional add-on excursions. Tours are limited to 16 people and are guided by naturalists. All accommodations are in small hotels, lodges, or tent camps.

Tico Travel (☎800/493-8426; www.ticotravel.com) has offices in both the United States and Costa Rica. It specializes in surfing and sportfishing pack-ages, but it can put together a wide range of tours.

In addition to these companies, many environmental organizations, including the **Sierra Club** (☎415/977-5500; www.sierraclub.org) and the **Smithsonian Institute** (☎877/338-8687; www.smithsonianjourneys.org), regularly offer or-ganized trips to Costa Rica.

ACTIVITIES A TO Z

Each listing in this section describes the best places to practice a particular sport or activity and lists tour operators and outfitters. If you want to focus on only one active sport during your Costa Rican stay, these companies are your best bets for quality equipment and knowledgeable service.

Adventure activities and tourism, by their very nature, carry certain risks and dangers. Over the years, there have been several deaths and dozens of mi-nor injuries in activities ranging from mountain biking to white-water rafting to canopy tours. I've tried to list only the most reputable and safest of companies. However, if you ever have any doubt as to the safety of the guide, equipment, or activity, it's better to be safe than sorry. Moreover, know your limits and abilities, and don't try to exceed them.

See "A Week of Adventures in Costa Rica," in chapter 4, for additional tour ideas.

Biking

There are several significant regional and international touring races in Costa Rica each year, but as a general rule the major roads are dangerous and inhospitable for cyclists. Roads are narrow, there's usually no shoulder, and most drivers show little care or consideration for those on two wheels. The options are much more appeal-ing for mountain bikers and off-track riders. If you plan to do a lot of biking and are very attached to your rig, bring your own. However, several companies in San José and elsewhere rent bikes, and the quality of the equipment is improving all the time. I've listed rental shops in each of the regional chapters that follow.

The area around **Lake Arenal** and **Arenal Volcano** wins my vote as the best place for mountain biking in Costa Rica. The scenery's great, with primary forests, waterfalls, and plenty of trails. And the hot springs at nearby Tabacón Grand Spa Thermal Resort is a perfect place for those with aching muscles to unwind at the end of the day. See chapter 9 for full details.

TOUR OPERATORS & OUTFITTERS

Bike Arenal ★ (☎866/465-4114 in U.S. and Canada, or 2479-7150; www. bikearenal.com) is based in La Fortuna and specializes in 1-day and multiday trips around the Arenal area.

Coast to Coast Adventures ★ (☎2280-8054; www.ctocadventures.com) offers mountain-biking itineraries among its many tour options.

Costa Rica Biking Adventures (☎2235-4982; www.bikingincostarica. com) is a local outfit offering day trips and multiday excursions around the country using high-quality Trek and Cannondale bikes.

ExperiencePlus! Specialty Tours ★★ (☎800/685-4565 or 970/484-8489 in the U.S.; www.experienceplus.com) offers guided group and assisted individual bike tours around the country. This is the only company I know of that uses touring bikes. It also offers guided group hiking tours.

Lava Tours (☎888/862-2424 in the U.S. and Canada, or 2281-2458; www.lava-tours.com) conducts a variety of fixed-date-departure and custom mountain-bike tours all over Costa Rica.

Serendipity Adventures ★ (☎877/507-1358 in the U.S. and Canada, or 2558-1030; www.serendipityadventures.com) offers several mountain-biking trips among its many other expeditions.

Bird-Watching

With more than 850 species of resident and migrant birds identified throughout the country, Costa Rica abounds with great bird-watching sites. Lodges with the best bird-watching include **Savegre Lodge,** in Cerro de la Muerte, off the road to San Isidro de El General (quetzal sightings are almost guaranteed); **La Paloma Lodge** in Drake Bay, where you can sit on the porch of your cabin as the avian parade goes by; **Arenal Observatory Lodge,** on the flanks of Arenal

Ruta de los Conquistadores

Each year, Costa Rica hosts what many consider to be the most challenging and grueling mountain-bike race on the planet. La Ruta de los Conquistadores (the Route of the Conquerors; www.adventurerace. com) retraces the path of the 16th-century Spanish conquistadores from the Pacific Coast to the Caribbean Sea—all in 4 days. The race usually takes place in mid-November, and draws hundreds of competitors from around the world.

Volcano; **La Selva Biological Station,** in Puerto Viejo de Sarapiquí; **Aviarios del Caribe** and **Selva Bananito Lodge,** both just north of Cahuita; **Lapa Ríos** and **Bosque del Cabo,** on the Osa Peninsula; **Playa Nicuesa Rainforest Lodge,** along the Golfo Dulce; **La Laguna del Lagarto Lodge,** up by the Nicaraguan border; and **Tiskita Lodge,** down by the Panamanian border.

Some of the best parks and preserves for serious birders are **Monteverde Biological Cloud Forest Reserve** (for resplendent quetzals and hummingbirds); **Corcovado National Park** (for scarlet macaws); **Caño Negro Wildlife Refuge** (for wading birds, including jabiru storks); **Wilson Botanical Gardens** and the **Las Cruces Biological Station,** near San Vito (the thousands of flowering plants here are bird magnets); **Guayabo, Negritos,** and **Pájaros Islands biological reserves** in the Gulf of Nicoya (for magnificent frigate birds and brown boobies); **Palo Verde National Park** (for ibises, jacanas, storks, and roseate spoonbills); **Tortuguero National Park** (for great green macaws); and **Rincón de la Vieja National Park** (for parakeets and curassows). Rafting trips down the Corobicí and Bebedero rivers near Liberia, boat trips to or at Tortuguero National Park, and hikes in any cloud forest also provide good bird-watching opportunities.

In San José your best bets are to head toward the lush grounds and gardens of the University of Costa Rica, or to Parque del Este, a little farther east in the foothills just outside of town.

COSTA RICAN TOUR AGENCIES

In addition to the agencies listed below, check in with the **Birding Club of Costa Rica** ★★ (costaricabirding@hotmail.com), which runs monthly outings and provides you with the opportunity to connect with local birders. These are also the folks to contact if you want to participate in the annual Christmas bird count. This event is part of a worldwide network of bird counts loosely coordinated by the Audubon Society.

Costa Rica Expeditions ★★ (℃2257-0766; www.costaricaexpeditions. com) and **Costa Rica Sun Tours** ★ (℃2296-7757; www.crsuntours.com) are well-established companies with very competent and experienced guides who offer a variety of tours to some of the better birding spots in Costa Rica.

INTERNATIONAL TOUR OPERATORS

Field Guides (℃800/728-4953 or 512/263-7295; www.fieldguides.com) is a specialty bird-watching travel operator. Its 16-day tour of Costa Rica costs $4,675, not including airfare. Group size is limited to 14 participants.

Tropical Birding ★ (℃800/348-5941 in the U.S. and Canada; www. tropicalbirding.com) is a leading operator specializing in birding tours around the world, which happens to be based in Ecuador. These folks specialize in small group tours, with highly skilled guides, and run periodic trips to Costa Rica.

Victor Emanuel Nature Tours ★★ (℃800/328-8368, or 512/328-5221 in the U.S.; www.ventbird.com) is a well-respected small-group tour operator specializing in bird-watching trips. Their 12-day "Best of Costa Rica" trip costs $4,480.

WINGS ★ (℃888/293-6443 or 520/320-9868; www.wingsbirds.com) is a specialty bird-watching travel operator with 30 years of experience in the field. Its 14-day Costa Rica trip covers the major bird-watching zones in the country and costs around $4,820, not including airfare. Group size is usually between 6 and 14 people.

WHERE TO SEE THE RESPLENDENT quetzal

Revered by pre-Columbian cultures throughout Central America, the resplendent quetzal has been called the most beautiful bird on earth. Ancient Aztec and Maya Indians believed that the robin-size quetzal protected them in battle. The males of this species have brilliant red breasts; iridescent emerald green heads, backs, and wings; and white tail feathers complemented by a pair of iridescent green tail feathers that are more than .5m (1¾ ft.) long.

The belief that these endangered birds live only in the dense cloud forests cloaking the higher slopes of Central America's mountains was instrumental in bringing many areas of cloud forest under protection as quetzal habitats. (Since then, researchers have discovered that the birds do not, in fact, spend their entire lives here.) After nesting between March and July, resplendent quetzals migrate down to lower slopes in search of food. These lower slopes have not been preserved in most cases, and now conservationists are trying to salvage enough lower-elevation forests to help the quetzals survive.

Although for many years **Monteverde Biological Cloud Forest Reserve** was *the* place to see quetzals, throngs of people crowding the reserve's trails now make the pursuit more difficult. Other places where you can see quetzals are in the **Los Angeles Cloud Forest Reserve** near San Ramón, in **Tapantí National Wildlife Refuge,** and in **Chirripó National Park.** Perhaps the best place to spot a quetzal is at one of the specialized lodges located along the Cerro de la Muerte between San José and San Isidro de El General.

Bungee Jumping

Tropical Bungee (☎2248-2212; www.bungee.co.cr) will let you jump off an 80m (262-ft.) bridge over the Río Colorado for $65, including transportation from San José and a video of your jump. A second jump will cost you another $30. The jump site is located on a small bridge over the Río Colorado about 37km (23 miles) northwest of San José, just off the Pan-American Highway. There are obvious and well-placed signs on the highway. Someone should be there from 9am to 3pm every day. They prefer for you to have a reservation, but if you show up on your own, they'll probably let you jump, unless huge groups are booked ahead of you.

Camping

Heavy rains, difficult access, and limited facilities make camping a challenge in Costa Rica. Nevertheless, a backpack and tent will get you far from the crowds and into some of the most pristine and undeveloped nooks and crannies of the country. Camping is forbidden in some national parks, so read the descriptions for each park carefully before you pack a tent.

If you'd like to participate in an organized camping trip, contact **Coast to Coast Adventures** (☎2280-8054; www.ctocadventures.com) or **Serendipity**

Adventures (☎877/507-1358 in the U.S. and Canada, or 2558-1030; www.serendipityadventures.com).

In my opinion, the best place to pop up a tent on the beach is in **Santa Rosa National Park** or at the Puerto Vargas campsite in **Cahuita National Park.** The best camping trek is, without a doubt, a hike through **Corcovado National Park** or a climb up **Mount Chirripó.**

Canopy & Canyoning Tours

Canopy tours are all the rage in Costa Rica, largely because they are such an exciting and unique way to experience tropical rainforests. It's estimated that some two-thirds of a typical rainforest's species live in the canopy (the upper-most, branching layer of the forest). From the relative luxury of Rain Forest Aerial Tram's high-tech funicular to the rope-and-climbing-gear rigs of more basic operations, a trip into the canopy will give you a bird's-eye view of a Neotropical forest. There are now canopy-tour operations in or close to nearly every major tourist destination in the country, including Monteverde, Manuel Antonio, La Fortuna, Tabacón, Montezuma, Punta Islita, Villablanca, and Rincón de la Vieja, as well as on Tortuga Island and around Guanacaste and the Osa Peninsula. There's even a small canopy tour in the La Sabana Park in downtown San José.

Most canopy tours involve strapping yourself into a climbing harness and being winched up to a platform some 30m (100 ft.) above the forest floor, or doing the work yourself. Many of these operations have a series of treetop platforms connected by taut cables. Once up on the first platform, you click your harness into a pulley and glide across the cable to the next (slightly lower) platform, using your hand (protected by a thick leather glove) as a brake. When you reach the last platform, you usually rappel down to the ground. (Don't worry—they'll teach even the most nervous neophyte.)

Although this can be a lot of fun, do be careful because these tours are popping up all over the place and there is precious little regulation of the activity. Some of the tours are set up by fly-by-night operators (obviously, I haven't listed any of those). Be especially sure that you feel comfortable and confident with the safety standards, guides, and equipment before embarking. Before you sign on to any tour, ask whether you have to hoist yourself to the top under your own steam, and then make your decision accordingly.

One of the country's more reputable operators is the **Original Canopy Tour** (☎2291-4465; www.canopytour.com), which has sites in Monteverde and Mahogany Park, about an hour outside of San José. The operation in **Monteverde** features an ascent up the hollow interior of a giant strangler fig tree.

Another option is to try one of the tram or gondola tours through the canopy. The folks at Rain Forest Aerial Tram (see below) currently have two such operations, and there's a ski-lift-style gondola ride at **Turu BaRi Tropical Park** (☎2428-6070; www.turubari.com) outside of San José. See "Side Trips from San José," in chapter 6, for more information.

Canyoning tours are even more adventurous. Hardly standardized, most involve hiking down along a mountain stream, river, and/or canyon, with periodic breaks to rappel down the face of a waterfall, or swim in a jungle pool. The best canyoning operations in Costa Rica are offered by **Pure Trek Canyoning ★★** (☎866/569-5723 in the U.S. and Canada, or 2479-1313; www.puretrekcosta rica.com) and **Desafío Expeditions ★★** (☎2479-9464; www.desafiocostarica.

com), both in La Fortuna; and **Psycho Tours ★★★** (☎8353-8619; www.psychotours.com), which operates outside of Puerto Jiménez. The latter is arguably my favorite adventure tour in the country.

Rain Forest Aerial Tram Caribbean ★ (☎2257-5961; www.rainforest tram.com) is located some 50 minutes from San José. For $55, this modern tram takes you on a 90-minute trip through the rainforest canopy in the comfort and safety of an enclosed cab. The entrance fee includes an additional guided hike and access to its trail system, butterfly garden, and other attractions. The best thing here isn't necessarily the tram ride, which I find somewhat disappointing, but the fact that this makes a good spot for a full-day excursion relatively close to San José. For an extra $15 per person, you can also take a spin on the zip-line canopy tour here. The outfit has a sister project on the central Pacific coast just outside of Jacó. See "Side Trips from San José," in chapter 6, and "Playa de Jacó, Playa Hermosa & Playa Herradura," in chapter 10, for more information.

Cruising

Cruising options in Costa Rica range from transient cruisers setting up a quick charter business to converted fishing boats taking a few guests out to see the sunset.

The most popular cruise option is a day trip from San José (the boats actually leave from Puntarenas) to **Tortuga Island** in the Nicoya Gulf (see "Side Trips from San José," in chapter 6). Alternatively, you can book a cruise to Tortuga from Playa Montezuma at the tip of the Nicoya Peninsula (see chapter 10 for details). It's cheaper from here (around $40–$50 per person), but the excursion doesn't include the gourmet lunch that's usually featured on cruises leaving from San José.

If diesel fumes and engine noise bother you, the best places to charter a sailboat are in Playa del Coco, Playa Hermosa, and Playa Flamingo in Guanacaste province (see chapter 7); Playa Herradura and Quepos along the central Pacific coast (see chapter 10); and Golfito along the southern Pacific coast (see chapter 11). You can get information about sailboat rides and charters at any one of the larger lodgings in these areas. My favorite place to charter a sailboat is **Golfito.** From here, it's a pleasant, peaceful day's sail around the Golfo Dulce (see chapter 11).

For information on cruise ships and cruise lines that ply the coasts and call on the ports of Costa Rica, see p. 54.

Diving & Snorkeling

Many islands, reefs, caves, and rocks lie off the coast of Costa Rica, providing excellent spots for underwater exploration. Visibility varies with season and location. Generally, heavy rainfall tends to swell the rivers and muddy the waters, even well offshore. Banana plantations and their runoff have destroyed most of the Caribbean reefs, although there's still good diving at **Isla Uvita,** just off the coast of Limón, and in **Manzanillo,** down near the Panamanian border. Most divers choose Pacific dive spots such as **Isla del Caño, Bat Island,** and the **Catalina Islands,** where you're likely to spot manta rays, moray eels, white-tipped sharks, and plenty of smaller fish and coral species. But the ultimate in Costa Rican dive experiences is 7 to 10 days on a chartered boat, diving off the coast of **Isla del**

Beach Blanket Bingo

If you plan to spend time at the beach, it's often a good idea to pack your own beach towel or mat. Many of the midrange and budget hotels in Costa Rica do not provide them.

Coco (see "Diving Trips to Isla del Coco [Cocos Island]," on p. 254).

Snorkeling is not incredibly common or rewarding in Costa Rica. The rain, runoff, and wave conditions that drive scuba divers well offshore tend to make coastal and shallow-water conditions less than optimal. If the weather is calm and the water is clear, you might just get lucky. Ask at your hotel or check the different beach listings in this book to find snorkeling options and operators up and down Costa Rica's coasts. The best snorkeling experience to be had in Costa Rica is on the reefs off **Manzanillo Beach** in the southern Caribbean coast, particularly in the calm months of September and October.

DIVING OUTFITTERS & OPERATORS

In addition to the companies listed below, check the listings at specific beach and port destinations in the regional chapters.

Aggressor Fleet Limited ★★ (☎800/348-2628 in the U.S., or 2257-0191; www.aggressor.com) runs the 36m (118-ft.) *Okeanos Aggressor* on regular trips out to Isla del Coco.

Diving Mania (☎2291-2936; www.divingmania.net) is a San José–based outfit that offers equipment rental, certification classes, and tours.

Diving Safaris de Costa Rica ★★ (☎2672-1260; www.costaricadiving.net) is perhaps the largest, most professional, and best-established dive operation in the country. Based out of the Sol Playa Hermosa Hotel in Playa Hermosa, this outfitter is also a local pioneer in nitrox diving.

Undersea Hunter ★★ (☎800/203-2120 in the U.S., or 2228-6613; www.underseahunter.com) offers the *Undersea Hunter* and its sister ship, the *Sea Hunter,* two pioneers of the live-aboard diving excursions to Isla del Coco.

Fishing

Anglers in Costa Rican waters have landed over 100 world-record catches, including blue marlin, Pacific sailfish, dolphin, wahoo, yellowfin tuna, *guapote,* and snook. Whether you want to head offshore looking for a big sail, wrestle a tarpon near a Caribbean river mouth, or choose a quiet spot on Arenal Lake to cast for *guapote,* you'll find it here. You can raise a marlin anywhere along the Pacific coast.

Many of the Pacific port and beach towns—Quepos, Puntarenas, Playa del Coco, Tamarindo, Flamingo, Golfito, Drake Bay, Zancudo—support large charter fleets and have hotels that cater to anglers; see chapters 7, 9, 10, and 11 for recommended boats, captains, and lodges. Costs for fishing trips usually range between $400 and $1,600 per day (depending on the size of the boat) for boat, captain, tackle, drinks, and lunch, so the cost per person depends on the size of the group.

Costa Rica Outdoors ★ (☎800/308-3394 in the U.S. or 2231-0306; www.costaricaoutdoors.com) is a well-established operation founded by local fishing legend and outdoor writer Jerry Ruhlow, specializing in booking fishing trips around the country.

5

ACTIVE VACATION PLANNER | Activities A to Z

FISHING LODGES

Aguila de Osa Inn ★ (☎866/924-8452 in the U.S. and Canada, or 2296-2190; www.aguiladeosainn.com) is a luxury lodge in Drake Bay. See p. 406.

The **Río Colorado Lodge** (☎800/243-9777 in the U.S. and Canada, or 2232-4063; www.riocoloradolodge.com) is located at the Barra del Colorado National Wildlife Refuge. See p. 440.

Silver King Lodge ★★ (☎800/847-3474 in the U.S., or 2711-0708; www.silverkinglodge.net) is a luxury lodge at Barra del Colorado. See p. 441.

The **Zancudo Lodge** ★★ (☎800/854-8791 in the U.S., or 2776-0008; www.thezancudolodge.com) is located in Playa Zancudo. See p. 431.

Golfing

Costa Rica is not one of the world's great golfing destinations—at least not yet, anyway. There are currently seven regulation 18-hole courses open to the public and visitors, but several others are either under construction or in the planning stages, with a potential boom shaping up in Guanacaste.

Currently, the best option for golfers staying in and around San José is **Parque Valle del Sol** ★ (☎2282-9222; www.vallesol.com), an 18-hole course in the western suburb of Santa Ana. Greens fees are $94, including a cart. The **Cariari Country Club** ★★ (☎2293-3211; www.clubcariari.com), just outside of San José, is a private course and not open to the public. However, guests at the **Marriott Costa Rica** and some neighboring hotels can play. If you can wrangle an invitation, or are staying at a hotel with an agreement with the club, greens fees are $60, including a mandatory caddy. You should expect to tip your caddy around $20, and pay an extra $25 for a cart.

The Meliá chain also runs the **Garra de León course** ★★ at the **Paradisus Playa Conchal** resort (☎2654-4123; www.solmelia.com) up in Guanacaste. Greens fees here are $200, including a cart. With advance notice and depending on available tee times, this course is currently open to guests at other hotels in the region.

Another major resort course is at the **Los Sueños Marriott Ocean & Golf Resort** ★★ in Playa Herradura (☎800/228-9290 in the U.S., or 2630-9028; www.marriott.com). Greens fees, including a cart, run around $160 for the general public, and guests pay slightly less.

Hacienda Pinilla ★ (☎2680-7000; www.haciendapinilla.com) is an 18-hole links-style course located south of Tamarindo. This might just be the most challenging course in the country, and the facilities, though limited, are top-notch. Currently, the course is open to golfers staying at hotels around the area, with advance reservations. Greens fees run around $185 for 18 holes, including a cart.

Tai Chi in Paradise

For the past 20 years, tai chi master and two-time U.S. national champion Chris Luth has been leading weeklong retreats to Costa Rica, combining intensive classes in this ancient Chinese martial art with rainforest hikes, river rafting, and just enough beach time. For more information, contact **T'ai Chi in Paradise** (☎858/259-1396; www.taichiinparadise.com).

The **Papagayo Golf & Country Club** (☎2697-1313; www.papagayo-golf.com), on the outskirts of Playa del Coco, offers up a full 18-hole course, with a pro shop, driving range, and rental equipment. It costs $95 in greens fees, including a cart.

The most spectacular course in Costa Rica is at **Four Seasons Resort** ★★★ (☎212/688-2440 in the U.S., or 2696-0871; www.fourseasons.com), but it is open only to hotel guests. Greens fees run around $210.

Golfers who want the most up-to-date information, or those who are interested in a package deal that includes play on a variety of courses, should contact **Costa Rica Golf Adventures** ★ (☎877/258-2688; www.golfcr.com).

Hang Gliding, Paragliding & Ballooning

Paragliding with a pilot in a tandem rig is taking off (pardon the pun) in the cliff areas around Caldera, just south of Puntarenas, as well as other spots around Costa Rica. If you're looking to paraglide, check in with the folks at the **Costa Rican Association of Free Flying** (call Miguel Dib at ☎8842-9644; www.parapente-costa-rica.org).

Serendipity Adventures (☎877/507-1358 in the U.S. and Canada, or 2558-1000; www.serendipityadventures.com) will take you up, up, and away in a hot-air balloon on a variety of single- or multiday tours, either in Turrialba, in Naranjo, or near Arenal Volcano. A basic flight costs around $345 per passenger, with a two-person minimum, and a five-person or 800-pound maximum.

Hang Glide Costa Rica (☎8353-5514; www.hangglidecr.com) offers about a half-hour of gentle hang gliding in a tandem rig, which begins with a tow by an ultralight, for $99 to $150 per person.

Horseback Riding

Costa Rica's rural roots are evident in the continued use of horses for real work and transportation throughout the country. Visitors will find that horses are easily available for riding, whether you want to take a sunset trot along the beach, ride through the cloud forest, or take a multiday trek through the northern zone.

Most travelers simply saddle up for a couple of hours, but those looking for a more specifically equestrian-based visit should check in with the following folks.

Coast to Coast Adventures (☎2280-8054; www.ctocadventures.com) specializes in 2-week trips spanning the country via horseback, raft, or mountain bike, as well as on foot, with no motor vehicles involved. Other trips are also available.

Nature Lodge Finca Los Caballos ★ (☎/fax 2642-0124; www.naturelodge.net) specializes in horse tours and has the healthiest horses in the Montezuma area.

Serendipity Adventures (☎877/507-1358 in the U.S. and Canada, or 2558-1030; www.serendipityadventures.com) offers horseback treks and tours.

Motorcycling

Visiting bikers can either cruise the highways or try some off-road biking around Costa Rica. All the caveats about driving conditions and driving customs in Costa Rica apply equally for bikers. If you want to rent a Harley-Davidson for cruising around the country, **María Alexandra Tours** (☎2289-5552; www.mariaalexandra.com) conducts guided bike tours and rents well-equipped late-model

Harleys by the day or the week. If your tastes run to off-road riding, **MotoAdventures** (☎440/256-8508 in the U.S., or 2228-8494 in Costa Rica; www.motoadventuring.com) runs guided multiday tours on Honda dirt bikes. Bike rental rates run between $70 and $150 per day.

Rock Climbing

Although this is a nascent sport in Costa Rica, the possibilities are promising. There are several challenging rock formations close to San José and along the Cerro de la Muerte, as well as great climbing opportunities on Mount Chirripó. The folks at **Tropical Bungee** (☎2248-2212; www.bungee.co.cr) are the most dependable operators in this field, and they regularly organize climbing outings. Alternatively, you could visit **Mundo Aventura** (☎2221-6934; www.maventura. com), an adventure- and climbing-gear store with an indoor climbing wall and in-house tour company.

Spas & Yoga Retreats

Hotel Borinquen Mountain Resort, Cañas Dulces (☎2690-1900; www. borinquenresort.com; p. 204), on the flanks of the Rincón de la Vieja volcano, has the setting, natural hot springs, volcanic mud pots, and luxurious accommodations to be a world-class destination spa. But, despite being in operation for several years, they've so far been unable to get their spa operation up to snuff.

The **Four Seasons Resort ★★★** (☎800/819-5053 in the U.S., or 2696-0000; www.fourseasons.com/costarica; p. 212) on the Papagayo Peninsula has ample and luxurious facilities and treatment options, as well as scheduled classes in yoga, aerobics, and other disciplines.

Luna Lodge ★ (☎888/409-8448 in the U.S. and Canada, or 8380-5036; www.lunalodge.com) is a gorgeous lodge located on a hillside overlooking Playa Carate, on the border with Corcovado National Park. These folks run a fairly full schedule of dedicated yoga and wellness programs and have a good little spa on-site.

Samasati ★, Puerto Viejo de Talamanca (☎800/563-9643 in the U.S., or 2750-0315; www.samasati.com), is a lovely yoga retreat in some dense forest on a hillside above the Caribbean. Accommodations here range from budget to rustically luxurious. See "Puerto Viejo," in chapter 12.

Serenity Spa ★ (☎2643-4094) started out with a little storefront spa in Jacó but now contracts out the spa services at several large resorts up and down the Pacific coast. At last count, it was running the spas at Villa Caletas (p. 353), Hotel Sí Como No (p. 373), and Villa Blanca (p. 314).

Sueño Azul Resort ★★, Las Horquetas de Sarapiquí (☎2764-1048; www.suenoazulresort.com; p. 295), is a nature lodge and retreat center with regular programs and retreats in a wonderful setting at the juncture of two rivers.

Tabacón Grand Spa Thermal Resort ★★★, Tabacón (☎877/277-8291 in the U.S. and Canada, or 2519-1900; www.tabacon.com; p. 308), is a top-notch spa with spectacular hot springs, lush gardens, and a volcano view. A complete range of spa services and treatments is available at reasonable prices.

Xandari Resort & Spa ★★, Alajuela (☎866/363-3212 in the U.S., or 2443-2020; www.xandari.com; p. 144), is a unique and distinctive little luxury hotel that has some top-notch spa facilities and services. This is a good choice if you're looking for a day or two of pampering, or for day treatments while staying in San José. Xandari has also opened a sister resort on the Central Pacific coast, for those looking for a beach spa retreat (p. 357).

Surfing

When *Endless Summer II,* the sequel to the all-time surf classic, was filmed, the production crew brought its boards and cameras to Costa Rica. Point and beach breaks that work year-round are located all along Costa Rica's immense coastline. **Playas Hermosa, Jacó,** and **Dominical,** on the central Pacific coast, and **Tamarindo** and **Playa Guiones,** in Guanacaste, are becoming mini surf meccas. **Salsa Brava** in Puerto Viejo is a steep and fast wave that peels off both right and left over shallow coral. It has a habit of breaking boards, but the daredevils keep coming back for more. Beginners and folks looking to learn should stick to the mellower sections of **Jacó** and **Tamarindo**—surf lessons are offered at both beaches. Crowds are starting to gather at the more popular breaks, but you can still stumble onto secret spots on the **Osa** and **Nicoya peninsulas** and along the northern **Guanacaste** coast. Costa Rica's signature wave is still found at **Playa**

IN SEARCH OF turtles

Few places in the world have as many sea-turtle nesting sites as Costa Rica. Along both coasts, five species of these huge marine reptiles come ashore at specific times of the year to dig nests in the sand and lay their eggs. Sea turtles are endangered throughout the world due to over-hunting, accidental deaths in fishing nets, development on beaches that once served as nesting areas, and the collection and sale (often illegally) of their eggs. International trade in sea-turtle products is already prohibited by most countries (including the U.S.), but sea-turtle numbers continue to dwindle.

Among the species of sea turtles that nest on Costa Rica's beaches are the **olive ridley** (known for their mass egg-laying migrations, or *arribadas*), **leatherback, hawksbill, green,** and **Pacific green turtle.** Excursions to see nesting turtles have become common, and they are fascinating, but please make sure that you and/or your guide do not disturb the turtles. Any light source (other than red-tinted flashlights) can confuse female turtles and cause them to return to the sea without laying their eggs. In fact, as more development takes place on the Costa Rican coast, hotel lighting may cause the number of nesting turtles to drop. Luckily, many of the nesting beaches have been protected as national parks.

Here are the main places to see nesting sea turtles: **Santa Rosa National Park** (near Liberia), **Las Baulas National Marine Park** (near Tamarindo), **Ostional National Wildlife Refuge** (near Playa Nosara), and **Tortuguero National Park** (on the northern Caribbean coast).

See the regional chapters for descriptions of the resident turtles and their respective nesting seasons, as well as listings of local tour operators and companies that arrange trips to see sea turtles nesting.

Pavones, which is reputed to have one of the longest lefts in the world. The co-gnoscenti, however, also swear by places such as **Playa Grande, Playa Negra, Matapalo, Malpaís,** and **Witch's Rock.** An avid surfer's best bet is to rent a dependable four-wheel-drive vehicle with a rack and take a surfin' safari around the breaks of Guanacaste.

If you're looking for an organized surf vacation, contact **Tico Travel** (☏800/493-8426 in the U.S.; www.ticotravel.com), or check out **www.crsurf.com**. For swell reports, general surf information, live wave-cams, and great links pages, point your browser to **www.surfline.com**. Although killer sets are possible at any particular spot at any time of the year, depending upon swell direction, local winds, and distant storms, in broad terms, the northern coast of Guanacaste works best from December to April; the central and southern Pacific coasts work best from April to November; and the Caribbean coast's short big-wave season is December through March.

White-Water Rafting, Kayaking & Canoeing

Whether you're a first-time rafter or a world-class kayaker, Costa Rica's got some white water suited to your abilities. Rivers rise and fall with the rainfall, but you can get wet and wild here even in the dry season. The best white-water rafting ride is still the scenic **Pacuare River;** although there has been talk about damming it to build a hydroelectric plant, the project has thankfully failed to materialize. If you're just experimenting with river rafting, stick to Class II and III rivers, such as **Reventazón, Sarapiquí, Peñas Blancas,** and **Savegre.** If you already know which end of the paddle goes in the water, there are plenty of Class IV and V sections to run.

Die-hard river rats should get *Chasing Jaguars: The Complete Guide to Costa Rican Whitewater,* by Lee Eudy, a book loaded with photos, technical data, and route tips on almost every rideable river in the country.

Aventuras Naturales ★★ (☏800/321-8410 in the U.S., or 2225-3939; www.toenjoynature.com) is a major rafting operator that runs daily trips on the most popular rivers in Costa Rica. Its Pacuare Jungle Lodge is pretty plush, and a great place to spend the night on one of its 2-day rafting trips.

Canoe Costa Rica (☏/fax 732/736-6586 in the U.S., or 2282-3579; www.canoecostarica.com) is the only outfit I know of that specializes in canoe trips; it works primarily with custom-designed tours and itineraries, although it does have several set departure trips each year.

Exploradores Outdoors ★ (☏2222-6262; www.exploradoresoutdoors.com) is another good company run by a longtime and well-respected river guide. They run the Pacuare, Reventazón, and Sarapiquí rivers, and even combine a 1-day river trip with onward transportation to or from the Caribbean coast, or the Arenal volcano area, for no extra cost.

If you're out on the Osa Peninsula, hook up with **Escondido Trex ★** (☏/fax 2735-5210; www.escondidotrex.com).

Pacuare River Tours (☏888/472-3827 in the U.S. and Canada, or 2291-6844 in Costa Rica; www.pacuarerivertours.com) is a small, new river company with good guides and a profit-sharing plan they're very proud of.

Rio Locos (☏2556-3500; www.whiteh2o.com) is a small company based in Turrialba. These folks are a good option for hard-core kayakers, small custom group tours, and folks who find themselves in Turrialba.

Ríos Tropicales ★ (☎866/722-8273 in the U.S. and Canada, or 2233-6455 in Costa Rica; www.riostropicales.com) is one of the major operators in Costa Rica, with tours on most of the country's popular rivers. Accommodation options include a very comfortable lodge on the banks of the Río Pacuare for the 2-day trips.

Windsurfing & Kiteboarding

Windsurfing is not very popular on the high seas here, where winds are fickle and rental options are limited, even at beach hotels. However, **Lake Arenal** is considered one of the top spots in the world for high-wind boardsailing. During the winter months, many of the regulars from Washington's Columbia River Gorge take up residence around the nearby town of Tilarán. Small boards, water starts, and fancy gibes are the norm. The best time for windsurfing on Lake Arenal is between December and March. The same winds that buffet Lake Arenal make their way down to **Bahía Salinas** (also known as Bolaños Bay), near La Cruz, Guanacaste, where you can get in some good windsurfing. Both spots also have operations offering lessons and equipment rentals in the high-action sport of kiteboarding. See "La Cruz & Bahía Salinas," in chapter 7, and "Along the Shores of Lake Arenal," in chapter 9, for details.

COSTA RICA'S TOP NATIONAL PARKS & BIORESERVES

Costa Rica has 28 national parks, protecting more than 12% of the country. They range in size from the 212-hectare (524-acre) Guayabo National Monument to the 189,696-hectare (468,549-acre) La Amistad National Park. Many of these national parks are undeveloped tropical forests, with few services or facilities available for visitors. Others, however, offer easier access to their wealth of natural wonders.

Most of the national parks charge a $10 per-person per-day fee for any foreigner, although Chirripó National Park costs $15 per day. Costa Ricans and foreign residents continue to pay just $1. At parks where camping is allowed, there is usually an additional charge of around $2 per person per day.

This section is not a complete listing of all of Costa Rica's national parks and protected areas, but rather a selective list of those parks that are of greatest interest and accessibility. They're popular, but they're also among the best. You'll find detailed information about food and lodging options near some of the individual parks in the regional chapters that follow. As you'll see from the descriptions, Costa Rica's national parks vary greatly in terms of attractions, facilities, and accessibility.

If you're looking for a camping adventure or an extended stay in one of the national parks, I recommend **Santa Rosa, Rincón de la Vieja, Chirripó, Corcovado,** or **Cahuita.** Any of the others are better suited for day trips or guided hikes, or in combination with your travels around the country.

For more information, call the national parks information line at ☎192, or the main office at ☎2283-8004. You can also stop by the **National Parks Foundation office** (☎2257-2239) in San José, located between Calle 23 and Avenida 15. Both offices are open Monday through Friday from 8am to 5pm.

San José/Central Valley Area

GUAYABO NATIONAL MONUMENT This is the country's only significant pre-Columbian archaeological site. It's believed that Guayabo supported a population of about 10,000 people some 3,000 years ago. The park is set in a forested area rich in flora and fauna, although the ruins are quite small and limited when compared to sites in Mexico, Guatemala, and South America. **Location:** 19km (12 miles) northeast of Turrialba, which is 53km (33 miles) east of San José. See "Side Trips from San José," in chapter 6.

IRAZU VOLCANO NATIONAL PARK ★ Irazú Volcano is the highest (3,378m/11,080 ft.) of Costa Rica's four active volcanoes and a popular day trip from San José. A paved road leads right up to the crater, and the lookout also has a view of both the Pacific and the Caribbean on a clear day. The volcano last erupted in 1963 on the same day U.S. President John F. Kennedy visited the country. There are an information center, picnic tables, restrooms, and a parking area here. **Location:** 55km (34 miles) east of San José. See "Holy Smoke! Choosing the Volcano Trip That's Right for You," in chapter 6.

POAS VOLCANO NATIONAL PARK ★★ Poás is the other active volcano close to San José. The main crater is more than 1.6km (1 mile) wide, and it is constantly active with fumaroles and hot geysers. I slightly prefer Poás to Irazú because it is surrounded by dense cloud forests, and there are some nice gentle trails to hike here. Although the area around the volcano is lush, much of the growth is stunted due to the gases and acid rain. On January 8, 2009, a 6.1 magnitude earthquake struck Costa Rica, with its epicenter very close to Poás. The park was closed for several days, and an uptick in volcanic activity was noted. The park still sometimes closes when the gases get too feisty. There are nature trails, picnic tables, restrooms, and an information center. **Location:** 37km (23 miles) northwest of San José. See "Holy Smoke! Choosing the Volcano Trip That's Right for You," in chapter 6.

Guanacaste & the Nicoya Peninsula

BARRA HONDA NATIONAL PARK Costa Rica's only underground national park, Barra Honda features a series of limestone caves that were once part of a coral reef some 60 million years ago. Today the caves are home to millions of bats and impressive stalactite and stalagmite formations. Only Terciopelo Cave is open to the public. A camping area, restrooms, and an information center are here, as well as trails through the surrounding tropical dry forest. **Location:** 335km (208 miles) northwest of San José. See "Playa Sámara," in chapter 8.

PALO VERDE NATIONAL PARK A must for bird-watchers, Palo Verde National Park is one of Costa Rica's best-kept secrets. This part of the Tempisque River lowlands supports a population of more than 50,000 waterfowl and forest bird species. Various ecosystems here include mangroves, savanna brush lands, and evergreen forests. There are camping facilities, an information center, and some nice accommodations at the Organization for Tropical Studies (OTS) research station here. **Location:** 200km (124 miles) northwest of San José. Be warned that the park entrance is 28km (17 miles) off the highway down a very rugged dirt road; it's another 9km (5½ miles) to the OTS station and campsites. For more information, call the OTS (☎ 240-6696; reservas@cro.ots.ac.cr). See "Liberia," in chapter 7.

RINCON DE LA VIEJA NATIONAL PARK ★★ This large tract of parkland experiences high volcanic activity, with numerous fumaroles and geysers, as well as hot springs, cold pools, and mud pots. You'll find excellent hikes to the upper craters and to several waterfalls. You should hire a guide for any hot-spring or mud-bath expeditions as inexperienced visitors have been burned. Camping is permitted at two sites, each of which has an information center, a picnic area, and restrooms. **Location:** 266km (165 miles) northwest of San José. See "Liberia," in chapter 7.

SANTA ROSA NATIONAL PARK ★ Occupying a large section of Costa Rica's northwestern Guanacaste province, Santa Rosa has the country's largest area of tropical dry forest, important turtle-nesting sites, and the historically significant La Casona monument. There are also caves for exploring. The beaches are pristine and have basic camping facilities, and the waves make them quite popular with surfers. An information center, a picnic area, and restrooms are at the main campsite and entrance. **Location:** 258km (160 miles) northwest of San José. For more information, you can call the park office at ☎ 666-5051. See "La Cruz & Bahía Salinas," in chapter 7.

The Northern Zone

ARENAL NATIONAL PARK ★★ This park, created to protect the ecosystem that surrounds Arenal Volcano, has few services or attractions. Basically, the government has set up a tollbooth on the access road leading to an up-close view of the volcano's lava flows. Most travelers and tour operators choose to forgo the entrance fee and watch the volcano from spots along the dirt road leading to the Arenal Observatory Lodge, or from the road to Tabacón, where the view is arguably as good as it is inside the park. However, there are several excellent hiking trails inside the park that explore cooled-off lava flows and the neighboring rainforest. **Location:** 129km (80 miles) northwest of San José. See "Arenal Volcano & La Fortuna," in chapter 8.

BRAULIO CARRILO NATIONAL PARK Braulio Carillo, which occupies a large area of the nation's central mountain range, is the park you pass through on your way from San José to the Caribbean coast. A deep rainforest, Braulio Carrillo receives an average of 177 inches of rain per year. There are beautiful rivers, majestic waterfalls, and more than 6,500 species of plants and animals. The park has an information center, picnic tables, restrooms, and hiking trails. Camping is allowed but is not common or recommended. Be careful here. Make sure you park your car in and base your explorations from the park's main entrance, not just anywhere along the highway. There have been several robberies and attacks against visitors reported at trails leading into the park from the highway. This park also seems to have the highest incidence of lost hikers. **Location:** 22km (14 miles) north of San José. See "Puerto Viejo de Sarapiquí," in chapter 9.

CAÑO NEGRO NATIONAL WILDLIFE REFUGE ★ A lowland swamp and drainage basin for several northern rivers, Caño Negro is excellent for bird-watching.

There are a few basic cabinas and lodges in this area, but the most popular way to visit is on a combined van and boat trip from the La Fortuna/Arenal area. **Location:** 20km (12 miles) south of Los Chiles, near the Nicaraguan border. See "Arenal Volcano & La Fortuna," in chapter 9.

MONTEVERDE BIOLOGICAL CLOUD FOREST RESERVE ★★★ This private reserve might be the most famous patch of forest in Costa Rica. It covers some 26,000 acres of primary forest, mostly mid-elevation cloud forest, with a rich variety of flora and fauna. Epiphytes thrive in the cool, misty climate. The most famous resident is the spectacular resplendent quetzal. There is a well-maintained trail system, as well as some of the best-trained and most experienced guides in the country. Nearby you can visit both the Santa Elena and Sendero Tranquilo reserves. **Location:** 167km (104 miles) northwest of San José. See "Monteverde," in chapter 9.

Central Pacific Coast

CARARA NATIONAL PARK ★★ Located just off the highway near the Pacific coast, on the road to Jacó, this is one of the best places in Costa Rica to see scarlet macaws. Several trails run through the park, including one that is wheelchair accessible. The park is comprised of various ecosystems, ranging from rainforests to transitional forests to mangroves. **Location:** 102km (63 miles) west of San José. See "Playa de Jacó, Playa Hermosa & Playa Herradura," in chapter 10.

CHIRRIPO NATIONAL PARK ★★ Home to Costa Rica's tallest peak, 3,761m (12,336-ft.) Mount Chirripó, Chirripó National Park is a hike, but on a clear day you can see both the Pacific Ocean and the Caribbean Sea from its summit. There are a number of interesting climbing trails here, and camping is allowed. **Location:** 151km (94 miles) southeast of San José. See "San Isidro de El General: A Base for Exploring Chirripó National Park," in chapter 10.

MANUEL ANTONIO NATIONAL PARK ★★ Though relatively small, Manuel Antonio is the most popular national park and supports the largest number of hotels and resorts. This lowland rainforest is home to a healthy monkey population, including the endangered squirrel monkey. The park is best known for its splendid beaches. **Location:** 129km (80 miles) south of San José. See "Manuel Antonio National Park," in chapter 10.

The Southern Zone

CORCOVADO NATIONAL PARK ★★★ The largest single block of virgin lowland rainforest in Central America, Corcovado National Park receives more than 200 inches of rain per year. It's increasingly popular but still very remote. (It has no roads; only dirt tracks lead into it.) Scarlet macaws live here, as do countless other Neotropical species, including two of the country's largest cats, the puma and the endangered jaguar. There are camping facilities and trails throughout the park. **Location:** 335km (208 miles) south of San José, on the Osa Peninsula. See "Puerto Jiménez: Gateway to Corcovado National Park," in chapter 11.

The Caribbean Coast

CAHUITA NATIONAL PARK ★ A combination land and marine park, Cahuita National Park protects one of the few remaining living coral reefs in the country. The topography here is lush lowland tropical rainforest. Monkeys and numerous bird species are common. Camping is permitted, and there are basic facilities at the Puerto Vargas entrance to the park. If you want to visit for only the day, however, enter from Cahuita village because the local community has taken over that entrance and is asking for only a voluntary donation, in lieu of the normal $6 fee. **Location:** On the Caribbean coast, 42km (26 miles) south of Limón. See "Cahuita," in chapter 12.

TORTUGUERO NATIONAL PARK ★★ Tortuguero National Park has been called the Venice of Costa Rica due to its maze of jungle canals that meander through a dense lowland rainforest. Small boats, launches, and canoes carry visitors through these waterways, where caimans, manatees, and numerous bird and mammal species are common. The extremely endangered great green macaw lives here. On the beaches green sea turtles nest here every year between June and October. The park has a small but helpful information office and some well-marked trails. **Location:** 258km (160 miles) northeast of San José. See "Tortuguero National Park," in chapter 12.

TIPS ON HEALTH, SAFETY & ETIQUETTE IN THE WILDERNESS

Much of what is discussed here is common sense. For more detailed information, see "Health," in chapter 3. Although most tours and activities are safe, there are risks involved in any adventure activity. Know and respect your own physical limits before undertaking any strenuous activity. Be prepared for extremes in temperature and rainfall and for wide fluctuations in weather. A sunny morning hike can quickly become a cold and wet ordeal, so it's usually a good idea to carry along some form of rain gear when hiking in the rainforest, or to have a dry change of clothing waiting at the end of the trail. Be sure to bring along plenty of sunscreen when you're not going to be covered by the forest canopy.

If you do any backcountry packing or camping, remember that it really *is* a jungle out there. Don't go poking under rocks or fallen branches. Snakebites are very rare, but don't do anything to increase the odds. If you encounter a snake, stay calm, don't make any sudden movements, and *do not* try to handle it. Also avoid swimming in major rivers unless a guide or local operator can vouch for their safety. Although white-water sections and stretches in mountainous areas are generally safe, most mangrove canals and river mouths in Costa Rica support healthy crocodile and caiman populations.

Bugs and bug bites will probably be your greatest health concern in the Costa Rican wilderness, and even they aren't as big of a problem as you might expect. Mostly, bugs are an inconvenience, although mosquitoes can carry malaria or dengue (see "Health," in chapter 3, for more information). A strong repellent and proper clothing minimize both the danger and the inconvenience; you might also want to bring along some cortisone or Benadryl cream to soothe itching. ***And remember:*** Whenever you enter and enjoy nature, you should tread lightly and try not to disturb the natural environment. There's a popular slogan well known to most campers that certainly applies here: "Leave nothing but footprints; take nothing but memories." If you must take home a souvenir, take photos. Do not cut or uproot plants or flowers. Pack out everything you pack in, and *please* do not litter.

VOLUNTEER & STUDY PROGRAMS
Language Immersion

As more people travel to Costa Rica with the intention of learning Spanish, the number of options for Spanish immersion vacations increases. You can find courses of varying lengths and degrees of intensiveness, and many that include cultural activities and day excursions. Many of these schools have reciprocal relationships with U.S. universities, so, in some cases, you can even arrange for college credit. Most Spanish schools can arrange for home stays with a middle-class Tico family for a total-immersion experience. Classes are often small, or even one-on-one, and can last anywhere from 2 to 8 hours a day. Listed below are some of the larger and more established Spanish-language schools, with approximate costs. Most are located in San José, but there are also schools in Monteverde, Manuel Antonio, Playa Flamingo, Malpaís, Playa Nosara, and Tamarindo. (I'd certainly rather spend 2 weeks or a month in one of these spots than in San José.) Contact the schools for the most current price information.

Adventure Education Center (AEC) Spanish Institute ★ (☎800/237-2730 in the U.S. and Canada, or 2258-5111 in Costa Rica; www.adventure spanishschool.com) has branches in La Fortuna, Dominical, and Turrialba, and specializes in combining language learning with adventure activities. A 1-week course here with 4 hours of classes each day, including room and board with a Costa Rican family, costs $450.

Centro Lingüístico Conversa ★ (☎888/669-1664 in the U.S. and Canada, or 2221-7649; www.conversa.net) has classes in both San José and Santa Ana (a suburb of the capital city). A 1-week course here with 4 hours of classes each day, including room and board with a Costa Rican family, costs between $530 and $760, depending on which campus you choose.

Centro Panamericano de Idiomas (CPI) ★ (☎877/373-3116 in the U.S., or 2265-6306; www.cpi-edu.com) has three campuses: one in the quiet suburban town of Heredia, another in Monteverde, and one at the beach in Playa Flamingo. A 1-week program, with 4 hours of class per day and a home stay with a Costa Rican family, costs $465.

Costa Rican Language Academy ★ in San José (☎866/230-6361 in the U.S., or 2280-1685; www.spanishandmore.com) has intensive programs with classes held Monday to Thursday to give students a chance for longer weekend excursions. The academy also integrates Latin dance and Costa Rican cooking classes into the program. A 1-week class with 4 hours of class per day, plus a home stay, costs $337.

Costa Rica Spanish Institute (COSI; ☎2234-1001; www.cosi.co.cr) offers small classes in the San Pedro neighborhood of San José, as well as a program at Manuel Antonio. The weekly cost of $495 includes a home stay.

Forester Instituto Internacional ★ (☎2225-3155 or 2225-0135; www. fores.com), is 75m (246 ft.) south of the Automercado in the Los Yoses district

monkey **BUSINESS**

No trip to Costa Rica would be complete without at least one monkey sighting. Home to four distinct species of primates, Costa Rica offers the opportunity for one of the world's most gratifying wildlife-viewing experiences. Just listen for the deep guttural call of a howler or the rustling of leaves overhead—telltale signs that monkeys are in your vicinity.

Costa Rica's most commonly spotted monkey is the white-faced or **capuchin monkey** (*mono cara blanca* in Spanish), which you might recognize as the infamous culprit from the film *Outbreak*. Contrary to that film's plot, however, capuchins are native to the New World tropics and do not exist in Africa. Capuchins are agile, medium-size monkeys that make good use of their long, prehensile tails. They inhabit a diverse collection of habitats, ranging from the high-altitude cloud forests of the central region to the lowland mangroves of the Osa Peninsula. It's almost impossible not to spot capuchins at Manuel Antonio (see chapter 10), where they have become a little too dependent on fruit and junk-food feedings by tourists. Please do not feed wild monkeys (and try to keep your food away from them—they're notorious thieves), and boycott establishments that try to attract both monkeys and tourists with daily feedings.

Howler monkeys (*mono congo* in Spanish) are named for their distinct and eerie call. Large and mostly black, these monkeys can seem ferocious because of their physical appearance and deep, resonant howls that can carry for more than a mile, even in dense rainforest. Biologists believe that male howlers mark the bounds of their territories with these deep, guttural sounds. In the presence of humans, however, howlers are actually a little timid and tend to stay higher up in the canopy

than their white-faced cousins. Howlers are fairly common and easy to spot in the dry tropical forests of coastal Guanacaste and the Nicoya Peninsula (see chapter 7).

Even more elusive are **spider monkeys** (*mono araña* in Spanish). These long, slender monkeys are dark brown to black and prefer the high canopies of primary rainforests. Spiders are very adept with their prehensile tails but actually travel through the canopy with a hand-over-hand motion frequently imitated by their less graceful human cousins on playground monkey bars around the world. I've had my best luck spotting spider monkeys along the edges of Tortuguero's jungle canals (see chapter 12), where howlers are also quite common.

The rarest and most endangered of Costa Rica's monkeys is the tiny **squirrel monkey** (*mono tití* in Spanish). These small, brown monkeys have dark eyes surrounded by large white rings, white ears, white chests, and very long tails. In Costa Rica, squirrel monkeys can be found only at Manuel Antonio (see chapter 10) and the Osa Peninsula (see chapter 11). These seemingly hyperactive monkeys are predominantly fruit eaters and often feed on bananas and other fruit trees near hotels in both of the above-mentioned regions. Squirrel monkeys usually travel in large bands, so if you do see them, you'll likely see quite a few.

of San José. I've received glowing reports from satisfied customers here. The cost of a 1-week language course with a home stay and excursions is approximately $505.

Institute for Central American Development Studies (ICADS) ★★ near San Pedro (℃2225-0508; www.icads.org) has one of the best and most extensive fieldwork and volunteer programs in Costa Rica, as well as quality Spanish-language immersion programs. A 4-week course with home stay costs $1,950.

International House Costa Rica ★ (℃2234-9054; www.instituto britanico.co.cr), formerly the Instituto Britanico, is a venerable institution with installations in the Los Yoses neighborhood of San José. A bit more attention seems to be paid to teacher training and selection here than at other institutions around town. A 2-week course with 40 hours of classes and a home stay costs $685.

Escuela D'Amore ★ (℃800/261-3203 in the U.S. and Canada, or ℃/fax 2777-1143; www.escueladamore.com) is situated in the lush surroundings of Manuel Antonio National Park. A 2-week conversational Spanish course, including a home stay and two meals daily, costs $995. This is a much nicer environment than San José for learning Spanish (for most everything else too, in fact).

Wayra Instituto de Español (℃/fax 2653-0359; www.spanish-wayra. co.cr) is located in the beach town of Tamarindo. A week of classes, 4 hours per day, will run you $420 including a home stay.

Sustainable Volunteer Projects

Below are some institutions and organizations that are working on ecology and sustainable development projects in Costa Rica.

APREFLOFAS (Association for the Preservation of the Wild Flora and Fauna; ℃2574-6816; www.preserveplanet.org) is a pioneering local conservation organization that accepts volunteers and runs environmentally sound educational tours around the country.

Asociación de Voluntarios para el Servicio en las Areas Protegidas (ASVO) ★ (℃2258-4430; www.asvocr.org) organizes volunteers to work in Costa Rican national parks. A 2-week minimum commitment is required, as is a basic ability to converse in Spanish. Housing is provided at a basic ranger station, and there is a $17 daily fee to cover food, which is basic Tico fare.

Caribbean Conservation Corporation (℃800/676-2018 in the U.S., or 2278-6058; www.cccturtle.org) is a nonprofit organization dedicated to sea turtle research, protection, and advocacy. Their main operation in Costa Rica is headquartered in Tortuguero, where volunteers can aid in various scientific studies, as well as nightly patrols of the beach during nesting seasons to prevent poaching.

Costa Rica Rainforest Outward Bound School (℃800/676-2018 in the U.S., or 2278-6058; www.crrobs.org) is the local branch of this well-respected international adventure-based outdoor-education organization. Courses range from 2 weeks to a full semester, and offerings include surfing, kayaking, tree climbing, and learning Spanish.

Eco Teach (℃800/626-8992 in the U.S.; www.ecoteach.com) works primarily in facilitating educational trips for high school and college student groups.

Trips focus on Costa Rican ecology and culture. Costs run around $1,495 to $1,675 per person for a 10-day trip, including lodging, meals, classes, and travel within the country. Airfare to Costa Rica is extra.

Global Volunteers (☎800/487-1074 in the U.S.; www.globalvolunteers. org) is a U.S.-based organization that offers a unique opportunity to travelers who've always wanted a Peace Corps–like experience but can't make a 2-year commitment. For 2 to 3 weeks, you can join one of its working vacations in Costa Rica. A certain set of skills, such as engineering or agricultural knowledge, is helpful but by no means necessary. Each trip is undertaken at a particular community's request, to complete a specific project. However, be warned: These "volunteer" experiences do not come cheap. You must pay for your transportation as well as a hefty program fee, around $2,395 for a 2-week program.

Habitat for Humanity International (☎2296-3436; www.habitat costarica.org) has several chapters in Costa Rica and sometimes runs organized Global Village programs here.

The **Institute for Central American Development Studies** ★ (☎2225-0508; www.icads.org) offers internship and research opportunities in the areas of environment, agriculture, human rights, and women's studies. An intensive Spanish-language program can be combined with work-study or volunteer opportunities.

The **Monteverde Institute** (☎2645-5053; www.mvinstitute.org) offers study programs in Monteverde and also has a volunteer center that helps in placement and training of volunteers.

The **Organization for Tropical Studies** ★ (☎2524-0607; www.three paths.co.cr) represents several Costa Rican and U.S. universities. This organization's mission is to promote research, education, and the wise use of natural resources in the Tropics. Research facilities include La Selva Biological Station near Braulio Carrillo National Park and Palo Verde, and the Wilson Botanical Gardens near San Vito. Housing is provided at one of the research facilities. There's a wide variety of programs, ranging from full-semester undergraduate programs to specific graduate courses (of varying duration) to its tourist programs. (These are generally sponsored/run by established operators such as Costa Rica Expeditions or Elderhostel.) Programs range in duration from 3 to 10 days, and costs vary greatly. Entrance requirements and competition for some of these courses can be demanding.

Vida (☎2221-8367; www.vida.org) is a local nongovernmental organization working on sustainable development and conservation issues; it can often place volunteers. However, their website is entirely in Spanish, and some reasonable Spanish language skills are recommended for working with them.

6

SAN JOSE

F or as long as I've written this book, my stock advice to tourists has been to get in and out of San José as quickly as possible. In most cases, this remains good counsel. Still, San José is the country's only major urban center, with varied and active restaurant and nightlife scenes, several museums and galleries worth visiting, and a steady stream of theater, concerts, and other cultural events that you won't find elsewhere in the country.

At first blush, San José comes across as little more than a chaotic jumble of cars, buses, buildings, and people. The central downtown section of the city exists in a near-constant state of gridlock. Antiquated buses spewing diesel fumes and a lack of emission controls have created a brown cloud over the city's sky. Sidewalks are poorly maintained and claustrophobic, and street crime is a serious problem. Most visitors quickly seek the sanctuary of their hotel room and the first chance to escape the city.

Still, things have improved in recent years. Mayor Johnny Araya has led ambitious campaigns to rid the narrow sidewalks of impromptu and illegal vendors, to reduce the clutter of billboards and overhead signs, and to bury a good share of the city's electrical and phone cables.

This chapter helps you plan whatever time you intend for the capital and ease your way through the pitfalls inherent in such a rough-and-tumble little city.

ORIENTATION
Arriving
BY PLANE

Juan Santamaría International Airport (℡2437-2626 for 24-hr. airport information; airport code SJO) is near the city of Alajuela, about 20 minutes from downtown San José. A taxi into town costs between $12 and $22, and a bus is only 75¢. The Alajuela–San José buses run frequently and will drop you off anywhere along Paseo Colón or at a station near the Parque de la Merced (downtown, btw. calles 12 and 14 and avs. 2 and 4). There are two separate lines: **Tuasa** (℡2442-6900) buses are red; **Station Wagon** (℡8388-9263) buses are beige/yellow. At the airport you'll find the bus stop directly in front of the main terminal, beyond the parking structure. Be sure to ask whether the bus is going to San José, or you'll end up in Alajuela. If you have a lot of luggage, you should probably take a cab.

Most car-rental agencies have desks and offices at the airport, although if you're planning to spend a few days in San José itself, a car is a liability. (If you're heading off immediately to the beach, though, it's much easier to pick up your car here than at a downtown office.)

FACING PAGE: **A San José street performer.**

At press time the airport was still in the midst of a major renovation and expansion, a process that has been plagued by work stoppages, delays, contract disputes, bickering between the government and the international company in charge of the work, and financing problems. So far, the first phase of the new terminal has been completed, and all of the major airlines have moved their desks into the terminal. Unfortunately, the new baggage claim and Customs and Immigration areas, which are modern and spacious, are not necessarily fast and efficient. Moreover, despite the major remodeling, chaos and confusion continue to greet arriving passengers the second they step out of the terminal. You must abandon your luggage carts just before exiting the building and then face a gauntlet of aggressive taxi drivers and people offering to carry your bags. (Moreover, there's often really nowhere for them to have to carry your bags because the line of waiting taxis and shuttles is just steps away.) Fortunately, the official airport taxi service (see below) has a booth inside the terminal after you clear Customs. Most porters or skycaps wear a uniform identifying them as such, but sometimes "improvised" porters will try to earn a few dollars here. *Tip:* Keep a very watchful eye on your bags: Thieves have historically preyed on newly arrived passengers and their luggage. You should tip porters about 50¢ per bag.

The entire airport renovation and expansion should be completed sometime in mid-2010. There is hope that things will improve once the work is done and new facilities are opened.

In terms of taxis, you should stick with the official airport taxi service, **Taxis Unidos Aeropuerto** (☏ **2221-6865;** www.taxiaeropuerto.com), which operates a fleet of orange vans and sedans. These folks have a kiosk in the no man's land just outside the exit door for arriving passengers. Here they will assign you a cab. These taxis now use meters, and fares to most downtown hotels should run $12 to $22. Despite the fact that Taxis Unidos has an official monopoly at the airport, you will usually find a handful of regular cabs (in traditional red sedans) and "pirate" cabs, driven by freelancers using their own vehicles. You could use either of these latter options, and "pirate" cabs tend to charge a dollar or two less, but I recommend using the official service for safety and standardized prices.

You have several options for **exchanging money** when you arrive at the airport. There's an ATM in the baggage claim area, which is connected to both the PLUS and Cirrus networks. There's also a **Global Exchange** money exchange booth just as you clear Customs and Immigration. It's open whenever there are arriving flights; however, these folks exchange at more than 10% below the official rate. There's a branch of the **Banco de San José** inside the main terminal, on the second floor across from the airline check-in counters, as well as a couple more ATMs up there. The taxi company and rental-car agencies accept U.S. dollars. See "Money & Costs," in chapter 3, for more details.

Tip: There's really no pressing need to exchange money the minute you arrive. Taxis Unidos accepts dollars. You can wait until after you settle into your hotel, and see if the hotel will give you a good rate of exchange, or use one of the many downtown banks or ATMs.

If you arrive in San José via Nature Air, private aircraft, or another small commuter or charter airline, you might find yourself at the **Tobías Bolaños International Airport** in Pavas (SYQ; ☏ **2232-2820**). This small airport is on the western side of downtown San José, about 10 minutes by car from the center.

There are no car-rental desks here, so unless you have a car or a driver waiting for you here, you will have to take a cab into town, which should cost between $10 and $20.

BY BUS

If you're coming to San José by bus, where you disembark depends on where you're coming from. (The different bus companies have their offices, and thus their drop-off points, all over downtown San José. When you buy your ticket, ask where you'll be let off.) Buses arriving from Panama pass first through Cartago and San Pedro before letting passengers off in downtown San José; buses arriving from Nicaragua generally enter the city on the west end of town, on Paseo Colón. If you're staying here, you can ask to be let off before the final stop.

BY CAR

For those of you intrepid readers arriving by car, you'll enter San José via the Interamerican Highway. If you arrive **from Nicaragua and the north,** the highway brings you first past the airport and the city of Alajuela, to the western edge of downtown, right at the end of Paseo Colón, where it hits Parque La Sabana (La Sabana Park). The area is well marked with large road signs that direct you either to downtown (CENTRO) or to the western suburbs of Rohrmoser, Pavas, and Escazú. If you're heading toward downtown, follow the flow of traffic and turn left on Paseo Colón.

For those of you entering **from Panama and the south,** things get a little more complicated. The Interamerican Highway first passes through the city of Cartago and then through the San José suburbs of Curridabat and San Pedro before reaching downtown. This route is relatively well marked, and if you stick with the major flow of traffic, you should find San José without any problem.

A *mirador* outside San José.

Visitor Information

There's an **Instituto Costarricense de Turismo** (**ICT**; **℡2443-1535**; www. visitcostarica.com) desk at the Juan Santamaría International Airport, located in the baggage claims area, just before Customs. You can pick up maps and browse brochures, and they might even lend you a phone to make or confirm a reservation. It's open daily from 9am to 10pm. If you're looking for the **main ICT visitor information center** in San José, it's located below the Plaza de la Cultura, at the entrance to the Gold Museum, on Calle 5 between avenidas Central and 2 (**℡2222-1090**). The people here are helpful, although the information they have to offer is rather limited. This office is open Monday through Saturday from 9am to 5pm.

"I KNOW THERE'S GOT TO BE A number HERE SOMEWHERE . . . "

This is one of the most confusing aspects of visiting Costa Rica in general, and San José in particular. Although there are often street addresses and building numbers for locations in downtown San José, they are almost never used. Addresses are given as a set of coordinates such as "Calle 3 between avenidas Central and 1." It's then up to you to locate the building within that block, keeping in mind that the building could be on either side of the street. Many addresses include additional information, such as the number of meters from a specified intersection or some other well-known landmark. (These "meter measurements" are not precise but are a good way to give directions to a taxi driver. In basic terms, 100m = 1 block, 200m = 2 blocks, and so on.) These landmarks are what become truly confusing for visitors to the city because they are often simply restaurants, bars, and shops that would be familiar only to locals.

Things get even more confusing when the landmark in question no longer exists. The classic example of this is "the Coca-Cola," one of the most common landmarks used in addresses in the blocks surrounding San José's main market. The trouble is, the Coca-Cola bottling plant that it refers to is no longer there; the edifice is long gone, and one of the principal downtown bus depots stands in its place. Old habits die hard, though, and the address description remains. You might also try to find someplace near the *antiguo higuerón* ("old fig tree") in San Pedro. This tree was felled years ago. In outlying neighborhoods, addresses can become long directions such as "50m (½ block) south of the old church, then 100m (1 block) east, then 20m (two buildings) south." Luckily for visitors, most downtown addresses are more straightforward.

Oh, and if you're wondering how letter carriers manage, well, welcome to the club. Some folks actually get their mail delivered this way, but most people and businesses in San José use a post office box. This is called an *apartado* and is abbreviated "Apdo." or "A.P." in mailing addresses.

City Layout

Downtown San José is laid out on a grid. *Avenidas* (avenues) run east and west, while *calles* (streets) run north and south. The center of the city is at **Avenida Central** and **Calle Central.** To the north of Avenida Central, the avenidas have odd numbers beginning with Avenida 1; to the south, they have even numbers beginning with Avenida 2. Likewise, calles to the east of Calle Central have odd numbers, and those to the west have even numbers. The main downtown artery is **Avenida 2,** which merges with Avenida Central on either side of the downtown area. West of downtown, Avenida Central becomes **Paseo Colón,** which ends at Parque La Sabana and feeds into the highway to Alajuela, the airport, Guanacaste, and the Pacific coast. East of downtown, Avenida Central leads to San Pedro and then to Cartago and the Interamerican Highway heading south. **Calle 3** takes you out of town to the north, onto the Guápiles Highway that leads to the Caribbean coast.

The Neighborhoods in Brief

San José is divided into dozens of neighborhoods known as *barrios.* Most of the listings in this chapter fall within the main downtown area, but there are a few outlying neighborhoods you'll need to know about.

Panoramic view of San José.

DOWNTOWN In San José's busy downtown, you'll find most of the city's museums, as well as a handful of small urban parks and open-air plazas, and the city's main cathedral. There are also many tour companies, restaurants, and hotels here. Unfortunately, traffic noise and exhaust fumes make this one of the least pleasant parts of the city. Streets and avenues are usually bustling and crowded with pedestrians and vehicular traffic, and street crime is most rampant here. Still, the sections of Avenida Central between Calle 6 and Calle 7, as well as Avenida 4 between Calle 9 and Calle 14, have been converted into pedestrian malls, slightly improving things on these stretches.

BARRIO AMON/BARRIO OTOYA These two picturesque neighborhoods, just north and east of downtown, are the site of the greatest concentration of historic buildings in San José. Some of these have been renovated and turned into boutique hotels and atmospheric restaurants. If you're looking for character and don't mind the noise and exhaust fumes from passing cars and buses, this neighborhood makes a good base for exploring the city.

LA SABANA/PASEO COLON Paseo Colón, a wide boulevard west of downtown, is an extension of Avenida Central and ends at Parque La Sabana. It has several good, small hotels and numerous restaurants. This is also where several of the city's car-rental agencies have their in-town offices. Once the site of the city's main airport, the Parque La Sabana is San José's largest public park, with ample green areas, an urban "canopy tour," sport facilities, and the Museo de Arte Costarricense (Costa Rican Art Museum).

Colonial-era building in San José.

Parque La Sabana.

SAN PEDRO/LOS YOSES Located east of downtown San José, Los Yoses is an upper-middle-class neighborhood that is home to many diplomatic missions and embassies. San Pedro is a little farther east and is the site of the University of Costa Rica. Numerous college-type bars and restaurants are all around the edge of the campus, and several good restaurants and small hotels are in both neighborhoods.

ESCAZU/SANTA ANA Located in the hills west of San José, Escazú and Santa Ana are two fast-growing suburbs. Although the area is only 15 minutes from San José by car or taxi, it feels much farther away because of its relaxed and suburban atmosphere. This area also has a large expatriate community with many bed-and-breakfast establishments and excellent restaurants.

HEREDIA/ALAJUELA/AIRPORT AREA Heredia and Alajuela are two colonial-era cities that lie closer to the airport than San José. Alajuela is closest to the airport; Heredia is about midway between Alajuela and the capital. For more information on Heredia, see "Side Trips from San José," later in this chapter. Several quite nice high-end boutique hotels are in this area, and several large hotels and one chain hotel are located on, or just off, the Interamerican Highway close to the airport.

GETTING AROUND
By Bus

Bus transportation around San José is cheap—the fare is usually somewhere around 10¢ to 50¢—although the Alajuela/San José buses that run in from the airport cost 75¢. The most important buses are those running east along Avenida 2 and west along Avenida 3. The **Sabana/Cementerio** bus runs from Parque La Sabana to downtown and is one of the most convenient buses to use. You'll find a bus stop for the outbound Sabana/Cementerio bus near the main post office on Avenida 3 near the corner of Calle 2, and another one on Calle 11 between avenidas Central and 1. This bus also has stops all along Avenida 2. **San Pedro** buses leave from Avenida Central between calles 9 and 11, in front of the Cine Capri,

Bus stop in San José.

and take you out of downtown heading east. **Escazú-** and **Santa Ana–bound** buses leave from the Coca-Cola bus station, as well as from Avenida 1 between calles 24 and 28. Alternatively, you can pick up both the Escazú and Santa Ana buses from the busy bus stop on Calle 42, just north of Gimnasio Nacional.

The city's bus drivers can make change, although they don't like to receive large bills. Be especially mindful of your wallet, purse, or other valuables, because pickpockets often work the crowded buses.

By Taxi

Although taxis in San José have meters *(marías)*, the drivers sometimes refuse to use them, particularly with foreigners, so you'll occasionally have to negotiate the price. Always try to get them to use the meter first (say *"ponga la maría, por favor"*). The official rate at press time is around 80¢ for the first kilometer (½ mile) and around 60¢ for each additional kilometer. If you have a rough idea of how far it is to your destination, you can estimate how much it should cost from these figures. After 10pm taxis are legally allowed to add a 20% surcharge. Some of the meters are programmed to include the extra charge automatically, but be careful: Some drivers will use the evening setting during the daytime or (at night) to charge an extra 20% on top of the higher meter setting.

Depending on your location, the time of day, and the weather (rain places taxis at a premium), it's relatively easy to hail a cab downtown. You'll always find taxis in front of the Teatro Nacional (albeit at high prices) and around the Parque Central at Avenida Central and Calle Central. Taxis in front of hotels and the El Pueblo tourist complex usually charge more than others, although this is technically illegal. Most hotels will gladly call you a cab, either for a downtown excursion or for a trip back out to the airport. You can also get a cab by calling **Coopetaxi** (**☎2235-9966**), **Coopeirazu** (**☎2254-3211**), **Coopetico** (**☎2224-7979**), or **Coopeguaria** (**☎2227-9300**). **Cinco Estrellas Taxi** (**☎2228-3159**) is another company that is based in Escazú but services the entire metropolitan area and airport, and claims to always have an English-speaking operator on call.

On Foot

Downtown San José is very compact. Nearly every place you might want to go is within a 15-by-4-block area. Because of traffic congestion, you'll often find it faster to walk than to take a bus or taxi. Be careful when walking the streets any time of day or night. Flashy jewelry, loosely held handbags or backpacks, and expensive camera equipment tend to attract thieves. **Avenida Central** is a pedestrian-only street from Calle 6 to Calle 7, and has been redone with interesting paving stones and the occasional fountain in an attempt to create a comfortable pedestrian mall. A similar pedestrian-only walkway runs along **Avenida 4,** between Calle 9 and Calle 14.

By Train

In mid-2005, urban commuter train service was reopened in downtown San José. A single line connecting the western neighborhood of Pavas with the eastern suburb of San Pedro passes right through the downtown, with prominent stops at, or near, the U.S. Embassy, Parque La Sabana, the downtown court area, and the Universidad de Costa Rica (University of Costa Rica) and Universidad Latina (Latin University). The train runs in each direction roughly every 2 hours between 5am and 6pm. The fare ranges from 20¢ to 70¢ depending on the length of your ride.

By Car

It will cost you between $45 and $140 per day to rent a car in Costa Rica (the higher prices are for 4WD vehicles). Many car-rental agencies have offices at the airport. If not, they will usually either pick you up or deliver the car to any San José hotel. If you decide to pick up your rental car in downtown San José, be prepared for some very congested streets.

The following companies have desks at Juan Santamaría International Airport, as well as offices downtown: **Alamo** (☎800/462-5266 toll-free within Costa Rica, or 2242-7733 for central reservations; www.alamocostarica.com), **Adobe Rent A Car** (☎2442-2422 at the airport, or 2258-4242 in downtown San José; www.adobecar.com), **Avis** (☎800/331-1084 in the U.S., or 2293-2222 central reservation number in Costa Rica; www.avis.com), **Budget** (☎800/527-0700 in the U.S., 2436-2000 at the airport, or 2255-4750 in downtown San José; www.budget.co.cr), **Dollar** (☎2443-2736 at the airport, or 257-1585 in downtown San José; www.dollarcostarica.com), **Hertz** (☎800/011-0362 in the U.S., 2443-4645 at the airport, or 2221-1818 in downtown San José; www.hertz.com), **National Car Rental** (☎877/862-8227 toll-free in the U.S. and Canada; 2442-7878 at the airport, or

> ### Car-Rental Advice
>
> If you plan to rent a car, I recommend reserving it in advance from home. All the major international agencies and many local companies have toll-free numbers and websites. Sometimes you can even save a bit on the cost by reserving in advance. Costa Rica's car-rental fleet is not sufficient to meet demand during the high season when rental cars run at a premium. Sometimes this allows agencies here to gouge last-minute car-rental shoppers.

2290-8787 in downtown San José; www.natcar.com), **Payless Rent A Car** (☎**2257-0026** main reservations office in downtown San José, 2441-9366 at the airport; www.paylesscr.com), **Thrifty** (☎**800/847-4389** in the U.S., 2442-8585 at the airport, or 2257-3434 in downtown San José; www.thrifty.com), and **Toyota Rent A Car** (☎**2441-1411** at the airport, or 2258-5797 in downtown San José; www.toyotarent.com).

There are dozens of other car-rental agencies in San José, and most will arrange for airport or hotel pickup or delivery. One of the more dependable agencies is **Hola! Rent A Car,** across the street from (west of) Denny's, La Uruca, San José (☎**2520-0100;** www.hola.net). For more advice on renting cars, see "Getting There & Getting Around," in chapter 3.

As part of the new highway to Caldera project, the Prospero Fernandez highway (CR27) has been greatly improved between San José and the western suburbs of Escazú, Santa Ana, and Ciudad Colón. This improvement comes at a cost, however; drivers will pay 310 colones (55¢) each way between San José and Escazú, and an additional 160 colones (28¢) between Escazú and Ciudad Colón. The toll station is just beyond the main exit to Escazú, if you are coming from San José.

[FastFACTS] SAN JOSE

American Express American Express Travel Services is represented in Costa Rica by **ASV Olympia,** Oficentro La Sabana, Sabana Sur (☎**2242-8585;** www.asvolympia.com), which can issue traveler's checks and replacement cards and provide other standard services. To report lost or stolen Amex traveler's checks within Costa Rica, call the number above or call ☎**2295-9000,** or call collect to 336/393-1111 in the U.S.

Bookstores Seventh Street Books, Calle 7 between avenidas 1 and Central (☎**2256-8251**), has a wide range of new and used books in English, with an excellent selection of tropical biology, bird, and flora books; it's open

daily from 9am to 7pm. For a wide selection of new books in English and Spanish, check out **Librería Internacional** (☎**2257-2563;** www.libreriainternacional.com), which has stores in downtown San José, Santa Ana, Zapote, Alajuela, Rohrmoser, Heredia, Barrio Escalante, and inside most major malls around the metropolitan area.

Car Rentals See "Getting Around," above.

Dentists Call your embassy, which will have a list of recommended dentists. Many bilingual dentists also advertise in the *Tico Times.* Because treatments are so inexpensive in Costa Rica, dental tourism has become a popular option for people needing extensive work.

Doctors Contact your embassy for information on doctors in San José, or see "Hospitals," below.

Drugstores There are countless pharmacies and drugstores in San José. Many of them deliver at little or no extra cost. The pharmacy at the **Hospital Clínica Bíblica,** Avenida 14 between calles Central and 1 (☎**2522-1000**), is open 24 hours every day. The pharmacy (☎**2208-1080**) at the **Hospital CIMA** in Escazú is also open 24 hours daily. **Farmacia Fischel** (☎**2295-7555;** www.fischel.co.cr) has numerous branches around the metropolitan area.

Embassies & Consulates See chapter 13.

Emergencies In case of any emergency, dial ☎911 (which should have an English-speaking operator); for an ambulance, call ☎128; and to report a fire, call ☎118.

Express Mail Services Many international courier and express-mail services have offices in San José, including **DHL,** on Paseo Colón between calles 30 and 32 (☎2209-0000; www.dhl.com); **EMS Courier,** with desks at the principal metropolitan post offices (☎800/900-2000 in Costa Rica; www.correos.go.cr); **FedEx,** which is based in Heredia but will arrange pickup anywhere in the metropolitan area (☎800/463-3339; www.fedex.com); and **United Parcel Service,** in Pavas (☎2290-2828; www.ups.com).

Eyeglasses Look for the word *óptica*. **Optica Vision** (☎2255-2266) is a widespread and dependable chain with stores all around San José and the rest of the country. They can do everything from eye exams to eyeglass repairs.

Faxes Most hotels can send a fax for you. You can send telegrams and faxes from either the **ICE office** on Avenida 2 between calles 1 and 3 (www.grupoice.com; daily 7am–10pm), or **Racsa** (Av. 5 and Calle 1; ☎2287-0087; www.racsa.co.cr; Mon–Fri

7:30am–5pm, Sat 9am–1pm), as well as from most **post office** branches (☎800/900-2000 toll-free in Costa Rica; www.correos.go.cr).

Hospitals Clínica Bíblica, Avenida 14 between calles Central and 1 (☎2522-1000; www.clinicabiblica.com), is conveniently located close to downtown and has several English-speaking doctors. The **Hospital CIMA** (☎2208-1000; www.hospitalsanjose.net), located in Escazú on the Próspero Fernández Highway, which connects San José and the western suburb of Santa Ana, has the most modern facilities in the country.

Internet Access Internet cafes are all over San José. Rates run between 50¢ and $2 per hour. Many hotels have their own Internet cafe or allow guests to send and receive e-mail. And many have added wireless access, either for free or a small charge. You can also try **Racsa,** Avenida 5 and Calle 1 (☎2287-0087; www.racsa.co.cr), the state Internet monopoly, which sells prepaid cards in 5-, 10-, and 15-hour denominations for connecting your laptop to the Web via a local phone call. Some knowledge of configuring your computer's dial-up connection is necessary, and you'll want to factor

in the phone call charge if calling from a hotel.

Laundry & Dry Cleaning Self-service laundromats are uncommon in Costa Rica, and hotel services can be expensive. **Aqua Matic** (☎2291-2847) and **Tyson** (☎2215-2362) are two dependable laundry and dry-cleaning chains with outlets all over town. The latter will even pick up and deliver your clothes free of charge.

Maps The Costa Rican Tourist Board (ICT; see "Visitor Information," earlier in this chapter) can usually provide you with decent maps of both Costa Rica and San José. Also try **Seventh Street Books,** Calle 7 between avenidas Central and 1 (☎2256-8251); **Librería Lehmann,** Avenida Central between calles 1 and 3 (☎2522-4848); and **Librería Universal,** Avenida Central and calles Central and 1 (☎2222-2222).

Newspapers & Magazines See chapter 13.

Photographic Needs In the age of digital photography, travelers using film cameras are getting more and more rare. However if you are traveling with a film camera, you can process photos at **Rapi Foto** (☎2223-7640) or **IFSA-Kodak** (☎2223-1444), both of which have several

Fast Facts: San José

SAN JOSE

storefronts around downtown. For more serious photographic needs (equipment, repairs, and so on), try **Dima,** Avenida Central between calles 3 and 5 (☎**2222-3969**). Keep in mind that film is generally more expensive in Costa Rica, as is film processing.

Police Dial ☎**911** or 2222-1365 for the police. They should have someone available who speaks English.

Post Office The main post office (*correo*) is on Calle 2 between avenidas 1 and 3 (☎**800/900-2000** toll-free in Costa Rica, or 2202-2900; www.correos. go.cr). See "Mail," on p. 484, for more information.

Restrooms Public restrooms are rare to nonexistent, but most big hotels and public restaurants will let you use their restrooms. Downtown, you can find public restrooms at the entrance to the Museos del Banco Central de Costa Rica (p. 158).

Safety Pickpockets and purse slashers are rife in San José, especially on public buses, in the markets, on crowded sidewalks, near hospitals, and lurking outside of bank offices and ATMs. Leave most of your money and other valuables in your

hotel safe, and carry only as much as you really need when you go out. If you do carry anything valuable with you, keep it in a money belt or special passport bag around your neck. Day packs are a prime target of brazen pickpockets throughout the city. One common scam involves someone dousing you or your pack with mustard or ice cream. Another scamster (or two) will then quickly come to your aid—they are usually much more interested in cleaning you out than cleaning you up.

Stay away from the red-light district northwest of the Central Market. Also be advised that the Parque Nacional is not a safe place for a late-night stroll. Other precautions include walking around corner vendors, not between the vendor and the building. The tight space between the vendor and the building is a favorite spot for pickpockets. Never park a car on the street, and never leave anything of value in a car, even if it's in a guarded parking lot. Don't even leave your car unattended by the curb in front of a hotel while you dash in to check on your reservation. With these precautions in mind, you should have a safe visit to San José. Also, see "Safety," in chapter 3.

Taxes See "Taxes," in chapter 13, for info.

Taxis See "Getting Around," above.

Telephones See "Staying Connected," in chapter 3. There are no city or area codes to dial from within Costa Rica; use the country code, 506, only when dialing a San José number from outside Costa Rica. (To call San José from the U.S., dial the international access code [011], then 506, and then the eight-digit number.)

Time Zone San José is on Central Standard Time (same as Chicago and St. Louis), 6 hours behind Greenwich Mean Time.

Useful Telephone Numbers For directory assistance, call ☎**113;** for international directory assistance, call ☎**124;** and for the exact time (in Spanish), call ☎**112.**

Weather The weather in San José (including the Central Valley) is usually temperate, never getting extremely hot or cold. May through November is the rainy season, although the rain usually falls only in the afternoon and evening.

WHERE TO STAY

In San José, your hotel choices range from expensive luxury resorts to budget pensions charging only a few dollars a night. However, these two extremes are the exceptions, not the norm. The vast number of accommodations, and the best deals, are in the $90 to $160 price range. Within this relatively moderate bracket, you'll find restored homes that have been turned into small hotels and bed-and-breakfasts, modern hotels with pools and exercise rooms, and older downtown business hotels.

While, in general, there are plenty of rooms to go around in San José, the small boutique hotels and better-run establishments (including those recommended here) are often booked well in advance during the high season.

CHOOSING WHERE TO STAY Downtown hotels, many of which are in beautifully restored homes, are convenient to museums, restaurants, and shopping, but they can be noisy. Many people are also bothered by the exhaust fumes that permeate downtown streets. Moreover, because the streets of downtown are not especially safe, particularly at night, you should plan on taking taxis whether you stay downtown or in a nearby neighborhood or suburb. **Barrio Amón** is the downtown neighborhood with the most character and remnants of colonial architecture. If you want clean air and a peaceful night's sleep, consider staying out in the suburbs. **Escazú** and **Santa Ana** are both quiet yet modern suburbs, and many of the hotels there have great views. Heading east from downtown, **Los Yoses** is fairly close to the center of the action yet is still quiet. If you've rented a car, make sure your hotel provides secure parking or you'll have to find (and pay for) a nearby lot. If you plan to take some day tours, you can just as easily arrange these from a hotel situated outside the downtown area.

If you're heading out to Guanacaste, the central Pacific, or the northern zone, you might consider a hotel or bed-and-breakfast either near or beyond the airport. Sure, you give up proximity to downtown, but you can cut as much as an hour off your travel time to any of these destinations. Many car-rental companies will even deliver to or pick up cars from these establishments.

ALTERNATIVES TO HOTELS If you plan to be in town for a while or are traveling with family or several friends, you might want to consider staying in an *apartotel,* a cross between an apartment complex and a hotel. You can rent by the day, week, or month, and you get a furnished apartment with a full kitchen, plus housekeeping. Options include **Apartotel El Sesteo ★** (☎877/623-3198 in the U.S. and Canada, or 2296-1805; fax 2296-1865; www.sesteo.com), **Apartotel La Sabana ★** (☎877/722-2621 in the U.S. and Canada, or 2220-2422; fax 2231-7386; www.apartotel-lasabana.com), **Apartotel María Alexandra** (☎2228-1507; fax 2289-5192; www.maria alexandra.com), and **Apartotel Los Yoses** (☎888/790-5264 in the U.S. and Canada, or 2225-0033; fax 2225-5595; www.apartotel.com).

Downtown San José/Barrio Amón

EXPENSIVE

Aurola Holiday Inn Situated directly across the street from the attractive downtown Parque Morazán, this is San José's only high-rise business-class hotel. The rooms are everything you might expect from a prominent international chain

San José

Av. 17
Av. 15
PASO DE LA VACA
Av. 13
Av. 11
COCA-COLA
MEXICO
Av. 7
Av. 7
Av. 5
Av. 5
Av. 5
Av. 3
Av. 3
Av. 3
Av. 1
Paseo Colón
Coca-Cola Bus Terminal
Av. 1
PARQUE LA SABANA
Av. Central
Av. 2
Av. 2
Av. 4
Av. 4
Av. 6
Av. 6
Av. 8
MERCED
Av. 10
Av. 10
SANTA LUCIA

NICARAGUA
CARIBBEAN SEA
SAN JOSÉ
PACIFIC OCEAN
PANAMA

ACCOMMODATIONS

Aurola Holiday Inn **23**
Clarion Amón Plaza **19**
Crowne Plaza Corobicí **2**
Gran Hotel Costa Rica **31**
Hotel 1492
  Jade y Oro **44**
Hotel Aranjuez **16**
Hotel Britannia **21**
Hotel Cacts **7**
Hotel Del Rey **28**
Hotel Don Carlos **24**

Hotel Grano de Oro **10**
Hotel Le Bergerac **45**
Hotel Parque del Lago **5**
Hotel Posada
  del Museo **38**
Hotel Presidente **34**
Hotel Rosa del Paseo **9**
Hotel Santo Tomas **22**
Pension de la Cuesta **36**
Radisson Europa Hotel **13**
Raya Vida Villa **17**
Taylor's Inn **20**

in this price range—but nothing more. Service can be somewhat hit-or-miss, and the restaurants here leave lots to be desired. Still, the location is great for exploring downtown on foot, and if you get one of the upper-floor rooms on the north side, you'll have one of the best views in the city.

Av. 5 and Calle 5 (A.P. 7802-1000), San José. ☎ **800/465-4329** in the U.S. and Canada, or 2523-1000. Fax 2248-3101. www.holiday-inn.com. 200 units. $130 double; $175 junior suite; $255 suite. Internet rates available. AE, DC, MC, V. Free parking. **Amenities:** 2 restaurants; bar; poolside snack bar; executive-level rooms; exercise room; Jacuzzi; indoor pool; room service; sauna; smoke-free rooms. *In room:* A/C, TV, hair dryer, minibar, free Wi-Fi.

DINING

Café del Teatro
  Nacional **33**
Café Mundo **26**
Cafeteria
  1930 **31**
Chelles **35**
Del Mar **28**
Grano de Oro
  Restaurant **10**
Jurgen's **42**

La Piazetta **6**
Machu Picchu **8**
Olio **43**
Park Café **1**
Restaurante
  Nuestra Tierra **46**
Soda Tapia **4**
Tin Jo **39**
Vishnu **29, 40**
Whappin' **41**

ATTRACTIONS

Centro Nacional de
  Arte y Cultura **27**
El Pueblo **14**
Mercado Central **11**
Museo de Arte
  Costarricense **3**
Museo de Jade Marco
  Fidel Tristán **25**
Museo de
  los Niños **12**

Museos del Banco Central
  de Costa Rica **32**
Museo Nacional de
  Costa Rica **37**
Parque Zoologico
  Simon Bolivar **18**
Spirogyra Butterfly
  Garden **15**
Teatro Melico Salazar **30**
Teatro Nacional **33**

Clarion Amón Plaza ★ On the north edge of the historic Barrio Amón neighborhood, this hotel is a dependable business-class option. There's nothing distinctive about the property or rooms here; however, in terms of service, location, and price, it gets my nod over the nearby Holiday Inn. The rooms are good sized, well kept, and come with plenty of amenities. And you are close to all the downtown action. I recommend paying the upgrade for one of the executive-floor rooms, which get you free happy hour food and drinks, and a separate lounge area. While the food is merely average, the ambience of their little outdoor, sidewalk cafe, El Cafetal de la Luz, is delightful. There's also a fairly swank casino on-site. You can usually do a bit better than the rack rates listed below if you book through www.choicehotels.com.

Av. 11 and Calle 3 bis (A.P. 4192-1000), San José. ☎877/424-6423 in the U.S. and Canada, or 2523-4600 in Costa Rica. Fax 2523-4614. www.hotelamonplaza.com. 87 units. $130–$160 double; $220 suite. AE, DC, MC, V. Free parking. **Amenities:** Restaurant; bar; lounge; casino; babysitting; executive-level rooms; small exercise room; Jacuzzi; sauna; smoke-free rooms. *In room:* A/C, TV, hair dryer, free Wi-Fi.

Radisson Europa Hotel ★★   This hotel is geared mainly to business travelers, but is a good choice for anyone wanting a big, dependable hotel near downtown San José. Angular window nooks and other small architectural details give these rooms an edge over those in the Holiday Inn and Clarion Amón Plaza, although it's not as convenient for walking around downtown. For a modest price increase, you can opt for an executive room, which is basically a standard room with a cof-feemaker, a scale, terry-cloth bathrobes, and an extra telephone in the bathroom. The junior suites come with all the above amenities, as well as a desk and chair, in-room fax machine, and small balcony. This hotel is particularly well-located if you are driving to or from the Caribbean coast, as it is set right off the main downtown entrance to the highway to Guapiles.

Calle Blancos, behind La República building (A.P. 538-2120), San José. ☎888/201-1718 in the U.S., or 2257-3257. Fax 2257-8221. www.radisson.com. 210 units. $180 double; $230 executive room; $280 junior suite. Rates include continental breakfast. AE, DC, MC, V. Free parking. **Amenities:** 2 restaurants; bar; lounge; casino; executive-level rooms; extensive health club; outdoor pool; room service; smoke-free rooms. *In room:* A/C, TV, hair dryer, minibar, free Wi-Fi.

MODERATE

In addition to the hotels listed below, the **Sleep Inn** (Av. 3 btw. calles 9 and 11; ☎2222-0101; www.choicehotels.com) is a modern, American-style chain hotel in the heart of downtown, while **Hotel Doña Inés** (☎2222-7443; www.donaines. com), on Calle 11 between avenidas 2 and 6, and **Hotel Rincón de San José** (☎2221-9702; www.hotelrincondesanjose.com), on the corner of Avenida 9 and Calle 15, are two little boutique hotels that are also good options.

Gran Hotel Costa Rica   The Gran Hotel Costa Rica has arguably the best loca-tion of any downtown hotel (bordering the Teatro Nacional and the Plaza de la Cultura), and a major remodeling has finally brought the rooms and amenities al-most up to snuff. Most of the rooms here are fairly large. However, they still feel a bit spartan and dated. Although it's set a half-block from busy Avenida 2, some find the street noise a problem here. The Cafeteria 1930, reviewed separately later in this chapter, is perhaps the hotel's greatest attribute. It's memorable not so much for its food as for its atmosphere—it's an open-air patio that overlooks the Teatro Nacional, street musicians, and all the activity of the Plaza de la Cultura.

Av. 2, btw. calles 1 and 3, San José. ☎800/949-0592 in the U.S., or 2221-4000. Fax 2221-3501. www.grandhotelcostarica.com. 104 units. $85–$107 double; $149–$185 suite. Rates include breakfast buffet. AE, DC, MC, V. Free parking. **Amenities:** 2 restaurants, including Cafeteria 1930 (p. 148); bar; small gym; room service. *In room:* TV, minibar, free Wi-Fi.

Hotel Britannia ★ 🕯   This is the most elegant of the small hotels that have been created from restored old houses in downtown San José. Built in 1910, the large, low building, with its wraparound veranda, is one of the most attractive in the neighborhood. In the lobby, tile floors, large stained-glass picture windows, a brass chandelier, and reproduction Victorian decor all help set a tone of tropical opulence. Along with restoring the old home, the owners have built a four-story addition, which is separated from the original building by a narrow atrium. Rooms in the original home have hardwood floors and furniture; high ceilings and fans help keep them cool. Although the streetside rooms have double glass, light sleepers will still want to avoid them. The quietest rooms are those toward the back of the addition. The hotel's breakfast, along with afternoon tea and happy-hour drinks, is served in a sky-lit room adjacent to the restaurant.

Calle 3 and Av. 11 (A.P. 3742-1000), San José. **800/263-2618** in the U.S. or 2223-6667. Fax 2223-6411. www.hotelbritanniacostarica.com. 24 units. $89–$105 double; $117 junior suite. AE, MC, V. Parking nearby. **Amenities:** Restaurant; bar; room service; all rooms smoke-free. *In room:* A/C (in suites), TV, hair dryer, minibar (in suites), free Wi-Fi.

Hotel Del Rey You can't miss the Del Rey: It's a massive pink corner building with vaguely colonial styling. The lobby continues the facade's theme with pink-tile floors and stone columns. Inside, a carved hardwood door marks every guest room. The rooms vary in size and comfort: There are quiet interior rooms that have no windows, and larger rooms with windows (but also street noise). Try for a sixth-floor room with a balcony. The hotel's main restaurant is across the street in an old restored home, with plenty of stained glass. The hotel's 24-hour lobby bar and cafe serves respectable U.S.-style deli sandwiches, seafood, steaks, and pasta dishes. Much of the first floor is taken up with a bustling casino and the neighboring Blue Marlin Bar, which is very popular with tourists, expatriates, and prostitutes. The hotel's owners also manage the popular Key Largo Bar, just across the street.

Av. 1 and Calle 9 (A.P. 6241-1000), San José. **866/765-8037** in the U.S. and Canada, or 2257-7800. Fax 2221-0096. www.hoteldelrey.com. 104 units. $90–$130 double; $170 suite. AE, MC, V. Parking nearby. **Amenities:** Restaurant; bar; room service. *In room:* A/C, TV, hair dryer, minibar, Wi-Fi.

Hotel Don Carlos ★★ 🛅 If you're looking for a small downtown hotel that is unmistakably Costa Rican and hints at the days of the planters and coffee barons, this is the place for you. Located in an old residential neighborhood, only blocks from the business district, the Don Carlos was a former president's mansion. Inside you'll find a slew of arts-and-crafts works and archaeological re-productions, as well as orchids, ferns, palms, and parrots. The rooms are distinct and vary greatly in size, so be specific when you reserve, or ask if it's possible to see a few when you check in. Breakfast is served in an outdoor orchid garden and atrium. The gift shop here is one of the largest in the country.

779 Calle 9, btw. avs. 7 and 9, San José. **2221-6707.** Fax 2258-1152. www.doncarloshotel.com. 33 units. $80–$90 double. Rates include continental breakfast. AE, MC, V. Free parking. **Amenities:** Restaurant; bar; Jacuzzi; room service. *In room:* TV, hair dryer, free Wi-Fi.

Hotel Presidente This business-class hotel is a good midrange option in the heart of downtown. Although the hotel's eight stories practically qualify it for skyscraper status, few of the rooms have any view to speak of; those with north-facing windows are your best bet. Rooms are all well-kept and feature the ameni-ties you'd expect; upgrades have updated both furnishings and decor. If you want more space, opt for one of the junior suites. Rooms and suites with a "spa" des-ignation come with a private Jacuzzi. The master suite is a massive two-bedroom affair, featuring a widescreen TV in the living room and a private eight-person Jacuzzi. There's a very popular casual cafe-style restaurant just off the street.

While similar in style and vibe, the Presidente is a bit more tranquil and subdued than the Del Rey (see above), especially after dark.

Av. Central and Calle 7 (A.P. 2922-1000), San José. **2222-3022.** Fax 2221-1205. www.hotel-presidente.com. 100 units. $101–$111 double; $135–$175 junior or spa suite; $350–$360 master suite. Rates include full breakfast buffet. AE, MC, V. Free parking. **Amenities:** Restaurant; bar; casino; babysitting; small gym; rooftop Jacuzzi and sauna; room service. *In room:* A/C, TV, hair dryer, minibar, free Wi-Fi.

Hotel Santo Tomás 🍃 Even though it's on a busy downtown street, this converted mansion is a quiet oasis inside. Built more than 100 years ago by a coffee baron, the house has been lovingly restored and maintained by its owner, Thomas Douglas. Throughout the hotel you'll enjoy the deep, dark tones of well-aged and well-worked wood. The rooms vary in size, but most are fairly spacious and have a small table and chairs. Skylights in some bathrooms will brighten your morning, and firm beds provide a good night's sleep. There's also a small outdoor pool with a Jacuzzi above it; the two are solar heated and connected by a tiny water slide. The staff and management are extremely helpful, and the restaurant here is excellent. This neighborhood is a little bit sketchy after dark, so you'd be advised to take a taxi to and from the hotel for any evening excursions.

Av. 7, btw. calles 3 and 5, San José. **877/446-0658** in the U.S. or 2255-0448. Fax 2222-3950. www.hotelsantotomas.com. 20 units. $80–$110 double. Rates include breakfast buffet. MC, V. Parking nearby. **Amenities:** Restaurant; bar; lounge; exercise room; Jacuzzi; small outdoor pool; all rooms smoke-free. *In room:* TV, hair dryer, free Wi-Fi.

Raya Vida Villa ★ Located behind a big iron gate at the end of a narrow, dead-end lane, this little bed-and-breakfast is so secluded that it seems to be in a world all its own, yet it's in downtown San José. Behind the gate, in a shady old garden, is a miniature villa. The restored old stucco home is furnished with the owners' eclectic collection of crafts from around the world, and in the living room you'll find a grand piano and fireplace. Guest rooms are all different in style and decor. One features a four-poster bed with carved pineapples on the top of each post. The upstairs rooms have the largest bathrooms, and one even has a Jacuzzi tub. However, I like the downstairs room that opens onto a small open-air patio with a fountain.

Barrio Amón (A.P. 2209-2100), San José. **2223-4168.** Fax 2223-4157. www.rayavida.com. 4 units. $95 double. Rates include full breakfast. MC, V. Free parking. *In room:* TV, no phone.

Taylor's Inn Here's yet another lovely converted old downtown home turned bed-and-breakfast. The rooms are all arranged around the interior courtyard, which features flowering ginger and other tropical flora—a perfect place for breakfast. Most rooms have one single and one double bed, although a few have sleeping lofts and are good for families. All are very clean and feature artwork from prominent Costa Rican artists. The suite is a bit bigger. Don't expect a sense of hermetic privacy here, though—most of the rooms open onto the courtyard, and the old wooden construction guarantees that you hear the conversations of other guests passing by your door.

Av. 13, btw. calles 3 and 3 bis (A.P. 531-1000), San José. **2257-4333.** Fax 2221-1475. www.taylorinn.com. 12 units. $60 double. Rates include continental breakfast. Rates slightly lower in the off season. AE, MC, V. **Amenities:** Lounge; smoke-free rooms. *In room:* TV.

INEXPENSIVE

In addition to the places listed below, **Kap's Place** (☎2221-1169; www.kapsplace.com), across from the Hotel Aranjuez on Calle 19 between avenidas 11 and 13, is another good choice, while real budget hounds might want to try either **Tranquilo Backpackers** (☎2222-2493; www.tranquilobackpackers.com), on Calle 7 between avenidas 9 and 11, or **Costa Rica Backpackers** (☎2221-6191; www.costaricabackpackers.com), on Avenida 6 between calles 21 and 23.

Hotel Colonial ★ (Calle 11 btw. avs. 4 and 6; ☎2223-0109; www.hotelcolonialcr.com) is a good boutique hotel in a restored Victorian-style home a couple of blocks south of the city center, with rooms that fall into the upper end of this price range.

Hotel Aranjuez ★ 🎈 This is probably the best and deservedly most popular budget option close to downtown. On a quiet and safe street in the Barrio Amón neighborhood, this humble hotel is made up of five contiguous houses. All rooms are simple and clean, and some are a little dark. Rooms and bathrooms vary greatly in size, so ask when reserving, or try to see a few rooms when you arrive. The nicest features here, aside from the convivial hostel-like atmosphere, are the lush and shady gardens; the hanging orchids, bromeliads, and ferns decorating the hallways and nooks; and the numerous open lounge areas furnished with chairs, tables, and couches—great for lazing around and sharing travel tales with your fellow guests. The hotel has a couple of computers, as well as a free Wi-Fi network, and provides free local calling.

Calle 19, btw. avs. 11 and 13 (A.P. 457-2070), San José. ☎877/898-8663 in the U.S. or 2256-1825. Fax 2223-3528. www.hotelaranjuez.com. 36 units, 6 with shared bathroom. $26 double with shared bathroom; $40–$47 double with private bathroom. Rates include breakfast buffet. V. Free parking. **Amenities:** Restaurant; bar; several lounge areas. *In room:* TV, free Wi-Fi.

Hotel Posada del Museo Located just across busy Avenida 2 from the Museo Nacional, this place offers up clean and cheerful rooms in the heart of downtown. The Victorian-style building dates to 1928 and has been immaculately restored. Rooms are large and feature either varnished wood or original ornate tile floors. The small restaurant here is set on a small pedestrian mall that leads to the Costa Rican Court complex, and features a few outdoor tables perfect for people-watching. The only downside here is the fact that Avenida 2 is one of the city's busiest and loudest streets, with a steady stream of bus, truck, and even train traffic struggling up the steep hill that crests right at this hotel. Even the rooms farthest from the street are susceptible to street noise.

Av. 2 and Calle 17, San José. ☎2258-1027. ☎/fax 2257-9414. www.hotelposadadelmuseo.com. 10 units. $61–$84 double. Rates include full breakfast. AE, DC, MC, V. Free parking. **Amenities:** Restaurant; lounge. *In room:* TV, free Wi-Fi.

Pensión de la Cuesta 🎈 If you don't mind a clean communal bathroom down the hall from your room, this little bed-and-breakfast on the hill leading up to the Parque Nacional is a real bargain and definitely worth considering. It was once the home of Otto Apuy, a well-known Costa Rican artist, and original artwork abounds. The building itself is a classic example of a tropical wood-frame home and has been painted an eye-catching pink with blue and white trim. Some rooms are a bit dark and very simply furnished, but there's a sunny and cheery

IT'S IN THE beans

San José was built on the profits of the coffee-export business. Between the airport and downtown, you'll pass working coffee farms. Glance up from almost any street in the city and on the surrounding volcanic mountains you'll see a patchwork quilt of farm fields, most of which are planted with the *grano de oro* (golden bean), as it's known here. San José was a forgotten backwater of the Spanish empire until the first shipments of the local beans made their way to sleepy souls in Europe late in the 19th century. Soon San José was riding high. Coffee planters, newly rich and craving culture, imposed a tax on themselves to build the Teatro Nacional (National Theater), San José's most beautiful building. Coffee profits also built the city a university. Today you can wake up and smell the coffee roasting as you wander the streets near the Central Market (Mercado Central), and in any cafe or restaurant you can get a hot cup of sweet, milky *café con leche* to taste the bean that built San José.

Part of the reason the coffee grows so well here is the climate. The Central Valley, in which the city sits, has what's often been described as a perfect climate. At 1,125m (3,690 ft.) above sea level, San José enjoys springlike temperatures year-round. The pleasant climate, along with the beautiful views of lush green mountainsides, makes San José a memorable city to visit. All you have to do is glance up at those mountains to know that this is one of the most beautifully situated capitals in Central America. And if a glance isn't enough for you, you'll find that it's extremely easy to get out into the countryside. Within an hour or two, you can climb a volcano, go white-water rafting, hike through a cloud forest, and stroll through a butterfly garden—among many other activities.

sunken lounge/courtyard area in the center of the house. Most rooms have one double and a set of bunk beds. Overall, the place feels a lot like a hostel. The owners give you free run of the kitchen and offer free use of their Internet connection. They also rent out a fully furnished apartment.

1332 Cuesta de Núñez, Av. 1 btw. calles 11 and 15, San José. **2256-7946** or /fax 2255-2896. www.pensiondelacuesta.com. 15 units, none with private bathroom. $28 double. Rates include continental breakfast. Children 11 and under stay free in parent's room. AE, MC, V. Parking nearby. **Amenities:** Lounge w/cable TV. *In room:* No phone, free Wi-Fi.

La Sabana/Paseo Colón

EXPENSIVE

Crowne Plaza Corobicí ★ Just past the end of Paseo Colón and on the edge of Parque La Sabana, the Corobicí is a sleek business-class option. The lobby is a vast expanse of marble floor faced by blank walls, although the Art Deco furnishings lend a bit of character. Guest rooms are contemporary and comfortable, with firm beds and walls of glass through which, on most floors, you get good views of the valley and surrounding mountains. Joggers will enjoy the nearby Parque La Sabana. The Corobicí has a large, modern spa, where you will find a well-equipped gym featuring a large exercise room, on-staff trainers, and regular classes. The Fuji restaurant here is one of the better Japanese and sushi restaurants in San José.

Autopista General Cañas, Sabana Norte (A.P. 2443-1000), San José. **800/227-6963** in the U.S. or 2232-8122. Fax 2231-5698. www.crowneplaza.com. 213 units. $150 double; $167–$366 suite; $556 presidential suite. AE, MC, V. Free parking. **Amenities:** 2 restaurants; bar; lounge; casino; babysitting; extensive health club and spa; Jacuzzi; midsize pool; room service; sauna; all rooms smoke-free. *In room:* A/C, TV, hair dryer, minibar, free Wi-Fi.

Hotel Grano de Oro ★★ 🏠 San José boasts dozens of old homes that have been converted into hotels, but the Grano de Oro tops them all in terms of design, comfort, and service. On a quiet side street off Paseo Colón, it offers a variety of room types to fit a range of budgets and tastes. I favor the patio rooms, which have French doors opening onto private patios. Throughout all the guest rooms, you'll find attractive hardwood furniture. The Vista de Oro suite is the hotel's crown jewel, with its own private staircase and wonderful views of the city and surrounding mountains. If you don't grab one of the suites (which have whirlpool tubs), you still have access to the hotel's two rooftop Jacuzzis. The restaurant serves excellent international cuisine and some of the city's best desserts. The hotel owners support a noble shelter for young, unwed mothers, Casa Luz. Feel free to inquire as to how you can help.

Calle 30, no. 251, btw. avs. 2 and 4, 150m (1½ blocks) south of Paseo Colón, San José (mailing address: SJO 36, P.O. Box 025216, Miami, FL 33102). **2255-3322.** Fax 2221-2782. www.hotel granodeoro.com. 40 units. $115–$165 double; $210–$305 suite. AE, MC, V. Free parking. **Amenities:** Restaurant (p. 150); bar; lounge; concierge; 2 rooftop Jacuzzis; room service; all rooms smoke-free. *In room:* TV, minibar, free Wi-Fi.

Hotel Parque del Lago ★ This midsize business-class hotel is located on the western edge of busy Paseo Colón, right near the Costa Rican Art Museum and

Parque La Sabana. Rooms are large and modern, but have a somewhat sober decor. The junior suites are especially spacious, with a comfortable couch, sitting area, wet bar, and microwave oven. There's wireless Internet throughout the hotel, and an elegant little restaurant and bar area just off the lobby. This hotel is convenient to both downtown and the western suburbs of Escazú and Santa Ana, with easy access to the country's major highways.

Calle 40, btw. Av. 2 and Paseo Colón, San José. **2257-8787.** Fax 2223-1617. www.parquedellago. com. 40 units. $125 double; $155–$175 junior suite; $350 penthouse. Rates include buffet breakfast. AE, MC, V. Free parking. **Amenities:** Restaurant; bar; lounge; small exercise room and spa; Jacuzzi; room service; sauna; smoke-free rooms. *In room:* A/C, TV, hair dryer, minibar, free Wi-Fi.

MODERATE

Hotel Rosa del Paseo ★ This hotel is housed in one of San José's most beautiful old stucco homes, right on busy Paseo Colón. However, the rooms are all located away from the street and are pretty well insulated against the noise. Built more than 116 years ago, this old home has received regular upkeep and upgrading, yet remains richly appointed and evocative of 19th-century Costa Rica. I'd definitely try to grab one of the rooms on the second floor, which feature wooden floors and front doors that open onto the open-air central courtyard. The master suite comes with its own balcony and Jacuzzi. Beautiful details are spread throughout the hotel, including transoms, ornate stucco door frames, and polished hardwood floors.

2862 Paseo Colón, btw. calles 28 and 30 (A.P. 287-1007, Centro Colón), San José. **2257-3225.** Fax 2223-2776. www.rosadelpaseo.com. 19 units. $85 double; $100–$140 suite. Rates include continental breakfast. AE, DC, MC, V. Limited free parking. **Amenities:** Bar; lounge; babysitting; smoke-free rooms. *In room:* A/C, TV.

INEXPENSIVE

Hotel Cacts Housed in an attractive tropical contemporary home on a business and residential street, this is one of the more interesting and unusual budget hotels in San José. The seemingly constantly expanding complex is a maze of rooms and hallways on several levels. Rooms vary considerably in size, so it's always best to check out a few first if possible. The deluxe rooms here come with televisions and telephones, whereas the standard rooms lack both of these amenities. There's a small pool and separate Jacuzzi, in a lush garden patio. The third-floor open terrace serves as the breakfast area. The staff here is very helpful, and the hotel will receive mail and faxes, change money, and store baggage for guests.

Av. 3 bis, no. 2845, btw. calles 28 and 30 (A.P. 379-1005), San José. **2221-2928** or 2221-6546. Fax 2221-8616. www.hotelcacts.com. 25 units. $45–$60 double. Rates include breakfast buffet. MC, V. Free parking. **Amenities:** Lounge; Jacuzzi; small outdoor pool; all rooms smoke-free. *In room:* TV (in deluxe rooms), no phone (in standard rooms), free Wi-Fi.

San Pedro/Los Yoses

MODERATE

In addition to the places listed below, the **Hotel Boutique Jade** (**2224-2455;** www.hotelboutiquejade.com) is a modern business-class hotel with an excellent restaurant, while the **Hotel Don Fadrique** (**2225-8186;** www.

hoteldonfadrique.com) is another good option in a converted home, bedecked in interesting artwork.

Hotel 1492 Jade y Oro Housed in a restored old home on a quiet street in the heart of the Barrio Escalante neighborhood just east of the city center, this little bed-and-breakfast makes a good base for exploring the city or this side of town. The rooms are simple and tastefully done with locally crafted wooden furniture, plenty of light, local art on the walls, and a homey feel, but some are pretty small. Breakfast is served in an open-air rancho overlooking a lovely little garden. The hotel is run by a Costa Rican family who demonstrate a commitment to sustainability, and you really get the feel that you are staying in a typical Tico home here.

Av. 1, no. 2985, btw. calles 31 and 33, Barrio Escalante. ☎ **2256-5913.** Fax 2280-6206. www. hotel1492.com. 10 units. $70 double; $80–$90 suite. Rates include full breakfast. AE, MC, V. Free parking. **Amenities:** Smoke-free rooms. *In room:* TV, hair dryer, free Wi-Fi.

Hôtel Le Bergerac ★★ 🏠 With charm and sophistication, the Hôtel Le Bergerac has ingratiated itself over the years with business travelers and members of various diplomatic missions. Still, you don't have to be a diplomat or business traveler to enjoy this hotel's charms. Le Bergerac is composed of three houses with courtyard gardens in between. Almost all the rooms are fairly large, and each is a little different. I favor those with private patio gardens. In the evenings candlelight and classical music set a relaxing and romantic mood. The hotel's long-standing L'Ile de France restaurant serves gourmet French and continental dinners for guests and the public by reservation only.

Calle 35 no. 50 (A.P. 1107-1002), San José. ☎ **2234-7850.** Fax 2225-9103. www.bergerachotel.com. 26 units. $90–$145 double. Rates include full breakfast. AE, DC, MC, V. Free parking. **Amenities:** Restaurant; lounge; concierge. *In room:* TV, hair dryer.

Hotel Milvia ★ 🏠 Art lovers should definitely look into this offbeat little hotel. This old converted home is chock-full of paintings and sculptures by a wide range of contemporary Costa Rican artists. One of the owners, Florencia Urbina, is one of these artists. But you'll also find works by Mario Maffioli and Fabio Herrera, among others. My favorite pieces are the large-scale sculptures by Leda Astorga, including two functional and funny chairs. The rooms are bright and airy, and most are plenty spacious. The hotel has a mix of courtyards and gardens that seem to beckon one to linger with a book or sketch pad in hand.

1 block north and 2 blocks east of the Muñoz y Nanne Supermarket, San Pedro. ☎ **2225-4543.** Fax 2225-7801. www.hotelmilvia.com. 9 units. $69 double. Rates include continental breakfast. AE, MC, V. **Amenities:** Restaurant; lounge. *In room:* TV, free Wi-Fi.

Escazú & Santa Ana

Located about 15 minutes west of San José and about the same distance from the international airport, these affluent suburbs have experienced rapid growth in recent years, as the metropolitan area continues its urban sprawl. Both Escazú and Santa Ana are popular with the Costa Rican professional class and North American retirees and expatriates, and quite a few hotels have sprung up to cater to their needs. It's relatively easy to commute between Escazú or Santa Ana and downtown via bus or taxi. Taxi fare should run around $10 to $15, each way. A bus costs around 35¢.

VERY EXPENSIVE

Real InterContinental San José ★ This is a modern and luxurious large-scale business-class hotel, with three five-story wings. The large, open lobby has a beautiful flagstone-and-mosaic floor. The rooms are all well-appointed, with either one king-size or two double beds, a working desk, a sitting chair and otto-man, and a large armoire. The hotel is just across from a large, modern shopping-mall complex, which is nice if you want access to shopping, restaurants, and a six-plex movie theater. Overall, the InterContinental offers many of the same features and amenities as the Marriott (p. 143), although the latter gets my nod in terms of service, restaurants, and ambience.

Autopista Próspero Fernández, across from the Multiplaza mall, Escazú. ☎ **2208-2100.** Fax 2208-2101. www.gruporeal.com. 261 units. $250–$330 double; $750–$2,000 suite. AE, MC, V. Free parking. **Amenities:** 3 restaurants; 2 bars; lounge; concierge; good-size health club and spa; Jacuzzi; large free-form pool; room service; smoke-free rooms; outdoor tennis court. *In room:* A/C, TV, hair dryer, minibar, free Wi-Fi.

EXPENSIVE

Alta Hotel ★★ This small boutique hotel is infused with old-world charm. Curves and high arches abound. My favorite touch is the winding interior alley-way that snakes down from the reception through the hotel. Most of the rooms here have wonderful views of the Central Valley from private balconies; the others have pleasant garden patios. The rooms are all up to modern resort stan-dards, although some have slightly cramped bathrooms. The suites are consider-ably larger, each with a separate sitting room with its own television, as well as large Jacuzzi-style tubs in spacious bathrooms. The master suite has a steam bath as well. If you opt to rent the entire upper floor, the penthouse becomes a three-bedroom, full-floor extravaganza, with a massive living room and open-air rooftop patio. The hotel's La Luz restaurant is one of the more elegant and creative din-ing spots in the Central Valley.

Alto de las Palomas, old road to Santa Ana. ☎ **888/388-2582** in the U.S. and Canada or 2282-4160. Fax 2282-4162. www.thealtahotel.com. 23 units. $149 double; $179 junior suite; $199 master suite; $820 penthouse. Rates include continental breakfast and round-trip airport transfers. AE, DC, MC, V. Free parking. **Amenities:** Restaurant, La Luz (p. 154); bar; concierge; small exercise room; Jacuzzi; midsize outdoor pool; room service; sauna. *In room:* A/C, TV, hair dryer, minibar, free Wi-Fi.

Corteza Amarilla Art Lodge & Spa ★ 👔 Artistic touches abound in this whimsical hotel. Most of the rooms are classified as junior suites, although they really are just good-size rooms, with no separate sitting area, or other distinguish-ing factors that I usually associate with a junior. These are found in a series of individual and duplex buildings spread around the hotel's lush grounds. All come with wood floors, stone showers, and artsy tile work on the bathroom sinks and counters. I prefer no. 4 through no. 7, which have higher ceilings. The two master suites are in the main building, and are larger, and come with flatscreen television sets and a good-size private patio garden. A variety of treatments and therapies are offered at the small spa here, and the in-house restaurant is excel-lent. This hotel is located just outside of Santa Ana, on the main road to Ciudad Colón.

Prospero Fernández Hwy., just outside of Santa Ana. ☎**800/961-0419** in the U.S. and Canada, or 2203-7503 in Costa Rica. Fax 2282-6641. www.cortezaamarillalodge.com. 12 units. $150 junior suite; $180 master suite. Rates include full breakfast. AE, MC, V. **Amenities:** Restaurant; bar; Jacuzzi; small spa. *In room:* A/C, TV, hair dryer, minibar.

MODERATE

In addition to the hotels listed below, the **Courtyard San José** (☎**888/236-2427** in the U.S. and Canada, or 2208-3000; www.marriott.com) and **Quality Hotel Santa Ana** (☎**877/424-6423** in the U.S. and Canada, or 2204-6700; www.choicehotels.com) are both modern business-class hotels a few miles from each other, right on the western Próspero Fernández Highway connecting Santa Ana and Escazú with San José.

Casa de las Tías 📷 This old Victorian-style home is comfortable and brimming with local character. The rooms are homey and simply decorated in a sort of Costa Rican country motif. The hotel has a wonderful covered veranda for sitting and admiring the well-tended gardens, as well as a TV room and common areas inside the house. The owners live on-site and are extremely helpful and friendly—you really get the sense of staying in someone's home here. Though it's on a quiet side street, Casa de las Tías is nonetheless just a block away from a busy section of Escazú, where you'll find scores of restaurants and shops, and easy access to public transportation. The hotel is 100m (1 block) south and 150m (1½ blocks) east of El Cruce de San Rafael de Escazú.

San Rafael de Escazú. ☎**2289-5517.** Fax 2289-7353. www.hotels.co.cr/casatias.html. 5 units. $82–$92 double. Rates include full breakfast. AE, MC, V. *In room:* Free Wi-Fi.

Hotel Casa Alegre 📷 Housed in a converted home on a residential side street just a couple of blocks from Santa Ana's central square and church, this hotel offers spacious, comfortable rooms. The decor leans heavily on Southwest American artwork and design touches, combined with Guatemalan textiles and locally made heavy wooden furniture. My favorite rooms are the upstairs units. Rooms nos. 3 and 4 even have skylights in their bathrooms. A midsize outdoor pool, which is good for lap swimming, takes up much of the backyard, but there's also a shady lounge area out back as well.

Santa Ana. ☎/fax **2203-7467.** www.hotelcasaalegre.com. 8 units. $70–$87 double. Rates include full breakfast. AE, MC, V. **Amenities:** Pool. *In room:* TV, free Wi-Fi.

INEXPENSIVE

Hotel Mirador Pico Blanco There's nothing fancy about the rooms here, but most offer absolutely fabulous views, at a good value. Some rooms have high ceilings, creating an appearance of spaciousness, and almost all of them have balconies (albeit small ones) with good views. Most are pretty spartan in decor. The restaurant and bar also have stunning views. A few resident macaws fly around the hillsides during the day but come home here each evening.

1km (½ mile) south of the church in San Antonio de Escazú (A.P. 900), Escazú. ☎**2228-1908.** Fax 2289-5189. www.hotelpicoblanco.com. 25 units. $50–$70 double. MC, V. Free parking. **Amenities:** Restaurant; bar; babysitting; room service. *In room:* TV, no phone.

Finca Rosa Blanca.

Heredia & Alajuela (Airport Area)

Alajuela and Heredia, two colonial-era cities that lie much closer to the airport than San José, are two great places to find small, distinct, and charming hotels. To learn more about Heredia, see "Side Trips from San José," later in this chapter. If you plan to get yourself to a remote beach or rainforest lodge as quickly as possible and to use San José and the Central Valley purely as a transportation hub, or if you just detest urban clutter, noise, and pollution, you might do well to choose one of the hotels listed below.

VERY EXPENSIVE

Finca Rosa Blanca Coffee Plantation & Inn ★★★ 📖 Finca Rosa Blanca is an eclectic architectural gem set amid the lush, green hillsides of a coffee plantation. There's a turret atop the main building, walls of glass, arched windows, and curves instead of corners at almost every turn. Throughout, the glow of polished hardwood blends with white stucco walls and brightly painted murals. If breathtaking bathrooms are your idea of luxury, consider splurging on the Rosa Blanca suite, which has a stone waterfall that cascades into a tub in front of a huge picture window, and a spiral staircase that leads to the top of the turret. All of the suites and villas have the same sense of eclectic luxury, with beautiful tile work, fabulous views, and creative design touches. The restaurant and spa here are top-notch, and the owners have a real and noticeable dedication to sustainable practices. The hotel has 14 hectares of organic coffee under cultivation, and their in-house coffee tour is not to be missed.

Santa Bárbara de Heredia (mailing address: SJO 3475, P.O. Box 25369, Miami, FL 33102). **☎2269-9392.** Fax 2269-9555. www.fincarosablanca.com. 13 units. $290–$450 double. Rates include breakfast. AE, MC, V. Free parking. **Amenities:** Restaurant; bar; lounge; babysitting; concierge; small exercise room; small free-form pool set in the hillside; room service; full-service spa; all rooms smoke-free. *In room:* Minibar, free Wi-Fi.

Marriott Costa Rica Hotel ★★★ For my money, the Marriott remains the best large luxury resort hotel in the San José metropolitan area. The hotel is designed in a mixed colonial style, with hand-painted Mexican tiles, antique red-clay roof tiles, weathered columns, and heavy wooden doors, lintels, and trim. The centerpiece is a large open-air interior patio that somewhat replicates Old Havana's Plaza de Armas. All rooms are plush and well-appointed, with either a king-size or two double beds, a working desk, an elegant wooden armoire, plenty of closet space, a comfortable sitting chair and ottoman, and a small "Juliet" balcony. The bathrooms are up to par but seem slightly small for this price. The casual Antigua restaurant serves well-prepared Costa Rican and international dishes, and there's a more upscale Spanish restaurant and tapas bar. The large lobby-level bar features daily piano music and weekend jazz nights, with both indoor and patio seating.

San Antonio de Belén (A.P. 502-4005). ☎ **888/236-2427** in the U.S. and Canada or 2298-0844 in Costa Rica. Fax 2298-0033. www.marriott.com. 299 units. $260 double; $310 executive level; $450 master suite; $1,000 presidential suite. AE, DC, MC, V. Free valet parking. **Amenities:** 3 restaurants; bar; lounge; free airport transfers; babysitting; concierge; golf driving range; small but well-appointed health club; Jacuzzi; 2 outdoor pools; room service; sauna; 3 tennis courts; smoke-free rooms. *In room:* A/C, TV, hair dryer, minibar, Wi-Fi.

Peace Lodge ★★ 🏠 Part of the popular La Paz Waterfall Gardens, the rooms here are some of the most impressive in the country. All are quite large and feature sparkling wood floors, handcrafted four-poster beds, beautiful stone fireplaces, intricately sculpted steel light fixtures, and a host of other creative details—along

Marriott Costa Rica Hotel.

with a private balcony fitted with a mosaic-tiled Jacuzzi. The deluxe bathrooms come with a second oversize Jacuzzi set under a skylight in the middle of an immense room that features a full interior wall planted with ferns, orchids, and bromeliads and fed by a functioning waterfall system. Guests here have full access to all the tours and attractions of the La Paz Waterfall Gardens (p. 162) during normal operating hours and beyond. Peace Lodge was right near the epicenter of a major 6.2 earthquake in January 2009. However, the installations here and at the Waterfall Gardens escaped with very minor damage.

6km (3¾ miles) north of Varablanca on the road to San Miguel. **954/727-3997** in the U.S., or 2482-2720 or 2225-0643 in Costa Rica. www.waterfallgardens.com. 17 units. $245–$305 double; $395 villa. Rates include breakfast and entrance to La Paz Waterfall Gardens. AE, MC, V. **Amenities:** Restaurant; bar; Jacuzzi; 2 outdoor swimming pools. *In room:* A/C, TV, minibar, free Wi-Fi.

Xandari Resort & Spa ★★ Set on a hilltop above the city of Alajuela, Xandari commands wonderful views of the surrounding coffee farms and the Central Valley below. The owners are artists, and their original works and innovative design touches abound. The villas are huge private affairs with high-curved ceilings, stained-glass windows, living rooms with rattan sofas and chairs, as well as small kitchenettes. All come with both an outdoor patio with a view and a private covered palapa, as well as a smaller interior terrace with chaise longues. Most have king-size beds; the rest have two queen-size beds. The adjacent "spa village" features a series of private thatch-roofed treatment rooms; a wide range of fitness classes is offered, too. The hotel grounds contain several miles of trails that pass by at least five jungle waterfalls, as well as lush gardens and fruit orchards. Some of the land has been set aside as a permanent nature reserve, and they are reforesting other areas that were formerly dedicated to agriculture. These folks have a sister lodge on the Pacific Coast (p. 357).

Alajuela (A.P. 1485-4050). **866/363-3212** in the U.S. or 2443-2020. Fax 2442-4847. www. xandari.com. 22 villas. $230–$315 villa for 2. Rates include continental breakfast. $25 for extra person; children 3 and under stay free in parent's room. DC, MC, V. **Amenities:** Restaurant; bar; lounge; several Jacuzzis; 2 lap pools; full-service spa. *In room:* Kitchenette, minibar.

EXPENSIVE

Doubletree Cariari By Hilton ★★ With its stone walls, open-air lobby, and lush garden plantings, the Cariari has a warm tropical feel. The rooms, which are done in subdued tones, have either one king-size bed or two double beds, although I find most of the bathrooms a bit small. The suites are similarly appointed, but are more spacious and have larger bathrooms. The Royal Service rooms come with plenty of extra perks, including personalized butler service. There's a full complement of facilities and services here, and families can take advantage of the dependable babysitting, game room, children's menus, and easy access to the modern mall nearby.

Autopista General Cañas, Ciudad Cariari (A.P. 737-1007, Centro Colón), San José. **800/222-8733** in the U.S. and Canada or 2239-0022. Fax 2239-2803. www.cariarisanjose.doubletree.com. 222 units. $149–$189 double; $219–$449 suite; $1,000 presidential suite. AE, DC, MC, V. Free valet parking. **Amenities:** 2 restaurants; 2 bars; lounge; casino; free airport transfers; babysitting; concierge; small exercise room and spa; large pool w/swim-up bar; room service; smoke-free rooms. *In room:* A/C, TV, hair dryer, minibar, Wi-Fi.

Hampton Inn & Suites If familiarity, comfort, and proximity to the airport are important to you, then the Hampton Inn is a good bet. The rooms are what you'd expect from a well-known chain. The hotel has both standard rooms and suites. Breakfast is served, but no other dining options are on-site; a Denny's and a separate Costa Rican fast-food chicken joint are just across the parking lot, as is a large swank casino, with a popular bar. This is a good choice if your plane arrives very late or leaves very early and you don't plan to spend any time in San José. Free local calls, high-speed Internet access in all rooms, and Wi-Fi in public areas are perks that will appeal to business travelers and vacationers alike.

Autopista General Cañas, by the airport (A.P. 195-4003), San José. ☎800/426-7866 in the U.S. or 2436-0000. Fax 2442-2781. www.hamptoninn.com. 100 units. $164 double; $185 suite. Rates include buffet breakfast and airport shuttle. AE, DC, MC, V. Free parking. **Amenities:** Bar; free airport transfers; babysitting; small exercise room; small pool; smoke-free rooms. *In room:* A/C, TV, minifridge (in suites), hair dryer, free Wi-Fi.

Vista del Valle Plantation Inn ★★ 🏨 Individual and duplex villas are spread around the grounds here, which command an impressive view over the Río Grande and its steep-walled canyon. The architecture has a strong Japanese influence, from the open and airy villas to the comfortable wraparound decks. My favorite rooms are the Mona Lisa and Ilan-Ilan suites, which are octagonal affairs set on the edge of the bluff with great views and private outdoor showers. The grounds are wonderfully landscaped, with several inviting seating areas among a wealth of flowering tropical plants. There are stunning views from the restaurant, which features a regularly changing menu of fine international cuisine prepared with local ingredients. The hotel is 20 minutes north of the Juan Santamaría Airport, and staying here can cut as much as an hour off your travel time if you're heading out to the Pacific coast beaches, Arenal Volcano, and the Monteverde Cloud Forest.

A.P. 185-4003, Alajuela (mailing address: SJO 1994, P.O. Box 025216, Miami, FL 33102). ☎2450-0800. ☎/fax 2451-1165. www.vistadelvalle.com. 11 units. $100 double; $150–$175 villa. Rates include full breakfast. AE, MC, V. **Amenities:** Restaurant; Jacuzzi; midsize tile pool w/interesting fountain/ waterfall; room service; tennis court. *In room:* Kitchenette (in some), minibar, free Wi-Fi.

MODERATE

In addition to the places listed below, **Viña Romantica** (☎2430-7621; www. vinaromantica.com) is a cozy bed-and-breakfast in the hills just above Alajuela, which is earning strong praise for its amiable hosts and excellent restaurant, while **Pura Vida Hotel** (☎2441-1157; www.puravidahotel.com) is a popular Alajuela inn that's also convenient to the airport. Finally, the new **Holiday Inn Express** (☎2443-0043; www.hiexpress.com) is actually a rebranding of the former Garden Court, with some remodeling and updating, located right beside Hampton Inn, near the airport.

El Rodeo Country Inn ★ Located around the "backside" of the airport, in San Antonio de Belén, this long-standing hotel features spacious rooms and expansive grounds. Rooms feature sturdy beds with artistic wood-and-metal headboards adorned with sculpted calla lilies. Most have wood floors and large bathrooms. I'd ask for one either in the new section, or on the second floor of the older building. The suites have a Jacuzzi tub and sitting area. There are several lounge areas spread around the rambling structure, as well as a pool table on a large open second-floor veranda. The namesake El Rodeo steakhouse restaurant here is excellent.

San Antonio de Belén. **2293-3909.** Fax 2293-3464. www.elrodeohotel.com. 29 units. $115 double; $175 suite. Rates include buffet breakfast. AE, DC, MC, V. Free parking. **Amenities:** 2 restaurants; bar; Jacuzzi; midsize pool; room service; unlit outdoor tennis court. *In room:* A/C, TV, hair dryer, minibar, free Wi-Fi.

Hotel Bougainvillea ★ 🦋 The Hotel Bougainvillea is an excellent choice—a great value if you're looking for a hotel in a quiet residential neighborhood not far from downtown. It offers most of the amenities of the more expensive resort hotels around the Central Valley, but it charges considerably less. Rooms are carpeted and have small triangular balconies oriented to the wonderful views across the valley. The hillside property's gardens are beautifully designed and well tended, with pretty-good bird-watching. The hotel has an extensive recycling program and is working hard to implement sustainable tourism practices. A complimentary hourly downtown shuttle bus will take you in and out of town.

In Santo Tomás de Santo Domingo de Heredia, 100m (1 block) west of the Escuela de Santo Tomás (A.P. 69-2120), San José. **2244-1414.** Fax 2244-1313. www.hb.co.cr. 81 units. $103–$120 double; $128–$140 suite. AE, DC, MC, V. Free parking. **Amenities:** Restaurant; bar; babysitting; Jacuzzi; midsize pool in attractive garden; room service; sauna; smoke-free rooms; 2 lighted tennis courts. *In room:* TV, hair dryer, free Wi-Fi.

Orquídeas Inn This boutique inn is just 10 minutes from the airport on the road heading out of Alajuela to Grecia and the Poás Volcano. The rooms are all spacious, with tile floors, private bathrooms, and colorful Guatemalan bedspreads. The deluxe rooms are in a separate building up on a hill, and most of these offer wonderful views, particularly those with balconies facing one of the nearby volcanoes. There are a few larger minisuites located around the small pool, as well as a separate geodesic dome with a king-size bed in a loft reached by a spiral staircase, a large sunken tub in the bathroom, and a full kitchen and living-room area. The entire grounds are lush and tropical. The Marilyn Monroe bar serves up good drinks, *bocas* (appetizers), and some seriously spicy Buffalo wings.

A.P. 394, Alajuela. **2433-7128.** Fax 2433-9740. www.orquideasinn.com. 27 units. $79–$99 double; $130–$160 suite. Rates include breakfast buffet. AE, MC, V. Free parking. **Amenities:** Restaurant; bar; concierge; Jacuzzi; pool. *In room:* A/C, TV (in some), hair dryer.

Shameless Plug

If you want a more comprehensive guide to the restaurant scene in San José and around the country, pick up a copy of my *Tico Times Restaurant Guide to Costa Rica,* which is now in its fourth edition and features reviews of some 400 restaurants around Costa Rica, indexed by location, cuisine type, and overall quality. The guide is available in local bookstores, supermarkets, and gift shops, as well as online at **www.ticotimes.net.**

WHERE TO DINE

In broad terms, Costa Rican cuisine is easily disparaged and dismissed. Rice and beans are served at nearly every meal, the selection of other dishes is minimal, and Ticos generally don't go for spicy food. In recent years, though, some contemporary and creative chefs have been trying to educate and enlighten the Costa Rican palate, particularly in San José, and the results are promising. Still, most visitors to the capital city quickly tire of Tico fare, even in its more chichi incarnations, and start seeking out the many local restaurants serving international cuisines. They are richly rewarded.

San José has a rather amazing variety of restaurants serving cuisines from all over the world. Most restaurants fall into the moderate price range, although prices have crept up in recent years, and unless you stick to simple local joints, you probably won't find many true bargains. Service can be indifferent at many restaurants because the gratuity is already tacked on to the check, and tipping is not common among locals.

FRUIT VENDORS There's a fruit vendor on almost every street corner in downtown San José. If you're lucky enough to be in town between April and June, you can sample more varieties of mangoes than you ever knew existed. I like buying them already cut up in a little bag; they cost a little more this way, but you don't get nearly as messy. Be sure to try a green mango with salt and chili peppers—it's guaranteed to wake up your taste buds. Another common street food that you might be wondering about is called *pejibaye,* a bright orange palm nut about the size of a plum. They're boiled in big pots on carts; you eat them in much the same way you eat an avocado, and they taste a bit like squash.

LATE-NIGHT BITES San José has quite a few **24-hour restaurants.** The best of these is **Cafeteria 1930,** which is described below. Another popular place, which is definitely a bit seedier, is **Chelles,** on Avenida Central and Calle 9 (see "San José After Dark," later in this chapter, for more information). Then there's **Del Mar,** which belongs to and is across from the Hotel Del Rey (p. 133); with stained-glass windows and efficient service, this is a good option, although the food is rather pedestrian and uninspired. Finally, you'll find a **Denny's (℃2231-3500),** at the Best Western Irazú, on the highway out to the airport (there's another beside the Hampton Inn at the airport).

Vendor selling *pejibaye.*

Downtown San José

In addition to the places listed below, in a city awash in Argentine-style steak-houses, **La Esquina de Buenos Aires** (☎2223-1909; Calle 11 and Av. 4) stands out for its jovial and authentic *porteño* vibe and cuisine.

MODERATE

Café Mundo ★ 🍴 INTERNATIONAL This popular place mixes contemporary cuisine with an ambience of casual elegance. Wood tables and Art Deco wrought-iron chairs are spread spaciously around several rooms in this former colonial mansion. Additional seating can be had on the open-air front veranda and in the small gardens both in front and out back. The appetizers include vegetable tempura, crab cakes, and chicken satay alongside more traditional Tico standards such as *patacones* (fried plantain chips) and fried yuca. There's a long list of pastas and pizzas, as well as more substantial main courses, nightly specials, and delicious desserts. One room here boasts colorful wall murals by Costa Rican artist Miguel Casafont. This place is almost always filled with a broad mix of San José's gay, bohemian, theater, arts, and university crowds.

Calle 15 and Av. 9, 200m (2 blocks) east and 100m (1 block) north of the INS building. ☎2222-6190. Reservations recommended. Main courses $6–$14. AE, MC, V. Mon–Thurs 11am–10:30pm; Fri 11am–midnight; Sat 5–10:30pm.

Cafeteria 1930 📷 INTERNATIONAL With veranda and patio seating directly fronting the Plaza de la Cultura, this is one of the most atmospheric spots for a casual bite and some good people-watching. A wrought-iron railing, white columns, and arches create an old-world atmosphere; on the plaza in front of the cafe, a marimba band performs and vendors sell handicrafts. Stop by for the breakfast and watch the plaza vendors set up their booths, or peruse the *Tico Times* over coffee while you have your shoes polished. The menu covers a lot of ground, and the food is respectable, if unspectacular, but there isn't a better place downtown to bask in the tropical sunshine while you sip a beer or have a light lunch, and it's a great place to come before or after a show at the Teatro Nacional.

At the Gran Hotel Costa Rica, Av. 2, btw. calles 1 and 3. ☎2221-4011. Sandwiches $6.50–$12; main courses $7–$32. AE, DC, MC, V. Daily 24 hr.

La Piazzetta ★ ITALIAN With a long menu and formal service, this restaurant reminds me of the Italian restaurants of old in New York's Little Italy. The menu includes quite a few risotto dishes, as well as several lobster offerings and some Sicilian fare. The veal scaloppini in a truffle sauce is excellent. Salads are colorful and artistically arranged. For dessert, sample a classic chocolate mousse or tiramisu. The wine list is quite extensive, with good and reasonably priced offerings from Italy, and most other prominent wine-producing regions around the world.

Paseo Colón near Calle 40 (opposite Banco de Costa Rica). ☎2221-8451. Reservations recommended. Main courses $5.50–$28. AE, MC, V. Mon–Fri noon–2pm and 6–11pm; Sat 5–11pm.

Tin Jo ★★ 🍴 CHINESE/PAN-ASIAN San José has hundreds of Chinese restaurants, but most simply serve up tired takes on chop suey, chow mein, and fried rice. In contrast, Tin Jo has a wide and varied menu, with an assortment of Cantonese and Szechuan staples, as well as a range of Thai, Japanese, and

Malaysian dishes, and even some Indian food. Some of the dishes are served in edible rice-noodle bowls, and the pineapple shrimp in coconut-milk curry is served in the hollowed-out half of a fresh pineapple. Dishes not to miss include the salt-and-pepper shrimp, beef teriyaki, and Thai curries. For dessert, try the sticky rice with mango, or banana tempura. The decor features artwork and textiles from across Asia, and you'll have real tablecloths and cloth napkins. Tin Jo is also a great option for vegetarians, and even vegans.

Calle 11, btw. avs. 6 and 8. **2221-7605** or 2257-3622. Main courses $6–$15. AE, MC, V. Mon–Sat 11:30am–3pm and 5:30–10pm (Fri–Sat kitchen open 'til 11pm); Sun 11:30am–10pm.

INEXPENSIVE

In addition to the places listed below, the **Q'Café** (**2221-0707**) is a delightful little European-style cafe with a pretty perch above the busy corner of Avenida Central and Calle 2. Try to grab a seat overlooking the action on the street below.

Café del Teatro Nacional ★ CAFE/COFFEEHOUSE Even if there's no show on during your visit, you can enjoy a light meal, sandwich, dessert, or a cup of coffee here, while soaking up the neoclassical atmosphere. The theater was built in the 1890s from the designs of European architects, and the Art Nouveau chandeliers, ceiling murals, and marble floors and tables are pure Parisian. The ambience is French-cafe chic, but the marimba music drifting in from outside the open window and the changing art exhibits by local artists will remind you that you're still in Costa Rica. On sunny days, there's outdoor seating at wrought-iron tables on the side of the theater. In addition to the regular hours of operation listed below, the cafe is open until 8pm any evening that there is a performance in the theater.

In the Teatro Nacional, Av. 2 btw. calles 3 and 5. **2221-1329.** Sandwiches $4–$7; main courses $5–$12. AE, MC, V. Mon–Sat 9am–4:30pm.

Restaurante Nuestra Tierra 📷 COSTA RICAN Sure it's touristy, but if you want a *casado* or some *gallo pinto,* anytime of the day or night, this is the place to come. The decor seeks to imitate a humble country ranch kitchen, with heavy wooden tables, chairs, and paneling, and strings of fresh onions and bunches of bananas hung from the rafters and columns. Service is friendly and efficient; dressed in typical *campesino* outfits, servers periodically break out into traditional folkloric dances. The biggest downside here is that the restaurant fronts the very busy Avenida 2, so head for a second-floor table away from the traffic.

Av. 2, and Calle 15. **2258-6500.** Main courses $4–$8. MC, V. Daily 24 hr.

Vishnu VEGETARIAN Vegetarians will likely find their way to this Vishnu restaurant or one of its many sister outlets around the city. The vibe's a little too plastic, too loud, and too brightly lit for my tastes in a vegetarian joint. However, most people just come for the filling *plato del día* that includes soup, salad, veggies, an entree, and dessert for under $4. The menu also offers bean burgers and cheese sandwiches on whole-wheat bread. At the cashier's counter you can buy natural cosmetics, honey, and bags of granola. There's another Vishnu (**2223-3095**) on the north side of Avenida 8, between calles 11 and 9.

Av. 1, btw. calles 1 and 3. **2256-6063.** Main courses $4–$6. MC, V. Daily 8am–7pm.

La Sabana/Paseo Colón

EXPENSIVE

Grano de Oro Restaurant ★★★ INTERNATIONAL Set around the lovely interior courtyard of the wonderful Hotel Grano de Oro (p. 137), this restaurant manages to have an atmosphere that's intimate, relaxed, and refined, all at the same time. The menu features a wide range of meat and fish dishes. The *lomito piemontes* is two medallions of filet mignon stuffed with Gorgonzola cheese in a sherry sauce, while the *pernil de conejo* is a rabbit thigh stuffed with a mushroom pâté and served with a Dijon mustard sauce. If you opt for fish, I recommend the macadamia-encrusted corvina, which is served with a light and tangy orange sauce. Be sure to save room for the "Grano de Oro pie," a decadent dessert with various layers of chocolate and coffee mousses and creams. This place also has a good wine list, including a range of options by the glass.

Calle 30, no. 251, btw. avs. 2 and 4, 150m (1½ blocks) south of Paseo Colón. ☎2255-3322. Reservations recommended. Main courses $12–$44. AE, MC, V. Daily 6am–10pm.

Park Café ★★★ 🍴 FUSION Having opened and run a Michelin two-star restaurant in London and another one-star joint in Cannes, Richard Neat now finds

DINING UNDER THE stars

Although there are myriad unique experiences to be had in Costa Rica, one of my favorites is dining on the side of a volcano with the lights of San José shimmering below. These hanging restaurants, called *miradores,* are a resourceful response to the city's topography. Because San José is set in a broad valley surrounded on all sides by volcanic mountains, people who live in these mountainous areas have no place to go but up—so they do, building roadside cafes vertically up the sides of the volcanoes.

The food at most of these establishments is not spectacular, but the views often are, particularly at night, when the wide valley sparkles in a wash of lights. The town of **Aserri,** 10km (6¼ miles) south of downtown San José, is the king of *miradores,* and **Mirador Ram Luna** (☎2230-3060) is the king of Aserri. Grab a window seat and, if you've got the fortitude, order a plate of *chicharrones* (fried pork rinds). There's often live music. You can hire a cab for around $12 or take the Aserri bus at Avenida 6 between calles Central and 2. Just ask the driver where to get off.

There are also *miradores* in the hills above Escazú and in San Ramón de Tres Ríos and Heredia. The most popular is **Le Monestère** (☎2289-4404; closed Sun), an elegant converted church serving somewhat overrated French and Belgian cuisine in a spectacular setting above the hills of Escazú. I recommend coming here just for the less formal **La Cava Grill** ★, which often features live music, mostly folk-pop but sometimes jazz. I also like **Mirador Tiquicia** (☎2289-5839), which occupies several rooms in a sprawling old Costa Rican home and has live folkloric dance shows on Thursday.

himself turning out his fusion cuisine in an intimate space spread around the interior patio courtyard of a stately old downtown mansion, which also doubles as an antiques and imported furniture store. The menu changes regularly but might feature roasted scallops with ricotta tortellini in a pumpkin jus, or some expertly grilled quail on a vegetable purée bed, topped with poached quail egg. Presentations are artfully done, and often served in such a way as to encourage sharing. The well-thought-out and fairly priced wine list is a perfect complement to the cuisine.

Sabana Norte, 1 block north of Rostipollos. ☎2290-6324. Reservations recommended. Main courses $13–$22. V. Tues–Sat noon–3pm and 7–10pm.

MODERATE

El Chicote ★ COSTA RICAN/STEAK This is one of San José's most venerable and popular steakhouses. The large room is divided by half-walls planted with tropical flora and a bevy of hanging ferns, and heavy wooden beams and plenty of varnished-wood accents are used throughout. True meat aficionados should order the imported rib-eye or pound-and-a-half T-bone. There's an extensive se- lection of fish and poultry dishes as well. Everything comes with a choice of baked or mashed potatoes, black beans, and fresh tortillas. The wine list features a broad range of Italian, Spanish, French, and Californian wines. Waiters wear black jackets, white shirts, and black bow ties—typical of the unusually formal (for Costa Rica) service.

Av. Las Américas, 400m (4 blocks) west of the ICE building, Sabana Norte. ☎2232-0936 or 2232-3777. Reservations recommended. Main courses $10–$21. AE, MC, V. Mon–Fri 11am–3pm and 6–11pm; Sat–Sun 11am–11pm.

Machu Picchu ★ PERUVIAN/INTERNATIONAL Machu Picchu is an un- pretentious little restaurant that is perennially one of the most popular places in San José. The menu is classic Peruvian. One of my favorite entrees is the *causa limeña,* lemon-flavored mashed potatoes stuffed with shrimp. The *ceviche* here is excellent, as is the *ají de gallina,* a dish of shredded chicken in a fragrant cream sauce, and octopus with garlic butter. For main dishes, I recommend *corvina a lo macho,* sea bass in a slightly spicy tomato-based seafood sauce. Be sure to ask for a pisco sour, a classic Peruvian drink made from pisco, a grape liquor. These folks have a sister restaurant over in San Pedro (☎2283-3679), set on a hillside with a great view over the valley below.

Calle 32, btw. avs. 1 and 3, 150m (1½ blocks) north of the KFC on Paseo Colón. ☎2222-7384. Reser- vations recommended. Main courses $8–$16. AE, DC, MC, V. Mon–Sat 11am–3pm and 6–10pm.

INEXPENSIVE

Soda Tapia COSTA RICAN The food is unspectacular, dependable, and quite inexpensive at this very popular local diner. There's seating inside the brightly lit dining room, as well as on the sidewalk-style patio fronting the parking area. Dour but efficient waitstaff take the order you mark down on your combination menu/bill. This is a great place for late-night eats or for before or after a visit to Parque La Sabana or the Museo de Arte Costarricense. These folks also have another site in a small strip mall in Santa Ana (☎2203-7174).

Calle 42 and Av. 2, across from the Museo de Arte Costarricense. ☎2222-6734. Sandwiches $2–$4; main dishes $4.50–$9. MC, V. Daily 7am–midnight.

San Pedro/Los Yoses

In addition to the restaurants listed below, local and visiting vegetarians swear by the little **Comida Para Sentir Restaurante Vegetariano San Pedro** (☎2224-1163), located 125m (1¼ blocks) north of the San Pedro Church. Despite the massive size and popularity of the nearby **Il Pomodoro,** I prefer **Pane E Vino** (☎2280-2869), an excellent pasta-and-pizza joint on the eastern edge of San Pedro.

For Peruvian cuisine, try the branch of **Machu Picchu** (☎2283-3679; see above for a review) in San Pedro. Finally, if you're hankering for sushi, try **Ichiban ★** (☎2253-8012) in San Pedro, or **Matsuri ★** (☎2280-5522), a little farther east in Curridabat.

MODERATE

Donde Carlos ★★ ARGENTINE/STEAK Bold architectural touches abound in this stylish restaurant, yet the food is built primarily around simple, expertly grilled meats and fresh fish. You pass the wood-burning Argentine-style charcoal grill as you enter. I like the outdoor tables on the second-floor balcony when the weather permits. Most folks stick to the hearty steak options, but you can also order a wide range of sausages and offal meats, as well as fresh tuna. Don't pass on the apple pancake dessert—it's delicious. All portions are huge, and this place has a good and reasonably priced wine list to boot.

1 block north of the Fatima Church in Los Yoses. ☎**2225-0819.** Main courses $14–$35. AE, MC, V. Mon–Fri noon–3pm; Mon–Thurs 6:30–10:30pm; Fri 6:30–11pm; Sat noon–11pm; Sun noon–7pm.

Jurgen's ★★ INTERNATIONAL Housed in a boutique business-class hotel, this elegant little restaurant serves excellent European-style continental fare in a refined atmosphere. The lighting is low and service extremely professional. You'll find poached salmon with a dill sauce, and grilled tilapia with a Dijon mustard sauce. The steaks are top cuts of beef, perfectly prepared. This place has one of the more extensive wine lists in town. The owner, Jurgen Mormel, also has several gourmet specialty food shops around San José.

Inside Hotel Jade, 2½ blocks north of the Subaru dealership, Los Yoses. ☎**2283-2239.** Main courses $9–$25. AE, MC, V. Mon–Fri noon–2pm and 6–10pm; Sat 6–10:30pm.

Olio ★ 🍴 MEDITERRANEAN Exposed brick walls, dark wood wainscoting, and stained-glass lamps imbue this place with character and romance. Couples will want to grab a table in a quiet nook, since groups tend to dominate the large main room or crowd the bar. The extensive tapas menu features traditional Spanish fare, as well as bruschetta, antipasti, and a Greek *mezza* plate. For a main dish, I recommend the chicken Vesuvio, which is marinated first in a balsamic vinegar reduction and finished with a creamy herb sauce; or the *arrollado siciliano,* which is a thin filet of steak rolled around spinach, sun-dried tomatoes, and mozzarella cheese and topped with a pomodoro sauce. The midsize wine list features very reasonably priced wines from Italy, France, Spain, Germany, Chile, Greece, and even Bulgaria. Nonsmokers be forewarned: The bar and dining areas here are often tightly packed and smoke-filled.

Barrio California, 200m (2 blocks) north of Bagelman's. ☎**2281-0541.** Main courses $5–$12. AE, DC, MC, V. Mon–Fri noon–midnight; Sat 6pm–midnight.

INEXPENSIVE

Whappin' ★ 🎁 COSTA RICAN/CARIBBEAN You don't have to go to Limón or Cahuita to get good home-cooked Caribbean food. In addition to *rondon,* a coconut milk–based stew or soup (see "That Rundown Feeling," on p. 478), you can also get the classic rice and beans cooked in coconut milk, as well as a range of fish and chicken dishes from the coastal region. I like the whole red snapper covered in a spicy sauce of sautéed onions. There's a small bar at the entrance and some simple tables spread around the restaurant, with an alcove here and there. Everything is very simple, and prices are quite reasonable. After a dinner of fresh fish, with rice, beans, and *patacones,* the only letdown is that the beach is some 4 hours away.

Barrio Escalante, 200m (2 blocks) east of El Farolito. ☎2283-1480. Main courses $6.50–$14. AE, MC, V. Mon–Sat 11:30am–2:30pm and 6–10pm.

Escazú & Santa Ana

These two suburbs on the western side of town have the most vibrant restaurant scene in San José. Although there's high turnover and sudden closings, this remains a good area to check out for a variety of dining experiences. A good one-stop option to consider is the Plaza Itskatzu shopping center, just off the highway and sharing a parking lot with the Courtyard San José. Here you'll find a wide variety of moderately priced restaurant options, including **Tutti Li** (☎2289-8768), a good Italian restaurant and pizzeria; **Chancay** (☎2289-6964), which serves Peruvian and Peruvian/Chinese cuisine; **La Guagua** (☎2288-5112), serving up tasty Cuban food; **Las Tapas de Manuel** ★ (☎2288-5700), a Spanish-style tapas restaurant; and franchise outlets of both **Hooters** (☎2289-3498) and **Outback Steakhouse** (☎2288-0511). In addition, **Il Panino** ★ (☎2228-3126) is an upscale sandwich shop and cafe, located in the Centro Comercial El Paco.

EXPENSIVE

Bacchus ★★★ 🎁 ITALIAN My favorite Italian restaurant in San José, this place is housed in a historic home that is over a century old. Nevertheless, this place somehow seamlessly blends the old with the new in an elegant atmosphere. The best tables are on the covered back patio, where you can watch the open kitchen and wood-burning pizza oven in action. The regularly changing menu features a range of antipasti, pastas, pizzas, and main dishes. Everything is perfectly prepared and beautifully presented. The desserts are also excellent, and the wine list is extensive and fairly priced.

Downtown Santa Ana. ☎2282-5441. Reservations required. Main courses $8–$24. AE, MC, V. Tues–Sat noon–3pm and 6–11pm; Sun noon–9pm.

Barbecue Los Anonos ★ COSTA RICAN/STEAK Good steaks and well-prepared Costa Rican cuisine have made this homey restaurant something of an institution. Most of the seating is at rustic wooden tables covered with red-and-white checkered tablecloths, and long and rustic booths set under the shelter of low interior red-tile roofs. Aged Angus beef is served, and this is *the* place to come if you're craving a 16-ounce T-bone on the west side of town. There are also a host of chicken, pork, and fish options; I recommend the mixed-grill plate for two, which comes with a little bit of everything.

600m (6 blocks) west of the Los Anonos bridge in San Rafael de Escazú, next to the Sarretto Market. ☎2228-0180. Reservations recommended. Main courses $9–$26. AE, MC, V. Tues–Sat noon–3pm; Tues–Thurs 6–10pm; Fri–Sat 6–11pm; Sun 11:30am–9pm.

La Luz ★ CALIFORNIAN/FUSION La Luz was one of the first fusion restaurants in Costa Rica, and it continues to serves up excellent food in an elegant, eye-catching setting. I keep coming back for the fiery garlic prawns, which are sautéed in ancho-chili oil and sage and served over a roasted-garlic potato mash. The whole thing is served with a garnish of fried leeks and a tequila-lime butter and cilantro-oil sauce. I also enjoy the passion fruit–glazed duck breast. On top of an extensive menu, there are nightly specials and a wide selection of inventive appetizers and desserts. The glass-walled dining room offers up a stunning view of the Central Valley lights at night. The Sunday brunch here is delightful and very filling.

In the Alta Hotel (p. 140), on the old road to Santa Ana. ☎2282-4160. Reservations recommended. Main courses $12–$24. AE, DC, MC, V. Daily 6:30am–10pm.

La Mar Cebicheria ★★ PERUVIAN/FUSION The growing international empire of famed Peruvian chef and restaurateur Gaston Acurio has touched down in Costa Rica. A refined take on Lima's typical street food and *ceviche* restaurants, you can get a variety of marinated seafood concoctions here. I recommend the Nikkei, which features chunks of raw tuna in a tangy sesame-soy marinade. While there are a host of main dishes on the menu, the strong suit here are the fusion takes on a range of traditional Peruvian appetizers—*tiraditos, anticuchos, causas*—which makes this a great place to pick and share among friends, while enjoying the tasty (and strong) pisco sours.

Plaza Momentum, Santa Ana. ☎2282-6856. Reservations recommended. Main courses $9–$18. AE, DC, MC, V. Sun–Mon 11:45am–4:30pm; Tues–Sat 11:45am–3:30pm and 7–10pm.

MODERATE

La Cava Grill ★ 🎁 COSTA RICAN/STEAK This place is a cozy and warm spot built underneath the popular yet overpriced and overrated Le Monestère restaurant. While the decor is much less ornate, the service much less formal, and the menu much less French, the view is just as spectacular. Grab a window seat on a clear night and enjoy the sparkle of the lights below. The menu features a range of simply prepared meat, poultry, and fish. More adventurous diners can try the *tepezquintle* (a large rodent, also called a *paca*), which is actually quite tasty. There's live music and a festive party most weekend nights in the attached bar. My big complaint here is that the wine list is borrowed from the upstairs restaurant, and is pretentious and expensive.

1.5km (1 mile) south of Centro Comercial Paco; follow the signs to Le Monestère. ☎2289-4404. Reservations recommended. Main courses $6–$22. AE, MC, V. Mon–Sat 6pm–1:30am.

Taj Mahal ★ 🎁 INDIAN If you're craving Indian cuisine in San José, this is the place to come. The menu is quite extensive and covers most of the traditional bases with *biryanis, vindaloos, tikka masalas*, and a variety of curries. They have an authentic tandoor oven, and the tandoori meats are excellently prepared. The restaurant is spread out through several rooms in a converted home. The decorations and furniture are mostly imported from India. I like the few outdoor tables in the backyard, especially for lunch. Like Tin Jo, this is a great choice for vegetarians.

On the old road to Santa Ana, 1km (½ mile) west of Centro Comercial Paco. **2228-0980.** Reservations recommended. Main courses $7–$16. AE, MC, V. Tues–Sun noon–3pm and 6–11pm.

WHAT TO SEE & DO

Most visitors to Costa Rica try to get out of the city as fast as possible so they can spend more time on the beach or off in the rainforests. But there are a few attractions in San José to keep you busy. Some of the best and most modern museums in Central America are here, with a wealth of fascinating pre-Columbian artifacts. Standouts include the remodeled Museo de Jade Marco Fidel Tristán (Jade Museum) and the centrally located Centro Nacional de Arte y Cultura (National Center of Arts and Culture), featuring yet another museum and several performing-arts spaces.

Sculpture at Museo de Arte Costarricense.

There are also several great things to see and do just outside San José in the Central Valley. If you start doing day trips out of the city, you can spend quite a few days in this region. See "San José in 3 Days," in chapter 4, for additional touring ideas.

ORGANIZED TOURS There really isn't much reason to take a tour of San José. It's so compact that you can easily visit all the major sights on your own, as described below. However, if you want to take a city tour, which will run you between $20 and $50, here are some companies you can use: **Horizontes Travel** ★★, Calle 32 between avenidas 3 and 5 (**2222-2022;** www.horizontes.com); **Gray Line Tours,** Avenida 7 between calles 6 and 8, with additional offices at the Hampton Inn and Best Western Irazú (**2220-2126;** www.graylinecostarica.com); and **Swiss Travel Service** (**2282-4898;** www.swisstravelcr.com). These same companies also offer a complete range of day trips out of San José (see "Side Trips from San José," later in this chapter). Almost all of the major hotels have tour desks, and most of the smaller hotels will also help arrange tours and day trips.

The Top Attractions

In addition to the attractions listed below, you might consider a quick stop at San José's main **cathedral.** The church and its interior are largely unspectacular. However, you'll see a pretty garden, as well as a massive marble statue of Pope Juan Pablo II, with a woman and child, carved by celebrated Costa Rican sculptor Jorge Jiménez Deredia. Deredia also has a work at the Vatican. The cathedral is located at the corner of Avenida 2 and Calle Central.

Centro Nacional de Arte y Cultura (National Center of Art and Culture) ★ 🎁 Occupying a full city block, this was once the National Liquor Factory (FANAL). Now it houses the offices of the Cultural Ministry, several performing-arts centers, and the Museum of Contemporary Art and Design. The latter has done an excellent job of promoting cutting-edge Costa Rican and Central American artists, while also featuring impressive traveling international exhibits, including large retrospectives by prominent Latin American and international art stars. If you're looking for modern dance, experimental theater, or a lecture on Costa Rican video, this is a good place to check out. Allow around 2 hours to take in all the exhibits here.

Calle 13 btw. avs. 3 and 5. ☎2257-7202 or 2257-9370. Admission $1, 60¢ for students with valid ID, free for seniors and children 11 and under, free for everyone on Mon. Museum Mon–Sat 9:30am–4:45pm.

Museo de Arte Costarricense (Costa Rican Art Museum) ★★ *Note:* This museum was closed in early 2009 for a major restoration. It remains closed as the book goes to press, but is expected to open in early 2010.

This small museum at the end of Paseo Colón in Parque La Sabana was originally the country's principal airport terminal. Today it houses a collection of works in all media by Costa Rica's most celebrated artists. On display are some exceptionally beautiful pieces in a wide range of styles, demonstrating how Costa Rican artists have interpreted and imitated the major European movements over the years. In addition to the permanent collection of sculptures, paintings, and prints, there are rotating temporary exhibits. If the second floor is open during your visit, have a look at the conference room's bas-relief walls, which chronicle the history of Costa Rica from pre-Columbian times to the present with evocative images of its people. Be sure to visit the outdoor sculpture garden, which features works by José Sancho, Jorge Jiménez Deredia, Max Jiménez, and Francisco Zuñiga. Moreover, the outdoor setting is lovely. You can easily spend an hour or two at this museum—more if you take a stroll through the neighboring park.

Calle 42 and Paseo Colón, Parque La Sabana Este. ☎2222-7155. www.musarco.go.cr. Admission $5 adults, $3 for students with valid ID, free for children and seniors, free for everyone Sun. Tues–Fri 9am–5pm; Sat–Sun 10am–4pm.

Museo de Jade Marco Fidel Tristán (Jade Museum) ★ Jade was the most valuable commodity among the pre-Columbian cultures of Mexico and Central America, worth more than gold. Located on the first floor of the INS (National Insurance Company) building, this popular museum houses a huge collection of jade artifacts dating from 500 B.C. to A.D. 800. Most are large pendants that were parts of necklaces and are primarily human and animal figures. A fascinating display illustrates how the primitive peoples of this region carved this extremely hard stone.

The museum also possesses an extensive collection of pre-Columbian polychrome terra-cotta vases, bowls, and figurines. Some of these pieces are amazingly modern in design and exhibit a surprisingly advanced technique. Particularly fascinating is a vase that incorporates real human teeth, and a display that shows how jade was embedded in human teeth merely for decorative reasons. All of the explanations are in English and Spanish. Allot at least an hour to tour this museum.

Av. 7 btw. calles 9 and 9B, INS Building. ☎2287-6034. Admission $7, free for children 11 and under. Mon–Fri 8:30am–3:30pm; Sat 9am–1pm.

Art displays at Museo de Jade Marco Fidel Tristán.

Museo de Los Niños (Children's Museum) ☺ If you're traveling with children, you'll definitely want to come here, and you might want to visit even if you aren't. A former barracks and then a prison, this museum houses an extensive collection of exhibits designed to edify and entertain children of all ages. Experience a simulated earthquake or make music by dancing across the floor. Many exhibits encourage hands-on play. The museum sometimes features limited shows of "serious" art and is also the home of the National Auditorium. You can spend anywhere from 1 to 4 hours here, depending on how long your children linger at each exhibit. Be careful, though: The museum is large and spread out; it's easy to lose track of a family member or friend.

This museum is a few blocks north of downtown, on Calle 4. It's within easy walking distance, but you might want to take a cab because you'll have to walk right through the worst part of the red-light district.

Calle 4 and Av. 9. ☎2258-4929. www.museocr.com. Admission $2 adults, $1.20 students and children 17 and under. Tues–Fri 8am–4:30pm; Sat–Sun 10am–5pm.

Museo Nacional de Costa Rica (National Museum) ★ Costa Rica's most important historical museum is housed in a former army barracks that was the scene of fighting during the civil war of 1948. As you approach the building, or walk around it, you can still see hundreds of bullet holes on the turrets at its corners. Inside this traditional Spanish-style courtyard building, you will find displays on Costa Rican history and culture from pre-Columbian times to the present. In the pre-Columbian rooms, you'll see a 2,500-year-old jade carving that is shaped like a seashell and etched with an image of a hand holding a small animal.

Among the most fascinating objects unearthed at Costa Rica's numerous archaeological sites are many *metates*, or grinding stones. This type of grinding stone is still in use today throughout Central America; however, the ones on display here are more ornately decorated than those that you will see anywhere else. Some of the *metates* are the size of a small bed and are believed to have been part of funeral rites. A separate vault houses the museum's collection of pre-Columbian gold jewelry and figurines. In the courtyard you'll be treated to a wonderful view of the city and see some of Costa Rica's mysterious stone spheres. It takes about 2 hours to take in the lion's share of the collection here.

Museo Nacional de Costa Rica.

Calle 17, btw. avs. Central and 2, on the Plaza de la Democracia. ☎2257-1433. www.museocostarica. go.cr. Admission $6 adults, $3 students and children 11 and under. Tues–Sat 8:30am–4:30pm; Sun 9am–4:30pm. Closed Jan 1, May 1, Dec 25, and Holy Thursday, Good Friday, and Easter Sunday.

Museos del Banco Central de Costa Rica (Gold Museum) ★★ Located directly beneath the Plaza de la Cultura, this unusual underground museum houses one of the largest collections of pre-Columbian gold in the Americas. On display are more than 20,000 troy ounces of gold in more than 2,000 objects. The sheer number of pieces can be overwhelming and seem redundant, but the unusual display cases and complex lighting systems show off every piece to its utmost. This complex also includes a gallery for temporary art exhibits, separate numismatic and philatelic museums (coins and stamps, for us regular folks), a modest gift shop, and a branch of the Costa Rican Tourist Institute's info center. Plan to spend an hour or two here.

Calle 5, btw. avs. Central and 2, underneath the Plaza de la Cultura. ☎2243-4202. www.museosdelbancocentral.org. Admission $9 adults, $4 students, 80¢ children 11 and under. Daily 9:30am–5pm.

Parque Zoológico Simón Bolívar ☺ This zoo no longer suffers from the overwhelming sense of neglect and despair that once plagued it, though it's still pretty lackluster and depressing. Why spend time here when you could head out into the forests and jungles? You won't see the great concentrations of wildlife available in one stop here at the zoo, but you'll see the animals in their natural habitats, not yours. The zoo is really geared toward locals and school groups, with a collection that includes Asian, African, and Costa Rican animals. There's a children's discovery area, a snake-and-reptile house, and a gift shop. You can easily spend a couple of hours here.

Artwork at Museos del Banco Central.

Av. 11 and Calle 7, in Barrio Amón. ☎ **2256-0012.** Admission $3 adults, $1.50 children, free for children 2 and under. Mon–Fri 8am–4pm; Sat–Sun 9am–4:30pm.

Spirogyra Butterfly Garden This butterfly garden is smaller and less elaborate than the Butterfly Farm (see below), but it provides a good introduction to the life cycle of butterflies. It's also a calm and quiet oasis in a noisy and crowded city, quite close to downtown. Plan on a half-hour to several hours here, depending on whether they have lunch or refreshments at the small coffee shop and gallery. You'll be given a self-guided-tour booklet when you arrive, and an 18-minute video show runs continuously throughout the day. You'll find Spirogyra near El Pueblo, a short taxi ride from the center of San José. This is a convenient place to visit in combination with some shopping and a meal at El Pueblo.

100m (1 block) east and 150m (1½ blocks) south of El Pueblo Shopping Center. ☎/fax **2222-2937.** www.infocostarica.com/butterfly. Admission $6. Daily 8am–4pm (cafe 'til 7:30pm).

Outside San José

The **Museo Historico Cultural Juan Santamaría,** Avenida 3 between calles Central and 2 (☎ **2441-4775**), isn't worth a trip of its own, but if you're planning an afternoon in Alajuela, you may want to stop here before or after Zoo Ave. (p. 162). The museum commemorates Costa Rica's national hero, Juan Santamaría, who gave his life defending the country against a small army led by William Walker, a U.S. citizen who invaded Costa Rica in 1856, attempting to set up a slave state. The museum is open Tuesday through Sunday from 10am to 6pm; admission is free.

To locate the attractions below, see "The Central Valley" map on p. 179.

Butterfly Farm ★ At any given time, you might see around 30 of the 80 species of butterflies raised at this butterfly farm south of Alajuela. The butterflies live in

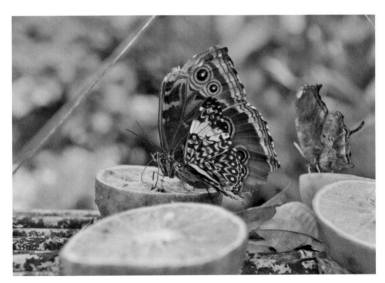

Butterflies at Spirogyra Butterfly Garden.

enclosed garden similar to an aviary and flutter about the heads of visitors during tours of the gardens. You should be certain to spot glittering blue morphos and a large butterfly that mimics the eyes of an owl. Admission includes a 2-hour guided tour. In the demonstration room you'll see butterfly eggs, caterpillars, and pupae. There are cocoons trimmed in a shimmering gold color and cocoons that mimic a snake's head to frighten away predators. The last guided tour of the day begins at 3pm.

If you reserve in advance, the Butterfly Farm has three daily bus tours that run from many major San José hotels. The cost, including round-trip transportation and admission to the garden, is $35 for adults, $30 for students, and $20 for children 5 to 12. Buses pick up passengers at more than 20 different hotels in the San José area.

In front of Los Reyes Country Club, La Guácima de Alajuela. ☏ **2438-0400.** www.butterflyfarm. co.cr. Admission $15 adults, $10 students, $7 children 5–11, free for children 4 and under. Daily 8:45am–3pm.

Café Britt Farm ★ Although bananas are the main export of Costa Rica, most people are far more interested in the country's second-most-important export crop: coffee. Café Britt is one of the leading brands here, and the company has put together an interesting tour and stage production at its farm, which is 20 minutes outside of San José. Here, you'll see how coffee is grown. You'll also visit the roasting and processing plant to learn how a coffee "cherry" is turned into a delicious roasted bean. Tasting sessions are offered for visitors to experience the different qualities of coffee. There are also a restaurant and a store where you can buy coffee and coffee-related gift items. The entire tour, including transportation, takes about 3 to 4 hours. Allow some extra time and an extra $10 for a visit to their nearby working plantation and mill. You can even strap on a basket and go out coffee picking during harvest time.

North of Heredia on the road to Barva. ☏ **2277-1600.** www.coffeetour.com. Admission $20 adults, $16 children 6–11; $37 adults and $33 children, including transportation from downtown San José and a coffee drink. Add $15 for a full buffet lunch. Tour daily at 11am. Store and restaurant daily 8am–5pm year-round.

Else Kientzler Botanical Garden ★★ ☺ Located on the grounds of an ornamental flower farm, on the outskirts of the tourist town Sarchí, these are extensive, impressive, and

Else Kientzler Botanical Garden.

INBio Park.

lovingly laid out botanical gardens. Over 2.5km (1½ miles) of trails run through a collection of more than 2,000 species of flora. All of the plants are labeled with their Latin names, with some further explanations around the grounds in both English and Spanish. There's a topiary labyrinth, as well as a variety of lookouts, gazebos, and shady benches on the grounds. A children's play area features some water games, jungle gym setups, and a child-friendly little zip-line canopy tour. Over 40% of the gardens are wheelchair accessible.

Tuan (℡**2258-2004**) buses leave San José about five times throughout the day for Sarchí from Calle 18 between avenidas 5 and 7. The fare is $1.25. Alternatively, you can take any Grecia bus from this same station. In Grecia they connect with the Alajuela-Sarchí buses, leaving every 30 minutes from Calle 8 between avenidas Central and 1 in Alajuela.

Sarchí, Alajuela. ℡**2454-2070.** www.elsegarden.com. Admission $14, $6 students with valid ID and children 5–12. A guided tour costs an extra $15 per guide per hour, for a group of up to 15 persons. Advance reservations are necessary for guided tours. Daily 8am–4pm. About 6 blocks north of the central football (soccer) stadium in the town of Sarchí.

INBio Park ★★ ☺ Run by the National Biodiversity Institute (Instituto Nacional de Biodiversidad, or INBio), this place is part museum, part educational center, and part nature park. In addition to watching a 15-minute informational video, visitors can tour two large pavilions explaining Costa Rica's biodiversity and natural wonders, and hike on trails that re-create the ecosystems of a tropical rainforest, dry forest, and premontane forest. A 2-hour guided hike is included in the entrance fee, and self-guided-tour booklets are also available. There's a good-size butterfly garden, as well as a Plexiglas viewing window into the small lagoon. One of my favorite attractions here is the series of wonderful animal sculptures donated by one of Costa Rica's premiere artists, José Sancho. There's a simple cafeteria-style restaurant here for lunch, as well as a coffee shop and gift shop. You can easily spend 2 to 3 hours here.

400m (4 blocks) north and 250m (2½ blocks) west of the Shell station in Santo Domingo de Heredia. ℡**2507-8107.** www.inbio.ac.cr. Admission $23 adults, $13 children 12 and under. Daily 8am–6pm (admission closes at 4pm). INBio Park can arrange round-trip transportation from downtown for $18 per person.

Lankester Gardens ★★ Costa Rica has more than 1,400 varieties of orchids, and almost 800 species are cultivated and on display at this botanical garden in Cartago province. Created in the 1940s by English naturalist Charles Lankester, the gardens are now administered by the University of Costa Rica. The primary goal is to preserve the local flora, with an emphasis on orchids and bromeliads. Paved trails meander from open, sunny gardens into shady forests. In each environment different species of orchids are in bloom. There's an information center and a gift shop, and the trails are well tended and well marked. Plan to spend between 1 and 3 hours here if you're interested in flowers and gardening; you could run through it more quickly if you're not. You can easily combine a visit here with a tour at Cartago and/or the Orosi Valley and Irazú Volcano. See "Side Trips from San José," later in this chapter.

Paraíso de Cartago. ☏ **2552-3247.** www.jardinbotanicolankester.org Admission $5 adults, $3.50 children 6-16. Daily 8:30am-5:30pm. Closed all national holidays. Take the Cartago bus from San José, and then the Paraíso bus from a stop 1 block south and ¾ block west of the Catholic church ruins in Cartago (ride takes 30-40 min.).

La Paz Waterfall Gardens ★★ ☺ The main attraction here consists of a series of trails through primary and secondary forests alongside the La Paz River, with lookouts over a series of powerful falls, including the namesake La Paz Fall. In addition to an orchid garden and a hummingbird garden, you must visit their huge butterfly garden, which is easily the largest in Costa Rica. A small serpentarium, featuring a mix of venomous and nonvenomous native snakes, and several terrariums containing various frogs and lizards, are added attractions. There's also a man-made trout pond where you can cast for trout, or just take a swim with them. While the admission fee is a little steep, everything is wonderfully done and the trails and waterfalls are beautiful. A buffet lunch at the large cafeteria-style restaurant costs an extra $12 for adults, or $6 for kids. This is a good stop after a morning visit to the Poás Volcano. Plan to spend 2 to 4 hours here. The hotel rooms (Peace Lodge; p. 143) are some of the nicest in the country.

6km (3¾ miles) north of Varablanca on the road to San Miguel. ☏ **2225-0643.** www.waterfall gardens.com. Admission $32 adults, $20 children and students with valid ID. Daily 8:30am-5:30pm. Take a Puerto Viejo de Sarapiquí bus from Calle 12 and Av. 9 (make sure it passes through Varablanca and La Virgen), and ask to be let off at the entrance. Buses are infrequent, and coordinating your return can be difficult, so it's best to come in a rental car or arrange transport.

Zoo Ave. ★ Dozens of scarlet macaws, reclusive owls, majestic raptors, several different species of toucans, and a host of brilliantly colored birds from Costa Rica and around the world make this one exciting place to visit. In total, over 115 species of birds are on display, including some 80 species found in Costa Rica. Bird-watching enthusiasts will be able to get a closer look at birds they might have seen in the wild. There are also large iguana, deer, tapir, ocelot, puma, and monkey exhibits—and look out for the 3.6m (12-ft.) crocodile. Zoo Ave. houses only injured, donated, or confiscated animals. It takes about 2 hours to walk the paths and visit all the exhibits here.

La Garita, Alajuela. ☏ **2433-8989.** www.zooave.org. Admission $15, $13 students with valid ID. Daily 9am-5pm. Catch a bus to Alajuela on Av. 2 btw. calles 12 and 14. In Alajuela, transfer to a bus to Atenas and get off at Zoo Ave. before you get to La Garita. Fare is 60¢.

OUTDOOR ACTIVITIES & SPECTATOR SPORTS

Due to the chaos and pollution, you'll probably want to get out of the city before undertaking anything too strenuous. But if you want to brave the elements, there are a few outdoor activities in and around San José.

Parque La Sabana (at the western end of Paseo Colón), formerly San José's international airport, is the city's center for active sports and recreation. Here you'll find everything from jogging trails, soccer fields, and a few public tennis courts to the National Stadium. All the facilities are free and open to the public. Families gather for picnics, people fly kites, and there's even an outdoor sculpture garden. If you really want to experience the local culture, try getting into a pickup soccer game here. However, be careful in this park, especially at dusk or after dark, when it becomes a favorite haunt for youth gangs and muggers.

For information on horseback riding, hiking, and white-water rafting trips from San José, see "Side Trips from San José," later in this chapter.

BIRD-WATCHING Serious birders will certainly want to head out of San José, but it is still possible to see quite a few species in the metropolitan area. Two of the best spots for urban bird-watching are the campus at the **University of Costa Rica,** in the eastern suburb of San Pedro, and **Parque del Este ★**, located a little farther east on the road to San Ramón de Tres Ríos. You'll see a mix of urban species, and if you're lucky, you might spy a couple of hummingbirds or even a blue-crowned motmot. To get to the university campus, take any San Pedro bus from Avenida Central between

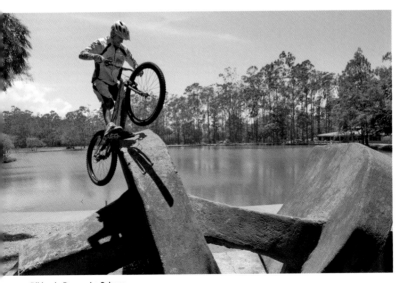

Biking in Parque La Sabana.

A Costa Rican bullfight.

calles 9 and 11. To get to Parque del Este, take the San Ramón/Parque del Este bus from Calle 9 between avenidas Central and 1. To hook up with fellow birders, e-mail the **Birding Club of Costa Rica** ★★ (costarica birding@hotmail.com), which frequently organizes expeditions around the Central Valley and beyond.

BULLFIGHTING Although I hesitate to call it a sport, **Las Corridas a la Tica (Costa Rican bullfighting)** is a popular and frequently comic stadium event. Instead of the blood-and-gore/life-and-death confrontation of traditional bullfighting, Ticos just like to tease the bull. In a typical *corrida* (bullfight), anywhere from 50 to 150 *toreadores improvisados* (literally, "improvised bullfighters") stand in the ring waiting for the bull. What follows is a slapstick scramble to safety whenever the bull heads toward a crowd of bullfighters. The braver bullfighters try to slap the bull's backside as the beast chases down one of his buddies.

You can see a bullfight during the various Festejos Populares (City Fairs) around the country. The country's largest Festejos Populares are held in Zapote, a suburb east of San José during Christmas week and the first week in January. Admission is $2 to $5. This is a purely seasonal activity and occurs in San José only during the Festejos. However, there are yearly *festejos* in nearly every little town around the country. These are spread out throughout the year. Ask at your hotel; if your timing's right, you might be able to take in one of these.

GOLF & TENNIS If you want to play tennis or golf in San José, your options are limited. If you're looking for a real local experience on some rough concrete courts, you can take a racket and some balls down to **Parque La Sabana.** However, the best facilities for visiting golfers and tennis players are found at **Parque Valle del Sol** ★ (☎2282-9222; www.vallesol.com), in the western suburb of Santa Ana. The 18-hole course here is open to the general public. Greens fees are $94 per golfer per day, including the cart and unlimited playing both on the course and driving range. The tennis courts here cost $8 per hour. Reservations are essential. The golf course at the Cariari Country Club is not open to the general public.

HOTEL SPAS & WORKOUT FACILITIES Most of the city's higher-end hotels have some sort of pool and exercise facilities. You'll find the best of these at the Marriott Costa Rica Hotel (p. 143) and Crowne Plaza Corobicí (p. 137). If you're looking for a good, serious workout, I recommend the **Multispa ★** (**2231-5542**), located in the Tryp Corobicí. Even if you're not a guest at the hotel, you can use the facilities here and join in any class for $13 per day. Multispa has five other locations around the Central Valley.

JOGGING Try **Parque La Sabana,** mentioned above, or head to **Parque del Este,** which is east of town in the foothills above San Pedro. Take the San Ramón/Parque del Este bus from Calle 9 between avenidas Central and 1. It's never a good idea to jog at night, on busy streets, or alone. Women should be particularly careful about jogging alone. And remember, Tico drivers are not accustomed to joggers on residential streets, so don't expect drivers to give you much berth.

SOCCER (*FÚTBOL*) Ticos take their *fútbol* seriously. Costa Rican professional soccer is some of the best in Central America, and the national team, or *Sele (selección nacional),* qualified for the World Cup in 2002 and 2006, although they made early exits both times. The soccer season runs from September to June, with the finals spread out over several weeks in late June and early July.

You don't need to buy tickets in advance. Tickets generally run between $2 and $15. It's worth paying a little extra for *sombra numerado* (reserved seats in the shade). This will protect you from both the sun and the more rowdy aficionados. Costa Rican soccer fans take the sport seriously, and several violent incidents, both inside and outside the stadiums, have marred the sport in recent years, so be careful. Other options include *sombra* (general admission in the shade), *palco* and *palco numerado* (general admission and reserved mezzanine), and *sol general* (general admission in full sun).

The main San José team is Saprissa (affectionately called El Monstruo, or "The Monster"). **Saprissa's stadium** is in Tibás (**2240-0002;** take any Tibás bus from Calle 2 and Av. 5). Games are often held on Sunday at 11am,

Fans at a *fútbol* match.

but occasionally they are scheduled for Saturday afternoon or Wednesday evening. Check the local newspapers for game times and locations.

SWIMMING If you aren't going to get to the beach anytime soon and your hotel doesn't have a pool, you can use the pool at the Multispa facility at the hotel **Crowne Plaza Corobicí** (☎**2231-5542**) for $13. Alternatively, for a real Tico experience, head to **Ojo de Agua** (☎**2441-2808**), on the road between the airport and San Antonio de Belén. The spring-fed waters are cool and refreshing, and even if it seems a bit chilly in San José, it's always several degrees warmer out here. This place is very popular with Ticos and can get quite crowded on weekends. Unfortunately, the place is perennially run-down and you have to keep an eye on your valuables here. Admission is $2. Buses leave almost hourly for Ojo de Agua from Avenida 2 and Calle 12.

SHOPPING

Serious shoppers will be disappointed in Costa Rica. Aside from coffee and oxcarts, there isn't much that's distinctly Costa Rican. To compensate for its own relative lack of goods, Costa Rica does a brisk business in selling crafts and clothes imported from Guatemala, Panama, and Ecuador.

THE SHOPPING SCENE San José's central shopping corridor is bounded by avenidas 1 and 2, from about Calle 14 in the west to Calle 13 in the east. For several blocks west of the Plaza de la Cultura, **Avenida Central** is a pedestrian-only street mall where you'll find store after store of inexpensive clothes for men, women, and children. Depending on the mood of the police that day, you might find a lot of street vendors as well. Most shops in the downtown district are open Monday through Saturday from about 8am to 6pm. Some shops close for lunch, while others remain open (it's just the luck of the draw for shoppers). You'll be happy to find that the sales and import taxes have already been figured into the display price.

MARKETS There are several markets near downtown, but by far the largest is the **Mercado Central,** located between avenidas Central and 1 and calles 6 and 8. Although this dark maze of stalls is primarily a food market, inside you'll find all manner of vendors, including a few selling Costa Rican souvenirs, crude leather goods, and musical instruments. Be especially careful about your wallet or purse or any prominent jewelry because very skilled pickpockets frequent this area. All the streets surrounding the Mercado Central are jammed with produce vendors selling from small carts or loading and unloading trucks. It's always a hive of activity, with crowds of people jostling for space on the streets. Your best bet is to visit on Sunday or on weekdays; Saturday is particularly busy. In the hot days of the dry season, the aromas can get quite heady.

There is also a daily street market on the west side of the **Plaza de la Democracia.** Here you'll find two long rows of outdoor stalls selling T-shirts, Guatemalan and Ecuadorian handicrafts and clothing, small ceramic *ocarinas* (a small musical wind instrument), and handmade jewelry. The atmosphere here is much more open than at the Mercado Central, which I find just a bit too claustrophobic. You might be able to bargain prices down a little bit, but bargaining is not a traditional part of the vendor culture

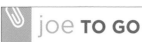

joe **TO GO**

Two words of advice: Buy coffee. Lots of it.

Coffee is the best shopping deal in all of Costa Rica. Although the best Costa Rican coffee is allegedly shipped off to North American and European markets, it's hard to beat the coffee that's roasted right in front of you here. Best of all is the price: One pound of coffee sells for around $3 to $6. It makes a great gift and truly is a local product.

can also try **Café Trébol,** on Calle 8 between avenidas Central and 1 (on the western side of the Central Market; **☎ 2221-8363**). It's open Monday through Saturday from 7am to 6:30pm and Sunday from 8:30am to 12:30pm.

Be sure to ask for whole beans; Costa Rican grinds are often too fine for standard coffee filters. The store will pack beans for you in whatever size bag you want. If you buy prepackaged coffee in a supermarket in Costa Rica, the whole beans will be marked either *grano* (grain) or *grano entero* (whole bean). If you opt for ground varieties *(molido),* be sure the package is marked *puro;* otherwise, it will likely be mixed with a good amount of sugar, the way Ticos like it.

One good coffee-related gift to bring home is a coffee sock and stand. This is the most common mechanism for brewing coffee beans in Costa Rica. It consists of a simple circular stand, made out of wood or wire, which holds a sock. Put the ground beans in the sock, place a pot or cup below it, and pour boiling water through. You can find the socks and stands at most supermarkets and in the Mercado Central. In fancier crafts shops, you'll find them made out of ceramic. Depending on its construction, a stand will cost you between $1.50 and $15; socks run around 30¢, so buy a few spares.

Café Britt is the big name in Costa Rican coffee. These folks have the largest export business in the country, and, although high-priced, their blends are very dependable. Café Britt is widely available at gift shops around the country, and at the souvenir concessions at both international airports. My favorites, however, are the coffees roasted and packaged in Manuel Antonio and Monteverde, by **Café Milagro** and **Café Monteverde,** respectively. If you visit either of these places, definitely pick up their beans.

In general, the best place to buy coffee is in any supermarket. Why pay more at a gift or specialty shop? You here, so you'll have to work hard to save a few dollars.

Finally, two other similar options downtown include **La Casona,** Calle Central between avenidas Central and 1 (☏**2222-7999**), a three-story warren of crafts and souvenir shops; and **El Pueblo,** a tourism complex built in the style of a mock colonial-era village, with a wide range of restaurants, gift shops, art galleries, bars, and discos.

Plaza de la Democracia street market.

MODERN MALLS With globalization and modernization taking hold in Costa Rica, much of the local shopping scene has shifted to large megamalls. Modern multilevel affairs with cineplexes, food courts, and international brand-name stores are becoming more ubiquitous. The biggest and most modern of these malls include the **Mall San Pedro, Multiplaza, Terra Mall,** and **Mall Real Cariari.** Although they lack the charm of small shops found around San José, they are a reasonable option for one-stop shopping; most contain at least one or two local galleries and crafts shops, along with a large supermarket, which is always the best place to stock up on local coffee, hot sauces, liquors, and other nonperishable foodstuffs.

Shopping A to Z
ART GALLERIES

Art lovers should check out Molly Keeler's 1-day **Art Tour ★** (☏**8359-5571** or 2288-0896; www.costaricaarttour.com), which includes scheduled visits to the studios and personal shops of prominent local artists working in a wide range of media.

Arte Latino This gallery carries original artwork in a variety of media, featuring predominantly Central American themes. Some of it is pretty gaudy, but this is generally a good place to find Nicaraguan and Costa Rican "primitive" paintings. The gallery also has storefronts in the Multiplaza Mall in Escazú and at the Mall Cariari, which is on the Interamerican Highway, about halfway between the airport and downtown, across from the Hotel Herradura. Calle 5 and Av. 1.
☏**2258-7083.**

Galería Amón ★ Located in a stylish old house in the historic Barrio Amón district, this gallery features contemporary artists from Central and South America. Feature exhibits are mixed with a regularly rotating collection of works from a stable of artists. The spaces are ample and well-lit, giving this place almost a museum-like feel. No. 937 Calle 7 btw. Av. 7 and 9. ☏**2223-9725.** www.amon937.com.

Galería 11'12 ★★★ This outstanding gallery deals mainly in high-end Costa Rican art, from neoclassical painters such as Teodorico Quirós to modern masters such as Francisco Amighetti and Paco Zuñiga, to current stars such as Rafa Fernández, Rodolfo Stanley, Fernando Carballo, and Fabio Herrera. Plaza Itzkatzu, off the Prospero Fernández Hwy., Escazú. ☏**2288-1975.** www.galeria11-12.com.

Galería Jacobo Karpio This excellent gallery handles some of the more adventurous modern art to be found in Costa Rica. Karpio has a steady stable of prominent Mexican, Cuban, and Argentine artists, as well as some local talent. Av. 1, casa no. 1352, btw. calles 13 and 15. ☎**2257-7963.**

Galería Kandinsky Owned by the daughter of one of Costa Rica's most prominent modern painters, Rafa Fernández, this small gallery usually has a good selection of high-end contemporary Costa Rican paintings, be it the house collection or a specific temporary exhibit. Centro Comercial Calle Real, San Pedro. ☎**2234-0478.**

TEORetica ★★ This small downtown gallery is run by one of the more adventurous and internationally respected collectors and curators in Costa Rica, Virginia Pérez-Ratton. You'll often find very interesting and cutting-edge exhibitions here. Calle 7 btw. Av. 9 and 11. ☎**2233-4881.** www.teoretica.org.

BOOKS

For English-language novels, field guides and general guidebooks, and natural history books, head to either **Seventh Street Books** (☎**2256-8251;** Calle 7 btw. avs. 1 and Central), or **Librería Internacional** (☎**2253-9553;** www.libreriainternacional.com). Librería Internacional has several outlets around San José, including storefronts in most of the major modern malls.

HANDICRAFTS

In downtown San José, try the outdoor market on the **Plaza de la Democracia,** although prices here tend to be high and bargaining can be difficult. If you prefer to do your crafts shopping in a flea-market atmosphere, head over to **La Casona** on Calle Central between avenidas Central and 1.

Notable exceptions to the city's generally meager crafts offerings include the fine wooden creations of **Barry Biesanz** ★★ (☎**2289-4337;** www.biesanz.com). His work is sold in many of the finer gift shops around and at his own shop (see below), but beware: Biesanz's work is often imitated, so make sure that what you buy is the real deal (he generally burns his signature into the bottom of the piece). **Lil Mena** is a local artist who specializes in working with and painting on handmade papers and rough fibers. You'll find her work in a number of shops around San José.

Cecilia "Pefi" Figueres ★★ makes practical ceramic wares that are lively and fun. Look for her brightly colored abstract and figurative bowls, pitchers, coffee mugs, and more at some of the better gift shops around the city.

Scores of shops around San José sell a wide variety of crafts, from the truly tacky to the divinely inspired. Here are some that sell more of the latter and fewer of the former.

Biesanz Woodworks ★ 🎁 Biesanz makes a wide range of high-quality items, including bowls, jewelry boxes, humidors, and some wonderful sets of wooden chopsticks. Biesanz Woodworks is actively involved in local reforestation, too. Bello Horizonte, Escazú. ☎**2289-4337.** www.biesanz.com. Call for directions and off-hour appointments.

Boutique Annemarie ★ Occupying two floors at the Hotel Don Carlos (p. 133), this shop has an amazing array of wood products, leather goods, papiermâché figurines, paintings, books, cards, posters, and jewelry. You'll see most of this stuff at the other shops, but not in such quantities or in such a relaxed and pressure-free environment. At the Hotel Don Carlos, Calle 9, btw. avs. 7 and 9. ☎**2221-6063.**

Biesanz woodwork.

Boutique Kiosco ★★ This place features a range of original and one-off pieces of functional, wearable, and practical pieces made by contemporary Costa Rican and regional artists and designers. While the offerings are regularly changing, you'll usually find a mix of jewelry, handbags, shoes, dolls, furniture, and knickknacks. Often the pieces are made with recycled or sustainable materials. Calle 7 and Avenida 11, Barrio Amón. ☏ **2258-1829.**

Galería Namu ★★ Galeria Namu has some very high-quality arts and crafts, specializing in truly high-end indigenous works, including excellent Boruca and Huetar carved masks and "primitive" paintings. It also carries a good selection of more modern arts and craft pieces, including the ceramic work of Cecilia "Pefi" Figueres. This place organizes tours to visit various indigenous tribes and artisans as well. Av. 7 btw. calles 5 and 7. ☏ **2256-3412.** www.galerianamu.com.

Green Turtle This large shop has a vast selection of handicrafts and souvenirs. Most of it is of very standard to poor quality, but this does make a particularly convenient stop for some last-minute shopping on your way to the airport. In fact, if you call, they will provide free round-trip transport from and to the airport. 4 blocks north of Denny's, near the airport. ☏ **2430-0211.** www.greenturtlesouvenirs.com.

Las Garzas Handicraft Market This is an appealing collection of artisans' shops in a suburb on the outskirts of San José. It includes more than 25 shops selling wood, metal, and ceramic crafts, among a large variety of other items. There's a huge selection, and you can get some good buys here. In Moravia, 100m (1 block) south and 50m (½ block) east of the Red Cross Station. ☏ **2236-0037.** Ask a taxi driver to take you to Las Garzas Mercado de Artesanía in Moravia.

Suraska Among the selections here are ceramics, mobiles, and jewelry. This store tends to carry higher-quality items than most gift shops downtown. However, be warned that prices are accordingly more expensive. Calle 5 and Av. 3. ☏ **2222-0129.**

JEWELRY

Plaza Esmeralda Part working jewelry factory, part shopping center, part tourist trap, this is still a good place to come to buy replicas of pre-Columbian jewelry.

Galería Namu wares.

The several shops here carry a wide range of typical tourist souvenirs and locally produced arts and craftworks at fair prices. Visitors are treated to a 15-minute guided tour where you can see some of the jewelry being manufactured. Sabana Norte, 800m (8 blocks) north of Jack's in Pavas. ☎2296-0312.

Studio Metallo ★★ The outgrowth of a jewelry-making school and studio, this shop has some excellent handcrafted jewelry made in a range of styles, using everything from 18-karat white and yellow gold and pure silver, to some less exotic and expensive alloys. Some works integrate gemstones, while many others focus on the metalwork. 6½ blocks east of the Iglesia Santa Teresita, Barrio Escalante. ☎2281-3207. www.studiometallo.com.

LEATHER GOODS

In general, Costa Rican leather products are not of the highest grade or quality, and prices are not particularly low. **Del Río** (☎2262-1415) is a local leather goods manufacturer, with stores in most of the city's modern malls. It also offers free hotel pickup and transfer to its factory outlet in Heredia.

LIQUOR

The best prices I've seen for liquor are at any large supermarket, such as **Más × Menos.** There is a Más × Menos store on Paseo Colón and another on Avenida Central at the east end of town, just below the Museo Nacional de Costa Rica.

SAN JOSE AFTER DARK

Catering to a mix of tourists, college students, and just generally party-loving Ticos, San José has a host of options to meet the nocturnal needs of visitors and residents alike. You'll find plenty of interesting clubs and bars, a wide range of theaters, and some very lively discos and dance salons.

To find out what's going on in San José while you're in town, pick up a copy of the *Tico Times* (English) or *La Nación* (Spanish). The former is a good place to find out where local expatriates are hanging out; the latter's "Viva" and "Tiempo Libre" sections have extensive listings of discos, movie theaters, and live music.

The Performing Arts

Theater is very popular in Costa Rica, and downtown San José is studded with small theaters. However, tastes tend toward the burlesque, and the crowd pleasers are almost always simplistic sexual comedies. The **National Theater Company** (☏2221-1273) is an exception, tackling works from Lope de Vega to Lorca to Mamet. Similarly, the small independent group **Abya Yala** (☏2240-6071) also puts on several cutting-edge avant-garde shows each year. Almost all of the theater offerings are in Spanish, although the **Little Theater Group** (www.little theatregroup.org) is a long-standing amateur group that periodically stages works in English. Finally, **Britt Expresivo** (☏2277-1600) has been staging regular works ranging from original pieces to Shakespeare to Beckett, in both English and Spanish, at the small theater up at Café Britt (p. 160) in the hills above Heredia. Check the *Tico Times* to see if anything is running during your stay.

Costa Rica has a strong modern-dance scene. Both the **University of Costa Rica** and the **National University** have modern-dance companies that perform regularly in various venues in San José. In addition to the university-sponsored companies, there's a host of smaller independent companies worth catching; check local papers for details.

The **National Symphony Orchestra** is respectable by regional standards, although its repertoire tends to be rather conservative. Symphony season runs March through November, with concerts roughly every other weekend at the **Teatro Nacional,** Avenida 2 between calles 3 and 5 (☏2221-5341; www.teatronacional. go.cr), and the **Auditorio Nacional** (☏2256-5876) at the Museo de Los Niños (p. 157). Tickets cost between $3 and $30 and can be purchased at the box office.

Teatro Nacional.

Visiting artists stop in Costa Rica on a regular basis. Recent concerts have featured hard rockers Iron Maiden, Argentine pop star Fito Páez, operatic legend Placido Domingo, and Brazilian maestro Caetano Veloso. Many of these performances take place in San José's two historic theaters, the **Teatro Nacional** (see above) and the **Teatro Melico Salazar,** Avenida 2 between calles Central and 2 (**2221-4952**), as well as at the **Auditorio Nacional** (see above). Really large shows are usually held at soccer stadiums or large, natural amphitheaters.

Costa Rica's cultural panorama changes drastically every November when the country hosts large arts festivals. In odd-numbered years, **El Festival Nacional de las Artes** reigns supreme, featuring purely local talent. In even-numbered years, the month-long fete is **El Festival Internacional de las Artes,** with a nightly smorgasbord of dance, theater, music, and monologues from around the world. Most nights of the festival offer between 4 and 10 shows. Many are free, and the most expensive ticket is usually around $5. For exact dates and details, you can contact the **Ministry of Youth, Culture, and Sports** (**2255-3188;** www.mcjdcr.go.cr), although you might have trouble getting any information if you don't speak Spanish.

The Club, Music & Dance Scene

You'll find plenty of places to hit the dance floor in San José. Salsa and merengue are the main beats that move people here, and many of the dance clubs, discos, and salons feature live music on the weekends. You'll find a pretty limited selection, though, if you're looking to catch some small-club jazz, rock, or blues.

The daily "Viva" and Friday's "Tiempo Libre" sections of *La Nación* newspaper have weekly performance schedules. Some dance bands to watch for are Gaviota, Chocolate, Timbaleo, Son de Tikizia, Taboga Band, and Los Brillanticos. While Ghandi, Evolución, and Malpaís are popular local rock groups, Marfil is a good cover band, and both Harmony Roads and the Blind Pig Blues Band are outfits that play American-style rock, blues, and folk music. If you're looking for jazz, check out Editus, El Sexteto de Jazz Latino, or pianist Manuel Obregón. For a taste of something eclectic, look for Santos y Zurdo; Peregrino Gris; or Amarillo, Cyan y Magenta.

A good place to sample a range of San José's nightlife is in **El Pueblo,** a shopping, dining, and entertainment complex done up like an old Spanish village. It's just across the river to the north of town. The best way to get there is by taxi; all the drivers know El Pueblo well. Within the alleyways that wind through El Pueblo are a dozen or more bars, clubs, and discos—there's even an indoor soccer playing field. **Fiesta Latina** (**2222-8782**), **Twister** (**2222-5746**), and **Friends** (**2233-5283**) are happening party spots. Across the street, **Copacabana** (**2233-5516**) is a popular dance spot. For a mellower option, inside El Pueblo, try **Café Art Boruca** (**2221-3615**).

Most of the places listed below charge a nominal cover charge; sometimes it includes a drink or two.

Castro's ★ 🍸 This is a classic Costa Rican dance club. The music varies throughout the night, from salsa and merengue to reggaeton and occasionally electronic trance. There are several rooms and various types of environments, including some intimate and quiet corners, spread over a couple of floors. It's open daily from noon to anytime between 3 and 6am. Avenida 13 and Calle 22, Barrio Mexico. **2256-8789.**

Salsa dancing at a San José club.

Copacabana ★ This large, open, upscale disco has long been a favored dance venue for the young and beautiful of San José. The interior is designed to resemble a colonial plaza. Tunes come in sets that can range from salsa to merengue to reggae to electronic. This place pulls a younger crowd than many of the other spots around town; the party here is Wednesday through Saturday nights 'til around 4am. Admission is around $3. Across from the El Pueblo shopping center. ☎ **2233-5516.**

El Tobogán ★★ 🎁 The dance floor in this place is about the size of a football field, yet it still fills up. This is a place where Ticos come with their loved ones and dance partners. The music is a mix of classic Latin dance rhythms—salsa, cumbia, and merengue. It's open only on the weekends ('til about 2am), but there's always a live band here, and sometimes it's very good. 200m (2 blocks) north and 100m (1 block) east of the La República main office, off the Guápiles Hwy. ☎ **2257-3396.**

Salsa 54 This is the place to go to watch expert salsa dancers and to try some yourself. You can take formal Latin dance classes here, or you might learn something just by watching. This place is popular with Ticos, and tourists are a rare commodity here—tourists who can really dance salsa, even more so. It's open daily 'til 4am. Calle 3 btw. avs. 1 and 3. ☎ **2233-3814.**

Utopia In a modern strip mall on the road between the western suburbs of Santa Ana and San Antonio de Belén, this club is one of the hippest places to see and be seen. In fact, bouncers out front often screen the incoming clientele, admitting only the prettiest and best connected. The music is loud and modern, and the decor is minimal. It's open daily 'til 4am. Radial San Antonio de Belén-Santa Ana. ☎ **2221-6655.**

Vértigo Tucked inside a nondescript office building and commercial center on Paseo Colón, this club remains one of the more popular places for rave-style late-night dancing and partying. The dance floor is huge and the ceilings are high, and electronic music rules the roost. It's open daily 'til 4am. Edificio Colón, Paseo Colón. ☎ **2257-8424.**

The Bar Scene

There seems to be something for every taste here. Lounge lizards will be happy in most hotel bars in the downtown area, while students and the young at heart will have no problem mixing in at the livelier spots around town. Sports fans can find plenty of places to catch the most important games of the day, and there are even a couple of brewpubs that are drastically improving the quality and selection of the local suds.

The best part of the varied bar scene in San José is something called a *boca*, the equivalent of a tapa in Spain: a little dish of snacks that arrives at your table when you order a drink. Although this is a somewhat dying tradition, especially in the younger, hipper bars, you will still find *bocas* alive and well in the older, more traditional San José drinking establishments. In most, the *bocas* are free, but in some, where the dishes are more sophisticated, you'll have to pay for the treats. You'll find drinks reasonably priced, with beer costing around $2 to $3 a bottle, and mixed drinks costing $2 to $5.

Café Expresivo ★ Laid-back and funky, this cafe, restaurant, and gallery features occasional DJs spinning dance beats. When there's no act, this is a mellow place to have a drink and good conversation. It's open Tuesday through Friday from noon to midnight, and Saturday and Sunday from 5pm to midnight. 4 blocks east of the Santa Teresita Church, Barrio Escalante. ☎ **2224-1202.**

Chelles 👬 This classic downtown bar and restaurant makes up for its lack of ambience with plenty of tradition and a diverse and colorful clientele. The lights are bright, the chairs surround simple Formica-topped card tables, and mirrors adorn most of the walls. Simple sandwiches and meals are served, and pretty good *bocas* come with the drinks. It's open daily, round-the-clock. Av. Central and Calle 9. ☎ **2221-1369.**

El Cuartel de la Boca del Monte ★★ This popular bar, one of San José's best, began life as an artist-and-bohemian hangout, and has evolved into the leading meat market for the young and well-heeled. However, artists still come, as do foreign exchange students, visitors, and a broad cross section of San José's youth, so there's always a diverse mix. There's usually live music here on Monday, Wednesday, and Friday nights, and when there is, the place is packed shoulder to shoulder. From Monday to Friday it's open for lunch and again in the evenings; on weekends it opens at 4pm. On most nights it's open 'til about 1am, although the revelry might continue 'til about 3am on Friday or Saturday. One corner has been separated into a more bohemian-style bar or pub called La Esquina, or "The Corner." Av. 1 btw. calles 21 and 23 (50m/½ block west of the Cine Magaly). ☎ **2221-0327.**

El Observatorio ★★ 👬 It's easy to miss the narrow entrance to this hot spot across from the Cine Magaly. Owned by a local filmmaker, its decor includes a heavy dose of cinema motifs. The space is large, with high ceilings, and one of the best (perhaps only) smoke extraction systems of any popular bar, making the place bearable, even though most of the clientele are chain-smoking. There's occasional live music and movie screenings and a decent menu of appetizers and main dishes drawn from various world cuisines. It's open noon to 2am daily. Calle 23 btw. avs. Central and 1. ☎ **2223-0725.**

Key Largo ★ 👬 This meticulously restored downtown mansion is also one of San José's top prostitute pickup bars. Housed in a beautiful old building just off

Parque Morazán in the heart of downtown, Key Largo is worth a visit if only to take in the scene and admire the dark-stained carved wood ceilings. There are a couple of pool tables, there's usually a live band, and there are always working women—however, this is still an acceptable place for visiting couples and those not actively shopping the wares. It's open 11am to 3am daily. Calle 7 btw. avs. 1 and 3. **2221-0277.**

Shakespeare Bar Located next to, and somewhat underneath, the Sala Garbo movie theater, this quiet little spot is a good place to meet after a movie or a show at the Sala Garbo or Laurence Olivier Theater next door. Intimate and reserved, it's open daily 'til midnight. Av. 2 and Calle 28. **2258-6787.**

HANGING OUT IN SAN PEDRO

The funky 2-block stretch of **San Pedro** ★★ just south of the University of Costa Rica has been dubbed La Calle de Amargura, or the "Street of Bitterness," and it's the heart and soul of this eastern suburb and college town. Bars and cafes are mixed in with bookstores and copy shops. After dark the streets are packed with teens, punks, students, and professors barhopping and just hanging around. You can walk the strip until someplace strikes your fancy—you don't need a travel guide to find **Omar Khayyam** (**2253-8455**), **Marrakech Pool & Pizza** (**253-2049**), **Tavarua Surf & Skate Bar** (**2225-7249**), or **Caccio's** (**2224-3261**), which lie at the heart of this district—or you can try one of the places listed below. *Note:* La Calle de Amargura attracts a certain unsavory element. Use caution here. Try to visit with a group, and try not to carry large amounts of cash or wear flashy jewelry.

You can get here by heading out (east) on Avenida 2, and following the flow of traffic. You will first pass through the neighborhood of Los Yoses before you reach a large traffic circle with a big fountain in the center (La Fuente de la Hispanidad). The Mall San Pedro is located on this traffic circle. Heading straight through the circle (well, going around it and continuing on what would have been a straight path), you'll come to the Church of San Pedro, about 4 blocks east of the circle. The church is the major landmark in San Pedro. You can also take a bus here from downtown.

Jazz Café ★ The Jazz Café is consistently a great spot to find live music and one of the more happening spots in San Pedro. It remains one of my favorites, although low ceilings and poor air circulation make it almost unbearably smoky most nights. Wrought-iron chairs, sculpted busts of famous jazz artists, and creative lighting give the place ambience. There's live music here most nights. It's open daily 'til about 2am. There's a sister Jazz Café Escazu (**2288-4740**) on the western end of town. Next to the Banco Popular on Av. Central. **2253-8933.** www. jazzcafecostarica.com.

Mosaikos The entrance to this popular nightspot is a long, narrow corridor/bar that is generally packed solid. A larger room in the back has another bar, some tables, and some funky art. The crowd here is young and can get quite rowdy. They often have live DJs playing a mix of house, techno, and trance-style dance music, although you're also just as likely to hear reggae, ska, or hip-hop tunes blasting. It's open Monday through Saturday from 11am to 2am, Sunday from 5pm to 2am. 200m (2 blocks) east and 150m (1½ blocks) north of the Church in San Pedro. **2280-9541.**

Terra U Set on a busy corner in the heart of the university district, this two-story joint is one of the most popular bars in the area. Part of this is due to the inviting open-air street-front patio area, which provides a nice alternative to the all-too-common smoke-filled rooms found at most other trendy spots. It's open Monday through Saturday evenings 'til 2am. 200m (2 blocks) east and 150m (1½ blocks) north of the church in San Pedro. ☎**2225-4261.**

The Gay & Lesbian Scene

Because Costa Rica is such a conservative Catholic country, the gay and lesbian communities here are rather discreet. Homosexuality is not generally under attack, but many gay and lesbian organizations guard their privacy, and the club scene is changeable and not well publicized.

The most established and happening gay and lesbian bar and dance club in San José is **La Avispa** ★, Calle 1 between avenidas 8 and 10 (☎**2223-5343;** www.laavispa.co.cr). It is popular with both men and women, although it sometimes sets aside certain nights of the week or month for specific persuasions. There's also **Buenas Vibraciones** (☎**2223-4573**), out on Paseo de los Estudiantes; **Club Oh** (☎**2221-9341**), on Calle 2 between avenidas 14 and 16; **Pucho's Bar** (☎**2256-1147**), on Calle 11 and Avenida 8; **El Bochinche** (☎**2221-0500**), on Calle 11 between avenidas 10 and 12; and **Punto G** (☎**2280-3726**) in San Pedro, half a block southwest of the Higuerón. Out in the suburb of San Antonio de Belén is **Kashmir Cocktail Lounge** (☎**2293-0162**) located inside the La Ribera shopping center.

Casinos

Gambling is legal in Costa Rica, with casinos at virtually every major hotel. However, as with Tico bullfighting, there are some idiosyncrasies involved in gambling *a la Tica.*

If blackjack is your game, you'll want to play "rummy." The rules are almost identical, except that the house doesn't pay 1½ times on blackjack—instead, it pays double on any three of a kind or three-card straight flush.

If you're looking for roulette, what you'll find here is a bingolike spinning cage of numbered balls. The betting is the same, but some of the glamour is lost.

You'll also find a version of five-card-draw poker, but the rule differences are so complex that I advise you to sit down and watch for a while and then ask questions before joining in. That's about all you'll find. There are no craps tables or baccarat.

There's some controversy over slot machines—one-armed bandits are currently outlawed—but you will be able to play electronic slots and poker games. Most casinos here are casual and small by international standards. You may have to dress up slightly at some of the fancier hotels, but most are accustomed to tropical vacation attire.

SIDE TRIPS FROM SAN JOSE

San José makes an excellent base for exploring the beautiful Central Valley and the surrounding mountains. For first-time visitors, the best way to make the most of these excursions is usually to take a guided tour, but if you rent a car, you'll have greater independence. Some day trips also can be done by public bus.

Guided Tours & Adventures

A number of companies offer a wide variety of primarily nature-related day tours out of San José. The most reputable include **Costa Rica Expeditions ★★** (☎2257-0766; www.costaricaexpeditions.com), **Costa Rica Sun Tours ★** (☎2296-7757; www.crsuntours.com), **Horizontes Tours ★★** (☎2222-2022; www.horizontes.com), and **Swiss Travel Service** (☎2282-4898; www.swisstravelcr.com).

Before signing on for a tour of any sort, find out how many fellow travelers will be accompanying you, how much time will be spent in transit and eating lunch, and how much time will actually be spent doing the primary activity. I've had complaints about tours that were rushed, that spent too much time in a bus or on secondary activities, or that had a cattle-car, assembly-line feel to them. The tours below are arranged by type of activity. In addition to these, you'll find many other tours that combine two or three different activities or destinations.

BUNGEE JUMPING There's nothing unique about bungee jumping in Costa Rica, but the site here is quite beautiful. If you've always had the bug, **Tropical Bungee** (☎2248-2212; www.bungee.co.cr) will let you jump off an 80m (262-ft.) bridge for $65; two jumps cost $95. Transportation is provided free from San José twice daily. These folks also offer paragliding tours.

CANOPY TOURS & AERIAL TRAMS Getting off the ground and up into the treetops is the latest fad in Costa Rican tourism, and there are scores of such tours around the country. You have several options relatively close to San José, and one actually in the city center.

The quickest and easiest way to experience a zip-line canopy tour from San José is to head to the La Sabana park and take the **Urban Canopy Tour** (☎2215-2544). Given the fact that this tour is set on a relatively flat patch of city park, it is neither as extensive nor exciting as the other options listed in this section. Still, the tour has eight zip-line cables, with the longest being some 200m (650 ft.) long. The tour costs $20.

Another option is the **Rain Forest Aerial Tram Caribbean ★** (☎2257-5961; www.rainforesttram.com), built on a private reserve bordering Braulio Carrillo National Park. This pioneering tramway is the brainchild of rainforest researcher Dr. Donald Perry, whose cable-car system through the forest canopy at Rara Avis helped establish him as an early expert on rainforest canopies. The tramway takes visitors on a 90-minute ride through the treetops, where they have the chance to glimpse the complex web of life that makes these forests unique. Additional attractions include a butterfly garden, serpentarium, and frog collection. They also have their own zip-line canopy tour, and the grounds feature well-groomed trails through the rainforest and a restaurant—with all this on offer, a trip here can easily take up a full day. If you want to spend the night, there are 10 simple but clean and comfortable bungalows, which cost $150 per person per day (double occupancy), including three meals, three guided tours, taxes, two tram rides, and unlimited use of the rest of the facilities.

The cost for a full-day tour, including both the aerial tram and canopy tour, all the park's other attractions, and transportation from San José and either breakfast or lunch, is $105. Alternatively, you can drive or take one of the frequent Guápiles buses—they leave every half-hour throughout

The Central Valley

Butterfly Farm	**8**
Café Britt Farm	**6**
Elsie Kientzler	
Botanical Garden	**2**
INBio Park	**7**
Lankester Gardens	**9**
La Paz Waterfall	
Gardens	**4**
Rain Forest Aerial	
Tram Caribbean	**5**
Turu BaRi Tropical Park	**1**
Zoo Ave.	**3**

the day and cost $2—from the Caribbean bus terminal (Gran Terminal del Caribe) on Calle Central, 1 block north of Avenida 11. Ask the driver to let you off in front of the *teleférico*. If you're driving, head out on the Guápiles Highway as if driving to the Caribbean coast. Watch for the tram's roadside welcome center—it's hard to miss. For walk-ins, the entrance fee is $55; students and anyone under 18 pay $28. Because this is a popular tour for groups, I highly recommend that you get an advance reservation in the high season and, if possible, a ticket; otherwise you could wait a long time for your tram ride or even be shut out. The tram handles only about 80 passengers per hour, so scheduling is tight; the folks here try to schedule as much as possible in advance.

Turu BaRi Tropical Park (**☎2250-0705** or 2428-6070; www.turubari.com) is another similar attraction that aims to cover as many bases as possible. Located about 90 minutes outside San José, this park features a series of gardens, trails, and exhibits set in a deep valley that you can reach by means of a gondola-style ski lift, by cable and zip-line canopy tour, or on horseback. Down in the valley, you can wander around the botanical gardens, orchid gardens, and butterfly gardens, or grab a bite at the typical Costa Rican restaurant. You can even take a turn on their massive climbing wall. The gondola ride here actually features enclosed cabin cars (with windows that open) and doesn't provide nearly the sense of intimacy or contact with the forest that the Aerial Tram does. The basic fee admission is $60 for adults, $55 for students, and $40 for children; all the various adventure and activity options cost extra. However, various combination package tours, with or without transportation and meals, are available.

Rain Forest Aerial Tram Caribbean.

Finally, the folks at **Original Canopy Tour** ★ (**2291-4465;** www. canopytour.com) have their **Mahogany Park** operation, located about 1 hour outside of San José. The tour here features 10 platforms, and at the end you have the choice of taking a cable to a ground station or doing an 18m (60-ft.) rappel down to finish off. The tour takes about 2 hours and costs $45. Package tours with transportation from San José are also available.

DAY CRUISES Several companies offer cruises to lovely Tortuga Island in the Gulf of Nicoya. These full-day tours generally entail an early departure for the 2½-hour chartered bus ride to Puntarenas, where you board your vessel for a 1½-hour cruise to Tortuga Island. Then you get several hours on the uninhabited island, where you can swim, lie on the beach, play volleyball, or try a canopy tour, followed by the return journey.

The original and most dependable company running these trips is **Calypso Tours** ★ (**2256-2727;** www.calypsotours.com). The tour costs $119 per person and includes round-trip transportation from San José, a basic continental breakfast during the bus ride to the boat, all drinks on the cruise, and an excellent buffet lunch on the beach at the island. The Calypso Tours main vessel is a massive motor-powered catamaran. A second runs a separate tour to a private nature reserve at **Punta Coral** ★. The beach is much nicer at Tortuga Island, but the tour to Punta Coral is more intimate, and the restaurant, hiking, and kayaking are all superior here.

EXPLORING PRE-COLUMBIAN RUINS Although Costa Rica lacks the kind of massive pre-Columbian archaeological sites found in Mexico, Guatemala, or Honduras, it does have **Guayabo National Monument** ★, a small excavated town that today is just a small collection of building foundations, cobbled streets, aqueducts, and a small plaza. If you have a car or are an intrepid bus hound, you can do this tour on your own. Admission to the park is $10, and you can usually find a guide at the entrance for around $5. See the below section on Turrialba for more information on Guayabo.

HIKING Most of the tour agencies listed above offer 1-day guided hikes to a variety of destinations. In general, I recommend taking guided hikes to really see and learn about the local flora and fauna.

HORSEBACK RIDING Options are nearly endless outside of San José, but it's more difficult to find a place to saddle up in the metropolitan area. The **La Caraña Riding Academy** (**2282-6106;** www.lacarana.com) and **Centro Ecuestre Valle Yos Oy** (**2282-6934**) are both in Santa Ana, and offer riding classes as well as some guided trail rides.

MOUNTAIN BIKING The best bicycle riding is well outside of San José—on dirt roads where you're not likely to be run off the highway by a semi, or run head-on into someone coming around a blind curve in the wrong lane. Several companies run a variety of 1-day and multiday tours out of San José. The 1-day tours usually involve a round-trip bus or van ride out of downtown to the primary destination, such as the towns of Sarchí and Turrialba, and the Irazú and Poás volcanoes. Several of these tours are entirely or primarily descents. **Costa Rica Biking Adventure** (**2225-6591;** www. bikingincostarica.com) offers a variety of mountain-biking tours using high-end bikes and gear. A 1-day trip costs between $95 and $150 per person.

HOLY SMOKE! CHOOSING THE
volcano TRIP THAT'S RIGHT FOR YOU

Poás, Irazú, and Arenal volcanoes are three of Costa Rica's most popular destinations, and the first two are easy day trips from San José (see below). Although numerous companies offer day trips to Arenal, I don't recommend them because travel time is at least 3½ hours in each direction. You usually arrive when the volcano is hidden by clouds and leave before the night's darkness shows off its glowing eruptions. For more information on Arenal Volcano, see chapter 9.

Tour companies offering trips to Poás and Irazú include **Costa Rica Expeditions** ★★ (☎2257-0766), **Costa Rica Sun Tours** ★ (☎2296-7757), **Horizontes** ★★ (☎2222-2022), and **Swiss Travel Service** (☎2282-4898). Prices range from $30 to $50 for a half-day trip, and from $50 to $120 for a full-day trip.

The 3,378m (11,080-ft.) **Irazú Volcano** ★ (☎2551-9398) is historically one of Costa Rica's more active volcanoes, although it's relatively quiet these days. It last erupted on March 19, 1963, the day that President John F. Kennedy arrived in Costa Rica. There's a good paved road right to the rim of the crater, where a desolate expanse of gray sand nurtures few plants and the air smells of sulfur. The landscape here is often compared to that of the moon. There are magnificent views of the fertile Meseta Central and Orosi Valley as you drive up from Cartago, and if you're very lucky, you might be able to see both the Pacific Ocean and the Caribbean Sea. Clouds usually descend by noon, so get here as early in the day as possible.

The visitor center up here has information on the volcano and natural history. A short trail leads to the rim of the volcano's two craters, their walls a maze of eroded gullies feeding onto the flat floor far below. This is a national park, with an admission fee of $10 charged at the gate. Dress in layers; this might be the Tropics, but it can be cold up at the top if the sun's not out. The park restaurant, at an elevation of 3,022m (9,912 ft.), with walls of windows looking out over the valley far below, claims to be the highest restaurant in Central America.

If you don't want an organized tour, buses leave for Irazú Volcano daily at 8am from Avenida 2 between calles 1 and 3 (across the street from the entrance to the Gran Hotel Costa Rica). The fare is $7 round-trip, with the bus leaving the volcano at 12:30pm. This company is particularly fickle; to

Poás Volcano.

Irazú Volcano.

make sure that the buses are running, call ☎2530-1064, although that might not help much, since they often don't answer their phone, and speak only Spanish. If you're driving, head northeast out of Cartago toward San Rafael, and then continue driving uphill toward the volcano, passing the turnoffs for Cot and Tierra Blanca en route.

Poás Volcano ★★ (☎2482-2424) is 37km (23 miles) from San José on narrow roads that wind through a landscape of fertile farms and dark forests. As at Irazú, there's a paved road right to the top, although you'll have to hike in about 1km (½ mile) to reach the crater. The volcano stands 2,640m (8,659 ft.) tall and is located within a national park, which preserves not only the volcano but also dense stands of virgin forest. Poás's crater, said to be the second largest in the world, is more than a mile across. Geysers in the crater sometimes spew steam and muddy water 180m (590 ft.) into the air, making this the largest geyser in the world. There's an information center where you can see a slide show about the volcano, and

there are well-groomed and marked hiking trails through the cloud forest that rings the crater. About 15 minutes from the parking area, along a forest trail, is an overlook onto beautiful Botos Lake, which has formed in one of the volcano's extinct craters.

Be prepared when you come to Poás: This volcano is often enveloped in dense clouds. If you want to see the crater, it's best to come early and during the dry season. Moreover, it can get cool up here, especially when the sun isn't shining, so dress appropriately. Admission to the national park is $10.

In case you don't want to go on a tour, there's a daily bus (☎2442-6900 or 2222-5325) from Avenida 2 between calles 12 and 14 that leaves at 8am and returns at 2pm. The fare is $6 roundtrip. The bus is often crowded, so arrive early. If you're driving, head for Alajuela and continue on the main road through town and follow signs for Fraijanes. Just beyond Fraijanes you will connect with the road between San Pedro de Poás and Poasito; turn right toward Poasito and continue to the rim of the volcano.

Another company offering mountain-biking trips is **Coast to Coast Adventures ★** (✆2280-8054; www.ctoadventures.com), which, in addition to its 2-week namesake adventure, also designs customized mountain-biking trips of shorter durations.

A unique option is to take a **Railbike Tour** (✆8303-3300; www.rail bike.com). This tour involves a mountain bike rigged to a contraption that fits over abandoned railroad tracks, running through the countryside outside San José. The full-day tour costs $75 and includes all equipment, plus a light breakfast and full lunch.

RAFTING, KAYAKING & RIVER TRIPS Cascading down Costa Rica's mountain ranges are dozens of tumultuous rivers, several of which are very popular for white-water rafting and kayaking. If I had to choose just one day trip out of San José, it would be a white-water rafting trip. For between $75 and $120, you can spend a day rafting through lush tropical forests; multiday trips are also available. Some of the most reliable rafting companies are **Aventuras Naturales ★** (✆800/514-0411 in the U.S., or 2225-3939), **Exploradores Outdoors ★** (✆2222-6262), and **Ríos Tropicales ★** (✆2233-6455). These companies all ply a number of rivers of varying difficulties, including the popular Pacuare and Reventazón rivers. For details, see "White-Water Rafting, Kayaking & Canoeing," in chapter 5.

The Sarapiquí River is also a popular waterway for day trips outside of San José. **Ecoscapes Highlights Tour** (✆2297-0664; www.ecoscape tours.com) runs a jampacked trip here that combines a stop at the La Paz waterfall, a visit to a banana plantation, a rainforest hike, and a boat ride on the river for $83 per person, including round-trip transportation, breakfast, and lunch.

Perhaps the best-known river tours are those that go up to **Tortuguero National Park ★★**. It's possible to do this tour as a day trip out of San José, but it's a long, tiring, and expensive day. You're much better off doing it as a 1- or 2-night trip. See chapter 12 for details.

Cartago & the Orosi Valley

These two regions southeast of San José can easily be combined into a day trip. You might also squeeze in a visit to the Irazú Volcano (see box above for details).

CARTAGO

Located about 24km (15 miles) southeast of San José, **Cartago ★** is the former capital of Costa Rica. Founded in 1563, it was Costa Rica's first city—and was, in fact, its *only* city for almost 150 years. Irazú Volcano rises up from the edge of town, and although it's quiet these days, it has not always been

Lankester Gardens.

Cartago Basilica.

so peaceful. Earthquakes have damaged Cartago repeatedly over the years, so today few of the old colonial buildings are left standing. In the center of the city, a public park winds through the ruins of a large church that was destroyed in 1910 before it could be finished. Construction was abandoned after the quake, and today the ruins sit at the heart of a neatly manicured park, with quiet paths and plenty of benches. The ruins themselves are closed off, but the park itself is lovely. (The park is a free Wi-Fi hot spot as well.)

Cartago's most famous building is the **Basílica de Nuestra Señora de los Angeles (Basilica of Our Lady of the Angels)** ★, which is dedicated to the patron saint of Costa Rica and stands on the east side of town. Within the walls of this Byzantine-style church is a shrine containing the tiny carved figure of **La Negrita,** the Black Virgin, which is nearly lost amid its ornate altar. Legend has it that La Negrita first revealed herself on this site to a peasant girl in 1635. The walls of the shrine are covered with a fascinating array of tiny silver images left as thanks for cures affected by La Negrita. Amid the plethora of diminutive silver arms and legs, there are also hands, feet, hearts, lungs, kidneys, eyes, torsos, breasts, and—peculiarly—guns, trucks, beds, and planes. There are even dozens of sports trophies that I assume were left as thanks for helping teams win big games. Outside the church, vendors sell a wide selection of these trinkets, as well as little candle replicas of La Negrita.

More than 1km (½ mile) east of Cartago, on the road to Paraíso, you'll find **Lankester Gardens** ★★ (☎2552-3247; p. 162), a botanical garden known for its orchid collection.

GETTING THERE **Lumaca** buses (☎2537-0347) for Cartago leave San José every 3 to 5 minutes between 5am and 9pm, with slightly less frequent service until midnight, from Calle 3 and Avenida 2. You can also pick up one en route at any of the little covered bus stops along Avenida Central in Los Yoses and San Pedro. The length of the trip is 45 minutes; the fare is about 65¢.

OROSI VALLEY

The Orosi Valley, southeast of Cartago and visible from the top of Irazú on a clear day, is generally considered one of the most beautiful valleys in Costa Rica. The Reventazón River meanders through this steep-sided valley until it collects in the lake formed by the Cachí Dam. There are scenic overlooks near the town of Orosi, which is at the head of the valley, and in Ujarrás, which is on the banks of the lake. Near **Ujarrás** are the ruins of Costa Rica's oldest church (built in 1693), whose tranquil gardens are a great place to sit and gaze at the surrounding mountains. In the town of Orosi itself, there is yet another colonial church and convent, built in 1743. A small museum here displays religious artifacts.

Near the town of Cachí, you'll find **La Casa del Soñador** (**House of the Dreamer; (2577-1983**), the home and gallery of the late sculptor Macedonio Quesada and his sons, who carry on the family tradition.

From the Orosi Valley, it's a quick shot to the entrance to the **Tapantí National Park ★** (**(2552-4823**), where you'll find some gentle and beautiful hiking trails, as well as riverside picnic areas. The park is open daily from 8am to 4pm; admission is $10.

If you're interested in staying out here, check out the charming little **Orosi Lodge** (**(2533-3578;** www.orosilodge.com), which is right next to some simple hot spring pools.

GETTING THERE If you're driving, take the road to Paraíso from Cartago, head toward Ujarrás, continue around the lake, and then pass through Cachí and on to Orosi. From Orosi, the road leads back to Paraíso. It is difficult to explore this whole area by public bus because this is not a densely populated region and connections are often infrequent or unreliable. However, there are regular buses from Cartago to the town of Orosi. These buses run roughly every half-hour and leave the main bus terminal in Cartago. The trip takes 30 minutes, and the fare is 60¢. There are also guided day tours of this area from San José (call any of the companies listed under "Guided Tours & Adventures," earlier in this section).

Turrialba

This attractive little town 53km (33 miles) east of San José is best known as the starting point and home base for many popular white-water rafting trips. However, it's also worth a visit if you have an interest in pre-Columbian history or tropical botany.

Panorama of Orosi Valley.

La Casa del Soñador sculptures.

Guayabo National Monument ★ (**2559-1220**) is one of Costa Rica's only pre-Columbian sites that has been excavated and is open to the public. It's 19km (12 miles) northeast of Turrialba and preserves a town site that dates from between 1000 B.C. and A.D. 1400. Archaeologists believe that Guayabo might have supported a population of as many as 10,000 people, but there is no clue yet to why the city was eventually abandoned only shortly before the Spanish arrived in the New World. Excavated ruins at Guayabo consist of paved roads, aqueducts, stone bridges, and house and temple foundations. There are also gravesites and petroglyphs. The monument is open daily from 8am to 4pm. This is a national park, and admission is $10 at the gate. For information about other parks in this area, see "Costa Rica's Top National Parks & Bioreserves," in chapter 5.

Botanists and gardeners will want to pay a visit to the **Center for Agronomy Research and Development** (**CATIE;** www.catie.ac.cr), which is located 5km (3 miles) southeast of Turrialba on the road to Siquirres. This center is one of the world's foremost facilities for research into tropical agriculture. Among the plants on CATIE's 2,000 acres are hundreds of varieties of cacao and thousands of varieties of coffee. The plants here have been collected from all over the world. In addition to trees used for food and other purposes, there are plants grown strictly for ornamental purposes. CATIE is open Monday through Friday from 7am to 4pm. Guided tours are available with advance notice for $15 per person. Call **2556-2700** for reservations.

While you're in Turrialba, you might want to spend a little time at **Turrialtico** (**2538-1111;** www.turrialtico.com), a rustic yet beautiful open-air restaurant and small hotel high on a hill overlooking the Turrialba Valley. The view from here is one of the finest in the country, with lush greenery far below and volcanoes in the distance. Meals are quite inexpensive; a double room will cost you around $62 to $66 including breakfast and taxes. This place is popular with rafting companies that bring groups here for meals and for overnights before, during, and after multiday rafting trips. You'll find Turrialtico about 10km (6¼ miles) outside of Turrialba on the road to Siquirres.

If you're looking for more luxury in this area, check out **Casa Turire ★★** (**2531-1111;** www.hotelcasaturire.com), where well-appointed rooms and

Grecia church.

suites in an elegant country mansion run between $135 and $330. The hotel is set on the banks of the lake formed by the Angostura dam project, and you can take a kayak or paddleboat out on the lake here.

Since Turrialba is a main base for several rafting trips and rafting operators, the town has a healthy population of rafting guides living here, and as a result, it actually has a pretty active nightlife.

GETTING THERE **Transtusa** buses (☎ **2222-4464** or 2556-4233) leave San José hourly for Turrialba between 5am and 10pm from Calle 13 between avenidas 6 and 8. The fare is $2. If you're driving, take the road from Cartago to Paraíso, then through Juan Viñas, and on to Turrialba. It's pretty well marked. (Alternatively you can head toward the small town of Cot, on the road to Irazú Volcano, and then through the town of Pacayas on to Turrialba, another well-marked route.)

Turrialba itself is a bit of a jumble, and you will probably have to ask directions to get to locations outside of town. Guayabo is about 20km (12 miles) beyond Turrialba on a road that is paved the entire way except for the last 3km (1¾ miles). Around three buses also head to Guayabo daily from the main bus terminal in Turrialba.

Heredia, Grecia, Sarchí & Zarcero

All of these cities and towns are northwest of San José and can be combined into a long day trip (if you have a car), perhaps in conjunction with a visit to Poás Volcano and/or the Waterfall Gardens. The scenery here is rich and verdant, and the small towns and scattered farming communities are truly representative of Costa Rica's agricultural heartland and *campesino* tradition. This is a great area to explore on your own in a rental car, if you don't mind getting lost a bit (roads are narrow, winding, and poorly marked). If you're relying on buses, you'll be able to visit any of the towns listed below, but probably just one or two per day.

The road to Heredia turns north off the highway from San José to the airport. If you're going to Sarchí, take the highway west toward Puntarenas. Turn north to Grecia and then west to Sarchí. There'll be plenty of signs.

HEREDIA

Set on the flanks of the impressive Barva Volcano, this city was founded in 1706. Heredia is affectionately known as "The City of Flowers." A colonial church inaugurated in 1763 stands in the central park—the stone facade leaves no questions as to the age of the church. The altar inside is decorated with neon stars and a crescent moon surrounding a statue of the Virgin Mary. In the middle of the palm-shaded park is a music temple, and across the street, beside several tile-roofed municipal buildings, is the tower of an old Spanish fort. Of all the cities in the Meseta Central, Heredia has the most colonial feel to it—you'll still see adobe buildings with Spanish tile roofs along narrow streets. Heredia is also the site of the **National Autonomous University**, and you'll find some nice coffee shops and bookstores near the school.

Surrounding Heredia is an intricate maze of picturesque villages and towns, including Santa Bárbara, Santo Domingo, Barva, and San Joaquín de Flores. San Isidro de Heredia has a lovely, large church with an ornate facade. However, the biggest attraction up here is **INBio Park ★★** (☎2507-8107; p. 161). Located on 5 hectares (12 acres) in Santo Domingo de Heredia, this place is part museum, part educational center, and part nature park. This is also where you'll find the **Café Britt Farm ★** (☎2277-1600; p. 160). On the road to Barva, you'll find the small **Museo de Cultura Popular** (☎2260-1619), which is open Monday through Friday from 8am to 4pm and Saturday and Sunday from 10am to 5pm; admission is $2. Anyone with an interest in medicinal herbs should plan a visit to the **Ark Herb Farm ★** (☎8846-2694 or 2269-4847; www.arkherbfarm.com). These folks offer guided tours of their gardens, which feature more than 300 types of medicinal plants. The tour costs $12 per person, and includes a light snack and refreshments. Reservations are required.

Sarchí oxcart factory.

If you make your way to San Pedro de Barva de Heredia, stop in at **La Lluna de Valencia** ★★ (☏2269-6665), a delightful rustic Spanish restaurant with amazing paella, delicious sangria, and a very amiable host. And if you're looking to overnight, high in the hills of Heredia, near the Barva volcano, check out the new high-end B&B the **Orchid Lodge** (☏2260-2744; www.theorchid lodge.com).

Buses leave for Heredia every 5 minutes between 5am and 11pm from Calle 1 between avenidas 7 and 9, or from Avenida 2 between calles 12 and 14. Bus fare is 45¢.

GRECIA

The picturesque little town of Grecia is noteworthy for its unusual **metal church,** which is painted a deep red and has white gingerbread trim. Just off the central park, next to the Palacio Municipal, you'll find the humble **Grecia Regional Museum** (☏2494-6767; Mon–Fri 9am–5pm, Sat 9am–noon; free admission), which has some simple exhibits and information about the town's history. About 1km (½ mile) outside of Grecia, on the old road to Alajuela, you will find the **World of Snakes** (☏2494-3700). Open daily from 8am to 4pm, this serpentarium has more than 150 snakes representing more than 50 species. Admission, which includes a guided tour, is $11 for adults, and $6 for children 7 to 14.

Tuan (☏2258-2004) buses leave San José every half-hour for Grecia from Calle 18 between avenidas 5 and 7 (on the east side of the Abonos Agros building). The fare is $1.20. The road to Sarchí is to the left as you face the church in Grecia, but due to all the one-way streets, you'll have to drive around it.

SARCHI ★

Sarchí is Costa Rica's main artisan town. The colorfully painted miniature **oxcarts** that you see all over the country are made here. Oxcarts such as these were once used to haul coffee beans to market. Today, although you might occasionally see oxcarts in use, most are purely decorative. However, they remain a well-known symbol of Costa Rica. In addition to miniature oxcarts, many carved wooden souvenirs are made here with rare hardwoods from the nation's forests. There are dozens

Close-up of oxcart.

Topiary gardens in Zarcero.

of shops in town, and all have similar prices. Perhaps your best one-stop shop in Sarchí is the large and long-standing **Chaverri Oxcart Factory ★** (**2454-4411**), which is right in the center of things, but it never hurts to shop around and visit several of the stores.

Aside from handicrafts, there are other reasons to visit Sarchí. Built between 1950 and 1958, the town's main **church ★** is painted pink with aquamarine trim and looks strangely like a child's birthday cake. But my favorite attraction in Sarchí is the **Else Kientzler Botanical Garden ★★** (**2454-2070;** p. 160), which features an extensive collection of several thousand types of plants, flowers, and trees.

While there are no noteworthy accommodations in Sarchí itself, the plush **El Silencio Lodge & Spa** (**2291-3044;** www.elsilenciolodge.com; p. 314) is about a 35-minute drive away in a beautiful mountain setting.

Tuan (**2258-2004**) buses leave San José about five times throughout the day for Sarchí from Calle 18 between avenidas 5 and 7. The fare is $1.25. Alternatively, you can take any Grecia bus from this same station. In Grecia they connect with the Alajuela-Sarchí buses, leaving every 30 minutes from Calle 8 between avenidas Central and 1 in Alajuela.

ZARCERO

Beyond Sarchí, on picturesque roads lined with cedar trees, you'll find the town of Zarcero. In a small park in the middle of town is a **menagerie of sculpted shrubs** that includes a monkey on a motorcycle, people and animals dancing, an ox pulling a cart, a man wearing a top hat, and a large elephant. Behind all the topiary is a wonderful rural **church.** It's not really worth the drive just to see this park, but it's a good idea to take a break in Zarcero to walk the gardens, on the way to La Fortuna and Arenal Volcano.

Daily buses (**2255-0567**) for Zarcero leave from San José hourly from the Atlántico del Norte bus station at Avenida 9 and Calle 12. This is actually the Ciudad Quesada–San Carlos bus. Just tell the driver that you want to get off in Zarcero, and keep an eye out for the topiary. The ride takes around 1½ hours, and the fare is around $1.75.

GUANACASTE:
THE GOLD COAST

G uanacaste is also known as Costa Rica's "Gold Coast." And it's not because this is where the Spaniards found vast quantities of the shiny soft metal ore. Instead, it's because more and more visitors to Costa Rica are choosing Guanacaste as their first—and often only—stop. Beautiful beaches abound along this coastline. Several are packed with a mix of hotels and resorts, some are still pristine and deserted, and others are backed by small fishing villages. Choices range from long, broad stretches of sand stretching on for miles, to tiny pocket coves bordered by rocky headlands.

This is Costa Rica's most coveted vacation destination and the site of its greatest tourism development. The international airport in Liberia receives daily direct flights from several major U.S. and Canadian hub cities, allowing tourists to visit some of Costa Rica's prime destinations without having to go through San José.

This is also Costa Rica's driest region. The rainy season starts later and ends earlier, and overall it's more dependably sunny here than in other parts of the country. Combine this climate with a coastline that stretches south for hundreds of miles, from the Nicaraguan border, all the way to the Nicoya Peninsula, and you have an equation that yields beach bliss.

There is one caveat: During the dry season (mid-Nov to Apr), when sunshine is most reliable, the hillsides in Guanacaste turn browner than the chaparral of Southern California. Dust from dirt roads blankets the trees in many areas, and the vistas are far from tropical. Driving these dirt roads without air-conditioning and the windows rolled up tight can be extremely unpleasant.

On the other hand, if you happen to visit this area in the rainy season (particularly from May–Aug), the hillsides are a beautiful, rich green, and the sun usually shines all morning, giving way to an afternoon shower—just in time for a nice siesta.

Inland from the beaches, Guanacaste remains Costa Rica's "Wild West," a land of dry plains populated with cattle ranches and cowboys, who are known here as *sabaneros,* a name that derives from the Spanish word for "savanna" or "grassland." If it weren't for those rainforest-clad volcanoes in the distance, you might swear you were in Texas.

Guanacaste is home to several active volcanoes and some beautiful national parks, including **Santa Rosa National Park ★**, the home to massive sea turtle nestings and the site of a major battle to maintain independence, and **Rincón de la Vieja National Park ★★**, which features hot springs and bubbling mud pots, pristine waterfalls, and an active volcanic crater.

FACING PAGE: **Witch's Rock.**

LIBERIA

217km (135 miles) NW of San José; 132km (82 miles) NW of Puntarenas

Founded in 1769, Liberia is the capital of Guanacaste province, and although it can hardly be considered a bustling metropolis, it is growing rapidly, in large part as a business center to feed the growing coastal boom. Hardware stores, warehouses, malls, and shipping companies are setting up shop in Liberia, and the city is serving as a housing hub for the many workers needed to man the construction and tourism boom along the coast here.

Still, Liberia does boast more colonial atmosphere than almost any other city in the country. Its narrow streets are lined with charming old adobe homes, many of which have ornate stone accents on their facades, carved wooden doors, and aged red-tile roofs. Many have beautiful large, shuttered windows (some don't even have iron bars for protection) opening onto the narrow streets. The central plaza, which occupies 2 square blocks in front of the church, is still the city's social hub and principal gathering spot.

Liberia works well as a base for exploring this region or as an overnight stop as part of a longer itinerary. You'll find several moderately priced hotels in the city and its outskirts. Still, all things considered, it's usually preferable to base yourself either at the beach or at one of the mountain lodges in the area, and to visit the city on a day trip.

Essentials

GETTING THERE & DEPARTING By Plane: The **Daniel Oduber International Airport** (☎ **2668-1010** or 2688-1117; airport code LIR) in Liberia receives a steady stream of scheduled commercial and charter flights throughout the year. **Delta** (☎ **800/241-4141;** www.delta.com) has daily direct flights

Liberia central park.

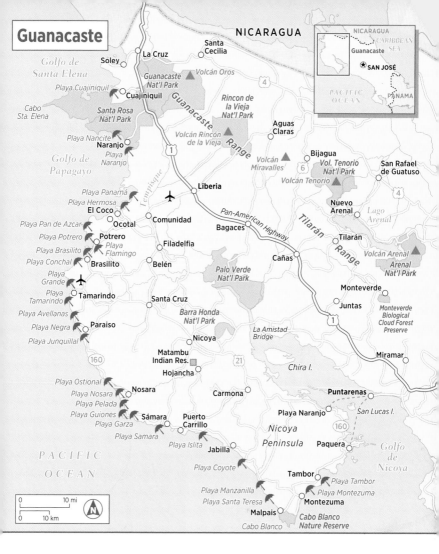

between its Atlanta hub and Liberia, twice-weekly direct flights from New York's JFK to Liberia; and a once-weekly direct flight between Los Angeles and Liberia; **American Airlines** (☎800/433-7300; www.aa.com) offers daily direct flights between Miami and Liberia, and twice-weekly flights between Dallas–Ft. Worth and Liberia; **Continental** (☎800/231-0856; www.continental.com) has daily direct flights between Houston and Liberia; and twice-weekly flights between Newark and Liberia; and **US Airways** (☎800/622-1015; www.usairways.com) has one weekly direct flight between Charlotte and Liberia. In addition, there are numerous commercial charter flights from various North American cities throughout the high season. Check with your travel agent.

Sansa (☎877/767-2672 in the U.S. and Canada, or 2290-4100 in Costa Rica; www.flysansa.com) has five daily flights to Liberia leaving between 6am and 11:40am from San José's Juan Santamaría International Airport. Return flights depart for San José between 7:40am and 12:40pm. During the high season, one late-afternoon flight is added. The fare for the 50-minute flight is $114 each way.

Nature Air (☎800/235-9272 in the U.S. and Canada, or 2299-6000; www.natureair.com) has four flights daily to Liberia at 6:30 and 11:20am, and 1:20 and 3:20pm from Tobías Bolaños International airport in Pavas (p. 118). Return flights leave Liberia at 7am and 12:40 and 4:45pm. Fares are $126 each way. Nature Air also has direct flights between Liberia and Arenal, Quepos, Tamarindo, and Tambor, as well as connections to just about every major destination in Costa Rica.

If you plan to fly here and rent a car to continue on to one of the nearby beaches and explore the region, the following companies all have local agencies: **Adobe** (☎2667-0608), **Alamo** (☎2668-1111), **Avis** (☎2668-1138), **Budget** (☎2668-1118), **Dollar** (☎2668-1061), **Economy** (☎2666-2816), **Hertz** (☎2668-1048), **Payless** (☎2667-0511), **Sol** (☎2666-2222), **Thrifty** (☎2665-0787), and **Toyota** (☎2668-1212). You can also reserve with these and most major international car-rental companies via their San José and international offices (see "Getting Around," in chapter 6).

Note: The official word is that the cramped, inefficient, and overcrowded terminals at the Daniel Oduber International Airport will be replaced with a major, modern new facility by mid-2009. If experience is any guide, I wouldn't start holding my breath for a couple years beyond that date, but don't be surprised if there is ongoing construction when you arrive.

An Interesting Stop on Your Way to Liberia

If you're driving to or from Guanacaste, be sure to take a brief break to check out the **Iglesia de Cañas (Cañas Church)** ★★ in Cañas. Well-known painter, installation artist, and local prodigal son Otto Apuy has designed and directed the envelopment of the entire church in colorful mosaic. The work uses whole and broken tiles in glossy, vibrant colors to depict both religious and abstract themes. The church's central tower, which is entirely covered in mosaic, is nearly 30m (100 ft.) tall. It is estimated that more than a million pieces of ceramic were used in the work. The church is located in the center of town, just a few blocks off the highway.

Colonial-era building in Liberia.

The airport is located 13km (8 miles) from downtown Liberia. Taxis await all incoming flights; a taxi into town should cost around $10. The ride takes around 10 minutes.

By Car: Take the Interamerican Highway west from San José, and follow the signs for Nicaragua and the Guanacaste beaches. Liberia is about a 3½- to 4-hour drive.

By Bus: Pulmitan express buses (☎2222-1650 in San José, or 2666-0458 in Liberia) leave **San José** roughly every hour between 6am and 8pm from Calle 24 between avenidas 5 and 7. The ride to Liberia takes 4 hours. A one-way fare costs around $5.25.

Gray Line (☎2220-2126; www.graylinecostarica.com) has a daily bus that leaves San José for Liberia at 7am. The fare is $45. **Interbus** (☎2283-5573; www.interbusonline.com) has two daily buses that leave San José for Liberia at 7am and 2:30pm; the fare is $39 to Liberia. The morning bus (for either company) makes connections to Rincón de la Vieja and Santa Rosa national parks. Both companies will pick you up at most San José–area hotels.

Buses depart for San José and most of the area beaches and national parks from the Liberia bus station on the edge of town, 200m (2 blocks) north and 100m (1 block) east of the main intersection on the Interamerican Highway. Express buses for San José leave roughly every hour between 4am and 8pm.

FAST FACTS There are several state and private bank offices clustered around downtown Liberia, as well as a branch of the **Banco de Costa Rica** inside the airport. The local **police** number is ☎2690-0129, and the **Liberia Hospital** number is ☎2666-0011. If you need a taxi, dial ☎2666-3330. There are a host of Internet cafes on the blocks surrounding and just off the central plaza.

On the southern outskirts of the city is a modern shopping mall, the place to come for a food court fix or to catch a semi-late-run movie at the local multiplex. Smaller, contemporary shopping centers can be found near the airport, and right at the major intersection between the Interamerican highway and the road to the beaches.

Exploring the Town

The central plaza in Liberia is a great place to people-watch, especially in the early evenings and on weekends. Grab a seat on one of the many concrete benches, or join the families and young lovers as they leisurely stroll around. If you venture off for a few blocks down **Calle Real** ★, you'll see fine examples of the classic Spanish colonial architecture—adobe buildings with ornate wooden doors, heavy beams, central courtyards, and faded, sagging, red-tile roofs.

While the Catholic church that anchors the central plaza is unspectacular, if you head several blocks east of the plaza, you will come to **Iglesia La Ermita de la Agonía** ★, which was built in 1865, and is still in pretty decent shape.

Outdoor Adventures near Liberia

EXPLORING RINCON DE LA VIEJA NATIONAL PARK ★★

This national park begins on the flanks of the Rincón de la Vieja Volcano and includes this volcano's active crater. Down lower you'll find an area of geothermal activity similar to that of Yellowstone National Park in the United States. Fumaroles, geysers, and hot pools cover this small area, creating a bizarre, otherworldly landscape. In addition to hot springs and mud pots, you can explore waterfalls, a lake, and volcanic craters. The bird-watching here is excellent, and the views across the pasturelands to the Pacific Ocean are stunning.

The main entrance is 25km (16 miles) northeast of Liberia, down a badly rutted dirt road. The park entrance fee is $10 per person per day, and the park is open daily from 7am to 3pm.

Camping will cost you an extra $2 per person per day. There are actually two entrances and camping areas here: **Santa María** and **Las Pailas** (also called Las Espuelas; ℂ**2661-8139**) ranger stations. The latter is by far the more popular and accessible, and it's closer to the action. These small camping areas are near each other. I recommend the one closer to the river, although the bathroom and shower facilities are about 90m (295 ft.) away, at the other site. For those seeking a less rugged tour of the park, there are several lodges located around the perimeter of the park; all offer guided hikes and horseback rides into the park.

GETTING THERE To reach the Las Pailas (Las Espuelas) entrance, drive about 5km (3 miles) north of Liberia and turn right on the dirt road to the park. The turnoff is well marked. In about 12km (7½ miles), you'll pass through the small village of Curubandé. Continue on this road for another 6km (3¾ miles) until you reach the Hacienda Guachipelin. The lodge is private property, and the owners charge vehicles a $2 toll to pass through their gate and continue on to the park. I'm not sure if this is legal or mandatory, but it's not worth the hassle to protest. Pay the toll, pass through the gate, and continue for another 4km (2½ miles) until you reach the park entrance.

La Cangrejo Waterfall.

Rincón de la Vieja National Park mud pots.

There are two routes to the **Santa María entrance.** The principal route heads out of the northeastern end of Liberia toward the small village of San Jorge. This route is about 25km (16 miles) long and takes about 45 minutes. A four-wheel-drive vehicle is required. Alternatively, you can reach the entrance on a turnoff from the Interamerican Highway at Bagaces. From here, head north through Guayabo, Aguas Claras, and Colonia Blanca. The road is paved up to Colonia Blanca, but again a four-wheel-drive vehicle is required for the final, very rough 10km (6¼ miles) of gravel road.

HIKING IN THE PARK There are several excellent trails inside the Rincón de la Vieja National Park. More energetic hikers can tackle the 8km (5 miles) up to the **summit** and explore the several craters and beautiful lakes up here. On a clear day you'll be rewarded with a fabulous view of the plains of Guanacaste and the Pacific Ocean below. The easiest hiking is the gentle **Las Pailas loop ★**. This 3km (1.75-mile) trail is just off the Las Espuelas park entrance and passes by several bubbling mud pots and steaming fumaroles. This trail crosses a river, so you'll have to either take off your shoes or get them wet. The whole loop takes around 2 hours.

My favorite hike here is to the **Blue Lake** and **La Cangrejo Waterfall ★★**. This 5km (3-mile) trail passes through several different life zones, including dry forest, transitional moist forest, and open savanna. A variety of birds and mammals are commonly sighted. Pack a lunch; at the end of your 2-hour hike in, you can picnic at the aptly named Blue Lake, where a 30m (98-ft.) waterfall empties into a small pond whose crystal-blue hues are amazing.

LLANO DE CORTES WATERFALL ★

Located about 25km (16 miles) south of Liberia, the Llano de Cortes Waterfall is a beautiful and wide jungle waterfall with an excellent pool at the base for cooling off and swimming. At roughly 12m (40 ft.) wide, the falls are actually slightly wider than they are tall. This is a great spot for a picnic. The turnoff for the dirt road to the falls is well marked and about 3km (1¾ miles) north of the crossroads for Bagaces. From the turnoff, you must drive a rough dirt road to the parking area and then hike down a short steep trail to the falls. Admission is free.

BACK TO AFRICA

Since the landscape is postcard-perfect, especially in the dry season, you shouldn't be too surprised to see antelope, zebra, giraffe, and elands roaming the grassy plains of Guanacaste. **Africa Mia** (**My Africa;** ☎ **2666 1111;** www. africamia.net) offers safari-style open-jeep tours through its 100-hectare (247-acre) private reserve, which is populated with a wide range of nonnative (predominantly African) species. All of the animals are herbivores, so don't expect to see any lions, hyenas, or cheetahs. Still, the trip does provide some of the sense of being on the Serengeti or some other African plain. The animals have plenty of room to roam. Admission, which is $16 for adults, and $11 for children 11 and under, includes a 90-minute guided tour. Other more extensive tours are offered, including those that get you closer to the animals. Africa Mia is located just off the Interamerican Highway, 8km (5 miles) south of Liberia. The park is open daily from 8am to 6pm.

BIRDING

The **Río Tempisque Basin** ★, southwest of town, is one of the best places in the country to spot marsh and stream birds by the hundreds. This area is an important breeding ground for gallinules, jacanas, and limpkins, as well as a common habitat for numerous heron and kingfisher species. Several tour operators offer excursions and a wide range of tours in the region from Liberia. **Swiss Travel Services** (☎ **2282-4898;** www.swisstravelcr.com) is the largest and most reliable of the major operators here.

One of the most popular tours is a boat tour down the Bebedero River to **Palo Verde National Park** ★, which is south of Cañas and is best known for its migratory bird populations. Some of the best bird-watching requires no more than a little walking around the Biological Station in the park.

RAFTING TRIPS

Leisurely raft trips (with little white water) are offered by **Safaris Corobicí** (☎/fax **2669-6191;** www.nicoya.com), about 40km (25 miles) south of Liberia. It has 2-hour ($38), 3-hour ($46), and half-day ($62) trips that are great for

FROM LEFT: **Africa Mia; Roseate spoonbill.**

Hacienda Guachipelín horseback riding.

families (children 13 and under are half-price) and bird-watchers. Along the way you may see many of the area's more exotic animal residents: howler monkeys, iguanas, caimans, coatimundis, otters, toucans, parrots, motmots, trogons, and many other species of birds. Aside from your binoculars and camera, a bathing suit and sunscreen are the only things you'll need. Safaris Corobicí is based on the main highway, just before the Restaurant Rincón Corobicí (p. 205). For a much wetter and wilder ride, the folks at **Hacienda Guachipelín** (see below) offer white-water inner-tube trips on the narrow Río Negro.

ONE-STOP ADVENTURE SHOP

Hacienda Guachipelín (see below) offers up a range of adventure tour options, including horseback riding, hiking, white-water river inner-tubing, a waterfall canyoning and rappel tour, and a more traditional zip-line canopy tour. The most popular is the hacienda's **1-Day Adventure pass ★★**, which allows you to choose as many of the hotel's different tour options as you want and fit them into 1 adventure-packed day. The price for this is $80, including a buffet lunch and transportation. Almost all of the beach hotels and resorts of Guanacaste offer day trips here, or you can book directly with the lodge. **Be forewarned:** During the high season, there's a bit of a cattle-car feel to the whole operation, with busloads of day-trippers coming in from the beach. Also, I have found the inner-tube adventure to be fairly dangerous when the river is high, particularly during or just after the rainy season.

HOT SPRINGS & MUD BATHS

Even if you're not staying at the Hacienda Guachipelín, you can take advantage of the hot spring pools and hot mud pools at their **Simbiosis Spa (☎2666-8075;** www.simbiosis-spa.com). A $25 entrance fee gets you a stint in a sauna, self-application of the hot volcanic mud, and free run of the pools. **Be forewarned:** The pools are better described as warm, not hot, mud pools, and mud is the operative word here. A wide range of massages, mud wraps, facials and other treatments are available at reasonable prices.

Shopping

On the road to the beaches, just west of the airport, are several large souvenir shops. These are popular stopping points on organized tours throughout this region. The best of the bunch for a one-stop shop is **Kaltak Arts & Craft Market** (☎2667-0696). However, you might find better selection and prices, especially for Guaitíl pottery, at some of the smaller makeshift roadside kiosks that line the road between Liberia and the Guanacaste beaches.

Where to Stay in Town

In addition to the places listed below, **El Punto Bed & Breakfast** (☎2665-2986; www.elpuntohotel.com) is a cute little boutique option, located close to the main highway intersection in Liberia.

MODERATE

Best Western El Sitio Hotel & Casino Located just out of town, about 1 block west of the main intersection on the road to Santa Cruz and the beaches, this hotel has seen better days. It is primarily used by Costa Ricans as a conference center or weekend getaway. The hotel is actually pretty from the outside, with a Spanish-influenced hacienda style, and an open, breezy layout. There's a large, shady pool, as well as a fairly well-equipped little gym. However, rooms feel worn and dated, and upkeep and service can be pretty spotty. If you're looking for a more contemporary and familiar option, I recommend the Hilton Garden Inn, across from the airport.

Liberia (A.P. 134-5000), Guanacaste. ☎800/780-7234 in the U.S. and Canada, or 2666-1211 in Costa Rica. Fax 2666-2059. www.bestwestern.com. 52 units. $108 double. Rates include full breakfast. AE, MC, V. **Amenities:** 2 restaurants; 2 bars; exercise room; large pool; Jacuzzi; room service. *In room:* A/C, TV, free Wi-Fi.

Hilton Garden Inn Liberia Airport ★ Long overdue, Liberia now has a modern, business-class airport hotel. That said, with most of Guanacaste's beaches under an hour drive away (some much closer), unless your flight arrives very late, or leaves very early, there's little need to stay near the airport. Rooms and suites are up-to-date, with 32-inch hi-def televisions, MP3 docking stations, a large desk, and complimentary Wi-Fi. They also all come with a fridge, microwave, and coffeemaker. The hotel is located directly across the street from the airport, and a shopping mall is currently being built just next door.

Across from the airport, Liberia, Guanacaste. ☎877/STAY-HGI in the U.S. and Canada, or 2690-8888 in Costa Rica. Fax 2690-8889. www.hgi.com. 169 units. $79–$149 double. Rates include breakfast buffet. AE, DC, DISC, MC, V. **Amenities:** Restaurant; bar; exercise room; Jacuzzi; outdoor pool; room service; all rooms smoke-free. *In room:* A/C, TV, minifridge, hair dryer, free Wi-Fi.

Hotel Boyeros 🍃 Located just off the highway, on the outskirts of town, this long-standing local place remains a good value, and reasonable alternative to the aforementioned Best Western and Hilton chain hotels. Arches with turned wooden railings and a red-tile roof give this place a colonial Spanish feel. The best and coolest rooms are on the second floor of the east wing. There's a large central courtyard with two swimming pools, some basic playground equipment, and a massive shade tree.

Liberia (A.P. 85-5000), Guanacaste. ☎2666-0722 or 2666-0809. Fax 2666-2529. www.hotel boyeros.com. 70 units. $67 double. AE, MC, V. **Amenities:** Restaurant; bar; midsize pool and children's pool; room service. *In room:* A/C, TV, free Wi-Fi.

INEXPENSIVE

Hotel Guanacaste This basic, economical choice is primarily a hostel catering to young travelers on a tight budget. In addition to the small and simply furnished rooms—almost all of which have bunk beds with thin foam mattresses—there's a basic *soda* (diner) serving inexpensive meals. The management here can help arrange trips to nearby national parks and tell you about other budget accommodations around the country. The best rooms have double beds, private bathrooms, and air-conditioning, and these cost slightly more. Camping is also allowed, for $6 per person.

A.P. 251-5000 (1 block north and 2 blocks east of the intersection of the Interamerican Hwy. and the beach highway), Liberia, Guanacaste. **2666-0085.** Fax 2666-2287. www.higuanacaste. com. 27 units. $34 double. Discounts for students and those holding a valid hostel ID. AE, MC, V. **Amenities:** Restaurant; bike rental. *In room:* No phone.

Posada del Tope This rustic little pension is nothing fancy, but the rooms and shared bathrooms are kept clean, the owners are friendly and helpful, and it's a real bargain. Only a couple of rooms have double beds; the rest have one, two, or three twin beds. The nicest thing about Posada del Tope is that it's housed in a wonderfully restored traditional colonial home with high ceilings, big shuttered windows facing the street, and hefty wooden trim all around. These folks also run another simple hotel in another old home, Casa Real, located directly across the street. This annex has more rooms and a basic restaurant serving inexpensive Tico cuisine.

Calle Real (1½ blocks south of the central park), Liberia, Guanacaste. /fax **2666-3876.** 22 units, 13 with shared bathroom. $19 double with shared bathroom; $22 double with private bathroom. AE, MC, V. Free parking. **Amenities:** Restaurant; bike rental. *In room:* TV, no phone, free Wi-Fi.

Where to Stay near Rincón de la Vieja National Park

In addition to the hotels listed below, there are a couple of other good choices by the park. On Cañas Dulces road, **Buena Vista Lodge** ★ (**2665-7759;** www. buenavistalodgecr.com) is set on the edge of the national park and offers a wide range of activities and attractions.

If you want easy access to the Tenorio volcano and Rio Celeste waterfall, I recommend the delightful **La Carolina Lodge** ★ (**8380-1656;** www.la carolinalodge.com), which is on a working farm, next to a clear flowing river. Another option is the new **Celeste Mountain Lodge** (**2786-628;** www. celestemountainlodge.com), a beautiful, sustainable lodge, with great views of the surrounding volcanoes.

Hacienda Guachipelin ★ Set on the edge of Rincón de la Vieja National Park, this lodge is built around a still-operational 19th-century cattle-and-horse ranch. The best rooms are housed in a series of long buildings enclosing a large lawn and garden area. All are spacious and modern and come with a wide shared veranda. The older rooms are still clean and comfortable, but generally smaller, and more rustic. In addition to the lodge's good-size pool, nearby creeks and rivers offer up a couple of natural swimming holes. These folks have implemented a range of sustainable practices ranging from the use of solar energy for hot water and electricity to reforestation to on-site generation of bio-gas. Meals are buffet affairs, although you can opt out of the meal plan and go a la carte. This place does a brisk business as a day-tour destination for a variety of hotels and resorts around Guanacaste, and there can be a cattle-car feel to the operation at times. See "One Stop Adventure Shop," above, for a description of their many tour offerings.

Rincón de la Vieja (23km/14 miles northeast of Liberia). ☎2665-3303 for reservations, or 2666-8075 at the lodge. Fax 2665-2178. www.guachipelin.com. 52 units. $169 double; $180 superior double. Rates include 3 meals and taxes. Rates higher during peak periods. AE, MC, V. Follow the directions/signs to Curubandé and Rincón de la Vieja National Park. A 4WD vehicle is required in the rainy season (May to mid-Nov) and strongly recommended at other times. **Amenities:** Restaurant; pool; small spa. *In room:* No phone, free Wi-Fi.

Hotel Borinquen Mountain Resort ★ This is the fanciest resort in the Rincón de la Vieja area. Individual and duplex bungalows are set on a hillside above the main lodge, restaurants, and hot springs. While the individual bungalow units are slightly larger, every room is large and comes with two queen-size beds, high ceilings, heavy wooden furniture, and a plush bathroom. Each has an ample wooden deck with a view over the valley and surrounding forests. In the foot of the valley are several natural hot-spring pools of varying temperatures, a natural sauna, and an area for full-body mud baths given with hot volcanic mud; a good-size free-form man-made swimming pool is on-site as well. There are good hiking and horseback riding trails here and some nice waterfalls nearby, and golf carts are available to shuttle you around. Despite the amazing facilities, the hotel's service and food have always been lacking, and the spa has yet to be fully developed.

Cañas Dulces (A.P. 108-5000), Liberia. ☎2690-1900. Fax 2690-1903. www.borinquenresort.com. 33 units. $185 double villa; $206–$286 double bungalow; $323 junior suite. Rates include breakfast and unlimited use of the hot springs, sauna, and mud baths. AE, MC, V. Drive 26km (16 miles) north of Liberia along the Interamerican Hwy., take the turnoff toward Cañas Dulces, and follow the signs. The hotel is approximately 18km (11 miles) from the highway and 3.5km (2¼ miles) beyond Cañas Dulces. **Amenities:** Restaurant; bar; large swimming pool; small spa. *In room:* A/C, TV, minibar, free Wi-Fi.

Rincón de la Vieja Mountain Lodge This is the closest lodge to the Las Pailas mud pots and the Azufrale hot springs. Rooms vary in size, and the best are the individual cabins, which come with hammocks on their private balconies. In all rooms, the furnishings and decor are simple, rustic, and feel dated. Quite a few come with one queen-size and one set of bunk beds. Meals are served in a large open-air rancho in the middle of the complex. The lodge offers numerous daylong tours either on foot, by mountain bike, or on horseback. It also runs an extensive canopy tour, which takes you on a high-wire ride over a couple dozen different treetop platforms, beginning with a manual ascent up a towering ceiba tree. This place is geared toward backpackers, students, and nature enthusiasts.

Rincón de la Vieja (A.P. 164-5000, Liberia), Guanacaste. ☎2200-0238. Fax 2666-2441. www.rincondelaviejalodge.net. 40 units. $70–$79 double. Rates include breakfast. Student discounts and off-season rates available. AE, MC, V. If you're driving, follow the directions to the Hacienda Lodge Guachipelin and continue driving on this dirt road for another 7km (4⅓ miles), bearing right at the turnoff for the park entrance. **Amenities:** Restaurant; bar; small pool. *In room:* No phone.

Where to Dine

There are plenty of standard Tico dining choices in Liberia. In town, the most popular alternative is **Pizzería Pronto** (☎2666-2098), which serves a wide range of wood-oven pizzas and assorted pasta dishes, in a restored old colonial home. Another favorite of mine is **El Café Liberia ★** (☎2665-1660), a little French-style coffee shop and bistro that morphs into a sort of European-style hip lounge and bar at night. For some local flavor, choose one of the *sodas* around the central park. The best of these is **Restaurante Paseo Real** (☎2666-3455). However, for a taste of history, check out the new **Casa Antigua ★** (☎2666-1224; www.casaantigualiberia.com), a simple coffee house, located in an immaculately restored colonial home on Calle Real, just next to La Posada del Tope.

For seafood and a good bar scene, try **LIB** (☎2665-7106), which sometimes features live music and dancing at night, and is located in the Centro Comercial Santa Rosa, at the main highway crossroads.

If you want fast food, you can find both **Burger King** and **Papa John's** in a small shopping complex on the northwest corner of the main intersection of the Interamerican Highway and the road to the beaches, as well as an even bigger food court with more fast-food options at the mall on the southern outskirts of town.

Restaurant Rincón Corobicí COSTA RICAN This roadside tourist restaurant can be packed with tour groups, and the food is far from memorable. But the setting on the banks of the Corobicí River is wonderful. Although plenty of covered seating is available in the main open-air dining room, try to get a table on the wooden deck overlooking the river. The sound of rushing water tumbling over the rocks in the riverbed is a soothing accompaniment to the simple but filling meals. The whole fried fish is your best choice here, although you can also have steaks, lobster, shrimp, sandwiches, and even a couple of lamb dishes. This restaurant makes an ideal lunch stop if you're heading to or coming from Liberia, or if you have just done a rafting trip on the Corobicí River. Be sure to try the fried yuca chips; they're excellent.

Interamerican Hwy., 5km (3 miles) north of Cañas. ☎**2669-6262.** Main courses $5.50–$16. AE, DC, MC, V. Daily 8am–5pm.

LA CRUZ & BAHIA SALINAS

277km (172 miles) NW of San José; 59km (37 miles) NW of Liberia; 20km (12 miles) S of Peñas Blancas

Near the Nicaraguan border, La Cruz is a tiny hilltop town that has little to offer beyond a fabulous view of Bahía Salinas (Salinas Bay), but it does serve as a gateway to the nearly deserted beaches down below, a few mountain lodges bordering the nearby Santa Rosa and Guanacaste national parks, and the Nicaraguan border crossing at Peñas Blancas.

There's little reason to stay in La Cruz, but if you must, check out either **Hotel La Mirada Inn** (☎2679-9084; www.hotellamirada.com) or **Hotel Bella Vista** (☎2679-8060). Both are simple hotels, and both have small pools and good views of the bay. (Instead of staying in town, I recommend you check out the listings below for places to stay on the shores of the beaches below.)

Essentials

GETTING THERE & DEPARTING By Plane: The nearest airport with regular service is in Liberia (see "Liberia," earlier in this chapter).

  By Car: Take the Interamerican Highway west from San José and follow the signs for Nicaragua and the Guanacaste beaches. When you reach Liberia, head straight through the major intersection, following signs to Peñas Blancas and the Nicaraguan border. Allow approximately 5 hours to get from San José to La Cruz.

  By Bus: Transportes Deldú buses (☎**2256-9072** in San José, or 2677-0091 in La Cruz) leave San José at least every hour (often more frequently) between 4am and 7pm for **Peñas Blancas** from Calle 20 and Avenida 1. These buses stop in La Cruz and will also let you off at the entrance to Santa Rosa National Park. The ride to La Cruz takes 5½ hours; a one-way fare costs around $6. Additional buses are often added on weekends.

  Local buses leave Liberia for Peñas Blancas periodically throughout the day. The ride to La Cruz takes about 1 hour and costs $2. Buses depart for San José from Peñas Blancas daily between 5am and 5:30pm, passing through La Cruz about 20 minutes later. Buses leave Liberia for San José roughly every hour between 5am and 7pm.

ORIENTATION The highway passes slightly to the east of town. You'll pass the turnoffs to Santa Rosa National Park and Playa Caujiniquil before you reach the town. To reach the beaches of Bahía Salinas, head into La Cruz and take the road that runs along the north side of the small central park and then follow the signs down to the water and Bahía Salinas.

Exploring Santa Rosa National Park

Known for its remote, pristine beaches (reached by several kilometers of hiking trails or a 4WD vehicle), **Santa Rosa National Park ★** (☎**2666-5051**) is a great place to camp on the beach, surf, or (if you're lucky) watch sea turtles nest. Located 30km (19 miles) north of Liberia and 21km (13 miles) south of La Cruz on the Interamerican Highway, Costa Rica's first national

Surfers approaching Witch's Rock.

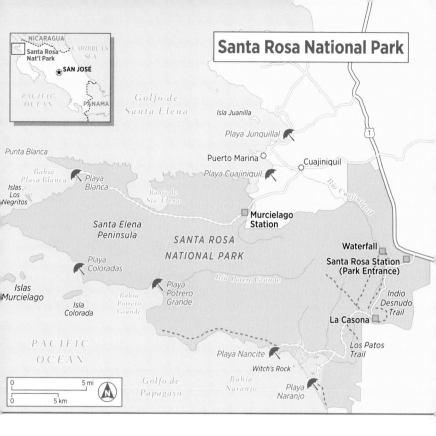

park blankets the Santa Elena Peninsula. Unlike other national parks, it was founded not to preserve the land but to save a building, known as **La Casona,** which played an important role in Costa Rican independence. It was here, in 1856, that Costa Rican forces fought the decisive Battle of Santa Rosa, forcing the U.S.-backed soldier of fortune William Walker and his men to flee into Nicaragua. La Casona was completely destroyed by arson in 2001, but it has been rebuilt, very accurately mimicking the original building, and now houses a small museum.

It costs $10 per person to enter the park. Camping is allowed at several sites within the park. A campsite costs $2 per person per day. There's camping near the entrance and principal ranger station, as well as near La Casona and down by playas Naranjo and Nancite.

THE BEACHES ★★ Eight kilometers (5 miles) west of La Casona, down a rugged road that's impassable during the rainy season (it's rough on 4WD vehicles even in the dry season), is **Playa Naranjo.** Four kilometers (2½ miles) north of Playa Naranjo, along a hiking trail that follows the beach, you'll find **Playa Nancite. Playa Blanca** is 21km (13 miles) down a dirt road from Caujiniquil, which itself is 20km (12 miles) north of the park entrance.

None of these three beaches has shower or restroom facilities. (Playa Nancite does have some facilities, but they're in a reservation-only camping area.) Bring along your own water, food, and anything else you'll need, and expect to find things relatively quiet and deserted.

Playa Nancite is known for its *arribadas* ("arrivals," grouped egg-layings) of olive ridley sea turtles, which come ashore to nest by the tens of thousands each year in October. Playa Naranjo is legendary for its perfect surfing waves. In fact, this spot is quite popular with day-trippers who come in by boat from the Playa del Coco area to ride the waves that break around **Witch's Rock,** which lies just offshore.

La Casona at Santa Rosa National Park.

On the northern side of the peninsula is **Playa Blanca,** a beautiful, remote white-sand beach with calm waters. This beach is reached by way of the small village of Caujiniquil and is accessible only during the dry season.

If you reach Caujiniquil and then head north for a few kilometers, you'll come to a small annex to the national park system at **Playa Junquillal** (**2679-9692**), not to be confused with the more-developed beach of the same name farther south in Guanacaste. This is a lovely little beach that is also often good for swimming. You'll have to pay the park entrance fee ($10) to use the beach, and $2 more to camp here. There are basic bathroom and shower facilities.

Fun on & over the Waves

The waters of Bahía Salinas are buffeted by serious winds from mid-November through mid-May, and this area is a prime spot for windsurfing and kiteboarding. The folks at **Ecoplaya Beach Resort** (see below) have the best windsurfing operation and rental equipment in the area. If you want to try your hand at the sport of kiteboarding, check in with the folks at the **Kitesurfing Center,** who operate out of the **Blue Dream Hotel** (**8826-5221;** www.bluedreamhotel. com) in Playa Copal.

Note: If you're coming to this area and aren't interested in windsurfing or kitesurfing, the winds can make your beach time rather unpleasant during the peak wind months. If you're just looking for a beach-resort vacation, I recommend heading to one of the beaches farther south in Guanacaste.

Where to Stay near La Cruz

Ecoplaya Beach Resort This is the most comfortable beach hotel in the area. (However, aside from a facile attempt to cash in on a trend, I see no reason to use "eco" in the name.) The rooms are classified as either studios or junior, master, or luxury suites. Opt for one of the suites because the studios are somewhat cramped. Inside they all have high ceilings, tile floors, and plenty of varnished wood accents. The dark sand beach here is calm, although the winter winds really howl. To take advantage of this, the hotel features a fully equipped windsurf center, offering rentals and classes. This is a decent option if you're looking for isolation, or to combine some beach time with excursions to Santa Rosa National Park and/or neighboring Nicaragua, although most folks will be much happier at the more popular Guanacaste beach destinations described below.

La Coyotera Beach, Salinas Bay. **☎2228-7146.** Fax 2289-4536. www.ecoplaya.com. 35 units. $98–$114 double; $182–$245 suite. Rates include taxes. AE, MC, V. From La Cruz, take the dirt road that passes to the right of El Mirador Ehecatl restaurant (as you face the water), and then follow signs to the hotel. **Amenities:** Restaurant; bar; 2 Jacuzzis; midsize pool; extensive watersports equipment rental. *In room:* A/C, TV, kitchenette.

PLAYA HERMOSA, PLAYA PANAMA & PAPAGAYO ★

258km (160 miles) NW of San José; 40km (25 miles) SW of Liberia

While most of Costa Rica's coast is highly coveted by surfers, the beaches here are mostly protected and calm, making them good destinations for families with kids. **Playa Hermosa ★** means "beautiful beach," which is an appropriate name for this crescent of sand. Surrounded by steep forested hills, this curving gray-sand beach is long and wide and the surf is usually quite gentle. Fringing the beach is a swath of trees that stays surprisingly green even during the dry season. The shade provided by these trees, along with the calm protected waters, is a big part of the beach's appeal. Rocky headlands jut out into the surf at both ends of the beach, and at the base of these rocks, you'll find fun tide pools to explore.

Beyond Playa Hermosa you'll find **Playa Panamá ★** and, farther on, the calm waters of **Bahía Culebra ★**, a large protected bay dotted with small, private patches of beach and ringed with mostly intact dry forest. Around the north end of Bahía Culebra is the **Papagayo Peninsula ★**, which is currently the home to two large all-inclusive resorts and one championship golf course. This peninsula has a half-dozen or so small to midsize beaches, the nicest of which might just be **Playa Nacascolo ★★**, which is inside the domain of the Four Seasons Resort here—but all beaches in Costa Rica are public, so you can still visit, albeit after passing through security and parking at the public parking lot.

Essentials

GETTING THERE & DEPARTING By Plane: The nearest airport with regularly scheduled service is in Liberia (p. 194). From there you can arrange a taxi to bring you the rest of the way. The ride takes about 25 minutes and should cost $35 to $50.

By Car: Follow the directions for getting to Liberia (described earlier in this chapter), and then head west toward Santa Cruz. The turnoff for the Papagayo Peninsula is prominently marked 8km (5 miles) south of the Liberia airport. At the corner here you'll see a massive Do It Center hardware store and lumber yard. If you're going on to Playa Hermosa, continue on a little farther and, just past the village of Comunidad, turn right. In about 11km (6¾ miles) you'll come to a fork in the road; take the right fork. The drive takes about 4½ hours from San José.

If you are going to the Pagagayo Peninsula, turn at the Do It Center and follow the paved road out and around the peninsula. If you are going to Playa Panamá or Playa Hermosa, you might consider taking the shortcut that leads from a turnoff on the Papagayo Peninsula road, just beyond the Do It Center, directly to Playa Hermosa.

These roads are all relatively well marked, and a host of prominent hotel billboards should make it easy enough to find the beach or resort you are looking for.

By Bus: A **Tralapa** express bus (☎2221-7202) leaves San José daily at 3pm from Calle 20 and Avenida 3, stopping at Playa Hermosa and Playa Panamá, 3km (1¾ miles) farther north. One-way fare for the 5-hour trip is around $8.

Gray Line (☎2220-2126; www.graylinecostarica.com) has a daily bus that leaves San José at 8am for all beaches in this area. The fare is $45. **Interbus** (☎2283-5573; www.interbusonline.com) has two daily buses that leave San José at 2:30pm for all beaches in this area. The fare is $39. Both companies will pick you up at most San José–area hotels.

You can take a bus from San José to Liberia (see "Essentials," earlier in this chapter) and then take a bus from Liberia to Playa Hermosa and Playa Panamá. Local buses (☎2666-0042) leave Liberia for Playa Hermosa and Playa Panamá at least a half-dozen times throughout the day between 5am and 6pm. The trip lasts 40 minutes because the bus stops frequently to drop off and pick up passengers. The one-way fare costs $1.80. These bus schedules change from time to time, so it's always best to check in advance. During the high season and on weekends, extra buses from Liberia are sometimes added. You can also take a bus to Playa del Coco, from which playas Hermosa and Panamá are a relatively quick taxi ride away. Taxi fare should run between $5 and $10.

One direct bus departs for San José daily at 5am from Playa Panamá, with a stop in Playa Hermosa along the way. Buses to Liberia leave Playa Panamá regularly between 6am and 7pm, stopping in Playa Hermosa a few minutes later. Ask at your hotel about current schedules, and where to catch the bus.

ORIENTATION From the well-marked turnoff for the Papagayo Peninsula (near the prominent Do It Center hardware store), a paved road leads around to the Allegro Papagayo and Four Seasons resorts. If you are heading to the beaches a little farther south, continue on to the well-marked turnoff for Playa del Coco and Playa Hermosa. This road forks before reaching Playa del Coco. You'll come to the turn-off for Playa Hermosa first. Playa Panamá is located a few kilometers farther along the same road. The road ends at the Hilton Papagayo Resort. There is also a connecting road between the Papagayo Peninsula road and Playa Panamá. This 11km (6¾-mile) shortcut is definitely your quickest route to Playa Panamá.

Playa Hermosa is about a 450m (1,476-ft.) stretch of beach, with all the hotels laid out along this stretch. From the main road, which continues on to Playa Panamá, three access roads head off toward the beach. All the hotels are well marked, with signs pointing guests down the right access road. Playa Panamá is the least developed of the beaches out here. Somewhat longer than Playa Hermosa, it also has several access roads heading in toward the beach from the main road, which is slightly inland.

Fun on & Under the Water

Most of the beaches up here are usually quite calm and good for swimming.

If you want to do some diving, check in with **Diving Safaris de Costa Rica ★** (**2672-1259;** www.costaricadiving.net), which is headquartered on the principal access road into Playa Hermosa, about 137m (450 ft.) before you hit the beach. This is a long-established and respected dive operation. It has a large shop and offers a wide range of trips to numerous dive spots, and it also offers night dives, multiday packages, certification classes, and Nitrox dives. These folks also offer multiday live-aboard and dive trips on their 14m (48-ft.) yacht.

Alternatively, you can check out **Resort Divers** (**2672-0106;** www.resortdivers-cr.com), which has set up shop at the Hilton Papagayo Resort.

Both of the above-mentioned companies will accept divers from any of the hotels in the area, and can arrange transport. A two-tank dive should run between $70 and $140 per person, depending primarily on the distance traveled to the dive sites.

In the middle of Playa Hermosa, **Aqua Sport** (**2672-0050**) is where to go for watersports equipment rental in Playa Hermosa. Kayaks, sailboards, canoes, bicycles, beach umbrellas, snorkel gear, and parasails are available for rental at fairly reasonable rates. You'll also find here a small supermarket, public phones, and a restaurant.

Because the beaches in this area are relatively protected and generally flat, surfers should look into boat trips to nearby **Witch's Rock ★★** and **Ollie's Point ★**. Diving Safaris de Costa Rica (**2672-1259**), **Hotel Finisterra** (**2672-0227**), and **Aqua Sport** (**2672-0050**) all offer trips for up to six surfers for around $60 per hour. Most of these companies also offer fishing trips for between $240 to $280 for groups of two to four anglers.

If you're interested in wind power, check in with the folks at the **El Velero Hotel** (see below), or **Tahini Yacht Tours** (**2672-1037**). Both offer a range of full- and half-day tours, with snorkel stops, as well as sunset cruises.

Other Options

Other activities in the area include horseback riding, all-terrain quad tours, canopy tours, and trips to other major attractions in the Guanacaste region. **Swiss Travel Service** (**2668-1020**) has operations in the area and offers a wide range of activities and tours,

Surfers at Playa Hermosa.

including trips to Santa Rosa or Rincón de la Vieja national parks, and rafting on the Corobicí River. These folks have desks at many of the hotels around here and will pick you up at any hotel in the area.

The best zip-line canopy tour in this area is the **Witch's Rock Canopy Tour** (☎**2667-0661**), just before the Allegro Papagayo Resort. The 2½-hour tour covers 3km (1¾ miles) of cables touching down on 23 platforms and costs $65.

Finally, the Arnold Palmer–designed championship course at the Four Seasons Resort (see below) is hands down the most beautiful and challenging **golf course** in the country. However, it is open only to guests at the Four Seasons.

Take It Easy

If you're looking for some pampering, whether it be a massage, facial, or body scrub, check out **Spa Aguas de Hermosa** (☎**2672-1386**), which is located in the Hermosa Heights Resort Community, and offers up a wide range of treatment options.

Where to Stay

VERY EXPENSIVE

Four Seasons Resort Costa Rica ★★★ ☺ Set on a narrow spit of land between two stunning white-sand beaches, this is the most luxurious and impressive resort in Costa Rica. The architecture is unique, with most buildings featuring flowing roof designs and other touches imitating the forms of turtles, armadillos, and butterflies. Rooms are very spacious, with beautiful furnishings, fixtures and decorations from around the world, and marble bathrooms with deep tubs and separate showers. Each has a large private balcony with a sofa, a table, and a couple of chairs. Rooms on the third and fourth floors have the best views and are priced accordingly. Suites and villas have even more space and either a private pool, Jacuzzi, or an open-air gazebo for soaking in the views. The resort features the Four Seasons' renowned service (including family-friendly amenities such as kid-size bathrobes and childproof rooms), one of the best-equipped spas in the country, and a spectacular golf course that offers ocean views from 15 of its 18 holes. Despite being such a large resort, these folks have been granted "4 Leaves" by the CST Sustainable Tourism program.

Papagayo Peninsula, Guanacaste. ☎**800/819-5053** in the U.S. or 2696-0000. Fax 2696-0500. www.fourseasons.com/costarica. 153 units. $815–$955 double; $1,480–$9,500 suites and villas. Children stay free in parent's room. AE, DC, DISC, MC, V. **Amenities:** 4 restaurants; 2 bars; lounge; babysitting; children's programs; concierge; championship 18-hole golf course; 3 free-form pools; room service; smoke-free rooms; full-service spa; 2 tennis courts; watersports equipment. *In room:* A/C, TV/DVD, hair dryer, MP3 docking station, Wi-Fi.

Grand Papagayo ★★ The Grand Papagayo is the highest-end all-inclusive resort of the Occidental Hotel chain in Costa Rica. The rooms are spread over a broad and contoured hillside overlooking the ocean, but not all rooms come with an ocean view. The resort is geared toward couples, and the vast majority of the rooms come with just one king-size bed, although there are some with two queen-size. I like the Grand Concierge rooms, which are close to the pool and restaurants, and feature marble floors. However, the Royal Club rooms and

Four Seasons Resort.

suites are the best rooms, and they come with beefed up concierge services. The beach here is very protected and calm, although it almost entirely disappears at peak high tide. A host of scheduled activities and entertainment options are offered, and a wide range of additional tours and activities can be added on.

Papagayo Peninsula, Guanacaste. ☎**800/858-2258** in the U.S. and Canada, 2672-0191 for reservations inside Costa Rica. Fax 2672-0057. www.occidentalhotels.com. 169 units. $426–$470 per person double occupancy; $747–$1,160 Royal Club room double. Rates include food, drinks, a range of activities, and taxes. AE, DC, MC, V. **Amenities:** 4 restaurants; 2 bars; lounge; babysitting; large health club and spa; 2 large free-form pools; smoke-free rooms; 1 lighted tennis court; watersports equipment. *In room:* A/C, TV, hair dryer, stocked minibar, Wi-Fi.

Hilton Papagayo Resort ★ ☺ The very first all-inclusive resort in the Guanacaste region, this place has changed its name and management at least four times, most recently in 2008, being taken over by the Hilton group. Most of the duplex villas can be separated into two rooms or shared by a family or two couples. Inside, one room is equipped with a king-size bed; the other has two queens. All rooms have marble floors, large bathrooms, and small private patios or balconies. The resort is quite spread out, so if you don't want to do a lot of walking or wait for the minivan shuttles, request a room near the main pool and restaurants. If you want a good view, ask for one on the hill overlooking the bay. The hotel has a large, modern, and plush spa facility. It also has its own small crescent-shape swath of beach, which is very calm and protected for swimming.

Playa Panamá, Guanacaste. ☎**800/445-8667** in the U.S. and Canada, or 2672-0000 in Costa Rica. Fax 2672-0181. www.hilton.com. 202 units. $229–$579 double; $530–$630 junior suite. Rates include food, drinks, activities, and taxes. AE, DC, DISC, MC, V. **Amenities:** 3 restaurants; 2 bars; babysitting; children's programs; well-equipped health center and spa; Jacuzzi; 3-tiered main pool, small lap pool, and resistance lap pool; tennis court; watersports equipment. *In room:* A/C, TV, hair dryer, minibar, free Wi-Fi.

Villas Sol Hotel & Beach Resort Set on a steep hillside at the north end of the beach, the Villas Sol is part of a long-standing project that has changed hands several times, divided, and grown over the years. The hotel is at the top of the hill, inland from the beach. You'll need to be in good shape to stay here, or you'll spend some time waiting for the sporadic jitney service. Luckily, the two pools are both at the top of the hill if you want to opt out of the trip to and from the beach. The hotel rooms are all well maintained and most have excellent views. (Given their placement just off the entrance, though, not all of the villas have spectacular views.) All villa rooms have kitchenettes, satellite TVs, and contemporary furnishings. About a third of them have their own small swimming pool or Jacuzzi.

Playa Hermosa, Guanacaste. **800/572-9934** in the U.S. and Canada, or 2257-0607 reservations in San José, or 2672-0001 at the hotel. Fax 2223-3086. www.villassol.com. 54 units, 120 villas. $179 double; $548–$1,170 villa. Rates include food, drinks, activities, and taxes. AE, DC, MC, V. **Amenities:** 3 restaurants; 2 bars; 2 pools; small spa; 2 lighted tennis courts; limited watersports equipment rental. In room: A/C, TV, minifridge, hair dryer, free Wi-Fi.

EXPENSIVE

Hotel Playa Hermosa Bosque del Mar ★★

Following a major rebuild, this place has emerged as the premier beachfront boutique hotel in the area. The oceanfront suites here are plush, and feature outdoor Jacuzzis. The garden-view suites are very similar but an indoor sauna replaces the Jacuzzi. In both cases, second floor units have better views and higher ceilings. The junior suites are all cozy and well-equipped. The whole complex was built around and among the lush existing gardens and trees, and employs sustainable practices wherever possible. Trees come up and through the main lobby and restaurant, and through some of the decks off the rooms. Three of the suites are handicapped accessible. The second-floor bar and lounge has great views through the trees to the sea.

Playa Hermosa, Guanacaste. **2672-0046.** Fax 2672-0019. www.hotelplayahermosa.com. 32 units. $175 junior suite; $225–$275 suite. AE, MC, V. **Amenities:** Restaurant; bar; pretty outdoor pool w/sculpted waterfall; free Wi-Fi. In room: A/C, TV, hair dryer.

MODERATE

El Velero Hotel ★

This place is one of my top choices right on the beach in Playa Hermosa, especially at this price. White walls and polished tile floors give El Velero a Mediterranean flavor. The rooms are large, and those on the second floor have high ceilings. The furnishings are simple, though, and some of the bathrooms are a bit small. The hotel has its own popular little restaurant, which offers a good selection of meat, fish, and shrimp dishes, as well as weekly barbecue fests. Various tours, horseback riding, and fishing trips can be arranged through the hotel; however, the most popular excursions are the full-day and sunset cruises on the hotel's namesake sailboat.

Playa Hermosa (A.P. 49-5019), Guanacaste. **2672-1017.** Fax 2672-0016. www.costaricahotel.net. 22 units. $89 double. AE, MC, V. **Amenities:** Restaurant; bar; small pool. In room: A/C, TV, hair dryer, free Wi-Fi.

Hotel Finisterra

This hillside hotel offers neat, spacious accommodations on the southern end of Playa Hermosa. All rooms are located on the second floor and come with either one queen-size bed or two double beds. Large picture windows face either a forested hillside or the Pacific Ocean. A large open-air restaurant and lounge takes up most of the first floor, and a refreshing little pool has good views. The beach is about 270m (886 ft.) away, down the steep driveway.

The folks here can arrange a wide variety of tours, including sportfishing and surf trips to Witch's Rock.

Playa Hermosa, Guanacaste. ☎/fax **2672-0227.** www.lafinisterra.com. 10 units. $110 double. Rates include full breakfast. AE, MC, V. **Amenities:** Restaurant; bar; babysitting; small pool; room service. *In room:* A/C, no phone, free Wi-Fi.

Villa del Sueño Hotel ★ Villa del Sueño offers cozy rooms at a good price, and one of the best restaurants in Playa Hermosa. All the rooms have cool tile floors, high hardwood ceilings, ceiling fans, and well-placed windows for cross ventilation. The second-floor superior rooms have more space and larger windows. More expensive rooms come with air-conditioning and televisions. Although this hotel isn't right on the beach (it's about 1 block inland), its well-groomed lawns and gardens feel like an oasis in the dust and heat of a Guanacaste dry season. There's a small pool and open-air bar in the center courtyard. In addition to fine meals, the restaurant features live music, by a variety of local acts, during much of the high season. Also under this hotel's management is the neighboring "El Oasis" condominium development, which has additional apartment and efficiency units available for nightly and weekly rentals, as well as its own pool.

Playa Hermosa, Guanacaste. ☎**800/378-8599** in the U.S. and Canada, or 2672-0026 in Costa Rica. Fax 2672-0021. www.villadelsueno.com. 45 units. $75–$105 double; $130–$255 condo. AE, MC, V. **Amenities:** Restaurant (p. 215); bar; small pool. *In room:* A/C, free Wi-Fi.

Dining & After Dark Diversions

For nightlife, find out whether the **Villa del Sueño Restaurant** (see below) has live music. Two Saturdays a month, Villa del Sueño hosts larger concerts, featuring prominent Costa Rican acts, in its spiffy open-air amphitheater.

In addition to the places listed below, you'll find good restaurants at both the **El Velero Hotel** and the **Hotel Finisterra** (see "Where to Stay," above). For U.S.-style bar food and entertainment, try the **Upper Deck Sports Bar** (☎**2672-1276**), just off the main road.

Ginger ★★ 🍴 INTERNATIONAL/TAPAS In this most creative restaurant in the area, the architecture and decor are stylish and modern, with sharp angles and loads of chrome and glass. The food is an eclectic mix of modern takes on wide-ranging international fare, all served as tapas, meant to be shared while sampling some of the many cocktails and wines served here. Still, it's easy to make a full meal. Order the house special ginger-glazed chicken wings, along with some spring rolls, and a plate of fresh mahimahi marinated in vodka and Asian spices. There are also more traditional Mediterranean and Spanish-style tapas, as well as delicious desserts.

On the main road, Playa Hermosa. ☎**2672-0041.** Tapas $4.50–$8. MC, V. Tues–Sun 5–10pm.

Villa del Sueño Restaurant ★ INTERNATIONAL A mellow yet refined atmosphere presides under slow-turning ceiling fans at this simple open-air restaurant. In addition to lots of fresh fish, there are well-prepared pasta dishes, as well as meat and poultry options. A small selection of specials is offered nightly. Live music is available many nights during high season.

At the Villa del Sueño Hotel. ☎**2672-0026.** Main courses $14–$25. AE, MC, V. Daily 7am–9:30pm.

PLAYA DEL COCO & PLAYA OCOTAL

253km (157 miles) NW of San José; 35km (22 miles) W of Liberia

Playa del Coco is one of Costa Rica's busiest and most built-up beach destinations. With a large modern mall and shopping center anchoring the eastern edge of town, you'll pass through a tight jumble of restaurants, hotels, and souvenir shops for several blocks before you hit the sand and sea; homes, condos, and hotels have sprouted up along the beach in either direction. This has long been, and remains, a popular destination with middle-class Ticos and weekend revelers from San José. It's also a prime jumping-off point for some of Costa Rica's best scuba diving. The beach, which has grayish-brown sand and gentle surf, is quite wide at low tide and almost nonexistent at high tide. The crowds that come here like their music loud and constant, so if you're in search of a quiet retreat, stay away from the center of town. Still, if you're looking for a beach with a wide range of inexpensive hotels, lively nightlife, and plenty of cheap food and beer close at hand, you'll enjoy Playa del Coco.

More interesting still, in my opinion, is **Playa Ocotal ★**, which is a couple of kilometers to the south. This tiny pocket cove features a small salt-and-pepper beach bordered by high bluffs and is quite beautiful. When it's calm there's good snorkeling around some rocky islands close to shore here.

Essentials

GETTING THERE & DEPARTING By Plane: The nearest airport with regularly scheduled flights is in Liberia (p. 194). From there you can arrange for a taxi to take you to Playa del Coco or Playa Ocotal, which is about a 25-minute drive, for $30 to $40.

By Car: From Liberia, head west toward Santa Cruz. Just past the village of Comunidad, turn right. In about 11km (6¾ miles) you'll come to a fork in the road. Take the left fork. It takes about 4½ hours from San José.

By Bus: Pulmitan express buses (✆2222-1650) leave San José for Playa del Coco at 8am and 2 and 4pm daily from Calle 24 between avenidas 5 and 7. Allow 5 hours for the trip. A one-way ticket is $6.25. From Liberia, buses (✆2666-0458) to Playa del Coco leave regularly throughout the day between 5am and 7pm. A one-way ticket for the 40-minute trip costs around $1. These bus schedules change frequently, so it's always best to check in

---

Charlie Don't Surf, But Ollie Does

Ollie's Point is named after Oliver North, the famous and felonious former lieutenant colonel at the center of the Iran-Contra scandal. The beaches and ports of northern Guanacaste were a staging ground for supplying the Nicaraguan Contra rebels. Legend has it that during a news broadcast of an interview with North, some surfers noticed a fabulous point break going off in the background. Hence, the discovery and naming of Ollie's Point.

Playa Ocotal.

advance. During the high season and on weekends, extra buses from Liberia are sometimes added. The direct bus for San José leaves Playa del Coco daily at 8am and 2 and 4pm. Local buses for Liberia leave between 5am and 7pm.

Gray Line (☎2220-2126; www.graylinecostarica.com) has a daily bus that leaves San José at 8am for Playa del Coco. The fare is $33. **Interbus** (☎2283-5573; www.interbusonline.com) has two daily buses that leave San José at 7:45am. The fare is $39. Both companies will pick you up at most San José–area hotels.

Depending on demand, the Playa del Coco buses sometimes go as far as Playa Ocotal; it's worth checking beforehand. Otherwise, a taxi should cost around $5.

ORIENTATION Playa del Coco is a compact and busy beach town. Most of its hotels and restaurants are either on the water, on the road leading into town, or on the road that heads north, about 100m (328 ft.) inland from and parallel to the beach.

Playa Ocotal, which is south of Playa del Coco on a paved road that leaves the main road about 183m (600 ft.) before the beach, is a small collection of vacation homes, condos, and a couple of hotels. It has one bar and one restaurant on the beach.

GETTING AROUND You can rent cars from any number of rental companies. Most are based in Liberia, or at the airport. See "Essentials," under "Liberia," for details and contact information.

If you can't flag down a **taxi** easily on the street, call ☎2670-0408.

FAST FACTS The nearest major hospital is in Liberia (☎2666-0011). For the local **health clinic,** call ☎2670-0987; and for the local **pharmacy** call ☎2670-1186. For the local **police,** dial ☎2670-0258.

There's a branch of the state-run **Banco Nacional** (☎2670-0801) on the main road into town, about 3 blocks before you hit the beach.

Boats at sea at Playa del Coco.

Fun on & off the Beach

Plenty of boats are anchored here at Playa del Coco, and that means plenty of opportunities to go fishing, diving, or sailing. Still, the most popular activities, especially among the hordes of Ticos who come here, are hanging out on the beach, hanging out in the *sodas,* and cruising the bars and discos at night. If you're interested, you might be able to join a soccer match. (The soccer field is in the middle of town.) You can also arrange horseback rides; ask at your hotel.

BEACH CLUB If you're staying at a hotel without a pool, or just want a sense of exclusivity on the beach, you might check out **Café de Playa Beach & Dining Club** (℡2670-1621; www.cafedeplaya.com). In addition to having an excellent restaurant (see below), this place offers up day passes for $15 that allow access to their pool and private grassy lawn fronting the beach, and spread with comfortable teak chaise longues. They also have a host of watersports equipment rental and tour options, and a small spa on-site, offering a broad range of massages and treatments.

GOLF Located about 10km (6¼ miles) outside Playa del Coco, the **Papagayo Golf & Country Club** (℡2697-1313; www.papagayo-golf.com) offers up a full 18-hole course, with a pro shop, driving range, and rental equipment. It costs $95 in greens fees, including a cart.

GYM If you want to work out while in town, head to the **Coco Gym** (℡8362-3355; www.cocogym.com), which is located on the road between Playa del Coco and Ocotal. Weights, cardio machines, and a range of classes are all offered. A day pass here costs $10.

SAILING Several cruising sailboats and longtime local salts offer daily sailing excursions. The 47-foot **Kuna Vela** (℡8301-3030; www.kunava.com) is a spacious ketch plying the waters off Playa del Coco. A full-day cruise with lunch and drinks runs $70 per person. The trip includes a couple of snorkel stops and an open bar. You could also book a ride on the **Don Bosco** (℡8378-7170 or 8365-4993), a 65-foot ketch, that includes a beach barbecue and party as part of its daily cruise itinerary ($70–$120 per person, full day). Both of these boats also offer half-day cruises and sunset sails.

SCUBA DIVING Scuba diving is the most popular watersport in the area, and dive shops abound. **Ocotal Diving** (☎2670-0321; www.ocotaldiving. com), **Summer Salt** (☎2670-0308; www.summer-salt.com), and **Rich Coast Diving** (☎800/434-8464 in the U.S. and Canada, or 2670-0176 in Costa Rica; www.richcoastdiving.com) are the most established and offer equipment rentals and dive trips. A two-tank dive, with equipment, should cost between $70 and $140 per person, depending on the distance to the dive site. The more distant dive sites visited include the Catalina Islands and Bat Island. All of these operators also offer PADI certification courses.

SPORTFISHING Full- and half-day sportfishing excursions can be arranged through any of the hotel tour desks, or with **Tranquilamar** (☎8814-0994; www.tranquilamar.com). A half-day of fishing, with boat, captain, food, and tackle, should cost between $450 and $600 for two to four passengers; a full day should run between $600 and $1,600.

SURFING There's no surf whatsoever in Playa del Coco. But this is a popular jumping-off point for daily boat trips to Witch's Rock or Roca Bruja, and Ollie's Point up in Santa Rosa National Park (p. 206). Most of the above-mentioned sportfishing and dive operations also offer trips to ferry surfers up to these two isolated surf breaks. Alternatively, you can contact **Roca Bruja Surf Operations** (☎2670-1020). A boat that carries six surfers for a full day, including lunch and beer, should run around $300. *Tip:* Both Witch's Rock and Ollie's Point are technically within Santa Rosa National Park. Permits are sometimes required, and boats without permits are sometimes turned away. If you decide to go, be sure your boat captain is licensed and has cleared access to the park. You may also have to pay the park's $10 entrance fee.

Moray eel.

Where to Stay

EXPENSIVE

El Ocotal Beach Resort ★ This is the most luxurious and complete resort hotel in the Playa del Coco area. The guest rooms vary considerably in size and styling. Each of the six duplex bungalows shares a small oceanview plunge pool. Those at the top of the hill overlook a dramatic stretch of rocky coastline and have fabulous views, although if you want quick access to the beach, choose one of the lower units. The third-floor suite, no. 520, is the best room in the house, with a large wraparound balcony and private Jacuzzi. El Ocotal's hilltop restaurant is one of its greatest assets, with loads of open air seating and stunning views. This is a great place to come for sunset and a drink. *Note:* It's a steep, vigorous hike from bottom to top at this resort.

Playa del Coco (A.P. 1), Guanacaste. ☎ **877/862-6825** in U.S. and Canada, or 2670-0321 in Costa Rica. Fax 2670-1122. www.ocotalresort.com. 42 units, 12 bungalows, 5 suites. $180 double; $278 bungalow; $341 suite. Rates include full breakfast. AE, DC, MC, V. **Amenities:** 2 restaurants; babysitting; exercise room; Jacuzzi; 3 outdoor swimming pools and 3 plunge pools; lighted tennis court. *In room:* A/C, TV, minifridge, hair dryer, free Wi-Fi.

The Suites at Café de Playa ★ While simple and understated, the five suites here are the plushest beachfront rooms you'll find right in Playa del Coco. The design and decor are minimalist, with contemporary fixtures, furnishings, and art. Rooms are arranged around a central pool area and come with either one or two queen-size beds. The best thing about these rooms is the fact that they are just a few steps from the sand, and allow you access to the facilities and services available at Café de Playa.

Playa del Coco, Guanacaste. ☎ **2670-1621** or 2670-1554. www.cafedeplaya.com. 5 units. $160 double. AE, DC, MC, V. **Amenities:** Restaurant; outdoor pool; small spa. *In room:* A/C, TV, free Wi-Fi.

MODERATE

Coco Bay Hotel & Casino This two-story hotel is the biggest thing in Playa del Coco and is an acceptable choice if you're looking for a cookie-cutter-style room close to the beach, restaurants, and action. The bland rooms are identical in size but have a variety of bedding options for singles, couples, and families. They all share a common veranda, which gets blasted by the hot afternoon sun. The casino here is the best in Playa del Coco. You can't miss this large building on your right, on the main road into Playa del Coco—about 2 blocks before you hit the beach.

Playa del Coco, Guanacaste. ☎ **2670-0494.** Fax 2670-0555. 33 units. $79–$107 double. V. **Amenities:** Restaurant; bar; casino; small pool; small spa. *In room:* A/C, TV, hair dryer.

Hotel Villa Casa Blanca ★ With friendly staff, beautiful gardens, and attractive rooms, this bed-and-breakfast inn is one of my favorite options in the area. Located about 500m (1,640 ft.) inland from the beach at Playa Ocotal, it's built in the style of a Spanish villa. All the guest rooms feature fine furnishings and are well kept. Some are a tad small, but others are quite roomy and even have kitchenettes. The suites are higher up and have ocean views. My favorite has a secluded patio with lush flowering plants all around. A little rancho serves as an open-air bar and breakfast area, and beside this is a pretty little lap pool with a bridge over it. Another separate rancho serves as a sort of lounge/recreation area and they have a little, in-house day spa.

Playa Ocotal (A.P. 176-5019), Playa del Coco, Guanacaste. ☎**2670-0518.** Fax 2670-0448. www. hotelvillacasablanca.com. 10 units. $105 double; $125 double suite. Rates include breakfast buffet. AE, MC, V. **Amenities:** Outdoor lounge and bar; Jacuzzi; small pool; small day spa. *In room:* A/C, free Wi-Fi.

Villa del Sol B&B This bed-and-breakfast, located 1km (½ mile) north of Playa del Coco village, is a friendly family-run joint. There are seven rooms in the original building here. All are spacious and clean and receive plenty of light. The most interesting room has a round queen-size bed, high ceilings, and views of the gardens. Still, the nicest rooms here are the six studios, each with a small kitchenette, private bathroom, television, and telephone. Those on the second floor even have a bit of an ocean view from their shared veranda. There's an inviting small pool with a covered barbecue area. Tasty dinners from a small menu of European-influenced dishes are prepared nightly for guests.

Playa del Coco (A.P. 52-5019), Guanacaste. ☎**866/793-9523** in the U.S. or ☎/fax 2670-0085 in Costa Rica. www.villadelsol.com. 13 units, 11 with private bathroom. $65–$75 double; $87 studio apt. Rates include taxes, and full breakfast (for rooms only, not studio apts). AE, MC, V. **Amenities:** Restaurant; small pool. *In room:* A/C, no phone, free Wi-Fi.

Where to Dine

There's a clutch of basic open-air *sodas* at the traffic circle in the center of El Coco village. These restaurants serve Tico standards, with an emphasis on fried fish. Prices are quite low—and so is the quality, for the most part.

In addition to the places listed below, you can get excellent Italian food at **Sol y Luna,** at the Hotel La Puerta del Sol (☎**2670-0195**), 200m (2 blocks) north and 100m (1 block) east of the main road at the turnoff just beyond the Coco Beach Hotel, before you hit the beach, and at **La Dolce Vita** (☎**2670-2142;** www.ladolcevitacostarica.com), in the little El Pueblito strip mall on the road running north and parallel to the beach.

Right on the main strip, you'll also find the neighboring Papagayo and Louisiana operations. Growing out of the success of their seafood restaurant, **Papagayo Seafood** (☎**2670-0298**) has opened both the **Papagayo Steak House** (☎**2670-0605**) and **Papagayo Sushi** (☎**2670-0298**), in an attempt to cover all possible bases. For another sushi option, try **Coco Sushi** (☎**2670-0153**), at the Coco Palms hotel, right across from the soccer field.

Café de Playa ★★ 🏮 INTERNATIONAL/FUSION This hip restaurant is the most elegant and enjoyable spot in Playa del Coco. The creative menu covers a lot of ground, with influences from Italy and across Asia most prevalent. Appetizers range from an octopus carpaccio to a cold Thai beef salad. There are several pasta choices, and a very tasty oriental rice salad with smoked tuna, caviar, and avocado. Lobster is served several ways, as are tenderloin filets. For dessert be sure to try the passion-fruit ice cream. Heavy teak tables and chairs are spread around the ample open-air dining room, or out under the open sky (either sun or stars, depending upon the hour). These folks also have an excellent wine list, with plenty of Italian and French choices, in addition to the more common Chilean and Argentine fare.

On the beach, Playa del Coco. ☎**2670-1621.** Reservations recommended. Main courses $12–$20. MC, V. Daily 7am–10pm.

Picante INTERNATIONAL This is a large, open-air, poolside restaurant at the Bahía Pez Vela resort and condominium project. Beyond the pool and down a steep little hill, you can see the Pacific Ocean. The menu is pretty simple and straightforward, with a selection of fresh seafood dishes, big burgers, excellent fish sandwiches, and large creative salads. There are also daily chalkboard specials, which are usually more creative and eclectic, ranging from sesame-seared tuna to mahimahi topped with a homemade curry sauce.

At Bahía Pez Vela resort, Playa Ocotal. ☎**2670-0901.** Reservations recommended. Main courses $9–$18. MC, V. Daily 9am–9:30pm.

Playa del Coco After Dark

Playa del Coco is one of Costa Rica's liveliest beach towns after dark. Most of the action is centered along a 2-block section of the main road into town, just before you hit the beach. Here you'll find the **Lizard Lounge ★**, which has recently expanded and taken on a bigger party vibe. Just across the street is the new, large, open-air **Zi Lounge.** For some neo-European style, check out **Zouk Santana ★**, which features electronic dance and lounge music and often has a DJ spinning, while those looking for a Gringo-influenced sports-bar hang-out can try **Coconuts.**

If you head north on the dirt road running parallel to the beach you'll find **Café de Playa,** which often has live music and concerts, with major acts from San José, as well as local talent filling the bills. For a Middle Eastern–inspired mellow lounge scene, you can head to **Kashbar,** in the Pueblito shopping center, located on this same road.

On the south end of the beach, reached via a rickety footbridge over the estuary, you'll find **La Vida Loca,** a lively beachfront bar with a pool table, Ping-Pong table, and foosball table, as well as occasional live bands.

Cocomar is the main disco in town. It's just off the little park fronting the beach. (If these directions don't get you there, just follow the loud music.) Finally, if you want to test your luck, head to the casino at the **Coco Bay Hotel & Casino** (see above).

PLAYAS FLAMINGO, POTRERO, BRASILITO & CONCHAL

280km (174 miles) NW of San José; 66km (41 miles) SW of Liberia

For a time this was the epicenter of Costa Rica's beach tourism. Today it lives, in many senses, in the shadow of Tamarindo to the south and the Papagayo peninsula to the north. However, this area still has numerous charms and attractions.

Playa Conchal ★★ is the first in a string of beaches stretching north along this coast. This beach is almost entirely backed by the massive Paradisus Playa Conchal resort and Reserva Conchal condominium complex. The unique beach here was once made up primarily of soft crushed shells. Nearly every place you could walk, turn, or lay down your towel was a shell-collectors' heaven. Unfortunately, as Conchal has developed and its popularity spread, unscrupulous

Playa Conchal.

builders have brought in dump trucks to haul away the namesake seashells for landscaping and construction, and the impact is noticeable.

Just beyond Playa Conchal to the north, you'll come to **Playa Brasilito,** a tiny beach town and one of the few real villages in the area. The soccer field is the center of the village, and around its edges you'll find a couple of little *pulperías* (general stores). There's a long stretch of beach, and though it's of gray sand, it still has a quiet, undiscovered feel to it.

Playa Flamingo ★★ is in my opinion the prettiest beach in the region. A long, broad stretch of pinkish white sand, it is located on a long spit of land that forms part of Potrero Bay. At the northern end of the beach is a high rock outcropping upon which most of Playa Flamingo's hotels and vacation homes are built. There are great views from this rocky hill.

If you continue along the road from Brasilito without taking the turn for Playa Flamingo, you'll come to **Playa Potrero.** The sand here is a brownish gray, but the beach is long, clean, deserted, and very protected for swimming. You can see the hotels of Playa Flamingo across the bay. Drive a little farther north and you'll find the still-underdeveloped beaches of **Playa La Penca ★** and, finally, **Playa Pan de Azúcar ★**, or **Sugar Beach.**

Essentials

GETTING THERE & DEPARTING By Plane: The nearest airport with regularly scheduled flights is in Tamarindo (see "Essentials," earlier in this chapter), although it is also possible to fly into Liberia (p. 194). From either of these places, you can arrange for a taxi to drive you to any of these beaches. Playas Brasilito and Conchal are about 25 minutes from Tamarindo and 40 minutes from Liberia (add about 5 min. for Flamingo and 10 min. for Potrero). A taxi from Tamarindo should cost around $30 to $45, and between $40 and $60 from Liberia.

By Car: There are two major routes to the beaches. The most direct is by way of the La Amistad Bridge over the Tempisque River. Take the Interamerican Highway west from San José. Forty-seven kilometers (29 miles) past the turnoff for Puntarenas, you'll see signs for the turnoff to the bridge. After crossing the Tempisque River, follow the signs for Nicoya, continuing north to Santa Cruz. About 16km (10 miles) north of Santa Cruz, just before the village of Belén, take the turnoff for playas Flamingo, Brasilito, and Potrero. After another 20km (12 miles), at the town of Huacas, take the right fork to reach these beaches. The drive takes about 4½ hours.

Alternatively, you can drive here via Liberia. When you reach Liberia, turn west and follow the signs for Santa Cruz and the various beaches. Just beyond the town of Belén, take the turnoff for playas Flamingo, Brasilito, and Potrero, and continue following the directions given above. This route takes around 5 hours.

By Bus: Tralapa express buses (☎2221-7202 in San José, or 2654-4203 in Flamingo) leave San José daily at 8 and 10:30am and 3pm from Calle 20 between avenidas 3 and 5, stopping at playas Brasilito, Flamingo, and Potrero, in that order. The ride takes around 5½ hours. A one-way ticket costs $7.

Alternatively, the same company's buses to Santa Cruz (☎2680-0392) connect with one of the several buses from Santa Cruz to Playa Potrero. Buses depart San José for Santa Cruz roughly every 2 hours between 7am and 6pm from Calle 20 between avenidas 3 and 5. Trip duration is around 4 hours; the fare is $5.80. From Santa Cruz, the ride is about 90 minutes; the fare is $2.

Gray Line (☎2220-2126; www.graylinecostarica.com) has a daily bus that leaves San José for Playa Flamingo at 7am. The fare is $35. **Interbus** (☎2283-5573; www.interbusonline.com) has two daily buses that leave San José for Playa Flamingo at 7:30am and 2:30pm. The fare is $39. Both companies will pick you up at most San José–area hotels.

Express buses depart **Playa Potrero** for San José at 3 and 9am and 2pm, stopping a few minutes later in playas Flamingo and Brasilito. Ask at your hotel where to catch the bus. Buses to **Santa Cruz** leave Potrero at regular intervals throughout the day and take about 90 minutes. If you're heading north toward Liberia, get off the bus at Belén and wait for a bus going north. Buses leave Santa Cruz for San José roughly every hour between 6am and 6pm.

GETTING AROUND Economy Rent A Car (☎2654-4543) has an office in Playa Flamingo.

ORIENTATION The pavement ends just beyond Playa Conchal as you leave the small village of Brasilito. The rest of these beaches are strung out over several kilometers of rough dirt roads. Playa Flamingo is by far the most developed town in this region. There's a small collection of shops in a couple of minimalls at the crossroads in the center of Playa Flamingo. Here you'll find a branch of **Banco de Costa Rica,** as well as the **Santa Fe Pharmacy and Medical Center** (☎2654-9000).

Fun on & off the Beach

Playa Flamingo ★★ is a long and beautiful stretch of soft white sand, although the surf can sometimes get a bit rough here. There isn't much shade on the

Playa Flamingo.

beach, so be sure to use plenty of sunscreen and bring an umbrella if you can. If you're not staying here, there are parking spots all along the beach road where you can park your car for the day—although remember not to leave anything of value inside.

Playa Potrero has the gentlest surf and, therefore, is the best swimming beach. However, the beach is made up of hard-packed dark sand that is much less appealing than that found at other spots mentioned here. The water at **Playa Brasilito** is often fairly calm, which makes it another good swimming choice.

Playa Conchal ★★, which is legendary for its crushed seashells, is also stunningly beautiful, but the drop-off is quite steep, making it notorious for its strong riptides. My favorites for a full day of swimming and sunbathing are **Playa La Penca ★★** and **Playa Pan de Azúcar ★★**, both of which are north of Playa Potrero.

Tip: All beaches in Costa Rica are public property. But the land behind the beaches is not, and the Meliá company owns almost all of it in Playa Conchal, so the only public access is along the soft-sand road that follows the beach south from Brasilito. Before the road reaches Conchal, you'll have to ford a small river and then climb a steep, rocky hill, so four-wheel-drive is recommended.

GOLF The **Paradisus Playa Conchal ★★** (☎2654-4123) is home to an excellent golf course featuring a few wonderful views of the ocean. This Robert Trent Jones–designed resort course is open to the walk-in public from neighboring hotels and resorts. It costs $200 in greens fees for as many rounds as you can squeeze into 1 day, including a cart. If you tee off after 1pm, the price drops to $160.

HORSEBACK RIDING You can arrange a horseback ride with the **Flamingo Equestrian Center** (☎2654-4089), **Casagua Horses** (☎2653-8041), or **Brasilito Excursions** (☎2654-4237). This latter place works out of the Hotel Brasilito. Depending on the size of your group, it should cost between $25 and $40 per person per hour.

LEARN THE LANGUAGE The **Centro Panamericano de Idiomas** (☎2654-5002; www.cpi-edu.com), which has schools in San José and Monteverde,

The Flamingo marina, usually a hub for sportfishing charters, has been closed down by the municipal and county authorities for operating without proper permits (it had been built and set up a decade or so ago). Currently it's tied up in a slow process of public bidding, and there's been no word on when or if it will reopen. The harbor just outside the marina breakwall is big, deep, and well protected; all boats are just working from there and are kept at anchor instead of at dock.

has a branch in Flamingo, across from the Flamingo Marina, facing Potrero Bay. A 1-week course with 4 hours of classes per day, including a home stay, costs $315. Longer course options are available.

OTHER ADVENTURE TOURS You can sign up for a **sea kayaking or surf trip** with the **Edge Adventure Company.** Alternatively, check in with the tour desk at the **Flamingo Marina Resort Hotel and Club,** which offers a host of tours to other nearby destinations, as well as hiking and rafting trips.

SCUBA DIVING Scuba diving is quite popular here. The **Edge Adventure Company** (☎2654-4946) and **Costa Rica Diving** (☎/fax **2654-4148;** www.costarica-diving.com) both have shops in Flamingo and offer trips to the Catalina and Bat islands for between $80 and $120. Both also offer PADI certification courses, as well as multiday packages. Alternatively, you can check in at the **Flamingo Marina Resort Hotel and Club** (p. 228).

SPORTFISHING & SAILBOAT CHARTERS Although the Flamingo Marina remains in a state of legal limbo and turmoil (see above), you still have plenty of sportfishing and sailboat charter options here. Jim McKee, the former force behind the Flamingo Marina, manages a fleet of boats. Contact him via his company, **Oso Viejo** (☎8827-5533 or 2653-8437; www.flamingo beachcr.com). A full-day fishing excursion costs between $700 and $2,500, depending on the size and quality of the boat, and distance traveled to the fishing grounds. Half-day trips cost between $500 and $700.

If you're looking for a full- or half-day sail or sunset cruise, check in with **Oso Viejo** (see above) to see what boats are available, or ask about the 52-foot cutter *Shannon.* The 52-foot ketch *Samonique III* (☎8388-7870; www.costarica-sailing.com) and the 43-foot catamaran **Seabird Sailing** (☎8381-1060; www.seabirdsailing.com) are two other good options. Prices range from around $50 to $120 per person, depending on the length of the cruise. Multiday trips are also available.

Alternatively, you can contact the **Edge Adventure Company** or the **Flamingo Marina Resort Hotel and Club.**

Where to Stay

If you plan to be here for a while or are coming down with friends or a large family, you might want to consider renting a condo or house. For information and reservations, contact the folks at **Emerald Shores Realty** (☎2654-4554; www. emeraldshoresrealty.net) or **Century 21 Marina Trading Post** (☎2654-4004; www.century21costarica.net).

VERY EXPENSIVE

Paradisus Playa Conchal ★★ This sprawling all-inclusive resort is still the largest in Costa Rica. From the massive open-air reception building down to the free-form swimming pool, everything here is on a grand scale. All rooms are suites and come with either one king-size bed or two double beds in a raised bedroom nook. The bathrooms feature marble tiles, full tubs, and bidets. Each unit has a garden patio or a small balcony. While the rooms are almost exactly the same, the Royal level suites come with butler service and access to a private, adults-only pool. Very few rooms here have ocean views. Unlike most all-inclusives, most of the restaurants are sit-down a la carte affairs, although they are decidedly mediocre. The golf course, with its ponds and wetlands, allows for healthy populations of parrots, roseate spoonbills, and wood storks. Because the hotel owns so much land behind Playa Conchal, guests have almost exclusive access to this crushed-seashell beach.

Playa Conchal (A.P. 499-4005, San Antonio de Belén), Guanacaste. ☎888/336-3542 in the U.S. or 2654-4123. Fax 2654-4181. www.solmelia.com. 406 suites. $319–$443 double; $419–$503 Royal suite; $990 Presidential suite. Rates include all meals, drinks, taxes, a wide range of activities, and use of nonmotorized land and watersports equipment. Golf and spa services extra. AE, MC, V. **Amenities:** 8 restaurants; 3 bars; 2 lounges; casino; babysitting; bike rental; children's programs; concierge; Robert Trent Jones II–designed 18-hole golf course and pro shop; modest exercise facilities and spa; massive free-form pool w/several Jacuzzis, another large outdoor pool for Royal Level suites; room service; smoke-free rooms; 4 lighted tennis courts; watersports equipment rental. In room: A/C, TV, hair dryer, minibar, free Wi-Fi.

EXPENSIVE

Bahía del Sol ★ This small resort hotel sits right on the water's edge at the heart of Playa Potrero. The rooms are all large and feature contemporary decor with bright primary colors at every turn, although the furnishings are rather sparse. All have either a private balcony or shared veranda, and most of these are strung with hammocks. They also have fully equipped studio and two-bedroom apartments that are a good bet for longer stays. The midsize pool is set in a small grassy lawn, just beyond the beach. The pool features a Jacuzzi above it, whose water cascades down a faux-waterfall into it. The large open-air restaurant serves fresh seafood and international fare, and offers wonderful views of Potrero Bay.

Playa Potrero, Guanacaste. ☎866/223-2463 in the U.S. and Canada, or 2654-4671 in Costa Rica. Fax 2654-5182. www.bahiadelsolhotel.com. 28 units. $165–$195 double; $250–$375 suite. Rates include full breakfast. AE, MC, V. **Amenities:** Restaurant; bar; Jacuzzi; large pool; room service; all rooms smoke-free; small spa. In room: A/C, TV, hair dryer.

Flamingo Beach Resort Located right across the road from the best section of beach at Playa Flamingo, this large resort boasts an enviable location fronting a gorgeous section of beach. The hotel is constructed in a horseshoe shape around a large pool and opens out onto the ocean. Half of the rooms have clear views of the ocean across a narrow dirt road. I definitely prefer the pool and oceanview rooms. Others, which are termed "mountain view" rooms, aren't quite as desirable. All the rooms are clean and cool, with tile floors and comfortable bathrooms. The suites are larger and better equipped, with full-size refrigerators, kitchenettes, and 27-inch television sets.

Playa Flamingo, Guanacaste. ☎2654-4444. Fax 2654-4060. www.resortflamingobeach.com. 120 units. $119–$165 double; $279–$399 suite. Rates include full breakfast. AE, MC, V. **Amenities:** 2 restaurants; 2 bars; casino; exercise room; large pool; room service; small spa; outdoor lighted tennis court. *In room:* A/C, TV, minifridge, hair dryer, kitchenette (in suites).

Hotel Sugar Beach ★★ Hotel Sugar Beach is on a beautiful, semiprivate salt-and-pepper beach about a 10-minute drive north of Playa Potrero along a rough dirt road. It's the only hotel in the immediate area, and that's what gives it most of its charm, in my opinion—lots of seclusion and privacy. The beach is on a small cove surrounded by rocky hills. Nature lovers will be thrilled to find that howler monkeys and iguanas abound on the grounds. Snorkelers should be happy here too; this cove has some good snorkeling in the dry season. My favorite rooms are the oceanfront standard rooms, which have great views and easy access to the beach. However, the deluxe rooms and suites are larger and more luxurious, and some have excellent ocean views from their private balconies. If you don't land one of the rooms with a sea view, the main lodge and restaurant have commanding views from a hillside perch.

Playa Pan de Azúcar (A.P. 90, Santa Cruz), Guanacaste. ☎2654-4242. Fax 2654-4239. www.sugar-beach.com. 30 units. $125–$155 double; $195–350 suite; $475–$660 villa. Rates include breakfast. AE, MC, V. **Amenities:** Restaurant; bar; small kidney-shape pool set on the hillside; watersports equipment rental. *In room:* A/C, TV, minifridge.

MODERATE

Flamingo Marina Resort Hotel and Club ★ Uphill from the beach, the Flamingo Marina Hotel is a midsize resort with a good mix of facilities and amenities. The entire complex has received steady upkeep and makeovers over the years. Most rooms have white tile floors, bright bedspreads, and lots of light. The suites have leather couches and a wet bar in the seating area, as well as private whirlpool tubs. Condo units have full kitchenettes. All the rooms have patios or balconies, and most have pretty good bay views. This place caters to fishermen and scuba divers, and a host of tours and adventures are offered. While not directly on the beach (like Flamingo Beach Resort or Sugar Beach, see above), the hotel is close to Flamingo's principal beach, as well as all of the town's restaurants and nightlife options.

Playa Flamingo (A.P. 321-1002, San José), Guanacaste. ☎800/276-7501 in the U.S. and Canada, or 2654-4141. Fax 2654-4035. www.flamingomarina.com. 45 units, 44 apts. $119 double; $169–$189 suite; $209–$280 apt. AE, DC, MC, V. **Amenities:** Restaurant; snack bar; bar; exercise room; Jacuzzi; 4 small pools; tennis court; watersports equipment rental. *In room:* A/C, TV, free Wi-Fi, kitchenette (in condos).

INEXPENSIVE

A string of inexpensive cabinas line the main road leading into Brasilito, just before you hit the beach. It's also possible to camp on playas Potrero and Brasilito.

At the former, contact **Maiyra's** (☏**2654-4213**); at the latter, try **Camping Brasilito** (☏**2654-4452**). Both of these places offer some budget rooms as well. Each charges around $8 to $10 per person to make camp and use the basic bathroom facilities or around $10 to $15 per person to stay in a rustic room.

Hotel Brasilito ☝ This hotel, just across a sand road from the beach, offers pretty basic and small rooms that are nonetheless quite clean and well maintained. There's also a bar and a big open-air restaurant that is excellent. Even with Playa Brasilito's glut of budget options, this is one of the best values in town and is the closest to the water. The best rooms have nice balconies with ocean views, and air-conditioning. The hotel rents snorkeling equipment, kayaks, body boards, and horses and can arrange a variety of tours.

Playa Brasilito, Santa Cruz, Guanacaste. ☏**2654-4237**. Fax 2654-4247. www.brasilito.com. 15 units. $39–$56 double. Rates include taxes. V. **Amenities:** Restaurant; watersports equipment rental. *In room:* No phone, free Wi-Fi.

Where to Dine

In addition to the places listed below, you'll find good fresh seafood and international fare at the **Happy Snapper** (☏**2654-4413**) in Brasilito. Out in Playa Potrero, **El Castillo** (☏**2654-4271**) is the most happening spot, with a wideranging menu of bar food and main courses.

Camarón Dorado 🍴 SEAFOOD With a series of tables and kerosene torches set right in the sand just steps from the crashing surf, this is one of the most perfectly placed beach restaurants in the country. There are more tables in a simple, open-air dining room, for those who don't want sand in their shoes. The service is semiformal, and at times can be anything from lax to rude. The seafood is fresh, well-prepared, and reasonably priced. When I asked to see the wine list, two waiters came over carrying about 12 different bottles between them, held precariously between the straining fingers of each hand.

Playa Brasilito. ☏**2654-4028.** Reservations recommended in high season. Main courses $6–$23. MC, V. Daily 11am–10pm.

Marie's ★ COSTA RICAN/SEAFOOD This long-standing local restaurant is a large open-air affair, with a soaring thatch roof and tall, thick columns all around. The menu has grown steadily over the years, although the best option here is always some simply prepared fresh fish, chicken, or meat. Check the blackboard for the daily specials, which usually highlight the freshest catch, such as mahi-mahi *(dorado)*, marlin, and red snapper. You'll also find such Tico favorites as *casados* (rice-and-bean dish), rotisserie chicken, and *ceviche,* as well as burritos and quesadillas.

Playa Flamingo. ☏**2654-4136.** Reservations recommended for dinner during the high season. Sandwiches $3.25–$6; main courses $7.50–$25. V. Daily 6:30am–9:30pm.

Mar y Sol ★★ 🍴 INTERNATIONAL/SEAFOOD Seventh-generation Catalan chef Alain Taulere has prepared food for regular folk and royalty. For visitors to his hilltop restaurant in Flamingo Beach, he offers a small, well-executed, and pricey selection of fresh seafood and meats. The ambience is casually formal, with the open-air main dining room dimly lit by old-fashioned lamp posts and covered by a thatch roof. Along with a surf-and-turf combo featuring filet

A sailboat cruise near Tamarindo.

mignon and either lobster tails or jumbo shrimp, menu highlights include rich and creamy lobster bisque, and a hearty bouillabaisse. I recommend the duck served with passion-fruit-cognac sauce. For starters, try the escargot in puff pastry. Call in advance for free transportation from and back to your hotel.

Playa Flamingo. ☎2654-4151. Reservations recommended for dinner in high season. Main courses $17–$39. AE, DC, MC, V. Nov–Apr daily 10am–3:30pm and 5–10pm; May–Aug daily 2–10pm. Closed Sept–Oct.

Outback Jack's Australian Roadkill Grill & Beach Bar ☺ INTERNA-TIONAL The menu here is almost as long, eclectic, and varied as the name. Still, at heart, this is a simple beachside bar and grill. You can get nachos, quesadillas, and spicy wings, as well as fresh seafood in a variety of preparations. For something more adventurous, try the grilled tuna with an eggplant *caponata,* served over some spaghetti with pesto. There's even a full children's menu, which is hard to come by in these parts. A few tables are set in the sand in front of the joint, facing the beach and Brasilito bay. Inside, there's a thatched Tiki-style bar and some large-screen televisions for sporting events, and a host of heavy wooden tables set on a polished concrete floor. The whole restaurant is a free Wi-Fi hot spot.

Playa Brasilito. ☎2654-5463. Main courses $6–$14. AE, MC, V. Daily 11am–10pm.

Playa Flamingo After Dark

With both a disco and casino, **Amberes,** which is located just slightly up the hill at the north end of town, is the undisputed hot spot in this area; however, there's also a casino at the **Flamingo Beach Resort** (see above). Over in Brasilito, you might also see if there's any live music or sporting events on the televisions at the **Happy Snapper** (see above) or **Outback Jack's Australian Roadkill Grill & Beach Bar** (see above). In Playa Potrero, locals and tourists alike gather at **El Castillo,** which sometimes has live bands. All of the other beaches and towns here are rather quiet.

PLAYA TAMARINDO ★
& PLAYA GRANDE ★★

295km (183 miles) NW of San José; 73km (45 miles) SW of Liberia

Tamarindo is the biggest boomtown in Guanacaste—and personally, I think the boom went a bit too far, a bit too fast. The main road into Tamarindo is a helter-skelter jumble of strip malls, surf shops, hotels, and restaurants. Ongoing development is spreading up the hills inland from the beach and south beyond Punta Langosta. None of it seems regulated or particularly planned out.

Still, the wide range of accommodations, abundant restaurants, and active nightlife, along with very dependable surf have established Tamarindo as one of the most popular beaches on this coast. The beautiful beach here is a long, wide swath of white sand that curves gently from one rocky headland to another. Fishing boats bob at their moorings and brown pelicans fish just beyond the breakers.

A sandy islet off the southern end of the beach makes a great destination if you're a strong swimmer; if you're not, it makes a great foreground for sunsets. Tamarindo is very popular with surfers, who ply the break right here or use the town as a jumping-off place for beach and point breaks at playas Grande, Langosta, Avellanas, and Negra.

Just to the north of Tamarindo lies **Playa Grande,** one of the principal nesting sites for the giant leatherback turtle, the largest turtle in the world. This beach is often too rough for swimming, but the well-formed and consis-

Surfing in Tamarindo.

tent beach break is very popular with surfers. I almost hate to mention places to stay in Playa Grande because the steady influx of tourists and development has apparently doomed it as a turtle-nesting site.

Behind all the beaches in this area are low, dry hills that can be a dreary brown in the dry season but that instantly turn green with the first brief showers of the rainy season.

Essentials

GETTING THERE & DEPARTING **By Plane: Sansa** (☎877/767-2672 in the U.S. and Canada, or 2290-4100 in Costa Rica; www.flysansa.com) has seven daily flights to Tamarindo from San José's Juan Santamaría International Airport, with the first flight leaving at 6am and the last flight departing at 1:50pm. The flight takes 55 minutes. The fare is $115 each way. During the high season, a later afternoon flight is added.

Nature Air (☎800/235-9272 in the U.S. and Canada, or 2299-6000; www.natureair.com) flies to Tamarindo daily at 6:30, 10, and 10:10am, and 12:25 and 4:30pm from Tobías Bolaños International Airport in Pavas. The fare is $126 each way. The flight takes 55 minutes. Nature Air also has connections between Tamarindo and Arenal, Liberia, and Quepos.

Whether you arrive on Sansa or Nature Air, a couple of cabs or minivans are always waiting for arriving flights. It costs $3 to $6 for the ride into town.

Sansa flights leave Tamarindo for San José between 7am and 3pm. Nature Air flights leave for San José at 7:25 and 11:25am, and 2:25 and 4:35pm.

If you're flying into Liberia, a taxi should cost around $50 to $70. Alternately, you can use **Tamarindo Shuttle** (☎2653-1326; www. tamarindoshuttle.com), which charges $18 per person one-way.

By Car: The most direct route is by way of the La Amistad bridge. Take the Interamerican Highway west from San José. Forty-seven kilometers (29 miles) past the turnoff for Puntarenas, you'll see signs for the turnoff to the bridge. After crossing the river, follow the signs for Nicoya and Santa Cruz. Continue north out of Santa Cruz, until just before the village of Belén, where you will find the turnoff for Tamarindo. In another 20km (12 miles) take the left fork for Playa Tamarindo at Huacas and continue on until the village of Villareal, where you make your final turn into Tamarindo. The trip should take around 4½ hours.

You can save a little time, especially in the dry season, by taking a more direct but rougher route: You turn left just after passing the main intersection for Santa Cruz at the turnoff for playas Junquillal and Ostional. The road is paved until the tiny village of Veintesiete de Abril. From here, it's about 20km (12 miles) on a rough dirt road until the village of Villareal, where you make your final turn into Tamarindo.

Alternatively, you can drive here via Liberia. When you reach Liberia, turn west and follow the signs for Santa Cruz and the various beaches. Just beyond the town of Belén, take the turnoff for playas Flamingo, Brasilito, and Tamarindo, and then follow the directions for the second option above. This route takes around 5½ hours.

By Bus: Tracopa-Alfaro express buses (☎2222-2160) leave San José daily for Tamarindo at 8:30 and 11:30am and 3:30pm, departing from Calle 14 between avenidas 3 and 5. **Tralapa** (☎2221-7202) also has one daily direct bus to Tamarindo leaving at 4pm from their main terminal at Calle 20 between avenidas 3 and 5. The trip takes 5 hours, and the one-way fare is around $6.50.

Alternatively, you can catch a bus to Santa Cruz from either of the above bus companies. Buses leave both stations for Santa Cruz roughly every 2 hours between 6am and 6pm. The trip's duration is 4 hours; the one-way fare is around $5.80. Buses leave Santa Cruz (☎2680-0392) for Tamarindo roughly every 1½ hours between 6am and 6pm; the one-way fare is $1.80.

Gray Line (☎2220-2126; www.graylinecostarica.com) has a daily bus that leaves San José for Tamarindo at 8am. The fare is $35. **Interbus** (☎2283-5573; www.interbus

Yo Quiero Hablar Español

If you want to try an intensive immersion program or just brush up on your rusty high school Spanish, check in with the folks at **Wayra Instituto de Español** (☎/fax 2653-0359; www.spanish-wayra.co.cr). This place is located up a side street from the dirt road that connects Tamarindo to Playa Langosta.

Tamarindo

Isla Capitán

To Airport

Bahía Tamarindo

Punta San Francisco

Playa Tamarindo

Playa Langosta

Calle Principal

Calle Pasatiempo

Calle Langosta

Langosta Loop

NICARAGUA
CARIBBEAN SEA
★ SAN JOSÉ
Tamarindo
PACIFIC OCEAN
PANAMA

1/4 mi
1/4 km

DINING

Cala Moresco **4**
Carolina's Restaurant & Grill **8**
Dragonfly Bar & Grill **11**
Jaw's **27**
La Caletta **4**
La Laguna del Cocodrilo Bistro **27**
Mama's Deli **19**
Noguí's Café **16**
Season's by Shlomy **9**
Walter's **17**

NIGHTLIFE

Aqua **25**
Bar 1 **13**
Barceló Playa Langosta Casino **1**
Crazy Monkey Bar **26**
Jazz Casino **21**
Sharky's **15**
Voodoo Lounge **14**

ACCOMMODATIONS

15 Love Bed & Breakfast **31**
Best Western Tamarindo Vista Villas **26**
Cabinas Marielos **24**
El Diriá **20**
Hostal La Botella de Leche **10**
Hotel Arco Iris **9**
Hotel and Villas Cala Luna **4**
Hotel Capitan Suizo **5**

(cont.)

Hotel El Jardin del Eden **22**
Hotel Pasatiempo **12**
Hotel Pueblo Dorado **29**
Hotel Zully Mar **18**
Sueño del Mar **3**
Tito's Camping **6**
Tsunami Backpackers **28**
Villa Alegre **2**

ATTRACTIONS

Agua Rica Diving Center **21**
Hightide Adventures **14**
Iguana Surf **23**
Papagayo Excursions **21**
Tamarindo Tennis Club **30**
Wayra Instituto de Español **7**

233

online.com) has two daily buses that leave San José for Tamarindo at 7am and 2pm. The fare is $39. Both companies will pick you up at most San José–area hotels.

Direct buses leave Tamarindo for San José daily at 3:30 and 5:45am and 2 and 4pm. Buses to Santa Cruz leave roughly every 1½ hours between 6am and 6pm. In Santa Cruz you can transfer to one of the frequent San José buses.

ORIENTATION The road leading into town runs parallel to the beach and ends in a small cul-de-sac just past Zully Mar. A couple of side roads off this main road lead farther on, to playa Langosta. You'll find several of the newer hotels mentioned below off these side roads. To reach playas Avellanas, Negra, and Junquillal, you have to first head out of town and take the road toward Santa Cruz.

FAST FACTS The local **police** can be reached at ☎**2653-0283.** In the event of a medical emergency, call **Pacific Emergencies** (☎**8378-8265**).

There's a **Banco Nacional** branch at the little mall across from El Diria, and a branch of the **Banco de Costa Rica** in the Plaza Conchal mall. There are also several Internet cafes and a couple of pharmacies in town. You'll find the **Mariposa Laundry** (no phone) just past the turnoff for Playa Langosta.

GETTING AROUND Adobe (☎2653-0031), Alamo (☎2653-0727), Budget (☎2436-2000), Economy (☎2653-0752), Europcar (☎2653-1809), Hertz (☎2653-1358), Payless (☎2653-0015), and Thrifty (☎2653-0829) have rental car offices in Tamarindo.

The town itself is very compact and you should be able to walk most places. Aside from that, a large fleet of taxis are usually cruising around town, or hanging out at principal intersections and meeting points. If you need to, you can call a **taxi** at ☎**2653-0751,** 8836-7783, or 2653-0586.

Fun on & off the Beach

Tamarindo is a long, white-sand beach. Still, you have to be careful when and where you swim. The calmest water and best swimming are always down at the far southern end of the beach, toward Punta Langosta. Much of the sea just off the busiest part of the town is best for surfing. When there's any swell, you'll find scores of surfers in the water here. Be careful: There are rocks just offshore in several places, some of which are exposed only at low tide. An encounter with one of these rocks could be nasty, especially if you're bodysurfing. I also advise that you avoid swimming near the estuary mouth, where the currents can carry you out away from the beach.

BIKING Bikes are available for rent at several locations in Tamarindo. Check around; you'll probably find your best bikes at the **Blue Trax Bike Shop ★** (☎2653-1705), which rents high-end Trek and Specialized mountain bikes for around $20 per day. These folks also offer guided mountain-bike tours and excursions.

FOUR-WHEELING Hightide Adventures (☎2653-0108; www.tamarindo adventures.net) offers a variety of guided ATV tours that range in duration from 1 to 3 hours and in price from $78 to $150 per person. This company

Hacienda Pinilla golf course.

also rents dirt bikes, snorkel equipment, surf and boogie boards, and jet skis and offers a full menu of other guided tours around the region. Similar ATV tours are offered by **Fourtrax Adventures** (☎2653-4040; www.fourtrax adventure.com), which charges $95 for its 3-hour outing.

Another alternative is to sign up for a tour with **Off Road Costa Rica** (☎2653-1969; www.offroadcostarica.com), which employs a fleet of open-air restored Toyota Land Cruisers, and head into the backcountry and hinterlands. A wide range of outings are offered, from a couple of hours to several days. The jeeps are taken through rivers, mud, and forests and over deserted stretches of beach. Their standard half-day tour costs $75 person, but a wide range of custom tours can be arranged.

GOLF Hacienda Pinilla ★★ (☎2680-7000; www.haciendapinilla.com) is a beautiful 18-hole links-style course located south of Tamarindo. The course is currently accepting golfers staying at all of the hotels around the area, with advance reservation. Greens fees run around $185 for 18 holes, including a cart. Many folks staying in Tamarindo also play at the **Paradisus Playa Conchal** ★★, an excellent resort course (p. 227).

HORSEBACK RIDING Although some will be disappointed, I think it's a very good thing that horses are no longer allowed on the beach. Fortunately, you'll find plenty of opportunities to ride in the hills and forests around Tamarindo. You can go riding with **Casagua Horses** ★ (☎2653-8041), **Hightide Adventures** (☎2653-0108; www.tamarindoadventures.net), **Iguana Surf** (☎2653-0148; www.iguanasurf.net), or **Papagayo Excursions** (☎2653-0254). Rates for horse rental, with a guide, are around $30 to $65 per hour.

SAILBOAT CHARTERS There are several boats offering cruises offshore from Tamarindo; the 50-foot schooner *Lemuria* (☎8831-8875; www.tamarindosailing.com), and the 40-foot catamaran *Blue Dolphin* (☎2653-0446; www.sail bluedolphin.com) are both good choices. Options range from sunset cruises to weeklong trips out to Isla del Coco. A half-day snorkel or shorter sunset cruise should cost $55 to $75 per person, and a full day should run between $80 and $130 per person. This usually includes an open bar and snacks on the half-day and sunset cruises, and all of that plus lunch on the full-day trip.

SCUBA DIVING If you want to do any scuba diving or snorkeling while you're here, check in with **Agua Rica Diving Center ★** (☎2653-0094; www. aguarica.net). These folks are the best and longest running operators in Tamarindo, and have a full-service dive shop. They offer day trips, multiday dive cruises, and standard resort and full-certification courses.

SPORTFISHING A host of captains offer anglers a chance to go after the "big ones" that abound in the waters offshore here. From the Tamarindo estuary, it takes only 20 minutes to reach the edge of the continental shelf, where the waters are filled with mostly marlin and sailfish. Although fishing is good all year, the peak season for billfish is between mid-April and August. You can contact **Tamarindo Sportfishing** (☎2653-0090; www. tamarindosportfishing.com), **Capullo Sportfishing** (☎2653-0048; www. capullo.com), or **Osprey Sportfishing** (☎2653-0162; www.osprey-sport fishing.com).

TENNIS You can rent court time and equipment at the **Tamarindo Tennis Club** (☎2653-0898), which features two lighted outdoor courts on the back road on the way to the Hotel El Jardín del Edén. It is open daily from 7:30am to 9pm, and court time runs $10 per hour. You can also play at **Hacienda Pinilla** (see above) for $5 per hour during the day, and $10 per hour at night.

TOURS GALORE **Hightide Adventures, Papagayo Excursions,** and **Iguana Surf** (see above for all) all offer a host of tour and activity options. Papagayo Excursions probably offers the widest selection of full- and multiday trips, including outboard or kayak tours through the nearby estuary and mangroves, excursions to Santa Cruz and Guaitíl, raft floats on the Corobicí River, and tours to Palo Verde and Rincón de la Vieja national parks. Rates run between $30 and $140, depending on the length of the tour and group size.

There's no longer a canopy tour available right in Tamarindo, but the **Santa Rosa Canopy Tour** (☎2653-0926) and **Cartagena Canopy Tour** (☎2675-0801) are nearby. Both charge $35 per person and include transportation from Tamarindo. Of these two, I recommend the Cartagena tour, which has a much more lush forest setting, but I think your best bet is to take a day trip to Hacienda Guachipelin (p. 203) and do the "Canyon Tour" there.

WATCHING NESTING SEA TURTLES On nearby **Playa Grande,** leatherback sea turtles nest between early October and mid-February. The turtles come ashore to lay their eggs only at night. During the nesting season, you'll be inundated with opportunities to sign up for nightly tours, which usually cost $35 to $50 per person. No flash photography or flashlights are allowed because any sort of light can confuse the turtles and prevent them from laying their eggs; guides must use red-tinted flashlights.

Note: Turtle nesting is a natural, unpredictable, and increasingly rare event. Moreover, things have gotten worse here in recent years. All indications are that excessive building and lighting close to the beach are the culprits. Even during heavy nesting years you sometimes have to wait your turn for hours, hike quite a way, and even accept the possibility that no nesting mothers will be spotted that evening.

If your hotel can't set it up for you, you'll see signs all over town offering tours. Make sure you go with someone licensed and reputable.

Leatherback turtle hatchling in Tamarindo Bay.

Do-it-yourselfers can drive over to Playa Grande and book a $25 tour directly with the **National Parks Service** (☎2653-0470). The Parks Service operates out of a small shack just before the beach, across from the hotel Las Tortugas. It opens each evening at around 6pm to begin taking reservations. They sometimes answer their phone during the day, and it's best to make a reservation in advance because only a limited number of people are allowed on the beach at one time. Spots fill up fast, and if you don't have a reservation, you may have to wait until really late, or you may not be able to go out onto the beach.

WATERSPORTS If you want to try snorkeling, surfing, or sea kayaking while in Tamarindo, **Iguana Surf** and **Hightide Adventures** (see above) both rent snorkeling equipment, boogie boards, sea kayaks, and surfboards. They have half-day and hourly rates for many of these items.

If you want to learn to catch a wave while in Tamarindo, check in with the **Tamarindo Surf School** (☎2653-0923; www.tamarindosurfschool.com), **Banana Surf Club** (☎2653-1270; www.bananasurfclub.com), or **Witch's Rock Surf Camp** ★ (☎2653-1262; www.witchsrocksurfcamp.com).

WELLNESS CENTERS Several of the higher-end hotels have their own spas, and most hotels can call you a massage therapist. But if you're looking for a local day spa experience, try **Domaniti's Day Spa** (☎2653-0995), which has a wide range of treatments and packages, from facials and pedicures to two-therapist Balinese-style massages.

Shopping

Tamarindo is awash in souvenir stands, art galleries, jewelry stores, and clothing boutiques. The modern **Garden Plaza** shopping center is located near the entrance to town, and has several high-end shops, as well as a massive and modern **Automercado** supermarket.

Pretty Pots

The lack of any long-standing local arts and crafts tradition across Costa Rica is often lamented. One of the outstanding exceptions to this rule is the small village of Guaitíl, located on the outskirts of the provincial capital of Santa Cruz. The small central plaza—actually a soccer field—of this village is ringed with craft shops and artisan stands selling a wide range of ceramic wares. Most are low-fired relatively soft clay pieces, with traditional Chorotega indigenous design motifs. All of the local tour agencies offer day trips to Guaitíl, or you can drive there yourself, by heading first to Santa Cruz, and then taking the well-marked turnoff for Guaitíl, just south of the city, on the road to Nicoya.

Where to Stay

IN TOWN

In addition to the hotels listed below, Tamarindo and Playa Grande have a wide range of beach houses and condos for rent by the night, the week, or the month. For more information on this option, check out **Remax Tamarindo** (☎**2653-0073;** www.remax-oceansurf-cr.com) or **Century 21** (☎**866/978-4492** in the U.S. and Canada, or 2653-0030 in Costa Rica; www.costarica1realestate.com).

Very Expensive

Hotel and Villas Cala Luna ★★ If you're looking for serious luxury in Tamarindo, stay in one of the two- or three-bedroom villas here. The living rooms are huge, with high-peaked ceilings, couches, tables and chairs, satellite televisions, and complete sound systems. The large kitchens are fully equipped and come with fancy cappuccino machines. You even get a washer-dryer. If this isn't enough, each villa has its own private swimming pool. Bedrooms are spacious and elegant, with either a king-size bed or two double beds. Everything is done in soft pastels with hand-painted accents, and the red-tile roofs and Mexican tile floors add a sense of tropical elegance. Rooms in the hotel are similarly well done, with their own terraces, but you'll have to share the hotel's main swimming pool with the rest of the guests. The hotel isn't right on the beach; you have to cross the street and walk a short path to reach the ocean.

Playa Langosta, Guanacaste. ☎**800/503-5202** in the U.S. and Canada, or 2653-0214 in Costa Rica. Fax 2653-0213. www.calaluna.com. 20 units, 18 villas. $185 double; $370–$470 villa. Rates for rooms, but not villas, include continental breakfast. AE, MC, V. **Amenities:** 2 restaurants; bar; babysitting; bike rental; large free-form pool w/poolside bar; room service; watersports equipment rental. *In room:* A/C, TV, hair dryer, minibar, free Wi-Fi.

Expensive

In addition to the places listed below, tennis lovers (and anyone else) might want to check out the new **15 Love Bed & Breakfast** (☎**2653-0898;** www.15love bedandbreakfast.com), which is attached to the Tamarindo Tennis Club (see above).

El Diriá ★ This is Tamarindo's largest beachfront resort. Wedged into a narrow piece of land planted with tropical gardens and palm trees, the Diriá has an enviable spot, smack-dab in the middle of Tamarindo's long beach. The rooms in the main building are done in pastel colors with red-tile floors. Some have separate seating areas, and all come with a small bathroom. I especially recommend the second- and third-floor "sunset deluxe" rooms, which feature oceanview private balconies. However, some rooms are across the street from the beach, so be sure you know what type of room you are booking when you reserve. The hotel has several swimming pools, as well as a lighted outdoor tennis court. They also have a large, open-air amphitheater that they use for weddings, private parties, and the occasional public concert, as well as a golf driving range on the outskirts of town.

Playa Tamarindo (A.P. 476-1007, San José), Guanacaste. ☎**866/603-4742** in the U.S. and Canada, or 2653-0031 in Costa Rica. Fax 2653-0848. www.tamarindodiria.com. 182 units. $157–$198 double. Rates include breakfast buffet. AE, MC, V. **Amenities:** 2 restaurants; 2 bars; 3 pools; watersports equipment rental. *In room:* A/C, TV, hair dryer, minibar (in some), free Wi-Fi.

Hotel Capitán Suizo ★★ ☺ This well-appointed beachfront hotel sits on the quiet southern end of Tamarindo. The rooms are housed in a series of two-story buildings. The lower rooms have air-conditioning and private patios; the upper units have plenty of cross ventilation, ceiling fans, and cozy balconies. All have large bathrooms and sitting rooms with fold-down futon couches. In effect, all the rooms are really suites, with separate sitting/living room areas. The spacious bungalows are spread around the shady grounds; these all come with a tub in the bathroom and an inviting outdoor shower among the trees. The hotel's free-form pool is a delight, with tall shade trees all around. The shallow end slopes in gradually, imitating a beach, and there's also a separate children's pool. Perhaps the greatest attribute here is that it's just steps from one of the calmer and more isolated sections of Playa Tamarindo, making it a good family pick.

Playa Tamarindo, Guanacaste. **2653-0353** or 2653-0075. Fax 2653-0292. www.hotelcapitan suizo.com. 22 units, 8 bungalows. $175–$195 double; $235–$275 bungalow; $360 suite. Rates include breakfast buffet. AE, MC, V. **Amenities:** Restaurant; bar; babysitting; small exercise room; midsize pool and children's pool. *In room:* Minifridge.

Hotel El Jardín del Edén It isn't right on the beach, but this is one of the more stylish hotels in Tamarindo. There are splendid views from many of the guest rooms, which are in Mediterranean-style buildings on a hill 136m (446 ft.) from and high above the beach. Almost all have balconies or private terraces with views of the Pacific. Those with large stone-tiled terraces, in particular, give you the sense that you're staying at your own private villa. Steady upkeep and remodeling continue to keep this place a top choice in town.

Playa Tamarindo, Guanacaste. **2653-0137.** Fax 2653-0111. www.jardindeleden.com. 36 units, 2 apts. $135–$185 double; $165–$220 apt or suite. Rates include full breakfast. AE, MC, V. **Amenities:** Restaurant; bar; small exercise room; Jacuzzi; 2 small adjoining pools; room service. *In room:* A/C, TV, hair dryer, minibar.

Sueño del Mar ★ On Playa Langosta, Sueño del Mar has charming little touches and innovative design: four-poster beds made from driftwood; African dolls on the windowsills; Kokopeli candleholders; and open-air showers with sculpted angelfish, hand-painted tiles, and lush tropical plants. Fabrics are from Bali and Guatemala. Somehow all of this works well together, and the requisite chairs, hammocks, and lounges nestled under shade trees right on the beach add the crowning touch. The two casitas have their own kitchens, veranda, and sleeping loft. The honeymoon suite is a spacious second-floor room, with wraparound windows, a delightful open-air shower, and commanding ocean views. The beach right out front is rocky and a bit rough, but it does reveal some nice, quiet tidal pools at low tide; it's one of the better sunset-viewing spots in Costa Rica.

Playa Langosta, Guanacaste. /fax **2653-0284.** www.sueno-del-mar.com. 4 units, 2 casitas. $195 double; $195–$295 suite or casita. Rates include full breakfast. No children 11 and under. MC, V. **Amenities:** Small pool; free use of snorkel equipment and boogie boards; free Wi-Fi. *In room:* A/C, hair dryer, kitchens (in casitas).

Villa Alegre This small bed-and-breakfast on Playa Langosta is a well-located and homey option. The owners' years of globetrotting have inspired them to decorate each room in the theme of a different country. In the main house, Guatemala, Mexico, and the United States are all represented. Of these, Mexico is the most spacious, with a large open-air bathroom and shower. The smallest are Guatemala and the California casita. The latter room is quite small, in fact. Every room has its own private patio, courtyard, or balcony. The villas are spacious and luxurious, with kitchenettes. My favorite is the Japanese unit, with its subtle design touches and great woodwork. The Russian villa and the United States rooms are truly wheelchair accessible and equipped, with ramps and modified bathrooms with handrails. The beach is just a short stroll away through the trees. Breakfasts are delicious and abundant.

Playa Langosta, Guanacaste. ☎2653-0270. Fax 2653-0287. www.villaalegrecostarica.com. 5 units, 2 villas. $170–$185 double; $230 villa. Rates include full breakfast. AE, MC, V. **Amenities:** Mid-size pool. *In room:* A/C, no phone, free Wi-Fi, kitchenettes (in villas).

Moderate

In addition to the places listed here, **Hotel Pueblo Dorado** (☎2653-0008; www.pueblodorado.com) is a well-located option just across from the beach.

Best Western Tamarindo Vista Villas This place was originally conceived as a condo project and then converted into a hotel and taken over by a local surfer and businessman and is marketed as part of the Best Western chain. This mixed breeding shows in the wide range of accommodations here, from the simple garden-view rooms to the Tropical and Corona suites. The former are basic budget motel-like affairs. The latter are split-level one-bedroom affairs with full kitchens, large living rooms (with two couches that can double as single beds), and either a private patio or a balcony with fabulous views of the Pacific Ocean. This hotel really caters to surfers, and there is often a lively, spring break–like atmosphere around the pool and at the bar—in fact, scenes from E! TV's *Wild On* were shot here.

Playa Tamarindo, Guanacaste. ☎800/536-3241 in the U.S. and Canada, or 2653-0114 in Costa Rica. Fax 2653-0115. www.tamarindovistavillas.com. 33 units. $89–$119 double; $159–$229 suite. AE, DC, MC, V. **Amenities:** Restaurant; bar; midsize free-form pool w/swim-up bar and a waterfall. *In room:* A/C, TV, free Wi-Fi, kitchens (in suites).

Hotel Arco Iris ★ Under new management, and entirely rebuilt, this place is a great option in this price category. Rooms feature a slightly minimalist contemporary Asian decor. The deluxe rooms are more spacious than the bungalows, and I especially like the second-floor deluxe units. The hotel is located a few blocks inland from the beach, but at times there's not much impetus to leave, as there's a small rectangular pool, and the restaurant here, Season's by Shlomy (see below), is one of the best in town.

Playa Tamarindo, Santa Cruz, Guanacaste. ☎/fax **2653-0330.** www.hotelarcoiris.com. 10 units. $89–$99 double. AE, MC, V. **Amenities:** Restaurant; bar; small pool. *In room:* A/C, TV, minibar, free Wi-Fi.

Hotel Pasatiempo ★ A long-standing and dependable option, this hotel is set back from the beach a couple of hundred meters in a grove of shady trees. Most rooms are housed in duplex buildings, but each room has its own private patio with a hammock or chairs. Every room has plenty of space, and all have received regular upkeep and remodeling over the years. The suites are cushy and well-equipped, with separate sitting rooms. A small and inviting pool sits in the center of the complex. The restaurant serves excellent fresh fish, as well as pizza and Tex-Mex specialties. This popular rancho-style affair also has a pool table, a nightly happy hour, cable TV with live sporting events, good snacks, and occasional live music.

Playa Tamarindo, Santa Cruz, Guanacaste. ☎2653-0096. Fax 2653-0275. www.hotelpasatiempo. com. 17 units. $109–$139 double. AE, MC, V. **Amenities:** Restaurant; bar; midsize pool. *In room:* A/C, no phone, free Wi-Fi.

Inexpensive

In addition to the cabinas listed below, **Hostal La Botella de Leche** (☎2653-0189; www.labotelladeleche.com) and **Tsunami Backpackers** (☎2653-0956) are two popular budget options, and the latter also allows camping. Just off the beach, out toward Hotel Capitán Suizo, **Tito's Camping** (no phone) charges $5 to $8 per person for camping.

Cabinas Marielos ★ This place is located up a palm-shaded driveway across the road from the beach just before the center of town. Rooms are clean and well maintained, although most are small and simply furnished. Most have air-conditioning. Some of the bathrooms are quite small, but they're clean. There's a kitchen that guests can use, and the lush gardens are beautiful and provide some welcome shade. Common verandas and balconies are cool places to sit and read a book. The staff and owners are incredibly helpful and will make you feel like part of the family—in fact many of them are already family to each other.

Playa Tamarindo, Guanacaste. ☎/fax **2653-0141.** www.cabinasmarieloscr.com. 20 units. $45–$60 double. Rates include taxes. AE, MC, V. **Amenities:** Surfboard rentals. *In room:* No phone.

Hotel Zully Mar The Zully Mar has long been a favorite of budget travelers, although they've upgraded their rooms and upped their prices over the years. The best rooms here are in a two-story white-stucco building with a wide, curving staircase on the outside. They have air-conditioning, tile floors, long verandas or balconies, overhead or standing fans, large bathrooms, and doors that are hand-carved with pre-Columbian motifs. The less expensive rooms are smaller and darker and just have ceiling fans. There is a small free-form pool that's refreshing if you don't want to walk across the street to the beach. This place is set on the busiest intersection in Tamarindo, smack-dab in the center of things, and noise can be a problem at times.

Playa Tamarindo, Guanacaste. ☎/fax **2653-0140.** Fax 2653-0028. www.zullymar.com. 25 units. $46–$79 double. AE, MC, V. **Amenities:** Restaurant; small pool. *In room:* A/C (in some), mini-fridge, no phone.

IN PLAYA GRANDE

In addition to the places listed below, **Hotel Bula Bula** ★ (☎877/658-2880 in the U.S. and Canada, or 2653-0975 in Costa Rica; www.hotelbulabula.com) is another excellent inland option, while the **Playa Grande Surf Camp** (☎2653-1074; www.playagrandesurfcamp.com) is geared toward surfers and budget travelers.

Hotel Las Tortugas ★ 🏨 The owners of this place have led the local fight to protect the leatherback turtles that nest here, and have the surrounding area declared Las Baulas National Park. Still, this beach is extremely popular with surfers, who make up a large share of the clientele at this beachfront hotel. Several of the rooms are quite large, and most have interesting stone floors and shower stalls. The upper suite has a curving staircase that leads to its second room. As part of the hotel's turtle-friendly design, a natural wall of shrubs and trees shields the beach from the restaurant's light and noise, and the swimming pool is shaped like a turtle. These folks also have a collection of fully equipped apartments located a few blocks inland from the water, and available for weekly or monthly rental.

Playa Grande (A.P. 164, Santa Cruz), Guanacaste. ☎**2653-0423** or ☎/fax 2653-0458. www.lastortugashotel.com. 11 units. $90 double; $120 suite. MC, V. **Amenities:** Restaurant; bar; Jacuzzi; small pool. *In room:* A/C, no phone.

Ripjack Inn ★ This hotel is located about 100m (328 ft.) inland from the beach, which is reached via a short path. The rooms are all clean and cool, with tile floors, air-conditioning, and private bathrooms. The rooms come in several sizes and a mix of bed arrangements. They feature various Indonesian-inspired and imported design touches. The hotel's restaurant and bar, which is located on the second floor of the octagonal main building, is one of the best restaurants in Playa Grande. The hotel has a large yoga studio, with regular classes for guests and the local community.

Playa Grande, Guanacaste. **800/808-4605** in the U.S. and Canada, or 2653-0480 in Costa Rica. Fax 2652-9272. www.ripjackinn.com. 8 units. $80–$100 double. MC, V. **Amenities:** Restaurant; bar. *In room:* A/C, no phone, free Wi-Fi.

Where to Dine

Tamarindo has a glut of restaurants. **Nogui's Café** ★ (**2653-0029**) is one of the more popular places in town—and rightly so. This simple open-air cafe just off the beach on the small traffic circle serves hearty breakfasts and well-prepared salads, sandwiches, burgers, and casual meals. **Mama's Deli** (**2653-0178**) is another good beachfront joint, although these folks specialize in pizzas, panini, pastas, and other Italian fare. **Jaw's** (**2653-3896**), which also specializes in panini, as well as salads and a limited selection of more hearty fare, operates during lunchtime out of the **La Laguna del Cocodrilo Bistro** (see below).

The **Cala Moresco** ★ (**2653-0214**) restaurant, at the Hotel and Villas Cala Luna (p. 238), is the place to go if you're looking for some slightly fancier Italian and Mediterranean cuisine served up in an elegant open-air atmosphere. The folks at Cala Luna also have a sushi bar, **La Caletta** (**2653-0214**).

Meanwhile, over on Playa Grande, try **Upstairs** ★, the restaurant at the Ripjack Inn (see above), or **Great Waltini's** ★, at the Hotel Bula Bula (see above). Both are excellent restaurants serving fresh seafood and prime meats, cooked with care and creativity.

Carolina's Restaurant & Grill ★★ INTERNATIONAL/FUSION Housed in a large, enclosed space that feels like an old colonial-era home, this elegant restaurant is run by a Costa Rican–Swiss couple that met at culinary school. The red clay tile ceiling is exposed through heavy wood beams, and tables feature white cloths and glass candle holders. Start things off with the hot ginger and papaya soup, and follow it up with some sesame seared tuna. The pastas here are also excellent. Or you can opt for one of the nightly four- or five-course tasting menus. Presentations are artful, service is impeccable, and they boast an excellent wine list.

On the road to Playa Langosta. **2653-1946** or 8379-6834. Reservations recommended. Main courses $12–$24. AE, MC, V. Daily 6–11pm.

Dragonfly Bar & Grill ★★ 🏠 INTERNATIONAL/FUSION Tucked away on a back street, this restaurant has earned ample praise and a loyal following with its excellent food and cozy ambience. The menu mixes and matches several cuisines, with the southwestern United States and Pacific Rim fusion being the strongest influences. There are daily seafood specials, which might range from seared tuna to wood-fired red snapper. If you're in the mood for meat, try the thick-cut pork chop with chipotle apple chutney. The restaurant space itself is a simple open-air affair, with a concrete floor and rough wood tree trunks as support columns. There's an open wood-fired oven on one side, and a popular bar toward the back. They even offer free Wi-Fi throughout the restaurant.

Down a dirt road behind the Hotel Pasatiempo. ☏2653-1506. Reservations recommended. Main courses $10–$16. AE, MC, V. Mon–Sat 6–10pm.

La Laguna del Cocodrilo Bistro ★★ INTERNATIONAL/FUSION Yet another option for fine dining and fusion cuisine, this small open-air restaurant has impressed me every time I've eaten here. When weather permits, tables are set up under the trees in their beachfront garden area. Beautiful presentations and creative use of ingredients are the norm. The menu changes regularly, but the chefs always focus on using the freshest and best ingredients available. One of the best options is the nightly tasting menu, which will feature anywhere from five to seven courses, including dessert (which is always excellent here). The restaurant also has a good wine list, and they keep their bottles properly cool, to compensate for the often unforgiving heat of Guanacaste.

On the main road, toward the north end of Tamarindo. ☏2653-3897. Reservations recommended. Main courses $12–$29. MC, V. Mon–Sat 7:30am–9pm.

Season's by Shlomy ★★ INTERNATIONAL This is another of Tamarindo's standout restaurants. Chef and owner Slomy Koren has earned a fond and faithful following for both his consistency and creativity. For years he held court at the local restaurant Pachanga and he continues to please at this restaurant, located on the poolside patio of the Hotel Arco Iris (see above). The contemporary cuisine carries a heavy Mediterranean influence: The seared tuna in a honey chili marinade is always a favorite, as is the seafood pasta with an unexpected lemon vinaigrette sauce. Desserts often feature homemade ice creams and sorbets.

Inside the Hotel Arco Iris. ☏8368-6983. Reservations recommended. Main courses $13–$15. No credit cards. Mon–Sat 6–10pm.

Walter's COSTA RICAN/SEAFOOD This place has one of the most enviable locations, right on the beach and facing the bay, in the center of Tamarindo. The food and menu are not fancy, nor extensive, but the fresh seafood specials are all well prepared and reasonably priced. You can also get a range of Costa Rican standards, as well as decent pizzas. The restaurant is a simple, open-air affair, but there are quite a few tables with good views of the sea.

On the beach, across from the Hotel Zully Mar. ☏2653-0023. Main courses $5–$11. MC, V. Daily 7am–10pm.

Tamarindo After Dark

As a popular surfer destination, Tamarindo has a sometimes raging nightlife. The most happening bars in town are **Bar 1** ★★, a second-floor affair located about a block inland, on the road leading towards Playa Langosta, and **Aqua** ★, on the main road through town. Other popular spots that go on throughout the week include the **Crazy Monkey Bar** at the Best Western Tamarindo Vista Villas (p. 240), and the bar at the **Hotel Pasatiempo** (p. 240). Both of these places have televisions for sporting events and sometimes feature live music. For a chill-out dance scene try the **Voodoo Lounge,** while those looking for a sports bar blasting '80s rock can head to **Sharky's.** These latter two places are located just across from each other, just a little up the road that heads to Playa Langosta.

For those looking for some gaming, there are two casinos in town: the **Jazz Casino,** across from the El Diriá hotel (p. 238), and the casino at the **Barceló Playa Langosta** resort down in Playa Langosta.

En Route South: Playa Avellanas & Playa Negra

Heading south from Tamarindo are several as-yet-undeveloped beaches, most of which are quite popular with surfers. Beyond Tamarindo and Playa Langosta are **Playa Avellanas** and **Playa Negra,** both with a few basic cabinas catering to surfers.

WHERE TO STAY

In addition to the places listed below, the **Mono Congo Lodge** (☎2658-8261; www.monocongolodge.com), just outside of Playa Negra, is a rustically plush option in a lush, forested setting a few hundred yards from the water.

About a 15- to 20-minute drive inland is **Los Altos de Eros ★** (☎8850-4222; www.losaltosdeeros.com), a small, adults-only, luxury hotel and spa.

In addition to the JW Marriott (see below), the large golf, residential, and vacation resort complex of **Hacienda Pinilla** (☎2680-3000; www.haciendapinilla.com) features a couple of small hotels and condo rental units.

Very Expensive

JW Marriott Guanacaste Resort & Spa ★★★ The newest large-scale resort in Costa Rica is also one of its best. The rooms, facilities, restaurants, amenities, and service here are all top-of-the-line. All have large flatscreen televisions, a separate tub and shower, and a spacious balcony or patio, with a cooling retractable shade screen. Of the limited number of beachfront rooms, the Marimba suite (#339), a corner, view unit, is probably the best in the house. The spa here is large, modern, and luxurious. The Mansita beach just out front is a bit rocky, but beautiful stretches of Playa Avellanas lie a short walk or shuttle ride away, and the hotel also boasts having the largest pool in Central America—edging out the Paradisus Playa Conchal for the honor.

Hacienda Pinilla, Guanacaste. ☎888/236-2427 in the U.S. and Canada, or 2681-2000. Fax 2681-2001. www.marriott.com. 310 units. $225–$369 double; $425–$769 suite; $1,625–$1,770 presidential suite. AE, DC, DISC, MC, V. **Amenities:** 4 restaurants; 3 bars; lounge; babysitting; children's programs; concierge; championship 18-hole golf course nearby; large, modern health club and spa; massive free-form pool; room service; smoke-free rooms; tennis courts nearby; watersports equipment. *In room:* A/C, TV/DVD, hair dryer, minibar, MP3 docking station, Wi-Fi.

Moderate

Cabinas Las Olas This collection of duplex cabins is a popular surf lodge set in the shade of some tall trees, a couple hundred meters inland from the beach and bordering a mangrove reserve. The rooms are simple but clean and are a good value. Each comes with a private little veranda with a table and some chairs and a hammock. The beach is a long stretch of almost always uncrowded white sand. There are good beach breaks for surfers up and down the shoreline, especially toward the northern end and the Langosta estuary. Mountain bikes and sea kayaks are available for rent.

Playa Avellanas, Santa Cruz, Guanacaste. ☎2658-9315. Fax 2658-9331. www.cabinaslasolas.co.cr. 10 units. $80 double. MC, V. **Amenities:** Restaurant; bar; bike rentals; limited watersports equipment rentals. *In room:* No phone.

Hotel Playa Negra These thatch-roofed bungalows are set right in front of the famous Playa Negra point break. Even if you're not a surfer, you'll appreciate the beautiful beach and coast with its coral and rock outcroppings and calm tide pools. The round bungalows each have one queen-size and two single beds, two desks, a ceiling fan, and a private bathroom. Although they have concrete floors, everything is painted in contrasting pastels and feels quite comfortable. Still, they're a bit pricey for what you get, unless all you're after is proximity to the waves. The restaurant is close to the ocean in a large open-air rancho and serves as a social hub for guests and surfers staying at more basic cabinas inland from the beach.

Playa Negra (A.P. 31-5150, Santa Cruz), Guanacaste. ☎2652-9134. Fax 2652-9035. www.playa negra.com. 10 units. $88 double. AE, MC, V. **Amenities:** Restaurant; bar; midsize oval pool; free Wi-Fi. *In room:* No phone.

WHERE TO DINE

Lola's ★★★ 🍴 INTERNATIONAL/SEAFOOD Long loved by locals, the secret is out on Lola's. Named after the owner's recently departed massive pet pig, this place serves up top-notch fresh fare in a beautiful open-air beachfront setting. Most of the heavy, homemade wooden tables and chairs are set in the sand, under the intermittent shade of palm trees and large canvas umbrellas. The fresh seared tuna, big healthy salads, and Belgian french fries are the favorites here, alongside the fresh fruit smoothies and delicious sandwiches on just-baked bread. You'll have to come early on weekends to get a seat.

On the beach, Playa Avellanas. ☎2652-9097. Reservations not accepted. Main courses $4.50–$13. No credit cards. Tues–Sun 8am–sunset.

PLAYA JUNQUILLAL ★

30km (19 miles) W of Santa Cruz; 20km (12 miles) S of Tamarindo

A long, windswept beach that, for most of its length, is backed by grasslands, Playa Junquillal remains a mostly undiscovered gem on an increasingly crowded coast. There's really no village to speak of here and the road is rough, so it's a good place to get away from it all and enjoy some unfettered time on a nearly deserted beach. The long stretch of white sand is great for strolling, and the sunsets are superb. When the waves are big, this beach is great for surfing, but can be a little dangerous for swimming. When it's calm, jump right in.

Essentials

GETTING THERE & DEPARTING By Plane: The nearest airport with regularly scheduled flights is in Tamarindo (see earlier in this chapter). You can arrange a taxi from the airport to Playa Junquillal. The ride should take around 40 minutes and cost about $40 to $60.

By Car: Take the Interamerican Highway from San José. Forty-seven kilometers (29 miles) past the turnoff for Puntarenas, you'll see signs and the

Playa Junquillal.

turnoff for the La Amistad Bridge. After crossing the river, follow the signs for Nicoya and Santa Cruz. Just after leaving the main intersection for Santa Cruz, you'll see a marked turnoff for Playa Junquillal, Ostional, and Tamarindo. The road is paved for 14km (8½ miles), until the tiny village of Veintesiete de Abril. From here, it's another rough 18km (11 miles) to Playa Junquillal.

From Liberia, head south to Santa Cruz on the main road to all the beach towns, passing through Filadelfia and Belén. Then follow the directions above from Santa Cruz.

By Bus: To get here by bus, you must first head to Santa Cruz and, from there, take another bus to Playa Junquillal. Buses depart San José for Santa Cruz roughly every hour between 6am and 6pm from the **Tralapa** bus station (**2221-7202**) at Calle 20 between avenidas 3 and 5, and from the **Tracopa-Alfaro** bus station (**2222-2666**) at Calle 14 between avenidas 3 and 5. Trip duration is around 4 hours; the fare is $6. Buses leave Santa Cruz for Junquillal at 5 and 10am, and 2:30 and 5:30pm from the town's central plaza. The ride takes about 1 hour, and the one-way fare is $2. Buses depart Playa Junquillal for Santa Cruz daily at 6 and 9am, and 12:30 and 4:30pm.

Always check with your hotel in advance as the schedule of buses between Junquillal and Santa Cruz is notoriously fickle. If you miss the connection, or there's no bus running, you can hire a taxi for the trip to Junquillal for $30 to $40. From Tamarindo, a taxi should cost $40 to $60.

What to See & Do

Other than walking on the beach, surfing, swimming when the surf isn't too strong, and exploring tide pools, there isn't much to do here—which is just fine with me. This beach is ideal for anyone who wants to relax without any distractions. Bring a few good books. You can rent bikes at the Iguanazul Hotel (see below), which is a good way to get up and down to the beach; horseback-riding tours are also popular. If you have a car, you can explore the coastline just north and south of here, as well.

For surfers, the beach break right in Junquillal is often pretty good. I've also heard that if you look hard enough, there are a few hidden reef and point breaks around.

Several sportfishing boats operate out of Playa Junquillal. Inquire at your hotel or ask at the Iguanazul Hotel. To rent a mountain bike, you can also check in at the Iguanazul. If you want to ride a horse on the beach, call **Paradise Riding** (**☎2658-8162;** www.paradiseriding.com). The cost is $55 per person for a 2-hour ride and $65 per person for a 3-hour ride.

Where to Stay & Dine

All of the hotels listed below have their own restaurants. You can get good pizza, homemade pasta, and fresh seafood at **Pizzería Tatanka** (**☎2658-8426**), which also offers simple rooms at very reasonable rates. It's near the Iguanazul Hotel on your left as you come into Junquillal, and also has good ocean and sunset views. For a more elegant dining experience, also featuring Italian cuisine, try **La Puesta del Sol** (**☎2658-8442**), which is on a hillside overlooking the sea. This is a great place for sunsets. For a change of pace, try **Lak Ampu** (**☎2658-8339**), which serves up Peruvian fare.

MODERATE

Iguanazul Hotel Set on a windswept, grassy bluff above a rocky beach, Iguanazul is the biggest, best-equipped, and most happening hotel in Junquillal. The pool—which features a tiny island with a palm tree growing on it—is large, as is the surrounding patio area, and there's also a volleyball court. If you're feeling mellow, head down to one of the quiet coves or grab a hammock set in a covered palapa on the hillside. Guest rooms are spacious and nicely decorated with basket lampshades, wicker furniture, red-tile floors, high ceilings, and blue-and-white-tile bathrooms. Even if you're not staying here, it's a good place to dine and the sunset views are phenomenal. These folks can also rent out fully equipped houses and condos for longer stays at their neighboring residential project.

Playa Junquillal (A.P. 130-5150, Santa Cruz), Guanacaste. **☎2658-8123** or **☎**/fax 2658-8235. www.iguanazul.com. 24 units. $70–$110 double. Rates include continental breakfast. AE, MC, V. **Amenities:** Restaurant; bar; bike rental; pool; small spa; watersports equipment rental. *In room:* A/C, TV, free Wi-Fi.

INEXPENSIVE

In addition to the hotel listed below, **Camping Los Malinches** (**☎2658-8429**) has wonderful campsites on fluffy grass amid manicured gardens set on a bluff above the beach. Camping costs $6 per person, and includes bathroom and shower privileges. You'll see a sign on the right as you drive toward Playa Junquillal, a little bit beyond the Iguanazul Hotel. The campground is about 1km (½ mile) down this dirt road. These folks also have some simple, rustic rooms.

Hotel Hibiscus 🏷 Although the accommodations here are simple, the friendly German owner makes sure that everything is always in top shape. The grounds are pleasantly shady, with plenty of flowering tropical flora, and the beach is just across the road. The rooms have cool Mexican-tile floors and firm beds. The service and ambience are excellent for the price range. The restaurant serves very well-prepared international cuisine and fresh seafood at reasonable prices.

Playa Junquillal (A.P. 163-5150, Santa Cruz), Guanacaste. **☎**/fax **2658-8437.** www.adventure-costarica.com/hibiscus. 4 units. $50 double. Rates include full breakfast and taxes. MC, V. **Amenities:** Restaurant. *In room:* No phone.

PUNTARENAS & THE NICOYA PENINSULA

The beaches of the Nicoya peninsula don't get nearly as much attention or traffic as those to the north in Guanacaste. However, they are just as stunning, varied, and rewarding. **Montezuma,** with its jungle waterfalls and gentle surf, is the original beach destination out this way. However, it's getting a concerted run for its money from the up-and-coming hot spots of **Malpaís** and **Santa Teresa.**

Farther up the peninsula lie the beaches of **Playa Sámara** and **Playa Nosara.** With easy access via paved roads and the time-saving La Amistad bridge, Playa Sámara is one of the coastline's more popular destinations, especially with Ticos looking for a quick and easy weekend getaway. Just north of Sámara, Nosara and its neighboring beaches remain remote and sparsely visited, thanks in large part to the horrendous dirt road that separates these distinctly different destinations. However, Nosara is widely known and coveted as one of the country's top **surf spots,** with a host of different beach and point breaks from which to choose.

Nearby **Puntarenas** was once Costa Rica's principal Pacific port. The town bustled and hummed with commerce, fishermen, coffee brokers, and a weekend rush of urban dwellers enjoying some sun and fun at one of the closest beaches to San José. Today, Puntarenas is a run-down shell of its former self. Still, it remains a major fishing port, and the main gateway to the isolated and coveted beaches of the Nicoya Peninsula.

PUNTARENAS

115km (71 miles) W of San José; 191km (118 miles) S of Liberia; 75km (47 miles) N of Playa de Jacó

They say you can't put lipstick on a pig, and this has proven true for Puntarenas. Despite serious investment and the steady influx of cruise ship passengers, Puntarenas has yet to shed its image as a rough-and-tumble, perennially run-down port town. While the seafront **Paseo de los Turistas (Tourist Walk)** has a string of restaurants and souvenir stands, there's really little in this town to interest visitors, and the beach here pales in comparison to almost any other beach destination in the country.

A 16km (10-mile) spit of land jutting into the Gulf of Nicoya, Puntarenas was once Costa Rica's busiest port, but that changed drastically when the government inaugurated nearby Puerto Caldera, a modern container port facility. After losing its shipping business, the city has survived primarily on commercial fishing.

There's a good highway leading all the way from San José, so you can reach Puntarenas (on a good day, with little traffic) in little more than 2 hours by car, which makes it one of the closest beaches to San José at least in elapsed time, if not in distance. A long, straight stretch of sand with gentle surf, the beach is backed for most of its length by the Paseo de los Turistas. Across a wide boulevard

FACING PAGE: **A beach outside Montezuma.**

A Colorful Festival

If you're in Puntarenas on the Saturday closest to July 16, you can witness the Fiesta of the Virgin of the Sea. During this festival a regatta of colorfully decorated boats carries a statue of Puntarenas's patron saint. Boats run all along the waterfront, but the Paseo de los Turistas makes for a good place to catch the action.

from the Paseo de los Turistas are hotels, restaurants, bars, discos, and shops. The sunsets and the views across the Gulf of Nicoya are quite beautiful, and there's usually a cooling breeze blowing in off the water. All around town you'll find unusual old buildings, reminders of the important role that Puntarenas once played in Costa Rican history. It was from here that much of the Central Valley's coffee crop was once shipped, and while the coffee barons in the highlands were getting rich, so were the merchants of Puntarenas.

Puntarenas is primarily popular as a weekend holiday spot for Ticos from San José and is at its liveliest on weekends. Puntarenas is also where you must pick up the ferries to the southern Nicoya Peninsula, and some folks like to arrive the night before and get an early start.

Essentials

GETTING THERE & DEPARTING **By Car:** Head west out of San José on the Interamerican Highway, passing the airport and Alajuela, and follow the signs to Puntarenas. The drive takes between 2 and 2½ hours. To reach Puntarenas from Liberia, just take the Interamerican Highway south, to the well-marked exit for Puntarenas.

By Bus: Empresarios Unidos express buses (☎2222-0064) leave San José daily every hour between 6am and 7pm from Calle 16 and Avenida 12. Trip duration is 2½ hours; the fare is $3. Buses to **San José** leave the main station daily every hour between 6am and 9pm. Buses to **Quepos** (Manuel Antonio) leave the main station daily at 5, 8, and 11am and 12:30, 2:30, and 4:30pm. The main Puntarenas bus station is cater-cornered to the main pier on the Paseo de los Turistas.

The bus to **Santa Elena** leaves daily at 2:15pm from a stop across the railroad tracks from the main bus station.

By Ferry: See "Playa Tambor" or "Playa Montezuma," below, for information on crossing to and returning from Puntarenas from Paquera or Naranjo on the Nicoya Peninsula.

By Train: One unique option for getting here is to take the train. Although Costa Rica's train system is for the most part nonoperational, the **Tico Train Tour** (☎2233-3300; www.americatravelcr.com) runs the 87km (54-mile) stretch between San José and the nearby port city of Caldera. The train runs very infrequently and only when there's sufficient demand, but it usually runs most weekends, especially in the high season. The round-trip ride, which leaves at 7am and returns at 4pm, costs $39, including a snack and refreshments.

ORIENTATION Puntarenas is built on a long, narrow sand spit that stretches 16km (10 miles) out into the Gulf of Nicoya and is marked by only five

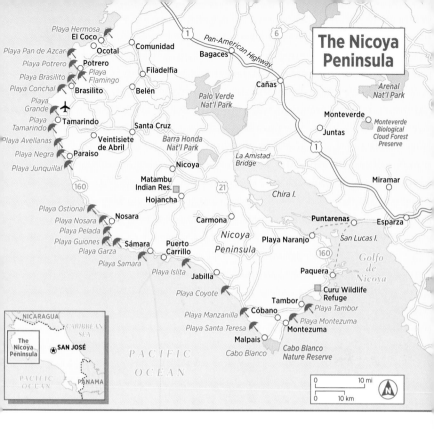

The Nicoya Peninsula

streets at its widest. The ferry docks for the Nicoya Peninsula are near the far end of town, as are the bus station and market. The north side of town faces an estuary, and the south side faces the mouth of the gulf. The Paseo de los Turistas is on the south side of town, beginning at the pier and extending out to the point.

FAST FACTS There are several banks, Internet cafes, and general markets all located within a 2-block radius of the town's small church and central park. If you need a taxi, call **Coopetico (☎2663-2020)**.

What to See & Do

Take a walk along the **Paseo de los Turistas,** which feels rather like a Florida beach town out of the 1950s. The hotels here range in style from converted old wooden homes with bright gingerbread trim to modern concrete monstrosities to tasteful Art Deco relics that need a new coat of paint.

If you venture into the center of the city, be sure to check out the **central plaza around the Catholic church.** The large, stone church itself is interesting because it has portholes for windows, reflecting the city's maritime tradition. It's also one of the few churches in the country with a front entry facing east, as most face west. Here you'll also find the city's cultural center, **La Casa de la Cultura (☎2661-1394)**, and the **Museo Histórico Marino (☎2661-5036)**, a small museum on the city's maritime history, with exhibits in both English and

Spanish. Admission is free, and it's open Monday to Saturday from 8am to 4pm. If you're looking for a shady spot to take a break, some inviting benches are in a little park off the north side of the church.

The biggest attraction in town is the **Parque Marino del Pacífico** (**Pacific Marine Park; (**2661-5272; www.parque marino.org), a modest collection of saltwater aquariums highlighting the sea life of Costa Rica. There are 22 separate tanks, with the largest dedicated to re-creating the undersea environment of Isla del Coco. Despite only being a few years old, this park already has a rather neglected and run-down feel to it. This place is located 2 blocks east of the main cruise ship terminal and is open Tuesday through Sunday from 9am to 5pm. Admission is $7 for adults, and $4 for children 13 and under.

Puntarenas building detail.

If you want to go swimming, the ocean waters are now said to be perfectly safe (pollution was a problem for many years), although the beach is still not very attractive. Your best bet is to head back down the spit; just a few kilometers out of town, you'll find **Playa Doña Aña,** a popular beach with picnic tables, restrooms and changing rooms, and a couple of *sodas* (diners). If you head a little farther south, you will come to **Playa Tivives,** which is virtually unvisited by tourists but quite popular with Ticos, many of whom have beach houses up and down this long, brown-sand beach. Surfers can check out the beach break here or head to the mouth of the Barranca River, which boasts an amazingly long left break. Still, surfers and swimmers should be careful; there are crocodiles in both the Barranca and Tivives river mouths, and I'd be wary of pollution in the waters emptying out of the rivers here.

Puntarenas isn't known as one of Costa Rica's prime sportfishing ports, but a few charter boats are usually available. Check at your hotel or head to the docks and ask around. Rates (for up to six people) are usually between $400 and $600 for a half-day and between $800 and $1,600 for a full day.

You can also take a yacht cruise through the tiny, uninhabited islands of the Guayabo, Negritos, and Pájaros Islands Biological Reserve. These cruises include a lunch buffet and a relaxing stop on beautiful and undeveloped **Tortuga Island ★**, where you can swim, snorkel, and sunbathe. The water is clear blue, and the sand is bright white. However, this trip has surged in popularity, and many of the tours here have a cattle-car feel. Several San José–based companies offer these excursions, with round-trip transportation from San José, but if you're already in Puntarenas, you might receive a slight discount by boarding here.

Calypso Tours ★ (**(**2256-8585; www.calypsotours.com) is the most reputable company that cruises out of Puntarenas. In addition to **Tortuga Island** trips, Calypso Tours takes folks to its own private nature reserve at **Punta Coral** and even on a sunset cruise that includes dinner and some guided stargazing. Either cruise will run you $119 per person. These prices are the same whether you join them in San José or Puntarenas. If you ask around at the docks, you might find some other boats that ply the waters of the Nicoya Gulf. Some of these companies also offer sunset cruises with live music, snacks, and a bar.

Where to Stay

In addition to the places mentioned below, the former Fiesta Premier Beach Resort has been taken over, remodeled, and rechristened as the **Double Tree Resort Puntarenas** (☎800/222-8733 in the U.S. and Canada, or 2663-0808 in Costa Rica; www.puntarenas.doubletree.com). The all-inclusive resort sits on a decidedly unspectacular patch of sand, just south of the Puntarenas peninsula. I never much cared for it in its previous incarnation, and while accommodations and service have definitely improved, it's still not a top beach resort pick in my book.

MODERATE

Hotel Alamar ★ This hotel is the most contemporary and luxurious option in town. Located toward the end of the Paseo de los Turistas, more than half of its units are one- or two-bedroom apartments, with fully equipped kitchens. All the rooms are spacious, clean, and modern. Walls are painted in bright primary colors and pastels. The furniture and decor are contemporary. In the center of the hotel complex are a refreshing pool and Jacuzzi. Ample breakfast buffets are served poolside. The best rooms here feature water-facing balconies and Jacuzzi tubs.

Paseo de los Turistas (A.P. 195-5400), Puntarenas. ☎2661-4343. Fax 2661-2726. www.alamarcr. com. 34 units. $110–$140 double. Rates include buffet breakfast. AE, DC, MC, V. **Amenities:** Restaurant; bar; Jacuzzi; small pool. *In room:* A/C, TV, minifridge, hair dryer, free Wi-Fi.

Hotel Las Brisas Out near the end of the Paseo de los Turistas, you'll find this older, yet well-kept hotel with large air-conditioned rooms, a small pool out front, and the beach right across the street. All the rooms have tile floors, double or twin beds, and small televisions and tables. Large picture windows keep the rooms sunny and bright during the day. There's complimentary coffee and a secure parking lot. The hotel's small open-air restaurant serves Greek specialties, fresh seafood, and other international fare. Personally, I find the rooms here a little more cheery and better maintained than those at the Tioga, but not as nice as those at Alamar.

Paseo de los Turistas (A.P. 83-5400), Puntarenas. ☎2661-4040. Fax 2661-2120. www.lasbrisas hotelcr.com. 27 units. $125 double. AE, DC, MC, V. **Amenities:** Restaurant; bar; small gym; Jacuzzi; small pool. *In room:* A/C, TV, free Wi-Fi.

Hotel Tioga This 1950s-style hotel was once the standard-bearer beachfront accommodation option in Puntarenas. It's still dependable, but shows its age. The interior courtyard with a pool that's just inside the entrance feels slightly claustrophobic. Rooms vary in size and view. The larger, most expensive rooms are attractive, with huge closets, modern bathrooms, and private balconies with a view of the ocean. The smaller, less expensive rooms have louvered, frosted-glass windows to let in lots of light and air while maintaining some privacy. The hotel runs a small casino next door. The beach is across the street, and plenty of restaurants are nearby.

Paseo de los Turistas (A.P. 96-5400), Puntarenas. ☎2661-0271 or 2255-3115. Fax 2661-0127. www.hoteltioga.com. 52 units. $75–$118 double. Rates include breakfast. Rates for extended stays. AE, DC, MC, V. **Amenities:** Restaurant; bar; casino; small pool; room service. *In room:* A/C, TV, free Wi-Fi.

INEXPENSIVE

Hotel La Punta Most budget lodgings in Puntarenas are real port-town dives. This place isn't for rock-bottom backpackers, but it's the most appealing and comfortable hotel I've found for those looking for a relatively inexpensive room. The rooms are spread around the two-story building here. Some are a bit small and spartan. You have to pay a little more for air-conditioning, but you'll almost definitely need it. There's a small pool for cooling off in during the day, as well as safe parking and easy access to the ferry terminal and docks.

A.P. 228, Puntarenas (50m/164 ft. south of the ferry terminal). **2661-0696.** 11 units. $50 double. MC, V. **Amenities:** Restaurant; bar; small pool. *In room:* A/C (extra fee), no phone.

DIVING TRIPS TO isla del coco (COCOS ISLAND)

This little speck of land located some 480km (300 miles) off the Pacific coast was a prime pirate hide-out and refueling station. Robert Louis Stevenson most likely modeled *Treasure Island* on Cocos.

Sir Francis Drake, Captain Edward Davis, William Dampier, and Mary Welch are just some of the famous corsairs who dropped anchor in the calm harbors of this Pacific pearl. They allegedly left troves of buried loot, although scores of treasure hunters over several centuries have failed to unearth more than a smattering of the purported bounty. The Costa Rican flag was first raised here on September 15, 1869. Throughout its history, Isla del Coco has provided anchorage and fresh water to hundreds of ships and has entertained divers and dignitaries. (Franklin Delano Roosevelt visited it three times.) In 1978 it was declared a national park and protected area.

The clear, warm waters around Cocos are widely regarded as one of the most rewarding **dive destinations ★★★** on this planet. This is a prime place to see schooling herds of scalloped hammerhead sharks. On a recent shallow-water checkout dive—normally, a perfunctory and uninspiring affair—I spotted my first hammerhead lurking just 4.5m (15 ft.) below me within 15 seconds of flipping into the water. Soon there were more, and soon they came much, much closer.

Other denizens of the waters around Isla del Coco include white- and

Where to Dine

You're in a seaport, so try some of the local catch. Corvina (sea bass) is the most popular offering, and it's served in various forms and preparations. My favorite dish on a hot afternoon is *ceviche,* and you'll find that just about every restaurant in town serves this savory marinated seafood concoction.

The most economical option is to pull up a table at one of the many open-air *sodas* along the Paseo de los Turistas, serving everything from sandwiches, drinks, and ice cream to fish meals. Sandwiches are priced at around $2, and a fish filet with rice and beans should cost around $4. If you want some seafood in a slightly more formal atmosphere, try the **Jardin Cervecero** or **Casa de los Mariscos,** or the open-air **Restaurant Aloha,** all located on the Paseo de los Turistas.

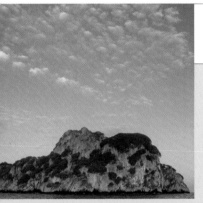

silver-tipped reef sharks; marbled, manta, eagle, and mobula rays; moray and spotted eels; octopi; spiny and slipper lobsters; hawksbill turtles; squirrel fish, trigger fish, and angelfish; surgeon fish, trumpet fish, grouper, grunts, snapper, jack, and tangs; and more. Two of the more spectacular underwater residents here include the red-lipped batfish and the frogfish.

Most diving at Cocos is relatively deep (26–35m/85–115 ft.), and there are often strong currents and choppy swells to deal with—not to mention all those sharks. This is not a trip for novice divers.

The perimeter of Isla del Coco is ringed by steep, forested cliffs punctuated by dozens of majestic waterfalls cascading down in stages or steady streams for hundreds of feet. The island itself has a series of trails that climb its steep hills and wind through its rainforested interior. There are several endemic bird, reptile, and plant species here, including the ubiquitous Cocos finch, which I spotted soon after landing onshore, and the wild Isla del Coco pig.

With just a small ranger station housing a handful of national park guards, Isla del Coco is essentially uninhabited. Visitors these days come on private or charter yachts, fishing boats, or one of the few live-aboard dive vessels that make regular voyages out here. It's a long trip: Most dive vessels take 30 to 36 hours to reach Cocos. Sailboats are even slower.

Both **Aggressor Fleet Limited** (&800/348-2628 in the U.S. and Canada, or 2257-0191 in Costa Rica; www.aggressor.com) and **Undersea Hunter** (&800/203-2120 in the U.S., or 2228-6613 in Costa Rica; www.underseahunter.com) regularly run dive trips to Isla del Coco from Puntarenas.

La Yunta Steakhouse ★ 🏛 STEAK/SEAFOOD This airy place bills itself as a steakhouse, but it has an ample menu of seafood dishes as well. Most of the tables are located on a two-tiered covered veranda at the front of the restaurant, overlooking the street and the ocean just beyond. Overall, this restaurant has the nicest ambience in town. The portions are immense, and the meat is tender and well prepared.

Paseo de los Turistas. **☎2661-3216.** Reservations recommended in high season and on weekends. Main courses $5.50–$28. AE, MC, V. Daily 9am–midnight.

PLAYA TAMBOR

150–168km (93–104 miles) W of San José (not including ferry ride); 20km (12 miles) S of Paquera; 38km (24 miles) S of Naranjo

Playa Tambor is home to Costa Rica's first large-scale all-inclusive resort, the Barceló Playa Tambor Beach Resort. Despite big plans, the resort and surrounding area have never really taken off. Though this beach and the two hotels listed below were chosen as the prime locations for the TV show *Temptation Island 2* and got lots of international television exposure, Tambor still has a forgotten, isolated feel to it.

Playa Tambor itself is a long, gently curving stretch of beach protected on either end by rocky headlands. These headlands give the waters ample protection from Pacific swells, making this a good beach for swimming. However, the sand is a rather hard-packed, dull gray-brown color, which often receives a large amount of flotsam and jetsam brought in by the sea. I find this beach much less attractive than those located farther south along the Nicoya Peninsula.

Tambor is the site of the only major commuter airport on the southern Nicoya peninsula, and you'll be arriving and departing here if you choose to visit Montezuma, Malpaís, or Santa Teresa by air.

Essentials

GETTING THERE & DEPARTING By Plane: Sansa (**☎877/767-2672** in the U.S. and Canada, or 2290-4100 in Costa Rica; www.flysansa.com) flies six times daily to **Tambor airport** (TMU; no phone) from San José's Juan Santamaría International Airport, with the first flight at 7:45am and the last flight at 4:20pm. Flights begin departing for San José at 8:30am, with the last flight out at 5:05pm. Flight duration is 30 minutes; the fare is $94 each way.

Nature Air (**☎800/235-9272** in the U.S. and Canada, or 2299-6000; www.natureair.com) flies to Tambor daily at 8am and 2pm from Tobías Bolaños International Airport in Pavas. Flight duration is 30 minutes; the fare is $99 each way. Return flights for San José leave at 8:35am and 2:35pm. Nature Air also has either direct flights or connecting flights between Tambor and Liberia, Tamarindo, Quepos, Palmar Sur, and Puerto Jiménez.

Taxis are generally waiting to meet most regularly scheduled planes, but if they aren't, you can call Gilberto (**☎2642-0241**) or Ronald (**☎8822-0610**) for a cab. The short ride into Tambor should cost around $8.

By Car: The traditional route here is to take the Interamerican Highway from San José to Puntarenas and catch the ferry to either Naranjo

Boating at Playa Tambor.

or Paquera. Tambor is about 30 minutes south of Paquera and about an hour and 20 minutes south of Naranjo. The road from Paquera to Tambor is paved and usually in pretty good shape, and taking the Paquera ferry will save you time and some rough, dusty driving. The road from Naranjo to Paquera is all dirt and gravel and often in very bad shape.

Naviera Tambor (☎2661-2084) car ferries to Paquera leave Puntarenas roughly every 2 hours daily between 5am and 9pm. The trip takes 1½ hours. The fare is $12 per car, including the driver; $1.50 for each additional adult, and 80¢ for children. I recommend arriving early during the peak season and on weekends because lines can be long; if you miss the ferry, you'll have to wait around 2 hours or more for the next one. Moreover, the ferry schedule changes frequently, with fewer ferries during the low season, and the occasional extra ferry added during the high to meet demand. It's always best to check in advance.

The car ferry from Paquera to Puntarenas leaves roughly every 2 hours between 8am and 9pm. **Note:** If you have to wait for the ferry, do not leave your car unattended, since break-ins are common.

The **Naranjo ferry** (☎2661-1069) leaves daily at 6:30 and 10am and 2:30 and 7:30pm. The trip takes 1½ hours. Return ferries leave Naranjo for Puntarenas daily at 8am and 12:30, 5:30, and 9pm. The fare is $11 per car, including the driver; $1.50 for each additional adult; and 90¢ for children.

Another option is to drive via the La Amistad Bridge over the Tempisque River. I only recommend this route when the ferries are on the fritz, or when the wait for the next ferry that your car will fit on is over 2 hours. (When the lines are long, you may not find room on the next departing ferry.) Although heading farther north and crossing the bridge is more circuitous, you will be driving the whole time, which beats waiting around in the midday heat of Puntarenas. To go this route, take the Interamerican Highway west from San José. Forty-seven kilometers (29 miles) past the turnoff for Puntarenas, turn left for the La Amistad Bridge. After you cross the Tempisque River, head to Quebrada Honda and then south to Route 21, following signs for San Pablo, Jicaral, Lepanto, Playa Naranjo, and Paquera.

To drive to Tambor from Liberia, head out of town on the main road to the Guanacaste beaches, passing through Filadelfia, Santa Cruz, and Nicoya on your way toward the turnoff for the La Amistad Bridge. Continue straight at this turnoff, and follow the directions for this route as listed above.

By Bus & Ferry: Transportes Rodriguez Hermanos (☎2642-0219) runs three daily direct buses between San José and Cobano, dropping passengers off in Tambor en route. The buses leave from the Coca-Cola bus terminal at Calle 12 and Avenida 5 at 6am and 2pm. The fare is around $12, including the ferry ride, and the trip takes a little over 4 hours.

Alternately, it takes two buses and a ferry ride to get to Tambor. **Empresarios Unidos** express buses (☎2222-0064) leave San José daily every hour between 6am and 7pm from Calle 16 and Avenida 12. Trip duration is 2½ hours; the fare is $3.

From Puntarenas, you can take one of the car ferries mentioned above or the passenger launch, *Don Bernadino* (☎2641-0515, or 2641-0746), which leaves from the pier behind the market at 11:30am and 4pm. Ferry-trip duration is 1½ hours; the fare is 90¢. A bus south to Montezuma (this will drop you off in Tambor) will be waiting to meet the ferry when it arrives in Paquera. The bus ride takes about 35 minutes; the fare is around $2. Be careful not to take the Naranjo ferry because it does not meet with regular onward bus transportation to Tambor.

When you're ready to head back, buses originating in Montezuma, Cobano, or Malpaís pass through Tambor roughly every 2 hours between 6am and 4:30pm. The Paquereña ferry returns for Puntarenas at 7:30am and 2pm, but you can also hop on any of the car ferries listed above. Total trip duration is 3½ hours. Buses to San José leave Puntarenas daily every hour between 5am and 8pm.

ORIENTATION Although there's a tiny village of Tambor, through which the main road passes, the hotels themselves are scattered along several kilometers, with Tango Mar (see below), definitively outside Tambor proper. You'll see signs for all these hotels as the road passes through and beyond Playa Tambor. If you want to rent a car, **Europcar** (☎2683-0067; www.europcar.co.cr) has an office here.

If you need a bank, pharmacy, or post office, you'll have to head to nearby Cóbano.

Fun on & off the Beach

Curú Wildlife Refuge ★ (☎2641-0004; www.curuwildliferefuge.com), 16km (10 miles) north of Tambor, is a private reserve that has several pretty, secluded beaches, as well as forests and mangrove swamps. This area is extremely rich in wildlife. Howler and white-faced monkeys are often spotted here, as are quite a few species of birds. You can usually spot scarlet macaws, and the refuge is actively involved in a macaw protection and re-population effort. Admission for the day is $8 per person. Horses are available to rent for $10 per hour. There are also some rustic cabins available with advance notice for $22 per person per day, including the entrance and three square meals. If you don't have a car, you should arrange pickup with the folks who manage this refuge. Or you could hire a taxi in Paquera to take you there for around $8.

Both the hotels listed below offer horseback riding and various tours around this part of the peninsula and can arrange fishing and dive trips.

Woodpecker.

Where to Stay & Dine

Aside from the hotels listed here, there are a few inexpensive cabinas available near the town of Tambor, at the southern end of the beach. Most are very rustic and basic, and charge around $10 per person. Another option is **Costa Coral ★** (**2683-0105;** www.costacoral.com), a very attractive place with a good restaurant. This place would be my top choice in Tambor, except it's unfortunately set right off the busy main road here, several hundred meters from the beach.

The **Barceló Playa Tambor Beach Resort** (**2683-0303;** www.barcelo.com) was Costa Rica's first all-inclusive resort, but its beach is mediocre at best, and the Barceló company has been accused of violating Costa Rica's environmental laws, ignoring zoning regulations, and mistreating workers. So although this resort is a major presence here, I don't recommend it; there are much better all-inclusive options available farther north in Guanacaste.

Tambor Tropical ★ Rooms here are located in five two-story octagonal buildings, and the whole place is an orgy of varnished hardwoods, with purple heart and cocobolo offsetting each other at every turn. The rooms are enormous and come with large, complete kitchens and a spacious sitting area. The walls are, in effect, nothing but shuttered picture windows, which give you the choice of gazing out at the ocean or shutting in for a bit of privacy. The upstairs rooms have large wraparound verandas, and the lower rooms have garden-level decks. The beach is only steps away. Plenty of coconut palms and flowering plants provide a very tropical feel.

Tambor, Puntarenas (mailing address: 867 Liberty St. NE, Salem, OR 97301). **866/890-2537** in the U.S., or 2683-0011 in Costa Rica. Fax 2683-0013. www.tambortropical.com. 12 units. $140–$190 double. Rates include continental breakfast. AE, MC, V. No children 15 and under. **Amenities:** Restaurant; bar; small free-form tile pool and Jacuzzi; small spa. *In room:* Fridge, kitchenette, no phone, free Wi-Fi.

Tango Mar Resort ★★ Tango Mar was *the* original luxury resort in this neck of the woods, and it's still a great place to get away from it all. With only 18 rooms and scattered suites and villas, there are never any crowds. If you choose to go exploring, you'll find seaside cliffs and a beautiful nearby waterfall. The rooms have big balconies and glass walls to soak up ocean views; some have their own Jacuzzis. The suites are set back among shade trees and flowering vegetation. Most come with carved four-poster canopy beds and indoor Jacuzzis. The villas are all different, spacious, and relatively secluded. Some suites and villas are a bit far from the beach and main hotel, so you'll need either your own car or one of the hotel's golf carts. In addition to a 9-hole par-3 golf course and two tennis courts, the hotel has a small spa and yoga space to keep you fit and busy.

Playa Tambor, Puntarenas. **866/770-7383** in the U.S., or 2683-0001 in Costa Rica. Fax 2683-0003. www.tangomar.com. 18 units, 17 suites, 3 villas. $190 double; $240 suite; $450–$999 villa. Rates include breakfast. Rates slightly lower during the off season, higher during peak weeks. AE, DC, MC, V. **Amenities:** Restaurant; bar; bike rental; 9-hole par-3 golf course ($20 full-day greens fee) w/wonderful sea views; 3 small pools; room service; small spa; 2 lighted tennis courts; limited watersports equipment rental. *In room:* A/C, TV, minibar.

PLAYA MONTEZUMA ★★

166–184km (103–114 miles) W of San José (not including the ferry ride); 36km (22 miles)
SE of Paquera; 54km (33 miles) S of Naranjo

Montezuma still feels worlds apart from most other beach destinations in
Guanacaste and Nicoya. For years, this remote village and its surrounding beaches,
forests, and waterfalls have enjoyed near-legendary status among backpackers,
UFO seekers, hippie expatriates, and European budget travelers. Although it
maintains its alternative vibe, Montezuma is a great destination for all manner of
travelers looking for a beach retreat surrounded by some stunning scenery. As with
the rest of Guanacaste and Nicoya, the town is booming, and there are lodgings
of value and quality in all price ranges. Active pursuits abound, from hiking in the
Cabo Blanco Absolute Nature Reserve to horseback riding to visiting a beachside
waterfall. The natural beauty, miles of almost abandoned beaches, rich wildlife,
and jungle waterfalls here are what first made Montezuma famous, and they
continue to make this one of my favorite beach towns in Costa Rica.

Essentials

GETTING THERE & DEPARTING By Plane: The nearest airport is in Tambor,
17km (11 miles) away (see "Playa Tambor," above, for details). Some of the
hotels listed below might pick you up in Tambor for a reasonable fee. If
not, you'll have to hire a taxi, which could cost anywhere between $20 and
$30. **Taxis** are generally waiting to meet most regularly scheduled planes,
but if they aren't, you can call Gilberto (☎2642-0241) or Ronald (☎8822-
0610) for one.

   By Car: The traditional route here is to take the Interamerican
Highway from San José to Puntarenas and catch the ferry to either Naranjo
or Paquera. Montezuma is about 30 minutes south of Tambor, 1 hour south
of Paquera, and about 2 hours south of Naranjo. The road from Paquera to
Tambor is paved and usually in pretty good shape, and taking the Paquera
ferry will save you time and some rough, dusty driving. The road from
Naranjo to Paquera is all dirt and gravel and often in very bad shape.

   For info on car ferries, see p. 257.

   To drive to Montezuma from Liberia, head out of town on the main
road to the Guanacaste beaches, passing through Filadelfia, Santa Cruz, and
Nicoya on your way toward the turnoff for the La Amistad bridge. Continue
straight at this turnoff, and follow the directions for this route as listed
above.

   By Bus & Ferry: Transportes Rodriguez Hermanos (☎2642-
0219) runs two daily direct buses between San José and Montezuma. The
buses leave from the Coca-Cola bus terminal at Calle 12 and Avenida 5 at
6am and 2pm. The fare is around $12, including the ferry ride, and the trip
takes a little over 4 hours.

   Alternately, it takes two buses and a ferry ride to get to Montezuma.
Empresarios Unidos express buses (☎2222-0064) to Puntarenas leave
San José daily every hour between 6am and 7pm from Calle 16 and Avenida
12. Trip duration is 2½ hours; the fare is $3.

   From Puntarenas, you can take one of the car ferries mentioned
on p. 257 or the passenger launch *Don Bernardino* (☎2641-0515 or

Playa Montezuma swimming hole.

2641-0746), which leaves from the pier behind the market at 11:30am and 4pm. Ferry-trip duration is 1½ hours; the fare is 90¢. A bus south to Montezuma will be waiting to meet the ferry when it arrives in Paquera. The bus ride takes about 55 minutes; the fare is $2.50. Be careful not to take the Naranjo ferry because it does not meet with regular onward bus transportation to Montezuma.

Buses are met by hordes of locals trying to corral you to one of the many budget hotels. Remember, they are getting a commission for everybody they bring in, so their information is biased. Not only that, they are often flat-out lying when they tell you the hotel you wanted to stay in is full.

When you're ready to head back, direct buses leave Montezuma daily at 6:15am and 2:45pm. Regular local buses to Paquera leave Cóbano roughly every 2 hours throughout the day starting around 4am. The Paquereña ferry returns for Puntarenas at 7:30am and 2pm. Total trip duration is 3½ hours. Buses to San José leave Puntarenas daily every hour between 5am and 8pm.

ORIENTATION As the winding mountain road that descends into Montezuma bottoms out, you turn left onto a small dirt road that defines the village proper. On this 1-block road, you will find El Sano Banano Village Cafe and, across from it, a small shady park with plenty of tall trees, as well as a basketball court and children's playground. The bus stops at the end of this road. From here, hotels are scattered up and down the beach and around the village's few sand streets.

There are several tour agencies and Internet cafes clustered among the restaurants and souvenir stores around the center of town.

Fun on & off the Beach

The ocean here is a gorgeous royal blue, and beautiful beaches stretch out along the coast on either side of town. Be careful, though: The waves can occasionally be too rough for casual swimming, and you need to be aware of stray rocks at your feet. Be sure you know where the rocks and tide are before doing any bodysurfing. The best places to swim are a couple hundred meters north of town in front of **El Rincón de los Monos,** or several kilometers farther north at Playa Grande.

If you're interested in more than simple beach time, head for the **Montezuma waterfall ★** just south of town—it's one of those tropical fantasies where water comes pouring down into a deep pool. It's a popular spot, and it's a bit of a hike up the stream. There are actually a couple of waterfalls up this stream, but the upper falls are by far the more spectacular. You'll find the trail to the falls just over the bridge south of the village (on your right just past Las Cascadas restaurant). At the first major outcropping of rocks, the trail disappears and you have to scramble up the rocks and river for a bit. A trail occasionally reappears for short stretches. Just stick close to the stream and you'll eventually hit the falls.

Note: Be very careful when climbing close to the rushing water, and also if you plan on taking any dives into the pools below. The rocks are quite slippery, and several people each year get very scraped up, break bones, and otherwise hurt themselves here.

Another popular local waterfall is **El Chorro ★**, located 8km (5 miles) north of Montezuma. This waterfall cascades down into a tide pool at the edge of the ocean. The pool here is a delightful mix of fresh- and seawater, and you can bathe while gazing out over the sea and rocky coastline. When the water is clear and calm, this is one of my favorite swimming holes in all of Costa Rica. However, a massive landslide in 2004 filled in much of this pool and also somewhat lessened the drama and beauty of the falls. Moreover, the pool here is dependent upon the tides—it disappears entirely at very high tide. It's about a 2-hour hike along the beach to reach El Chorro. Alternatively, you can take a horseback tour here with any of the tour operators or horseback riding companies in town.

ON THE WING For an intimate look at the life cycle and acrobatic flights-of-fancy of butterflies, head to the **Mariposario Montezuma Gardens** (☎8888-4200). This is perhaps the most wild and natural feeling of all the butterfly gardens in Costa Rica. Wooden walkways wind through thick vegetation under black screen meshing. Most of the butterflies in the enclosure are self-reproducing, and there are trails through open forested areas outside the enclosure, where you can also see butterflies and other wildlife. Located along the dirt road heading up the hill just beyond the entrance to the waterfall trail, this place is open daily from 8am to 4pm. Admission is $7.20, and includes a guided tour. These folks also have a few pretty rooms they rent out, or give to volunteers in exchange for work around the gardens.

HORSEBACK RIDING Several people around the village will rent you horses for around $10 to $20 an hour, although most people choose to do a guided 4-hour horseback tour for $30 to $50. Any of the hotels or tour agencies in town can arrange it for you, or you can look for "Roger, the horse guy"—any local can direct you to him. However, you'll find the best-cared-for and best-kept horses at **Finca Los Caballos ★** (☎2642-0124), which is up the hill on the road leading into Montezuma.

OTHER ACTIVITIES There are some shops in the center of the village where you can rent a bicycle by the day or hour, as well as boogie boards and snorkeling equipment (although the water must be very calm for snorkeling).

A range of guided tour and adventure options is available in Montezuma. **CocoZuma Traveller** (☎2642-0911; www.cocozuma.com) and **Montezuma Travel Adventures** (☎2642-0808; www.montezuma traveladventures.com) can both arrange horseback riding, boat excursions, scuba-dive and snorkel tours, ATV outings, and rafting trips; car and motorcycle rentals; airport transfers; international phone, fax, and Internet service; and currency exchange.

One popular tour option here is the **Waterfall Canopy Tour ★** (☎8823-6111 or 2642-0808), which is built right alongside Montezuma's famous falls. The tour, which features nine cables connecting 12 platforms, includes a swim at the foot of the falls and costs $40 per person.

Cabo Blanco Absolute Nature Reserve.

There are plenty of simple souvenir stores, as well as itinerant artisans selling their wares on the street, but it's worth stopping in at **Piedra Colorado ★** (☎**2642-0612** or 8841-5855) to check out their impressive silver, stone, and polished-shell creations. This place is located in the tiny strip mall in the center of Montezuma.

An Excursion to Cabo Blanco Nature Reserve

As beautiful as the beaches around Montezuma are, the beaches at **Cabo Blanco Absolute Nature Reserve ★★** (☎**2642-0093**), 11km (6¾ miles) south of the village, are even more stunning. At the southernmost tip of the Nicoya Peninsula, Cabo Blanco is a national park that preserves a nesting site for brown pelicans, magnificent frigate birds, and brown boobies. The beaches are backed by a lush tropical forest that is home to howler monkeys. You can hike through the preserve's lush forest right down to the deserted, pristine beach, which is 4km (2½ miles) away. Or you can take a shorter 2km (1¼-mile) loop trail through the primary forest here. This is Costa Rica's oldest official bioreserve and was set up thanks to the pioneering efforts of conservationists Karen Mogensen and Nicholas Wessberg. Admission is $10; the reserve is open Wednesday through Sunday from 8am to 4pm.

On your way out to Cabo Blanco, you'll pass through the tiny village of **Cabuya.** There are a couple of private patches of beach to discover in this area, off some of the deserted dirt roads, and a small offshore island serves as the town's cemetery. Snorkel and kayak trips around this island are offered out of Montezuma.

Shuttle buses head from Monte-zuma to Cabo Blanco roughly every 2 hours beginning at 8am, and then turn around and bring folks from Cabo Blanco to Montezuma; the last one leaves Cabo Blanco around 5pm. The fare is $2 each way. These shuttles often don't run during the off season. Alternatively, you can share a taxi: The fare is around $15 to $20 per taxi, which can hold four or five passengers. Taxis tend to hang around Montezuma center. One dependable *taxista* is **Gilberto Rodríguez** (☎**2642-0241**).

Where to Stay

VERY EXPENSIVE

Ylang Ylang Beach Resort ★★ 🏨 Set in a lush patch of forest just steps away from the sand, this hotel offers accommodations in a variety of shapes

> ## Buy the Book . . . or Just Borrow It
>
> **If you came unprepared or ran out of reading material, check in at Librería Topsy (☎2642-0576),** which, in addition to selling books, runs a lending library and serves as the local post office. These folks also have a branch up in Cabuya.

and sizes. Coco Joe's Bungalow is the largest and features a luscious wraparound balcony and a small sleeping loft. But I also like the smaller ferroconcrete geodesic domes, which look like igloos and have outdoor garden showers. There are suites with private balconies and sleeping lofts in a separate building, with standard rooms on the ground floor below them, as well as "jungalows"—large tents set on wooden platforms, featuring an indoor sink, small fridge, ceiling fan, and a private deck. These units share nearby bathrooms and showers. A beautiful swimming pool with a sculpted waterfall is on-site, and the whole operation is set amid lush gardens. You cannot drive in and out of the hotel, so arrival and check-in are handled at the downtown El Sano Banano Village B&B (see below). The owners here are committed environmentalists and are actively involved in local and regional conservation efforts; the restaurant serves both vegan and raw food dishes and as much locally grown organic produce as possible.

Montezuma, Cóbano de Puntarenas. ☎2642-0636. Fax 2642-0068. www.ylangylangresort. com. 26 units. $160–$295 double. Rates include breakfast and dinner. AE, MC, V. **Amenities:** Restaurant; bar; midsize outdoor pool; smoke-free rooms. *In room:* A/C (except jungalows), fridge, hair dryer, no phone, free Wi-Fi.

MODERATE

The El Sano Banano folks also run an in-town B&B (☎2642-0636; www.el banano.com), just off the popular restaurant (see below). The rooms here feature air-conditioning and satellite televisions; because of the design, you are basically forced to use the air-conditioning. Rooms here go for $75 per double, including breakfast.

Amor de Mar ★ This hotel has an idyllic setting, with a wide expanse of neatly trimmed grass sloping down to the sea, tide pools (one of which is as big as a small swimming pool), and hammocks slung from the mango trees. The rooms are housed in a pretty two-story building, which abounds in varnished hardwoods. Although simply appointed, most rooms have plenty of space and receive lots of sunlight. Five of them have air-conditioning. My favorite room is no. 5, which has exclusive access to a long second-floor balcony with a superb ocean view. Breakfast and lunch only are served on a beautiful open-air patio overlooking the sea. The breakfast specialties include big banana pancakes and fresh homemade whole-wheat French bread. These folks also rent out a large fully equipped two-story, four-bedroom house next to the hotel.

Montezuma (A.P. 22, Cóbano de Puntarenas). ☎/fax **2642-0262.** www.amordemar.com. 11 units, 9 with private bathroom. $50–$60 double with shared bathroom; $70–$95 double with private bathroom; $200 house. V. **Amenities:** Restaurant. *In room:* A/C (in some), no phone.

El Jardín Set on a steep hill, right on the crossroads leading into "downtown," this is a good choice if you're looking for a comfortable and well-equipped room close to the action. The rooms are located in a series of different buildings spread

Montezuma

To Cóbano

Playa Grande

(cont.)

Hotel Los Mangos **15**
Hotel Lucy **16**
Ylang-Ylang
  Beach Resort **1**

DINING
Cocolores **4**
El Sano Banano
  Village Cafe **8**
Hotel Moctezuma **7**
Organico **12**
Pizzería L'Angulo
  Allegro **9**
Playa de los Artistas **14**
Ylang-Ylang **1**

NIGHTLIFE
Chico's Bar **6**
Hotel Moctezuma **7**
El Sano Banano
  Village Café **8**

SHOPPING
Piedra Colorado **13**

ATTRACTIONS
Cabo Blanco Absolute
  Nature Reserve **21**
El Rincón de los Monos **2**
Mariposario
  Montezuma Gardens **20**
Montezuma waterfall **18**
Waterfall Canopy Tour **19**

ACCOMMODATIONS
Amor de Mar **17**
Cabinas Mar y Cielo **5**
El Jardín **11**
El Pargo Felíz **3**
El Sano Banano Village
  Bed & Breakfast **8**
Hotel La Aurora **10**

NICARAGUA
CARIBBEAN SEA
SAN JOSÉ
Montezuma
PACIFIC OCEAN
PANAMA

160

PACIFIC OCEAN

0   300 yds
0   300 m

---

across the hillside. Number 9 is my favorite, with pretty stone work in the bathroom, a greater sense of privacy than some of the others, and a good view from its private terrace. There's a two-level pool and Jacuzzi in a relaxing little garden area. Although the hotel doesn't have a restaurant, the town and its many dining options are just steps away.

Montezuma. /fax **2642-0074** or 2642-0548. www.hoteleljardin.com. 15 units. $65–$75 double. MC, V. **Amenities:** Jacuzzi; small pool. *In room:* A/C, minifridge, no phone.

Hotel Los Mangos Across the road from the water, a bit before the waterfall on the road toward Cabo Blanco, this place takes its name from the many mango trees under which the bungalows are built. (If mango is your passion, come in May, when it's in season.) The shared-bathroom budget rooms are very basic and a bit worn, but they are a decent value and you do get access to the pool. The octagonal hardwood bungalows are the better accommodations here. Each has a small porch with rocking chairs, a thatch roof, a good amount of space, and ceiling fans. Still, even these are pretty spartan. The swimming pool is built to resemble a natural pond, with an artificial waterfall flowing into it—and there's a separate Jacuzzi. The former restaurant here has been converted into a yoga studio, and daily yoga classes are offered.

Montezuma, Cóbano de Puntarenas. **2642-0076.** Fax 2642-0259. www.hotellosmangos.com. 10 units, 6 with private bathroom; 9 bungalows. $35 double with shared bathroom; $75 double with private bathroom; $95 bungalow. AE, DC, MC, V. **Amenities:** Jacuzzi; small pool. *In room:* No phone.

Nature Lodge Finca Los Caballos ★ This lodge is on a high ridge about 3km (1¾ miles) above Montezuma. The rooms are simple, with Spanish-style tile roofs, hardwood trim, stone floors, and some pretty paintings and decorative accents. Every room has a private patio or balcony with either a garden, jungle, or ocean view. The Superior Pacific rooms are the best bet, with beautiful ocean views out across the forested hills below. There's a small pool here, and plenty of hammocks strung around for relaxing.

Finca Los Caballos translates to "horse ranch," and riding is taken seriously by the hotel. The owners have 16 hectares (40 acres) of land and access to many neighboring ranches and trail systems. *Be forewarned:* If you stay here, it's a quick car ride, but very hefty hike, especially on the way back, to the beach.

Montezuma (A.P. 22, Cóbano de Puntarenas). ☎ **2642-0124.** ☎/fax 2642-0664. www.nature lodge.net. 12 units. $86–$138 double. Rates include breakfast. MC, V. **Amenities:** Restaurant; small pool. *In room:* Minifridge, no phone.

INEXPENSIVE

In addition to the places mentioned below, **El Pargo Feliz** (☎ **2642-0065**) and **Cabinas Mar y Cielo** (☎ **2642-0261**) are two good budget options right in the center of town.

Hotel La Aurora Just to the left as you enter the village of Montezuma, you'll find this long-standing budget hotel. The rooms are spread out over three floors in two neighboring buildings fronting the village's small park and playground. All rooms are clean and well-kept. A two-room apartment is set on the third floor here, with a private balcony and a bit of an ocean view through the treetops. The hotel also features a couple of common sitting areas, a small lending library, some hammocks and comfortable chairs for chilling out in, a communal kitchen, and flowering vines growing up the walls. In fact, there are plants and vines all over La Aurora, which keeps things cool and gives the place a fitting tropical feel. Fresh coffee, tea, and hearty breakfasts are served each morning.

Montezuma (A.P. 2), Cóbano de Puntarenas. ☎/fax **2642-0051.** www.playamontezuma.net. 18 units. $45–$70 double. Rates include taxes. AE, MC, V. **Amenities:** Lounge. *In room:* A/C, TV, minifridge, no phone.

Hotel Lucy ✦ Situated on a pretty section of beach a bit south of town, in front of Los Mangos, this converted two-story wooden home has the best location of any budget lodging in Montezuma. If you can snag a second-floor room with an ocean view, like room no. 19, you'll be in budget heaven. While very rustic and basic, the rooms are kept clean. The beach here is a bit rough and rocky for swimming, but the sunbathing and sunsets are beautiful.

Montezuma, Cóbano de Puntarenas. ☎ **2642-0273.** 17 units, 6 with bathroom. $22 double with shared bathroom; $25 double with private bathroom. No credit cards. **Amenities:** Restaurant. *In room:* No phone.

Where to Dine

In addition to the places listed below, you'll find several basic *sodas* and casual restaurants right in the village. My favorite of these is the **Pizzería L'Angulo Allegro** (☎ **2642-1430**), which is at the crossroads into town and serves good thin-crust pizzas, calzones, and pastas. You might also want to check out the Spanish cuisine and fabulous setting at the downtown **Hotel Moctezuma**

($\mathbf{2642\text{-}0657}$), or the varied international fare at **Cocolores** ($\mathbf{2642\text{-}0348}$). For breakfast, coffee, and light meals, **Organico** ($\mathbf{8359\text{-}4197}$) is a good option, with a range of healthy sandwiches, daily specials, and freshly baked goods.

El Sano Banano Village Cafe ★★ VEGETARIAN/INTERNATIONAL
Delicious vegetarian meals, including nightly specials, sandwiches, and salads, are the specialty of this perennially popular Montezuma restaurant, although there's also a variety of fish and chicken dishes. Lunches feature hefty sandwiches on whole-wheat bread and filling fish and vegetarian *casados*. The natural yogurt fruit shakes are fabulous, but I like to get a little more decadent and have one of the mocha chill shakes. El Sano Banano also doubles as the local movie house. Nightly DVD releases are projected on a large screen; the selection ranges from first-run to quite artsy, and there's a constantly growing library of more than 1,000 movies. The movies begin at 7:30pm and require a minimum purchase of $5.50.

On the main road into the village. $\mathbf{2642\text{-}0944}$. Main courses $4–$21. AE, MC, V. Daily 6am–10pm.

Playa de los Artistas ★★★ 🛍 ITALIAN/MEDITERRANEAN This open-air restaurant is housed in the back garden of an old house fronting the beach, and there are only a few tables, so arrive early. If you don't get a seat and you feel hearty, try the low wooden table surrounded by tatami mats on the sand. Meals are served in large creative plates, in broad wooden bowls set on ceramic-ringed coasters, or on large wooden planks lined with banana leaves. The menu changes nightly but always features several fish dishes. The fresh grouper in a black-pepper sauce is phenomenal, as is the *moscardini* polenta, a tasty appetizer of polenta pieces topped with grilled calamari tentacles and pecorino cheese. The outdoor brick oven and grill turns out consistently spectacular grilled seafood. All meals come with plenty of fresh bread for soaking up the delicious sauces.

Across from Hotel Los Mangos. $\mathbf{2642\text{-}0920}$. Reservations recommended. Main courses $6.50–$14. No credit cards. Mon–Wed 5–9:30pm; Thurs–Sat 11:30am–10pm.

Ylang Ylang ★★ INTERNATIONAL Located at the Ylang Ylang Beach Resort, this attractive, open-air affair features a covered dining area, as well as outdoor tables under broad canvas umbrellas, and a sculpted bar with indigenous and wildlife motifs. The menu is ample, with a prominent Asian influence, ranging from sushi to vegetarian teriyaki stir-fry. There are also several crepe and pasta options and plenty of fresh seafood dishes. For lunch you can have a bruschetta or some cool gazpacho and be just a few steps from the sand when you're done.

At the Ylang Ylang Beach Resort. $\mathbf{2642\text{-}0402}$ or 8833-4106. Reservations recommended. Main courses $10–$25. AE, MC, V. Daily 7am–9:30pm.

Montezuma After Dark

Montezuma has had a tough time coming to terms with its nightlife. For years, local businesses banded together to force most of the loud, late-night activity out of town. This has eased somewhat, and there's currently quite an active nightlife in Montezuma proper. The local action seems to base itself either at **Chico's Bar** ★ or at the bar at the **Hotel Moctezuma** (p. 266). Both are located on the main strip in town facing the water. If your evening tastes are mellower, **El Sano Banano Village Cafe** (p. 267) doubles as the local movie house, with nightly late-run features projected on a large screen.

MALPAIS & SANTA TERESA ★★

150km (93 miles) W of San José; 12km (7½ miles) S of Cóbano

Malpaís (or Mal País) means "badlands," and, while this may have been an apt moniker several years ago, it no longer accurately describes this booming beach area. Malpaís is a bucket term often used to refer to a string of neighboring beaches running from south to north, and including Malpaís, Playa Carmen, Santa Teresa, Playa Hermosa, and Playa Manzanillo. To a fault, these beaches are long, wide expanses of light sand dotted with rocky outcroppings. Currently, this area is one of Costa Rica's hottest spots, and hotels and restaurants are opening at a dizzying pace. Still, it will take some time before this place is anything like more developed destinations like Tamarindo or Manuel Antonio. In Malpaís and Santa Teresa today, you'll find a mix of beach hotels and resorts, restaurants, shops, and private houses, as well as miles of nearly deserted beach, and easy access to some nice jungle and the nearby **Cabo Blanco Nature Reserve** (p. 263).

Essentials

GETTING THERE & DEPARTING By Plane: The nearest airport is in Tambor (see "Playa Tambor," p. 256, for flight details). Some of the hotels listed below might be willing to pick you up in Tambor for a reasonable fee. If not, you'll have to hire a taxi, which could cost anywhere between $40 and $45. **Taxis** are generally waiting to meet most regularly scheduled planes, but if they aren't, you can call **Miguel** (☏8819-9021 or 2640-0261) or **Richard** (☏8317-7614 or 2640-0003) for a cab.

By Car: Follow the directions above to Montezuma (see "Playa Montezuma," earlier in this chapter). At Cóbano follow the signs to Malpaís and Playa Santa Teresa. It's another 12km (7½ miles) down a rough dirt road that requires four-wheel-drive much of the year, especially during the rainy season.

To drive to Malpaís from Liberia, head out of town on the main road to the Guanacaste beaches, passing through Fila-delfia, Santa Cruz, and Nicoya on your way toward the turnoff for the La Amistad Bridge. Continue straight at this turnoff, and follow the directions for this route as listed above.

By Bus & Ferry: Transportes Rodriguez Hermanos (☏2642-0219) has two daily buses from San José's Coca-Cola bus station to Malpaís. The buses leave at 6am and 2pm, and the fare is $12, including the ferry passage. The ride takes a little over 5 hours. The return buses leave Malpaís at 6am and 2pm.

Alternately, you can follow the directions above for getting to Montezuma, but get off in

Santa Teresa surfer.

Santa Teresa.

Cóbano. From Cóbano, there are daily buses for Malpaís and Santa Teresa at 10:30am and 2:30pm. The fare is $1.50. Buses return daily to Cóbano at 7 and 11:30am and 3:30pm. **Be forewarned:** These bus schedules are subject to change according to demand, road conditions, and the whim of the bus company.

 If you miss the bus connection in Cóbano, you can hire a cab to Malpaís for around $20.

ORIENTATION Malpaís and Santa Teresa are two tiny beach villages. As you reach the ocean, the road forks; Playa Carmen is straight ahead, Malpaís is to your left, and Santa Teresa is to your right. If you continue beyond Santa Teresa, you'll come to the even-more-deserted beaches of playas Hermosa and Manzanillo (not to be confused with beaches of the same names to be found elsewhere in the country). To get to playas Hermosa and Manzanillo you have to ford a couple of rivers, which can be tricky during parts of the rainy season.

FAST FACTS There are currently no banks in Malpaís or Santa Teresa, but there is an ATM (by Frank's Place, see below), along with several general stores, public phones, and a few Internet cafes. You'll find **Farmacia Amiga** (℡ 2640-0539) in the Playa Carmen Commercial Center.

 If you need a taxi, call **Miguel** (℡ 8819-9021 or 2640-0261) or **Richard** (℡ 8317-7614 or 2640-0003). If you want to do the driving yourself, you can contact the local offices of **Alamo** (℡ 2640-0526) or **Budget Rent A Car** (℡ 2640-0418). Or you can head to **Malpaís ATV Rentals** (℡ 2640-0195), which has a large stock of ATVs.

Fun on & off the Beach

If you decide to do anything here besides sunbathe on the beach and play in the waves, your options include nature hikes, horseback riding, ATV tours, scuba diving, and snorkeling, which most hotels can help arrange. Surfing is a major draw here. There are miles of beach breaks to choose from and a few points to boot. If you want to rent a board or take a lesson, check out the **Malpaís Surf Shop** (℡ 2640-0173), which charges $30 per hour for private lessons, and less for groups.

For canopy adventures, head to **Canopy del Pacífico** (☎**2640-0360**), which is toward the southern end of Malpaís and just slightly inland. A 2-hour tour over the nearly 1km (½ mile) of cables touches down on eight platforms, features two rappels, and offers good views of both the forest and the ocean below. The cost is $35.

Finally, any hotel in the area can arrange a horseback-riding or ATV trip into the hills and along the beaches of this region, a guided hike through **Cabo Blanco Nature Reserve,** a sportfishing excursion out onto the high seas, or a trip over to Montezuma.

Where to Stay

VERY EXPENSIVE

Florblanca Resort ★★★ 🛎 This lush and plush hotel is the most luxurious option in this neck of the woods and one of the top boutique hotels in the country. The individual villas are huge, with a vast living area opening onto a spacious veranda. The furnishings, decorations, and architecture boast a mix of Latin American and Asian influences. Most overlook lush gardens, and about half have views through to the sea. Every unit features a large open-air bathroom with a garden shower and teardrop-shape tub set amid flowering tropical foliage. Despite the luxury on display here, the owners and management are committed to sustainable tourism ideals. There's a modern, full-service spa, as well as a full-size and active dojo on the grounds, where complimentary classes like yoga are regularly offered. The beautiful free-form pool is on two levels, with a sculpted waterfall connecting them and a shady Indonesian-style gazebo off to one side.

Florblanca Resort.

Playa Santa Teresa, Cóbano, Puntarenas. ☎**2640-0232.** Fax 2640-0226. www.florblanca.com. 16 units. $475–$600 double; $650–$750 2-bedroom villa for 4; $850 honeymoon house. Transfer to and from Tambor airstrip is included. AE, DC, MC, V. No children 13 and under. **Amenities:** Restaurant; bar; bike rental; small open-air gym; pool; room service; spa; watersports equipment rental. *In room:* A/C, kitchenette, free Wi-Fi.

EXPENSIVE

Milarepa ★ Named after a Buddhist sage, this small collection of individual bungalows is spread around shady grounds fronting the beach, just next door to Flor Blanca. The bungalows are simple, roomy, and understated. All have wooden floors, a mix of teak and bamboo furniture, beds with mosquito netting, and a private porch. An overhead fan keeps things cool, and there are plenty of windows for cross ventilation. The more expensive units are closest to the beach and have ocean views. There's a midsize pool for when the surf is too rough. The restaurant here is excellent.

Playa Santa Teresa, Cóbano, Puntarenas. ☎2640-0023. Fax 2640-0168. www.milarepahotel.
com. 10 units. $194–$225 double. Rates include full breakfast and taxes. AE, MC, V. **Amenities:**
Restaurant; bar; pool. *In room:* No phone, free Wi-Fi.

Moana Lodge ★ Set on a steep hillside, the rooms here are all decorated in
some variation of an African theme. A couple of the higher-situated units have
a bit of an ocean view. In addition to being larger, the deluxe rooms come with
a stocked minibar, four-poster queen-size bed, and ceiling fan. There's a pretty
free-form pool here, with a shady gazebo beside it, as well as some mattresses
hung like swings under another shade structure. Though the lodge doesn't have
a restaurant, breakfasts are served and guests can use the communal kitchen and
barbecue areas.

Malpaís, Cóbano de Puntarenas. ☎2640-0230. Fax 2640-0632. www.moanalodge.com. 10
units. $115–$140 double; $195–$295 suite. Rates include breakfast and taxes. MC, V. **Amenities:**
Bar; Jacuzzi; outdoor pool. *In room:* A/C, hair dryer, no phone, free Wi-Fi.

MODERATE

In addition to the hotels listed below, the mix of rooms and bungalows at the
Place (☎/fax **2640-0001;** www.theplacemalpais.com) are stylish and reasonably
priced. And, I've been getting good reports about the new **Beija Flor Resort**
(☎**2640-1007;** www.beijaflorresort.com), in Malpaís.

Trópico Latino Lodge ★ One of the first hotels in the area, this well-located
beachfront spread is still a good choice and value. The best accommodations are
the private beachfront bungalows, which have artistic tile work and finishings
and views of the ocean. The older rooms are housed in four duplex units. These
are huge—the king-size bamboo bed barely makes a dent in the floor space.
There's also a separate sofa bed, as well as a small desk, a wall unit of shelves,
and closet space galore. Although none of the older rooms has any ocean view
to speak of, they all have private patios with a hammock. The shady grounds are
rich in the native pochote tree, which is known for its spiky trunk. The restaurant
here serves up excellent fresh fish and plenty of pasta dishes.

Playa Santa Teresa, Cóbano, Puntarenas. ☎2640-0062. Fax 2640-0117. www.hoteltropicolatino.
com. 16 units. $103–$155 double. MC, V. **Amenities:** Restaurant; bar; Jacuzzi; small free-form
pool; small spa. *In room:* A/C, no phone, free Wi-Fi.

INEXPENSIVE

Budget travelers can check out **Tranquilo Backpackers** (☎2640-0589; www.
tranquilobackpackers.com), which is an outgrowth of a popular San José hostel.
This place is located a bit inland off the road running toward Santa Teresa and
has a mix of dorm-style and private rooms.

You can also pitch a tent at several spots and makeshift campsites here.
Look for camping signs; you should get bathroom and shower access for a few
bucks.

Frank's Place These folks offer a hodgepodge of rooms in a variety of styles,
price ranges, and configurations. Nine rooms are very basic and feature a shared
bathroom; four units come with private bathrooms, a minifridge, and a tiny television set. Only four rooms feature double beds, although a few come with complete kitchenettes, and some have air-conditioning. The midrange rooms are a
decent value and the hotel is well located, but I don't think the higher-priced

rooms here are worth it—you can certainly do better for the money. There's a small pool at the center of the complex, as well as an unheated Jacuzzi. The restaurant is a glorified *soda,* but it does serve good Costa Rican cuisine, fresh fish, and a smattering of international dishes. It's also one of the most popular hangouts in Malpaís.

Malpaís, Cóbano de Puntarenas (at the crossroads of Malpaís and Playa Carmen). ☎/fax **2640-0096.** www.franksplacecr.com. 33 units, 9 with shared bathroom. $40 double with shared bathroom; $75–$95 double with private bathroom. AE, MC, V. **Amenities:** Restaurant; bar; bike rental; Jacuzzi; small pool; watersports equipment rental. *In room:* No phone, free Wi-Fi.

Malpaís Surf Camp & Resort There's a wide range of accommodations here, reflected in the equally wide range of prices. The most basic rooms are open-air ranchos with gravel floors, lathe-and-bamboo walls, bead curtains for a door, and shared bathrooms. They'll also let you set up a tent for around $10 per tent, with bathroom and shower access included. From here, your options get progressively more comfortable, ranging from shared-bathroom bunk-bed rooms to deluxe poolside villas. There's a refreshing free-form tile pool in the center of the complex, and the large, open main lodge area serves as a combination restaurant, bar, lounge, and surfboard-storage area. As the name implies, this place is run by and caters to surfers, and the overall vibe here is loose and funky. The restaurant serves filling, fresh, and, at times, quite creative cuisine, depending on how accomplished the itinerant surf-chef-of-the-month is. Surf rentals, lessons, and video sessions are all available.

Malpaís, Cóbano de Puntarenas. ☎**2640-0031.** ☎/fax 2640-0061. www.malpaissurfcamp.com. 16 units, 8 with shared bathroom. $35 per person with shared bathroom; $95–$115 double with private bathroom. AE, MC, V. **Amenities:** Restaurant; bar; babysitting; bike rental; small exercise room; midsize pool; watersports equipment rental. *In room:* No phone.

Where to Dine

In addition to the places listed below, you might try **Mary's** (☎2640-0153), which is a very popular open-air joint that features wood-oven baked pizzas and fresh seafood, and is located toward the northern end of Malpaís. For a coffee break, breakfast, or light bistro-style meal, there's **Artemis Café** (☎2640-0579; www.artemiscafe.com) in the Playa Carmen Commercial Center. I'm also getting good early reports about the new **Azucar Restaurant** (☎2640-0071; www.cafeazucar.net) at Frank's Place, and the **Beija Flor Resort** (☎2640-1007; www.beijaflorresort.com).

VERY EXPENSIVE

Nectar ★★★ 🍴 FUSION The dimly lit open-air setting of this poolside and beachfront restaurant is elegant yet casual. There's a Pacific Rim influence to the fusion cuisine served. You can almost always start with some sushi or sashimi made with the daily catch. In addition to fresh seafood and several vegetarian entrees, you might also find lamb, rabbit, or duck on the regularly changing menu. Between 4 and 6pm they specialize in sushi and *bocas,* the local term for *tapas.* The creativity, service, and presentation are some of the best you'll find in Costa Rica.

At Flor Blanca Resort in Santa Teresa. ☎**2640-0232.** Reservations recommended. Main courses $18–$35. AE, MC, V. Daily 7am–9:30pm.

INEXPENSIVE

Soda Piedra Mar 🍴 COSTA RICAN/SEAFOOD This simple open-air restaurant is set on a rocky outcropping just steps away from the sea. The place is little more than a zinc-roofed shack that seems as if a stiff breeze would quickly level it. There are only a few tables here under the low roof; weather permitting, more tables are set in the sand under the sun or stars. The fare is simple, but the fish is guaranteed fresh, the portions are hearty, and the setting and sunsets are wonderful.

On the beach in Malpaís. 📞**2640-0069.** Main courses $4–$17. No credit cards. Daily 8am–8pm.

Malpaís & Santa Teresa After Dark

There's not much in the way of raging nightlife here. Some folks make the long and arduous journey over to Montezuma. The most popular bar in Malpaís is **D&N ★**, which stands for Day & Night, and is located about 1 block north of the crossroads into town, off the main road. You might try **Artemis Café** (see above) for a mellower scene. Surfers and other travelers also tend to gather in the evenings at **Frank's Place** and the **Malpaís Surf Camp** (see above for both). In Santa Teresa, **La Lora** is the most happening spot. This is definitely the place to come on Saturday night, to dance some salsa and merengue with the locals.

PLAYA SAMARA ★

35km (22 miles) S of Nicoya; 245km (152 miles) W of San José

Playa Sámara is a long, broad beach on a gently curved horseshoe-shape bay. Unlike most of the other beaches along this stretch of the Pacific coast, the water here is usually calm and perfect for swimming because an offshore island and rocky headlands break up most of the surf. Playa Sámara is popular both with Tico families seeking a quick and inexpensive getaway and with young Ticos looking to do some serious beach partying. On weekends, in particular, Sámara can get crowded and rowdy. Still, the calm waters and steep cliffs on the far side of the bay make this a very attractive spot, and the beach is so long that the crowds are usually well dispersed. Moreover, if you drive along the rugged coastal road in either direction, you'll discover some truly spectacular and isolated beaches.

Essentials

GETTING THERE & DEPARTING By Plane: Sansa (📞**877/767-2672** in the U.S. and Canada, or 2290-4100 in Costa Rica; www.flysansa.com) flies to **Carrillo airport** (RIK; no phone; 15 min. south of Sámara) daily at 8:23am from San José's Juan Santamaría International Airport. The flight might stop first at either Punta Islita or Nosara and takes approximately 1 hour; the fare is $117 each way. The Sansa flight leaves Carrillo for San José at 9:43am.

Most hotels will arrange to pick you up in Carrillo. If not, you'll have to hire a cab for between $6 and $10.

Nature Air (📞**800/235-9272** in the U.S. and Canada, or 2299-6000; www.natureair.com) also has one flight daily to Punta Islita that leaves at 9:30am from Tobías Bolaños International Airport in Pavas (p. 118). The fare is $129 each way. The return flight for San José leaves at 10:25am.

Nature Air also flies between Punta Islita and Liberia, Puerto Jiménez, and Quepos.

By Car: Take the Inter-american Highway from San José. Forty-seven kilometers (29 miles) past the turnoff for Puntarenas, you'll see signs and the turnoff for the new La Amistad bridge. After crossing the bridge, continue north to Nicoya. In Nicoya, head more or less straight through town until you see signs for Playa Sámara. From here, it's a well-marked and paved road all the way to the beach.

To drive to Sámara from Liberia, head out of town on the main road to the Guanacaste beaches, passing through Filadelfia, Santa Cruz, and Nicoya. Once you reach Nicoya, follow the directions outlined above.

By Bus: Alfaro express buses (☎ 2222-2666) leave San José daily at noon and 6pm from Avenida 5 between calles 14 and 16. The trip lasts 5 hours; the one-way fare is $7. Extra buses are sometimes added on weekends and during peak periods, so it's always wise to check.

Alternatively, you can take a bus from this same station to Nicoya and then catch a second bus from Nicoya to Sámara. **Alfaro** buses leave San José nearly every hour between 6am and 5pm. The fare is $5. The trip can take between 4 and 5½ hours, depending if the bus goes via Liberia or the La Amistad bridge. The latter route is much faster and much more frequent. **Empresa Rojas** (☎ 2685-5032) buses leave Nicoya for Sámara and Carrillo regularly throughout the day, between 5am and 9pm. The trip's duration is 1½ hours. The fare to Sámara is $1.50; the fare to Carrillo is $2.25.

Express buses to San José leave daily at 4 and 8am. Buses for Nicoya leave throughout the day between 5am and 9pm. Buses leave Nicoya for San José nearly every hour between 5am and 5pm.

Interbus (☎ 2283-5573; www.interbusonline.com) has a daily bus that leaves San José for Playa Sámara at 8:15am. The fare is $39 and they will pick you up at most San José–area hotels.

ORIENTATION Sámara is a busy little town at the bottom of a steep hill. The main road heads straight into town, passing the soccer field before coming to an end at the beach. Just before the beach is a road to the left that leads to most of the hotels listed below. This road also leads to Playa Carrillo (see below) and the Hotel Punta Islita (p. 279). If you turn right 3 blocks before hitting the beach, you'll hit the coastal road that goes to playas Buena Vista, Barrigona, and eventually Nosara.

FAST FACTS In case of an emergency, dial ☎ 911. To reach the local police, dial ☎ 2656-0436. There's a small medical clinic in Sámara (☎ 2656-0166). A branch of **Banco Nacional** (☎ 2656-0086) is on the road to Playa Buena Vista,

Horses on Playa Sámara.

Playa Carrillo.

just as you head out of town. For full service laundry, head to **Green Life Laundry** (☎2656-1051) located about 3 blocks west of the Banco Nacional.

If you need a ride around Sámara, or to one of the nearby beaches, you can hire a taxi by calling **Jorge** (☎8830-3002). Rides in town should cost $2 to $4; rides to nearby beaches might run $8 to $20, depending upon the distance.

Fun on & off the Beach

Aside from sitting on the sand and soaking up the sun, the main activities in Playa Sámara seem to be hanging out in the bars and *sodas* and dancing into the early morning hours. But if you're looking for something more, there's horseback riding either on the beach or through the bordering pastureland and forests. Other options include sea kayaking in the calm waters off Playa Sámara, sportfishing, snorkeling and scuba diving, boat tours, mountain biking, and tours to Playa Ostional to see the mass nesting of olive ridley sea turtles. You can inquire about and book any of these tours at your hotel.

You'll find that the beach is nicer and cleaner down at the south end. Better yet, head about 8km (5 miles) south to **Playa Carrillo ★★**, a long crescent of soft, white sand. There's almost no development here, so the beach is almost always deserted and there are loads of palm trees providing shade. If you've got a good four-wheel-drive vehicle, ask for directions at your hotel and set off in search of the hidden gems of **Playa Buena Vista** and **Playa Barrigona ★★**, which are north of Sámara, less than a half-hour drive away. In late 2007, actor Mel Gibson bought a large estate overlooking Playa Barrigona, and many locals say he actually bought the entire beach. Although his plans for this patch of paradise are still unclear, all beaches in Costa Rica are public property, and access must be provided.

A taxi to Playa Carrillo should cost about $6 to $10 each way. Because it's a bit farther and the roads are a little rougher, expect to pay a little more to reach Playa Buena Vista, and even more for Playa Barrigona.

The folks at **Wingnuts Canopy Tours** (☎2656-0153) offer zip-line and harness "canopy tours." The 2-hour outing costs $55 per person. You'll find their office by the giant strangler fig tree, or *matapalo,* toward the southern end of the beach.

Almost every hotel in the area can arrange sportfishing trips, or you could contact **Samara Sport Fishing** (☎2656-0589) or **Kingfisher ★** (☎2656-0091;** www.costaricabillfishing.com). Rates run from $250 to $500 for a half-day and $500 to $1,200 for a full day outing.

To learn how to surf, or to rent a board, check in with **C & C Surf Shop and School** (☎2656-00590). Surfboard rentals run $20 per day. Private lessons cost $40 per hour, including a free hour of board rental after your lesson. And, if you want to head out and try some scuba diving or a snorkel excursion, call **Samara Diving** (☎2656-0235). A two-tank dive, with equipment, will run you $80 to $100.

For a bird's-eye view of the area, head over to the **Flying Crocodile** (☎2656-8048 or 8827-8858; www.flying-crocodile.com) in Playa Buena Vista. A 20-minute flight will run you $75.

All of the hotels here can help you arrange any number of tour options, including horseback rides, boat trips, sea kayaking, scuba diving, and snorkeling outings. You might also contact **Tío Tigre Tours** (☎2656-1060), a good all-around local tour company.

LEARN THE LANGUAGE

If you want to acquire or polish some language skills while here, check in with the **Intercultura Language School** (☎866/978-6668 in the U.S. and Canada, or 2656-0127 in Sámara; www.samaralanguageschool.com). These folks offer a range of programs and private lessons and can arrange for a home stay with a local family. The facility even features classes with ocean views, although that might be a detriment to your language learning.

Going Down Under

Cavers will want to head 62km (38 miles) northeast of Playa Sámara on the road to the La Amistad bridge. If you don't have a car, your best bet is to get to Nicoya, which is about a half-hour away by bus, and then take a taxi to the park, which should cost about $15. Here, at **Barra Honda National Park ★** (☎2685-5267 or 2659-1551), there's an extensive system of caves, some of which reach more than 200m (656 ft.) in depth. Human remains and indigenous relics have been found in other caves, but those are not open to the public. Because this is a national park, you'll have to pay the $10 entrance fee.

If you plan to descend the one publicly accessible cave, you'll also need to rent (or bring your own) equipment and hire a local guide at the park entrance station. Depending upon your group size and bargaining abilities, expect to pay between $20 to $36 per person for a visit to the **Terciopelo Cave,** including the guide, harness, helmet, and flashlight. Furthermore, the cave is open only during the dry season (mid-Nov to Apr). You begin your tour with a descent of 19m (62 ft.) straight down a wooden ladder with a safety rope attached. Inside you'll see plenty of impressive stalactites and stalagmites while visiting several chambers of varying sizes. Even if you don't descend, the trails around Barra Honda and its prominent limestone plateau are great for hiking and bird-watching. Be sure to make a stop at **La Cascada,** a gentle waterfall that fills and passes through a series of calcium and limestone pools, some of them large enough to bathe in. The entire thing is slightly reminiscent of Ocho Rios in Jamaica.

Terciopelo Cave at Barra Honda National Park.

Where to Stay

EXPENSIVE

Hotel Guanamar ★ Set on a high bluff overlooking Playa Carillo, this place offers great views, large well-equipped rooms, and easy access to one of the best beaches in the region. New management has done a good job of reviving this long neglected hotel. Once a dedicated fishing resort, it's now geared towards a broad spectrum of travelers, including sport fishers. The pool has the best vantage point on the property, with large, broad wooden decks all around, and the open-air restaurant and bar share the view from under soaring thatch roofs. I recommend grabbing one of the rooms built into the hillside, in two long rows of buildings. These are the newer units and each features a private balcony facing the sea. However, there are also some good options, including the suites, set higher up behind the pool and restaurants. Of these, I recommend #116, which has a great private balcony.

Puerto Carillo. ☎2656-0054. Fax 2232-6678. www. guanamar.net. 41 units. $123–$158 double; $239 suite. Rates include continental breakfast. AE, DC, MC, V. **Amenities:** Restaurant; bar; large outdoor pool; room service; small spa; free Wi-Fi in main building and around pool. *In room:* A/C, TV, fridge.

MODERATE

In addition to the places listed below, **Tico Adventure Lodge** (☎2656-0628; www.ticoadventurelodge.com) is another good option, about 2 blocks from the beach, in the heart of town, while **Casitas Laz Divaz** (☎2656-0295; www. lazdivaz.com) is an intimate B&B offering up three individual cabins, right on the beach.

Fenix Hotel ★ Set right on the beach, the rooms here are all really studio apartments, with fully equipped kitchenettes. The rooms are simple, but they are kept clean. For cooling off, the hotel has a postage stamp–size pool and some coconut trees for shade. Hammocks are hung in the shade and the ocean is just steps away. The owners are personable and accommodating, and the full kitchens are a boon for families and those looking for longer stays.

Playa Sámara, Nicoya, Guanacaste. ☎2656-0158. Fax 2656-0162. www.fenixhotel.com. 6 units. $90 double. No credit cards. **Amenities:** Small pool. *In room:* A/C, kitchenette, no phone.

Hotel Belvedere ★ 🐾 This long-standing German-run option is located a few blocks inland and uphill from the beach. Rooms are housed in the older main building, and a new annex, another block or so inland. Those in the annex feature modern split A/C units, one queen and one twin bed, a coffeemaker, and little fridge. The rooms in the older section are somewhat more basic, although everything is well-maintained and immaculate. Some have a small kitchenette, and so are geared towards longer stays and families. There's a pool at each of the building sites. Only breakfast is served, although they run a snack bar throughout most of the day, and there's an honor bar system for beverages.

Playa Sámara. ☎/fax **2656-0213.** www.belvederesamara.net. 21 units. $66–$105 double. Rates include breakfast. MC, V. **Amenities:** Lounge; Jacuzzi; 2 outdoor pools. *In room:* A/C, TV (in some), fridge.

Hotel Giada This neat little Italian-owned hotel is on the left-hand side of the main road into town, about 150m (492 ft.) before the beach. The rooms are all very clean and comfortable and even have small balconies. Breakfast is served in a cool, shady central gazebo. The management is very helpful and can arrange diving or fishing expeditions and horseback-riding trips. Still, the hotel is located roadside at perhaps the busiest section of street in town.

Playa Sámara, Nicoya, Guanacaste. ☎**2656-0132.** Fax 2656-0131. www.hotelgiada.net. 24 units. $90 double. Rates include breakfast. AE, DC, MC, V. **Amenities:** Restaurant; bar; small pool. *In room:* A/C, TV.

Samara Tree House Inn ★★ Set right on the beach in the heart of town, this hotel is my top choice in Sámara. The individual units are really small studio apartments. The four namesake rooms are built on raised stilts, made from varnished tree trunks. Inside, they are awash in varnished wood. There's a small sitting area, with large picture windows and a great view up above. And the open-air area underneath each unit is outfitted with a couple of hammocks, a table and chairs, some chaise longues, and a barbecue. There's also a ground-floor unit, which is handicap accessible and quite beautiful in its own right. There's no air-conditioning, but fans are found in every bedroom. No children 11 and under are allowed in the pool at anytime, although they are not prohibited from staying at the hotel.

Playa Sámara, Guanacaste. ☎**2656-0733.** www.samaratreehouse.com. 5 units. $80–$100 pool-front double; $130 beachfront double. Rates include breakfast. AE, MC, V. **Amenities:** Jacuzzi; small outdoor pool. *In room:* TV, free Wi-Fi.

INEXPENSIVE

You'll find a slew of very inexpensive places to stay along the road into town and around the soccer field. Many of the rooms at these places are less accommodating than your average jail cell.

Casa del Mar 🗝 On the inland side of the beach-access road, 1 block south of the downtown, Casa del Mar is just 50m (164 ft.) from the beach. The rooms here are kept immaculate, and most of them are quite spacious. The place feels like a cool oasis from the harsh Guanacaste sun, with its open-air restaurant, shady central courtyard, and small pool/Jacuzzi. Although the units with shared bathrooms are the best bargains here, I'd opt for a second-floor room with a private bathroom. The owners and staff members are extremely friendly and helpful.

Playa Sámara, Nicoya, Guanacaste. ☎**2656-0264.** Fax 2656-0129. www.casadelmarsamara.com. 17 units, 11 with private bathroom. $30 double with shared bathroom; $75 double with private bathroom and A/C. Rates include full breakfast and taxes. AE, MC, V. **Amenities:** Bar; unheated pool/Jacuzzi. *In room:* No phone.

Casa Valeria This is the best beachfront budget option in town. The rooms are quite basic and much more rustic than those at Casa del Mar, but you don't have to cross the road to reach the sand and surf. The best bets here are the four individual bungalows. There's a basic restaurant, as well as some tables, chairs, and plenty of hammocks set in the shade of tall coconut palms. This place is popular with European backpackers, and there's a hostel-like feel to the whole operation.

Playa Sámara, Nicoya, Guanacaste. ☎**2656-0511.** Fax 2656-0317. 9 units. $30–$70 double. Rates include breakfast. V. **Amenities:** Restaurant. *In room:* A/C, minifridge, no phone.

A NEARBY LUXURY HOTEL

Hotel Punta Islita ★★★ 🎁 Set on a high bluff between two mountain ridges that meet the sea, this is one of the most exclusive and romantic luxury resorts in Costa Rica. The rooms here are done in a Santa Fe style, with red Mexican floor tiles, and adobe-colored walls. Suites come with a separate sitting room and a private two-person plunge pool or Jacuzzi; the villas have two or three bedrooms, their own private swimming pools, and full kitchens. The beach below the hotel is a small crescent of gray-white sand with a calm, protected section at the northern end. It's about a 10-minute hike, but the hotel will shuttle you up and back if you don't feel like walking. There's a rancho bar and grill down there for when you get hungry or thirsty, and a lap pool for when the waves are too rough.

Punta Islita is very involved with the local community, and has sponsored a wide-ranging art program that brings in prominent Costa Rican artists to teach the local residents art and craft skills, while often creating large public works in the process.

Playa Islita (A.P. 242-1225, Plaza Mayor, San José), Guanacaste. ☎**866/446-4053** in the U.S. and Canada, or 2231-6122 in Costa Rica, 2661-4044 at the hotel. Fax 2231-0715. www.hotelpunta islita.com. 20 units, 17 villas. $300 double; $420–$480 suite; $625–$920 villa. Rates include continental breakfast. AE, MC, V. **Amenities:** 3 restaurants; bar; bike rental; 9-hole golf course and driving range; small exercise room and spa; Jacuzzi; small tile pool and lap pool; room service; smoke-free rooms; 2 lit tennis courts; watersports equipment rental. *In room:* A/C, TV, hair dryer, minibar, free Wi-Fi.

Where to Dine

There are numerous inexpensive *sodas* in Sámara, and most of the hotels have their own restaurants. If you want to eat overlooking the water, check out **El Ancla** (☎**2656-0716**) or **Shake Joe's** (☎**2656-0252**). Both of these are located right on the beach a bit south of downtown.

El Lagarto ★★ 🎁 STEAK/GRILL The first thing you notice as you enter this rustic, open-air restaurant—unless you come via the beach—is the two massive grill stations gravity-fed with fresh glowing wood coals via metal troughs from a huge overhead fire. The almost as massive menu features every form of meat, poultry, or fish you could imagine cooked to order over these fresh coals. The rustic open-air dining room features heavy wooden tables and chairs, some under a roof, others in the sand under shade trees and coconut palms. At night, atmospheric lighting gives this place a very romantic vibe.

On the beach, north end of Playa Sámara. ☎**2656-0750.** Reservations recommended. Main courses $8.50–$29. AE, MC, V. Daily 10am–11pm. Closed Sept 16–Oct 31.

Las Brasas SPANISH/SEAFOOD This two-story, open-air affair serves authentic Spanish cuisine and well-prepared fresh seafood. The whole fish *a la catalana* is excellent, as is the paella. For something lighter, try the gazpacho Andaluz, a refreshing lunch choice on a hot afternoon. If you have a big party, and order a day or so in advance, they'll roast a whole pig for you. There's a good selection of Spanish wines, a rarity in Costa Rica. Service is attentive yet informal.

On the main road into Sámara, about 90m (295 ft.) before the beach. **☎2656-0546.** Reservations recommended in the high season. Main courses $5–$32. V. Sat–Thurs 3–11pm.

Playa Sámara After Dark

After dark the most happening place in town is **La Góndola Bar,** which has a pool table, dartboards, and board games, and is located just before the soccer field on the main road into town. If you're looking for loud music and dancing, head to the beachfront **Tutti Frutti.** You might also try the lounge scene at **Shake Joe's, La Vela Latina,** or **Wana Wana Acuario,** all right near the center of the action, on the main road running parallel to the beach off the center of town. Or you could head a little farther south to **Sol Azteca,** a Mexican bar and restaurant, with a lively nightlife scene and occasional live music.

PLAYA NOSARA ★★

55km (34 miles) SW of Nicoya; 266km (165 miles) W of San José

As is the case in Malpaís, **Playa Nosara** is a bucket term used to refer to several neighboring beaches, spread along an isolated stretch of coast. In addition to the namesake beach, **Playa Guiones, Playa Pelada, Playa Garza,** and (sometimes) **Playa Ostional** are also lumped into this area. In fact, the village of Nosara itself is several kilometers inland from the beach. Playa Nosara marks the northern limit of the Nicoya Peninsula.

Playa Guiones is one of Costa Rica's most dependable beach breaks, and surfers come here in good numbers throughout the year. There's even a tiny strip mall at the crossroads to Playa Guiones; however, the waves are still much less crowded than you would find in and around Tamarindo.

The best way to get to Nosara is to fly, but, with everything so spread out, that makes getting around difficult after you've arrived. The roads to, in, and around Nosara are almost always in very rough shape, and there's little sign that this will improve anytime soon.

Essentials

GETTING THERE & DEPARTING By Plane: Sansa (☎877/767-2672 in the U.S. and Canada, or 2290-4100 in Costa Rica; www.flysansa.com) has two daily flights to **Nosara airport** (NOB; no phone), departing from San José's Juan Santamaría International Airport (p. 117) at 11:18am and 2:13pm. The one-way fare for the 50-minute flight is $114.

Nature Air (☎800/235-9272 in the U.S. and Canada, or 2299-6000; www.natureair.com) also has two flights daily leaving at 9:30am and 9:30am from Tobías Bolaños International Airport in Pavas (p. 118). The fare is $126 each way. The return Sansa flights to San José depart Nosara at 12:32am and 3:38pm and the Nature Air flights leave at 10:45am and 2:55pm.

Playa Guiones.

Taxis wait for every arrival; fares range between $5 and $10 to most hotels in Nosara.

By Car: Follow the directions for getting to Playa Sámara (see "Playa Sámara," earlier in this chapter), but watch for a well-marked fork in the road a few kilometers before you reach that beach. The right-hand fork leads to Nosara over another 22km (14 miles) of rough dirt road.

By Bus: An **Alfaro** express bus (☎2222-2666 in San José, or 2682-0297 in Nosara) leaves San José daily at 6am from Avenida 5 between calles 14 and 16. The trip's duration is 5½ hours; the one-way fare is $8.

You can also take an Alfaro bus from San José to Nicoya and then catch a second bus from Nicoya to Nosara. **Alfaro** buses leave San José nearly every hour between 6am and 5pm. The fare is $5. The trip can take between 4 and 5½ hours, depending if the bus goes via Liberia or the La Amistad bridge. The latter route is much faster and much more frequent. **Empresa Rojas** buses (☎2685-5032) leave Nicoya for Nosara daily at 5 and 10am, noon, and 3pm. Trip duration is 2 hours; the one-way fare is $1.90.

The direct Alfaro bus to San José leaves daily at 12:30pm. Buses to Nicoya leave Nosara daily at 5 and 7am, noon, and 3pm. Buses leave Nicoya for San José nearly every hour between 5am and 5pm.

Interbus (☎2283-5573; www.interbusonline.com) runs a daily bus from San José to Playa Nosara at 8:15am; the fare is $45.

ORIENTATION The village of Nosara is about 5km (3 miles) inland from the beach. The small airstrip runs pretty much through the center of town; however, most hotels listed here are on or near the beach itself. You'll find the **post office** and **police station** right at the end of the airstrip. There's an **EBAIS** medical clinic (☎2682-0226) and **Farmacia San Boutique** (☎2682-0168) in the village as well. Both **Banco Popular** and **Banco Nacional** have offices in Nosara, with ATMs.

If you want to rent a car, both **Alamo** (☎2242-7733) and **National** (☎2242-7878) have offices here. Because demand often outstrips supply, I recommend you reserve a car in advance. Alternatively, you can rent an ATV from several operators around town. If you need a taxi, call **José** (☎8833-3752) or **Miguel** (☎8895-7154).

There's an **Internet cafe** in the village and others at Café de Paris (p. 285), Frog Pad (☎2682-4039), and Harbor Reef Lodge (p. 284).

This area was originally conceived and zoned as a primarily residential community. The maze of dirt roads and lack of any single defining thoroughfare can be confusing for first-time visitors. Luckily, a host of hotel and restaurant signs have gone up in recent years pointing lost travelers in the general direction of their final destination.

Fun on & off the Beach

Among the several beaches at Nosara are the long, curving **Playa Guiones ★★**, **Playa Nosara ★**, and the diminutive **Playa Pelada ★**. Because the village of Nosara is several miles inland, these beaches tend to be clean, secluded, and quiet. Surfing and bodysurfing are good here, particularly at Playa Guiones, which is garnering quite a reputation as a consistent and rideable beach break. Pelada is a short white-sand beach with three deep scallops, backed by sea grasses and mangroves. There isn't too much sand at high tide, so you'll want to hit the beach when the tide's out. At either end of the beach, rocky outcroppings reveal tide pools at low tide.

With miles of excellent beach breaks and relatively few crowds, this is a great place to learn how to surf. If you want to try to stand up for your first time, check in with the folks at **Safari Surf School** (☎866/433-3355 in the U.S. and Canada, or 2682-0573; www.safarisurfschool.com), **Coconut Harry's Surf Shop** (☎2862-0574; www.coconutharrys.com), or **Corky Carroll's Surf School** (☎888/454-7873 in the U.S. and Canada, or 2682-0385; www.surf school.net). All of the above offer hourly solo or group lessons, multiday packages with accommodations and meals included, and board rental.

When the seas are calm, there's some decent snorkeling around the rocks and reefs just offshore. You can rent masks, snorkels, and fins at Café de Paris (p. 285) or Coconut Harry's.

BIRD & SEA TURTLE WATCHING Bird-watchers should explore the mangrove swamps around the estuary mouth of the Río Nosara. Just walk north from Playa Pelada and follow the riverbank; explore the paths into the mangroves.

If you time your trip right, you can do a night tour to nearby **Playa Ostional** to watch nesting olive ridley sea turtles. These turtles come ashore by the thousands in a mass egg-laying phenomenon known as an *arribada*. These *arribadas* take place 4 to 10 times between July and December; each occurrence lasts between 3 and 10 days. Consider yourself very lucky if you happen to be around during one of these fascinating natural phenomena. Even if it's not turtle-nesting season, you might want to look into visiting Playa Ostional just to have a long, wide expanse of beach to yourself. However, be careful swimming here because the surf and riptides can be formidable. During the dry season (mid-Nov to Apr), you can usually get here in a regular car, but during the rainy season you'll need four-wheel-drive. This beach is part of Ostional National Wildlife Refuge. At the northwest end of the refuge is **India Point,** which is known for its tide pools and rocky outcrops.

The *arribadas* are so difficult to predict that no one runs regularly scheduled turtle-viewing trips, but when the *arribada* is in full swing, several local tour guides and agencies offer tours. Your best bet is to ask the staff at your hotel or check in with Joe at **Iguana Expeditions** (☎2682-4089; www.iguanaexpeditions.com).

FISHING CHARTERS & OTHER OUTDOOR ACTIVITIES All the hotels in the area can arrange fishing charters for $200 to $500 for a half-day, or $400 to $1,200 for a full day. These rates are for one to four people and vary according to boat size and accouterments.

HORSEBACK RIDING The folks at **Boca Nosara Tours** (☎2682-0280) have a large stable of well-cared-for horses and a range of beach, jungle, and

Instructor at Nosara Yoga Institute.

waterfall rides to choose from. Rates run between $55 and $95 per person, depending on the size of your group and the length of the tour.

KAYAK TOURS Based out of the Gilded Iguana hotel and restaurant, **Iguana Expeditions** ★ (✆2682-4089; www.iguanaexpeditions.com) offers a range of full- and half-day tours around the area. Explore the inland coastal mangroves, or combine some open-water paddling with a snorkel break at San Juanillo. These folks also offer hikes to waterfalls and can arrange inexpensive fishing outings in a *panga* (small craft) with a local fisherman. Half-day tours cost about $50; full-day tours run $100.

YOGA & MORE If you want to spend some time getting your mind and body together, check in with the **Nosara Yoga Institute** (✆2682-0360; www.nosarayoga.com), which offers intensive and daily yoga classes, teacher trainings, and a host of custom-designed "retreat" options. This is an internationally recognized retreat and teacher training center. Their daily, open, 90-minute classes cost just $10, and they even provide a mat.

You might also check in to see if anything is being offered up at the Harmony Hotel & Spa (see below).

Where to Stay

In addition to the places listed below, the **Nosara Beach House** ★ (✆2682-0019; www.thenosarabeachhouse.com) on Playa Guiones, has clean and comfortable rooms and a swimming pool—and it's right on the beach to boot. **Giardino Tropicale** (✆2682-4000; www.giardinotropicale.com) is a similar choice, although a bit farther from the beach. For a more intimate option that's also a very good deal, check out the **Nosara B&B** (✆2682-0209; www.nosarabandb.net).

One final hotel that needs mentioning is the **Nosara Beach Hotel** (✆2682-0121; www.nosarabeachhotel.com). You can't miss the giant Russian-style dome topping this hillside hotel, which is the tallest and most striking structure in town. The location and view here are top-notch. However, the place has been in a constant state of construction for over a decade, rooms are pretty run-down, and service is gruff at times and spotty at best.

VERY EXPENSIVE

The Harmony Hotel & Spa ★ This cozy hotel sits right in front of the beach break on Playa Guiones. The room decor is simple but attractive, with white-tile floors, contemporary furnishings, and well-designed bathrooms. All the rooms have patios or wooden decks. In fact, even the most basic rooms here, their "Coco" rooms, feature large private wooden decks out back, with an outdoor shower. The hotel is geared toward couples, and all are equipped with just one king-size bed, although roll-in beds are available for families or buddies. The bungalows are two-bedroom affairs, with a king-size bed and fold-out sofa in each room and large shared deck area. The lush hotel grounds have been planted to be adapted to the dry Guanacaste conditions, and the hotel boasts a gray water irrigation system and organic gardens. The hotel has a well-run, pretty spa, with various treatment options and regular yoga classes. The best perk here is the location only about 90m (295 ft.) away from the beach, which is reached via a short path through some sea grass and dunes.

Playa Nosara, Guanacaste. ☎2682-4113. Fax 2682-4114. www.harmonynosara.com. 16 units, 10 bungalows. $220 double; $280 bungalow; $425 2-bedroom bungalow. Rates include breakfast buffet. AE, MC, V. **Amenities:** Restaurant; bar; midsize pool; spa; lighted tennis court; watersports equipment rental. *In room:* A/C, TV, minifridge, free Wi-Fi.

L'Acqua Viva ★★ This new resort hotel has the most architecturally stunning and well-equipped facilities in the Nosara area. The name translates roughly as "Living Water," and you'll find pools and water elements all around. Rooms are large, beautifully appointed, and feature LCD televisions. The restaurant, reception, lobby, and other public areas are also attractively done, with soaring thatch roofs and Balinese-inspired furnishings and decor. The biggest drawbacks here are the fact that the beach is a 10-minute drive away, and the whole complex is built close to the area's main dirt road and during the dry season dust can be a problem.

Playa Guiones, Guanacaste. ☎2682-1087. Fax 2682-0420. www.lacquaviva.com. 35 units. $205 double; $310–$341 suite; $525–$735 villa. Rates include continental breakfast. AE, MC, V. **Amenities:** Restaurant; bar; Jacuzzi; 2 large outdoor pools; room service; full-service spa; free Wi-Fi. *In room:* A/C, TV, hair dryer, minibar.

EXPENSIVE

Harbor Reef Lodge ★ This hotel caters to surfers, fishermen, and all-around vacationers, with clean, spacious rooms close to the beach (about 182m/597 ft. inland from Playa Guiones). The suites come with separate sitting rooms, and a couple even have kitchenettes. There's a cool, oasis-like feel to the lush grounds. The best rooms are the Surf City rooms and suites, which are set around the hotel's second and larger pool, which is reserved for hotel guests—the other pool, which is just off the restaurant, is open to diners and walk-ins. The hotel offers surf lessons and sportfishing outings and even has a small general store and Internet cafe on the grounds. They also rent out a variety of private homes and villas.

Playa Nosara, Guanacaste. ☎2682-0059. Fax 2682-0060. www.harborreef.com. 22 units. $119–$129 double; $159–$239 suite. AE, MC, V. **Amenities:** Restaurant; bar; bike rental; 2 small pools; watersports equipment rental. *In room:* A/C, TV, fridge, free Wi-Fi.

MODERATE

Café de Paris ★ On the main road into Nosara, where it branches off to Playa Guiones, this popular bakery and bistro (reviewed separately below) has some equally popular rooms out back, set behind the restaurant and pool in a series of duplex buildings. All have high ceilings and plenty of room; about half have kitchenettes. A few shady ranchos are spread around the grounds for afternoon lazing. These folks also rent a couple of luxury villas with fabulous views atop a steep hill across the street. In 2007, the owners began focusing solely on weeklong rentals for all their rooms, bungalows, and villas. During the off season, however, you should be able to negotiate a daily rate.

Playa Nosara, Guanacaste. ☎2682-0087. Fax 2682-0089. www.cafedeparis.net. 14 units. $360–$480 per week; $700–$1,200 bungalow or villa per week. AE, MC, V. **Amenities:** Restaurant; bar; small pool. *In room:* A/C, no phone.

Lagarta Lodge Located on a hillside high over the Nosara River, this small lodge is an excellent choice for bird-watchers and other travelers who are more interested in flora and fauna than the beach. The rooms are spartan but acceptable. The lodge borders its own private reserve, which has trails along the riverbank and through the mangrove and tropical humid forests here. There are spectacular views from the restaurant and most rooms over the river and surrounding forest, with the beaches of Nosara and Ostional in the distance. You'll want to have your own vehicle if you stay here: The beach is a good 10- to 15-minute hike away, and it's uphill on the way back.

Playa Nosara (A.P. 18-5233), Guanacaste. ☏**2682-0035.** Fax 2682-0135. www.lagarta.com. 6 units. $70 double. AE, MC, V. **Amenities:** Restaurant; bar; midsize pool. *In room:* No phone.

INEXPENSIVE

The Gilded Iguana ★ This long-standing hotel and restaurant began with a few very basic budget rooms. However, it now has a swimming pool, with a high waterfall emptying into it, and six newer, more luxurious rooms. The new rooms have very high ceilings, lots of space, air-conditioning, and minifridges. They are set back from the pool in a row, and sit among some shade trees. The older rooms are much more rustic, and located close to the road, just off the hotel's popular restaurant. These lack air-conditioning, but are more economical. The restaurant here is deservedly popular (see below), and in addition to feeding its guests, draws a lot of the local expatriate community to watch sporting events and listen to the occasional live band.

Playa Guiones, Guanacaste. ☏**2682-0259.** www.thegildediguana.com. 12 units. $45–$55 double; $65–$80 suite. AE, MC, V. **Amenities:** Restaurant; bar; midsize pool. *In room:* Minifridge, no phone.

Where to Dine

In addition to the places mentioned below, **Marlin Bill's** (☏**2682-0458**) is a popular and massive open-air haunt on the hillside on the main road, just across from Café de Paris (see below). You can expect to get good, fresh seafood and American classics here. For Mexican food, try **Pancho's** (☏**2682-0591**) or **Foony's** (☏**2682-0385**), both in Playa Guiones. For Italian, **La Dolce Vita** ★ (☏**2682-0107**), on the outskirts of town on the road to Playa Sámara, serves up excellent Italian fare nightly, while closer to town, **Giardino Tropicale** (☏**2682-4000**) also has good Italian fare and brick-oven pizzas. Finally, for local flavor, head to **Doña Olga's** (no phone), a simple Costa Rican *soda,* located right on the beach in Playa Pelada.

Finally, if you're looking to beat the heat, head to **Robin's Ice Cream** ★ (☏**2682-0617**), on the road to the beach in Guiones, for some homemade ice cream.

Café de Paris ★ BAKERY/BISTRO This popular place has wonderful fresh-baked goods and a wide assortment of light bites and full-on meals. You can get pizza or

Yo Quiero Hablar Español

You can brush up on or start up your Spanish at the **Rey de Nosara Language School** (☏/fax 2682-0215; www.reydenosara.itgo.com). It offers group and private lessons according to demand, and can coordinate week or multiweek packages.

nachos or filling sandwiches on fresh baguettes. There are also hearty salads, as well as fish, meat, and chicken dishes. I enjoy stopping in for a cup of espresso and a fresh almond croissant, and breakfasts are excellent here. Sporting events or movie videos are shown nightly, and there's even a pool table and Internet cafe.

On the main road into Nosara. ☎2682-0087. Baked goods 75[ce]–$4; main courses $4–$18. AE, MC, V. Daily 7am–11pm.

The Gilded Iguana ★ SEAFOOD/GRILL This simple restaurant serves fish so fresh that it's still wiggling: The owner's husband, Chiqui, is a local fisherman. There are also great burgers, Costa Rican *casados,* and a list of nightly specials. If you're in town fishing, they'll cook your catch. Sporting events are shown on a not-quite-big-enough television. There's a separate bar area, on the other side of their pool, where you can also dine. Overall, the vibe is sociable and lively. Most of the tables and chairs here are low-lying affairs; plus-size travelers might find the chairs a bit challenging to get in and out of.

About 90m (295 ft.) inland from the beach at Playa Guiones. ☎2682-0259. Main courses $5–$17. V. Daily 7am–9:30pm.

La Luna ★ 🍴 INTERNATIONAL With an enviable location overlooking the water at Playa Pelada and a casually elegant ambience, this little restaurant is an excellent choice. I especially like grabbing one of the outdoor tables closest to the waves for breakfast or lunch. However, it's also quite beautiful at night, with candles spread around generously. The chalkboard menu changes regularly, but will usually include some Thai or Indian curry, as well as pasta dishes and hearty steaks. Prices are on the high side, and service and hospitality can be spotty at times, but this is still probably the best beachside dining to be had in Nosara.

Playa Pelada. ☎2682-0122. Main courses $8–$36. MC, V. Daily 5am–9pm.

Nosara After Dark

When evening rolls around, don't expect a major party scene. Nightlife near the beach seems to center on the **Café de Paris, Marlin Bill's,** and **Casa Tucán,** which are all near the main intersection leading to Playa Guiones. While you also might head further north to **Blew Dogs** or the **Gilded Iguana.** Casa Tucán and Gilded Iguana often have live music. In "downtown" Nosara, you'll probably want to check out either the **Tropicana,** the town's long-standing local disco, or the **Legends Bar,** a U.S.-style bar with big-screen televisions, and pool and foosball tables.

North of Nosara

Just north of Nosara lies Playa Ostional, famous for its massive nestings of olive ridley sea turtles (see above). At the northern edge of Playa Ostional where it meets Playa San Juanillo, a few hotels have sprung up. The best of these is **Hotel Luna Azul** ★ (☎8821-0075; www.hotellunaazul.com), which features beautiful individual bungalows and a great view of the ocean—although the beach is a good distance away.

THE NORTHERN ZONE:
MOUNTAIN LAKES, CLOUD FORESTS & A VOLCANO

C osta Rica's northern zone is home to several prime ecotourist destinations, including the misty and mysterious **Monteverde Cloud Forest Reserve ★★★** and the astoundingly active **Arenal Volcano ★★**. There are rainforests and cloud forests, jungle rivers, mountain lakes, lowland marshes, and an unbelievable wealth of birds and other wildlife. Slight changes in elevation create unique microclimates and ecosystems throughout the region. In addition to these natural wonders, this region also provides an intimate glimpse into the rural heart and soul of Costa Rica. Small, isolated lodges flourish, and towns and villages remain predominantly small agricultural communities.

This area is also a must for adventure travelers. The northern zone has one of the best windsurfing spots in the world, on **Lake Arenal ★**, as well as excellent opportunities for mountain biking, hiking, canyoning, and river rafting. Zipline canopy tours and suspended forest bridges abound. And if you partake in any number of adventure activities, you'll also find several soothing natural hot springs in the area to soak your tired muscles.

PUERTO VIEJO DE SARAPIQUI ★

82km (51 miles) N of San José; 102km (63 miles) E of La Fortuna

The Sarapiquí region, named for the principal river that runs through this area, lies at the foot of the Cordillera Central mountain range. To the west is the rainforest of **Braulio Carrillo National Park,** and to the east are **Tortuguero National Park ★★** and **Barra del Colorado National Wildlife Refuge ★**. In between these protected areas lay thousands of acres of banana, pineapple, and palm plantations. Here you see the great contradiction of Costa Rica: On the one hand, the country is known for its national parks, which preserve some of the largest tracts of rainforest left in Central America; on the other hand, nearly every acre of land outside of these parks, save a few private reserves, has been clear-cut and converted into plantations—and the cutting continues.

Within the remaining rainforest are several lodges that attract naturalists (both amateur and professional). Two of these lodges, **La Selva** and **Rara Avis,** are famous for the research that's conducted on their surrounding reserves. Birdwatching and rainforest hikes are the primary attractions, but more adventure-oriented travelers will find plenty of activities available here, including canopy tours and boating and rafting trips along the Sarapiquí River.

PREVIOUS PAGE: **Selvatura hanging bridge.**

The Northern Zone

Essentials

GETTING THERE & DEPARTING By Car: The Guápiles Highway, which leads to the Caribbean coast, heads north out of downtown San José on Calle 3 before heading east. Turn north before reaching Guápiles on the road to Río Frío, and continue north through Las Horquetas, passing the turnoffs for Rara Avis, La Selva, and El Gavilán lodges before reaching Puerto Viejo.

A more scenic route goes through Heredia, Barva, Varablanca, and San Miguel before reaching Puerto Viejo. This route passes very close to the Poás Volcano and directly in front of the La Paz waterfall. If you want to take this route, head west out of San José, then turn north to Heredia and follow the signs for Varablanca. *Tip:* If you plan to stop on the way to see the **La Paz Waterfall Gardens** (p. 162) or ride the **Rain Forest Aerial Tram** (p. 178), budget at least 2 hours to visit either attraction.

By Bus: Empresarios Guapileños buses (☎2222-0610 in San José, or 2710-7780 in Puerto Viejo) leave San José roughly every hour between 6:30am and 6pm from the **Gran Terminal del Caribe,** on Calle Central, 1 block north of Avenida 11. The buses are marked RIO FRIO, PUERTO VIEJO, or both. There are two routes to Puerto Viejo de Sarapiquí. The faster route heads out on the Guápiles Highway, through Braulio Carrillo National Park and then past Las Horquetas. The slower but more scenic route heads out through Heredia, Varablanca, and La Virgen, passing between the Barva and Poás volcanoes. If you're heading to La Selva, Rara Avis, or El Gavilán lodges, be sure you're on a bus going through Braulio Carrillo and Las Horquetas. The trip takes between 2 and 3 hours, depending on the route taken, the condition of the roads, and the frequency of stops; the fare is around $3. Buses for San José leave Puerto Viejo roughly every hour between 6am and 6pm.

ORIENTATION Puerto Viejo is a very small town, at the center of which is a soccer field. If you continue past the soccer field on the main road and stay on the paved road, and then turn right at the Banco Nacional, you'll come to the Río Sarapiquí and the dock, where you can look into arranging a boat trip.

What to See & Do

BOAT TRIPS For the adventurous, Puerto Viejo is a jumping-off point for trips down the Río Sarapiquí to Barra del Colorado National Wildlife Refuge and Tortuguero National Park on the Caribbean coast. A boat for up to 10 people will cost you around $200 to $300 to Barra del Colorado or $250 to $375 to Tortuguero. If you're interested in this trip, it's worth checking at your hotel or with **Oasis Nature Tours** (☎2766-6108; www.oasisnaturetours. com). Alternatively, you can head down to the town dock on the bank of the Sarapiquí and see if you can arrange a less expensive boat trip on your own by tagging along with another group or, better yet, with a bunch of locals.

In addition to the longer trips, you can take shorter trips on the river for between $10 and $20 per person per hour. A trip down the Sarapiquí, even if it's for only an hour or two, provides opportunities to spot crocodiles, caimans, monkeys, sloths, and dozens of bird species.

CANOPY TOUR & MORE Hacienda Pozo Azul (☎877/810-6903 in the U.S. and Canada, or 2761-1360 in Costa Rica; www.pozoazul.com) is a working cattle farm and one-stop shop for a wide range of adventure activities. These folks have an extensive zip-line canopy tour operation, with 17 platforms connected by 12 different cable runs, in addition to offering white-water rafting and kayaking, horseback riding, guided hikes, and mountain bike tours. They even run a tent-camp and separate rustic lodge, in deep rainforest sites here. Several differently priced combo packages are offered, and the property is open daily from 9am to 5pm.

GO BANANAS The local community of Nogal and Chiquita banana company have combined to offer an interpretive tour of a regional banana plantation. Part theater, part educational presentation, and part site inspection, the tour even features dancing girls. The 2-hour tour is offered every Tuesday at 1:30pm, or by reservation (☎8862-5780; www.chiquitabananashow.com), and costs $15.

HIKING & GUIDED TOURS Anyone can take advantage of the 56km (35 miles) of well-maintained **trails at La Selva ★** (p. 293). If you're not staying there, however, you'll have to take a guided hike, led by experienced and well-informed naturalists. Half- and full-day hikes ($30 and $38, respectively) are offered daily, but you must reserve in advance (☎2524-0607 or 2424-0607; www.threepaths.co.cr). The half-day tours leave at 8am and 1:30pm daily.

My favorite hike starts off with the Cantarrana ("singing frog") trail, which includes a section of low bridges over a rainforest swamp. From here, you can join up with either the near or far circular loop trails—**CCC** and **CCL.** Another good hiking option is the trails and suspended bridges at the **Centro Neotrópico SarapiquíS** (p. 294).

Finally, if you want to visit the Sarapiquí region on a day trip from San José, call either **Costa Rica Fun Adventures** (☎2290-6015; www.cr funadventures.com) or **Ecoscapes Highlights Tour** (☎2297-0664; www. ecoscapetours.com), which run jampacked day trips that combine a bus ride and stop at the Poás Volcano, La Paz waterfall, a visit to a coffee farm, a rainforest hike, and a boat ride on the river for around $90 per person.

FROM LEFT: La Paz Waterfall Gardens; Red-eyed tree frog.

A NATURAL-HISTORY THEME PARK The **Sarapiquís Rainforest Lodge** (p. 294) is a multifaceted natural-history project and tourist attraction. The **Alma Ata Archaeological Park** is basically an ongoing dig of a modest pre-Columbian gravesite; so far, 12 graves, some petroglyphs, and numerous pieces of ceramic and jewelry have been unearthed. Plans for the park include the reconstruction of a small indigenous village. The hotel also has a small museum that displays examples of the ceramics, tools, clothing, and carvings found here, as well as other natural-history exhibits. Just across the hotel's driveway, you'll find the Chester Field Biological Gardens, which feature well-tended and displayed examples of local medicinal and ornamental plants and herbs, as well as food crops. Admission to the archaeological park, museum, and gardens costs $30. If you just want to visit the museum, the cost is $15; it's open daily from 8am to 5pm. A self-guided walk through the botanical gardens is free.

Across the river from the Sarapiquís Rainforest Lodge is the 300-hectare (741-acre) private **Tirimbina Rainforest Center** ★ (✆2761-1579; www.tirimbina.org), which features a small network of trails and several impressive suspension bridges, both over the river and through the forest canopy. A self-guided walk of the bridges and trails of the reserve costs $15 per person, and a 2-hour guided tour costs $22 per person—definitely worth the extra few bucks. The center is open daily from 7am to 5pm, and from 7:30 to 9:30pm for night tours; specialized bird-watching tours are also available.

PINEAPPLE PRODUCTION Similar to the above-mentioned banana tour, you can visit a working pineapple plantation on the **Colin Street Bakery's Pineapple Tour** (✆8820-6489). Located between Puerto Viejo and La Virgin, near La Quinta de Sarapiquí Country Inn, these folks have over 3,000 acres under cultivation, including conventional, organic, and ornamental fields. The tour includes a trip through the plantation, explanations and demonstrations of the processes involved, and a sampling of the fruit. Admission is $24 for adults; $18 for students; $13 children 4 to 11.

RAFTING & KAYAKING If you want a fast, wild ride on the river, check in with **Aguas Bravas** (✆2292-2072; www.aguas-bravas.co.cr) or **Aventuras del Sarapiquí** ★ (✆2766-6768; www.sarapiqui.com). Both companies run trips on a variety of sections of the Sarapiquí and Puerto Viejo rivers, ranging from Class I to Class IV. Trips cost between $50 and $80 per person. Aventuras del Sarapiquí also runs mountain-biking and horseback riding tours in the area. They rent kayaks, give kayaking classes, and offer kayak trips for more experienced and/or daring river rats, and offer inner-tube floats for those with lesser skill sets still looking to get wet.

SNAKES UNDER GLASS Just a few blocks west of the Centro Neotrópico Sarapiquís, you'll find **Jardin de Seprientes** (Snake Garden; ✆2761-1059), a collection of over 50 snakes, both venomous and nonvenomous, and other reptiles and amphibians. One of the prize attractions here, although not native, is a massive, yellow Burmese python. All are kept in clean, well-lit displays. Admission is $6 adults, $4 children and it's open daily from 9am to 5pm.

ONE MAJOR ATTRACTION EN ROUTE If you're driving to Puerto Viejo de Sarapiquí via the Guápiles Highway, you might want to stop at the **Rain Forest Aerial Tram** ★. You'll see the entrance on your right shortly after passing

Eyelash viper.

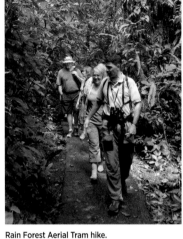

Rain Forest Aerial Tram hike.

through the Zurquí tunnel. For more information, see "What to See & Do" and "Side Trips from San José," in chapter 6.

Where to Stay & Dine

All the lodges listed below arrange excursions throughout the region, including boat trips on the Sarapiquí, guided hikes in the rainforest, and horseback or mountain-bike rides. Also note that rates for the lodges in the "Expensive" category include all meals, taxes, and usually a tour or two, greatly reducing their real cost. In addition to the hotels listed below, **Peace Lodge** (p. 143), located at the La Paz Waterfall Gardens, is almost close enough to be considered lodging in this region.

EXPENSIVE

La Selva Biological Station ★ This place caters primarily to students and researchers but also accepts visitors seeking a rustic rainforest adventure. The atmosphere is definitely that of a scientific research center. La Selva, which is operated by the Organization for Tropical Studies (OTS), covers 1,480 hectares (3,656 acres) and is contiguous with Braulio Carrillo National Park. There are miles of well-maintained hiking trails to explore. Rooms are basic but large, and the high ceilings help keep them cool. Most have bunk beds and shared bathrooms, although eight have private bathrooms and twin beds, and the two-room family units have a mix of twin and queen-size beds. There's no price difference, so be specific when reserving a room. Rates are pretty high for what you get, but you can take some solace in the fact that you're helping to support valuable and valiant research and conservation efforts.

Puerto Viejo (A.P. 676-2050, San Pedro, Costa Rica). ☎ **2524-0607** reservations office in San José, or 2766-6565 at the lodge. Fax 2524-0608. www.threepaths.co.cr. 24 units, 16 with shared bathroom. $84 per person double occupancy. Rates include all meals, half-day tour, and taxes. Rates lower for researchers and student groups. MC, V. **Amenities:** Restaurant; kayak rentals. *In room:* No phone.

Selva Verde Lodge ★ ☺ This is one of the pioneering ecotourist ventures in Costa Rica. The main lodge is a series of buildings connected by covered walkways that keep you dry even though this area receives more than 150 inches of rain each year. The bungalows are across the road and 500m (1,640 ft.) into the forest; they're not as close to the main compound as the lodge rooms, but they offer more privacy, as well as air-conditioning and a private screened veranda. Meals are served buffet-style in a beautiful large dining room that overlooks the river. Across the river is a large rainforest preserve. There are trails on the grounds, a wonderful suspension bridge with a separate zip-line adventure across the river to more trails, and modest butterfly and botanical gardens. There's also a pretty free-form pool and separate children's pool, as well as a natural swimming hole right on the river.

Chilamate (A.P. 55-3069), Sarapiquí. **☎800/451-7111** in the U.S. and Canada, or 2766-6800. Fax 2766-6011. www.selvaverde.com. 40 units, 5 bungalows. $187–$216 double. Rates include 3 meals daily and taxes. AE, DC, DISC, MC, V. **Amenities:** Restaurant; bar; outdoor pool; smoke-free rooms. *In room:* Hair dryer.

MODERATE

Although I highly recommend you choose one of the more atmospheric nature lodges listed in this section, if you absolutely must, or for some reason prefer to, stay in Puerto Viejo de Sarapiquí proper, **Hotel El Bambú** (**☎2766-6005;** www.elbambu.com) is a clean, comfortable, and almost modern option.

In addition to the places outside town that are reviewed below, the **Tirimbina Rainforest Center** ★ (**☎2761-1579;** www.tirimbina.org) now has rooms.

Rara Avis 🎁 Rara Avis is one of the first, most responsible, biologically rich, and isolated ecolodge operations in Costa Rica. There are several options here, but the Waterfall Lodge is by far the most comfortable and popular. It has rustic but comfortable rooms in a two-story building near the main lodge, dining room, and namesake waterfall. Each unit here is a corner room with a wraparound porch. For those who want a closer communion with nature, Rara Avis has a two-room cabin set deep in the forest beside a river, about a 10-minute hike from the main lodge, as well as three more rustic two-bedroom cabins with shared bathrooms, located in a small clearing about a 5-minute walk from the lodge. Meals are basic Tico-style dishes with lots of beans and rice. *Bird-watchers, take note:* More than 362 species of birds have been sighted here, and the lodge consistently has excellent guides and naturalists.

When making reservations, be sure to get directions for how to get to Las Horquetas and information on coordinating your ride on the lodge's tractor. The tractor leaves just once daily for the very bumpy and plodding 3-hour ride to the lodge.

15km (9⅓ miles) from Las Horquetas (A.P. 8105-1000, San José). **☎2764-1111** for reservations or 2710-8032 at the lodge. Fax 2764-1114. www.rara-avis.com. 16 units, 10 with private bathroom. $50 per person with shared bathroom; $150–$170 double with private bathroom. Rates include transportation from Las Horquetas, guided hikes, all meals, and taxes. AE, MC, V. **Amenities:** Restaurant. *In room:* No phone.

Sarapiquís Rainforest Lodge ★ On a high bluff fronting the Sarapiquí River, this complex is the most unique project in the Sarapiquí region. Rooms are housed in three large, round buildings, or *palenques*, based on the traditional pre-Columbian constructions of the area. Each *palenque* has a towering thatch roof.

All rooms are of good size, although a little dark. Each has a door leading out to the shared veranda that encircles the building. The hotel has several interesting attractions, including a small natural-history museum, an on-site excavation of a pre-Columbian graveyard, and a well-marked botanical garden. Just across the river lies the 300-hectare (741-acre) Tirimbina Rainforest Center, with a small network of trails and several impressive suspension bridges, both over the river and through the forest canopy.

A.P. 86-3069, La Virgen de Sarapiquí. **2761-1004.** Fax 2761-1415. www.sarapiquis.org. 36 units. $104 double. V. **Amenities:** Restaurant; bar; babysitting; room service; smoke-free rooms.

Sueño Azul Resort ★ ★ ☺ This lodge and wellness retreat offers the best accommodations in the area. Set at the juncture of two rivers and backed by forested mountains, the setting's pretty sweet, as well. All rooms are spacious, with high ceilings, large bathrooms, and a private porch overlooking either one of the rivers or a small lake. Junior suites come with a private outdoor Jacuzzi. Meals served in an open-air dining room set to take in the view, and a pool, Jacuzzi, and bar are down by the rivers' edge. The best place to cool off is in the massive outdoor pool, fed and filled by river water, although there's a traditional freshwater pool, and you can simply swim in the river at various spots. A wide range of spa treatments, tours, and activities is offered, including rainforest hikes, horseback riding, mountain biking, and fly-fishing.

Las Horquetas de Sarapiquí (A.P. 3630-1000, San José). **2253-2020** reservation number in San José, 2764-1048 at the lodge. Fax 2224-3552. www.suenoazulresort.com. 65 units. $125 double; $180 suite. Rates include taxes. Add $20 for air-conditioning. MC, V. **Amenities:** Restaurant; Jacuzzi; 2 outdoor pools; room service. *In room:* A/C (in some), hair dryer, minibar.

INEXPENSIVE

In addition to the places listed below, budget travelers might want to check out the **Posada Andrea Cristina** (**2766-6265;** www.andreacristina.com), which is just on the outskirts of Puerto Viejo and is run by Alex Martínez, an excellent local guide and pioneering conservationist in the region. You may also consider staying at the jungle tent camp or isolated Magsasay Lodge at **Hacienda Pozo Azul** (**877/810-6903** in the U.S. and Canada, or 2438-2616; www.pozoazul.com).

Gavilán Sarapiquí River Lodge On the banks of the Río Sarapiquí just south of Puerto Viejo, Gavilán is surrounded by 100 hectares (247 acres) of forest reserve (secondary forest) and 14 hectares (35 acres) of gardens planted with lots of flowering ginger, heliconia, orchids, and bromeliads. Guest rooms are basic and simply furnished. All have fans and hot water, and there are always fresh-cut flowers. The four "superior" rooms have much more contemporary appointments and amenities. There's an unheated Jacuzzi in the garden and several open-air ranchos, some of which have hammocks strung up for afternoon siestas. Tico and Continental meals are served buffet-style, and there are always plenty of fresh fruits and juices. Guided hikes through the forest, horseback rides, and river trips are all offered for around $30 per person.

Puerto Viejo de Sarapiquí (A.P. 445-2010, San José). **2234-9507** or 2766-6743. Fax 2253-6556. www.gavilanlodge.com. 17 units. $60 double; $75 superior double. MC, V. **Amenities:** Restaurant; bar; Jacuzzi. *In room:* No phone.

La Quinta de Sarapiquí Country Inn This small, family-run lodge makes a good base for exploring the Sarapiquí region. Located on the banks of the Sardinal River about 15 minutes west of Puerto Viejo, La Quinta caters primarily to nature lovers and bird-watchers. The rooms are located in a half-dozen buildings dispersed around the grounds among richly flowering gardens and connected by covered walkways. They're simple but clean, with good lighting and comfortable bathrooms. Each room has a small patio with a sitting chair or two for gazing out into the garden. The superior rooms have air-conditioning. A small gift shop, a butterfly garden, a frog garden, an extensive insect display, and a vegetable garden and reforestation project are also on hand. Meals are served either buffet- or family-style in the main lodge.

Chilamate (A.P. 43-3069), Sarapiquí. ☎2761-1300. Fax 2761-1395. www.laquintasarapiqui.com. 31 units. $80 double; $95 superior double; $125 suite. Children 11 and under stay free in parent's room. AE, MC, V. **Amenities:** Restaurant; bar; small outdoor pool.

ARENAL VOLCANO & LA FORTUNA ★★

140km (87 miles) NW of San José; 61km (38 miles) E of Tilarán

I've visited scores of times, and I never tire of watching red lava rocks tumble down the flanks of **Arenal Volcano,** and listening in awe to its deep rumbling. If you've never experienced them firsthand, the sights and sounds of an active volcano are awe-inspiring. Arenal is one of the world's most regularly active volcanoes. In July 1968, the volcano, which had lain dormant for hundreds of years, surprised everybody by erupting with sudden violence. The nearby village of Tabacón was destroyed, and nearly 80 of its inhabitants were killed. Since that eruption, 1,607m (5,271-ft.) Arenal has been Costa Rica's most active volcano. Frequent powerful explosions send cascades of red-hot lava rocks down the volcano's steep slopes. During the day these lava flows smoke and rumble. However, at night the volcano puts on its most mesmerizing show. If you are lucky enough to be here on a clear and active night—not necessarily a guaranteed occurrence—you'll see the night sky turned red by lava spewing from Arenal's crater. In the past few years, the forests to the south of the volcano have been declared Arenal National Park. Eventually, this park should stretch all the way to Monteverde Biological Cloud Forest Reserve.

Lying at the eastern foot of this natural spectacle is the tiny farming community of **La Fortuna.** This town has become a magnet for volcano watchers, adventure tourists, and assorted travelers from around the world. A host of budget and moderately priced hotels are in and near La Fortuna, and from here you can arrange night tours to the best volcano-viewing spots, which are 17km (11 miles) away on the western slope, on the road to and beyond the Tabacón Grand Spa Thermal Resort.

Essentials

GETTING THERE & DEPARTING By Plane: Nature Air (☎800/235-9272 in the U.S. and Canada, or 2299-6000; www.natureair.com) flies to Arenal/ La Fortuna daily at 11:20am from Tobías Bolaños International Airport in

Arenal Volcano at night.

Pavas. The flight duration is 30 minutes. Return flights depart for San José at 1:20pm. One-way fares are $94. Nature Air also has connecting flights between Arenal and other major destinations in the country.

Sansa (☎877/767-2672 in the U.S. and Canada, or 2290-4100 in Costa Rica; www.flysansa.com) has one daily flight to Arenal La Fortuna from San José's Juan Santamaría International airport at 7:10am. The flight takes 30 minutes. The fare is $68 each way. The return flight leaves Arenal at 9:30am. Sansa also has one daily direct flight from Liberia to Arenal at 8:55am, returning at 7:50am.

Taxis are sometimes waiting for all arriving flights. If not, you can call one at ☎2479-9605 or 2479-8522. The fare to La Fortuna runs around $20. Alternately, Nature Air can arrange to have a van waiting for you, for $57 for up to seven people.

By Car: There are several routes to La Fortuna from San José. The most popular is to head west on the Interamerican Highway and then turn north at Naranjo, continuing north through Zarcero to Ciudad Quesada. From Ciudad Quesada, one route goes through Jabillos, while the other goes through Muelle. The former route is better marked, more popular, slightly shorter, and generally better maintained, but the severe weather and heavy traffic quickly take their toll, and the roads up here can be notoriously bad for long stretches. This route offers wonderful views of the San Carlos valley as you come down from Ciudad Quesada; and Zarcero, with its topiary gardens and quaint church, makes a good place to stop, stretch your legs, and snap a few photos (see "Side Trips from San José," in chapter 6, for more information).

You can also stay on the Interamerican Highway until San Ramón (west of Naranjo) and then head north through La Tigra. This route is also very scenic and passes the Villa Blanca Cloud Forest & Spa (p. 314). The travel time on any of the above routes is between 2½ and 3½ hours.

Finally, if you combine your visit here with a stop at the Poás Volcano and La Paz Waterfall, or if you stay at a lodge closer to Aguas Zarcas, you can go first to Alajuela or Heredia and then head north to Varablanca before continuing on to San Miguel, where you turn west toward Río Cuarto and

boats, **HORSES & TAXIS**

You can travel between La Fortuna and Monteverde by boat and taxi, or on a combination boat, horseback, and taxi trip. A 10- to 20-minute boat ride across Lake Arenal cuts out hours of driving around its shores. From La Fortuna to the put-in point is about a 25-minute taxi ride. It's about a 1½-hour four-wheel-drive taxi ride between the Río Chiquito dock on the other side of Lake Arenal and Santa Elena. These trips can be arranged in either direction for between $25 and $50 per person, all-inclusive.

You can also add on a horseback ride on the Santa Elena/Monteverde side of the lake. There are several routes and rides offered. The steepest heads up the mountains and through the forest to the town of San Gerardo, which is only a 30-minute car ride from Santa Elena. Other routes throw in shorter sections of horseback riding along the lakeside

lowlands. With the horseback ride, this trip runs around $50 to $75 per person. *Warning:* The riding is often rainy, muddy, and steep. Many find it much more arduous than awe-inspiring. Moreover, I've received numerous complaints about the condition of the trails and the treatment of the horses, so be very careful and demanding before signing on for this trip. Find out what route you will be taking, as well as the condition of the horses if possible. **Desafío Expeditions** (☎2479-9464; www.desafiocostarica.com) is one of the more reputable operators. They will even drive your car around for you while you take the scenic (and sore) route.

If you're looking to make the ride just by taxi and boat, check in with **Jeep Boat Jeep** (☎2479-9955), which has two daily fixed departures in each direction at 7am and 4pm for $30 per person.

Aguas Zarcas. From Aguas Zarcas, continue west through Muelle to the turnoff for La Fortuna. This is the longest route.

By Bus: Buses (☎2255-0567) leave San José for La Fortuna roughly every 2 hours between 5am and 7:30pm from the **Atlántico del Norte** bus station at Avenida 9 and Calle 12. The trip lasts 4 hours; the fare is $3.70. The bus you take might be labeled TILARAN. Make sure it passes through Ciudad Quesada. If so, it passes through La Fortuna; if not, you'll end up in Tilarán via the Interamerican Highway, passing through the Guanacaste town of Cañas, a long way from La Fortuna.

Alternatively, you can take a bus from the same station to Ciudad Quesada and transfer there to another bus to La Fortuna. These buses depart roughly every 30 minutes between 5am and 7:30pm. The fare for the 2½-hour trip is $3. Local buses between Ciudad Quesada and La Fortuna run regularly through the day, although the schedule changes frequently, depending on demand. The trip lasts an hour; the fare is $1.50.

Buses depart **Monteverde/Santa Elena** for Tilarán every day at 7am. This is a journey of only 35km (22 miles), but the trip lasts 2½ hours because the road is in such horrendous condition. People with bad backs should think twice about making the trip, especially by bus. The return bus from Tilarán to Santa Elena leaves at 12:30pm. The fare is $2.30. Buses

9

from Tilarán to La Fortuna depart daily at 8am and 4:30pm, and make the return trip at 7am and 12:30pm. The trip is 3 to 4 hours; the fare is $2.75.

Buses depart La Fortuna for San José roughly every 2 hours between 5am and 5:30pm; in some instances, you might have to transfer in Ciudad Quesada. From there, you can catch one of the frequent buses to San José.

Gray Line (☎2220-2126; www.graylinecostarica.com) has two daily buses from San José to La Fortuna at 6:30 and 7am and 3:30pm. The fare is $35. **Interbus** (☎2283-5573; www.interbusonline.com) also has two buses daily leaving San José for La Fortuna at 8am and 2pm. The fare is $39. Both companies will pick you up at most San José–area hotels. And both companies also run routes from La Fortuna with connections to most other major destinations in Costa Rica.

ORIENTATION & FAST FACTS As you enter La Fortuna, you'll see the massive volcano directly in front of you. La Fortuna is only a few streets wide, with almost all the hotels, restaurants, and shops clustered along the main road that leads out of town toward Tabacón and the volcano. There are several information and tour-booking offices and Internet cafes, as well as a couple of pharmacies, general stores, and laundromats on the streets that surround the small central park that fronts the Catholic church. There's a Banco de Costa Rica as you enter La Fortuna, just over the Río Burío bridge, and a Banco Nacional in the center of town, across the park from the church. Both have ATMs.

GETTING AROUND If you don't have a car, you'll need to either take a cab or go on an organized tour if you want to visit the hot springs or view the volcano eruption. There are tons of taxis in La Fortuna (you can flag one down practically anywhere), and there is always a line of them ready and waiting along the main road beside the central park. A taxi between La Fortuna and Tabacón should cost around $6. Another alternative is to rent a car when you get here. **Alamo** (☎2479-9090; www.alamocostarica.com) and **Poás** (☎2479-8027; www.carentals.com) both have offices in La Fortuna.

There are also several places to rent scooters and ATVs around town. Provided it's not raining too heavily, this is a good way to get around. Rates run around $35 to $50 per day for a scooter, and $50 to $90 for an ATV.

What to See & Do

While in the town of La Fortuna, be sure to spend some time simply people-watching from a bench or grassy spot on the central plaza. It's also worth a quick visit to tour the town's **Catholic church.** This modern church was designed by famous Costa Rican artist Teodorico Quirós, and features an interesting soaring front steeple and clock tower of concrete.

EXPERIENCING THE VOLCANO ★★

The first thing you should know is that Arenal Volcano borders a region of cloud forests and rainforests, and the volcano's cone is often socked in by clouds and fog. Many people come to Arenal and never get to see the exposed cone. Moreover, the volcano does go through periods when it is relatively quiet.

The second thing you should know is that you can't climb Arenal Volcano—it's not safe due to the constant activity. Several foolish people who have ignored this warning have lost their lives, and others have been severely injured. The most recent fatalities occurred in August 2000.

Still, waiting for and watching Arenal's regular eruptions is the main activity in La Fortuna and is best done at night when the orange lava glows against the starry sky. Although it's possible simply to look up from the middle of town and see Arenal erupting, the view is best from the north and west sides of the volcano along the road to Tabacón and toward the national park entrance. If you have a car, you can drive along this road, but if you've arrived by bus, you will need to take a taxi or tour.

Arenal National Park (☎2461-8499) constitutes an area of more than 2,880 hectares (7,114 acres), which includes the viewing and parking areas closest to the volcano. The park is open daily from 8am to 10pm and charges $10 admission per person. The trails through forest and over old lava flows inside the park are gorgeous and fun. (Be careful climbing on those volcanic boulders.) However, at night the view from inside the park is no better than on the roads just outside it.

If you don't have a car and are staying in La Fortuna, every hotel in town and several tour offices offer night tours to the volcano. (They don't actually enter the park; they stop on the road that runs between the park entrance and the Arenal Observatory Lodge.) These tours generally cost between $10 and $30 per person. Often these volcano-viewing tours include a stop at one of the local hot springs, and the price goes up accordingly (see "Taking a Soothing Soak in Hot Springs," below, for a description of the different options and fees).

Note: Although it's counterintuitive, the rainy season is often a better time to see the exposed cone of Arenal Volcano, especially at night. I don't know why this is, but I've had excellent volcano-viewing sessions at various points during the rainy season; during the dry season the volcano can often be socked in solid for days at a time. The bottom line is that catching a glimpse of the volcano's cone is never a sure thing.

La Fortuna with Arenal Volcano in background.

Lava flows in Arenal National Park.

Sky Tram canopy tour.

Canyoning tour.

OTHER ADVENTUROUS PURSUITS IN THE AREA

Aside from the impressive volcanic activity, the area around Arenal Volcano is packed with other natural wonders.

ATV The folks at **Fourtrax Adventures** (☎2479-8444; www.fourtraxadventure. com) offer a 3-hour adventure through the forests and farmlands around La Fortuna. The tour includes a stop at a jungle swimming hole, where you can cool off, as well as a visit to a butterfly farm. You get good views of the volcano, as well as the La Fortuna Waterfall. The cost is $85 per ATV. A second rider on the same ATV costs $25.

CANOPY TOURS & CANYONING There are numerous ways to get up into the forest canopy here. Perhaps the simplest way is to hike the trails and bridges of **Arenal Hanging Bridges** (☎2290-0469; www.hangingbridges.com). Located just over the Lake Arenal dam, this attraction is a complex of gentle trails and suspension bridges through a beautiful tract of primary forest. It's open daily from 7:30am to 4:30pm; admission is $22. Guided tours, early bird-watching tours, and transportation are also available.

Another option is the **Sky Tram** ★★ (☎2479-9944; www.skytrek. com), an open gondola-style ride that begins near the shores of Lake Arenal and rises up, providing excellent views of the lake and volcano. From here you can hike down their series of trails and suspended bridges. In the end you can hike down, take the gondola, or strap on a harness and ride their zip-line canopy tour down to the bottom. The zip-line tour here features several very long and very fast sections, with some impressive views of the lake and volcano. The cost is $60 for the combined tram ride up and zip-line down tour. It's $50 to ride the tram round-trip. The tram runs daily from 7:30am to 6pm.

There are several other zip-line canopy tours in the area, including the **Arenal Canopy Tour** (☎2479-9769) and **Ecoglide ★** (☎2479-7120; www.arenalecoglide.com). The hotel **Montaña de Fuego** (see later in this chapter), even has its own zip-line tour set up.

If you'd like a bigger rush than the canopy tours offer, you could go "canyoning" with **Pure Trek Canyoning** ★★ (☎866/569-5723 in the U.S. and Canada, or 2479-1313; www.puretrekcostarica.com) and **Desafío Expeditions** ★★ (☎2479-9464; www.desafiocostarica.com); both offer canyoning adventures. This adventure sport is a mix of hiking through and alongside a jungle river, punctuated with periodic rappels through and alongside the faces of rushing waterfalls. Pure Trek's trip is probably better for first-timers and families with kids, while Desafío's tour is just a bit more rugged and adventurous. Pure Trek charges $95, while Desafio charges $90. Both of these companies offer various combination full-day excursions, mixing canyoning with other adventure tours, and tend to have two to three daily departures, including one in the morning and one in the afternoon.

Finally, while nowhere near as natural, you can also take a bungee jump in La Fortuna at **Arenal Bungee** (☏**2479-7440;** http://arenal bungee.com). The bungee jump here is a 40m (130 ft.) fall from a steel

TAKING A SOOTHING SOAK IN
hot springs

Arenal Volcano has bestowed a terrific fringe benefit on the area around it: several naturally heated thermal springs.

Located at the site of the former village that was destroyed by the 1968 eruption, **Tabacón Grand Spa Thermal Resort ★★★** (☏**2519-1900;** www.tabacon.com) is the most extensive, luxurious, and expensive spot to soak your tired bones. A series of variously sized pools, fed by natural springs, are spread out among lush gardens. At the center is a large, warm, spring-fed swimming pool with a slide, a swim-up bar, and a perfect view of the volcano. One of the stronger streams flows over a sculpted waterfall, with a rock ledge underneath that provides a perfect place to sit and receive a free hydraulic shoulder massage. The grounds here are extensive and it's worth exploring. The pools and springs closest to the volcano are some of the hottest—makes sense, doesn't it? The resort also has an excellent spa on the grounds offering professional massages, mud masks, and other treatments, as well as yoga classes (appointments required). Most of the treatments are conducted in lovely open-air gazebos surrounded by

the rich tropical flora. The spa here even has several permanent sweat lodges, based on a Native American traditional design. A full-service restaurant, garden grill, and a couple of bars are available for those seeking sustenance.

Entrance fees are $85 for adults and $40 for children 11 and under. This rate includes either a buffet lunch or dinner, and allows admission for a full day. After 6pm, you can enter for $45 not including any meals. The hot springs are open daily from noon to 10pm (spa

Tabacón spa treatment.

tower constructed on the outskirts of downtown La Fortuna. You can even try a water landing, as well as a "rocket launch," which is kind of the equivalent of becoming a human sling shot. Jumps, falls, and rocket shots cost $50 each, with various packages available. This attraction is open 9:30am to 9:30pm daily, so you can partake in this fun day or night.

FISHING With Lake Arenal just around the corner, fishing is a popular activity here. The big fish here is *guapote,* a Central American species of rainbow bass. However, you can also book fishing trips to Caño Negro, where snook, tarpon, and other game fish can be stalked. Most hotels and adventure-tour companies can arrange fishing excursions. Costs run around $150 to $250 per boat, and a full day goes for around $250 to $500.

Eco Termales.

treatments can actually be scheduled as early as 8am, and hotel guests can enter at 10am). The pools are busiest between 2pm and 6pm. Management enforces a policy of limiting visitors, so reservations (which can be made online or by phone) are recommended. Spa treatments must be purchased separately, and reservations are required.

Baldi Hot Springs (☎ 2479-9651), next to the Volcano Look Disco, are the first hot springs you'll come to as you drive from La Fortuna toward Tabacón. This place has grown substantially over the years, with many different pools, slides, and bars and restaurants spread around the expansive grounds.

However, I find this place far less attractive than the other options mentioned here. There's much more of a party vibe at Baldi, with loud music often blaring at some of the swim-up bars. Admission is $34.

Just across the street from Baldi Hot Springs is the unmarked entrance of my current favorite local hot spring, **Eco Termales** ★★ (☎ 2479-8484). Smaller and more intimate than Tabacón, this series of pools set amid lush forest and gardens is almost as picturesque and luxurious, although there are far fewer pools, the spa services are much less extensive, and there is no view of the volcano. Reservations are absolutely necessary here, and total admissions are limited so that it is never crowded. Admission is $29. These folks have added a restaurant serving basic local fare, but I recommend just coming for the springs.

Finally, the newest entrant in the field is **Tikokú** (☎ 2479-1700), which is located right beside Baldi, and run by the folks at Arenal Kioro (p. 308). This spot features a row of eight descending sculpted pools. Admission is $24.

HIKING & HORSEBACK RIDING Horseback riding is a popular activity in this area, and there are scores of good rides on dirt back roads and through open fields and dense rainforest. Volcano and lake views come with the terrain on most rides. Horseback trips to the Río Fortuna waterfall are perhaps the most popular tours sold, but remember, the horse will get you only to the entrance; from there, you'll have to hike a bit. A horseback ride to the falls should cost between $20 and $40, including the entrance fee. Alternately, you

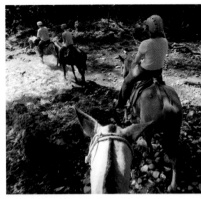

Horseback riding in Cerro Chato.

can check in with the folks at **Cabalgata Don Tobias** (☎2479-1212; www.cabalgatadontobias.com) which runs a 2½ hour tour on their private land, which is a mix of farmland and forest, with some great views of the volcano.

One popular and strenuous hike is to **Cerro Chato,** a dormant volcanic cone on the flank of Arenal. There's a pretty little lake up here. **Desafío Expeditions ★** (☎2479-9464; www.desafiocostarica.com) leads a 4- to 5-hour hike for $68, including lunch.

Aventuras Arenal (☎2479-9133; www.arenaladventures.com), **Desafío Expeditions ★★** (☎2479-9464; www.desafiocostarica.com), **Jacamar Tours** (☎2479-9767; www.arenaltours.com), and **Sunset Tours** (☎866/417-7352 in the U.S. and Canada, or 2479-9800 in Costa Rica; www.sunsettourcr.com) are the main tour operators. In addition to the above tours, each of these companies offers most of the tours listed in this section, as well as fishing trips and sightseeing excursions on the lake, and transfers to other destinations around Costa Rica.

LA FORTUNA FALLS Leading the list of side attractions in the area is the impressive **Río Fortuna Waterfall ★** (☎2479-8360), located about 5.5km (3½ miles) outside of town in a lush jungle setting. There's a sign in town to indicate the road that leads out to the falls. You can drive or hike to just within viewing distance. When you get to the entrance to the lookout, you'll have to pay a $6 entrance fee to actually check out the falls. It's another 15- to 20-minute hike down a steep and often muddy path to the pool formed by the waterfall. The hike back up will take slightly longer. You can swim, but stay away from the turbulent water at the base of the falls—several people have drowned here. Instead, check out and enjoy the calm pool just around the bend, or join the locals at the popular swimming hole under the bridge on the paved road, just after the turnoff for the road up to the falls. The trail to the falls is open daily from 8am to 4pm.

MOUNTAIN BIKING This region is very well suited for mountain biking. Rides range in difficulty from moderate to extremely challenging. You can combine a day on a mountain bike with a visit to one or more of the popular attractions here. **Bike Arenal** ★ (**866/465-4114** in the U.S. and Canada, or 2479-9454; www.bikearenal.com) is the only dedicated operator in the field, with an excellent collection of top-notch bikes and equipment and a wide range of tour possibilities.

WHITE-WATER RAFTING & CANOEING For adventurous tours of the area, check out **Desafío Expeditions** ★★ (**2479-9464**; www.desafiocosta rica.com) or **Wave Expeditions** ★★ (**2479-7262**; www.wave expeditions.com). Both companies offer daily raft rides of Class I to II, III, and IV to V on different sections of the Toro, Peñas Blancas, and Sarapiquí rivers. A half-day float trip on a nearby river costs around $65 per person; a full day of rafting on some rougher water costs $85 per person, depending on what section of what river you ride. Both companies also offer mountain biking and most of the standard local guided trips. If you want a wet and personal ride, try Desafío's tour in inflatable kayaks, or "duckies."

A more laid-back alternative is to take a canoe tour with **Canoa Aventura** (**2479-8200**; www.canoa-aventura.com), which offers half-, full-, and multiday excursions on a variety of rivers in the region, which range from $55 to $150 per person.

SIDE TRIPS FROM LA FORTUNA

La Fortuna is a great place from which to make a day trip to the **Caño Negro National Wildlife Refuge** ★. This vast network of marshes and rivers (particularly the Río Frío) is 100km (62 miles) north of La Fortuna near the town of Los Chiles. This refuge is best known for its amazing abundance of bird life, including roseate spoonbills, jabiru storks, herons, and egrets, but you can also see caimans and crocodiles. Bird-watchers should not miss this refuge, although keep in mind that the main lake dries up in the dry season (mid-Apr to Nov),

White-water rafting the Rio Toro.

which reduces the number of wading birds. Full-day tours to Caño Negro average between $55 and $65 per person. However, most of the tours run out of La Fortuna that are billed as Caño Negro never really enter the refuge but instead ply sections of the nearby Río Frio, which features similar wildlife and ecosystems. If you're interested in staying in this area and really visiting the refuge, check out the **Caño Negro Natural Lodge** (see "Where to Stay & Dine Farther Afield," later in this chapter).

Jabiru storks.

You can also visit the **Venado Caverns,** a 45-minute drive away. In addition to plenty of stalactites, stalagmites, and other limestone formations, you'll see bats and cave fish. Tours here cost around $45. All of the tour agencies and hotel tour desks can arrange or directly offer trips to Caño Negro and Venado Caverns.

Shopping

La Fortuna is chock-full of souvenir shops selling standard tourist fare. However, you'll find one of my favorite craft shops here. As you leave the town of La Fortuna toward Tabacón, keep your eye on the right-hand side of the road. When you see a massive collection of wood sculptures and a building reading **Original Grand Gallery** (no phone), slow down and pull over. This local artisan and his family produce works in a variety of styles and sizes. They specialize in faces, many of them larger than a typical home's front door. You can also find a host of animal figures, ranging in style from purely representational to rather abstract. Another good shop for higher-end arts and crafts is **Galería Lunática** (☎ **2479-8255**), on the main road in La Fortuna.

Where to Stay in La Fortuna

EXPENSIVE

Hotel Magic Mountain ★★ Located just on the outskirts of town—as you head toward Tabacón—this three-story hotel has large and luxurious rooms, with plenty of perks. All come with a private balcony facing the volcano. The junior suites are even bigger, with a separate sitting area, large shower with rainwater shower head, and private volcano-view in-room Jacuzzi. I like no. 506, which is an end unit with spectacular views. There's a spa and large free-form pool, with two separate outdoor Jacuzzis and separate children's pool, as well as the town's only sports bar.

La Fortuna, San Carlos. ☎ **2479-7246.** Fax 2479-7248. www.hotelmagicmountain.com. 42 units. $125 double; $175 suite. Rates include buffet breakfast. AE, MC, V. **Amenities:** Restaurant; bar; Jacuzzis; outdoor pool; spa. *In room:* A/C, TV, hair dryer, minibar, free Wi-Fi.

MODERATE

Hotel La Fortuna ★ This long-standing budget stalwart burned down several years ago and was quickly rebuilt near its original state. However, it was again razed (intentionally) and replaced with a massive and modern five-story building. Centrally located just 1 block south of the gas station, the Hotel La Fortuna now features large, spiffy rooms with a host of modern amenities. The best of these have volcano-view private balconies—ask for a room on the fourth or fifth floor with a volcano view. This hotel has 12 rooms designed for wheelchair accessibility.

La Fortuna, San Carlos. **☎2479-9197.** Fax 2479-8563. www.fortunainn.com. 44 units. $75–$85 double. Rates include buffet breakfast. MC, V. **Amenities:** Restaurant. *In room:* A/C, TV, hair dryer, no phone, free Wi-Fi.

Hotel San Bosco Located a block off La Fortuna's main street, the San Bosco offers some of the better rooms to be found right in town. The hotel actually has two styles of rooms. The least expensive rooms are all well maintained and feature tile floors and fans. However, these are standard budget-hotel affairs. The more expensive rooms are much more attractive and have stone walls, tile floors, reading lights, televisions, and benches on the veranda in front. There's an observation deck for volcano viewing on the top floor of the hotel, as well as a helpful front desk staff.

La Fortuna, San Carlos (200m/656 ft. north of the central park). **☎2479-9050.** Fax 2479-9109. www.arenal-volcano.com. 34 units. $72–$77 double. Rates include breakfast. AE, MC, V. **Amenities:** Small exercise room; Jacuzzi; small pool and separate children's pool. *In room:* A/C, TV, no phone, free Wi-Fi.

INEXPENSIVE

La Fortuna is a tourist boomtown; basic hotels have been popping up here at a phenomenal rate for several years running. Right in La Fortuna you'll find a score of budget options. If you have time, it's worth walking around and checking out a couple. One of the better options is **Arenal Backpackers Resort (☎2479-7000;** www.arenalbackpackers.com), which bills itself as a five-star hostel. It has both shared-bathroom dorm rooms, and more upscale private rooms, but even backpackers get to enjoy the large pool, Wi-Fi, and volcano views.

There are a couple places both in town and right on the outskirts of La Fortuna that allow camping, with access to basic bathroom facilities, for around $5 to $10 per person per night. If you have a car, drive a little bit out of town toward Tabacón and you'll find several more basic cabins and camping sites, some that even offer views of the volcano.

Hotel Las Colinas ★ 🌶 Like the Hotel La Fortuna (see above), this long-standing downtown hotel was torn down and rebuilt. Today, Las Colinas sits as the centerpiece of a minimall, which features some shops and a small spa. The rooms range from simple budget accommodations to spiffy junior suites with a private volcano-view balcony and Jacuzzi. The budget rooms come with televisions, but lack the other amenities found in the rest of the rooms. The best feature of the hotel is its ample rooftop terrace where breakfasts are served. Ecofriendly touches include solar-heated water.

La Fortuna (A.P. 06), San Carlos. **☎2479-9305.** Fax 2479-9160. www.lascolinasarenal.com. 19 units. $30 budget room double; $60–$78 double; $70 junior suite. Rates include breakfast and taxes. MC, V (5% surcharge). **Amenities:** Restaurant. *In room:* A/C, TV, minifridge, free Wi-Fi.

Where to Stay near the Volcano

While La Fortuna is the major gateway town to Arenal Volcano, for my money, the best places to stay are located on the road between La Fortuna and the National Park.

One other very unique alternative is to stay aboard the **Rain Goddess** (☎866/593-3168 in the U.S., or 2231-4299; www.bluwing.com). This luxurious houseboat has four staterooms, ample lounge and dining areas, and cruises around Lake Arenal.

VERY EXPENSIVE

Arenal Kioro ★★ Set on 27 acres of hilly land with two rivers and a small patch of forest, this place is extremely close to Arenal Volcano. The views from the rooms, grounds, pool, and restaurant of this hotel are truly astounding. The rooms themselves are massive, with soaring high ceilings, large picture windows and glass doors, and a private balcony or patio facing the action. Each has its own four-person modern Jacuzzi tub, with sculpted seats and numerous jets, set below a large picture window with a volcano view. The beds are also set to take in the view. There are trails through the grounds, and a host of tours and activities are offered. The pricey restaurant serves excellent international cuisine in a beautiful setting, with a giant wall of windows facing the volcano.

On the main road btw. La Fortuna and Lake Arenal, 10km (6 miles) from La Fortuna. ☎888/866-5027 in the U.S. and Canada, or 2461-1700. Fax 2461-1710. www.hotelarenalkioro.com. 53 units. $345 double. Rates include buffet breakfast. AE, DC, MC, V. **Amenities:** Restaurant; bar; exercise room; Jacuzzi; large outdoor pool; small spa. *In room:* A/C, TV, hair dryer, minibar.

The Springs Resort & Spa ★★★ Located on a large piece of land with a great view of the volcano, this new resort features plush, luxurious rooms, and some fabulous facilities. The five-story main lodge building is massive, with several restaurants, a large, full-service spa, modern exercise room, open-air casino, and much-needed elevator. At its base sit a series of sculpted hot and cold pools of various sizes, and below these you'll find the suites and villas. All of the rooms here are opulently appointed, and all have volcano views. The bathrooms are large, marble affairs with a huge Jacuzzi tub and separate shower. Food and service are excellent, as you would expect. The resort plans call for scores of more rooms and construction is ongoing, but in general, that does not impinge on the experience here. *Note:* Do not confuse this place with the Arenal Springs Resort.

Off the main road btw. La Fortuna and Lake Arenal, 10km (6 miles) from La Fortuna. ☎954/727-8333 in the U.S. and Canada, or 2461-1700 in Costa Rica. Fax 2401-3313. www.thespringscostarica.com. 20 units. $375–$440 suite; $950–$1,400 villa for 4. AE, DC, MC, V. **Amenities:** 4 restaurants; 3 bars; large, modern exercise room; several Jacuzzis; series of outdoor pools; room service; smoke-free rooms; full-service spa. *In room:* A/C, TV/DVD, movie library, CD player, hair dryer, minibar, MP3 docking station, free Wi-Fi.

Tabacón Grand Spa Thermal Resort ★★★ This is the most popular resort in the Arenal area—and for good reason. Many rooms have excellent, direct views of the volcano. Rooms on the upper floors of the 300-block building have the best vistas. However, quite a few of the rooms have obstructed, or no, views. Be sure to specify in advance if you want a view room. All rooms are large, with heavy, dark-stained wooden furniture. Most come with a private terrace or balcony with a table and a couple of chairs. Nine of the rooms are truly accessible to travelers with disabilities. Guests enjoy privileges at the spectacular hot-springs complex and spa across the street (see "Taking a Soothing Soak in Hot Springs," on p. 302), including slightly extended hours. When you consider the included entrance fee to the hot springs, the rates here are actually rather reasonable. This hotel has shown a committed and innovative approach to sustainable tourism. Guests are encouraged to make their stay carbon neutral, and the hotel is actively involved in a range of local development and conservation programs.

On the main road btw. La Fortuna and Lake Arenal, Tabacón (P.O. Box 181-1007, Centro Colón, San José). ☎ **877/277-8291** in the U.S. and Canada, or 2519-1900 reservations in San José, or 2460-2020 at the resort. Fax 2519-1940. www.tabacon.com. 114 units. $230–$310 double; $390–$450 suite. Rates higher during peak periods. AE, DC, MC, V. **Amenities:** 2 restaurants; 2 bars; exercise room; Jacuzzi; large pool w/swim-up bar; all rooms smoke-free; extensive hot springs and spa facilities across the street. *In room:* A/C, TV, hair dryer, Wi-Fi.

EXPENSIVE

Lost Iguana Resort ★ This place offers large and luxurious rooms with great volcano views, although you're a little farther away from the action here than at most of the other hotels mentioned in this section. The rooms are housed in a series of two-story buildings set on a hillside facing the volcano, and come with either one king or two twin beds on bamboo frames, attractive handmade wooden furniture, and interesting decorative touches. All feature a wall of glass letting out on a private balcony or porch, which in itself lets out onto the view. The suites are even larger and feature a Jacuzzi tub on the porch or balcony. The hotel has a small network of trails on its own 40 hectares (100 acres) of land, as well as a well-equipped spa set on the lush grounds below the hotel.

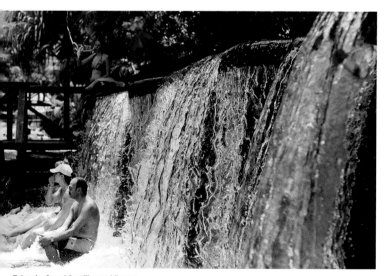

Tabacón Grand Spa Thermal Resort.

On the road to Arenal Hanging Bridges, just over the Lake Arenal dam and to the right. The hotel is about a mile up this road on rough gravel (mailing address: A.P. 63-4417, La Fortuna de San Carlos). ☎2267-6148 reservations office in San José, or 2461-0122 at the lodge. Fax 2267-7672. www.lostiguanaresort.com. 41 units. $185 double; $225 suite; $395 villa. Rates include breakfast. AE, MC, V. **Amenities:** Restaurant; bar; midsize 2-tiered pool w/swim-up bar; room service; spa. *In room:* A/C, TV, minifridge, hair dryer, free Wi-Fi.

Montaña de Fuego Inn ★ This midsize resort is a collection of individual and duplex cabins spread over hilly grounds. Most have marvelous volcano views from their spacious glass-enclosed porches. Some rooms even have back balconies overlooking a forested ravine, in addition to the volcano-facing front porch. The suites and junior suites all have a Jacuzzi tub. I actually prefer the juniors over the full suites, since the Jacuzzis in the juniors are set in front of a volcano-view picture window. Behind the hotel are some rolling hills that lead down to a small river surrounded by patches of gallery forest, where they conduct an adventurous horseback, hiking, and a zip-line canopy tour.

La Palma de la Fortuna (A.P. 82-4417), San Carlos. ☎2460-1220. Fax 2460-1455. www.montanafuegohotel.com. 69 units. $128 double; $154–$189 suite. Rates include buffet breakfast. MC, V. **Amenities:** Restaurant; 2 bars; 2 Jacuzzis; outdoor pool; room service; full-service spa. *In room:* A/C, TV, hair dryer, minibar.

MODERATE

In addition to the places listed below, there has been ongoing construction along the entire length of the road between La Fortuna and Tabacón over the past number of years. If you have a car and some time, you might want to stop and check out any new or interesting hotels or cabins that strike your fancy along the way.

Arenal Observatory Lodge ★★ This place is built on a high ridge very close to the volcano, with a spectacular view of the cone. The best rooms here are the junior suites below the restaurant and main lodge, as well as the four rooms in the Observatory Block, and the White Hawk villa. The "Smithsonian" rooms feature massive picture windows with a direct view of the volcano. The lodge offers a number of guided and unguided hiking options, including a free morning guided hike through their trails and gardens, as well as a wide range of other tours. Five rooms are truly equipped for wheelchair access, and a paved path extends almost 1km (½ mile) into the rainforest. When you're not hiking or touring the region, you can hang by the volcano-view swimming pool and Jacuzzi. The hotel maintains much of its land as part of a private nature reserve and is committed to sustainable and green tourism practices.

To get here, head to the national park entrance, stay on the dirt road past the entrance, and follow the signs to the Observatory Lodge. A four-wheel-drive vehicle used to be required for the 9km (5½-mile) dirt road up to the lodge, but two bridges now eliminate the need to ford any major rivers, and a traditional sedan will usually make it even in the rainy season—although you'll always be better off with the clearance afforded by a four-wheel-drive vehicle

On the flanks of Arenal Volcano (A.P. 13411-1000, San José). ☎2290-7011 reservations number in San José, or 2479-1070 at the lodge. Fax 2290-8427. www.arenalobservatorylodge.com. 42 units. $73 La Casona double; $98 standard double; $128 Smithsonian; $148 junior suite. Rates include breakfast buffet and are lower in off season. AE, MC, V. **Amenities:** Restaurant; bar; Jacuzzi; midsize outdoor pool; smoke-free rooms. *In room:* No phone.

Volcano Lodge ★ ☺ This place has grown from a small collection of duplex cabins in a single row, to a large and spread-out resort with a wide range of services and amenities. All of the rooms are large and tastefully decorated with heavy wooden furnishings. All come with a small terrace with a couple of wooden rocking chairs, and most of these have great views of the volcano. Several rooms are wheelchair accessible. There are two restaurants here, as well as two outdoor pools, each with a separate heated Jacuzzi and volcano views. One also features a children's pool and playground. A wide range of tours and activities are offered.

La Fortuna de San Carlos. ☎**866/208-9819** in the U.S. and Canada, or 2460-6080. Fax 2460-6020. www.volcanolodge.com. 70 units. $125 double. Rates include taxes and breakfast buffet. AE, MC, V. **Amenities:** 2 restaurants; 2 bars; Jacuzzis; 2 pools; small spa. *In room:* A/C, TV, hair dryer, free Wi-Fi.

INEXPENSIVE

While the hotels located along the road tend to be geared toward higher-end travelers, there are a few options for more budget-conscious travelers. In addition to the inexpensive options in La Fortuna, if you have a car, **Cabinas Los Guayabos** (☎/fax **2460-6644**) and **Palo Verde Resort** (☎**2460-9791**) are good, value options, with views and locations that rival some of the more expensive lodgings listed above.

Where to Dine in & Around La Fortuna

Dining in La Fortuna is nowhere near as spectacular as volcano viewing, although, given the area's popularity, there's no lack of options. The favorite meeting places in town are the **El Jardín Restaurant** (☎**2479-9360**) and **Lava Rocks** (☎**2479-8039**); both are on the main road, right in the center of La Fortuna. Other choices include **Rancho La Cascada** (☎**2479-9145**) and **Restaurante Nene's** (☎**2479-9192**) for Tico fare, and **Las Brasitas** (☎**2479-9819**) for a Mexican food fix. For good pizza and Italian cuisine, try either **Anch'io** (☎**2479-7560**), located near the heart of town, or **El Vagabundo** ★ (☎**2479-9565**), just on the outskirts.

Finally, for some fine and fancy dining, you can try **Los Tucanes** ★★ (☎**2460-2020**) restaurant at the Tabacón Grand Spa resort.

Don Rufino ★ COSTA RICAN/INTERNATIONAL Set on a busy corner in the heart of town, this restaurant is easily the best—and the busiest—option right in town. The front wall and bar area open on to the street and are often filled both with local tour guides and tourists. Try the *pollo al estilo de la abuela* (Grandma's chicken), which is baked and served wrapped in banana leaves, or one of the excellent cuts of meat. It's a good choice for breakfast, and the bar stays open most nights until 2am.

Downtown La Fortuna. ☎**2479-9997.** Main courses $6–$34. Reservations recommended during the high season. AE, MC, V. Daily 11am–11pm.

El Novillo del Arenal STEAK/COSTA RICAN This place is the definition of "nothing fancy." In fact, it's just some lawn furniture (tables and chairs) set on a concrete slab underneath a high, open zinc roof. Still, it is perennially popular. The steaks are large and well prepared. The chicken and fish portions are large, as well and also nicely done. Meals come with garlic bread, fries, and some slaw.

For a real local treat, order some fried yuca as a side. If the night is clear, you can get a good view of any volcanic activity from the parking lot here.

On the road to Tabacón, 10km (6¼ miles) outside of La Fortuna. **2479-1910.** Reservations recommended. Main courses $5.35–$14. MC, V. Daily 10am–10pm.

Lava Lounge ★ 🎁 INTERNATIONAL This humble downtown La Fortuna open-air restaurant combines a very simple setting with a sleek and somewhat eclectic menu. Healthy and hearty sandwiches, wraps, and salads are the main offerings here. You can get a traditional burger or one made with fresh grilled tuna. For more substantial fare, there's traditional Costa Rican *arroz con pollo,* and a *casado,* built around a thick pork chop. You can also get several different pasta dishes, and every evening there are dinner specials, which may include some coconut-battered shrimp with a mango salsa, or a prime sirloin steak in a green pepper or red-wine sauce. The decor consists of a series of rustic wooden tables with mostly bench seats.

Downtown La Fortuna, on the main road. **2479-7365.** Main courses $4.50–$20. AE, MC, V. Daily 11am–11:30pm.

La Fortuna After Dark

La Fortuna's biggest after-dark attraction is the volcano, but the **Volcano Look Disco** on the road to Tabacón is trying to compete. If you get bored of the eruptions and seismic rumbling, head here for heavy dance beats and mirrored disco balls. In town the folks at Luigi's Hotel have opened a midsize **casino** (**2479-9898**) next door to their hotel and restaurant, while the open-to-the-street bar at **Don Rufino** (see above) is a popular spot for a drink. Finally, there's a cozy new sports bar with a pool table and flatscreen televisions on the second floor at the **Hotel Magic Mountain** (see above).

Where to Stay & Dine Farther Afield

All of the hotels listed in the following three sections are at least a half-hour drive from La Fortuna and the volcano. Most, if not all, offer both night and day tours to Arenal and Tabacón, but they also hope to attract you with their own natural charms.

EAST OF LA FORTUNA

In addition to the places listed below, the new **Leaves & Lizards** (**888/828-9245** in the U.S. and Canada, or 2478-0023 in Costa Rica; www.leavesandlizards.com), near El Muelle, is winning high praise as an intimate, isolated getaway.

Termales del Bosque 🎁 The best thing about this hotel is its wonderful **natural hot springs ★★**. The series of sculpted pools is set in the midst of rich rainforest, on the banks of a small river. Down by the pools are a natural steam room (scented each day with fresh eucalyptus), a massage room, and a snack-and-juice bar. The trail down here winds through the thick forest, and, if you want to keep on walking, you can take guided or self-guided tours on a network of well-marked trails. Rooms are pretty simple and plain. Still, they are clean and spacious, and most feature a private or shared veranda with views over gardens and rolling hills. There is also a three-bedroom bungalow with a shared bathroom and kitchenette.

Termales del Bosque.

You can rent horses at the lodge, and a variety of tours are offered. If you aren't staying here, you can use the pools and hike the trails for $11.

On the road from San Carlos to Aguas Zarcas, just before El Tucano; Ciudad Quesada (A.P. 243-4400), San Carlos. ☎ **2460-4740.** Fax 2460-1356. www.termalesdelbosque.com. 51 units. $75–$152 double; $152 bungalow. Rates include full breakfast, unlimited use of the hot springs, and taxes. AE, DC, MC, V. **Amenities:** Restaurant; several hot-spring pools set beside a forest river; massage. *In room:* A/C, TV, no phone.

Tilajari Resort Hotel ★ ☺ This sprawling resort on the banks of the San Carlos River makes a good base for exploring the area and offers terrific bird-watching. Most rooms have views of the river; others open onto rich flowering gardens. All have a private balcony or terrace. Large iguanas are frequently sighted on the grounds, and crocodiles live in the river. There's also an orchid garden, a tropical fruit-and-vegetable garden, a medicinal herb garden, and a well-maintained butterfly garden. Tilajari is quite popular with Tico families, especially on weekends. This is a great place for your kids to have a chance to interact and play with their Costa Rican counterparts. The lodge arranges a wide range of tours of the region, and frequently hosts local tennis tournaments, too. Tilajari lies between La Fortuna, Aguas Zarcas, and Ciudad Quesada, and there are roads leading here from each of these towns.

Muelle (A.P. 81-4400), San Carlos. ☎ **2469-9091.** Fax 2469-9095. www.tilajari.com. 76 units. $99–$108 double; $113–$120 suite. Rates include full breakfast. AE, MC, V. **Amenities:** Restaurant; bar; bike rental; exercise room; Jacuzzi; large pool; sauna; 6 lighted tennis courts (2 indoors). *In room:* A/C, TV, hair dryer.

NORTH OF LA FORTUNA

Caño Negro Natural Lodge ★ This small nature lodge is the best option in the tiny village of Caño Negro, and it's well located right near the canals and lagoons. If you really want to visit the Caño Negro Wildlife Refuge, either for bird-watching and wildlife viewing or for fishing, this is a good choice. The hotel has spacious grounds full of flowering plants, tropical palms, and fruit trees. The rooms, housed in a series of duplex buildings, are all simple but roomy, clean, and comfortable, with much needed air-conditioning and tasteful decor. The hotel is proud of its small carbon footprint and contributions to local conservation and community development efforts. To get here, drive toward Los Chiles; several kilometers before Los Chiles, you'll see signs for this hotel and the wildlife refuge. From here, it's 18km (11 miles) on a flat dirt road to the village, refuge, and hotel.

Caño Negro. ☎ **2265-3302** for reservations in San José, or 2471-1426 direct to the lodge. Fax 2265-4310. www.canonegrolodge.com. 22 units. $100 double. Rates include continental breakfast. AE, DC, MC, V. **Amenities:** Restaurant; bar; midsize pool. *In room:* A/C.

SOUTH OF LA FORTUNA

El Silencio Lodge & Spa ★★ Built and run by the folks behind Punta Islita (p. 279), this luxurious lodge features a small collection of large and plush individual cabins, set on a hillside in an isolated mountain setting. Each room features a king-size bed with luscious bedding, a modern marble bathroom, and private outdoor Jacuzzi. The spa here offers a range of excellent treatments, and the restaurant specializes in healthy spa cooking—no red meat is served. Hiking around the grounds will take you through their organic gardens, and a relatively easy loop trail passes by three nearby waterfalls. Day tours to Sarchí, Puerto Viejo de Sarapiquí, and Arenal/La Fortuna are all offered. There are no televisions in the rooms, but the main lodge features a lounge area with a large plasma-screen set and modest DVD library.

To reach El Silencio, you must first get to the town of Sarchí. From the Pali supermarket in the center of town, head north and follow the signs. El Silencio is approximately 22km (13 miles) outside of Sarchí.

Bajos del Toro, Alajuela. **☎2291-3044.** Fax 2232-2183. www.elsilenciolodge.com. 16 units. $240 double. Rates include all meals, nonalcoholic drinks, taxes, and 1 daily hike. AE, DC, MC, V. **Amenities:** Restaurant; bar; small spa. *In room:* Hair dryer, minibar, free Wi-Fi.

Villa Blanca Cloud Forest & Spa ★★ This plush mountain-retreat hotel consists of a series of Tico-style casitas surrounded by 800 hectares (1,976 acres) of farm and forest. Each casita is built of adobe and has tile floors, open beamed ceilings, and whitewashed walls. Inside you'll find a fireplace in one corner, comfortable hardwood chairs, and either one queen-size or two twin beds covered with colorful bedspreads. The deluxe units and suites have a separate sitting area with a fold-out couch and bathrooms with a whirlpool bathtub and a separate shower. In many rooms the bathroom tubs look out through a wall of windows onto lush gardens. Some have private patios. Just outside are 11km (6.75 miles) of trails through the **Los Angeles Cloud Forest Reserve.** You can also rent horses or take an adventurous swing through the canopy on a canopy tour here. The hotel is a member of the "Green Hotels of Costa Rica" and was granted "5 Leaves" by the CST Sustainable Tourism program.

Villa Blanca is off the beaten track, but it is relatively close to San José, and if you're interested in bird-watching or exploring a cloud forest and want to avoid the crowds of Monteverde, this is a good choice. If you're driving, head west out of San José to San Ramón and then head north, following the signs to Villa Blanca. Or you can take a public bus from San José to San Ramón and then take a taxi for around $15.

San Ramón, Alajuela. **☎2461-0300.** Fax 2461-0302. www.villablanca-costarica.com. 34 units. $170 double; $192 deluxe; $215 suite. Rates include buffet breakfast. AE, DC, MC, V. **Amenities:** Restaurant; bar; small spa. *In room:* Stocked minifridge, Wi-Fi.

A REALLY REMOTE NATURE LODGE

La Laguna del Lagarto Lodge 🎁 Located near the Nicaraguan border, La Laguna del Lagarto Lodge is bordered by more than 480 hectares (1,186 acres) of virgin rainforest that is home to a rich variety of tropical flora and fauna. The accommodations are rustic yet comfortable. Most rooms open onto a balcony or veranda with sitting chairs and hammocks. The hotel is named after the two man-made lagoons that sit below the lodge buildings; canoes are available for paddling around these and several other nearby jungle waterways. There are more than 10km (6.25 miles) of well-maintained hiking trails, and the lodge offers trips on the San Carlos River, as well as horseback riding tours. More than 380 species of birds have been spotted here, and the hotel is involved in efforts to preserve the rare green macaw, which is frequently sighted in the area. In addition to the rainforest, the lodge sits on a small pepper plantation and has lands planted with palmito, pineapple, and other tropical fruits.

To get here, you head first to Pital and then continue on dirt roads to the town of Boca Tapada. It's another 6km (3¾ miles) to the lodge on more bumpy dirt roads. It's also possible to get here on public transportation (call for directions), or you can arrange for the lodge to handle your transportation from San José or La Fortuna (for a cost). Since anyone with four-wheel-drive can make the trip here independently, though, you're best off driving on your own.

Boca Tapada (A.P. 995-1007, San José). ☎**2289-8163.** Fax 2289-5295. www.lagarto-lodge-costa-rica.com. 20 units. $59 double. AE, MC, V (5% surcharge). **Amenities:** Restaurant; bar. *In room:* No phone.

ALONG THE SHORES OF LAKE ARENAL ★

200km (124 miles) NW of San José; 20km (12 miles) NW of Monteverde; 70km (43 miles) SE of Liberia

Despite possessing ample charms, this remains one of the least-developed tourism regions in Costa Rica. Lake Arenal, the largest lake in Costa Rica, is the

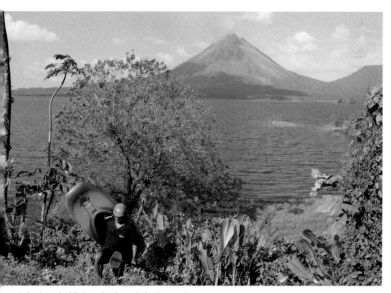
Lake Arenal with Arenal Volcano in background.

centerpiece here. A long beautiful lake, it is surrounded by rolling hills that are partly pastured and partly forested. There are loads of activities and adventures available both on the lake and in the hills and forests around it. While the towns of Tilarán and Nuevo Arenal remain quiet rural communities, there are several excellent hotels spread out along the shores of the lake.

Locals here used to curse the winds, which often come blasting across this end of the lake at 60 knots or greater. However, since the first sailboarders caught wind of Lake Arenal's combination of warm, fresh water, steady blows, and spectacular scenery, things have been changing quickly. Even if you aren't a fanatical sailboarder, you might enjoy hanging out by the lake, hiking in the nearby forests, riding a mountain bike on dirt farm roads and one-track trails, and catching glimpses of Arenal Volcano.

The lake's other claim to fame is its rainbow-bass fishing. These fighting fish are known in Central America as *guapote* and are large members of the cichlid family. Their sharp teeth and fighting nature make them a real challenge.

Essentials

GETTING THERE & DEPARTING By Car: From San José, take the Interamerican Highway north toward Puntarenas, and then continue on to Cañas. In Cañas, turn east toward Tilarán. The drive takes 4 hours. If you're continuing on to Nuevo Arenal, follow the signs in town, which will put you on the road that skirts the shore of the lake. Nuevo Arenal is about a half-hour drive from Tilarán. You can also drive here from La Fortuna, along a scenic road that winds around the lake. From La Fortuna, it's approximately 1 hour to Nuevo Arenal and 1½ hours to Tilarán.

By Bus: Transportes Tilarán buses (☎2258-5792 in San José, 2695-5611 in Tilarán) leave San José for Tilarán daily at 7:30 and 9:30am and 12:45, 3:45, and 6:30pm from Calle 20 and Avenida 3. The trip lasts from 4 to 5½ hours, depending on road conditions; the fare is $5.80.

There are also morning and afternoon buses from **Puntarenas** to Tilarán. The ride takes about 3 hours; the fare is $3. (For details on getting to Puntarenas, see "Puntarenas," in chapter 8.) From **Monteverde** (Santa Elena), there is a bus daily at 7am. The fare for the 2-hour trip is $2.30. Buses from **La Fortuna** leave for Tilarán daily at 8am and 4:30pm, returning at 7am and 12:30pm. The trip takes around 2 to 3 hours; the fare is $2.75.

Direct buses to San José leave from Tilarán daily at 5, 7, and 9:30am and 2 and 5pm. Buses to Puntarenas leave at 6am and 1pm daily. The bus to Santa Elena (Monteverde) leaves daily at 12:30pm. Buses also leave regularly for Cañas, and can be caught heading north or south along the Interamerican Highway.

ORIENTATION & FAST FACTS Tilarán is about 5km (3 miles) from Lake Arenal. All roads into town lead to the central park, which is Tilarán's main point of reference for addresses. If you need to exchange money, check at one of the hotels listed here, or go to the Banco Nacional. If you need a taxi to get to a lodge on Lake Arenal, call **Taxis Unidos Tilarán** (☎2695-5324). For a taxi in Nuevo Arenal, call **Taxis Nuevo Arenal** (☎2694-4415).

Along the Shores of Lake Arenal

Volcán Tenorio Nat'l Park

L. Coter

Nuevo Arenal

Lake Arenal

Tronadora

Tilarán

Quebrada Grande

Chiripa

Río Chiquito

Tabacón Hot Springs

Volcán Arenal

Arenal Nat'l Park

0   4 mi
0   4 km

ATTRACTIONS
Arenal Hanging Bridges **7**
San Luis Yacht Club **20**
Sky Tram **6**
Tico Wind **16**
Tilawa Windsurfing Center **17**

DINING
El Novillo de Arenal **3**
Mystica **15**
Willy's Caballo Negro **12**

SHOPPING
Casa Delagua **14**
Lucky Bug Gallery **12**

ACCOMMODATIONS
Arenal Kioro **2**
Arenal Observatory
  Lodge **5**
Cabinas Los Guayabos **1**
Cabinas Mary **19**
Ceiba Tree Lodge **10**
Chalet Nicholas **13**
Hotel Naralit **19**
Hotel Tilawa **18**

La Mansion
  Inn Arenal **9**
Lost Iguana Resort **8**
Lucky Bug Bed &
  Breakfast **12**
Tabacón Grand Spa
  Thermal Resort **4**
Mystica **15**
Villa Decary **11**

What to See & Do

ARTS, CRAFTS & DOWN-HOME COOKING About halfway between Nuevo Arenal and Tilarán is **Casa Delagua** ★ (☎2692-2101) the studio, gallery, and coffee shop of Costa Rican artist Juan Carlos Ruiz. These folks also have a good used book and DVD collection on sale.

The **Lucky Bug Gallery** ★★ is an excellent roadside arts-and-crafts and souvenir shop, attached to the Lucky Bug Bed & Breakfast (p. 319). This place features a host of functional and decorative pieces produced locally.

FISHING Ask at your hotel if you want to try your hand at fishing for *guapote*. A half-day fishing trip should cost around $150 to

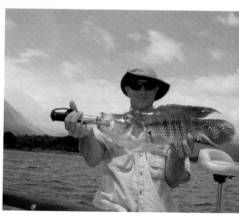

Fisherman with guapote at Lake Arenal.

317

Windsurfing Lake Arenal.

$250 per boat, and a full day goes for around $250 to $500. The boats used will usually accommodate up to three people fishing. If you're interested in fishing, I recommend you check in with Captain Ron at **Arenal Fishing Tours** (☎2694-4678; www.arenal fishing.com) or the **Puerto San Luis Yacht Club** (☎2695-5750; www.hotelpuertosan luiscr.com).

HORSEBACK RIDING Any of the hotels in the area can hook you up with a horseback-riding tour for around $10 to $20 per hour.

MOUNTAIN BIKING This is a great area to explore on a mountain bike. You can rent bikes from the **Hotel Tilawa** (see "Where to Stay," below).

SWIMMING & HIKING Up above Lake Arenal on the far side of the lake from Tilarán, you'll find the beautiful little heart-shape **Lake Coter.** This lake is surrounded by forest and has good swimming. (UFO watchers also claim that this is a popular pit stop for extraterrestrials.) A taxi to Lake Coter costs around $10.

If you feel like strapping on your boots, there are some hiking trails on the far side of Lake Arenal, near the smaller Lake Coter.

WINDSURFING & KITEBOARDING If you want to try windsurfing, **Tilawa Windsurfing Center** (☎2695-5050; www.windsurfcostarica.com) rents equipment at its facilities on one of the lake's few accessible beaches, about 8km (5 miles) from Tilarán on the road along the west end of the lake. Boards rent for around $55 per day, and lessons are available. These folks also offer classes and rentals for the high-octane sport of kiteboarding. Another option that is especially popular with serious sail- and kiteboarders is **Tico Wind** (☎2692-2002; www.ticowind.com), which sets up shop on the shores of the lake each year from December 1 to the end of April, when the winds blow. Rates run around $78 per day, including lunch, with multiday packages available. If you can't reach them via the phone or website, the folks at **Mystica** (see "Where to Stay," below) can hook you up.

WAKEBOARDING Lake Arenal is a big lake, and there are plenty of calm quiet corners to practice wakeboarding. If you're interested in lessons, or just a reliable pull on a wakeboard or water skis, contact **Fly Zone** (☎8339-5876; www.flyzone-cr.com). Simple pulls behind their specialized boat run around $85 per hour, including boards, skis, and any other necessary gear.

Where to Stay

In addition to the places listed below, the **Ceiba Tree Lodge** (☎2692-8050; www.ceibatree-lodge.com) is a small, simple lodge with a beautiful view and lovely gardens, located on a hill above the lake. **La Mansion Inn Arenal** (☎2692-8018; www.lamansionarenal.com) is an upscale option with a great setting and cozy cabins.

MODERATE

Hotel Tilawa ☺ Built to resemble the Palace of Knossos on the island of Crete, the Hotel Tilawa sits high on the slopes above the lake and has a sweeping vista down to the water. It's primarily a windsurfers' and kiteboarders' hangout, and there's often an untended or sloppy feel to the place, particularly in terms of service and upkeep. Unusual colors and antique paint effects give the hotel a weathered look; inside there are wall murals and other artistic paint treatments throughout. Rooms have dyed cement floors, Guatemalan bedspreads, and big windows. Some have kitchenettes. Tilawa can arrange windsurfing, kiteboarding, mountain-biking, horseback-riding, and fishing trips. There's even a small skate park for radical skateboarders and BMX freestyle bikers, which makes this a good place to bring teenagers.

On the road btw. Tilarán and Nuevo Arenal (A.P. 92-5710, Tilarán). **☎2695-5050.** Fax 2695-5766. www.hotel-tilawa.com. 28 units. $68–$110 double. MC, V. **Amenities:** Restaurant; bar; bike rental; Jacuzzi; outdoor pool; small spa; unlit outdoor tennis court; sailboard and kiteboard rental. *In room:* No phone, free Wi-Fi.

Lucky Bug Bed & Breakfast ★ An outgrowth of this family's successful restaurant and gift shop, this hotel boasts rooms that are artistic and cheery. Each features an animal motif, from the handmade wood and metal beds, to the hand-painted bathroom tiles, to the individual artworks and wall hangings. The Butterfly and Frog rooms are the best, and each comes with a small balcony. Most have one king-size bed. The largest room is the one ground-floor unit, although I prefer those on the second floor. The rooms are located just above the small lake that's behind the restaurant and gift shop. This lake is stocked with *guapote,* which you can fish for, and, if you're lucky, have cooked up for you at the restaurant.

Nuevo Arenal. **☎2694-4515.** Fax 2694-4418. www.luckybugcr.net. 5 units. $69–$120 double. Rates include full breakfast. MC, V. **Amenities:** Restaurant. *In room:* No phone, free Wi-Fi.

Mystica ★ 🍴 Set on a high hill above Lake Arenal (about midway btw. Nuevo Arenal and Tilarán), this establishment has simple but spacious and cozy rooms. The painted cement floors are kept immaculate, and the rooms get good ventilation from their large windows. All rooms open onto a long and broad shared veranda with a great view of the lake. There's also one private villa, with a kitchenette, fireplace, and beautiful open deck area. The owners can help you book a wide range of adventures and tours. The hotel has a large open-air yoga platform and sometimes hosts retreats. Perhaps the star attraction here is the hotel's excellent little Italian restaurant and pizzeria by the same name (p. 321).

On the road btw. Tilarán and Nuevo Arenal (A.P. 29-5710, Tilarán). **☎2692-1001.** Fax 2692-2097. www.mysticaretreat.com. 7 units. $100 double; $145 villa. Rates include continental breakfast. MC, V. **Amenities:** Restaurant; bar. *In room:* No phone.

Villa Decary ★ 💼 Named after a French explorer (and a rare palm species that he discovered and named), this small bed-and-breakfast is nestled on a hill above Lake Arenal, midway between the town of Nuevo Arenal and the Arenal Botanical Gardens. Each room comes with one queen-size and one twin bed, large picture windows, and a spacious private balcony with a lake view. The rooms get plenty of light, and the bright Guatemalan bedspreads and white-tile floors create a vibrant look. The separate casitas have full kitchens, more room, and even better views of the lake from their slightly higher perches. Breakfasts are extravagant, with a steady stream of fresh fruits and juice; strong coffee; homemade pancakes, waffles, or muffins; and usually an excellent omelet or soufflé. There's great bird-watching on the hotel grounds, and howler monkeys are common guests here as well.

Nuevo Arenal (5717 Tilarán, Guanacaste). **800/556-0505** in the U.S. and Canada, or 8383-3012 in Costa Rica, or /fax 2694-4330. www.villadecary.com. 5 units, 3 casitas. $99 double; $129–$149 casita for 2. Rates include full breakfast. Extra person $15. MC, V. *In room:* No phone, free Wi-Fi.

INEXPENSIVE

Cabinas Mary Right on Tilarán's large and sunny central park, Cabinas Mary is a basic but clean lodging, with a great location and secure parking. The rooms are located on the second floor, upstairs from the restaurant of the same name. All rooms are large, and most have plenty of windows. The restaurant downstairs serves grilled meats and local fare, and is a popular hangout for locals, travelers, and expats alike.

Tilarán (A.P. 89), Guanacaste. /fax **2695-5479.** 18 units. $22 double. Rates include breakfast. V. **Amenities:** Restaurant; bar. *In room:* TV, no phone.

Chalet Nicholas This friendly American-owned bed-and-breakfast is 2.5km (1½ miles) west of Nuevo Arenal and sits on a hill above the road. This converted home is set on 6 hectares (15 acres) and has pretty flower gardens, an organic vegetable garden, and an orchid garden. Behind the property are acres of forest through which you can hike in search of birds, orchids, butterflies, and other tropical beauties. The upstairs loft room is the largest unit, with its own private deck. All three rooms are nonsmoking and have a view of Arenal Volcano in the distance. Owners John and Catherine Nicholas go out of their way to make their guests feel at home, although their three Great Danes might intimidate you when you first drive up. All around, it's a really good deal. Three-hour horseback riding tours are offered for just $25 per person.

Tilarán (A.P. 72-5710), Guanacaste. **2694-4041.** www.chaletnicholas.com. 3 units. $65 double. Rates include full breakfast. No credit cards. *In room:* No phone.

Hotel Naralit This budget hotel is a good bet in Tilarán. The rooms are clean and comfortable, and some even come with air-conditioning. I'd try to land one of the three second-floor rooms that have a nice shared balcony, more natural light, and views of the town's church. The hotel is located across the street from one side of the church, and has its own fenced-in and guarded parking area.

Tilarán, Guanacaste. **2695-5393.** Fax 2695-6767. 26 units. $25–$32 double. MC, V. *In room:* TV, no phone.

Where to Dine

There are numerous inexpensive places to eat in the town of Tilarán, including the restaurant at Cabinas Mary. In Nuevo Arenal, try the pizzas and pastas at **Café del Lago Pizzeria** (**2694-4780**). For breakfast, snacks, lunch, and fresh-baked goods, check out **Tom's Pan German Bakery** (**2694-4547**).

Mystica ★ PIZZA/ITALIAN The restaurant in this Italian-run hotel has a wonderful setting high on a hill overlooking the lake. The large dining room features rustic wooden chairs and tables, varnished wood floors, colorful tablecloths, and abundant flower arrangements. The most striking features, aside from the view, are the large open fireplace on one end and, on the other, the large brick oven, in the shape of a small cottage, that turns out pizzas. The pastas and delicious main dishes are authentically northern Italian. Whenever possible, Mystica uses fresh ingredients from its own garden.

On the road btw. Tilarán and Nuevo Arenal. ☎2692-1001. Main courses $6.50–$12. MC, V. Daily noon–9pm.

Willy's Caballo Negro ★ 🎒 INTERNATIONAL/VEGETARIAN The German owners of this attractive little roadside cafe serve up two different types of schnitzel, bratwurst, veal *cordon bleu,* and a host of other old-world dishes. However, vegetarians are well served here, and will find several tasty and filling options on the menu, including stuffed potatoes, garden burgers, and eggplant Parmesan. The delicious pesto is made with locally grown organic macadamia nuts and cilantro. Wooden tables are set around the edges of the round dining room, with a high peaked roof. Candles and creative lighting give the place a cozy and warm feel. There's a small, picturesque lake behind the restaurant, a small B&B (Lucky Bug Bed & Breakfast; see above), and the very interesting Lucky Bug Gallery (see above), run by the owner's triplet daughters.

Nuevo Arenal (about 3km/1¾ miles out of town on the road to Tilarán). ☎2694-4515. Main courses $6–$14. MC, V. Daily 7am–8pm.

MONTEVERDE ★★

167km (104 miles) NW of San José; 82km (51 miles) NW of Puntarenas

Monteverde translates as "green mountain," and that's exactly what you'll find at the end of the steep and windy rutted dirt road that leads here. Next to Manuel Antonio, this is Costa Rica's most internationally recognized ecotourism destination. The fame, rapid growth, and accompanying traffic have led some to dub it the Monteverde Crowd Forest. Nevertheless, the reserve itself and the extensive network of private reserves around it are incredibly rich in biodiversity, and a well-organized infrastructure helps guarantee a rewarding experience for both first-time and experienced ecoadventurers.

The village of Monteverde was founded in 1951 by Quakers from the United States who wanted to leave behind a constant fear of war as well as an obligation to support continued militarism through paying U.S. taxes. They chose Costa Rica primarily because it had no standing

**Today's Forecast . . .
Misty & Cool**

Make sure you understand that the climatic conditions that make Monteverde such a biological hot spot can leave many tourists feeling chilled to the bone. More than a few visitors are unprepared for a cool, windy, and wet stay in the middle of their tropical vacation, and can find Monteverde a bit inhospitable, especially from August through November.

Monteverde Biological Cloud Forest Reserve.

army. Although Monteverde's founders came here to farm the land, they wisely recognized the need to preserve the rare cloud forest that covered the mountain slopes above their fields, and to that end they dedicated the largest adjacent tract of cloud forest as the Monteverde Biological Cloud Forest Reserve.

Cloud forests are a mountaintop phenomenon. Moist, warm air sweeping in off the ocean is forced upward by mountain slopes, and as this moist air rises, it cools, forming clouds. The mountaintops of Costa Rica are blanketed almost daily in dense clouds, and as the clouds cling to the slopes, moisture condenses on forest trees. This constant level of moisture has given rise to an incredible diversity of innovative life forms and a forest in which nearly every square inch of space has some sort of plant growing. Within the cloud forest, the branches of huge trees are draped with epiphytic plants: orchids, ferns, and bromeliads. This intense botanic competition has created an almost equally diverse population of insects, birds, and other wildlife. Monteverde Biological Cloud Forest Reserve covers 10,400 hectares (25,688 acres) of forest, including several different life zones characterized by different types of plants and animals. Within this small area are more than 2,500 species of plants, including 400 types of orchids, 400 species of birds, and 100 species of mammals. It's no wonder that the reserve has been the site of constant scientific investigations since its founding in 1972.

Tip: For many, the primary goal in visiting Monteverde is to glimpse the rare and elusive **quetzal,** a bird once revered by the pre-Columbian peoples of the Americas. However, if you just care about seeing a quetzal, you should also consider visiting other cloud forest areas. In particular, San Gerardo de Dota and Cerro de la Muerte areas are home to several specialty lodges (see "San Isidro de El General: A Base for Exploring Chirripó National Park," in chapter 10), where you'll find far fewer crowds and often better chances of seeing the famed quetzal.

Essentials

GETTING THERE & DEPARTING By Car: From San José, take the Interamerican Highway north. About 20km (12 miles) past the turnoff for Puntarenas, there will be a marked turnoff for Sardinal, Santa Elena, and Monteverde.

Monteverde

See inset

To San José

SANTA ELENA

Post Office

Bus Terminal

Santa Elena

Gas Station

▲ Cerro Plano

CASEM

MONTEVERDE

MONTEVERDE BIOLOGICAL CLOUD FOREST RESERVE

Park Entrance

Hummingbird Gallery

Río Guacimal

Quebrada Máquina

NICARAGUA
CARIBBEAN SEA
PANAMA
★ SAN JOSÉ
Monteverde
PACIFIC OCEAN

0 ——— 1/2 mi
0 ——— 1/2 km

ATTRACTIONS

Bajo del Tigre Trail **30**
Bat Jungle **32**
Butterfly Garden **26**
Centro Panamericano
  de Idiomas **25**
Ecological Sanctuary **27**
Frog Pond of Monteverde **12**
Monteverde Cheese Factory **34**
Monteverde Conservation
  League **29**
Monteverde Serpentarium **9**
Orchid Garden **7**
Reserva Sendero Tranquilo **33**
World of Insects **6**

ACCOMMODATIONS

Arco Iris Lodge **2**
El Establo Mountain Hotel **21**
Finca Valverde **8**
Hotel Belmar **24**
Hotel El Sapo Dorado **18**
Hotel El Viandante **17**
Hotel Fonda Vela **35**
Hotel Heliconia **23**
Hotel Poco a Poco **13**
Monteverde Lodge
  & Gardens **11**
Pensión Flor de Monteverde **10**
Pensión Santa Elena **1**
Treehouse Hotel **4**

DINING

Chimera **22**
Chunches **3**
El Sapo Dorado **18**
Flor de Vida **15**
Moon Shiva **19**
Morpho's Cafe **5**
Pizzeria de
  Johnny **16**
Restaurante De
  Lucia **14**
Sophia **20**
Stella's
  Bakery **31**
Tramonti **28**

Alternative Transport

You can travel between Monteverde and La Fortuna by boat and taxi, or on a combination boat, horseback, and taxi trip. See "Boats, Horses & Taxis," on p. 298, for details. Any of the trips described there can be done in the reverse direction departing from Monteverde. Most hotels and **Desafío Expeditions** (☎2645-5874; www.monteverde tours.com) can arrange this trip for you. Desafío also offers multiday hikes from Monteverde to Arenal; you spend the night in rustic re-search facilities inside the Bosque Eterno de los Niños.

From this turnoff, the road is paved almost as far as the tiny town of Guaci-mal. From here it's another 20km (12 miles) to Santa Elena. It should take you a little over 2 hours to reach the turnoff and another 1 hour or so from there.

An alternative route is to continue on the Interamerican Highway until just before the Río Lagarto Bridge. This turnoff isn't always well marked. From the Río Lagarto turnoff, it's 38km (24 miles) to Santa Elena and Monteverde.

Whichever route you take, the final going is slow because the roads into Santa Elena are rough, unpaved dirt-and-gravel affairs. However, once you arrive, the roads in and around Santa Elena are paved, including all the way to Cerro Plano, and about halfway to the Cloud Forest Preserve. Just before you enter the town of Santa Elena, you may be stopped at a little tollbooth collecting 200 colones. The money is ostensibly going to maintain the road, and payment is actually optional.

To drive from Monteverde to La Fortuna, head out of Santa Elena to-ward Sky Trek and the Santa Elena Cloud Forest Reserve. Follow signs for Tilarán, which are posted at most of the critical intersections. If there's no sign, stick to the most well-worn road. This is a rough dirt road, all the way to Tilarán. From Tilarán, you have mostly well-marked and okay paved roads around the lake, passing first through Nuevo Arenal, and then over the dam and through Tabacón, before reaching La Fortuna.

By Bus: Transmonteverde express buses (☎2222-3854 in San José, or 2645-5159 in Santa Elena) leave San José daily at 6:30am and 2:30pm from Calle 12 between avenidas 7 and 9. The trip takes around 4 hours; the fare is $4.45. Buses arrive at and depart from Santa Elena. If you're stay-ing at one of the hotels or lodges toward the reserve, you'll want to arrange pickup if possible, or take a taxi or local bus.

A daily Transmonteverde bus departs Puntarenas for Santa Elena at 2:15pm. The bus stop in Puntarenas is across the street from the main bus station. The fare for the 2½-hour trip is $2.50. There's also a daily bus from Tilarán (Lake Arenal) at 12:30pm. Trip duration, believe it or not, is 2 hours (for a 40km/25-mile trip); the fare is $2.30. The express bus departs for San José daily at 6:30am and 2:30pm. The bus from Santa Elena to Puntarenas leaves daily at 6am.

Gray Line (☎2220-2126; www.graylinecostarica.com) has a daily bus that leaves San José for Monteverde at 8am; the fare is $35. **Interbus**

(**☎2283-5573**; www.interbusonline.com) has two daily buses that leave San José for Monteverde at 8:15am and 2:30pm; the fare is $39. Either of the above companies will pick you up and drop you off at most San José and Monteverde area hotels.

If you're heading to Manuel Antonio, take the Santa Elena/Puntarenas bus and transfer in Puntarenas. To reach Liberia, take any bus down the mountain and get off as soon as you hit the Interamerican Highway. You can then flag down a bus bound for Liberia (almost any bus heading north). The Santa Elena/Tilarán bus leaves daily at 7am. Both **Gray Line** and **Interbus** offer routes with connections to most major destinations in Costa Rica.

GETTING AROUND There are some six buses daily between the town of Santa Elena and the Monteverde Biological Cloud Forest Reserve. The first bus leaves Santa Elena for the reserve at 6am and the last bus from the reserve leaves there at 4pm. The fare is $1.50. There's also periodic van transportation between the town of Santa Elena and the Santa Elena Cloud Forest Reserve. Ask around town and you should be able to find the current schedule and book a ride for around $2 per person. A **taxi** (**☎2645-6969** or 2645-6666) between Santa Elena and either the Monteverde Reserve or the Santa Elena Cloud Forest Reserve costs around $8 to $10 for up to four people. Count on paying between $3 and $8 for the ride from Santa Elena to your lodge in Monteverde. Finally, several places around town rent ATVs, or all-terrain vehicles, for around $45 to $70 per day. Hourly rates and guided tours are also available. If this is up your alley, try **Aventura** (**☎2645-6959**; www.cienporcientoaventura.com).

ORIENTATION As you approach Santa Elena, take the right fork in the road if you're heading directly to Monteverde. If you continue straight, you'll come

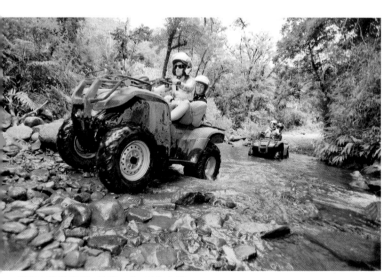

ATV on road between Monteverde and Santa Elena.

into the little village of **Santa Elena,** which has a bus stop, a health clinic, a bank, a general store, a laundromat, and a few simple restaurants, budget hotels, souvenir shops, and tour offices. **Monteverde,** on the other hand, is not a village in the traditional sense of the word. There's no center of town—only dirt lanes leading off from the main road to various farms. This main road has signs for all the hotels and restaurants mentioned here, and it dead-ends at the reserve entrance.

For a map of the Cloud Forest Reserve, see the inside front cover of this book.

FAST FACTS The telephone number for the **local clinic** is (2645-5076; for the **Red Cross,** (2645-6128; and for the **local police,** (911 or 2645-6248. There's a 24-hour gas station about halfway between the town of Santa Elena and the Monteverde Biological Cloud Forest Reserve. The **Farmacia Monteverde** ((2645-7110) is right downtown. There's a **Banco Nacional** ((2645-5610) in downtown Santa Elena and a **Coopemex** ((2645-6948) on the road out to Santa Elena, near Finca Valverde; both have 24-hour ATMs.

Exploring the Monteverde Biological Cloud Forest Reserve ★★★

The **Monteverde Biological Cloud Forest Reserve** ((2645-5122; www.cct.or.cr) is one of the most developed and well-maintained natural attractions in Costa Rica. The trails are clearly marked, regularly traveled, and generally gentle in terms of ascents and descents. The cloud forest here is lush and largely untouched. Still, keep in mind that most of the birds and mammals are rare, elusive, and nocturnal. Moreover, to all but the most trained of eyes, those thousands of exotic ferns, orchids, and bromeliads tend to blend into one large mass of indistinguishable green. However, with a guide hired through your hotel, or on one of the reserve's official guided 2- to 3-hour hikes, you can see and learn far more than you could on your own. At $17 per person, the reserve's tours might seem like a splurge, especially after you pay the entrance fee, but I strongly recommend that you go with a guide.

Perhaps the most famous resident of the cloud forests of Costa Rica is the quetzal, a robin-size bird with iridescent green wings and a ruby-red breast, which has become extremely rare due to habitat destruction. The male quetzal also has two long tail feathers that can reach nearly .6m (2 ft.) in length, making it one of the most spectacular birds on earth. The best time to see quetzals is

Seeing the Forest for the Trees, Bromeliads, Monkeys, Hummingbirds . . .

Because the entrance fee to Monteverde is valid for a full day, I recommend taking an early-morning walk with a guide and then heading off on your own either directly after that hike or after lunch. A guide will certainly point out and explain a lot, but there's also much to be said for walking quietly through the forest on your own or in very small groups. This will also allow you to stray from the well-traveled paths in the park.

early morning to midmorning, and the best months are February through April (mating season).

Other animals that have been seen in Monteverde, although sightings are extremely rare, include jaguars, ocelots, and tapirs. After the quetzal, Monteverde's most famous resident used to be the golden toad (*sapo dorado*), a rare native species. However, the golden toad has disappeared from the forest and is feared extinct. Competing theories of the toad's demise include adverse effects of a natural drought cycle, the disappearing ozone layer, pesticides, and acid rain.

ADMISSION, HOURS & TOURS The reserve is open daily from 7am to 4pm, and the entrance fee is $17 for adults and $9 for students and children. Because only 160 people are allowed into the reserve at any one time, you might be forced to wait for a while. Most hotels can reserve a guided walk and entrance to the reserve for the following day for you, or you can get tickets in advance directly at the reserve entrance.

Some of the trails can be very muddy, depending on the season, so ask about current conditions. If the mud is heavy, you can rent rubber boots at the reserve entrance for $2 per day. They might make your hike much more pleasant. Before venturing into the forest, have a look around the information center. There are several guidebooks available, as well as posters and postcards of some of the reserve's more famous animal inhabitants.

Night tours of the reserve leave every evening at 7:15pm. The cost is $17, including admission to the reserve, a 2-hour hike, and, most important, a guide with a high-powered searchlight. For an extra $2, they'll throw in round-trip transportation to and from your area hotel.

What to See & Do Outside the Reserve

BIRD-WATCHING & HIKING

You can also find ample bird-watching and hiking opportunities outside the reserve boundaries. Avoid the crowds at Monteverde by heading 5km (3 miles) north from the village of Santa Elena to the **Santa Elena Cloud Forest Reserve** ★★ (☎2645-5390; www.reservasantaelena.org). This 310-hectare (765-acre) reserve has a maximum elevation of 1,680m (5,510 ft.), making it the highest cloud forest in the Monteverde area. There are 13km (8 miles) of hiking trails, as well as an information center. Because it borders the Monteverde Reserve, a similar richness of flora and fauna is found here, although quetzals are not nearly as common. The $12 entry fee at this reserve goes directly to support local schools. The reserve is open daily from 7am to 4pm. Three-hour guided tours are available for $15 per person, not including the entrance fee. (Call the number above to make a reservation for the tour.) A night tour ($15) is also offered each evening at 7pm.

Sky Walk ★★ (☎2645-5238; www.skyadventures.travel) is a network of forest paths and suspension bridges that provides visitors with a view previously reserved for birds, monkeys, and the much more adventurous traveler. The bridges reach 39m (128 ft.) above the ground at their highest point, so acrophobia could be an issue. The Sky Walk and its sister attraction, **Sky Trek** (see "Canopy & Canyoning Tours," below), are about 3.5km (2¼ miles) outside the town of Santa Elena, on the road to the Santa Elena Cloud Forest Reserve. The Sky Walk is open daily from 7am to 4pm; admission is $17. For an extra

$13, a knowledgeable guide will point out the diverse flora and fauna on the walk. For $60 per person, you can do the Sky Trek canopy tour and then walk the trails and bridges of the Sky Walk. Reservations are recommended for the Sky Trek; round-trip transportation from Santa Elena is just $2 per person.

To learn even more about Monteverde, stop in at the **Monteverde Conservation League** (☎ **2645-5003;** www.acmcr.org), which administers the 22,000-hectare (54,000-acre) private reserve **Bosque Eterno de Los Niños (Children's Eternal Forest),** as well as the Bajo del Tigre Trail. The

Santa Elena Cloud Forest Reserve.

Conservation League has its office on the Cerro Plano road, 50m (164 ft.) before the Butterfly Garden. In addition to being a good source for information, it also sells books, T-shirts, and cards, and all proceeds go to purchase more land for the Bosque Eterno de Los Niños. The **Bajo del Tigre Trail ★** is a 3.5km (2.3-mile) trail that's home to several different bird species not usually found within the reserve. You can take several different loops, lasting anywhere from 1 hour to several hours. The trail starts a little past the CASEM artisans' shop (see "Shopping," below) and is open daily from 8am to 5pm. Admission is $8 for adults and $8 for students.

You can also go on guided 3-hour hikes at the **Reserva Sendero Tranquilo ★** (☎ **2645-7711**), which is run by the folks at the Sapo Dorado (p. 333) and has 80 hectares (198 acres) of land, two-thirds of which is in virgin forest. This reserve is located up the hill from the cheese factory (p. 332). Both day and night hikes are offered here, and the group size is always small. Prices run $35 for the 3- to 4-hour day tour, and $35 for the 2½-hour night tour.

Finally, you can walk the trails and grounds of the **Ecological Sanctuary ★** (☎ **2645-5869;** www.ecologicalsanctuary.com), a family-run wildlife refuge and private reserve located down the Cerro Plano road. This place has four main trails through a variety of ecosystems, and wildlife viewing is often quite good here. There are a couple of pretty waterfalls off the trails. It's open daily from 7:30am to 5pm; admission is $10 for self-guided hiking on the trails; $25 during the day for a 2-hour guided tour; and $20 for the 2-hour guided night tour that leaves at 5:30pm.

CANOPY & CANYONING TOURS

Selvatura Park ★★ (☎ **2645-5929;** www.selvatura.com), located close to the Santa Elena Cloud Forest Reserve, is the best one-stop shop for various adventures and attractions in the area. In addition to an extensive canopy tour, with 15 cables connecting 18 platforms, they also have a network of trails and suspended bridges, a huge butterfly garden, a hummingbird garden, a snake exhibit, and a wonderful insect display and museum. Prices vary depending upon how much you want to see and do. Individually, the canopy tour costs $45; the walkways and bridges, $25; the snake and reptile exhibit, $12; and the butterfly garden and the insect museum, $12 each. Packages to combine the various exhibits are available, although it's definitely confusing, and somewhat annoying, to pick the perfect package. For $121, you get the run of the entire joint, all the tours, lunch, and round-trip transportation from your Monteverde hotel. It's open daily from 7am to 4:30pm.

Another popular option is offered by the folks at **Sky Trek ★★ (℡2645-5238;** www.skyadventures.travel), which is part of a large complex of aerial adventures and hiking trails. This is one of the more extensive canopy tours in the country, with two very long cables to cross. The longest of these is some 770m (2,525 ft.) long, high above the forest floor. There are no rappel descents here, and you brake using the pulley system for friction. This tour costs $60.

One of the oldest canopy tours in the country is run by the **Original Canopy Tour ★ (℡2291-4465;** www.canopytour.com). This is one of the more interesting canopy tours in Costa Rica because the initial ascent is made by climbing up the hollowed-out interior of a giant strangler fig. The tour has 11 platforms and two rappels. The 2- to 2½-hour tours run three times daily and cost $45 for adults, $35 for students, and $25 for children 11 and under.

Finally, if you want to add a bit more excitement, and definitely more water, to your adventure, you can try the **Finca Modelo Canyoning Tour (℡2645-5581;** www.familiabrenestours.com). This tour involves a mix of hiking and then rappelling down the face of a series of forest waterfalls. The tallest of these waterfalls is around 39m (130 ft.). You will get wet on this tour. The cost is $60.

There's a glut of canopy tours in the Monteverde area, and I can only recommend those mentioned above. Anybody in average physical condition can do any of the adventure tours in Monteverde, but they're not for the fainthearted or acrophobic. Try to book directly with the companies listed above or through your hotel. Beware of touts on the streets of Monteverde, who make a small commission and frequently try to steer tourists to the operator paying the highest percentage.

HORSEBACK RIDING

There's excellent terrain for horseback riding all around Monteverde. **Meg's Riding Stables (℡2645-5560), La Estrella Stables (℡2645-5075), Palomina Horse Tours (℡2645-5479),** and **Sabine's Smiling Horses (℡2645-6894;** www.smilinghorses.com) are the more established operators, offering guided rides for around $15 to $20 per hour. As I mentioned earlier in "Boats, Horses & Taxis" (p. 298), there are horseback/boat trips linking Monteverde/Santa Elena with La Fortuna. This is certainly an exciting and adventurous means of connecting these two popular destinations, but I've received numerous complaints about the state of the trails and the treatment of the horses, so be very careful before undertaking this trip.

Another option is to set up a day tour and sauna at **El Sol ★ (℡2645-7214;** www.elsolnuestro.com). Located about a 10-minute car ride down the mountain from Santa Elena, these folks take you on a roughly 3-hour ride either to San Luis or to an isolated little waterfall with an excellent swimming hole. After the ride back, you'll find the wood-burning traditional Swedish sauna all fired up, with a refreshing and beautiful little pool beside it. The half-day tour costs $60 per person, including lunch. These folks also have two very rustically luxurious private cabins ($95–$125 double), with excellent views.

An orchid at the Orchid Garden.

OTHER ATTRACTIONS IN MONTEVERDE

It seems as if Monteverde has an exhibit or attraction dedicated to almost every type of tropical fauna. It's a pet peeve of mine, but I really wish these folks would band together and offer some sort of general pass. However, as it stands, you'll have to shell out for each individual attraction.

Butterflies abound here, and the **Butterfly Garden ★ (☎2645-5512)**, located near the Pensión Monteverde Inn, displays many of Costa Rica's most beautiful species. Besides the hundreds of preserved and mounted butterflies, there are a garden and a greenhouse where you can watch live butterflies. The garden is open daily from 9:30am to 4pm, and admission is $10 for adults and $8 for students and children, including a guided tour. The best time to visit is between 9:30am and 1pm, when the butterflies are most active.

If your taste runs toward the slithery, you can check out the informative displays at the **Monteverde Serpentarium (☎2645-5238;** www.snaketour.com), on the road to the reserve. It's open daily from 8am to 8:30pm and charges $8 for admission. The **Frog Pond of Monteverde ★ (☎2645-6320;** www.ranario. com), a couple of hundred meters north of the Monteverde Lodge, is probably a better bet. The $10 entrance gets you a 45-minute guided tour, and your ticket is good for 2 days. A variety of amphibian species populates a series of glass terrariums. In addition, these folks have a butterfly garden. It's open daily from 9am to 8:30pm. I especially recommend that you stop by at least once after dark, when the tree frogs are active.

Fans of invertebrates will want to head to **World of Insects (☎2645-6859)**, which features more than 30 terrariums filled with some of the area's more interesting creepy-crawlies. My favorites are the giant horned beetles. This place is 300m (984 ft.) west of the supermarket in Santa Elena. It's open daily from 9am to 7pm; admission is $9.

Finally, the newest entry in the field is the **Bat Jungle (☎2645-6566)**, an in-depth look into the world life and habits of these odd flying mammals. A visit here includes several different types of exhibits, from skeletal remains to a large enclosure where you get to see various live species in action—the enclosure and room are kept dark, and the bats have had their biological clocks tricked into thinking that it's night. It's quite an interesting experience. The Bat Jungle is open daily from 9am to 8pm. Admission is $10. In addition, there's a good gift shop and separate coffee shop, where they make homemade chocolate.

If you've had your fill of birds, snakes, bugs, butterflies, and bats, you might want to stop at the **Orchid Garden ★** (**2645-5308**; www.monteverdeorchid garden.com), in Santa Elena across from the Pension El Tucano. This small botanical garden boasts more than 450 species of orchids. The tour is fascinating, especially the fact that you need (and are given) a magnifying glass to see some of the flowers in bloom. Admission is $10 for adults and $7 for students. It's open daily from 8am to 5pm.

There are several options for those looking for a glimpse into the practices and processes of daily life in this region. My favorite is **El Trapiche Tour ★** (**2645-5834**; www.eltrapichetour.com), which gives you a glimpse into the traditional means of harvesting and processing coffee and sugar cane. The 2-hour tour also includes a ride in an ox-drawn cart, and a visit to their coffee farms. Depending upon the season, you may even get to pick a bushel of raw coffee beans. Back at the farmhouse you get to see how the raw materials are then turned into a variety of final products, including cane liquor, raw sugar, and roasted coffee. The tour costs $25 for adults, and $20 for children 6 through 10.

If your primary interest is java, you can take a tour of several different local coffee farms. The **Monteverde Coffee Tour** (**2645-5901**; www.monteverde-coffee.com) is run by the folks at the Cooperativa Santa Elena, a local Fair Trade coffee producer, with a shop right next to CASEM. They offer a 1½-hour tour close to Santa Elena for $22, and a 3-hour tour to a working coffee farm and mill for $30. **Don Juan Coffee Tour** (**2645-7100**; www.donjuancoffeetour.com) is a local, family farm operation, which offers a 2-hour tour for $25.

Because the vegetation in the cloud forest is so dense, most of the forest's animal residents are rather difficult to spot. If you were dissatisfied with your sightings, even with a naturalist guide leading you, you might want to consider attending a slide show of photographs taken in the reserve. Various daily slide shows are offered around Monteverde. The longest running of these takes place at

Sampling sugar cane on El Trapiche Tour.

the **Monteverde Lodge, Hotel El Sapo Dorado, Hotel Belmar** (see "Where to Stay," below), and **Hummingbird Gallery** (see below). Dates, showtimes, and admissions vary, so inquire at your hotel or one of the places mentioned above.

Almost all of the area hotels can arrange a wide variety of other tours and activities, including guided night tours of the cloud forest and night trips to the Arenal Volcano (a tedious 4-hr. ride, each way).

Learn the Language

The **Centro Panamericano de Idiomas ★** (**2645-5441**; www.spanishlanguageschool. com) offers immersion language classes in a wonderful setting. A 1-week program with 4 hours of class per day and a home stay with a Costa Rican family costs $465.

Shopping

The best-stocked gift shop in Monteverde is the **Hummingbird Gallery ★ (☎2645-5030)**. You'll find the gallery just outside the reserve entrance. Hanging from trees around it are several hummingbird feeders that attract more than seven species of these tiny birds. At any given moment, there might be several dozen hummingbirds buzzing and chattering around the building and your head. Inside you will

Birds at Hummingbird Gallery.

find many beautiful color prints of hummingbirds and other local flora and fauna, as well as a wide range of craft items, T-shirts, and other gifts. The Hummingbird Gallery is open daily from 7am to 6pm.

Another good option is **CASEM (☎2645-5190)**, on the right side of the main road, just across from Stella's Bakery. This crafts cooperative sells embroidered clothing, T-shirts, posters, and postcards with photos of the local flora and fauna, Boruca weavings, locally grown and roasted coffee, and many other items to remind you of your visit to Monteverde. CASEM is open Monday through Saturday from 8am to 5pm and Sunday from 10am to 4pm (closed Sun May–Oct). There is also a well-stocked **gift shop** at the entrance to the Monteverde Biological Cloud Forest Reserve. You'll find plenty of T-shirts, postcards, and assorted crafts here, as well as a selection of science and natural-history books.

Over the years, Monteverde has developed a nice little community of artists. Around town you'll see paintings by local artists such as Paul Smith and Meg Wallace, whose works are displayed at the Fonda Vela Hotel and Stella's Bakery, respectively. You might also check out **Casa de Arte ★ (☎2645-5275)**, which has a mix of arts and crafts in many media and is just off the main road to the reserve, as well as **Flor de Vida (☎2645-6328)**, which has some unique custom-made jewelry and clothing.

Finally, it's also worth stopping by the **Monteverde Cheese Factory (☎2645-5150)** to pick up some of the best cheese in Costa Rica. (You can even watch it being processed and get homemade ice cream.) The cheese factory is right on the main road about midway between Santa Elena and the reserve. They offer 1-hour tours at 9am and 2pm, at a cost of $10.

Where to Stay

When choosing a place to stay in Monteverde, be sure to check whether the rates include a meal plan. In the past almost all the lodges included three meals a day in their prices, but this practice is waning. Check before you assume anything.

EXPENSIVE

El Establo Mountain Hotel ★ From a working stable (*El Establo* translates as "the stable") owned by a local Quaker family, with just a handful of budget rooms, this place has morphed into what is the largest and most extravagant hotel in Monteverde. However, I think the vision here far exceeds the execution. The design and scale are somewhat out of place with the vibe and aesthetic of Monteverde, and the service and food can fall short. The rooms are all very large and have balconies or patios taking in spectacular views. The honeymoon suites have fabulous views and a private Jacuzzi, but the 400-block of rooms are my favorites. There's one midsize outdoor swimming pool and another slightly smaller pool built under a high open-air roof. El Establo owns 48 hectares (119 acres) of land backing the hotel, and half of that is primary forest. They also have an on-site canopy tour and spa.

Monteverde (A.P. 549-2050, San Pedro). ☎**2645-5110.** Fax 2645-5041. www.hotelelestablo.com. 115 units. $195 double; $273 suite. Rates include breakfast. AE, MC, V. **Amenities:** 2 restaurants; bar; babysitting; 2 pools; all rooms smoke-free; small spa. *In room:* TV, minifridge, hair dryer.

Hotel El Sapo Dorado ★ On a steep hill between Santa Elena and the reserve, El Sapo Dorado (named for Monteverde's famous golden toad) offers some of the more charming and comfortable accommodations in Monteverde. The cabins are built of hardwoods both inside and out and are surrounded by a grassy lawn and gardens, and backed by forest. Big windows let in lots of light, and high ceilings keep the rooms cool during the day. Some of the cabins have fireplaces, a welcome feature on chilly nights and during the rainy season. A remodeling in 2008 has left most cabins updated, with larger, more modern bathrooms, and livelier decor. My favorite rooms are the sunset suites, which have private terraces with views to the Gulf of Nicoya and wonderful sunsets. Not only does El Sapo Dorado own and manage the Reserva Sendero Tranquilo, but it also has a network of well-maintained trails into primary forest on-site.

Monteverde (A.P. 9-5655), Puntarenas. ☎**2645-5010.** Fax 2645-5180. www.sapodorado.com. 30 units. $122 double. Rates include breakfast and taxes. Lower rates in the off season. MC, V. **Amenities:** Restaurant; bar; free Wi-Fi. *In room:* Hair dryer.

MODERATE

In addition to the hotels listed below, **Hotel Heliconia** (☎**2240-7311** reservations office in San José, or 2645-5109 at the hotel; www.hotelheliconia.com) is another good option in this price range, as is **El Sol ★** (☎**2645-6672**; www.elsolnuestro.com), which is about 10 minutes south of Santa Elena, on the road to the Interamerican Highway. Also check out **Hotel Belmar** (☎**2645-5201**; www.hotelbelmar.net), a Swiss chalet–style hotel with moderate rates.

Arco Iris Lodge ★ 🖋 This is my favorite hotel in the town of Santa Elena and an excellent value to boot. The rooms are spread out in a variety of separate buildings, including several individual cabins. All have wood or tile floors and plenty of wood accents. My favorite is the "honeymoon cabin," which has a Jacuzzi tub and its own private balcony with a forest view and good bird-watching, although room nos. 16 and 17 are good choices, also with their own small private balconies. The management here is helpful, speaks five languages, and can arrange a wide variety of tours. Although they don't serve lunch or dinner, breakfast is offered in a spacious and airy dining and lounge building, where refreshments are available throughout the day and evening.

Monteverde (A.P. 003-5655), Puntarenas. ☎**2645-5067.** Fax 2645-5022. www.arcoirislodge.com. 19 units. $60–$120 double; $180 honeymoon cabin. AE, MC, V. **Amenities:** Lounge. *In room:* No phone.

Finca Valverde ★ This place is right on the outskirts of Santa Elena, yet once you head uphill to the rooms, you'll feel far from the hustle and bustle of the tiny burg. The standard rooms are set behind the main lodge and restaurant and are reached via a small suspension bridge over a small forest creek. Most have one queen-size and two twin beds. All share a broad common veranda. The junior suites and cabins are larger, more private, and feature bathtubs; these junior suites are the highest up the hill and also have televisions, small refrigerators, and coffeemakers. The grounds are lush and well tended, and meals are served in a large restaurant just off the main lobby.

Monteverde (A.P. 2-5655), Puntarenas. **2645-5157.** Fax 2645-5216. www.monteverde.co.cr. 22 units. $93–$111 double. Rates include continental breakfast. MC, V. **Amenities:** Restaurant; bar. *In room:* Free Wi-Fi.

Hotel Fonda Vela ★★ Although it's one of the older hotels here, Fonda Vela remains one of my top choices in Monteverde. Moreover, this is one of the closer lodges to the Cloud Forest Reserve, a relatively easy 15-minute walk away. Guest rooms are in a series of separate buildings scattered among the forests and pastures of this former farm, and most have views of the Nicoya Gulf. The junior suites all come with cable television. The newer block of junior suites, some of which have excellent views, are the best rooms in the house, and I prefer them to the older and larger junior suites. The dining room has great sunset views, and it sometimes even features live music. Throughout the hotel, you'll see paintings by co-owner Paul Smith, who also handcrafts violins and cellos and is a musician himself.

Monteverde (A.P. 70060-1000, San José). **2257-1413** reservations in San José, or 2645-5125 at the lodge. Fax 2257-1416. www.fondavela.com. 40 units. $110 double; $130 junior suite. Extra person $9. AE, MC, V. **Amenities:** Restaurant; bar. *In room:* TV, hair dryer, minibar.

Hotel Poco a Poco ★ Located just outside of the town of Santa Elena, this hotel provides many of the perks and comforts of a luxury hotel, at good prices. Some rooms are on the small side, but the beds are firm, and everything is kept neat and contemporary. The best rooms are higher up, away from the road, and have a small private balcony. All rooms come with DVD players, and the hotel maintains a movie-lending library of over 4,000 titles. A heated pool, children's pool, and Jacuzzi are on-site, and the restaurant is excellent.

Monteverde, Puntarenas. **2645-6000.** Fax 2645-6264. www.hotelpocoapoco.com. 30 units. $92 double. Rates include breakfast. MC, V. **Amenities:** Restaurant; bar; small outdoor pool. *In room:* TV/DVD, movie library, hair dryer, free Wi-Fi.

Monteverde Lodge & Gardens ★★ ☺ This was one of the first ecolodges in Monteverde, and it remains one of the best. Rooms are large and cozy. Most feature angled walls of glass with chairs and a table placed so that avid bird-watchers can do a bit of birding without leaving their rooms. The gardens and secondary forest surrounding the lodge have some gentle groomed trails and are home to quite a few species of birds. Perhaps the lodge's most popular attraction is the large hot tub in a big atrium garden just off the lobby. The dining room offers great views, good food, and excellent service. The adjacent bar is a popular gathering spot, and there are regular evening slide shows focusing on the cloud forest. Scheduled bus service to and from San José is available, as is a shuttle to the reserve, horseback riding, and a variety of optional tours.

Monteverde (mailing address: SJO 235, P.O. Box 25216, Miami, FL 33102-5216). **2257-0766** reservations office in San José, or 2645-5057 at the lodge. Fax 2257-1665. www.monteverdelodge. com. 28 units. $88–$148 double. Rates slightly lower in off season; higher during peak periods. AE, MC, V. **Amenities:** Restaurant; bar; Jacuzzi.

INEXPENSIVE

In addition to the hotels listed below, there are quite a few *pensiones* and backpacker specials in Santa Elena and spread out along the road to the reserve. The best of these are **Pensión Santa Elena** (☎2645-5051; www.pensionsantaelena.com) and **Pensión Flor de Monteverde** (☎2645-5758). A slightly more expensive and modern alternative is the **Hotel El Viandante** (☎2645-6475; www.hotelelviandante.com), which is near El Sapo Dorado.

Finally, it's possible to stay in a room right at the **Monteverde Biological Cloud Forest Reserve** (☎2645-5122; www.cct.or.cr). A bunk bed, shared bathroom, and three meals per day here run $53 per person. For an extra $11 you can get a room with a private bathroom. Admission to the reserve is included in the price.

Treehouse Hotel Housed in Santa Elena's first, and only, high-rise building, this hotel offers clean and spacious rooms in the center of town. Taking up the third—and highest—floor of this building, the rooms vary in size and the number of beds they feature. The best rooms come with small balconies overlooking the town, although these are also susceptible to street noise, particularly early in the morning and on weekend nights. All rooms feature bright white tile floors, colorful bedspreads, and sparse furnishings. Although the building is modern, it is built around a massive old fig tree, hence the hotel's name.

Santa Elena, Puntarenas. ☎2645-7475 or 8379-6908. 7 units. $56 double. MC, V. **Amenities:** Restaurant. *In room:* TV, hair dryer, no phone.

Where to Dine

Most lodges in Monteverde have their own dining rooms, and these are the most convenient places to eat, especially if you don't have a car. Because most visitors want to get an early start, they usually grab a quick breakfast at their hotel. It's also common for people to have their lodge pack them a bag lunch to take with them to the reserve, although there's now a decent little *soda* at the reserve entrance. If you're in the mood to eat out, there are several inexpensive restaurants scattered along the road between Santa Elena and Monteverde.

In addition to the places listed below, you can get good pizzas and pastas at **Tramonti** (☎2645-6120) and **Pizzeria de Johnny** (☎2645-5066), both located out along the road to the reserve. Also, the restaurant at the **Hotel Poco a Poco** (☎2645-6000) gets good marks with a wide range of international dishes. Finally, **Moon Shiva** (☎2645-6270), in Cerro Plano, serves a limited menu of Mediterranean and international fare and often features live music or movies.

A popular choice for lunch is **Stella's Bakery** (☎2645-5560), across from the CASEM gift shop. The restaurant is bright and inviting, with lots of varnished woodwork, as well as a few outdoor tables. The selection changes regularly but might include vegetarian quiche, eggplant parmigiana, and different salads. Stella's also features a daily supply of decadent baked goods.

Finally, Karen Nielsen, the force behind Chimera and Sofia (see below) recently opened yet another restaurant, called **Trio** (☎2645-7254) just below the supermarket, in the town of Santa Elena. It's geared more towards families and backpackers, but maintains her high culinary standards.

Chimera ★★ FUSION/TAPAS Building on the success of Sofia (see below), Karen Nielsen opened this creative, yet casual tapas restaurant. The small menu has a broad scope, with options available in the traditional categories of soups, salads, mains, sides, and dessert, and influences ranging from Asia to Latin America to the Old World. Standout dishes include slow-cooked pork with white beans and caramelized onions and the coconut shrimp "lollipops" with a mango-ginger dipping sauce. And for dessert, don't pass up the chocolate mousse with sangria syrup. A variety of creative and contemporary cocktails, as well as good wines, are also offered.

Cerro Plano, on the road btw. Santa Elena and the reserve, on your right. ☎ **2645-6081.** Reservations recommended during high season. Tapas $2.50–$8.50. AE, DC, DISC, MC, V. Daily 11:30am–9:30pm.

Shopping in Monteverde.

El Sapo Dorado ★ INTERNATIONAL High on a hill above the main road, the original restaurant at El Sapo Dorado continues to offer up great sunsets and food. The emphasis is on fresh ingredients and healthful preparation, and there are always nightly specials and vegetarian and vegan options as well. If you come in time for a sunset dinner, definitely grab a table in the large, covered dining room, which has full walls of picture windows for taking in the views, or, weather permitting, on their outdoor terrace. These folks have also opened another restaurant, La Guarida del Sapo, near the main road, in a large building that feels a bit like a church, with high ceilings, a tall central steeple, and plenty of stained glass and ironwork. The menu here is smaller and simpler, with an emphasis on healthy bar food, if such a thing is not too oxymoronic.

On the left as you go from Santa Elena toward the reserve. ☎ **2645-5010.** Reservations recommended during high season. Main courses $10–$18. AE, MC, V. Daily 6:30am–10pm.

Flor de Vida INTERNATIONAL/VEGETARIAN With large new digs, this long-standing local favorite continues to serve up some of the best and healthiest fare to be found in Monteverde. Large picture windows line the walls, and there's a small lounge area in one corner, with books, magazines, and board games. When it's cold and windy out, I like to start off with a bowl of their pumpkin-almond soup. For lunch, their veggie burger with roasted potatoes is hard to beat, and for dinner I tend to favor the Thai fish curry. In addition to the regular menu there are always daily specials.

On the road btw. Santa Elena and the reserve, on your right. ☎ **2645-6328.** www.flordevida.net. Reservations recommended during high season. Main courses $8–$12. MC, V. Daily 7am–10pm.

Morpho's Café 🐟 COSTA RICAN/INTERNATIONAL Probably the best and definitely the most popular restaurant in the town of Santa Elena, this simple second-floor affair serves up hearty and economical meals. There are soups, sandwiches, and *casados* (plates of the day) for lunch and dinner, and delicious fresh-fruit juices, ice-cream shakes, and home-baked desserts throughout the day. The tables and chairs are made from rough-hewn lumber and whole branches and trunks, and the place brims with a light convivial atmosphere. Morpho's is a very popular hangout for backpackers.

In downtown Santa Elena, across from the supermarket. ☎**2645-5607.** Main courses $4.50–$16. MC, V. Daily 11am–9pm.

Restaurante De Lucía COSTA RICAN/INTERNATIONAL De Lucía has earned a loyal following for its grilled-to-order meats and fresh fish. All meals come with fresh homemade tortillas and a full accompaniment of side orders and vegetables. They have a good wine selection, too. The sweet *plátanos* prepared on the open grill are delicious. Service is informal and friendly, as is the decor: Heavy wood tables and chairs are spread comfortably around the large dining room.

On the road down to the Butterfly Farm, on your right. ☎**2645-5337.** Reservations recommended during high season. Lunch $6–$12; main courses $8–$18. AE, MC, V. Daily 11–9pm.

Sofia ★★ 🎁 COSTA RICAN/FUSION This restaurant serves top-notch eclectic cuisine in a beautiful setting. Start everything off with a mango-ginger mojito and then try one of their colorful and abundant salads. Main courses range from seafood *chimichangas* to chicken breast served in a guava reduction. The tenderloin comes with a chipotle butter sauce, or in a roasted red-pepper and cashew sauce, either way served over a bed of mashed sweet potato. Everything is very well prepared and reasonably priced. There are two good-size dining rooms here; the best seats are close to the large arched picture windows overlooking the neighboring forest and gardens.

Cerro Plano, just past the turnoff to the Butterfly Farm, on your left. ☎**2645-7017.** Reservations recommended during high season. Main courses $12–$16. AE, DC, DISC, MC, V. Daily 11:30am–9:30pm.

Monteverde After Dark

The most popular after-dark activities in Monteverde are night hikes in one of the reserves and a natural-history slide show (see "Other Attractions in Monteverde," earlier in this chapter). However, if you want a taste of the local party scene, head to **La Taberna** ★, which is just outside of downtown Santa Elena before the Serpentarium. This place attracts a mix of locals and tourists, cranks its music loud, and often gets people dancing. Alternatively, **Flor de Vida** and **Moon Shiva** sometimes feature live music, theater, or open-mic jam sessions. **El Sapo Dorado** has been hosting live dance bands from San José most Monday evenings.

You'll also want to check to see if there's any live music or other performance at the **Monteverde Amphitheater** (☎**2645-6272**), a beautiful open-air performance space, up a steep driveway from Stella's Bakery, or the **Galeron Cultural Aspinall Murray** (☎**2645-6328**) a new theater and workshop space near Flor de Vida (see above).

Take a Break

If all of the activities in Monteverde have worn you out, stop in at **Chunches** (☎**2645-5147**), a bookstore with a small coffee shop and espresso bar that also doubles as a laundromat.

10

THE CENTRAL PACIFIC COAST:
WHERE THE MOUNTAINS
MEET THE SEA

A fter Guanacaste, the beaches of Costa Rica's central Pacific coast are the country's most popular. Options here range from the surfer and snowbird hangout of **Jacó,** to the ecotourist mecca of **Manuel Antonio,** to isolated and diminutive **Dominical,** with its jungle-clad hillsides and rainforest waterfalls. The region is also home to some spectacular national parks.

Jacó is the closest major beach destination to San José. It has historically been a top choice for young surfers and city-dwelling Costa Ricans. Just outside of Jacó sits **Carara National Park ★★**, one of the last places in Costa Rica where you can see the disappearing dry forest join the damp, humid forests that extend south down the coast. It's also a great place to see scarlet macaws in the wild.

For its part, Manuel Antonio remains one of the country's foremost ecotourist destinations, with a host of hotel and lodging options and an easily accessible national park that combines the exuberant lushness of a lowland tropical rainforest with several gorgeous beaches. **Manuel Antonio National Park ★★** is home to all four of Costa Rica's monkey species, as well as a wealth of other easily viewed flora and fauna.

If you're looking to get away from it all, **Dominical** and the **beaches south of Dominical ★** should be your top choice on this coast. Still a small village, the beach town of Dominical is flanked by even more remote and undeveloped beaches, including those found inside **Ballena Marine National Park ★**.

Finally, if you can tear yourself away from the beaches and coastline here, and head slightly inland, you'll find **Chirripó National Park ★★**, a misty cloud forest that becomes a barren *páramo* (a region above 3,000m/9,840 ft.) at the peak of its namesake, Mount Chirripó—the tallest peak in Costa Rica.

The climate here is considerably more humid than that farther north in Guanacaste, but it's not nearly as steamy as along the southern Pacific or Caribbean coasts.

PLAYA DE JACO, PLAYA HERMOSA ★ & PLAYA HERRADURA

Jacó: 117km (73 miles) W of San José; 75km (47 miles) S of Puntarenas

These beach towns are booming. While Jacó remains the center of the action here, the beaches just north and south of it are beginning to give it a run for its money. **Playa de Jacó** is a long stretch of beach strung with a dense hodgepodge of hotels in all price categories, souvenir shops, seafood restaurants, pizza joints, and rowdy bars. The main strip here, which runs parallel to the shoreline, is

FACING PAGE: **Keel-billed toucan.**

Jacó surf shop.

an overcrowded and congested collection of restaurants, shops, and small strip malls, where pedestrians, bicycles, scooters, cars, and ATVs vie for right of way both day and night.

The number-one attraction here is the surf, and this is definitely a surfer-dominated beach town. Surfers love the consistent beach break here. However, the beach itself is not particularly appealing. It consists of dark-gray sand with lots of little rocks, and it's often pretty rough for swimming. Still, given its proximity to San José, Jacó is almost always packed with a mix of foreign and Tico vacationers.

Just north of Jacó is **Playa Herradura,** a long stretch of brown sand that is home to the large Los Sueños Marriott Ocean & Golf Resort and its attached marina. North of Herradura, you'll find a few other small beaches and resorts, including the elegant boutique hotel Villa Caletas.

To the south of Jacó, **Playa Hermosa** is a black-sand beach with a fast and steep beach break. This is a spot for serious surfers. One of the hotels here has even installed a bank of klieg lights for night surfing. However, be careful; this break can be fierce and is known to break boards regularly and humble even experienced surfers.

In contrast to the dryness of Guanacaste, these are the first beaches on the Pacific coast to have a tropical feel. The humidity is palpable, and the lushness of the tropical forest is visible on the hillsides surrounding town. In hotel gardens, flowers bloom profusely throughout the year.

Essentials

GETTING THERE & DEPARTING By Car: There are several routes to this region. The most popular one is a narrow and winding two-lane road, the "old highway," over and through mountains, known locally as La Cuesta del Aguacate (Avocado Hill). This route is equal parts scenic and harrowing—it's not uncommon to encounter buses and trucks passing on blind curves, or to find yourself in a long line of cars stuck behind a slow-moving truck crawling up one of the steep hills. Begin this route by taking the Interamerican Highway west out of San José and exiting just west of Alajuela near the town of Atenas. Follow the numerous signs to any hotel in Jacó or Manuel Antonio.

The Central Pacific Coast

341

The old highway meets the Costanera Highway a few kilometers west of Orotina. From here it's a straight and flat shot down the coast to Jacó.

Alternatively, you can head out of San José on the highway to Escazú and Santa Ana. Continue to the town of Ciudad Colón; from here, follow signs to Puriscal and then Orotina. This is a similarly scenic and winding route through the mountains, with the same caveats, but it is less traveled and slightly more direct than the more popular route mentioned above. Finally, if you're coming from anywhere in northern Costa Rica, take the Interamerican Highway, get off at the Puntarenas exit, and follow signs to Caldera. From here, head south on the Costanera.

Note: Thirty years in the works, and seemingly endlessly delayed, a new highway is being built connecting San José with Orotina, via the western suburbs of Santa Ana and Ciudad Colón. When completed, this new toll highway is expected to reduce substantially the drive time to Jacó and the rest of the Central Pacific coast. The highway is slated to open in late 2009, but given its history, I wouldn't be surprised if it's somewhat delayed.

By Bus Transportes Jacó express buses (☎2223-1109 or 2643-3135) leave San José daily every 2 hours between 6am and 7pm from the Coca-Cola bus terminal at Calle 16 between avenidas 1 and 3. The trip takes between 2½ and 3 hours; the fare is $3.25. On weekends and holidays, extra buses are sometimes added, so it's worth calling to check.

Gray Line (☎2220-2126; www.graylinecostarica.com) has two buses that leave San José for Jacó daily at 7:30am and 4pm. **Interbus** (☎2283-5573; www.interbusonline.com) also has two buses that leave San José for Jacó daily at 8:15am and 2:30pm. Both companies charge $27 and will pick you up at most San José–area hotels. Both also have outgoing transportation with connections to most major tourist destinations in the country.

Buses from San José to **Quepos** and Manuel Antonio also pass by Jacó. (They let passengers off on the highway about 1km/½ mile from town.) However, during the busy months, some of these buses will refuse passengers getting off in Jacó or will accept them only if they pay the full fare to Quepos or Manuel Antonio. For information and departure times of these buses, see p. 58.

From **Puntarenas,** you can catch daily Quepos-bound buses at 5, 8, and 11am and 12:30, 2:30, and 4:30pm. The buses drop you off on the highway outside of town. The trip's duration is 1 hour; the fare is $2.

The Jacó bus station is at the north end of town, at a small mall across from the Jacó Fiesta Hotel. Buses for San José leave daily every 2 hours between 5am and 7pm. Buses returning to San José from Quepos pass periodically and pick up passengers on the highway. Because schedules can change, it's best to ask at your hotel about current departure times.

ORIENTATION Playa de Jacó is a short distance off the southern highway. One main road runs parallel to the beach, with a host of arteries heading toward the water; you'll find most of the town's hotels and restaurants off these roads.

GETTING AROUND Almost everything is within walking distance in Jacó, but you can call **Asotaxi** (☎2643-2020 or 2643-1919) for a cab.

You can also rent a bicycle or scooter from a variety of different shops and streetside stands along the main street. A bike rental should run you around $8 to $15 per day, and a scooter should cost between $30 and $55 per day.

For longer excursions, you can rent a car from **Alamo** (☎ 2643-2881), **Budget** (☎ 2643-2265), **Economy** (☎ 2643-1098), **National** (☎ 2643-1752), **Payless** (☎ 2643-3224), or **Zuma** (☎ 2643-3207). Expect to pay approximately $45 to $90 for a 1-day rental. You might also consider talking to a local taxi driver, who'd probably take you wherever you want to go for about the same price, saving you some hassle and headache.

FAST FACTS The **Banco Nacional** (☎ 2643-3072) and the **Banco de Costa Rica** (☎ 2643-3695) have branches in town on the main road. Also on the main road, you can find the **Farmacia Jacó** (☎ 2643-3205) and the well-stocked **Farmacia Fischel** (☎ 2643-2683), which is in the El Galeone shopping center. A gas station is on the main highway, between Playa Herradura and Jacó, and a 24-hour gas station, **El Arroyo,** is on the highway on the southern edge of Jacó. The **health center** (☎ 2643-3667) and **post office** (☎ 2643-2175) are at the Municipal Center at the south end of town. However, the best-equipped medical center is the **Clinica Santa Catalina** (☎ 2643-5059), located 4 blocks inland from the Pop's ice-cream shop.

A **public phone office,** where you can make international calls, is in the ICE building on the main road. This office is open Monday through Saturday from 8am to noon and 1 to 5pm. There are half a dozen or more **Internet cafes** in town, as well as several inexpensive full-service laundromats; a **Western Union office** in a small strip mall across from La Hacienda restaurant; a large **Más × Menos** supermarket on the main drag in the center of town; and an even larger and more modern **Automercado** supermarket in the strip mall on the main highway near the entrance to Playa Herradura.

Don't Feed the Crocs

The Costanera Highway passes over the Tárcoles River just outside the entrance to **Carara National Park,** about 23km (14 miles) south of Orotina. This is a popular spot to pull over and spot some gargantuan crocodiles. Some can reach 3.7 to 4.6m (12–15 ft.) in length. Usually anywhere from 10 to 20 are easily visible, either swimming in the water or sunning on the banks. But be careful. First, you'll be walking on a narrow sidewalk along the side of the bridge with cars and trucks speeding by. And second, there have been numerous car break-ins here, including the seemingly safe

restaurant parking lots at the north end of the bridge. Although a police post has somewhat reduced the risk, I recommend that you don't leave your car or valuables unguarded for long, or better yet, leave someone at the car and take turns watching the crocs.

Playa Esterillos.

Fun on & off the Beach

Jacó beach has a reputation for dangerous riptides (as does most of Costa Rica's Pacific coast). Even strong swimmers have been known to drown in the power rips. In general, the far southern end of the beach is the calmest and safest place to swim.

OTHER BEACHES AROUND JACO

As an alternative to Playa de Jacó, you may want to visit other nearby beaches. These beaches are easily reached by car, moped, or bicycle—if you've got a lot of energy. All are signposted, so you'll have no trouble finding them.

Playa Hermosa, 10km (6¼ miles) southeast of Jacó, where sea turtles lay eggs from July to December, is also well known for its great surfing waves. This beach is dark, made of nearly black, yet fine, volcanic sand. If you keep heading south (really southeast) you next come to **Playa Esterillos,** 22km (14 miles) south of Jacó, which is long and wide and almost always nearly deserted. Playa Esterillos is so long, in fact, that there are three separate entrances and sections, Esterillos Oeste, Centro, and Este—West, Center, and East, in order as you head away from Jacó. Just beyond Playa Esterillos is **Playa Bejuco,** another long, wide, nearly deserted stretch of sand.

Heading northwest from Jacó, the first beach you come to is **Playa Herradura,** a hard-packed brown-sand-and-rock beach ringed by lush hillsides. This is home to the Los Sueños Marriott Ocean & Golf Resort. However, the Marriott occupies only one end of the beach here; despite its presence, Playa Herradura still feels a lot more isolated and deserted than Jacó. Finally, **Punta Leona,** just a few kilometers north of Playa Herradura, is a cross between a

En Route to Jacó: An Isolated Boutique Beauty

If you're planning on heading to the beaches of the central Pacific coast via Ciudad Colón and Puriscal, you might consider a stop at **Ama Tierra Retreat & Wellness Center ★ (☎ 866/659-3805** in the U.S. and Canada, or 2419-0110 in Costa Rica; www.amatierra.com), a lovely little boutique hotel and retreat center located about 1½ hours outside of San José along this route, and approximately 1 hour from Jacó.

hotel, a resort, and a private country club, and it has some of the nicer beaches in the area. Although they effectively have restricted access to their beaches for years, this is technically illegal in Costa Rica, and you have the right to enjoy both playas **Manta** ★ and **Blanca** ★, two very nice white-sand beaches inside the Punta Leona complex. The public access road to these beaches is located south of the main Punta Leona entrance and is not very well marked.

Carara National Park ★★

A little more than 15km (9⅓ miles) north of Jacó is **Carara National Park** (**℡2637-1054** for visitor center), a world-renowned nesting ground for **scarlet macaws.** It has a few kilometers of trails open to visitors. There's a loop trail that takes about an hour, and another trail that's open only to tour groups. The macaws migrate daily, spending their days in the park and their nights among the coastal mangroves. It's best to view them in the early morning when they arrive, or around sunset when they head back to the coast for the evening, but a good guide can usually find them for you during the day. Whether or not you see them, you should hear their loud squawks. Among the other wildlife that you might see here are caimans, coatimundis, armadillos, pacas, peccaries, and, of course, hundreds of species of birds.

Be sure to bring along insect repellent or, better yet, wear light cotton long sleeves and pants. (I was once foolish enough to attempt a quick hike while returning from Manuel Antonio, still in beach clothes and flip-flops.) The reserve is open daily from 8am to 4pm. Admission is $10 per person at the gate.

Several companies offer tours to Carara National Park for around $59 to $65. Check at your hotel or contact **Gray Line Tours** (**℡2643-3231**) or **Superior Sightseeing** (**℡8393-6626**) to set one up. You can also hike the trails of Carara independently, but my advice is to take a guided tour; you'll learn a lot more about your surroundings.

Scarlet macaw.

The muddy banks of the Tárcoles River are home to a healthy population of American crocodiles. Just north of the entrance to the park is a bridge that's a prime spot for viewing both the crocs and the macaw migrations. In Jacó, several operators run daily crocodile tours on the Tárcoles River. These are simple tours in open skiffs or Boston whalers. Most of these companies bring along plenty of freshly killed chicken to attract the reptiles and pump up the adrenaline. Don't expect a highly trained naturalist guide or any semblance of respect for the natural world. Do expect to pay around $20 to $45 per person for the trip.

Finally, just beyond Carara National Park on the Costanera Sur in the direction of Jacó is a turnoff for some spectacular waterfalls (including a 180m/590-ft. fall) around the town of **Bijagual.** There are several ways to visit these falls, and people run tours from Jacó or from entrances both at the top and bottom of the falls. At the top a local family runs the **Complejo Ecológico La Catarata** (no phone), which features a basic restaurant and a campground, and offers horseback tours down to the falls for around $45. Alternatively, you can hike in from an entrance lower down. The hike takes about 45 minutes each way, and the entrance fee is $20 per person. While you're in this area, you can also visit **Pura Vida Botanical Gardens** (☎2645-1001). Admission for the gardens is $20. The fee includes free run of the gardens and trials, which lead to a couple of smaller local waterfalls. To get here, turn off at the signs for Hotel Villa Lapas. From there, it's a rough 8km (5 miles) up to the top of the falls.

Activities & Tours

ATV TOURS Several operations take folks out on ATV tours through the surrounding countryside. Tours range in length from 2 to 6 hours and cost between $85 and $165 per person. Contact **Four Trax Adventures** (☎2643-2373; www.fourtraxadventure.com), **Paraíso Adventures** (☎2643-2920; www.paraiso costarica.com), or **Jaguar Riders** (☎2643-0180; www.jaguariders.com).

BIKING You can rent a bike for around $8 to $15 per day or $2 to $3 per hour. Bikes are available from a slew of shops along the main road. Shop around, and make sure you get a bike that is in good condition and that is comfortable.

CANOPY TOURS The easiest way to get up into the canopy here is on the **Rain Forest Aerial Tram Pacific** (☎2257-5961; www.rfat.com). A sister project to the original Rain Forest Aerial Tram, this attraction features modified ski-lift type gondolas that take you through and above the transitional forests bordering Carara National Park. The $55 entrance fee includes the guided 40-minute tram ride, and a guided 45-minute hike on a network of trails. You can also hike the company's trails for as long as you like. These folks also have a zip-line canopy tour on the same grounds, and offer guided tours, including transportation from both San José and any hotel in the area. The Aerial Tram is located a few kilometers inland from an exit just north of the first entrance into Jacó.

There are quite a few zip-line and harness-style canopy tours in this area. **Chiclets Tree Tour** (☎2643-1880) offers up a canopy adventure ($60 per person) in nearby Playa Hermosa. This is an adventurous tour, with 13 platforms set in transitional forest, with some sweeping views of the Pacific. **Villa Lapas** (p. 353) has two different tours through the treetops outside of Jacó. The better and cheaper option is a guided hike on its network of trails and five suspended bridges ($20 per person). The operator also has a relatively low-adrenaline zip-line canopy tour ($35 per person), with seven platforms connected by six cables.

Finally, Jacó is also a good jumping-off point for a trip to **Turu BaRi Tropical Park** (☎2250-0705; www.turubari.com), near Orotina. See chapter 6 for details.

GOLF The excellent **La Iguana,** an 18-hole golf course at the **Los Sueños Marriott Ocean & Golf Resort** (☎2630-9000; www.golflaiguana.com), is open to nonguests. Greens fees are $160 for a full round. The price drops to $130 if you tee off after noon. Club and shoe rentals are available. Marriott guests pay slightly less to play here.

HORSEBACK RIDING Horseback-riding tours give you a chance to get away from all the development in Jacó and see a bit of nature. The best operator in the area, with the best horses, is **Discovery Horseback** (☎8838-7550 or 2637-0808) down in Playa Hermosa. It's $65 per person for a 2½-hour tour.

KAYAKING **Kayak Jacó** (☎2643-1233; www.kayakjaco.com) runs a couple of different trips. Tours range from gentle paddles and floats on the Tulin River to combination ocean-kayaking/snorkeling trips on calm Herradura Bay, to full-on kayak surfing at one of the local beach breaks. You can also do some moderate white-water kayaking in easy-to-use inflatable kayaks or try your hand in the ocean on one of the eight-person outrigger canoes. Most options run around 4 hours and include transportation to and from the put-in, as well as fresh fruit and soft drinks during the trip. The tours cost between $55 and $70 per person, depending on the particular trip and group size.

ORGANIZED TOURS FARTHER AFIELD If you'll be spending your entire Costa Rican visit in Jacó but would like to see some other parts of the country, you can arrange tours through the local offices of **Gray Line Tours** (☎2643-3231), which operates out of the Best Western Jacó Beach Resort (p. 350). Gray Line offers day tours to Arenal, Poás, and Irazú volcanoes; white-water rafting trips; cruises to Tortuga Island; and trips to Braulio Carrillo National Park and other places. Rates range from $36 to $120 for day trips. Overnight trips are also available. Thanks to improvements to the road, you can reach **Manuel Antonio** in about 1 hour from Jacó. In addition to the above-mentioned companies, many local operators offer a variety of tour options in Manuel Antonio, including trips to the national park, the Rainmaker Nature Refuge, and the Damas Island estuary. See the "Manuel Antonio National Park" section (later in this chapter) for more details on the types of tours and activities available there.

SPA The **Serenity Spa ★** (☎2643-1624; www.serenityspacr.net) offers massages, as well as mud packs, face and body treatments, and manicures and pedicures. The spa's Jacó branch is on the first floor, among a tiny little cul-de-sac of shops next to Zuma Rent-A-Car. These folks also have operations at Villa Caletas.

SPORTFISHING, SCUBA DIVING & SEABORNE FUN Since the Los Sueños Marriott Resort (p. 352) and its adjacent 250-slip marina opened, most local maritime activity has shifted over here. If you're interested in doing

Fishing vessels at dock at Los Sueños Marina.

some sportfishing, scuba diving, or any other waterborne activity, I recommend that you check with your hotel or at the marina. Dependable operators that have set up here include **Maverick Sportfishing Yachts** (☎866/888-6426 in the U.S., or 2637-8824 in Costa Rica; www.maverickyachtscostarica.com), **Costa Rica Dreams** (☎732/901-8625 in the U.S. and Canada, or 2637-8942 in Costa Rica; www.costaricadreams.com), and **Cuervo Sport Fishing** (☎800/656-1859 in the U.S. and Canada; www.costarica-fishingcharters.com). A half-day fishing trip for four people costs around $850 to $1,200, and a full day costs between $1,000 and $1,500.

SURFING The same waves that often make Playa de Jacó dangerous for swimmers make it one of the most popular beaches in the country with surfers. Nearby **Playa Hermosa, Playa Tulin,** and **Playa Escondida** are also excellent surfing beaches. Those who want to challenge the waves can rent surfboards for around $3 an hour or $10 to $15 per day, and boogie boards for $2 an hour, from any one of the numerous surf shops along the main road. If you want to learn how to surf, try the **Jacó Surf School** (☎6829-4697 [cell] or 6643-1905; www.jacosurfschool.com), or contact Johnny at **Superior Sightseeing** (☎8393-6626) or ask for him at Club del Mar (see below).

Shopping

If you try to do any shopping in Jacó, you'll be overrun with shops selling T-shirts, cut-rate souvenirs, and handmade jewelry and trinkets. Most of the offerings are of pretty poor quality. Two notable exceptions are **Guacamole ★** (☎2643-1120), a small clothing store that produces its own line of batik beachwear, and **La Galería Heliconia ★★** (☎2643-3613), which carries a superb selection of artworks and pottery. Both stores are on the main street through town, close to the center of town.

Where to Stay in Playa de Jacó

Because Punta Leona, Playa Herradura, Playa Hermosa de Jacó (not to be confused with either Playa Hermosa in Guanacaste, or Playa Hermosa on the Nicoya Peninsula), Playa Esterillos, and Playa Bejuco are close, many people choose accommodations in these beach towns as well. Selected listings for these towns follow this section.

Playa Jacó

To Playa Herradura and San José

Parque Lapa Verde

PACIFIC OCEAN

Soccer Field

Bus Stop

To Playa Hermosa & Quepos/Manuel Antonio

Soccer Field

ACCOMMODATIONS

Apartotel Flamboyant **14**
Apartotel Girasol **26**
Arenal Pacífico **28**
Best Western Jaco
  Beach Resort **4**
Blue Palms **19**
Club del Mar
  Condominiums
  & Resort **30**
Hotel Catalina **27**
Hotel Nine **29**
Hotel Mar de Luz **18**
Hotel Poseidon **7**
Hotel Zabamar **20**
Pochote Grande **1**

DINING

Caliche's Wishbone **11**
El Hicaco **21**
Lemon Zest **25**
Los Amigos **16**
Rioasis **13**
Taco Bar **17**

NIGHTLIFE

Beatle Bar **5**
Clarita's Beach Bar & Grill **2**
Congas **3**
Disco La Central **23**
Ganesha Lounge **15**
Hotel Copacabana **6**
Hotel Poseidon **7**

(cont.)
Jazz Casino **31**
Jungle Bar **8**
Le Loft **24**
Monkey Bar **9**
Tabacón **10**

SHOPPING

Guacamole **22**
La Galería Heliconia **12**

EXPENSIVE

Club del Mar Condominiums & Resort ★★ ☺ This has long been my top choice in Playa de Jacó, and it remains so. It has a fabulous location, friendly management, and attractively designed rooms. Club del Mar is at the far southern end of the beach, where the rocky hills meet the sand, and where the swimming is probably the safest in town. Most of the rooms are actually one- or two-bedroom condo units, with full kitchens. All are spacious and feature private balconies or porches. There are also eight rooms on the second floor of the large main building, as well as two huge and luxurious penthouse suites up on the third floor. All units come with an ocean view, although some are more open and expansive than others. The grounds are lush and chock-full of flowering heliconia and ginger. There's a midsize multipurpose pool and an excellent open-air restaurant, as well as some modest spa facilities.

Playa de Jacó (A.P. 107-4023), Puntarenas. **☎ 866/978-5669** in the U.S. and Canada, or 2643-3194 in Costa Rica. Fax 2643-3550. www.clubdelmarcostarica.com. 32 units. $153 double; $224–$320 condo; $383 penthouse. AE, DC, MC, V. **Amenities:** Restaurant; bar; babysitting; concierge; midsize free-form pool; room service; small spa; free Wi-Fi in main building and around pool. *In room:* A/C, TV, fridge.

Hotel Nine ★ 🎁 This new hotel features contemporary architectural design touches that would be right at home on Miami's South Beach. This is appropriate, as the "L"-shaped, two-story building fronts the sand towards the southern end of Jacó beach. Inside, the rooms are decorated with tropical-style wood and rattan furnishings and bold colors. The premium suites have two separate rooms and a small kitchenette with microwave oven. Laundry service and surfboards are both complimentary. The excellent restaurant here bills itself primarily as a steakhouse, but fresh seafood options are also available.

Playa de Jacó, Puntarenas. ☎2643-5335. www.hotelnine.com. 9 units. $130–$170 double; $220 suite. Rates include continental breakfast. AE, DC, MC, V. **Amenities:** Restaurant; bar; Jacuzzi; midsize pool; room service; all rooms smoke-free; free surfboards. *In room:* A/C, TV, minibar, free Wi-Fi.

MODERATE

In addition to the places listed below, the oceanfront **Apartotel Girasol ★** (☎800/923-2779 or 2643-1591; www.girasol.com), with 16 fully equipped one-bedroom apartments, is a good option, especially for longer stays. **Hotel Poseidon** (☎888/643-1242 in the U.S. and Canada, or 2643-1642; www.hotel-poseidon.com) is a pretty boutique hotel in the heart of downtown, while **Hotel Catalina** (☎2643-1237; www.hotelcatalinacr.com) is another good beachfront choice.

Apartotel Flamboyant Don't let the name fool you: The Flamboyant is actually rather quiet and intimate. The rooms are arranged around a small swimming pool and are only a few steps from the beach. They're all spacious, with simple furnishings, and most have kitchenettes. The more expensive rooms have air-conditioning, televisions, and private balconies. You'll find the hotel on a narrow lane leading toward the ocean, down from Caliche's Wishbone (p. 355).

Playa de Jacó (A.P. 18), Puntarenas. ☎2643-3146. Fax 2643-1068. www.apartotelflamboyant. com. 15 units. $75–$105 double. AE, MC, V. **Amenities:** Unheated Jacuzzi; outdoor pool. *In room:* No phone.

Arenal Pacífico ★ This is a good midrange option, and it's right on the beach to boot. The rooms are nothing special—and almost none offer an ocean view—but they are clean and cool, and most are pretty spacious. The grounds are lush by Jacó standards—you have to cross a shady bridge over a little stream to get from the parking lot and reception to the rooms and restaurant. I like the second-floor rooms, which have private balconies. The superior rooms are larger, and come with coffeemakers and minifridges. There are two outdoor pools—one with a little waterfall filling it, another with a round children's pool. The open-air restaurant serves standard Tico and international fare.

Playa de Jacó (A.P. 962-1000, San José), Puntarenas. ☎2643-3419. Fax 2643-3770. www.arenalpacifico.com. 22 units. $99 double; $129–$137 superior double; $240 junior suite. Rates include continental breakfast. AE, MC, V. **Amenities:** Restaurant; bar; bikes; 2 outdoor pools; surf- and boogie-board rental. *In room:* A/C, TV, free Wi-Fi.

Best Western Jacó Beach Resort Situated right on the beach, this five-story hotel offers all the amenities and services you could want at a pretty good price. Still, this is a cut-rate resort, and there's little in the way of charm, romance, or true ambience here. The hotel is often packed throughout the high season, and a party atmosphere pervades the place. The open-air lobby is surrounded by lush gardens, and covered walkways connect the hotel's buildings. Rooms are adequate and have tile floors and walls of glass facing balconies; however, not all of the rooms have good views (some face another building), and many of them show the wear and tear of age and heavy occupancy. Ask for a room on a higher floor and with an ocean view. A large percentage of guests opt for the all-inclusive package, even so, I think you'd do better to sample some of the many restaurants and dining options around Jacó.

Playa de Jacó (A.P. 962-1000, San José), Puntarenas. **800/528-1234** in the U.S. and Canada, or 2643-1000 in Costa Rica. Fax 2643-3833. www.bestwestern.com. 125 units. $96–$113 double. Rates include breakfast buffet. AE, DC, MC, V. **Amenities:** 2 restaurants; 2 bars; bikes; well-equipped gym; 2 circular pools; room service; tennis court; extensive watersports equipment rental. *In room:* A/C, TV, free Wi-Fi.

Hotel Mar de Luz ★ 🏄 This is one of Playa de Jacó's better deals and a comfortable alternative to the string of cut-rate cabinas you'll find crowding this popular beach town. All the rooms are immaculate and comfortable. Some feature stone walls, small sitting areas, and one or two double beds placed on a raised sleeping nook. My only complaint is that in most rooms, the windows are too small and mostly sealed, forcing you to use air-conditioning. In the gardens just off the pools are a couple of grills for guest use. A comfortable common sitting area has a selection of magazines and books, and there's a game room for the kids. The Dutch owner Victor Keulen seems driven to offer as much comfort, quality, and service as he can for the price. The hotel lies 50m (164 ft.) east of the Hotel Tangeri, right in the center of Jacó.

Playa de Jacó (A.P. 143), Puntarenas. 🗘/fax **2643-3259.** www.mardeluz.com. 29 units. $91 double. Rates include breakfast and taxes. V. **Amenities:** Babysitting; Jacuzzi; 2 small-to-midsize adult pools and children's pool; smoke-free rooms. *In room:* A/C, TV, minifridge, free Wi-Fi.

Pochote Grande 🏄 This well-kept hotel is located just off the beach toward the far north end of Jacó. All of the rooms are quite large, although sparsely furnished, and have white-tile floors, one queen-size and one single bed, a small fridge, and a balcony or patio. I prefer the second-floor rooms, which are blessed with high ceilings. The modest restaurant and snack bar serve a mixture of Tico, German, and American meals. (The owners are German by way of Africa.) The grounds here were once shady and lush, but encroaching construction all around has left this place feeling a bit exposed, and ongoing construction can be a nuisance and source of noise.

Playa de Jacó (A.P. 42), Puntarenas. 🗘**2643-3236.** Fax 2220-4979. www.hotelpochotegrande. net. 24 units. $80 double. Add $5 for a room with television. AE, MC, V. **Amenities:** Restaurant; bar; pool. *In room:* A/C, fridge, no phone, free Wi-Fi.

INEXPENSIVE

There are quite a few budget hotels around town. Most cater to itinerant surfers, backpackers, and Ticos. If you're looking to stay on the cheap, your best bet is to simply walk the strip and see who's got the best room at the best price. If you head several blocks inland from the center of town, the **Blue Palms** (🗘**2643-0099;** www.blue-palms.net) offers immaculate rooms and a small swimming pool at budget prices.

You can try camping at **El Hicaco** (🗘**2643-3004**), which is very centrally located and close to the beach, but it's also nearby the Disco La Central (p. 356), so don't expect to get much sleep if you stay here. In addition, you'll need to be very careful with your belongings; I've heard several complaints of robberies at the campsites here. Camping runs around $7 per person per night.

Hotel Zabamar ☺ The Zabamar is set back about 1 block from the beach in a shady compound. The best rooms are in a two-story building closest to the road. These are quite roomy and feature cool tile floors and air-conditioning. The rest of the rooms are also large and have red-tile floors, small refrigerators, ceiling fans, hammocks on their front porches, and *pilas* (laundry sinks) in little gravel-and-palm gardens behind them. There's a small swimming pool with two separate children's sections that's quite popular with Tico families staying here. Because of the proximity to the town's bars and restaurants, the rooms closest to the street can be noisy.

Playa de Jacó, Puntarenas. ☎2643-3174. Fax 2643-2645. 20 units. $53–$75 double. Rates include breakfast. Discounts for long-term stays. No credit cards. **Amenities:** Restaurant; small pool. *In room:* No phone, free Wi-Fi

Where to Stay in Playa Herradura & North of Playa de Jacó

VERY EXPENSIVE

In addition to its hotel rooms, the Los Sueños resort has scores of condominium units for rent. All come with kitchens, access to swimming pools, and rights to use the golf course here. These are excellent options for families who want to do some cooking, and for longer stays. If you want to rent a condo here, contact **Costa Rica Luxury Rentals** (☎866/525-2188 in the U.S. and Canada, or 2637-7105 in Costa Rica; www.crluxury.com). Rates run between $350 and $440 nightly for one- and two-bedroom units, to over $1,100 for some of the more luxurious three-bedroom units.

Los Sueños Marriott Ocean & Golf Resort ★★ ☺ This resort is done in a Spanish colonial style, with stucco walls, heavy wooden doors, and red-clay roof tiles. Every room has a balcony, but all are not created equal. Most have only small Juliet-style balconies. Those facing the ocean are clearly superior, and a few of the ocean-facing rooms even have large balconies with chaise longues and garden furniture. The pool is a vast, intricate maze built to imitate the canals of Venice, with private nooks and grottoes; kids love exploring it. Parents will appreciate the excellent children's program. The beach here is calm and good for swimming, although it's one of the least attractive beaches on this coast, with a mix of rocks and hard-packed, dark-brown sand. The golf course winds through some of the neighboring forest and is an excellent, if not particularly challenging, resort course. The Stellaris Casino is the largest and plushest I've found at a beach resort in Costa Rica.

Playa Herradura (A.P. 502-4005), San Antonio de Belén. ☎888/236-2427 in the U.S., 2298-0844 or 2630-9000 in Costa Rica. Fax 2630-9090. www.marriott.com. 201 units. $300–$350 double; $400–$700 suite; $1,300–$1,700 presidential suite. AE, MC, V. **Amenities:** 4 restaurants; coffee shop; 2 bars; lounge; babysitting; children's program; concierge; golf course and pro shop; 9-hole miniature golf course; extensive health club and spa; large pool; room service; smoke-free rooms; 4 outdoor lit tennis courts; Wi-Fi (for a fee) in most public areas. *In room:* A/C, TV, high-speed Internet for a fee, hair dryer, minibar.

Villa Caletas ★★★ 🎁 Perched above the sea, Villa Caletas enjoys commanding views of the Pacific over forested hillsides. The rooms are all elegantly appointed, but you'll want to stay in a villa or suite. All feature ornate neoclassical decor and a private terrace for soaking up the views. The larger junior suites come with their own outdoor Jacuzzis. The suites and master suites are larger still—and come with their own swimming pools. There are only two master suites, and one is a vigorous hike downhill from the main hotel building and restaurants. The same is true of some of the villas and juniors. The Zephyr Palace is a seven-suite addition, located a little bit apart from the main hotel and villas. The rooms here are immense and thematically designed—you can choose from an African suite, an Arabian suite, an Oriental suite, and more. All have beautiful ocean views, home theater systems, Jacuzzis, private balconies, and personal concierge service.

A.P. 12358-1000, San José. ☎**2630-3003.** Fax 2637-0404. www.hotelvillacaletas.com. 42 units. $178–$198 double; $230 villa; $300–$470 suite; $450–$600 Zephyr Palace suites. Rates slightly lower in off season; higher during peak periods. Extra person $35. AE, MC, V. **Amenities:** 2 restaurants; bar; concierge; 2 midsize pools w/spectacular view; spa. *In room:* A/C, TV, minibar.

EXPENSIVE

Villa Lapas Located on a lush piece of property along the Río Tarcolitos bordering Carara National Park, Villa Lapas is a good choice if you're looking to combine a bit of ecoadventure and bird-watching with some beach time. The spacious rooms have two double beds, cool red-clay tile floors, air-conditioning, and a shady veranda with wooden benches for taking in the scenery. The hotel's best feature is its massive, open-air restaurant and deck, which overlooks the river and where buffet-style meals are served. Villa Lapas has 217 hectares (536 acres) of land with excellent trails, a series of suspended bridges crossing the river, and its own canopy tour. The hotel also features a small re-creation of a typical Costa Rican rural village of times gone by. This riverside attraction also has three massive gift shops, an atmospheric old-style Costa Rican bar, and a small chapel. The hotel is about 15 to 25 minutes from the beaches of Jacó, Hermosa, and Herradura.

Tárcoles (A.P. 419-4005, San Antonio de Belén). ☎**2637-0232.** Fax 2637-0227. www.villalapas. com. 55 units. $121 per person. Rates include 3 meals daily and taxes. AE, MC, V. **Amenities:** 2 restaurants; 2 bars; small pool. *In room:* A/C, free Wi-Fi.

Where to Dine

Playa de Jacó has a wide range of restaurants. Many cater to surfers and budget travelers. In addition to the places listed below, if you're looking for simply prepared fresh seafood, **El Barco de Mariscos** (☎2643-2831) and **El Recreo** (☎2643-3012) are both good bets that serve standard Tico beach fare—fresh seafood, sandwiches, chicken, and steak. For a coffee break and newly baked pastries and breads, head to **Café del M@r** (☎2643-1250). **Wahoo Seafood Saloon** (☎2643-1876) offers fresh seafood and Mexican fare. The small restaurant at the **Hotel Poseidon** ★ (☎2643-1642) serves a regularly changing small menu of excellent Asian inspired fusion cuisine, while **Pili Pili** (☎2643-5535 or 8995-4946) also serves up fusion fare, with African and French flavors being dominant here. And sushi lovers should head to **Tsunami Sushi** (☎2643-3678), inside the El Galeone strip mall.

Over in Playa Herradura are several restaurants, including the Peruvian chain **Inka Grill** (☎2637-8510), in the strip mall on the highway near the entrance to the beach. Also, at the Los Sueños marina, you'll find several other options, including; **Bambu,** a sushi bar and Pan-Asian restaurant; **La Linterna,** a fancy Italian restaurant; and **Hook Up,** an excellent American-style grill and restaurant, serving great lunch and light fare, with a second-floor perch and good views. You can make reservations at any of the marina restaurants by calling ☎2630-4444.

Finally, **Steve & Lisa's** (☎2637-0594), located several miles outside of town, around Tárcoles, is a good place for lunch. The food here is standard Tico fare, but the oceanside setting and views set it apart from other simple *sodas*. **Note:** There's another restaurant on this road calling itself "Steve & Lisa's," but it's located inland with no view. Definitely head to the one on the water's edge.

VERY EXPENSIVE

El Galeón ★★ FUSION This is the top restaurant in a complex of restaurants found at the Los Sueños resort and marina. The setting is elegant, service refined, and the menu wide-ranging, creative, and eclectic. Appetizers range from an inventive plate of scallop sliders, to crisp Asian-spiced soft-shell crabs and sea bass *ceviche* served with avocado and a local salsa. For a main course, I recommend the pumpkin, ricotta, and basil–filled ravioli served with grilled Creole jumbo shrimp.

At the marina of the Los Sueños Marriott Resort (p. 352). ☎2630-4555 or 2637-8331. Reservations recommended. Main courses $19–$43. AE, MC, V. Daily 6–10pm.

El Nuevo Latino ★ LATIN FUSION The fanciest restaurant inside the Marriott Los Sueños Resort offers creative and modern takes on local and regional dishes. The dozen or so tables are set in a narrow room with a vaulted ceiling that features a glass wall running its length, fronting a gorgeous pool fed by a series of spouts from a story-high aqueduct. The service and setting are semiformal, but there's no dress code—they realize that you're at the beach and on vacation here. Standout dishes include local shrimp in a rum and sugar-cane glaze served with hearts of palm and rice, and tenderloin in a guava–black pepper sauce served with a yuca and bacon tart.

At the Los Sueños Marriott Resort (p. 352). ☎2630-9000. Reservations recommended. Main courses $19–$47. AE, MC, V. Daily 6–11pm. Closed Mon during the off season.

EXPENSIVE

El Hicaco ✋ SEAFOOD/COSTA RICAN This beachside restaurant has gotten too popular for its own good. There's a cattle-car feel to the entire operation, and the food is overpriced and quality has declined. But the setting is still wonderful: right on the edge of the beach, with the majority of the tables outdoors. At night you sit under the stars, surrounded by tall palm trees, with some interesting lighting overhead. If you do come here, stick with the freshly caught grilled seafood or lobster, although there are plenty of meat and chicken selections on the menu as well.

On the beach in downtown Jacó. ☎2643-3226. www.elhicaco.net. Reservations recommended during high season. Main courses $11–$45. AE, MC, V. Daily 11am–11pm.

Lemon Zest ★★ SEAFOOD/FUSION Culinary institute graduate and former Le Cordon Bleu instructor, chef Richard Lemon has set up shop in a second-floor space right along Jacó's main strip. The decor is elegant, with subdued lighting and white cloth-covered tables. I recommend starting things off with the lobster and manchego quesadilla, or the Korean BBQ satay skewers served with homemade banana ketchup. Seafood main courses include macadamia-crusted mahimahi and fresh seared tuna. For a splurge, try the sesame-and-panko-crusted lobster with a pineapple risotto and sweet chile sauce. There are also daily specials, and some outrageous desserts. The wine list here is well-priced, with several good selections offered by the glass.

Downtown Jacó. ☎**2643-2591.** www.lemonzestjaco.com. Reservations recommended during high season. Main courses $13–$20. AE, MC, V. Mon–Sat 5–10pm.

MODERATE

Los Amigos SEAFOOD/INTERNATIONAL Set on a large corner of a busy intersection in the heart of Jacó, this restaurant serves fresh seafood and adventurous international fare at very reasonable prices. Sturdy wooden tables are spread around the small dining room and open-air patio here. I prefer the patio seating, which looks out over flowering heliconia to the bustle of Jacó's main drag. Fresh tuna can be had Cajun-style or with a spicy mango salsa. There are also several traditional Thai dishes on the menu, as well as some wraps and hearty salads. At night, they play electronic music and have a lively bar scene.

On the main road in Jacó. ☎**2643-2961.** Main courses $7–$31. AE, MC, V. Daily 10am–11pm.

INEXPENSIVE

Caliche's Wishbone ★★ 📱 SEAFOOD/MEXICAN This casual spot is popular with surfers and offers Tex-Mex standards and homemade pizzas. However, you can also get perfectly prepared seafood dishes, as well as a variety of sandwiches served in homemade pita bread. The portions are huge. It almost always has fresh tuna lightly seared and served with a soy-wasabi dressing. The nicest tables are streetside on a covered veranda. Inside are more tables, as well as a bar with television sets showing surf videos.

On the main road in Jacó. ☎**2643-3406.** Reservations not accepted. Main courses $5.50–$27. V. Thurs–Tues 10am–10pm.

El Pelicano 📱 SEAFOOD/COSTA RICAN This simple beachfront restaurant is a lot like El Hicaco was before success went to its head. Heavy wooden tables and chairs are spread around a large, open-air dining room facing the beach and boats bobbing at anchor off Playa Herradura. The menu features a range of *ceviche* dishes, salads, and main courses, with a heavy—and logical—emphasis on fresh seafood. The *corvina al ajillo* (sea bass in garlic sauce) is excellent, as is the *arroz con mariscos* (rice with seafood). To get here, drive the Playa Herradura road until you hit the beach, and then turn left on the narrow sandy access road.

On the beach in Playa Herradura. ☎**2637-8910.** Reservations recommended during high season. Main courses $7–$45. MC, V. Daily 11:30am–10pm.

Rioasis PIZZA/MEXICAN Rioasis serves hearty burritos, simple pasta dishes, and a wide array of freshly baked wood-oven pizzas. My favorite item is the Greek pizza, with olives, feta cheese, and anchovies, but the barbecue chicken pizza is also delicious. There is both indoor and terrace seating, as well as a bar area, complete with a pool table, dartboards, and a couple of TVs for sports events and surf videos.

On the main road in Jacó. ☎2643-3354. Reservations not accepted. Main courses $6–$17. V. Daily noon–10pm.

Taco Bar ★ 🎁 MEXICAN/INTERNATIONAL This casual little open-air joint serves up excellent food at great prices. The best option here is to order a one-, two-, or three-taco plate with the accompanying salad bar. Choose from fresh fish, chicken, shrimp, calamari, or any combination of them. My favorites are the coconut shrimp and spicy fish fillings. The well-stocked salad bar features a wide range of stand-alone salads, as well as numerous toppings to finish off your tacos. You won't leave here hungry. A few wooden tables are set outdoors under large umbrellas, but most of the seating is around a large "U"-shaped bar. The seats are either high stools or wood planks hung from ropes, like swings. They also serve breakfast, as well as pizzas and a small selection of full entrees, and offer free Wi-Fi for diners.

A half-block inland from Pop's, central Jacó. ☎2643-0222 or 8836-2049. www.tacobar.info. Reservations not accepted. Main courses $5–$11. MC, V. Daily 7:30am–10pm.

Playa de Jacó After Dark

Playa de Jacó is the central Pacific's party town, with tons of bars and several discos. **Disco La Central** is packed every night of the high season and every weekend during the off season. La Central is right on the beach near the south end of town. There's a huge open-air hall that features the requisite 1970s flashing lights and suspended mirrored ball, as well as a garden bar in a thatch-roofed building that's a slightly quieter place to have a drink. For a more refined dance scene, try **Congas ★**, which often has live salsa bands, and is located toward the south end of town. Both discos charge a nominal cover fee.

Other popular bars in town are the **Beatle Bar, Jungle Bar,** and **Jaco Bar.** All of the aforementioned bars are located along the main strip through town. *Note:* There's a good amount of prostitution in Jacó. It's not uncommon to find working women at any of the above-mentioned places, particularly the Beatle Bar, as well as cruising other bars around town.

My favorite bar in town is the new beachfront **Ganesha Lounge ★★**, which has a laid-back Ibiza-like club vibe, while the similarly new **Le Loft ★**, on the beach and near the center of town, aims to attract a more sophisticated and chic clubbing crowd.

For a more casual atmosphere, head to either **Los Amigos** or **Tabacón ★** on the main street through Jacó, near the center of town. Los Amigos has nightly movies projected onto a large outdoor wall, while Tabacón has popular pool and foosball tables, and often has live music.

Sports freaks can catch the latest games at **Clarita's Beach Bar & Grill, Hotel Copacabana** (both are right on the beach toward the north end of town), or **Hotel Poseidon** (on a side street near the center of town). The first two serve up good reasonably priced burritos, burgers, and bar food, while the latter offers much the same, as well as some items from their much better restaurant downstairs.

If you're into gaming, head to the **Stellaris Casino ★★** at the Los Sueños Marriott Resort (p. 352), or the **Jazz Casino** (☏2643-2316) at the Hotel Amapola. The latter is a modest casino situated toward the southern end of the main road through Jacó (Av. Pastor Díaz), about a block beyond where it takes a sharp turn inland toward the Costanera Sur.

En Route South: Playas Hermosa, Esterillos & Bejuco

Playa Hermosa is the first beach you'll hit as you head south from Playa de Jacó. This is primarily a surfers' beach, but it is still a lovely spot to spend some beach time. In fact, even though the surf conditions here can be rather rough and unprotected, and the beach is made of dark volcanic sand, I find Playa Hermosa and the beaches south of it much more attractive than Jacó. After Playa Hermosa you will hit Esterillos, which is actually divided up by rivers into three sections, Esterillos Oeste, Esterillos Centro, and Esterillos Este, each with a separate well-marked entrance. Farther south (which because of how the coast turns here, is actually more easterly), lies Playa Bejuco.

Note: While beautiful, isolated, and expansive, the beaches of Hermosa, Esterillos, and Bejuco can be quite rough at times and dangerous for swimming. Caution is highly advised here.

WHERE TO STAY

In addition to the hotels listed below, there are a host of simple hotels and cabinas catering to surfers in Playa Hermosa. Prices, conditions, and upkeep can vary greatly. If you've got the time, your best bet is to visit a few until you find the best deal on the cleanest room. **Costa Nera** (☏2643-7044) and **Cabinas Las Arenas** (☏2643-7013; www.cabinaslasarenas.com) are two good options.

If you're looking for something even more remote and undeveloped, head to Playa Esterillos Este for the **Pelican Hotel** (☏2778-8105; www.pelican beachfronthotel.com), or head slightly farther south to the nearly deserted Playa Bejuco and the small **Delfin Beach Resort** (☏2778-8054; www.delfinbeach front.com).

Very Expensive

Xandari by the Pacific ★★★ 🎁 A sister to the popular, upscale boutique Xandari Resort & Spa (p. 144) in Alajuela, this beachfront boutique resort is very similar in terms of design, style, and aesthetics. All the accommodations here are large, private villas, with high, curved ceilings and loads of artistic touches. I especially like the open, mosaic tile showers that let out on to lush gardens. The Maxima villas are the top option and come with their own private plunge pool. Most of the villas are beachfront, but those that aren't have large gardens and a wonderful sense of seclusion and romance. *Note:* In order to encourage the enjoyment of the villas, beach, and surrounding nature, the rooms have no televisions. The open-air seafront restaurant serves excellent international fare, with an equal emphasis on healthy fresh ingredients and creative cooking combinations.

Playa Esterillos Centro (mailing address: A.P. 10-6300), Parrita. ☏866/363-3212 in the U.S. and Canada, or 2778-7070 in Costa Rica. Fax 2778-7878. www.xandari.com. 20 units. $235–$370 double. Rates include continental breakfast. AE, MC, V. **Amenities:** Restaurant; bar; Jacuzzi; 2 lap pools; room service; all rooms smoke-free; full-service spa. *In room:* A/C, kitchenette, minibar, free Wi-Fi.

Expensive

The Backyard This perennially popular bar and restaurant also has some of the most contemporary and comfortable accommodations in Playa Hermosa, although they're overpriced for what you get. The two-story building features large rooms with dark red terra-cotta tile floors and simple furnishings. The second-floor rooms are definitely better than those on the ground floor. The oceanfront end units are classified as suites. They are a bit bigger and do have excellent ocean views. The small pool features a little sculpted-rock waterfall and is quite refreshing on hot days. Despite the more elaborate facilities and amenities, this place is still quintessentially a surfer joint, and the main reason to stay here is that this hotel sits directly in front of the principal peaks on Playa Hermosa. At night most folks find their way to the raucous surfer bar here, with a pool table, darts, and hearty food.

Playa Hermosa de Jacó (A.P. 132), Jacó, Puntarenas. ☎/fax **2643-7011.** www.backyardhotel.com. 8 units. $150–$200 double. AE, MC, V. **Amenities:** Restaurant; bar; small pool. *In room:* A/C, TV.

Moderate

Hotel Fuego del Sol ★ This place is right on the beach and offers good value for someone looking for a clean, cool, and comfortable room, as well as easy access to the waves. (It's a better value than the Backyard, for example.) Most of the rooms are housed in a long, two-story block set perpendicular to the beach. Each comes with a queen-size and twin bed and a private balcony overlooking the free-form pool. Those closest to the water will also give you a glimpse of the sea. The suites come with king-size beds, a separate sitting room, and a fully stocked kitchenette. Everything is well maintained, and the restaurant here boasts a good view of the beach action.

Playa Hermosa, Jacó, Puntarenas. ☎**800/850-4532** in the U.S. and Canada, 2289-6060 reservations office in San José, or 2643-7171 at the hotel. Fax 2288-0123. www.fuegodelsolhotel.com. 22 units. $86–$116 double; $161–$182 suite. Rates include breakfast. Lower rates in off season. AE, MC, V. **Amenities:** Restaurant; bar; surf- and boogie-board rental. *In room:* A/C, TV (in some), kitchenette (in suites).

Hotel Playa Bejuco ★ ☺ Located a half-block off the beach at Playa Bejuco, this is a younger sister to the popular Mar de Luz hotel in Jacó (p. 351). The two-story hotel is an "L" shape around a central swimming pool and gardens and faces the ocean. The construction features various walls and details made from heavy, smooth river stones. Rooms are spacious and cool, with tile floors and simple wooden furnishings. The second-floor rooms are the biggest, and most feature high ceilings with sleeping lofts, making them good options for families with children.

Playa Bejuco, Puntarenas. ☎/fax **2778-8181.** www.hotelplayabejuco.com. 20 units. $105 double. Rates include breakfast and taxes. Lower rates in off season. AE, MC, V. **Amenities:** Restaurant; bar; outdoor pool. *In room:* A/C, TV, minifridge.

Terraza del Pacífico ★ Located just over the hill at the start of Playa Hermosa, this hotel has an excellent setting on a mostly undeveloped section of beach. In the middle of the complex is a circular pool with a swim-up bar and plenty of chaise longues for sunbathing and siestas. Red-tile roofs and faux-stucco walls give the buildings a Mediterranean look, and hardwood balcony railings add a touch of the Tropics. Each guest room has two double beds, a private bathroom, and either a patio or balcony. A couple of suites are considerably larger and even include a kitchenette. The hotel's restaurant and open-air bar are located within a few feet of the high-tide mark. Surfing is the major draw here, and the Terraza hosts several major tournaments each year and has even installed klieg lights on the beach for night surfing.

Playa Hermosa de Jacó (A.P. 168-4023), Jacó, Puntarenas. ☎**2643-3222** or 2440-6862. Fax 2430-7571. www.terrazadelpacifico.com. 62 units. $110 double; $199–$231 suite. Rates include full breakfast and taxes. AE, MC, V. **Amenities:** Restaurant; bar; pool w/swim-up bar. *In room:* A/C, TV, kitchenette (in suites), minibar, free Wi-Fi.

Inexpensive

Cabinas Las Olas This long-standing surfer joint sits just off the main road, on a small hill overlooking the beach. The best room here is the "Skybox Suite," located on the top floor, with a great view. Closer to the beach are three A-frame ranchos, each of which has a roomy bedroom on the second floor (in the peak of the A) and a single bed, a bunk bed, a kitchenette, and a bathroom on the ground floor. The remaining rooms are found in the main building by the road and parking lot. Between the main building and the ranchos is a pool with a small stone waterfall. Out by the ocean there's a restaurant that serves tasty, filling, and economically priced fare, as well as a comfortable, covered two-story palapa for watching the surf action.

Playa Hermosa (A.P. 258-4023), Jacó, Puntarenas. ☎/fax **2643-7021.** www.lasolashotel.com. 8 units. $45–$100 double. AE, MC, V. **Amenities:** Restaurant; bar; surf- and boogie-board rental. *In room:* Fridge, no phone, kitchenette (in ranchos).

MANUEL ANTONIO NATIONAL PARK ★★

140km (87 miles) SW of San José; 69km (43 miles) S of Playa de Jacó

Manuel Antonio was Costa Rica's first major ecotourist destination and remains one of its most popular. The views from the hills overlooking Manuel Antonio are spectacular, the beaches (especially those inside the national park) are idyllic, and its rainforests are crawling with howler, white-faced, and squirrel monkeys, among other forms of exotic wildlife. The downside is that you'll have to pay more to see it, and you'll have to share it with more fellow travelers than you would at other rainforest destinations around the country. Moreover, development has begun to destroy what makes this place so special. What was once a smattering of small hotels tucked into the forested hillside has become a long string of lodgings along the 7km (4⅓ miles) of road between Quepos and the national park entrance. Hotel roofs now regularly break the tree line, and there seems to be no control over zoning and unchecked ongoing construction. A jumble of snack shacks, souvenir stands, and makeshift parking lots choke the beach road just outside the park, making the entrance road look more like a shanty than a national park.

Still, this remains a beautiful destination, with a wide range of attractions and activities. Gazing down on the blue Pacific from high on the hillsides of

Squirrel monkey.

Palm plantation near Quepos.

Manuel Antonio, it's almost impossible to hold back a gasp of delight. Offshore, rocky islands dot the vast expanse of blue, and in the foreground, the rich, deep green of the rainforest sweeps down to the water. Even cheap disposable cameras regularly produce postcard-perfect snapshots. It's this superb view that keeps people transfixed on decks, patios, and balconies throughout the area.

One of the most popular national parks in the country, Manuel Antonio is also one of the smallest, covering fewer than 680 hectares (1,680 acres). Its several nearly perfect small beaches are connected by trails that meander through the rainforest. The mountains surrounding the beaches quickly rise as you head inland from the water; however, the park was created to preserve not its beautiful beaches but its forests, home to endangered squirrel monkeys, three-toed sloths, purple-and-orange crabs, and hundreds of other species of birds, mammals, and plants. Once, this entire stretch of coast was a rainforest teeming with wildlife, but now only this small rocky outcrop of forest remains.

Those views that are so bewitching also have their own set of drawbacks. If you want a great view, you aren't going to be staying on the beach—in fact, you probably won't be able to walk to the beach. This means that you'll be driving back and forth, taking taxis, or riding the public bus. Also keep in mind that it's hot and humid here, and it rains a lot. However, the rain is what keeps Manuel Antonio lush and green, and this wouldn't be the Tropics if things were otherwise.

If you're traveling on a rock-bottom budget or are mainly interested in sport-fishing, you might end up staying in the nearby town of **Quepos,** which was once a quiet banana port; the land to the north was used by Chiquita to grow its bananas. Disease wiped out most of the banana plantations, and now the land is planted primarily with African oil-palm trees. To reach Quepos by road, you pass through miles of these **oil-palm plantations.** Quepos is coming of age, and currently features a wide variety of restaurants, souvenir and crafts shops, and lively bars. Moreover, it stands to see even more improvement when a 270-slip marina project is completed in early 2010.

Essentials

GETTING THERE & DEPARTING **By Plane: Sansa** (☎877/767-2672 in the U.S. and Canada, or 2290-4100 in Costa Rica; www.flysansa.com) has nine daily flights to the **Quepos airport** (XQP; no phone) beginning at 6am, with the final flight departing at 4:20pm from San José's Juan Santamaría International Airport. The flight's duration is 30 minutes; the fare is $75 each way.

Nature Air (☎800/235-9272 in the U.S. and Canada, or 2299-6000; www.natureair.com) flies to Quepos daily at 9am and 2 and 4:20pm from Tobías Bolaños International Airport in Pavas (p. 118). The flight duration is 30 minutes; the fare is $80 each way.

Both Sansa and Nature Air provide minivan airport-transfer service co-ordinated with their arriving flights. The service costs around $9 per person each way, depending on where your hotel is located. Speak to your airline's agent when you arrive to confirm your return flight and coordinate a pickup at your hotel for that day if necessary. Taxis meet incoming flights as well. Expect to be charged between $8 and $12 per car for up to four people, depending on the distance to your hotel.

When you're ready to depart, **Sansa** (☎2777-1912 in Quepos) flights begin departing at 6:44am, with the final flight leaving at 5:06pm. **Nature Air** (☎2777-2548 in Quepos) flights leave for San José daily at 7:40 and 10:45am and 2:35 and 5pm.

By Car: From San José, the most popular route is to take the narrow and winding old highway, which turns off the Interamerican Highway just west of Alajuela near the town of Atenas and joins the Costanera Highway near Orotina. Just follow the many signs to hotels in either Jacó or Manuel Antonio. When you reach Jacó, it's a straight shot and another hour to Manuel Antonio.

Alternatively, you could try the route beginning in Ciudad Colón, a western suburb of San José, and then head out to Puriscal and join the Costanera Highway either near Parrita or Orotina. The route that heads to Parrita is the shortest route, but some sections are not paved and others are in rough shape. Nevertheless, locals often use it, especially during the dry season. Four-wheel-drive vehicles are recommended, but normal two-wheel-drive sedans can usually make it. The route to Orotina is paved the

Travel Tips

Despite the above caveats, Manuel Antonio is still a fabulous destination with a wealth of activities and attractions for all types and all ages. If you plan carefully, you can avoid many of the problems that detract from its appeal. If you steer clear of the peak months (Dec–Mar), you'll miss most of the crowds. If you must come during the peak months, try to avoid weekends, when the beach is packed with families and young Ticos from San José. If you visit the park early in the morning, you can leave when the crowds begin to show up at midday. In the afternoon you can lounge by your pool or on your patio.

entire way. It is slightly longer than the more popular route mentioned above and not as well marked, but since it passes over a narrow suspension bridge, there are never any trucks or commercial traffic.

Note: See p. 342 for info on a new highway that's being built connecting San José with Orotina, via the western suburbs of Santa Ana and Ciudad Colón.

If you're coming from Guanacaste or any point north, take the Interamerican Highway to the Puntarenas turnoff and head south on the Costanera Highway, the coastal road to Jacó. It's about a 4½-hour drive here from Liberia.

By Bus: Express buses (☎ 2223-5567) to Manuel Antonio leave San José daily at 6 and 9am, noon, and 2:30 and 7:30pm from the Coca-Cola bus terminal at Calle 16 between avenidas 1 and 3. Trip duration is 3½ hours; the fare is $5.50. These buses go all the way to the park entrance and will drop you off at any of the hotels along the way.

Regular buses (☎ 2223-5567) to Quepos leave San José daily at 7 and 10am and 2 and 4pm. Trip duration is 4½ hours; the fare is $4.40. These buses stop in Quepos. From here, if you're staying at one of the hotels on the road to Manuel Antonio, you must take a local bus or taxi to your hotel.

Gray Line (☎ 2220-2126; www.graylinecostarica.com) has two daily buses that leave San José for Quepos and Manuel Antonio at 7:30am and 4pm; the fare is $35. The return bus leaves at 10am and 1pm for San José. **Interbus** (☎ 2283-5573; www.interbusonline.com) has two daily buses that leave San José for Quepos and Manuel Antonio at 8:15am and 2:30pm; the fare is $39. Return buses leave at 8:30am and 1:45pm. Both companies will pick you up at most San José—and Manuel Antonio—area hotels and also offer connections to various other popular destinations around Costa Rica.

Buses leave **Puntarenas** for Quepos daily at 5, 8, and 11am and 12:30, 2:30, and 4:30pm. The ride takes 2½ hours; the fare is $3.

Many of the buses for Quepos stop to unload and pick up passengers in **Playa de Jacó.** If you're in Jacó heading toward Manuel Antonio, you can try your luck at one of the covered bus stops out on the Interamerican

Profitable Palms

On any drive to or from Quepos and Manuel Antonio you will pass through miles and miles of African palm plantations. Native to West Africa, *Elaeis guineensis* was planted along this stretch in the 1940s by United Fruit, in response to a blight that was attacking their banana crops. The palms took hold and soon proved quite profitable, being blessed with copious bunches of plumsize nuts that are rich in oil. This oil is extracted and processed in plantations that dot the road between Jacó and Quepos. The smoke and distinct smell of this processing is often easily noticed. The processed oil is then shipped overseas and used in a wide range of products, including soaps, cosmetics, lubricants, and food products.

Highway (see "Playa de Jacó, Playa Hermosa & Playa Herradura," earlier in this chapter).

When you're ready to depart, the Quepos bus station (☎2777-0263) is next to the market, which is 3 blocks east of the water and 2 blocks north of the road to Manuel Antonio. Express buses to San José leave daily at 4, 6, and 9am, noon, and 5pm. Local buses to San José (duration is 4 hr.) leave at 8am and 2 and 4pm.

In the busy winter months, tickets sell out well in advance, especially on weekends; if you can, purchase your ticket several days in advance. However, you must buy your Quepos-bound tickets in San José and your San José return tickets in Quepos. If you're staying in Manuel Antonio, you can buy your return ticket for a direct bus in advance in Quepos and then wait along the road to be picked up. There is no particular bus stop; just make sure you are out to flag down the bus and give it time to stop—you don't want to be standing in a blind spot when the bus comes flying around a tight corner.

Buses for **Puntarenas** leave daily at 4:30, 7:30, and 10:30am and 12:30, 3, and 5pm. Any bus headed for San José or Puntarenas will let you off in Playa de Jacó.

ORIENTATION Quepos is a little port town at the mouth of the Boca Vieja Estuary. After crossing the bridge into town, take the lower road (to the left of the high road). In 4 blocks, turn left; you'll be on the road to Manuel Antonio. This road winds through town a bit before starting over the hill to all the hotels and the national park. For a map of the national park, see the inside front cover of this book.

GETTING AROUND A taxi between Quepos and Manuel Antonio (or any hotel along the road toward the park) costs between $4 and $6, depending upon the distance. At night or if the taxi must leave the main road (for hotels such as La Mariposa, Parador, Makanda, and Arenas del Mar), the charge is a little higher. If you need to call a taxi, dial ☎2777-3080 or 2777-0425. Taxis are supposed to use meters, although this isn't always the case. If your taxi doesn't have a meter, or the driver won't use it, try to negotiate in advance. Ask your hotel desk what a specific ride should cost, and use that as your guide.

The bus between Quepos and Manuel Antonio takes 15 minutes each way and runs roughly every half-hour from 6am to 7pm daily, with one late bus leaving Quepos at 10pm and returning from Manuel Antonio at 10:30pm. The buses, which leave from the main bus terminal in Quepos, near the market, go all the way to the national park entrance before turning around and returning. You can flag down these buses from any point on the side of the road. The fare is 30¢.

You can also rent a car from **Adobe** (☎2777-4242), **Alamo** (☎2777-3344), **Economy** (☎2777-5260), **Hertz** (☎2777-3365), **National** (☎2777-0368), or **Payless Rent-a-Car** (☎2777-0115) for around $45 to $90 a day. All have offices in downtown Quepos, but with advance notice, someone will meet you at the airport with your car for no extra charge.

If you rent a car, never leave anything of value in it unless you intend to stay within sight of the car at all times. Car break-ins are common here.

There are now a couple of parking lots just outside the park entrance that cost around $3 for the entire day. You should definitely keep your car in one of these while exploring the park or soaking up sun on the beach. And although these lots do offer a modicum of protection and safety, you should still not leave anything of value exposed in the car. The trunk is probably safe, though.

If you want to rent a scooter, try **Fast Eddie's Scooter Rental** (☎2777-4127).

FAST FACTS The telephone number of the **Quepos Hospital** is ☎2777-0922. In the event of an emergency, you can also call the **Cruz Roja** (Red Cross; ☎2777-0116). For the **local police,** call ☎2777-1511 or 2777-2117.

The **post office** (☎2777-1471) is in downtown Quepos. There are several pharmacies in Quepos, as well as a pharmacy at the hospital, and another close to the park entrance. There are also a half-dozen or so laundromats and laundry services in town.

Several major Costa Rican banks have branches and ATMs in downtown Quepos, and a couple of ATMs have sprung up along the road to the national park. An ample array of **Internet cafes** can be found around Quepos and along the road to Manuel Antonio, and many hotels have them as well.

Exploring the National Park

Manuel Antonio is a small park with three major trails. Most visitors come primarily to lie on a beach and check out the white-faced monkeys, which sometimes seem as common as tourists. A guide is not essential here, but unless you're experienced in rainforest hiking, you'll see and learn a lot more with one. A 2- or 3-hour guided hike should cost between $25 and $45 per person. Almost any of the hotels in town can help you set up a tour of the park. Bird-watchers might want to book a tour with **Ave Natura** (☎2777-0973), a local tour agency that specializes in birding. If you decide to explore the park on your own, a basic map is usually available at the park entrances for $1.

ENTRY POINT, FEES & REGULATIONS The park (☎2777-5155) is closed on Monday but is open Tuesday through Sunday from 8am to 4pm year-round. The entrance fee is $10 per person. The principal park entrance is at **Playa Espadilla,** the beach at the end of the road from Quepos. To reach the park station, you must cross a small, sometimes polluted stream that's little more than ankle-deep at low tide but that can be knee- or even waist-deep at high tide. It's even reputed to be home to a crocodile or two. For years there has been talk of building a bridge over this stream; in the meantime you'll have to either wade it or pay a boatman a small voluntary tip for the very quick crossing. Just over the stream and over a small rise, you'll find a small ranger station. Another ranger station is located inland at the end of the side road that leads off perpendicular to **Playa Espadilla** just beyond Marlin Restaurant.

MINAE, the national ministry that oversees the park, has been frustratingly inconsistent about which entrance visitors must use. As of this writing, tickets are only being sold at the inland entrance. The trail from here begins with about 20 to 30 minutes of hiking along an often muddy

Manuel Antonio National Park trail. **Parasailing tour.**

access road before you get to the beach and principal park trails. If this is still the situation when you visit, I recommend buying your ticket here, then heading back to the principal beach entrance to begin your exploration of the park. The Parks Service allows only 600 visitors to enter each day, which could mean that you won't get in if you arrive in midafternoon during the high season. Camping is not allowed.

THE BEACHES **Playa Espadilla Sur** (as opposed to Playa Espadilla, which is just outside the park; see "Hitting the Water," below) is the first beach within the actual park boundaries. It's usually the least crowded and one of the best places to find a quiet shade tree to plant yourself under. However, if there's any surf, this is also the roughest beach in the park. If you want to explore further, you can walk along this soft-sand beach or follow a trail through the forest parallel to the beach. **Playa Manuel Antonio,** which is the most popular beach inside the park, is a short, deep crescent of white sand backed by lush rainforest. The water here is sometimes clear enough to offer good snorkeling along the rocks at either end, and it's usually fairly calm. At low tide Playa Manuel Antonio shows a very interesting relic: a circular stone turtle trap left by its pre-Columbian residents. From Playa Manuel Antonio, there's another slightly longer trail to **Puerto Escondido,** where a blowhole sends up plumes of spray at high tide.

THE HIKING TRAILS From either Playa Espadilla Sur or Playa Manuel Antonio, you can take a circular hike around a high promontory bluff. The farthest point on this hike, which takes about 25 minutes round-trip, is **Punta Catedral ★★**, where the view is spectacular. The trail is a little steep in places, but anybody in average shape can do it. I have done it in sturdy sandals, but you might want to wear good hiking shoes. This is a good place to spot monkeys, although you're more likely to see a white-faced monkey than a rare squirrel monkey. Another good place to see monkeys is the **trail inland** from Playa Manuel Antonio. This is a linear trail and mostly uphill, but it's not too taxing. It's great to spend hours exploring the steamy jungle and then take a refreshing dip in the ocean.

Finally, there's a trail that leads first to Puerto Escondido (see above) and **Punta Surrucho,** where there are some sea caves. Be careful when hiking beyond Puerto Escondido: What seems like easy beach hiking at low tide becomes treacherous to impassable at high tide. Don't get trapped.

Hitting the Water

BEACHES OUTSIDE THE PARK **Playa Espadilla,** the gray-sand beach just outside the park boundary, is often perfect for board surfing and bodysurfing. At times it's a bit rough for casual swimming, but with no entrance fee, it's the most popular beach with locals and visiting Ticos. Some shops by the water rent boogie boards and beach chairs and umbrellas. A full-day rental of a beach umbrella and two chaise longues costs around $10. (These are not available inside the park.) This beach is actually a great spot to learn how to surf, because there are several open-air shops renting surfboards and boogie boards along the road fronting the beach. Rates run between $5 and $10 per hour, and around $20 to $40 per day. If you want a lesson, check in with the **Manuel Antonio Surf School** (☎2777-4842; www.masurfschool.com), which has a roadside kiosk on the road to Manuel Antonio.

BOATING, KAYAKING, RAFTING & SPORTFISHING TOURS Adventure **Manuel Antonio** (☎2777-1084; www.adventuremanuelantonio.com) and **Iguana Tours** (☎2777-2052; www.iguanatours.com) are the most established and dependable tour operators in the area; both offer river rafting, sea kayaking, mangrove tours, and guided hikes.

The two above companies, as well as **Rios Tropicales** (☎2777-4092; www.aventurash2o.com), offer full-day rafting trips for around $85 to $110. Large multiperson rafts are used during the rainy season, and single-person "duckies" are broken out when the water levels drop. All of the above companies also offer half-day rafting adventures and sea-kayaking trips for around $65. Depending on rainfall and demand, they will run either the Naranjo or Savegre rivers. I very much prefer the **Savegre River** ★★ for its stunning scenery.

Another of my favorite tours in the area is a mangrove tour of the **Damas Island estuary.** These trips generally include lunch, a stop on Damas Island, and roughly 3 to 4 hours of cruising the waterways. You'll see loads of wildlife. The cost is usually around $60 to $80.

Among the other boating options around Quepos/Manuel Antonio are excursions in search of dolphins and sunset cruises. **Iguana Tours** (see above) and **Planet Dolphin** (☎/fax 2777-1647;

Helping Out

If you want to help efforts in protecting the local environment and the severely endangered squirrel monkey *(mono titi),* make a donation to the **Mono Titi Alliance** (☎2777-2306; www.monotiti.org), an organization supported by local businesses and individual donors, or to **Kids Saving The Rainforest** (☎2777-2592; www.kidssavingthe rainforest.org), which was started in 1999 by a couple of local children.

White-water rafting the Savegre River.

Damas Island boat tour.

www.planetdolphin.com) offer these tours for $75 per person, depending upon the size of the group and the length of the cruise. Most tours include a snorkel break and, if lucky, dolphin sightings. **Jungle Coast Jets** (☎2777-1706; www.junglecoastjets.com) offers 2-hour jet-ski tours for $105 per person. This tour plies the same waters and includes some snorkeling and the possibility of a dolphin encounter.

Quepos is one of Costa Rica's billfish centers, and sailfish, marlin, and tuna are all common in these waters. In the past year or so, fresh and brackish water fishing in the mangroves and estuaries has also become popular. If you're into sportfishing, try hooking up with **Blue Fin Sportfishing** (☎2777-0000; www.bluefinsportfishing.com), **Blue Water** (☎800/807-1585 in the U.S. and Canada, or 2777-4841; www.sportfishingincostarica.com), **High Tec Sportfishing** (☎2777-3465; www.hightecsportfishing.com), or **Luna Tours Sportfishing** (☎2777-0725; www.lunatours.net). A full day of fishing should cost between $400 and $1,800, depending on the size of the boat, distance traveled, tackle provided, and amenities. There's a lot of competition here, so shop around.

SCUBA DIVING & SNORKELING Oceans Unlimited ★ (☎2777-3171; www.oceansunlimitedcr.com) offers both scuba diving and snorkel outings, as well as certification and resort courses. Because of river run-off and often less-than-stellar visibility close to Quepos, the best trips involve some travel time. Tours around Manuel Antonio run $65 to snorkel, and $90 for a two-tank scuba dive.

However, **Isla del Caño** (p. 405) is only about a 90-minute ride (each way). This is one of the best dive sites in Costa Rica, and I highly recommend it. Trips to Isla del Cano are $149 for snorkeling and $220 for two-tank scuba diving.

Other Activities in the Area

ATV If you want to try riding a four-wheel ATV (all-terrain vehicle), check in with the folks at **Fourtrax Adventures** (☎2777-1829; www.fourtrax adventure.com). Their principal tour is a 3-hour adventure through African palm plantations, rural towns, and secondary forest to a jungle waterfall, where you stop for a dip. You cross several rivers and a long suspension bridge. Either breakfast or lunch is served, depending on the timing. The cost is $95 per ATV. A second rider on the same ATV costs $30.

BIKING If you want to do some mountain biking while you're here, contact **Estrella Tour** (☎2777-1286) in downtown Quepos. Well-maintained bikes rent for around $25 to $30 per day. You can also do a number of different guided tours according to skill level for between $50 and $120 per day, as well as multiday expeditions.

BUTTERFLY GARDEN **Fincas Naturales/The Nature Farm Reserve ★** (☎2777-1043; www.butterflygardens.co.cr) is just across from (and run by) Hotel Sí Como No (p. 373). A lovely bilevel **butterfly garden ★** is the centerpiece attraction here, but there is also a private reserve and a small network of well-groomed trails through the forest. A 1-hour guided tour of the butterfly garden costs $15 per person, or $35 when combined with a 1-hour guided hike through the forest. This is also a good place to do a night tour ($35).

Butterfly at Fincas Naturales.

CANOPY ADVENTURES There are several canopy tours in the area. The most adventurous is offered by **Canopy Safari ★** (☎2777-0100; www.canopysafari.com), which features 21 treetop platforms connected by a series of cables and suspension bridges. Adventurers use a harness-and-pulley system to "zip" between platforms, using a leather-gloved hand as their only brake. The **Titi Canopy Tour** (☎2777-3130; www.titicanopytours.com) is a similar but mellower setup. A canopy tour should run you between $50 and $70 per person.

About 20 minutes outside of Quepos is **Rainmaker Nature Refuge** (☎2777-3565; www.rainmakercostarica.org). The main attraction here is a system of connected suspension bridges strung through the forest canopy, crisscrossing a deep ravine. There are six bridges; the longest is 90m (295 ft.) across. There's also a small network of trails and some great swimming holes. A half-day tour, including a light breakfast, full lunch, round-trip transportation from Quepos, and a guide, costs $65 per person. Tours leave every morning, and most hotels in the area can book them for you.

HORSEBACK RIDING While you can still sometimes find locals renting horses on the beaches outside the national park, I discourage this, as there are just too many crowds, the beach is too short, and the droppings are a problem. Better yet, head back into the hills and forests. Both **Finca Valmy** (☎2779-1118; www.valmytours.com) and **Brisas del Nara** (☎2779-1235; www.horsebacktour.com) offer horseback excursions that pass through both primary and secondary forest and feature a swimming stop or two at a jungle waterfall. Full-day tours, including breakfast and lunch, cost between $70 and $90 per person. Finca Valmy also offers an overnight tour for serious riders, with accommodations in rustic, but cozy cabins in the Santa Maria de Dota mountains.

SOOTHE YOUR BODY & SOUL There are quite a few massage therapists around Manuel Antonio and a couple of day spas. The best of these are **Raindrop Spa** (☎ 2777-2880; www.raindropspa.com), **Spa Uno** ★ (☎ 2777-2607; www.spauno.com), and **Serenity Spa** ★ at the Hotel Sí Como No (p. 373). A wide range of treatments, wraps, and facials are available at all of the above.

   Sivana Yoga (☎ 2777-5268; www.sivanayoga.com) has open classes ($12) Monday through Friday at 8am above the Anaconda restaurant, across from the Hotel Costa Verde. Private classes are also offered.

TAKE A TOUR ON THE TICO SIDE ★ For a good taste of local Tico rural culture, mixed in with some fabulous scenery and adventure, sign up for the **Santa Juana Mountain Tour** (☎ 2777-0850). This full-day tour takes you to a local farming village about an hour outside of Quepos. Depending upon your needs and interests, you can tour coffee and citrus farms, take part in carbon-offset tree planting, hike the trails, swim in rainforest pools, fish for tilapia, see how sugar cane is processed, and/or ride horseback. A typical Tico lunch is included.

ULTRALIGHT TOUR If you want a really good view of Manuel Antonio's spectacular scenery, you might sign up with the folks at **Costa Rica Flying Boat** (☎ 2777-9208 or 8368-1426), who offer ultralight flights out of the Quepos airport. A 20-minute flight runs around $75.

Shopping

If you're looking for souvenirs, you'll find plenty of beach towels, beachwear, and handmade jewelry in a variety of small shops in Quepos and at impromptu stalls down near the national park. For a good selection, try **La Buena Nota** (☎ 2777-1002), which is on the road to Manuel Antonio, right near the Karahé hotel (p. 375). The shop is jampacked with all sorts of beachwear, souvenirs, used books, and American magazines and newspapers.

   For higher-end gifts, check out Hotel Sí Como No's **Regálame** (www.regalameart.com) gift shop, which has a wide variety of craft works, clothing, and original paintings and prints. Finally, one of my favorite shops from Jacó has opened a branch in Manuel Antonio. Look for handmade batik and tie-dye clothing at **Guacamole** (☎ 2777-2071) in the small Plaza Yara shopping center, along the road between Quepos and Manuel Antonio.

 Yo Quiero Hablar Español

Escuela D'Amore (☎/fax 2777-1143; www.escueladamore.com) runs language-immersion programs out of a former hotel with a fabulous view on the road to Manuel Antonio. A 2-week conversational Spanish course, including a home stay and two meals daily, costs $995. Or you can try the **Costa Rica Spanish Institute (COSI;** ☎ 800/771-5184 in the U.S. and Canada, 2234-1001 or 2777-0021 in Costa Rica; www. cosi.co.cr), which charges $940 for a similar 2-week program with a home stay.

Where to Stay

Take care when choosing your accommodations in Quepos/Manuel Antonio. There are very few true beachfront hotels in Manuel Antonio, so you won't have much luck finding a hotel where you can walk directly out of your room and onto the beach. In fact, most of the nicer hotels here are 1km (½ mile) or so away from the beach, high on the hill overlooking the ocean.

If you're traveling on a rock-bottom budget, you'll get more for your money by staying in Quepos and taking the bus to the beaches at Manuel Antonio every day. The rooms in Quepos might be small, but they're generally cleaner and more appealing than those available in the same price category closer to the park.

VERY EXPENSIVE

In addition to the places listed below, **Bella Vista Villas and Casas** (✆866/569-6241 in the U.S. and Canada, or 2777-9081 in Costa Rica; www.buenavista villas.net) is a current incarnation of the former Tulemar Resort, and, after years of ups-and-downs, they've finally got this superbly located property running in good shape.

If you're coming for an extended stay with your family or a large group, look into **Escape Villas** ★★ (✆877/533-8988 in the U.S., or 2777-5258 in Costa Rica; www.villascostarica.com), which rents a broad selection of very large and luxurious private villas with all the amenities and some of the best views in Manuel Antonio.

Arenas del Mar ★★★ 📷 This place has it all—direct beach access, a rainforest setting, fabulous views, and luxurious accommodations. Designed and built by the folks behind Finca Rosa Blanca (p. 142), Arenas del Mar is deeply

Downtown Quepos.

Manuel Antonio & Quepos

Area of inset below

Quepos

Bahía La Ceiba

NICARAGUA

CARIBBEAN SEA

⭐ SAN JOSÉ

Manuel Antonio & Quepos

PACIFIC OCEAN

PANAMA

Punta Quepos

Playa Espadilla

Bahía Manuel Antonio

Park Entrance

Park Entrance

MANUEL ANTONIO NATIONAL PARK

Playa Espadilla Sur

Playa Puerto Escondido

Punta Catedral

Playa Manuel Antonio

Punta Surrucho

| 0 | | 1/2 mi |
| 0 | | 1/2 km |

Quepos

Calle 2

Calle Central

Av. 1

Bus Station

Market

Calle 5

Calle 7

Av. Central

Av. 2

| 0 | | 1/8 mi |
| 0 | | 1/8 km |

ACCOMMODATIONS
Arenas del Mar **35**
Best Western Kamuk Hotel **6**
Buena Vista Villas & Casas **20**
El Mono Azul Hotel **15**
Gaia Hotel & Reserve **18**
Hotel Costa Verde **30**
Hotel La Mariposa **37**
Hotel Malinche **8**
Hotel Plinio **14**
Hotel Si Como No **28**
Hotel Verde Mar **33**
Karahé **31**
Makanda-by-the-Sea **36**
Villas Nicolás **27**
Widemouth Frog **12**

DINING
Agua Azul **25**
Barba Roja **23**
Café Milagro **2, 24**
El Avion **29**
El Gran Escape **3**
El Patio Bistro Latino **2**
Escalofrio **10**

(cont.)
Kapi Kapi **21**
La Hacienda **17**
La Luna **18**
Marlin Restaurant **34**
Mar Luna **19**
Mi Lugar
   (Ronny's Place) **13**
Pizza de Marco **17**
Plinio Restaurant **14**
Sunspot Bar & Grill **36**
Tropical Sushi **4**

NIGHTLIFE
Arco Iris **1**
Bambu Jam **16**
Billfish Sportbar
   & Grill **26**
Dos Locos **9**
Fish Head Bar **3**
Kamuk Casino **6**
Los Pescadores **7**
Salsipuedes **22**
Sargento Garcia's **11**
Wacky Wanda's **5**

SHOPPING
Guacamole **17**
La Buena Nota **32**
Plaza Yara **17**
Regaláme **28**

To Airport, Hospital & Dominical

committed to sustainability. Not all rooms have ocean views, so be sure to specify if you want one. However, all are spacious, with cool tile floors and stylish decorative accents. Most have outdoor Jacuzzi tubs on private balconies. The apartments are immense two-bedroom, three-bathroom affairs with a kitchenette, perfect for families and longer stays. The restaurant, lobby, and main pool are set on the highest point of land here, and several spots have fabulous views of Manuel Antonio's Punta Catedral. *Note:* The beautiful patch of beach right in front of Arenas has for decades been the town's de facto nude beach. Those who might find this offensive can walk farther down the beach or stick to the pools.

Manuel Antonio. ☎/fax **2777-2777.** www.arenasdelmar.com. 38 units. $260 double; $430 suite; $690 2-bedroom apt. Rates include full breakfast. AE, MC, V. **Amenities:** Restaurant; bar; snack bar; babysitting; concierge; 2 small outdoor pools; room service; spa. *In room:* A/C, TV, minibar, free Wi-Fi.

Gaia Hotel & Reserve ★★ Staking out the high-end luxury market, this hotel features chic, postmodern design and decor, with large, well-equipped rooms, tons of amenities, and personalized service. Set on a hilly patch of land, with its own private reserve, the rooms, spa, and restaurant are housed in a series of tall, blocky buildings. The large rooms all have wooden floors, contemporary furnishings, plasma-screen televisions with complete home theater systems, and elaborate bathrooms with massive Jacuzzi tubs. Each guest is assigned a personal concierge. The deluxe suites feature a private rooftop terrace, with a reflecting pool, and shaded lounge chairs. The immense Gaia suite features soaring ceilings, a huge sitting room, and a private pool. The spa is extensive and well-run, with a wide range of treatment options and free daily yoga classes. The restaurant serves excellent fusion cuisine. Despite the over-the-top luxury here, this hotel is dedicated to sustainable and green tourism practices and was granted "4 Leaves" by the CST Sustainable Tourism program.

Manuel Antonio. ☎ **800/226-2515** in the U.S., or 2777-9797 in Costa Rica. Fax 2777-9126. www.gaiahr.com. 17 units. $260–$330 double; $350–$495 suite; $840 Gaia suite. Rates include full breakfast. AE, MC, V. No children under 16 allowed. **Amenities:** Restaurant, bar; concierge; small gym; multilevel outdoor pool; room service; extensive spa. *In room:* A/C, TV/DVD, minibar, MP3 docking station, free Wi-Fi.

Hotel La Mariposa ★ ♨ Perched on top of the hill between Quepos and Manuel Antonio, La Mariposa (the Butterfly) commands a mountains-to-the-sea vista of more than 270 degrees. The sunsets here are knockouts, and the daytime views are pretty captivating, too. While this remains one of Manuel Antonio's premier accommodations, expansion and growth have cost this place much of its charm. The best accommodations are the Premier rooms, housed in two three-story buildings constructed over the foundation of a couple of the original villas. These are large, well equipped, and tastefully decorated, with excellent views. Each junior suite has a Jacuzzi out on the small balcony or just inside its sliding glass door. The rooms in the four-story addition to the hotel's main building are quite spacious and have great views, but lack charm, and are reached by a cumbersome spiral staircase. The few standard rooms are certainly acceptable, but lack the views.

Manuel Antonio (A.P. 4, Quepos). ☎ **800/549-0157** in the U.S. and Canada, or 2777-0355 in Costa Rica. Fax 2777-0050. www.lamariposa.com. 62 units. $205–$390 double; $440 penthouse suite.

Extra person $40. Children 9 and under stay free in parent's room. AE, MC, V. **Amenities:** Restaurant; bar; complimentary shuttle to and from the national park; babysitting; concierge; 4 small pools. *In room:* A/C, TV, free Wi-Fi.

Hotel Sí Como No ★★ 🏠 ☺ This local favorite is a lively, upscale, midsize resort that blends in with and respects the rainforests and natural wonders of Manuel Antonio. This is a place equally suited to families traveling with children and to couples looking for a romantic getaway. All the wood used is farm-grown, and while the rooms have energy-efficient air-conditioning units, guests are urged to use them only when necessary. The standard rooms are quite acceptable, but it's worth the splurge for a superior or deluxe room or a suite. Most of these are on the top floors of the two- to three-story villas, with spectacular treetop views out over the forest and onto the Pacific. There are a series of deluxe suites with lots of space and large garden bathrooms, some of which have private Jacuzzis. This hotel has earned "5 Leaves" in the CST Sustainable Tourism program, and the parent organization, Green Hotels of Costa Rica, was honored in 2009 as a corporate leader in sustainability by the Rainforest Alliance.

Manuel Antonio (mailing address: Mail Stop SJO 297, P.O. Box 02558216, Miami, FL 33102). ☎**2777-0777.** Fax 2777-1093. www.sicomono.com. 60 units. $210–$265 double; $305–$340 suite. Rates include breakfast buffet. Extra person $30. Children 5 and under stay free in parent's room. AE, MC, V. **Amenities:** 2 restaurants; 2 bars; babysitting; concierge; 2 Jacuzzis; 2 midsize pools, including 1 w/small water slide; all rooms smoke-free; modest spa. *In room:* A/C, hair dryer, minibar, free Wi-Fi.

Makanda by the Sea ★★ 🏠 A wonderful collection of studio apartments and private villas, Makanda is a great option for anyone looking for an intimate, romantic getaway in Manuel Antonio. If you combine villa no. 1 with the three studios, you get one very large four-bedroom villa, great for a family or a small group (although children 15 and under are not allowed, unless you rent out the entire hotel). Every choice comes with a full kitchenette, cable television, CD player, and either a terrace or a balcony. The grounds are well tended, and intermixed with tropical flowers and Japanese gardens. A full breakfast is delivered to your room each morning. The hotel's pool and Jacuzzi combine intricate and colorful tile work with a view of the jungle-covered hillsides and the Pacific Ocean. The hotel is set in thick forest, and, despite the name, is a hefty hike—or short drive—from the beach.

Manuel Antonio (A.P. 29, Quepos). ☎**888/625-2632** in the U.S., or 2777-0442 in Costa Rica. Fax 2777-1032. www.makanda.com. 11 units. $265 studio; $400 villa. Rates include full breakfast. AE, MC, V. **Amenities:** Restaurant; bar; bike rental; concierge; Jacuzzi; midsize pool; room service; massage and spa services; watersports equipment. *In room:* TV, kitchenette, stocked minibar, free Wi-Fi.

EXPENSIVE

Hotel Costa Verde ★ Located more than halfway down the hill to Manuel Antonio, about a 10-minute walk from the beach, Costa Verde has rooms in a wide range of sizes and prices. Some of the buildings are quite a hike from the hotel's reception and restaurants, so be sure you know exactly what type of room you'll be staying in and where it's located. The best rooms here have ocean views, kitchenettes, private balconies, and loads of space; some of these don't have air-conditioning, but that's no problem because they feature huge screened walls to encourage cross ventilation. There's also an enormous penthouse suite with a commanding view of the spectacular surroundings. Three small pools are set into the hillside, with views out to the ocean, and the hotel has a couple of miles of private trails through the rainforest.

Manuel Antonio (mailing address: SJO 1313, P.O. Box 025216, Miami, FL 33102). ☎ **866/854-7958** in the U.S. and Canada, or 2777-0584 in Costa Rica. Fax 2777-0560. www.costaverde.com. 63 units. $115–$350 double. AE, MC, V. **Amenities:** 2 restaurants; 3 bars; 3 small pools. *In room:* A/C (in some units), TV (in some units), no phone, free Wi-Fi.

Villas Nicolás ★ These large villas offer a lot of bang for your buck. Built as terraced units up a steep hill in deep forest, they really give you the feeling that you're in the jungle. Most are quite large and well appointed, with wood floors, throw rugs, and comfortable bathrooms; some rooms even have separate living rooms and full kitchenettes, which make longer stays comfortable. My favorite features, though, are the balconies, which come with sitting chairs and a hammock. Some of these balconies are massive and have incredible views. In fact, the rooms highest up the hill have views that I'd be willing to pay a lot more for, and a few of them even have air-conditioning. During the high season, the hotel opens an informal restaurant/bar near the pool that serves breakfast and sometimes lunch and dinner, depending on demand.

Manuel Antonio (A.P. 236, Quepos). ☎ **2777-0481.** Fax 2777-0451. www.villasnicolas.com. 20 units. $168 double; $192 suite. Weekly, monthly, and off season (May–Nov) rates available. AE, MC, V. **Amenities:** Small pool. *In room:* A/C (in some units), fridge.

MODERATE

In addition to the hotels mentioned below, the **Best Western Kamuk Hotel** (☎ **2777-0811;** www.kamuk.co.cr) is a dependable option right in downtown Quepos; it's popular with sportfishing enthusiasts.

El Mono Azul Hotel ◢ On the road to Manuel Antonio, just outside Quepos, the "Blue Monkey" offers clean and comfortable rooms at a good price. The more expensive rooms feature air-conditioning and/or a small television with cable. The villas have red-tile floors, separate sitting rooms, and a kitchenette. One room even has a Jacuzzi tub. Though all the rooms are rather spartan, the place has a lively, hostel-like vibe. The owners are active in a children's arts program aimed at helping preserve the local rainforest and the endangered squirrel monkey. In fact, 10% of your bill goes to this program. The restaurant/pizzeria here is quite popular. Staff members can arrange longer-term rentals of fully equipped apartments and villas.

Manuel Antonio (A.P. 297-6350, Quepos). ☎ **800/381-3578** in the U.S., or 2777-2572 in Costa Rica. Fax 2777-1954. www.monoazul.com. 29 units. $60–$85 double; $95–$160 villa. AE, DC, MC, V. **Amenities:** Restaurant; bar; lounge; small gym; 3 small pools. *In room:* A/C, TV, no phone, free Wi-Fi.

Hotel Plinio The Plinio hotel is built into a steep hillside, so it's a bit of a climb from the parking lot up to the guest rooms and restaurant. That's fitting, considering that rooms have the feel of a treehouse. Floors and walls are polished hardwood, there are rooms with tree-trunk pillars, and the whole complex is set in lush forest. The hotel's suites are the best value. These are built on either two or three levels. Both options have sleeping lofts; the three-story rooms also have rooftop decks. Behind the hotel is a private reserve with 15km (9⅓ miles) of trails and, at the top of the hill, a 15m-tall (49-ft.) observation tower with an incredible view. In addition to the popular **Plinio Restaurant** (p. 378), there's a poolside grill where lunches are served. Plinio is just outside of Quepos on the road toward the national park, so it's a bit far from the park entrance and beaches.

Manuel Antonio (A.P. 71-6350, Quepos). ☎**2777-0055.** Fax 2777-0558. www.hotelplinio.com. 12 units. $65–$75 double; $85–$110 suite or house. Rates include breakfast buffet in high season. V. **Amenities:** Restaurant; bar; small pool in lush garden setting. *In room:* No phone.

Hotel Verde Mar ★ This hotel is a great choice for proximity to the national park and the beach, and I recommend it much more than the similarly priced hotel Karahé. From your room it's just a short walk to the beach (Playa Espadilla) via a raised wooden walkway. All the rooms here have plenty of space, nice wrought-iron queen-size beds, tile floors, a desk and chair, a fan, and a small porch. All but two of the rooms come with a basic kitchenette. Some of the larger rooms even have two queen-size beds. The hotel has no restaurant, but plenty are within walking distance. There's also a small pool here, for when the surf is too rough.

Manuel Antonio (A.P. 348-6350), Quepos. ☎**877/872-0459** in the U.S. and Canada, or 2777-1805 in Costa Rica. Fax 2777-1311. www.verdemar.com. 24 units. $100 double; $110 suite. AE, MC, V. **Amenities:** Small pool. *In room:* A/C, kitchenette (in some), no phone.

Karahé The Karahé is one of the original beachfront hotels in Manuel Antonio. If you stay in one of the more expensive beachfront units, you'll have a plain room with tile floors, two double beds, and a small patio. The least-expensive rooms are just off the reception area and offer neither views nor easy access to the ocean. Be aware that if you opt for one of the villas, you'll have a steep uphill climb from the beach; on the other hand, a couple of these have great views. The gardens here are quite lush and have flowering ginger that often attracts hummingbirds. The hotel can arrange a wide variety of tours and charters, including sportfishing. Karahé is located on both sides of the road about 450m (1,476 ft.) before you reach Playa Espadilla.

Manuel Antonio (A.P. 100-6350, Quepos). ☎**877/623-3198** in the U.S. and Canada, or 2777-0170 in Costa Rica. Fax 2777-1075. www.karahe.com. 33 units. $100–$130 double. Rates include continental breakfast. AE, MC, V. **Amenities:** Restaurant; bar; exercise room; Jacuzzi; small pool. *In room:* A/C, no phone.

INEXPENSIVE

In addition to the place listed below, the **Widemouth Frog** (☎2777-2798; www.widemouthfrog.org) is a hostel option in downtown Quepos, which even has its own swimming pool.

Hotel Malinche A good choice for budget travelers, the Hotel Malinche has consistently been my top choice in this category right in Quepos. The standard rooms are small but have hardwood or tile floors and clean bathrooms. Some of those on the second floor even have small private balconies that open on to a small interior courtyard. The more expensive rooms are larger and have air-conditioning, TVs, and carpets.

Half-block west of downtown bus terminal, Quepos. ☎**2777-3723.** Fax 2777-0093. hotel malinche@racsa.co.cr. 24 units. $30–$60 double. AE, MC, V. *In room:* No phone.

Where to Dine

Scores of dining options are available around Manuel Antonio and Quepos, and almost every hotel has some sort of restaurant. For the cheapest meals around, try a simple *soda* in Quepos, or head to one of the open-air joints on the beach road before the national park entrance. The standard Tico menu prevails, with prices in the $4-to-$8 range. Of these, **Marlin Restaurant** (☎2777-1134), right in front of Playa Espadilla, and **Mar Luna** (☎2777-5107), on the main road just beyond Hotel La Colina, are your best bets. For simple pasta, pizzas, and Italian gelato, head to **Escalofrío** (☎2777-0833; downtown Quepos) or **Pizza de Marco** (☎2777-9400; in the Plaza Yara shopping center). In addition to the places listed below, another good option, on the outskirts of Quepos, is **Mi Lugar,** or **"Ronny's Place"** (☎2777-5120; www.ronnysplace.com).

For a taste of the high life, head to the **La Luna** restaurant at Gaia Hotel & Reserve (see above) for their sunset tapas menu. The views are great and the creative tapas are very reasonably priced.

After years of radical ups and downs, I can once again recommend **Barba Roja** (☎2777-0331; www.barbaroja.co.cr), which now features a creative fusion menu and sushi bar. As always, the sunsets and bar scene here are excellent.

Finally, one of my favorite hangouts has always been **Café Milagro** ★★ (☎2777-1707; www.cafemilagro.com), a homey coffeehouse and gift shop with two locations in the area. The folks here roast their own beans and also have a mail-order service to keep you in Costa Rican coffee year-round. The menu includes a daily selection of freshly baked sweets, simple sandwiches and breakfast items, and a wide range of coffee drinks. You'll find local art for sale on the walls and a good selection of Cuban cigars and international newspapers, too. The original storefront, just over the bridge on your left as you enter Quepos, is now expanded and there's another branch on the main road to Manuel Antonio right across from the turnoff for Hotel La Mariposa.

EXPENSIVE

El Avión SEAFOOD/INTERNATIONAL Set on the edge of Manuel Antonio's hillside with a great view of the ocean and surrounding forests, this restaurant is housed under some permanent tents and the starboard wing of a retired army transport plane, hence the name El Avión, which means "the Plane." This specific plane was actually shot down by the Sandinista army, leading to a scandal that uncovered illegal CIA supply missions to the Contra rebels in Nicaragua. Today you can enjoy a wide range of seafood and steaks as you take in the unique surroundings and glow of history. However, food quality and service can be inconsistent here—I've had both excellent and roundly disappointing meals—although the setting never falters. Inside the fuselage you'll also find a small bar.

Manuel Antonio. ☎2777-3378. Reservations recommended. Main courses $8.50–$35. MC, V. Daily noon–10pm.

El Patio Bistro Latino ★★★ NUEVO LATINO/FUSION This small bistro-style restaurant is an outgrowth of the popular coffeehouse and roasting company Café Milagro. The same attention to detail and focus on quality carries over here. By day you can get a wide range of coffee drinks and specialties, as well as full breakfasts, fresh-baked sweets, and a variety of salads, sandwiches, wraps, and light lunch dishes. By night, things get more interesting. The menu features inventive main dishes that take advantage of local ingredients and various regional culinary traditions. Fresh mahimahi comes steamed in a banana leaf with a spicy *mojo,* and the tenderloin features a tamarind glaze and is served over roasted local yuca puree. There are nightly specials, and you may even find some of their home-roasted coffee used as an ingredient in a glaze, sauce, or dessert.

Downtown Quepos. **2777-4982.** Reservations recommended. Main courses $8–$22. AE, MC, V. Daily 6am–10pm.

Kapi Kapi ★★ FUSION/NUEVO COSTA RICAN This new restaurant features elegant understated Asian-influenced decor. At night, the ample, open-air dining room is candlelit and romantic. Start things off with the Asian-spice glazed baby back ribs or some seared fresh yellow-fin tuna. Or, save the seared tuna for your main course, where it comes encrusted in peppercorns and served with a green papaya salad. For a sample of local flavors, order up the grilled shrimp, which are served on sugar-cane skewers, with a glaze made from local rum, tamarind, and coconut. For dessert try their Mango Foster or a hot chocolate soufflé. These folks have an excellent and very fairly priced wine list.

On the road btw. Quepos and Manuel Antonio. **2777-5049.** www.restaurantekapikapi.com. Reservations recommended. Main courses $14–$21. AE, MC, V. Daily 4–10pm.

La Hacienda ★ INTERNATIONAL Located on a jungle-facing open-air back patio of the Plaza Yara strip mall, this place is surprisingly intimate and atmospheric, especially at night. Subdued lighting and vines draping down from the high ceiling make you feel as if you are almost in the jungle. The menu is inventive and eclectic. I highly recommend starting things off with the quesadilla of caramelized onions, brie, and fresh mango. For a main dish, the mixed seafood grill for two features shrimp, squid, and fresh fish prepared on a wood-fired grill with a tropical fruit salsa on the side. The dessert menu changes regularly, but almost always features some rich chocolate concoction, as well as a flavored crème brûlée.

In the Plaza Yara, on the road btw. Quepos and Manuel Antonio. **2777-3473.** Reservations recommended in high season. Main courses $12–$28. AE, MC, V. Daily 11:30am–10pm.

Sunspot Bar & Grill ★★ 🎁 INTERNATIONAL Dining by candlelight under a purple canvas tent at one of the few poolside tables here is one of the most romantic dining experiences to be had in Manuel Antonio. The food's some of the best in town as well. The menu changes regularly but features prime meats and poultry and fresh fish, excellently prepared. The rack of lamb might get a light jalapeño-mint or mango chutney, and the chicken breast might be stuffed with feta cheese, kalamata olives, and roasted red peppers and topped with a blackberry sauce. There are nightly specials and a good selection of salads, appetizers, and desserts.

At Makanda by the Sea (p. 373). **2777-0442.** Reservations recommended. Main courses $10–$30. V. Daily 11am–10pm.

MODERATE

Agua Azul ★ 🎁 INTERNATIONAL With a fabulous perch and panoramic view, this open-air restaurant has changed names and owners steadily over the years. It finally seems to have settled down with a menu and management that may just be able to make this place live up to its fantastic setting. Tables by the railing fill up fast, so get here well before sunset if you want to snag one.

Start things off with a Tuna Margarita, an inventive version of *ceviche* with a lime-and-tequila marinade. Main dishes include coconut-crusted mahimahi and panko-crusted tuna. For lunch there are giant burgers and fresh fish sandwiches. The long wooden bar is a popular hangout, and a good place to order up some appetizers and drinks.

Manuel Antonio, near Villas del Parque. **2777-5082.** Reservations not accepted. Main courses $9–$18. V. Thurs–Tues 11am–10pm.

El Gran Escape ★★ SEAFOOD This Quepos landmark is consistently one of the top restaurants in the area. The fish is fresh and expertly prepared, portions are generous, and the prices are reasonable. If that's not enough of a recommendation, the atmosphere is lively, the locals seem to keep coming back, and the service is darn good for a beach town in Costa Rica. Sturdy wooden tables and chairs take up the large indoor dining room, and sportfishing photos and an exotic collection of masks fill up the walls. If you venture away from the fish, the menu features hearty steaks and giant burgers; there's also a wide assortment of delicious appetizers, including fresh tuna sashimi, and an excellent breakfast menu. El Gran Escape's Fish Head Bar is usually crowded and spirited, and if there's a game going on, it will be on the television here.

On the main road into Quepos, on your left just after the bridge. **2777-0395.** Reservations recommended in high season. Main courses $5–$20. Wed–Mon 8am–11pm.

Plinio Restaurant ★ INTERNATIONAL This is a long-standing, popular restaurant in Manuel Antonio, located at an equally popular hotel. The open-air restaurant is about three stories above the parking lot, so be prepared to climb some steps. It's worth it, though. The broad menu features an enticing mix of international dishes, with a distinct emphasis on Asian fare. The chef uses locally organically grown herbs and veggies. Thai, Indian, and Indonesian dishes are all excellently prepared, and there are always vegetarian options. The shrimp in coconut-milk curry sauce is excellent.

In the Hotel Plinio, 1km (½ mile) out of Quepos toward Manuel Antonio. **2777-0055.** Reservations recommended in high season. Main courses $7–$20. V. Daily 5–10pm.

Tropical Sushi SUSHI/JAPANESE As the name implies, the ambience here is decidedly tropical, with lively pastel colors and Caribbean architectural highlights, but don't let the surroundings fool you: This is still an excellent sushi joint. In addition to fresh tuna and grouper brought in daily by local fishermen, you can get maki, sushi, and sashimi made with Chilean salmon, smoked eel, and deep-fried soft-shell crabs. The sushi bar itself is tiny, and the main dining room is similarly small. The nicest seating here is in the open-air patio. Start things off with some *edamame,* an appetizer of steamed soybeans in their husks, and be sure to try the Crocodile Roll, with its mix of crab, eel, and avocado. The biggest problem here is that, when busy, the service can be excruciatingly slow.

On a side street next to El Gran Escape, Quepos. **2777-1710.** Reservations recommended. Maki rolls $5–$10; main courses $6–$12. V. Daily 4:30–11pm.

Manuel Antonio After Dark

The bars at the **Barba Roja** restaurant, about midway along the road between Quepos and Manuel Antonio, and the **Hotel Sí Como No** (see earlier in this chapter) are good places to hang out and meet people in the evenings. For shooting pool, I head to the **Billfish Sportbar & Grill ★** at the Byblos Resort (on the main road btw. Quepos and the park entrance). For tapas and local *bocas,* try **Salsipuedes** (roughly midway along the road btw. Quepos and the National Park entrance), which translates as "get out if you can." If you want live music, **Bambu Jam ★** (along the road btw. Quepos and the park entrance) and **Dos Locos** (in the heart of downtown) are your best bets. In downtown Quepos, **Los Pescadores, Sargento Garcia's, Wacky Wanda's,** and the **Fish Head Bar** at El Gran Escape (see above) are all popular hangouts.

Night owls and dancing fools have several choices here, although the bulldozing of Mar y Sombra down by the beach has really hurt the scene. The live music at **Bambu Jam** is often salsa and merengue, perfect for dancing. For real late-night action, the local favorite appears to be the **Arco Iris,** which is located just before the bridge heading into town. Admission is usually around $3.

If you enjoy gaming tables, the **Hotel Kamuk** in Quepos and the **Byblos Resort** on the road to Manuel Antonio both have small casinos and will even foot your cab bill if you try your luck and lay down your money.

If you want to see a flick, check what's playing at **Hotel Sí Como No**'s (see above) little theater, although you have to eat at the restaurant or spend a minimum at the bar to earn admission.

En Route to Dominical: Playa Matapalo

Playa Matapalo is a long expanse of flat beach that's about midway between Quepos and Dominical. It's an easy but bumpy 26km (16 miles) south of Quepos on the Costanera Sur. It's nowhere near as developed as either of those two beaches, but that's part of its charm. The beach here seems to stretch on forever, and it's usually deserted. The surf and strong riptides frequently make Matapalo too rough for swimming, although surfing and boogie-boarding can be good. Foremost among this beach's charms are peace and quiet.

WHERE TO STAY

Matapalo is a tiny coastal village, although the actual beach is about 1km (½ mile) away. A few very small and intimate lodges are located right on the beach. One of the more interesting is **Bahari Beach Bungalows** (☎2787-5014; www.baharibeach.com), which offers deluxe tents with private bathrooms, and more standard rooms, right on the beach, or **Dreamy Contentment** (☎2787-5223; www.dreamycontentment.com), a more traditional beachfront hotel option. If you're looking for a longer stay, check out **Jungle House** (☎/fax 2787-5005; www.junglehouse.com), which has a variety of private houses and bungalows for rent.

DOMINICAL ★

29km (18 miles) SW of San Isidro; 42km (26 miles) S of Quepos; 160km (99 miles) S of San José

With a stunning setting, and miles of nearly deserted beaches backed by rainforest-covered mountains, Dominical and the coastline south of it are excellent places to find uncrowded stretches of sand, spectacular views, remote jungle waterfalls, and abundant budget lodgings. The beach at Dominical itself is one of

Bodyboarding at Playa Hermosa.

the prime surf destinations in Costa Rica, with both right and left beach breaks. When the swell is big, the wave here is a powerful and hollow tube, and the town is often packed with surfers. In fact, while the beach at Dominical gets broad, flat, and beautiful at low tide, its primary appeal is to surfers. It is often too rough for casual bathers. However, you will find excellent swimming, sunbathing, and strolling beaches just a little farther south at **Dominicalito, Playa Hermosa,** and inside **Ballena Marine National Park ★**.

Leaving Manuel Antonio, the road south to Dominical runs by mile after mile of oil-palm plantations. However, just before Dominical, the mountains again meet the sea. From Dominical south, the coastline is dotted with tide pools, tiny coves, and cliff-side vistas. Dominical is the largest village in the area and has several small lodges both in town and along the beach to the south. The village enjoys an enviable location on the banks of Río Barú, right where it widens considerably before emptying into the ocean. There's good bird-watching along the banks of the river and throughout the surrounding forests.

Essentials

GETTING THERE & DEPARTING By Plane: The nearest airport with regular service is in Quepos (see "Essentials" under "Manuel Antonio National Park," earlier in this chapter). From there you can hire a taxi, rent a car, or take the bus.

By Car: From San José, head south (toward Cartago) on the Interamerican Highway. Continue on this road all the way to San Isidro de El General, where you turn right and head down toward the coast. The entire drive takes about 4 hours.

You can also drive here from Manuel Antonio/Quepos. Just take the road out of Quepos toward the hospital and airport. Follow the signs for Dominical. It's a straight, albeit bumpy, shot that takes a bit over an hour due to the poor state of the washboard-rutted dirt road. For nearly a decade, this road has been scheduled for paving. If this happens, it should take only a half-hour to cover the 40km (25 miles).

The road from Dominical heading south to Palmar Norte, passing all the beaches mentioned below, is in excellent shape.

By Bus: To reach Dominical, you must first go to San Isidro de El General or Quepos. Buses leave San José for San Isidro roughly every hour between 5:30am and 6:30pm. See "Getting There & Departing" in "San Isidro de El General: A Base for Exploring Chirripó National Park," later in this chapter. The trip takes 3 hours; the fare is $3.50. Leave no later than 9am if you want to be sure to catch the 1:30pm bus to Dominical.

From San Isidro de El General, **Transportes Blanco** buses (☎2771-4744) leave for Dominical at 7 and 9am and 1:30 and 4pm. The bus station in San Isidro for rides to Dominical is 1 block south of the main bus station and 2 blocks west of the church. Trip duration is 1½ hours; the fare is $1.50.

From **Quepos,** buses (☎2771-4744) leave daily at 5, 6:30, 9:30, and 11:30am, and 3:30 and 5:30pm. Trip duration is 2 hours; the fare is $3.

When you're ready to leave, buses depart Dominical for San Isidro at 6:30 and 7:15am and 2:30 and 3:30pm. If you want to get to San José the same day, you should catch the morning bus. Buses leave San Isidro for San José roughly every hour between 5am and 6pm. Buses to Quepos leave Dominical at approximately 5, 8, and 11:30am and 1:30 and 5:30pm.

The main bus stop in Dominical is in the heart of town, near the soccer field and San Clemente restaurant.

ORIENTATION Dominical is a small village on the banks of the Río Barú. The village is to the right after you cross the bridge (heading south) and stretches out along the main road parallel to the beach. As you first come into town, you'll see the small Pueblo Del Rio shopping center dead ahead of you, where the road hits a "T" intersection. On your left is the soccer field and the heart of the village. To the right, a rough road heads to the river and up along the riverbank. If you stay on the Costanera Highway heading south, just beyond the turnoff into town is a little strip mall, **Plaza Pacífica,** with a couple of restaurants, a pharmacy, bank, and a grocery store.

FAST FACTS If you need any medical care, contact **Dominical Doctor** (☎2787-0129 or 8865-4064), which is inside the Pueblo del Rio minimall. You'll also find a pharmacy in the same little mall.

The closest gas station is about 2km (1¼ miles) north of town on the road to Quepos. Since this road is pretty rough, it's often better to head south along the Costanera to Uvita, where you'll find another gas station. Taxis tend to congregate in front of the soccer field. If you need to call a cab, try **Nelson** (☎8835-9528) or **Erik** (☎8881-4220). To rent a car, contact **Alamo** (☎2787-0052) which has a desk inside the Villas Rio Mar resort.

You can purchase stamps and send mail from the **San Clemente Bar & Grill** (see below). In the little mall built beside this restaurant, you'll also find an Internet cafe, and they'll change dollars. There's also a small branch of the **Banco de Costa Rica,** with an ATM, at the Plaza Pacífica.

Exploring the Beaches & Ballena Marine National Park

The open ocean waters just in front of town and toward the river mouth are often too rough for swimming. However, you can swim in the calm waters of the Río Barú, just in from the river mouth, or head down the beach a few kilometers to the little sheltered cove at **Roca Verde.**

Ballena Marine National Park.

If you have a car, you should continue driving south, exploring beaches as you go. You will first come to **Dominicalito,** a small beach and cove that shelters the local fishing fleet and can be a decent place to swim, but continue on a bit. You'll soon hit **Playa Hermosa,** a long stretch of desolate beach with fine sand. As in Dominical, this is unprotected and can be rough, but it's a nicer place to sunbathe and swim than Dominical.

At the village of Uvita, 16km (10 miles) south of Dominical, you'll reach the northern end of the **Ballena Marine National Park ★**, which protects a coral reef that stretches from Uvita south to Playa Piñuela and includes the little Isla Ballena, just offshore. To get to **Playa Uvita** (which is inside the park), turn in at the village of Bahía and continue until you hit the ocean. The beach here is actually well protected and good for swimming. At low tide an exposed sandbar allows you to walk about and explore another tiny island. This park is named for the whales that are sometimes sighted close to shore in the winter months. If you ever fly over this area, you'll also notice that this little island and the spit of land that's formed at low tide compose the perfect outline of a whale's tail. An office at the entrance here regulates the park's use and even runs a small turtle-hatching shelter and program. Entrance to the national park is $10 per person. Camping is allowed here for $2 per person per day, with access to a public bathroom and shower.

Dominical is a major surf destination. The long and varied beach break here is justifiably popular. In general, the beach boasts powerful waves best suited for experienced surfers. Nevertheless, beginners should check in with the folks at the **Green Iguana Surf Camp** (☎2787-0157 or 8825-1381; www.green iguanasurfcamp.com), who offer lessons and comprehensive "surf camps." Rates run around $585 to $1,155 per person, based on double occupancy, for a 1-week program including accommodations, lessons, unlimited surfboard use, transportation to various surf breaks, and a T-shirt.

Other Activities in the Area

Although the beaches stretching south from Dominical should be beautiful enough to keep most people content, there are lots of other things to do. Several local farms offer horseback tours through forests and orchards, and at some of these farms you can even spend the night. **Hacienda Barú ★** (**☎2787-0003;** fax 2787-0057; www.haciendabaru.com) offers several different hikes and tours, including a walk through mangroves and along the riverbank (for some good bird-watching), a rainforest hike through 80 hectares (198 acres) of virgin jungle, an all-day trek from beach to mangrove to jungle that includes a visit to some Indian petroglyphs, an overnight camping trip, and a combination horseback-and-hiking tour. The operation, which is dedicated to conservation and reforestation, even has tree-climbing tours and a small canopy platform 30m (98 ft.) above the ground, as well as one of the more common zip-line canopy tours. Tour prices range from $20 for the mangrove hike to $60 for the jungle overnight. If you're traveling with a group, you'll be charged a lower per-person rate, depending on the number of people. In addition to its eco- and adventure tourism activities, Hacienda Barú also has six comfortable cabins with two bedrooms each, full kitchens, and even a living room ($60 double, including breakfast). Hacienda Barú is about 1.5km (1 mile) north of Dominical on the road to Manuel Antonio.

The jungles just outside of Dominical are home to two spectacular waterfalls. The most popular and impressive is the **Santo Cristo** or **Nauyaca Waterfalls ★**, a two-tiered beauty with an excellent swimming hole. Most of the hotels in town can arrange for the horseback ride up here, or you can contact **Don Lulo** (**☎2787-8013;** www.cataratasnauyaca.com) directly. A full-day tour, with both breakfast and lunch, should cost around $50 per person, including transportation to and from Dominical. The tour is a mix of hiking, horseback riding, and hanging out at the falls. It is also possible to reach these falls by horseback from an entrance near the small village of Tinamaste. (You will see signs on the road.) Similar tours (at similar prices) are offered to the **Diamante Waterfalls,** which are a three-tiered set of falls with a 360m (1,180-ft.) drop, but not quite as spacious and inviting a pool as the one at Santo Cristo.

Nauyaca Waterfalls.

If you're looking for a bird's-eye view of the area, **Skyline Ultralights** (☎2743-8037; www.flyultralight.com) offers a variety of airborne tours of the area. Near the beach in Uvita, these folks offer options ranging from a 20-minute introductory flight for $65 to a circuit exploring the Ballena Marine National Park and neighboring mangrove forests lasting a bit over an hour for $160.

Basilisk lizard.

If you want to take a scuba-diving trip out to the rocky sites off Ballena National Park or all the way out to Isla del Caño, call **Mystic Dive Center** (☎2786-5217; www.mysticdivecenter.com), which has its main office in a small roadside strip mall down toward Playa Tortuga and Ojochal. These folks are only open from December 1 through April 15, and prices for Ballena National Park are $55 for snorkeling and $90 for a two-tank dive; prices for Isla del Caño are $95 for snorkeling and $145 for a two-tank dive.

Other adventure activities offered in Dominical include kayak tours of the mangroves, river floats in inner tubes, day tours to Caño Island and Corcovado National Park, and sportfishing. To arrange any of these activities, check in with **Dominical Adventures** (☎2787-0191; at the San Clemente Bar & Grill), **Southern Expeditions** (☎2787-0100; www.southernexpeditionscr.com), or the folks at the **Hotel Roca Verde** (☎2787-0036).

For a fun side trip for anyone interested in snakes and other little critters, head to **Parque Reptilandia** (☎2787-8007; www.crreptiles.com), located a few miles outside of Dominical on the road to San Isidro. This place features over 50 terrariums or enclosed exhibits of snakes, frogs, turtles, and lizards, as well as crocodiles and caimans. It's open daily from 9am to 4:30pm; admission is $9.

Finally, if you're looking to learn or bone up on your Spanish, **Adventure Education Center** (☎2787-0023; www.adventurespanishschool.com), located right in the heart of town, offers a variety of immersion-style language programs.

Where to Stay

In addition to the places listed below, a host of beautiful private homes on the hillsides above Dominical regularly rent out rooms. Most come with several bedrooms and full kitchens, and quite a few have private pools. If you're here for an extended stay and have a four-wheel-drive vehicle (a must for most of these), check in with **Paradise Costa Rica** (☎800/708-4552 in the U.S. and Canada; www.paradisecostarica.com) or with the folks at **Cabinas San Clemente** or **Hotel Roca Verde** (see below for both of these).

EXPENSIVE

Hotel Diuwak This little complex offers the best-equipped rooms right near the surf break, although that's not necessarily saying much. The rooms are spartan, but bright. About half the rooms come with air-conditioning, and there are a few suites and bungalows for larger groups and families. Most have some sort of private or semiprivate veranda facing lush gardens. At the center of the complex, you'll find a refreshing pool, and in the adjacent shopping center, there's a minimarket. Located about 50m (164 ft.) inland from the beach, this place is a decent option for surfers seeking a little extra comfort just steps away from the waves. However, service and upkeep can be spotty here.

Dominical (mailing address: A.P. 7737-1000, San José). **☎2787-0087.** Fax 2787-0089. www. diuwak.com. 18 units. $75–$160 double. Rates include full breakfast. MC, V. **Amenities:** Restaurant; bar; Jacuzzi; midsize pool. *In room:* Free Wi-Fi.

MODERATE

Hotel Roca Verde ★ This popular hotel offers the best beachfront accommodations in Dominical. Located a bit south of town, the setting is superb—on a protected little cove with rocks and tide pools. The rooms are located in a two-story building beside the swimming pool. Each room comes with one queen-size and one single bed, and a small patio or balcony. A large open-air restaurant with a popular bar really gets going on Saturday nights. The rooms are a bit close to the bar, so it can sometimes be hard to get an early night's sleep, especially during the high season if the bar is raging.

1km (½ mile) south of Barú River Bridge in Dominical, just off the coastal highway. **☎2787-0036.** Fax 2787-0013. www.rocaverde.net. 10 units. $65 double. MC, V. **Amenities:** Restaurant; bar; small pool. *In room:* A/C, no phone.

Pacific Edge ★ This place is away from the beach, but the views from the individual bungalows are so stunning that you might not mind. Spread along a lushly planted ridge on the hillside over Dominical, these simple, comfortable cabins have wood floors, solar-heated water, and solar reading lights. Their

Dominical's coastline.

best feature is surely the private porch with a comfortable hammock in which to laze about and enjoy the view. The restaurant serves breakfast, and dinners are served upon request. A wide range of tours and activities also can be arranged here, and there's a refreshing swimming pool, if you're too tired or lazy to head down to the beach. Pacific Edge is 4km (2½ miles) south of Dominical and then another 1.2km (¾ mile) up a steep and rocky road; four-wheel-drive vehicles are recommended.

Dominical (A.P. 531-8000, Pérez Zeledón). ☎/fax **2787-8010.** www.pacificedge.info. 4 units. $58–$70 double. AE, MC, V. **Amenities:** Restaurant; midsize pool. *In room:* Minifridge, no phone.

INEXPENSIVE

As a popular surfer destination, budget lodgings abound in Dominical. I've tried to list the best below, but if you're really counting pennies, it's always a good idea to walk around and check out what's currently available. There are plenty of camping options as well. I recommend **Piramys** (☎**2787-0196;** piramys@hotmail.com) or **Camping Antorchas** (☎**2787-0307**), both of which offer basic rooms very close to the beach.

Cabinas San Clemente 🌶 In addition to running the town's most popular restaurant (see below) and serving as the social hub for the surfers, beach bums, and expatriates passing through, this place offers a variety of accommodations to fit most budgets. Located about 1km (½ mile) from the in-town restaurant, San Clemente has rooms in three separate buildings, right on the beach. Some of the second-floor rooms have wood floors and wraparound verandas and are a good deal in this price range. The grounds are shady, and there are plenty of hammocks. The cheapest rooms are bunk-bed hostel-style affairs in a separate building dubbed the **Dominical Backpacker's Hostel.** Rooms here come with access to a communal kitchen.

Dominical (A.P. 703-8000, Pérez Zeledón). ☎**2787-0026** or 2787-0055. Fax 2787-0158. 19 units, 16 with private bathroom. $10 per person with shared bathroom; $30–$40 double with private bathroom. AE, MC, V. **Amenities:** Restaurant; bar; bike rental; surf- and boogie-board rental. *In room:* No phone.

Domilocos This place offers basic, comfortable rooms at a reasonable price. Rooms are simply furnished and on the plain side, with bamboo furnishings, air-conditioning, and large bathrooms. All open onto a common veranda. In the small, central garden area, you'll find a large Jacuzzi. Since it's about 1 block inland from the beach, this hotel has an isolated location; still, the restaurant and bar are both popular here, so things can get lively.

Dominical. ☎**2787-0244.** www.domilocos.com. 25 units. $65 double. Rates include breakfast. MC, V. **Amenities:** Restaurant; bar; Jacuzzi. *In room:* A/C.

Tortilla Flats This long-standing surfer hotel is another good budget option on the beach. There are several styles of rooms located in a cluster of buildings, including rooms with fans, rooms with air-conditioning, and larger rooms fitted out for groups of surfers. I recommend the second-floor rooms with ocean views. Because the rooms differ so much in size and comfort levels, you should definitely take a look at a few of them before choosing one.

Dominical. ☎/fax **2787-0168.** www.tortillaflatsdominical.com. 18 units. $35–$60 double. AE, MC, V. **Amenities:** Restaurant; bar. *In room:* No phone.

Where to Dine

On the beach, **Tortilla Flats** (☎2787-0033) is the best and most happening spot, and their menu features some excellent fresh-fish dishes and a touch of fusion cuisine. If you head a bit south of town, you can check out the restaurant at the **Hotel Roca Verde** (p. 385), which is usually pretty good for grilled fish, steaks, and burgers. For healthy fare, try **Maracatú** (☎2787-0091), toward the southern end of town.

Soda Nanyoa (☎2787-0164) is a basic Tico restaurant on the main road, just down a bit from the soccer field, serving local food and fresh seafood at good prices.

Coconut Spice ★★ THAI/INDIAN   Near the mouth of the river, this place continues to serve up excellent and reasonably authentic Thai, Malaysian, Indonesian, and Indian cuisine. The lemon-grass soup and pad Thai are both excellent. Chicken, pork, and shrimp are all served up in a selection of red, green, yellow, and Panang curry sauces. The open-air dining room has wood floors and paneling, heavy wooden tables and chairs, and a smattering of Asian decorations.

In the Pueblo del Rio shopping complex, Dominical. ☎2787-0073 or 8834-8103. Reservations recommended during the high season. Main courses $7–$14. V. Daily 1:15–9pm.

ConFusione ★ ITALIAN/INTERNATIONAL   This place turns out very good Italian fare and pizzas, with some other Continental dishes to boot. Standout appetizers include a baked gratin of shrimp in brandy sauce and fried fresh mushrooms. There's a long list of pastas and main dishes, and the seafood is always fresh and well prepared. These folks have a modest and fairly priced wine list, and there's a popular bar, which is a pleasant place to hang out, either before or after a meal.

Inside the Domilocos Hotel. ☎2787-0244. Reservations recommended during the high season. Main courses $6–$30. MC, V. Daily 7am–11:30pm.

San Clemente Bar & Grill ★ MEXICAN/AMERICAN   The large wooden tables and bench seats at this convivial place fill up fast most nights. The menu has a large selection of Mexican-American fare ranging from tacos and burritos to sandwiches. You can get any of the former with fresh fish. There are also more substantial plates, as well as nightly specials and excellent breakfasts. Just off the restaurant is a large indoor space that has a pool and foosball table, and which becomes one of the town's more popular nightspots, particularly on Fridays. An interesting (and sobering) decorative touch here is the ceiling full of broken surfboards. If you break a board out on the waves, bring it in; they'll hang it and even buy you a bucket of beer.

Next to the soccer field, Dominical. ☎2787-0055. Reservations not accepted. Main courses $3.50–$8. MC, V. Daily 7am–10pm.

Dominical After Dark

The big party scenes shift from night to night. **Maracatú** (see above) hosts an open jam session every Tuesday and a reggae night every Thursday. The loud and late-night dancing scene usually takes place Fridays at **San Clemente** and Saturdays at **Roca Verde;** see above for info on both. In addition, **Thrusters** in the center of town is a popular surfer bar with pool tables and dartboards, and the bar at **Rio Lindo Resort,** which is several hundred meters inland along the Rio Baru, has a mellow scene, with occasional live concerts. The bar at **ConFusione** (see above) also sometimes has live music.

South of Dominical

The beaches south of Dominical are some of the nicest and most unexplored in Costa Rica. With the paving of the Costanera Sur, hotels and cabinas have begun popping up all along this route. This is a great area to roam in a rental car—it's a **beautiful drive** ★★. One good itinerary is to make a loop from San Isidro to Dominical, down the Costanera Sur, hitting several deserted beaches and then returning along the Interamerican Highway.

Among the beaches you'll find are **Playa Ballena, Playa Uvita, Playa Piñuela, Playa Ventanas,** and **Playa Tortuga.** *Tip:* Most of these beaches are considered part of **Ballena Marine National Park** and are subject to the national park entrance fee of $6 per person. If you're visiting several of these beaches in 1 day, save your ticket—it's good at all of them.

WHERE TO STAY DOWN SOUTH

In addition to the places listed here, you'll find a campground at Playa Ballena and a couple of basic cabinas in Bahía and Uvita. The best of these is the **Tucan Hotel** (☎2743-8140; www.tucanhotel.com), with a mix of private rooms and dorm accommodations and a friendly hostel-like vibe.

However, if you want to be closer to the beach, check out **Canto de Ballenas** (☎2743-8085), an interesting local cooperative with neat rooms located about .7km (a little less than a half-mile) from the national park entrance at Playa Uvita.

Just south of Dominical, on a point over Dominicalito beach, **La Parcela** (☎2787-0016; www.laparcela.net) offers up four simple, but ideally located individual cabins, for $105 double, per night, while the nearby **Coconut Grove** (☎2787-0130; www.coconutgrovecr.com) offers a mix of cottages and guesthouses with direct access to Dominicalito, for between $75 and $135 double.

Expensive

Cuna del Angel ★★ This hotel has the plushest accommodations along this stretch of coast. The name of this place translates roughly as the Angel's Cradle. All rooms are named after angels, and angel motifs are abundant, as are stained-glass windows and lampshades, carved wood details, tile mosaics, and other artistic touches. The hotel is a bit set in, away from the ocean, but there are pretty good sea views from many rooms and common areas, over the thick forest and gardens here. Rooms come with either an open front patio fronting the pool, or a private balcony. I prefer the second-floor rooms, with the balconies. A wide range of treatments is available at the spa, and they have several well-equipped boats for deep-sea sportfishing.

9km (5½ miles) south of Dominical, just off the coastal highway. ☎2787-8436. Fax 2787-8015. www.cunadelangel.com. 16 units. $97–$178 double. Rates include full breakfast. AE, MC, V. **Amenities:** Restaurant; bar; Jacuzzi; midsize outdoor pool; sauna; small spa. *In room:* A/C, TV, mini-fridge, hair dryer, free Wi-Fi.

La Cusinga Lodge 🏨 La Cusinga is a wonderful, low-impact sustainable lodge, with a true commitment to environmental protection and education. This should be a top choice for bird-watchers and those looking for a comfortable lodge that also feels entirely in touch with the natural surroundings. The individual and duplex cabins feature lots of varnished woodwork and large screened windows on all sides for cross ventilation. Most have interesting stone and tile work in their bathrooms. The small complex is set on a hill overlooking Ballena National Park and Playa Uvita. Heavy stone paths connect the main lodge to the various individual cabins. The "honeymoon cabin" is large, with a private garden sitting area and a large bathroom with rustic stonemasonry and its own Jacuzzi tub. At press time, the property was about to open a yoga studio/space.

Bahía Ballena (A.P. 41-8000). ☎/fax **2770-2549.** www.lacusingalodge.com. 7 units. $135–$160 double. Rates include breakfast. MC, V. **Amenities:** Restaurant; bar. *In room:* No phone.

Moderate

Costa Paraiso Lodge ★ This hotel offers spacious and functional individual rooms on a rocky point at the north end of Dominicalito beach. All but one of the units come with either a full kitchen or kitchenette, and most have high ceilings and plenty of light and ventilation. The Toucan Nest is the best room here, set off from the rest, with a private deck and great view of the ocean. There is a small swimming pool, as well as some beautiful tide pools right in front of the hotel; the beach is just a short walk away.

2km (1¼ miles) south of Dominical, just off the coastal highway, Dominicalito (A.P. 578-8000, Pérez Zeledón). ☎**2787-0025.** Fax 2787-0338. www.costa-paraiso.com. 5 units. $110–$140 double. Rates include full breakfast. AE, DC, MC, V. **Amenities:** Small pool. *In room:* A/C, fridge, kitchenette (in some), no phone, free Wi-Fi.

Hotel Villas Gaia ★ Located off the Costanera Sur just before the town of Ojochal, this small hotel is a collection of separate, spacious wood bungalows. Each bungalow has one single and one double bed, a private bathroom, a ceiling fan, and a small veranda with a jungle view. I prefer the bungalows farthest from the restaurant, up on the high hill by the swimming pool. The pool and pool area have wonderful views over forest to the sea. A large, open-air dining room down by the parking lot is too close to the highway for my taste but serves tasty, well-prepared international fare. A wide range of tours are available, including trips to Isla del Caño, Corcovado National Park, and Wilson Botanical Gardens.

Playa Tortuga (A.P. 11510-1000, San José). ☎/fax **2244-0316** reservations in San José, or 2786-5044 at the lodge. www.villasgaia.com. 14 units. $80 double. Rates include taxes. AE, MC, V. **Amenities:** Restaurant; bar; small pool. *In room:* A/C ($10 surcharge), no phone.

WHERE TO DINE DOWN SOUTH

In addition to the places mentioned below, you'll also find a charming French-inspired international restaurant, **Citrus** (☎**2786-5175**), in Ojochal. The newest kid on the block down here, also in Ojochal, is **Ylang-Ylang** (☎**2786-5054**) serving up Indonesian fare.

Exotica ★★ 🏨 FRENCH/INTERNATIONAL This place is tucked away along one of the dirt roads that run through Ojochal. With polished concrete floors, roll-up bamboo screens for walls, and only a few tree-trunk slab tables and plastic lawn chairs for furniture, it is nonetheless one of the most popular restaurants in the area. The chalkboard menu changes regularly but might feature such dishes as shrimp in a coconut curry sauce or Chicken Exotica, which is stuffed with bacon, prunes, and cheese and topped with a red-pepper coulis. The lunch menu is much more limited, with a selection of fresh salads and a few more filling mains.

1km (½ mile) inland from the turnoff for Ojochal. ☎2786-5050. Reservations recommended. Lunch $4–$16; main courses $7–$27. MC, V. Mon–Sat 8am–9pm.

La Parcela SEAFOOD/INTERNATIONAL This open-air restaurant has a lovely setting on a rocky bluff overlooking the ocean. Try to get one of the tables by the railing and you'll be able to watch the waves crashing on the rocks below. The menu features fresh seafood, meat, and poultry dishes, as well as a selection of pastas. The sauces and presentation are all interesting. Start things off with a tuna tartare tower, and then try either their fresh mahimahi with a mango relish, or the filet mignon in a porcini mushroom sauce. The restaurant is a free Wi-Fi hot spot; in fact, I'd venture to bet this is one of the prettiest views you'll ever have while surfing the Web.

At Punto Dominical. ☎2787-0016. Reservations recommended. Main courses $8–$31. V. Daily 7:30am–9pm.

SAN ISIDRO DE EL GENERAL: A BASE FOR EXPLORING CHIRRIPO NATIONAL PARK

120km (74 miles) SE of San José; 123km (76 miles) NW of Palmar Norte; 29km (18 miles) NE of Dominical

San Isidro de El General is located just off the Interamerican Highway in the foothills of the Talamanca Mountains and is the largest town in this region. Although there isn't much to do right in town, this is the jumping-off point for trips to Chirripó National Park. This is also the principal transfer point if you're coming from or going to Dominical, and most buses traveling the Interamerican Highway stop here.

Essentials

GETTING THERE & DEPARTING **By Car:** The long and winding stretch of the Interamerican Highway between San José and San Isidro is one of the most difficult sections of road in the country. Not only are there the usual car-eating potholes and periodic landslides, but you must also contend with driving over the 3,300m (10,824-ft.) **Cerro de la Muerte (Mountain of Death).** This aptly named mountain pass is legendary for its dense afternoon fogs, blinding torrential downpours, steep drop-offs, severe switchbacks, and unexpectedly breathtaking views. (Well, you wanted adventure travel, so here you go!) Drive with extreme care, and bring a sweater or sweatshirt—it's cold up at the top. It'll take you about 3 hours to get to San Isidro.

Tip: If you want a break from the road, stop for a coffee or meal at **Mirador Vista del Valle** (☎8384-4685 or 8836-3193; at Km 119), a rustic roadside joint with a great view, gift shop, hiking trails, and orchid collection. These folks also have a few rustic cabins, as well as a zip-line canopy tour.

By Bus: Plenty of daily buses will take you to San Isidro. **Musoc** buses (☎ 2222-2422 in San José, or 2771-3829 in San Isidro) leave from their modern terminal at Calle Central and Avenida 22 roughly hourly between 5:30am and 5:30pm. **Tracopa** (☎ 2221-4214 or 2771-0468) also runs express buses between San José and San Isidro that leave roughly every hour between 5am and 6pm from Calle 5, between avenidas 18 and 20. Whichever company you choose, the trip takes a little over 3 hours, and the fare is roughly $4.40. Return buses depart San Isidro for **San José** roughly every hour between 5:30am and 7:30pm.

Buses from **Quepos** to San Isidro leave daily at 5 and 11:30am and 3:30pm. Trip duration is 3 hours; the fare is $3. Buses to or from **Golfito** and **Puerto Jiménez** will also drop you off in San Isidro.

ORIENTATION Downtown San Isidro is just off the Interamerican Highway. A large church fronts the central park, and you'll find several banks, and a host of restaurants, shops, and hotels within a 2-block radius of this park. The main bus station is 2 blocks west of the north end of the central park.

Exploring Chirripó National Park ★★

At 3,759m (12,330 ft.) in elevation, Mount Chirripó is the tallest mountain in Costa Rica. If you're headed up this way, come prepared for chilly weather. Actually, dress in layers and come prepared for all sorts of weather: Because of the great elevations, temperatures frequently dip below freezing, especially at night. However, during the day, temperatures can soar—remember, you're still only 9 degrees from the equator. The elevation and radical temperatures have produced an environment here that's very different from the Costa Rican norm. Above 3,000m (9,840 ft.), only stunted trees and shrubs survive in páramos. If you're driving the Interamerican Highway between San Isidro and San José, you'll pass through a páramo on the Cerro de la Muerte.

Hiking up to the top of Mount Chirripó is one of Costa Rica's best adventures. On a clear day (usually in the morning), an unforgettable **view ★★★** is

Little Devils

If you're visiting the San Isidro area in February, head out to the nearby **Rey Curré** village for the **Fiesta of the Diablitos,** where costumed Boruca Indians perform dances representative of the Spanish conquest of Central America. The 3-day event also includes fireworks and an Indian handicraft market—this is *the* best place in Costa Rica to buy hand-carved Boruca masks. The date varies, so it's best to call the **Costa Rica Tourist Board**

(☎ 800/327-7033 in the U.S. and Canada) for more information.

Summit of Mount Chirripó.

your reward: You can see both the Pacific Ocean and the Caribbean Sea from the summit. You can do this trip fairly easily on your own if you've brought gear and are an experienced backpacker. Although it's possible to hike from the park entrance to the summit and back down in 2 days (in fact, some daredevils even do it in 1 day), it's best to allow 3 to 4 days for the trip in order to give yourself time to enjoy your hike fully and spend some time on top because that's where the glacier lakes and páramos are. For much of the way, you'll be hiking through cloud forests that are home to abundant tropical fauna, including the spectacular **quetzal,** Costa Rica's most beautiful bird. However, quetzal sightings on summit climbs are rare. If you really want to see one of these birds, head to one of the specialized lodges listed below.

There are several routes to the top of Mount Chirripó. The most popular, by far, leaves from **San Gerardo de Rivas.** However, it's also possible to start your hike from the nearby towns of **Herradura** or **Canaan.** All these places are within a mile or so of each other, reached by the same major road out of San Isidro. San Gerardo is the most popular because it's the easiest route to the top and has the greatest collection of small hotels and lodges, as well as the National Parks office. Information on all of these routes is available at the parks office.

When you're at the summit lodge, there are a number of hiking options. Just in front of the lodge are Los Crestones (the Crests), an impressive rock formation, with trails leading up and around them. The most popular, however, is to the actual summit (the lodge itself is a bit below), which is about a 2-hour hike that passes through the Valle de los Conejos (Rabbit Valley) and the Valle de los Lagos (Valley of Lakes). Other hikes and trails lead off from the summit lodge, and it's easy to spend a couple of days hiking around here. A few trails will take you to the summits of several neighboring peaks. These hikes should be undertaken only after carefully studying an accurate map and talking to park rangers and other hikers.

ENTRY POINT, FEES & REGULATIONS Although it's not that difficult to get to Chirripó National Park from nearby San Isidro, it's still rather remote. And to see it fully, you have to be prepared to hike. To get to the trail head, you have three choices: car, taxi, or bus. If you choose to drive, take the road out of San Isidro, heading north toward San Gerardo de Rivas, which is some 20km (12 miles) down the road. Otherwise, you can catch a bus in San Isidro that will take you directly to the trail head in San Gerardo de Rivas. Buses leave daily at 5am from the western side of the central park in San Isidro. It costs 80¢ one-way and takes 1½ hours. Another bus departs at 2pm from a bus station 200m (656 ft.) south of the park. Buses return to San Isidro daily at 7am and 4pm. A taxi from town should cost around $15 to $20. Because the hike to the summit of Mount Chirripó can take between 6 and 12 hours, depending on your physical condition, I recommend taking a taxi or the early bus so that you can start hiking when the day is still young. Better still, you should arrive the day before and spend the night in San Gerardo de Rivas (there are inexpensive cabinas and one nice hotel there) before setting out early the following morning.

Before climbing Mount Chirripó, you must make a reservation and check in with the **National Parks office** (**☎2742-5083;** fax 2742-5085) in San Gerardo de Rivas. The office is open from 6:30am to 4:30pm daily. Even if you have a reservation, I highly recommend checking in the day before you plan to climb if possible. If you plan to stay at the lodge near the summit, you must make reservations in advance because accommodations there are limited (see "Staying at the Summit Lodge," below). Note that camping is not allowed in the park. It's possible to have your gear carried up to the summit by horseback during the dry season (Dec–Apr). Guides work outside the park entrance in San Gerardo de Rivas. They charge between $20 and $30 per pack, depending on size and weight. In the rainy season the same guides work, but they take packs up by themselves, not by horseback. The guides like to take up the packs well before dawn, so arrangements are best made the day before.

The entrance fee to the national park is $15 per day.

STAYING AT THE SUMMIT LODGE Reservations for lodging on the summit of Mount Chirripó must be made with the National Parks office listed above. This is an increasingly popular destination, and you must reserve well in advance during the dry season. The lodge holds only 30 people and fills up quickly and frequently. *Tip:* Many of the local tour agencies prebook the lodge beds, making it often difficult to impossible to do so on your own. If you can't book a bed by yourself, ask at your hotel, or contact one of the tour agencies listed below in "Other Adventures in & Around San Isidro."

Once you get to the lodge, you'll find various rooms with bunk beds, several bathrooms and showers, and a common kitchen area. There is good drinking water at the lodge. However, blankets, lanterns, and cook stoves are no longer for rent up top, so you have to pack all your own gear, as well as food and water (for the hike up). *Note:* It gets cold up here at night, and the lodge seems to have been designed to be as cold, dark, and cavernous as possible. No consideration was made to take advantage of the ample solar potential. The showers are freezing. It costs $10 per person per night to stay here.

Warning: It can be dangerous for more inexperienced or out-of-shape hikers to climb Chirripó, especially by themselves. It's not very technical climbing, but it is a long, arduous hike. If you're not sure you're up for it, you can just take day hikes out of San Isidro and/or San Gerardo de Rivas, or ask at your hotel about guides.

Race to the Top

If simply climbing the tallest peak in Costa Rica is a bit too mundane for you, why not join the annual **Carrera Campo Traviesa Al Cerro Chirripó** (**☎2771-8731;** www.carrerachirripo.com). Held the third Saturday of February, this is a grueling 34km (21-mile) race from the base to the summit and back. The record time, to date, is 3 hours, 15 minutes, and 3 seconds.

Other Adventures in & Around San Isidro

If you want to undertake any other adventures while in San Isidro, contact **Costa Rica Trekking Adventures** (☎2771-4582; www.chirripo.com), or **CIPROTUR** (☎2771-6096; www.ecotourism.co.cr). Both offer organized treks through Chirripó National Park, as well as white-water rafting trips and other adventure tours and activities.

Just 7km (4⅓ miles) from San Isidro is **Las Quebradas Biological Center** (☎2771-4131), a community-run private reserve with 2.7km (1¾ miles) of trails through primary rainforest. There's a rustic lodge for visitors and researchers ($24 per person; $20 students, including three meals), and camping is also permitted. You can hike the trails here and visit the small information center on-site for $3. From San Isidro, you can take a local bus to Quebradas, but you'll have to walk the last mile to the entrance. You can also take a taxi for around $8. If you're driving, take the road to Morazán and Quebradas.

Where to Stay & Dine

There are no notable restaurants in San Isidro. The town has its fair share of local joints, but most visitors are content at their hotel restaurant; see below for ideas. If you do venture beyond your hotel, your best options are the **México Lindo** (☎2771-8222) and the **Pizzería El Tenedor** (☎2771-0881), both just off the central park. Although the food is mediocre, the second-floor, open-air balcony seating at **La Cascada** (☎2771-6479), right in the town center, offers some excellent opportunities for people-watching, and is a great place to mingle with locals.

Hotel Diamante Real ★ This three-story business-class hotel feels a little out of place in San Isidro. Still, it offers the best-equipped rooms in town, and at a pretty fair price. The rooms themselves lack any sense of style or flair, and could really use a painting or two on the walls. But they are of good size, and boast either a table or desk for working executive types. The deluxe rooms even have Jacuzzi tubs. The restaurant serves respectable, if unimpressive, international and local fare.

San Isidro de El General, 1 block west of the Musoc bus station. ☎2770-6230. Fax 2770-6250. www.hoteldiamantereal.com. 21 units. $42–$71 double. Rates include breakfast. AE, MC, V. **Amenities:** Restaurant; room service. *In room:* A/C, TV, hair dryer, free Wi-Fi.

Hotel Iguazú This is a popular budget choice in San Isidro, although I recommend you splurge and stay at either of the other hotels in this section if you can afford it. The rooms are basic and come in different sizes with different arrangements of beds. All have small televisions. The rooms are definitely in better shape than those at the even more popular budget choice, the Hotel Chirripó. The hotel is on the second and third floors of the Gallo Mas Gallo department store, half a block away from the Musoc bus station. Some might find this convenient; others might find it too noisy. In 2007, they opened an annex, El Nuevo Iguazú, which is several blocks away, and very similar, although all rooms here have private bathrooms.

San Isidro de El General (above the Gallo Mas Gallo store). ☎2771-2571. Fax 2771-0076. 22 units, 17 with private bathroom. $10 double with shared bathroom; $22 double with private bathroom. V. *In room:* TV.

Hotel Los Crestones This two-story hotel is a few blocks south of downtown, and away from most of the traffic noise of this busy little city, although it is still on the main route that heads out of town toward Dominical. All rooms are relatively large and come with air-conditioning, but it costs an extra $10 to use it. The televisions are also pretty small. I recommend the units on the second floor, which share a broad tiled veranda. There's a midsize outdoor swimming pool and Jacuzzi.

San Isidro de El General (southwest side of the stadium). ☎**2770-1200.** Fax 2770-5047. www. hotelloscrestones.com. 27 units. $52–$58 double. Rates include breakfast. MC, V. **Amenities:** Restaurant; Jacuzzi; outdoor pool. *In room:* A/C (for a fee), TV, free Wi-Fi.

WHERE TO STAY CLOSER TO THE TRAIL HEAD

If you're climbing Mount Chirripó, you'll want to spend the night as close to the trail head as possible. As mentioned above, several basic cabinas right in San Gerardo de Rivas charge between $5 and $15 per person. The best of these are **El Descanso** (☎2742-5061) and **Roca Dura** (☎**8363-7318;** luisrocadura@ hotmail.com). If you're looking for a little more comfort, check out the lodge listed below.

Talari Mountain Lodge ★ This small mountain getaway is nothing fancy, but it is one of the nicer options right around San Isidro, and it also makes a good base for exploring or climbing Mount Chirripó. The rooms are in two separate concrete-block buildings. Most come with one double and one single bed, although one room can handle a family of four in one double and two single beds. I prefer the four rooms that face the Talamanca Mountains. There are plenty of fruit trees around and good bird-watching right on the grounds. (They've identified more than 222 bird species here.) The hotel borders the Río General and maintains some forest trails. Talari is 8km (5 miles) outside of San Isidro, and a staff member picks you up in town for free with advance notice. This lodge is also about 11km (6¾ miles) from San Gerardo de Rivas, so you'll probably have to arrange transportation to and from the park entrance.

Rivas, San Isidro (A.P. 517-8000, Pérez Zeledón). ☎/fax **2771-0341.** 8 units. $72 double. Rates include full breakfast and taxes. AE, MC, V. Closed Sept 16–Oct 31. **Amenities:** Restaurant; bar; small pool and separate children's pool. *In room:* Fridge, no phone.

En Route to San José: Three Places to See Quetzals in the Wild

Between San Isidro de El General and San José, the Interamerican Highway climbs to its highest point in Costa Rica and crosses over the Cerro de la Muerte. This area is one of the best places in Costa Rica to see quetzals. March, April, and May is nesting season for these birds, and this is usually the best time to see them. However, it's often possible to spot them year-round here. On my first visit here, a 2-hour hike without a guide, my small group spotted eight of these amazing birds. I was hooked.

In addition to the places listed below, **Dantica Cloud Forest Lodge** (☎**2740-1067;** www.dantica.com) is a small collection of private bungalows in a beautiful forested setting in this region, near the town of San Gerardo de Dota.

Albergue Mirador de Quetzales This family-run lodge is also known as Finca Eddie Serrano. The rooms in the main lodge are quite basic, with wood floors, bunk beds, and shared bathrooms. Eight separate A-frames provide a bit more comfort and a private bathroom. Meals are served family-style in the main lodge. But quetzals, not comfort, are the main draw here, and if you come between December and May, you should have no trouble spotting plenty of them. There are good hiking trails through the cloud forest, and the Serrano family members are genial hosts and good guides. On a clear day you can see the peaks of five volcanoes from the hotel's lookout—but it's not clear that often.

Carretera Interamericana Sur Km 70 (A.P. 985-7050, Cartago), about 1km (½ mile) down a dirt road from the highway. ☎/fax **8381-8456.** 11 units. $50 per person. Rate includes breakfast and dinner, a 2-hr. tour, and taxes. AE, MC, V. **Amenities:** Restaurant; bar. *In room:* No phone.

Savegre Mountain Hotel This working apple-and-pear farm, which also has more than 240 hectares (593 acres) of primary forest, has a well-earned reputation for superb bird-watching—it's one of the best places in the country to see quetzals. The rooms are clean and comfortable, but spartan, but if you're serious about birding, this shouldn't matter. In addition to the quetzals, some 170 other species have been spotted here. Hearty Tico meals are served, and if you want to try your hand at trout fishing, you might luck into a fish dinner. The owners of this place are a local family dedicated to local conservation and community development efforts. You'll find the lodge 9km (5½ miles) down a dirt road off the Interamerican Highway. This road is steep and often muddy, and four-wheel-drive is recommended, although not necessary.

Carretera Interamericana Sur Km 80, San Gerardo de Dota (A.P. 482, Cartago). ☎**2740-1028.** Fax 2740-1027. www.savegre.co.cr. 41 cabins. $179–$254 double. Rates include all meals, nonalcoholic drinks, entrance to their reserve, and taxes. Rates slightly lower in the off season. AE, MC, V. **Amenities:** Restaurant; bar; free Wi-Fi.

Trogon Lodge ★ 🎒 This is the most attractive and comfortable of the lodges in the area. The rooms are still rather basic, but the grounds, setting, and overall decor are a bit nicer than those at the lodges listed above. The rooms are all of good size, with wood floors, wood walls, a shared veranda, and one double and one twin bed. Room nos. 15 and 16 are my favorites; they are the farthest from the main lodge and have great views of the river. The family-style meals often feature fresh trout from their well-stocked trout ponds; as at Savegre Mountain Hotel, more than half the fun is catching it yourself. These folks also have their own little zip-line canopy tour.

Carretera Interamericana Sur Km 80, San Gerardo de Dota (A.P. 10980-1000, San José). ☎**2293-8181** in San José, or 2740-1051 at the lodge. Fax 2239-7657. www.grupomawamba.com. 23 units. $79 double; $130 junior suite with Jacuzzi. A full meal package runs $35 per person. AE, MC, V. **Amenities:** Restaurant; bar; lounge. *In room:* No phone.

Rest Your Weary Muscles Here

If you're tired and sore from so much hiking, be sure to check out the small **Herradura Hot Springs** (no phone) located off the road between San Gerardo de Rivas and Herradura. The entrance to the springs is 1km (½ mile) beyond San Gerardo de Rivas. The entrance fee is $3.

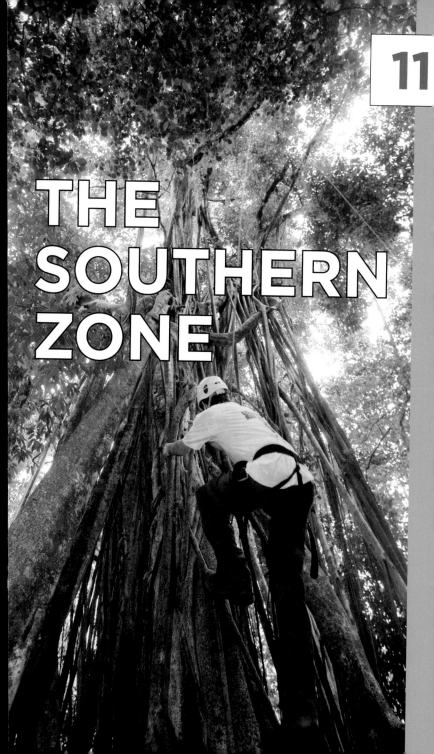

THE SOUTHERN ZONE

Costa Rica's southern zone is an area of jaw-dropping beauty, with vast expanses of virgin lowland rainforest, loads of wildlife, and few cities, towns, or settlements. Lushly forested mountains tumble into the sea, streams still run clear and clean, scarlet macaws squawk raucously in the treetops, and dolphins frolic in the **Golfo Dulce.** The **Osa Peninsula** is the most popular attraction in this region and one of the premier ecotourism destinations in the world. It's home to **Corcovado National Park ★★★**, the largest single expanse of lowland tropical rainforest in Central America, and its sister, **Piedras Blancas National Park ★★**. Scattered around the edges of these national parks and along the shores of the Golfo Dulce are some of the country's finest nature lodges. These lodges, in general, offer comfortable to nearly luxurious accommodations, attentive service, knowledgeable guides, and a wide range of activities and tours, all close to the area's many natural wonders.

But this beauty doesn't come easy. You must have plenty of time (or plenty of money—or, preferably, both) and a desire for adventure. It's a long way from San José, and many of the most fascinating spots can be reached only by small plane or boat—although hiking and four-wheeling will get you into some memorable surroundings as well. In many ways, this is Costa Rica's final frontier, and the cities of Golfito and Puerto Jiménez are nearly as wild as the jungles that surround them. Tourism is still underdeveloped here; there are no large resorts in this neck of the woods. Moreover, the heat and humidity are more than some people can stand. So it's best to put some forethought into planning a vacation down here, and it's usually wise to book your rooms and transportation in advance.

DRAKE BAY ★★

145km (90 miles) S of San José; 32km (20 miles) SW of Palmar

While Drake Bay remains one of the most isolated places in Costa Rica, the small town located at the mouth of the **Río Agujitas** has boomed in recent years. Most of that is due to the year-round operation of the small airstrip here, and the sometimes passable condition of the rough dirt road connecting Drake Bay to the coastal highway—just a handful of years ago there was no road, and the nearest regularly functioning airstrip was in Palmar Sur. That said, the village of Drake Bay is still tiny, and the lodges listed here remain quiet and remote getaways

PREVIOUS PAGE: **Climbing a Strangler fig.**

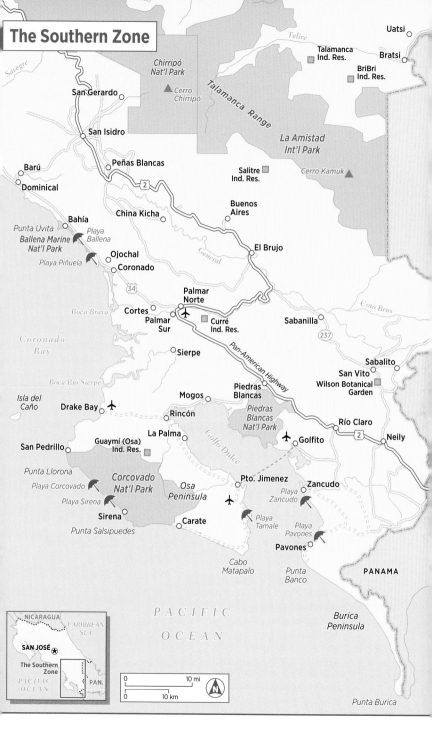

The Southern Zone

Uatsi

Talamanca
Ind. Res.

Bratsi

BriBri
Ind. Res.

Telire

Chirripó
Nat'l Park

Cerro
Chirripó

Savegre

San Gerardo

Talamanca Range

La Amistad
Int'l Park

San Isidro

Barú

Peñas Blancas

Salitre
Ind. Res.

Cerro Kamuk

Dominical

Buenos
Aires

China Kicha

Bahía

Punta Uvita

Playa
Ballena

El Brujo

Ballena Marine
Nat'l Park

General

Playa Piñuela

Ojochal

Coronado

Boca Brava

Cortes

Palmar
Norte

Coto Brus

Palmar
Sur

Curré
Ind. Res.

Sabanilla

Coronado
Bay

Sierpe

Pan-American Highway

Sabalito

Boca Río Sierpe

San Vito

Wilson Botanical
Garden

Isla del
Caño

Mogos

Piedras
Blancas

Drake Bay

Rincón

Piedras
Blancas
Nat'l Park

Río Claro

La Palma

San Pedrillo

Guaymí (Osa)
Ind. Res.

Golfo Dulce

Golfito

Neily

Punta Llorona

Corcovado
Nat'l Park

Playa Corcovado

Osa
Peninsula

Pto. Jimenez

Zancudo

Playa Sirena

Playa
Zancudo

Sirena

Carate

Playa
Tamale

Playa
Pavones

Punta Salsipuedes

Pavones

Cabo
Matapalo

Punta
Banco

PANAMA

Burica
Peninsula

PACIFIC
OCEAN

NICARAGUA

CARIBBEAN
SEA

SAN JOSÉ

The Southern
Zone

PACIFIC
OCEAN

PAN.

Punta Burica

0   10 mi
0   10 km

399

Common dolphin.

catering to naturalists, anglers, scuba divers, and assorted vacationers. Tucked away on the northern edge of the Osa Peninsula, Drake Bay is a great place to get away from it all.

The bay is named after Sir Francis Drake, who is believed to have anchored here in 1579. Emptying into a broad bay, the tiny Río Agujitas acts as a protected harbor for small boats and is a great place to do a bit of canoeing or swimming. It's here that many of the local lodges dock their boats, and many dolphin and whale-watching tours leave from here. Stretching south from Drake Bay are miles of deserted beaches and dense primary tropical rainforest. Adventurous explorers will find tide pools, spring-fed rivers, waterfalls, forest trails, and some of the best bird-watching in all of Costa Rica. If a paradise such as this appeals to you, Drake Bay makes a good base for exploring the peninsula.

South of Drake Bay lay the wilds of the **Osa Peninsula,** including **Corcovado National Park.** This is one of Costa Rica's most beautiful regions, yet it's also one of its least accessible. Corcovado National Park covers about half of the peninsula and contains the largest single expanse of virgin lowland rainforest in Central America. For this reason, Corcovado is well known among naturalists and researchers studying rainforest ecology. If you come here, you'll learn first-hand why they call them rainforests: Some parts of the peninsula receive more than 250 inches of rain per year.

Helping Out

If you want to help local efforts in protecting the fragile rainforests and wild areas of the Osa Peninsula, contact the **Corcovado Foundation** (📞2297-3013; www.corcovadofoundation.org) or the **Friends of the Osa** (📞2735-5756; www.osaconservation.org).

Moreover, if you're looking to really lend a hand, both of the aforementioned groups have volunteer programs ranging from trail maintenance to environmental and English-language education to sea-turtle-nesting protection programs.

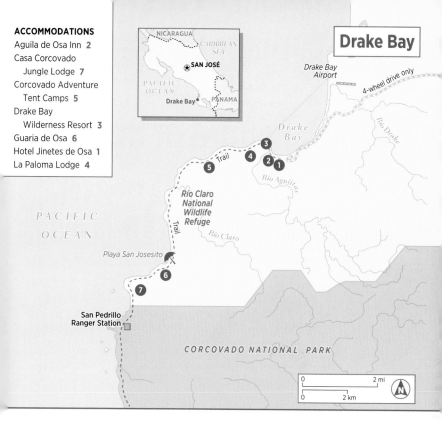

ACCOMMODATIONS

Aguila de Osa Inn **2**

Casa Corcovado
   Jungle Lodge **7**

Corcovado Adventure
   Tent Camps **5**

Drake Bay
   Wilderness Resort **3**

Guaria de Osa **6**

Hotel Jinetes de Osa **1**

La Paloma Lodge **4**

Puerto Jiménez (see later in this chapter) is the best base to choose if you want to spend a lot of time hiking in and camping inside Corcovado National Park. Drake Bay is primarily a collection of mostly high-end hotels, very isolated and mostly accessible only by boat. Travelers using these hotels can have great day hikes and guided tours into Corcovado Park, but Puerto Jiménez is the place if you want to have more time in the park or to explore independently. (It has a range of budget hotels, the parks office, and "taxi/bus" service to Carate and Los Patos, from which visitors can hike into the various stations.) From the Drake Bay side, you're much more dependent on a boat ride/organized tour from one of the lodges to explore the park; these lodges offer many other guided outings in addition to visits to the park.

Essentials

Because Drake Bay is so remote, I recommend that you have a room reservation and transportation arrangements (usually arranged with your hotel) before you arrive. Most of the lodges listed here are scattered along several kilometers of coastline, and it is not easy to go from one to another looking for a room.

Tip: A flashlight and rain gear are always useful to have on hand in Costa Rica; they're absolutely essential in Drake Bay.

Flowering banana plant.

GETTING THERE By Plane: Most people fly directly into the little airstrip at Drake Bay, although some tourists still fly to Palmar Sur: All lodges will either arrange transportation for you, or include it in their packages. **Sansa** (☎877/767-2672 in the U.S. and Canada, or 2290-4100 in Costa Rica; www.flysansa.com) flies directly to Drake Bay daily at 6:40 and 11am from San José's Juan Santamaría International Airport. The return flights leave Drake Bay at 7:45am and noon. The flight takes 50 minutes; the fare is $116 each way. Flights also depart San José daily at 9 and 9:30am for Palmar Sur; the fare is $106 each way.

Sansa also has a daily flight between Drake Bay and Puerto Jiménez. This 25-minute flight leaves Drake Bay at noon. The one-way fare is $62. The return flights from Puerto Jiménez don't actually stop down in Drake Bay.

Nature Air (☎800/235-9272 in the U.S. and Canada, or 2299-6000; www.natureair.com) has direct flights to Drake Bay departing daily from Tobías Bolaños International Airport in Pavas at 8:20 and 11:30am. The flight duration is 40 minutes; the fare is $128 each way. Return flights leave Drake Bay at 9:05am and 12:20pm. It also has a daily flight to Palmar Sur that departs at 9am and sometimes stops at Quepos en route. The flight takes a little over an hour, and the fare is $105 each way.

If your travels take you to Drake Bay via Palmar Sur, you must then take a 15-minute bus or taxi ride over dirt roads to the small town of **Sierpe.** This bumpy route runs through several **banana plantations** and quickly past some important archaeological sites. In Sierpe you board a small boat for a 40km (25-mile) ride to Drake Bay; see "By Taxi & Boat from Sierpe," below. The first half of this trip snakes through a maze of mangrove canals and rivers before heading out to sea for the final leg to the bay. **Warning:** Entering and exiting the Sierpe River mouth is often treacherous; I've had several very white-knuckle moments here.

By Bus: Tracopa buses (☎2221-4214 or 2258-8939) leave San José daily for the southern zone throughout the day, between 5am and 4pm from Calle 5 between avenidas 18 and 20. Almost all stop in Palmar Norte, although be sure to ask. The ride takes around 6 hours; the fare is $7.25.

Once in Palmar Norte, ask when the next bus goes out to Sierpe. If it doesn't leave for a while (buses aren't frequent), consider taking a taxi (see below).

By Taxi & Boat from Sierpe: When you arrive at either the Palmar Norte bus station or the Palmar Sur airstrip, you'll most likely first need to take a taxi to the village of Sierpe. The fare should be around $15. If you're booked into one of the main lodges, chances are your transportation is already included. Even if you're not booked into one of the lodges, a host of taxi and minibus drivers offer the trip. When you get to Sierpe, head to the dock and try to find space on a boat. This should run you another $20 to $40. If you don't arrive early enough, you might have to hire an entire boat, which usually runs around $90 to $150 for a boat that can carry up to six passengers. Make sure that you feel confident about the boat and skipper, and, if possible, try to find a spot on a boat from one of the established lodges in Drake Bay.

By Car: I don't recommend driving to Drake Bay. But if you insist, take the Interamerican Highway east out of San José (through San Pedro and Cartago) and continue south on this road. In about 3 hours you'll reach San Isidro de El General. Although you can continue on the Interamerican Highway all the way south, it is faster, smoother, and safer to turn off in San Isidro and head to Dominical, picking up the Southern Highway or Costanera Sur in Dominical. From here it's a fast and smooth shot down Palmar Norte, where you'll meet up again with the Interamerican Highway. South of Palmar take the turnoff for La Palma and Puerto Jiménez (at the town of Chacarita; it's clearly marked). Then at Rincón, turn onto the rough road leading into Drake Bay. This road fords some 10 rivers and is often not passable during the rainy season. Moreover, it only reaches into the small heart of the village of Drake Bay, though almost all of the hotels I've listed below are farther out along the peninsula, where only boats reach. In fact, the only hotels that you can actually drive up to are very basic cabins in town. For the rest, you'd have to find someplace secure to leave your car and either haul your bags quite a way or get picked up in a boat.

DEPARTING If you're not flying directly out of Drake Bay, have your lodge arrange a boat trip back to Sierpe for you. Be sure that the lodge also arranges for a taxi to meet you in Sierpe for the trip to Palmar Sur or Palmar Norte. (If you're on a budget, you can ask around to see whether a late-morning public bus is still running from Sierpe to Palmar Norte.) In the two Palmars you can make onward plane and bus connections. At the Palmar Norte bus terminal, almost any bus heading north will take you to San José, and almost any bus heading south will take you to Golfito.

What to See & Do

Beaches, forests, wildlife, and solitude are the main attractions of Drake Bay. Although Corcovado National Park (see "Puerto Jiménez: Gateway to Corcovado National Park," below) is the area's star attraction, there's plenty to soak up in and around Drake Bay. The Osa Peninsula is home to an unbelievable variety of plants and animals: more than 140 species of mammals,

Baird's tapir.

THOSE MYSTERIOUS
stone spheres

Although Costa Rica lacks the great cities, giant temples, and bas-relief carvings of the Maya, Aztec, and Olmec civilizations of northern Mesoamerica, its pre-Columbian residents did leave a unique legacy that continues to cause archaeologists and anthropologists to scratch their heads and wonder.

Over a period of several centuries, hundreds of painstakingly carved and carefully positioned granite spheres were left by the peoples who lived throughout the Diquis Delta, which flanks the Terraba River in southern Costa Rica. The orbs, which range from grapefruit size to more than 2m (6½ ft.) in diameter, can weigh up to 15 tons, and many reach near-spherical perfection.

Archaeologists believe that the spheres were created during two defined cultural periods. The first, called the Aguas Buenas period, dates from around A.D. 100 to 500. Few spheres survive from this time. The second phase, during which spheres were created in apparently greater numbers, is called the Chiriquí period and lasted from approximately A.D. 800 to 1500. The "balls" believed to have been carved during this time frame are widely dispersed along the entire length of the lower section of the Terraba River. To date, only one known quarry for the spheres has been discovered, in the mountains above the Diquis Delta, which points to a difficult and lengthy transportation process.

Some archaeologists believe that the spheres were hand-carved in a very time-consuming process, using stone tools, perhaps aided by some sort of firing process. However, another theory holds that granite blocks were placed at the bases of powerful waterfalls, and the hydraulic beating of the water eventually turned and carved the rock into these near-perfect spheres. And more than a few proponents have credited extraterrestrial intervention for the creation of the stone balls.

Most of the stone balls have been found at the archaeological remains of defined settlements and are associated with either central plazas or known burial sites. Their size and placement have been interpreted to have both social and celestial importance, although their exact significance remains a mystery. Unfortunately, many of the stone balls have been plundered and are currently used as lawn ornaments in the fancier neighborhoods of San José. Some have even been shipped out of the country. The **Museo Nacional de Costa Rica** (p. 157) has a nice collection, including one massive sphere in its center courtyard. It's a never-fail photo op. You can also see the stone balls near the small **airports in Palmar Sur** and **Drake Bay,** and on **Isla del Caño** (which is 19km/12 miles off the Pacific coast near Drake Bay).

Snorkelers at Caño Island Biological Reserve.

390 species of birds, and 130 species of amphibians and reptiles. You aren't likely to see anywhere near all of these animals, but you can expect to see quite a few, including several types of monkeys, coatimundis, scarlet macaws, parrots, and hummingbirds. Other park inhabitants include jaguars, tapirs, sloths, and crocodiles. If you're lucky, you might even see one of the region's namesake *osas*, or giant anteaters.

Around Drake Bay and within the national park are many miles of trails through rainforests and swamps, down beaches, and around rock headlands. All of the lodges listed below offer guided excursions into the park. It's also possible to begin a hike around the peninsula from Drake Bay.

One of the most popular excursions from Drake Bay is a trip out to **Isla del Caño** and the **Caño Island Biological Reserve ★★** for a bit of exploring and snorkeling or scuba diving. The island is about 19km (12 miles) offshore from Drake Bay and was once home to a pre-Columbian culture about which little is known. A trip to the island will include a visit to an ancient cemetery, and you'll also be able to see some of the stone spheres believed to have been carved by this area's ancient inhabitants (see the above box, "Those Mysterious Stone Spheres"). Few animals or birds live on the island, but the coral reefs just offshore teem with life and are the main reason most people come here. This is one of Costa Rica's prime **scuba spots ★★**. Visibility is often quite good, and there's even easily accessible snorkeling from the beach. All of the lodges listed below offer trips to Isla del Caño.

All lodges in the area also offer a host of half- and full-day tours and activities, including hikes in Corcovado National Park, horseback rides, and sportfishing. In some cases, tours are included in your room rate or package; in others, they must be bought a la carte. Other options include mountain biking and sea kayaking. Most of these tours run between $60 and $120, depending on the activity, with scuba diving ($90–$125 for a two-tank dive) and sportfishing ($450–$1,500, depending on the size of the boat and other amenities) costing a bit more.

One of the most interesting tour options in Drake Bay is a 2-hour **night tour ★★** (☎8382-1619; www.thenighttour.com; $35 per person) offered by Tracie Stice, who is affectionately known as the "Bug Lady." Equipped with flashlights, participants get a bug's-eye view of the forest at night. You might see reflections of some larger forest dwellers, but most of the tour is a fascinating

Humpback whale.

exploration of the nocturnal insect and arachnid world. Consider yourself lucky if she finds the burrow of a trap-door spider or large tarantula. Avoid this tour if you are helplessly arachnophobic. Any hotel in Drake Bay can book the tour for you. However, the travel distance makes it impossible for those staying at hotels outside of walking distance of the town.

Drake Bay is one of the best places to go **whale-watching** in Costa Rica; humpback whales are most commonly spotted in the area between late July and November and December through March. There are currently no dedicated whale-watching operators in the area, but all the hotels listed below can arrange whale-watching, as well as dolphin-spotting, trips. Two resident marine biologists, Shawn Larkin and Roy Sancho, are often hired by the better hotels, but depending on demand and availability, the hotels may send you out with one of their own guides and/or captains.

Where to Stay & Dine

Given the remote location and logistics of reaching Drake Bay, as well as the individual isolation of each hotel, nearly all of the hotels listed below deal almost exclusively in package trips that include transportation, meals, tours, and taxes. I've listed the most common packages, although all the lodges will work with you to accommodate longer or shorter stays. Nightly room rates are listed only where they're available and practical, generally at the more moderately priced hotels.

In addition to the places listed below, **Guaria de Osa** ★ (℡ **510/235-4313** in the U.S., or 8358-9788 in Costa Rica; www.guariadeosa.com) is a beautiful lodge near the Río Claro that specializes in yoga, spiritual, and educational retreats.

In addition to the hotels listed below, you could try **Corcovado Adventure Tent Camps** (℡ **831/345-8484** in the U.S., or 8384-1679 in Costa Rica; www.corcovado.com). A semipermanent tent, with three-squares per day and use of the facilities and watersports equipment, will run you around $80 per person, per day. Shared bathrooms are clean and the setting is beautiful, but meals and accommodations are a bit basic for the price.

VERY EXPENSIVE

Aguila de Osa Inn ★ This luxurious hillside lodge is a great choice for serious sportfishers and scuba divers, because it has a private fleet of sportfishing and dive vessels. Situated high on a hill overlooking Drake Bay and the Pacific Ocean, the Aguila de Osa Inn offers large, attractively decorated rooms, with hardwood or tile floors, ceiling fans, large bathrooms, and excellent views. Varnished wood and bamboo abound. A bar is built atop some rocks on the bank of the Río Agujitas, and the open-air dining room is set amid lush foliage with a partial view of the bay through the leaves, close to river level. Meals are excellent and filling, and the kitchen leaves a fresh Thermos of coffee outside each room every morning. Service, upkeep, and attention are top-notch here. The biggest drawback, however, is the lack of a swimming pool, which most of the other high-end places here have.

Drake Bay (mailing address: Interlink 898, P.O. Box 025635, Miami, FL 33102). **866/924-8452** in the U.S., or 2296-2190 in Costa Rica. Fax 2232-7722. www.aguiladeosainn.com. 13 units. $524–$648 for 3 days/2 nights; $789–$975 for 4 days/3 nights. Rates are per person based on double occupancy and include round-trip transportation from Palmar Sur, all meals, and taxes. Lower rates in off season. AE, MC, V. **Amenities:** Restaurant; bar; watersports rentals. *In room:* No phone.

Casa Corcovado Jungle Lodge ★ This very isolated jungle lodge is the closest to Corcovado National Park on this end of the Osa Peninsula. The rooms are all large private bungalows built on the grounds of an old cacao plantation on the jungle's edge. Family-style meals are served in the main lodge, although most guests take lunch with them to the beach or on one of the various tours available. Late afternoons are usually enjoyed from a high point overlooking the sea and sunset, with your beverage of choice in hand. Access is strictly by small boat, and sometimes the beach landing can be a bit rough and wet. When the sea is calm, the beach is great for swimming; when it is rough, it's a great place to grab a hammock in the shade and read a book. The lodge has two pretty swimming pools, both surrounded by thick rainforest, and a wide range of tours and activities are offered.

Osa Peninsula (mailing address: Interlink 253, P.O. Box 526770, Miami, FL 33152). **888/896-6097** in the U.S., or 2256-3181 in Costa Rica. Fax 2256-7409. www.casacorcovado.com. 14 units. $855 per person for 3 days/2 nights with 1 tour; $1,015–$1,165 for 4 days/3 nights with 2 tours. Rates are based on double occupancy and include round-trip transportation from San José, all meals, park fees, and taxes. Rates higher during peak weeks; lower in off season. AE, MC, V. **Amenities:** Restaurant; 2 bars; 2 outdoor pools. *In room:* Minibar, no phone.

Combing for Beaches

While the beach at Drake Bay itself is acceptable and calm for swimming, it's far from spectacular. The most popular swimming beach is a pretty small patch of sand, known locally as Cocalito beach, about a 7-minute hike down from La Paloma Lodge. The nicest beaches around involve taking a day trip to either Isla del Caño or San Josesito. The latter is a stunning beach farther south on the peninsula with excellent snorkeling possibilities.

La Paloma Lodge ★★★ On a steep hill overlooking the Pacific, with Isla del Caño in the distance, the luxurious bungalows at La Paloma offer expansive ocean views that make this my top choice in Drake Bay. All of the bungalows feature private verandas, and are set among lush foliage facing the Pacific. The large two-story Sunset Ranchos are the choice rooms here, with fabulous panoramic views. The other cabins are a tad smaller, but all are plenty spacious, beautifully appointed, and feature luxurious bathrooms and pretty good ocean views as well. Standard rooms, located in one long building, are smaller and less private than the cabins, but they're still attractive and have good views from their hammock-equipped balcony. The beach is about a 7-minute hike down a winding jungle path. Hearty and delicious meals are served family-style in the restaurant. The owners here are committed environmentalists and actively work on conservation and local development issues.

Drake Bay (mailing address: A.P. 97-4005, San Antonio de Belén). ☎ **2293-7502** or ☎/fax 2239-0954. www.lapalomalodge.com. 11 units. $1,115–$1,470 per person for 4 days/3 nights with 2 tours; $1,310–$1,700 per person for 5 days/4 nights with 2 tours. Rates are based on double occupancy and include round-trip transportation from San José, all meals, park fees, indicated tours, and taxes. Rates slightly lower in off season. AE, MC, V. **Amenities:** Restaurant; bar; small tile pool w/spectacular view; free Wi-Fi around the main lodge. *In room:* Minibar, no phone.

EXPENSIVE

Drake Bay Wilderness Resort ★ This is one of the best-located lodges at Drake Bay. It backs onto the Río Agujitas and fronts the Pacific. The rooms here are less fancy than those at the resort lodges listed above, but they are clean and comfortable, with ceiling fans, small verandas, good mattresses on the beds, and private bathrooms. The best room is a pretty, deluxe honeymoon suite on a little hill toward the rear of the property, with a great view of the bay. There are also five budget cabins that share bathroom and shower facilities. Because it's on a rocky spit, there isn't a good swimming beach on-site, but there's a saltwater pool in front of the bay, and, depending on the tide, you can bathe in a beautiful small tide pool formed by the rocks.

Drake Bay (A.P. 13710-1000, San José). ☎ **561/762-1763** in the U.S., or ☎/fax 2770-8012 in Costa Rica. www.drakebay.com. 25 units. $90 per person per day with shared bathroom; $130–$165 per person per day standard and deluxe. Rates include all meals and taxes. $770 per person for 4 days/3 nights with 2 tours, including all meals and taxes. AE, MC, V. **Amenities:** Restaurant; bar; small saltwater pool; free use of canoes and kayaks. *In room:* Hair dryer, no phone, free Wi-Fi.

MODERATE

Hotel Jinetes de Osa 🌶 This is a good option right in the village of Drake Bay, and a popular choice for serious divers and adventure tourists. Although no longer a budget lodging, it does offer a reasonable alternative to the more upscale options in the area. The best rooms here are spacious and well-appointed, and even have a view of the bay. The hotel is pretty close to the docks on the Río Agujitas, which is a plus for those traveling independently or with heavy bags. A wide range of tours and activities are available, as are dive packages, weekly packages, and PADI certification courses. For true budget travelers, camping is allowed just behind the main lodge.

Drake Bay (mailing address: 831 S. Newcombe Way, Lakewood, CO 80226). ☎ **866/553-7073** in the U.S. and Canada, or ☎/fax 2231-5806 in Costa Rica. www.drakebayhotel.com. 9 units, 7 with private bathroom. $132–$176 double. Rates include 3 meals daily. MC, V. **Amenities:** Restaurant; bar. *In room:* No phone, free Wi-Fi.

Casa Corcovado's shoreline.

PUERTO JIMENEZ: GATEWAY TO CORCOVADO NATIONAL PARK

35km (22 miles) W of Golfito by water (90km/56 miles by road); 85km (53 miles) S of Palmar Norte

Don't let its small size and languid pace fool you. **Puerto Jiménez ★** is actually a bustling little burg, where rough jungle gold-panners mix with wealthy ecotourists, budget backpackers, serious surfers, and a smattering of celebrities seeking a small dose of anonymity and escape. Located on the southeastern tip of the Osa Peninsula, the town itself is just a couple of streets wide in any direction, with a ubiquitous soccer field, a handful of general stores, some inexpensive *sodas* (diners), and several bars. Scarlet macaws fly overhead, and mealy parrots provide wake-up calls.

Corcovado National Park has its headquarters here, and this town makes an excellent base for exploring this vast wilderness area. Signs in English on walls around town advertise a variety of tours, including a host of activities outside of the park. If the in-town accommodations are too budget-oriented, you'll find several far more luxurious places farther south on the Osa Peninsula. This is also a prime surf spot. **Cabo Matapalo** (the southern tip of the Osa Peninsula) is home to several very dependable right point breaks. When it's working, the waves at Pan Dulce and Backwash actually connect, and can provide rides almost as long and tiring as those to be had in more famous Pavones (see "Playa Pavones: A Surfer's Mecca," later in this chapter).

Essentials

GETTING THERE & DEPARTING By Plane: Sansa (☎877/767-2672 in the U.S. and Canada, or 2290-4100 in Costa Rica; www.flysansa.com) has around seven daily flights to Puerto Jiménez from San José's Juan Santamaría International Airport. The cost is $114 each way. Some of the flights stop in Quepos en route. A direct flight takes around 55 minutes; add on about 10 minutes if there's a stop.

Nature Air (☎800/235-9272 in the U.S. and Canada, or 2299-6000; www.natureair.com) has flights to Puerto Jiménez departing from Tobías Bolaños International Airport in Pavas at 6, 8:30, and 11am and 3:15pm daily. The flight takes 50 minutes; the fare is $128 each way. Nature Air flights to San José depart daily at 7 and 9:30am, noon, and 5:25pm.

Note that due to the remoteness of this area and the unpredictable flux of traffic, both Sansa and Nature Air frequently improvise on scheduling. Sometimes this means an unscheduled stop in Quepos or Golfito either on the way to or from San José, which can add some time to your flight. Less frequently it might mean a change in departure time, so it's always best to confirm. Also, lodges down here sometimes run charters, so it pays to ask them as well.

Taxis are generally waiting to meet all incoming flights. A ride into downtown Puerto Jiménez should cost around $3. If you're staying at a hotel outside of downtown, it's best to have them arrange for a taxi to meet you. Otherwise you can hire one at the airstrip. Depending upon how far out on the peninsula you are staying, it could cost up to $80 for a rugged four-wheel-drive vehicle that can carry up to four people.

By Car: Take the Interamerican Highway east out of San José (through San Pedro and Cartago) and continue south on this road. In about 3 hours, you'll reach San Isidro de El General. Although you can continue on the Interamerican Highway all the way south, it is currently faster, smoother, and safer to turn off in San Isidro and head to Dominical, picking up the Southern Highway or Costanera Sur in Dominical. From here it's a fast and smooth shot down Palmar Norte, where you'll meet up again with the Interamerican Highway. Take the turnoff for La Palma, Rincón, and Puerto Jiménez. This road is paved at first, but at Rincón it turns to gravel. The last 35km (22 miles) are slow and rough, and, if it's the rainy season (mid-Apr to Nov), it'll be too muddy for anything but a four-wheel-drive vehicle.

By Bus: A **Transportes Blanco-Lobo** express bus (☎2257-4121 in San José or 2771-4744 in Puerto Jiménez) leaves San José daily at noon from Calle 12 between avenidas 7 and 9. The trip takes 8 hours; the fare is $7.50. Buses depart Puerto Jiménez for San José daily at 5am.

By Boat: Several speedboats work as boat taxis between Puerto Jiménez and Golfito. The fare is $5, and the ride takes a little under 30 minutes. These boats leave five or six times throughout the day, or whenever they fill up, beginning at around 5am and finishing up at around 5pm. Ask around town, or at the docks for current schedules.

There is also a daily passenger launch. This slower boat takes 1½ hours; and the fare is $3. The ferry leaves the public dock in Golfito at 6am for Puerto Jiménez. The return trip to Golfito leaves Puerto Jiménez's municipal dock at 11:30am. It's possible to charter a water taxi in Golfito for the trip across to Puerto Jiménez, as well. You'll have to pay between $40 and $80 for an entire launch, some of which can carry up to 12 people.

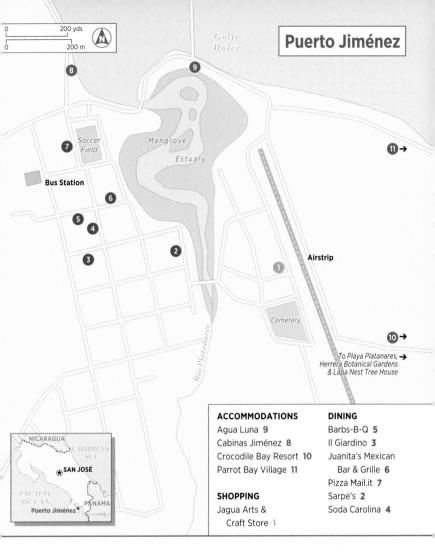

Puerto Jiménez

ACCOMMODATIONS	DINING
Agua Luna **9**	Barbs-B-Q **5**
Cabinas Jiménez **8**	Il Giardino **3**
Crocodile Bay Resort **10**	Juanita's Mexican
Parrot Bay Village **11**	Bar & Grille **6**
	Pizza Mail.it **7**
SHOPPING	Sarpe's **2**
Jagua Arts &	Soda Carolina **4**
Craft Store **1**	

ORIENTATION Puerto Jiménez is a dirt-lane town on the southern coast of the Osa Peninsula. The public dock is over a bridge past the north end of the soccer field; the bus stop is 2 blocks east of the center of town. You'll find a couple of Internet cafes in town; the best of these is **Cafe Net El Sol** (**☎2735-5719;** www.soldeosa.com), which is a great place to book tours and get information, and is also a Wi-Fi hot spot.

Four-wheel-drive taxis are actually fairly plentiful in Puerto Jiménez. You can usually find them cruising or parked along the main street in town. Alternatively, have your hotel or restaurant call one for you. You can even rent a car down here from **Solid Car Rental** (**☎2735-5777;** www.solid carrental.com).

Exploring Corcovado National Park ★★★

Exploring Corcovado National Park is not something to be undertaken lightly, but neither is it the expedition that some people make it out to be. The weather is the biggest obstacle to overnight backpacking trips through the park. Within a couple of hours of Puerto Jiménez (by 4WD vehicle) are several entrances to the park; however, there are no roads in the park, so once you reach any of the entrances, you'll have to start hiking. The heat and humidity are often quite extreme, and frequent rainstorms can make trails fairly muddy. If you choose the alternative—

Corcovado National Park trail.

hiking on the beach—you'll have to plan your hiking around the tides when often there is no beach at all and some rivers are impassable.

Because of its size and remoteness, Corcovado National Park is best explored over several days; however, it is possible to enter and hike a bit of it on day trips. The best way to do this is to book a tour with your lodge on the Osa Peninsula, from a tour company in Puerto Jiménez, or through a lodge in Drake Bay (see "Where to Stay & Dine," above).

GETTING THERE & ENTRY POINTS The park has four primary entrances, which are really just ranger stations reached by rough dirt roads. When you've reached them, you'll have to strap on a backpack and hike. Perhaps the easiest one to reach from Puerto Jiménez is **La Leona ranger station,** accessible by car, bus, or taxi.

If you choose to drive, take the dirt road from Puerto Jiménez to Carate (Carate is at the end of the road). From Carate, it's a 3km (1¾-mile) hike to La Leona. To travel there by "public transportation," pick up one of the collective buses (actually, a 4WD pickup truck with a tarpaulin cover and slat seats in the back) that leave Puerto Jiménez for Carate daily at 6am and 1:30pm, returning at 9am and 4pm. Remember, these "buses" are very informal and change their schedules regularly to meet demand or avoid bad weather, so always ask in town. The one-way fare is around $8. A small fleet of these pickups leaves just south of the bus terminal, and will stop to pick up anyone who flags them down along the way. Your other option is to hire a taxi to suit your schedule, which will charge approximately $70 to $90 each way to or from Carate.

En route to Carate, you will pass several campgrounds and small lodges as you approach the park. If you are unable to get a spot at one of the campsites in the park, you can stay at one of these and hike the park during the day.

You can also travel to **El Tigre,** about 14km (8¾ miles) by dirt road from Puerto Jiménez, where there's another ranger station. But note that trails from El Tigre go only a short distance into the park.

Corcovado National Park

The third entrance is in **Los Patos,** which is reached from the town of La Palma, northwest of Puerto Jiménez. From here, there's a 19km (12-mile) trail through the center of the park to **Sirena,** a ranger station and research facility (see "Beach Treks & Rainforest Hikes," below). Sirena has a landing strip that is used by charter flights.

The northern entrance to the park is **San Pedrillo,** which you can reach by hiking from Sirena or by taking a boat from Drake Bay or Sierpe (see "Beach Treks & Rainforest Hikes," below). It's 14km (8¾ miles) from Drake Bay.

If you're not into hiking in the heat, you can charter a plane in Puerto Jiménez to take you to Carate or Sirena. A five-passenger plane costs between $200 to $400 one-way, depending on your destination. Contact **Alfa Romeo Air Charters** (☎**2735-5353** or 2735-5112; www.alfaromeoair.com) for details.

Trail Distances in Corcovado National Park

It's 14km (8.5 miles) from La Leona to Sirena. From Sirena to San Pedrillo, it's 23km (14 miles) along the beach. From San Pedrillo, it's 20km (13 miles) to Drake Bay. It's 19km (12 miles) between Sirena and Los Patos.

FEES & REGULATIONS Park admission is $10 per person per day. Only the Sirena station is equipped with dormitory-style lodgings and a simple *soda*, but the others have basic campsites and toilet facilities. All must be reserved in advance by contacting the **ACOSA** (Area de Conservacion de Osa) in Puerto Jiménez (**☏2735-5036;** fax 2735-5276; pncorcovado@hotmail.com). For a good overview of the park and logistics, check out **www.corcovado.org**. Its offices are adjacent to the airstrip. Only a limited number of people are allowed to camp at each ranger station, so make your reservations well in advance.

BEACH TREKS & RAINFOREST HIKES The park has quite a few good hiking trails. Two of the better-known ones are the beach routes, starting at either the La Leona or San Pedrillo ranger stations. None of the hikes is easy, but the forest route from the Los Patos ranger station to Sirena, although long, is less taxing than either of the beach treks, which can be completed only when the tide is low. The route between the Los Patos/Sirena hike is 19km (12 miles) through beautiful rainforest.

Hummingbird.

Sirena is a fascinating destination. As a research facility and ranger station, it's frequented primarily by scientists studying the rainforest. One of the longest hikes, from San Pedrillo to Sirena, can be done only during the dry season. Between any two stations, the hiking is arduous and takes all day, so it's best to rest for a day or so between hikes if possible.

Remember, this is quite a wild area. Never hike alone, and take all the standard precautions for hiking in the rainforest. In addition, be especially careful about swimming in any isolated rivers or river mouths because most rivers in Corcovado are home to crocodiles.

Important Corcovado Tips

If you plan to hike the beach trails from La Leona or San Pedrillo, be sure to pick up a tide table at the park headquarters' office in Puerto Jiménez. The tide changes rapidly; when it's high, the trails and river crossings can be dangerous or impassable.

If you plan to spend a night or more in the park, you'll want to stock up on food, water, and other essentials while you're in Puerto Jiménez. There's a minimarket in Carate, but the selection is limited. Although most of the stations have simple *sodas,* you need to reserve in advance if you plan to take your meals at any of these.

WHERE TO STAY & DINE IN THE PARK: CAMPSITES, CABINS & CANTINAS Reservations are essential at the various ranger stations if you plan to eat or sleep inside the park (see "Fees & Regulations," above). **Sirena** has a modern research facility with dormitory-style accommodations for 28 persons, as well as a campground, *soda,* and landing strip for charter flights. There is also camping at the **La Leona, Los Patos,** and **San Pedrillo** ranger stations. Every ranger station has potable water, but it's advisable to pack in your own; whatever you do, don't drink stream water. Campsites in the park are $4 per person per night. A dorm bed at the Sirena station will run you $8—you must bring your own sheets, and a mosquito net is highly recommended—and meals here are another $40 per day. Everything must be reserved in advance.

Activities Outside the Park

While Puerto Jiménez has typically been a staging ground for adventures much farther out toward Carate and the park, quite a few activities and tours can be undertaken closer to town.

If you're looking to spend some time on the beach, head just east of town for a long pretty stretch of sand called **Playa Plantanares.** The waves are generally fairly gentle, and quite a few hotels have begun to pop up here. If you head farther out on the peninsula, you'll come to the beaches of **Pan Dulce, Backwash,** and **Matapalo,** all major surf spots with consistently well-formed right point breaks. When the waves aren't too big, these are excellent places to learn how to surf.

Kayaking trips around the estuary and up into the mangroves and out into the gulf are popular. Contact **Escondido Trex** ★ (**℡2735-5210;** www. escondidotrex.com), which has an office in the Soda Carolina (see "Where to Dine in Puerto Jiménez," below). There are daily paddles through the mangroves, as well as sunset trips where you can sometimes see dolphins. These folks also do guided rainforest hikes and can have you rappelling down the face of a jungle waterfall. More adventurous multiday kayak and camping trips are also available, in

Surfers at Backwash.

Kayaking with Escondido Trex.

price and comfort ranges from budget to luxury (staying at various lodges around the Golfo Dulce and Matapalo). They'll even take you gold-panning (although there are no guarantees that your panning will pay for the trip).

If you're in Puerto Jiménez, be sure to check out the **Herrera Botanical Gardens ★** (☎2735-5210). These gardens are just outside of town, and the entrance is across from Crocodile Bay. The whole project encompasses over 260 acres of botanical gardens, working permaculture gardens, and secondary forest. There are even a few platforms built high in the trees here and reached by climbing a ladder. A 2½-hour guided tour of the gardens costs $20, although you can wander the gardens yourself, with a self-guiding map, for $5.

For a real adventure, check in with **Psycho Tours ★★** (☎8353-8619; www.psychotours.com). These folks, who also call themselves Everyday Adventures, run a variety of adventure tours, but their signature combo trip features a free climb up (with a safety rope attached) the roots and trunks of a 200-foot-tall strangler fig. You can climb as high as your ability allows, but most try to reach a natural platform at around 18m (60 ft.), where you take a leap of faith into space and are belayed down by your guide. This is preceded by an informative hike through primary rainforest, often wading through a small river, and followed by a couple of rappels down jungle waterfalls, the highest of which is around 30m (100 ft.). You can do either one of the above adventures separately, but I recommend the 5- to 6-hour combo tour, which costs $120.

If you're interested in doing some **bill-fishing** or **deep-sea fishing,** you'll probably want to stay at or fish with **Crocodile Bay Lodge** (☎800/733-1115 in the U.S. and Canada, or 2735-5631 in Costa Rica; www.crocodilebay.com). This upscale fishing lodge is close to the Puerto Jiménez airstrip. Alternatively, you can check around the public dock for notices put up by people with charter boats. Rates can run between $400 and $2,400 for a full day, or between $150 and $900 for a half-day, depending on the boat, tackle, number of anglers, and fishing grounds.

If you want to learn to surf, contact **Pollo's Surf School ★** (☎8366-6559; rhoades_gretchen@hotmail.com), which is located near some excellent learning waves on Pan Dulce beach. A 2-hour lesson runs $55 per person.

To explore the rugged roads, trails, and beaches of this area by ATV or mountain bike, contact **Osa Discoveries** (☎2735-5260). **Osa Aventura**

(☎/fax **2735-5758** or 8830-9832; www.osaaventura.com), **Sol de Osa** (☎**2735-5702**; www.soldeosa.com), and **Tom Kayak's Osa Info** (☎**8838-2314**) are other local tour companies that offer a host of guided tours around the Osa Peninsula and into Corcovado National Park. Rates run between $35 and $120 depending upon group size and the tour or activity chosen.

Shopping

Jagua Arts & Craft Store ★★ (☎**2735-5267**) is near the airstrip, and is definitely worth a visit. Owner Karen Herrera has found excellent local and regional art and craft works, including some fine jewelry and blown glass. *Tip:* Many folks head to this store while waiting for their departing flight out of Puerto Jiménez. Be sure to give yourself enough time, as the store has a somewhat extensive collection.

Where to Stay in Puerto Jiménez

In addition to the places below, the **Lapa Nest Tree House** ★★ (☎**508/714-0622** in the U.S., or 8378-3013 in Costa Rica; www.treehouseincostarica.com) is a three-bedroom/two-bath concoction built up and around a giant Guanacaste tree in the midst of thick forest. Available for weekly rentals, this unique home is chock full of creative design touches.

VERY EXPENSIVE

Crocodile Bay Resort ★ Originally, and still primarily a sportfishing resort, this place also caters to other sorts of adventure travelers. The rooms are the best you'll find right in Puerto Jiménez, with tons of space and private balconies or verandas—try for a garden-facing second-floor unit. The hotel has excellent facilities and expansive grounds. In addition to a large modern fleet of fishing boats, with top-notch crew and equipment, they have a well-staffed activities and tour desk, and a large spa. The food and service here are also excellent.

Puerto Jiménez. ☎**800/733-1115** in the U.S. and Canada, or 2735-5631 in Costa Rica. www.crocodilebay.com. 40 units. $300 double. Rates include breakfast. A wide range of fishing and adventure-tour packages are available. AE, MC, V. **Amenities:** Restaurant; bar; Jacuzzi; outdoor swimming pool; large modern spa; watersports equipment rental. *In room:* A/C.

EXPENSIVE

Parrot Bay Village There's a small-resort feel to this collection of individual cabins—despite being just a short walk from town, it feels miles away. The smaller cabins are octagonal and have just one double bed, while the larger ones each feature a sleeping loft with a double and single bed above and a double bed below. Amenities include a small restaurant and bar, along with a large central deck with a view of the gulf and a pretty good sportfishing operation. The grounds include a semi-groomed trail through the mangroves. Perhaps the biggest plus here is the fact that the place sits on a pretty little patch of beach.

A.P. 91, Puerto Jiménez. ☎**866/551-2003** in U.S., or 2735-5180 in Costa Rica. Fax 2735-5568. www.parrotbayvillage.com. 9 units. $135 double. Rates include breakfast and local airport transfers. MC, V. **Amenities:** Restaurant; bar; watersports equipment rental and free kayak use. *In room:* A/C, hair dryer, no phone.

MODERATE

Agua Luna Agua Luna is located right at the foot of the town's public dock and backs up to a mangrove forest. The older rooms directly face the gulf across a fenced-in gravel parking area. The most surprising feature in each of these rooms is the bathroom, which includes both a shower and a tub facing a huge picture window that looks into the mangroves. There are two double beds in each room, and on the tiled veranda out front, you'll find hammocks for lounging. The newer rooms are a half-block away and are smaller and less attractive than those in the original building, although room nos. 4 and 5 in this building do overlook the mangroves.

In front of the public dock, Puerto Jiménez. 📞/fax **2735-5393.** 20 units. $60–$80 double. V. **Amenities:** Restaurant. *In room:* A/C, TV, minifridge.

INEXPENSIVE

In addition to the places listed below, you can camp or take advantage of some simple screened-in rooms at the beautiful **Herrera Botanical Gardens and Tent Camp** (📞**2735-5210**). Rates run around $12 to $15 per person to camp; it's $20 per person in a screened-in room, with access to a communal kitchen, bathroom, and shower facilities, and unlimited access to the trails and gardens. If you don't have your own tent, they can rent you one.

Cabinas Jiménez 🖌 Located right on the waterfront at the north end of the soccer field, this perennial budget favorite has improved with age. All of the rooms have air-conditioning, tile floors, hot-water showers, and hand-carved headboards and Guatemalan bedspreads on the beds. Some have little fridges and coffeemakers. Three units even have views of the water, with a broad shared veranda in front, and there's one private bungalow that's the choice room in the house. The wide range in prices, in fact, reflects the range in size and location of the rooms. But even the most basic standard room here is a good option.

Downtown, 50m (164 ft.) north of the soccer field, Puerto Jiménez, Puntarenas. 📞**2735-5090.** www.cabinasjimenez.com. 10 units. $50–$80 double. MC, V. *In room:* A/C, no phone, free Wi-Fi.

Where to Stay in Playa Plantanares

VERY EXPENSIVE

Iguana Lodge ★ This place has a variety of rooms and bungalows. The two-story casitas are their top option: These are set amid lush gardens just steps from the sand. Hardwood floors, bamboo furniture, and mosquito netting over orthopedic mattresses all add up to rustic tropical elegance. The lower units have delightful semi-outdoor garden showers, and all come with either a large covered balcony or veranda. Still, I prefer the second-floor rooms for their views and elevation. These folks also rent out a separate, private three-bedroom villa.

Playa Plantanares. 📞**8829-5865** or 8848-0752. Fax 2735-5436. www.iguanalodge.com. 19 units. $135 double club room; $310 casita double. Rates include breakfast. Rates of the casita include dinner as well. MC, V. **Amenities:** Restaurant; bar; watersports equipment rental. *In room:* No phone.

Where to Dine in Puerto Jiménez

In addition to the places listed below, I recommend the barbecue ribs, chicken, fish, and shrimp at **Barbs-B-Q** ★ (no phone), which is right downtown and

Puerto Jiménez.

managed by Barbara Burchkhardt, who used to run the excellent restaurant Jade Luna. You might also try the new **Sarpes** (☎ 2753-5373), next to the Bosque del Mar hotel, which serves up local seafood and other dishes done in a creative eclectic style.

For pizzas and homemade pastas, you should head to **Pizza Mail.it** (☎ 2753-5483), located next to the post office. You can also get pizzas and find the occasional sushi night at the open-air downtown Italian joint, **Il Giardino** (☎ 2735-5129).

Juanita's Mexican Bar & Grille ★ 🍴 MEXICAN This place offers good, hearty California-style Mexican food and seafood served up in a lively, convivial atmosphere. You can get fajitas with chicken, beef, fish, or even grilled vegetables. Juanita's also has pizza by the slice or pie, and will deliver, although I'm not sure how far out on the peninsula their drivers will go. There are nightly specials and a popular happy hour.

Downtown, Puerto Jiménez. ☎ **2735-5056.** Reservations not accepted. Main courses $4.80–$15. V. Daily 10am–midnight.

Soda Carolina 📷 COSTA RICAN Set in the center of the town's main street, and otherwise known as the "Bar, Restaurante y Cabinas Carolina," this is the town's main budget travelers' hangout and also serves as an unofficial information center. The walls are painted with colorful jungle and wildlife scenes. As for the fare, seafood is the way to go. There's good fried fish as well as a variety of *ceviche*. The black-bean soup is usually tasty, and the *casados* (plates of the day) are filling and cost around $4.30.

On the main street. ☎ **2735-5185.** Reservations not accepted. Main courses $3.50–$14. V. Daily 7am–10pm.

Where to Stay & Dine Around the Osa Peninsula

As with most of the lodges in Drake Bay, the accommodations listed in this section include three meals a day in their rates and do a large share of their bookings in package trips. Per-night rates are listed, but the price categories have been adjusted to take into account the fact that all meals are included. Ask about package rates if you plan to take several tours and stay awhile: They could save you money.

In addition to the lodges listed below, there are several other options, ranging from small bed-and-breakfasts to fully equipped home rentals. Surfers, in particular, might want to inquire into one of the several rental houses located close to the beach at Matapalo. Your best bet for alternative accommodations is to contact **Jimenez Hotels** (☎2735-5702; www.jimenezhotels.com), which also handles a host of house rentals around the area.

Finally, there's been a small boom of lodges out in Carate. In addition to the tent lodge listed below you can look into **La Leona Eco-Lodge** (☎2735-5705; www.laleonaecolodge.com), another tent camp option on the outskirts of the national park, and **Lookout Inn** (☎815/955-1520 in the U.S., or 2735-5431 in Costa Rica; www.lookout-inn.com), a more traditional lodge option right in Carate. Often used for yoga retreats, **Luna Lodge** ★ (☎888/409-8448 in the U.S., or 8380-5036; www.lunalodge.com) has luxurious rooms and private cabins with great views over the jungle, and they even have some permanent, large tents for more budget-conscious travelers. Among the various environmental and conservation causes she supports, the owner here is especially involved in White Hawk and Harpy Eagle monitoring and protection programs.

VERY EXPENSIVE

The following lodges are some of the best ecolodges Costa Rica has to offer, and most are pretty pricey. However, keep in mind that despite paying top dollar, there are no TVs, no in-room telephones, no air-conditioning, no discos, very limited shopping, and no paved roads. There are also no crowds and very few modern distractions.

Bosque del Cabo Rainforest Lodge ★★★ 💼 This secluded lodge is my favorite spot in this neck of the woods. The large individual cabins are attractively furnished, have wooden decks or verandas to catch the ocean views, and are set amid beautiful gardens. The deluxe cabins come with king-size beds and slightly larger deck space. The Congo cabin is my choice for its spectacular view of the sunrise from your bed. All cabins have indoor bathrooms; while tiled showers are set outdoors amid flowering heliconia and ginger. About half of the units also have outdoor bathtubs.

One trail leads to a jungle waterfall, and several others wind through the rainforests of the lodge's 260-hectare (650-acre) private reserve. If you're too lazy to hike down to the beach, there's a beautiful pool by the main lodge. Other attractions include a canopy platform 36m (118 ft.) up a Manu tree, reached along a 90m (295-ft.) zip line, as well as a bird- and wildlife-watching rancho set beside a little lake. These folks also rent out two separate, fully equipped houses that are quite popular, along with a couple of cabins set inland by their gardens. In addition to conservation and reforestation efforts, the owners here are actively involved in a host of local environmental and educational causes.

Osa Peninsula (mailing address: Interlink 528, P.O. Box 02-5635, Miami, FL 33102). ☎/fax **2735-5206** or 8389-2846. www.bosquedelcabo.com. 10 units. $350–$390 double. Rates include 3 meals daily and taxes. $25 round-trip transportation from Puerto Jiménez. **Amenities:** Restaurant; bar; midsize pool; surfboard rental. *In room:* No phone.

El Remanso ★★ This collection of individual cabins and two-story units is set in a deep patch of primary forest. The best view of the ocean, over and through thick forest, can be had from the two-story deluxe La Vanilla unit, which can be rented whole or split into two separate one-bedroom affairs. The upstairs room here is the best in the house, with plenty of space, varnished wood floors, and a spacious balcony. All of the private cabins feature polished cement floors, a queen-size bed, and separate fold-down futon. If you want an individual cabin, Azul de Mar has the best view. A host of adventure activities are available, including tree climbing, waterfall rappelling, and a zip-line canopy tour. They also have a large, open-air yoga platform, and frequently host yoga groups. For chilling out, there's a small oval pool set in a stone deck area with great views to the ocean. Breakfasts can be taken on a platform high atop a rainforest tree. The owners are committed to environmental protection. In fact, Joel and Belen Stewart met aboard the Greenpeace vessel *Rainbow Warrior,* which Joel captained for a number of years.

Osa Peninsula. (**2735-5569.** Fax 2735-5126. www.elremanso.com. 14 units. $320–$370 double. Rates include 3 meals daily and all taxes. MC, V. **Amenities:** Restaurant; bar; small outdoor pool. *In room:* No phone.

Lapa Ríos ★★ This is one of Costa Rica's pioneering ecolodges. Although half of a duplex, each spacious room is totally private and oriented toward the view, with open screen walls and a high-peaked thatch roof. A large deck and small tropical garden, complete with a hammock and outdoor shower, more than double the living space. There's an indoor shower as well, which features screen walls letting out on the view, so it's not all that different from being outdoors. **Note:** It's a bit of a hike back and forth from the main lodge to the farthest rooms.

The centerpiece of the lodge's large open-air dining room is a 15m (49-ft.) spiral staircase that leads to an observation deck tucked beneath the peak of the building's thatch roof. Just off the main lodge is a pretty little pool with great views. The beach, however, is a good 15-minute hike away. Lapa Ríos is surrounded by its own 400-hectare (988-acre) private rainforest reserve, which is home to scarlet macaws, toucans, parrots, hummingbirds, monkeys, and myriad other wildlife.

Osa Peninsula (mailing address: SJO-706, Box 025216, Miami, FL 33102). (**2735-5130.** Fax 2735-5179. www.laparios.com. 16 units. $325 double. Rates include 3 meals daily, round-trip transportation btw. the lodge and Puerto Jiménez, and taxes. Discounts for children 10 and under. AE, MC, V. **Amenities:** Restaurant; bar; small outdoor pool; all rooms smoke-free. *In room:* No phone.

Puerto Jiménez After Dark

If you're looking for any after-tours action in Puerto Jiménez, I recommend you start off at either **Juanita's Mexican Bar & Grille** or the **Soda Carolina.** You also might try **Sarpes,** or take a walk down along the water to see if anything is happening at **The Palms** ((**2735-5012**).

GOLFITO: GATEWAY TO THE GOLFO DULCE

87km (54 miles) S of Palmar Norte; 337km (209 miles) S of San José

Despite being the largest and most important city in Costa Rica's southern zone, Golfito, in and of itself, is neither a popular nor a particularly inviting tourist destination. In its prime, this was a major banana port, but following years of rising taxes, falling prices, and labor disputes, United Fruit pulled out in 1985. Things may change in the future, as rumors perennially abound about the potential construction of an international airport nearby, major marina right on the bay, or large-scale tuna farm just offshore. But for the moment, none of these megaprojects have gotten off the drawing board.

That said, Golfito is still a major sportfishing center and a popular gateway to a slew of nature lodges spread along the quiet waters, isolated bays, and lush rainforests of the Golfo Dulce, or "Sweet Gulf." In 1998, much of the rainforest bordering the Golfo Dulce was officially declared the **Piedras Blancas National Park ★★**, which includes 12,000 hectares (29,640 acres) of primary forests, as well as newly protected secondary forests and pasturelands.

Golfito is set on the north side of the Golfo Dulce, at the foot of lush green mountains. The setting alone gives Golfito the potential to be one of the most attractive cities in the country. However, the areas around the municipal park and public dock are somewhat seedy and the "downtown" section is quite run-down. Still, if you go a little bit farther along the bay, you come to the old United Fruit Company housing. Here you'll find well-maintained wooden houses painted bright colors and surrounded by neatly manicured gardens. Toucans are commonly sighted. It's all very lush and green and clean—an altogether different picture from that painted by most port towns in this country. When a duty-free zone was opened here, these old homes experienced a minor renaissance and several were converted into small hotels. Ticos come here in droves on weekends and throughout December to take advantage of cheap prices on name-brand goods and clothing at the duty-free zone; sometimes all these shoppers make finding a room difficult.

Essentials

GETTING THERE & DEPARTING By Plane: Sansa (☎877/767-2672 in the U.S. and Canada, or 2290-4100 in Costa Rica; www.flysansa.com) has four daily flights to Golfito, with the first one departing San José's Juan Santamaría

Golfito shoreline.

International Airport at 5:45am. The latest flight leaves at 3:15pm during the high season. The schedule is slightly reduced in the low season. Trip duration is 1 hour; the fare is $114 each way. Sansa flights return to San José daily beginning at 7am, with the last flight departing at 1:03pm in the low season, and 4:30pm in the high season.

Nature Air (✆800/235-9272 in the U.S. and Canada, or 2299-6000; www.natureair.com) has flights to Golfito departing daily from Tobías Bolaños International Airport in Pavas at 6am and 3:15pm. Flight duration is 50 minutes on the direct morning flight, and 70 minutes on the later flight, which stops first in Drake Bay; the fare is $124 each way.

By Car: Take the Interamerican Highway east out of San José (through San Pedro and Cartago) and continue south on this road. In about 3 hours, you'll reach San Isidro de El General. Although you can continue on the Interamerican Highway all the way south, it is currently faster, smoother, and safer to turn off in San Isidro and head to Dominical, picking up the Southern Highway or Costanera Sur in Dominical. From here it's a fast and smooth shot down to Palmar Norte, where you meet up again with the Interamerican Highway. When you get to Río Claro, you'll notice a couple of gas stations and quite a bit of activity. Turn right here and follow the signs to Golfito. If you end up at the Panama border, you've missed the turnoff by about 32km (20 miles). The complete drive takes about 6 hours. On most of the Interamerican Highway, you'll have to contend with potholes of sometimes gargantuan proportions. Just remember, if the road is suddenly smooth and in great shape, you can bet that around the next bend there will be a bottomless pothole that you can't swerve around. Take it easy.

By Bus: Express buses leave San José daily at 7am and 3:30pm from the **Tracopa** station on the Plaza Viquez at Calle 5 between avenidas 18 and 20 (✆2221-4214). The trip takes 7½ hours; the fare is $7.50. Buses depart Golfito for San José daily at 5am and 1:30pm from the bus station near the municipal dock.

By Boat: Several speedboats work as boat taxis between Golfito and Puerto Jiménez. The fare is $5, and the ride takes a little under 30 minutes. These boats leave five or six times throughout the day, or whenever they fill up, beginning at around 5am and finishing up at around 5pm. Ask at the *muellecito* (public dock) for current schedules.

There is also a daily passenger launch. This slower boat takes 1½ hours, and the fare is $3. The ferry leaves the public dock in Golfito at 6am for Puerto Jiménez. The return trip to Golfito leaves Puerto Jiménez's municipal dock at 11:30am.

It's also possible to charter a water taxi in Golfito for the trip across to Puerto Jiménez. You'll have to pay between $40 and $80 for an entire launch, some of which can carry up to 12 people.

GETTING AROUND Taxis are plentiful in Golfito, and are constantly cruising the main road, all the way from the entrance of town to the duty-free port. A taxi ride anywhere in town should cost around $1. Local buses also ply this loop. The fare for the bus is 15¢.

If you drive down here and head out to one of the remote lodges on the gulf, you can leave your car at Samoa del Sur (see "Where to Stay," below) for around $10 per day.

If you can't get to your next destination by boat, bus, commuter airline, or car, **Alfa Romeo Air Charters** (☎2735-5353 or 2735-5112; www.alfaromeoair.com) runs charters to most of the nearby destinations, including Carate, Drake Bay, Sirena, and Puerto Jiménez. A five-passenger plane should cost around $200 to $400 one-way, depending on your destination.

FAST FACTS To avoid the bureaucracy and frequently long lines at the banks, you can **exchange money** at the gas station, or "La Bomba," in the middle of town. A **laundromat** on the upper street of the small downtown charges around $3 for an average-size load.

Exploring the Area

You won't find any really good swimming beaches right in Golfito. The closest spot is **Playa Cacao,** a short boat ride away, although this is not one of my favorite beaches in Costa Rica. You should be able to get a ride here for around $5 per person from one of the boat taxis down at the public docks. However, you might have to negotiate hard because these boatmen like to gouge tourists whenever possible. If you really want some beach time, I recommend staying at one of the hotels in the Golfo Dulce (see "Where to Stay," below) or heading over to **Playa Zancudo** (see "Playa Zancudo," later in this chapter).

About a 20-minute drive over a rough dirt road from Golfito will bring you to the **Avellana Waterfall & Trails** (☎8877-4004). Admission to the site costs $5 and includes a 2-hour guided hike through the forests and a visit to a beautiful forest waterfall, with several refreshing pools perfect for swimming. A taxi should charge around $10 for the ride, one-way. Horseback riding is available, and they even have a zip-line canopy tour. Camping is also allowed, and meals are served by the friendly owners of the land, the local Gamba family. However, for most folks, the best way to visit this site is to go as part of an organized trip with **Land Sea Tours** (☎2775-1614).

The waters off Golfito also offer some of the best **sportfishing** in Costa Rica. If you'd like to try hooking into a possible world-record marlin or sailfish, contact **Banana Bay Marina** (☎800/245-1635 in the U.S. and Canada, or 2775-0838 in Costa Rica; www.bananabaymarina.com).   These folks have a full-service marina, a few waterside rooms for guests, and a fleet of sportfishing boats and captains. A full-day fishing trip costs between $800 and $2,000. You can also try the **Zancudo Lodge** (☎800/854-8791 in the U.S. and Canada, or 2776-0008 in Costa Rica; www.thezancudo lodge.com), which is based in nearby Playa Zancudo. The lodge can arrange pickup in Golfito, and I prefer the lodgings and scenery

Sportfishing vessel in Golfito.

Wilson Botanical Gardens.

out in Zancudo to what you'll find in Golfito.

There's no steady charter fleet here, but itinerant sailors often set up shop for a season or so. If you're looking to charter a sailboat, you should check with **Banana Bay Marina** or **Las Gaviotas Hotel** (p. 427).

About 30 minutes by boat out of Golfito, you'll find **Casa Orquídeas ★★**, a private botanical garden lovingly built and maintained by Ron and Trudy MacAllister. Most hotels in the area offer trips here, including transportation and a 2-hour tour of the gardens. During the tour, you'll sample a load of fresh fruits picked right off the trees. If your hotel can't, you can book a trip out of Golfito with **Land Sea Tours** (**℡2775-1614**). The entrance and guided tour is only $5 per person, but it will cost you between $50 and $60 to hire a boat for the round-trip ride.

If you have a serious interest in botanical gardens or bird-watching, consider an excursion to **Wilson Botanical Gardens ★★★** at the Las Cruces Biological Station (**℡2524-0607** in San José, or 2773-4004 at the gardens; www.threepaths.co.cr), just outside the town of San Vito, about 65km (40 miles) to the northeast. The gardens are owned and maintained by the Organization for Tropical Studies and include more than 7,000 species of tropical plants from around the world. Among the plants grown here are many endangered species, which make the gardens of interest to botanical researchers. Despite the scientific aspects of the gardens, there are so many beautiful and unusual flowers amid the manicured grounds that even a neophyte can't help but be astounded. All this luscious flora has attracted at least 360 species of birds. A full-day guided walk, including lunch, costs $41; a half-day guided walk costs $22. If you'd like to stay the night here, there are 12 well-appointed rooms. Rates, which include one guided walk, three meals, and taxes, run around $84 per person; you definitely need to make reservations if you want to spend the night, and it's usually a good idea to make a reservation for a simple day visit and hike. The gardens are about 6km (3¾ miles) before San Vito. To get here from Golfito, drive out to the Interamerican Highway and continue south toward Panama. In Ciudad Neily, turn north. A taxi from Golfito should cost around $40 each way.

Where to Stay

IN GOLFITO

Expensive

Casa Roland Marina Resort ★ If you want a plush room in Golfito, this new miniresort is probably your best bet. Located in the old banana company housing area, near the airport and duty-free zone, this place is geared equally towards business travelers, vacationers, and sport fishermen. However, the hotel is several blocks from the water, so I find the use of "marina" in the title a bit misleading. Still, the rooms are large and well equipped, with interesting art works and comfortable, heavy wood furnishings. The standard or corporate rooms only come with ceiling fans, and in this climate, that's a real handicap, so you'll want to upgrade to a luxury room or suite, which have air-conditioning.

Old American zone, near the duty-free zone, Golfito. ☎2775-0180. Fax 2775-3406. www.fishingmarinaresort.com. 53 units. $125–$165 double; $215–$260 suite. Rates include continental breakfast. AE, MC, V. **Amenities:** Restaurant; bar; midsize outdoor pool; room service. *In room:* A/C (in some), TV, free Internet, minibar.

Moderate

Centro Turístico Samoa del Sur This is the best-located hotel on the waterfront, and it features a popular restaurant and bar. The rooms are spacious and clean. Varnished wood headboards complement two firm and comfortable queen-size beds. With red-tile floors, modern bathrooms, and carved-wood doors, the rooms all share a long, covered veranda that's set perpendicular to the gulf, so the views aren't great. If you want to watch the water, you're better off grabbing a table at the restaurant, or walking out to the docks at their small marina. The hotel also has a swimming pool and a volleyball court that are popular with locals using it for a daily fee, as well as a large gift shop with an extensive shell-and-coral collection that they bill as a museum.

100m (328 ft.) north of the public dock, Golfito. ☎2775-0233. Fax 2775-0573. www.samoadelsur.com. 14 units. $60–$95 double. AE, MC, V. **Amenities:** Restaurant; bar; midsize outdoor pool; room service; kayak rentals. *In room:* A/C, TV.

Hotel Sierra This resort-style hotel is set right beside the airstrip, within walking distance to the duty-free zone. The Hotel Sierra was originally built as a business-class option geared toward middle-class Ticos in town to shop. It's currently trying to sell itself as a sportfishing and ecotourism lodge. The Sierra is constructed to be as open and breezy as possible, and covered walkways connect the hotel's various buildings. The rooms are large and have windows on two sides to let in plenty of light. The swimming pool is the largest and most appealing in town, and the restaurant serves good, affordable international fare. One of the biggest draws here is the small casino, which is popular with guests and locals alike.

Beside the airstrip (A.P. 37), Golfito. ☎2775-0666. Fax 2775-0506. www.hotelsierra.com. 72 units. $80 double. AE, MC, V. **Amenities:** Restaurant; bar; casino; midsize outdoor pool; room service. *In room:* A/C, TV.

Inexpensive

El Gran Ceibo 🎣 This little motel-like option at the entrance to Golfito is a good choice. It's named after the giant ceibo tree you'll see standing over it near the entrance. The rooms are clean, bright, comfortable, and relatively spacious.

All feature small verandas with some sitting chairs. About half of them come with air-conditioning and cable TV; although you pay more for these, they're still quite affordable. The others have just fans and cold-water showers. There are nice views over the gulf from the grounds and some of the rooms.

On the left, just as you enter Golfito. **2775-0403.** Fax 2775-2303. www.hotel-elgranceibo.com. 27 units. $20–$50 double. AE, MC, V. **Amenities:** Restaurant; bar; small outdoor pool. *In room:* A/C (in some units), TV (in some units), no phone.

Las Gaviotas Hotel Situated just at the start of Golfito proper—a short taxi or bus ride from the "downtown"—Las Gaviotas has long been a popular choice. The waterfront location is the hotel's greatest asset. There is a long pier that attracts the sailboat and sportfishing crowd. For landlubbers, there's a small pool built out near the gulf. Guest rooms all face the ocean, and although they're quite large, they're spartan and show their age. There are small, tiled patios in front of all the rooms, and the cabanas have little kitchens. A large, open-air restaurant looks over the pool to the gulf; it's a great view, but the food leaves much to be desired. Just around the corner is a large, open-air bar.

A.P. 12-8201, Golfito. **2775-0062.** Fax 2775-0544. 18 units, 3 cabanas. $50–$75 double; $95 cabana. AE, DC, MC, V. **Amenities:** Restaurant; bar; small pool; room service 7am–10pm. *In room:* A/C, TV.

WHERE TO STAY FARTHER AFIELD ON THE GOLFO DULCE

The lodges listed here are located on the shores of the Golfo Dulce. There are no roads into this area, so you must get to the lodges by boat. I recommend that you have firm reservations when visiting this area, so your transportation should be arranged. If worse comes to worst, you can hire a boat taxi at the *muellecito* (little dock), which is located on the water just beyond the gas station, or "La Bomba," in Golfito, for between $20 and $60, depending on which lodge you are staying at.

Both of the below hotels are extremely committed to environmental protection and education. Another excellent option, but with an emphasis on luxury, is **Villas Corcovado ★ (2296-8597;** www.villacorcovado.com).

Golfo Dulce Lodge ★ This small, Swiss-run lodge is just down the beach from Casa Orquídeas, about a 30-minute boat ride from Golfito. The five separate cabins and main lodge buildings are all set back away from the beach about 500m (1,640 ft.) into the forest. The cabins are spacious and airy, and feature either a twin and a double bed or three single beds. In addition, there are large bathrooms, solar hot-water showers, a small sitting area, and a porch with a hammock. The rooms are all comfortable and well appointed, and even feature private verandas, but they are not nearly as nice as the cabins. Meals are served in a two-story open rancho with an observation deck, located beside the small swimming pool. The lodge offers jungle hikes, river trips, and other guided tours. This lodge has been granted "4 Leaves" by the CST Sustainable Tourism program and is a member of the International Ecotourism Society.

Golfo Dulce (A.P. 137-8201, Golfito). **8821-5398.** Fax 2775-0573. www.golfodulcelodge.com. 8 units. $285–$345 per person double occupancy for 4-day/3-night stay. Rates include 3 meals daily and taxes. Add $25 per person for transportation to and from Golfito. No credit cards. **Amenities:** Restaurant; bar; small outdoor pool. *In room:* No phone.

Playa Nicuesa Rainforest Lodge ★★★ 🎁 Set on its own private bay, with a large stretch of black-sand beach, this is the most impressive lodge along the shores of the Golfo Dulce. While the four Mango Manor rooms are certainly very cozy, you'll definitely want to snag one of the individual cabins. These are all set amid dense forest and are made almost entirely of wood, with large open-air showers, private verandas, and a true sense of being in touch with nature. The main lodge building is a huge, open-air affair with an abundance of varnished wood and a relaxed inviting vibe that induces one to grab a book, board game, or chat with other guests. There's an excellent network of trails on the lodge's 66 hectares (165 acres), and a whole host of tours and activities are offered. The owners are dedicated environmentalists and have actively implemented a series of green and sustainable practices. Meals are served family-style and are inventive and tasty.

Golfo Dulce (A.P. 56, Golfito). ☏**866/504-8116** in the U.S., or 2258-8250 in Costa Rica. Fax 2735-5043. www.nicuesalodge.com. 8 units. $360–$400 double. Rates include all meals, taxes, and transfers to and from either Golfito or Puerto Jiménez. A 2-night minimum stay is required. Closed Oct 1–Nov 15. AE, MC, V. **Amenities:** Restaurant; bar; watersports equipment. *In room:* No phone.

Where to Dine

Bilge Bar, Restaurant & Grill ★ INTERNATIONAL/SEAFOOD This open-air restaurant attached to the Banana Bay Marina is the best restaurant in Golfito. The seafood is fresh and excellently prepared, but you can also get hearty steaks and great burgers. I personally recommend the fresh-fish burger. Breakfasts are also hearty and well-prepared. Grab a table toward the water and watch the boats bob up and down while you enjoy your meal.

At the Banana Bay Marina, on the waterfront in downtown Golfito. ☏**2775-0838.** Main courses $6–$18. AE, MC, V. Daily 7am–9pm.

Samoa del Sur INTERNATIONAL This large, open-air place features an extensive menu of Continental and French dishes (the owners are French), including such specialties as onion soup, salade niçoise, filet of fish meunière, and, in a nod to their southern neighbor, paella. There are also pizzas and spaghetti. In addition to the food, the giant rancho houses a pool table, several high-quality dartboards, and two big-screen TVs. The bar sometimes stays open all night.

100m (328 ft.) north of the public dock. ☏**2775-0233.** Reservations not accepted. Main courses $6–$28. AE, MC, V. Daily 7am–midnight.

Golfito After Dark

Golfito is a rough-and-tumble port town, and it pays to be careful here after dark. Right in town, about 1½ blocks inland and uphill from the *muellecito*, **Latitude 8** is the most popular spot. Another popular, if somewhat unlikely, spot is **La Pista** bar, located near the airstrip. Most folks stick pretty close to their hotel bar and restaurant. Of these, the bar/restaurants at **Las Gaviotas** and **Samoa del Sur** are, by far, the liveliest. If you're feeling lucky, you can head to the **casino** at the **Hotel Sierra.**

PLAYA ZANCUDO ★

19km (12 miles) S of Golfito by boat; 35km (22 miles) S of Golfito by road

Playa Zancudo is one of Costa Rica's most isolated and undeveloped beach destinations. If you're looking for a remote and low-key beach getaway, it's hard to beat Zancudo. It's pretty far from just about everything, and there are relatively few places to stay, so it's virtually never crowded. However, the small number of hotel rooms to be had means that the better ones, such as those listed here, can fill up fast in the high season. The beach itself is long and flat, and because it's protected from the full force of Pacific waves, it's one of the calmest beaches on this coast and relatively good for swimming, especially toward the northern end. There's a splendid view across the Golfo Dulce, and the sunsets are hard to beat.

Essentials

GETTING THERE By Plane: The nearest airport is in Golfito. See "Golfito: Gateway to the Golfo Dulce," earlier in this chapter, for details. To get from the airport to Playa Zancudo, your best bets are by boat or taxi.

By Boat: Water taxis can be hired in Golfito to make the trip out to Playa Zancudo; however, trips depend on the tides and weather conditions. When the tide is high, the boats take a route through the mangroves. This is by far the calmest and most scenic way to get to Zancudo. When the tide is low, they must stay out in the gulf, which can get choppy at times. It costs around $15 to $20 per person for a water taxi, with a minimum charge of $40. If you can round up any sort of group, be sure to negotiate. The ride takes about 30 minutes.

Also, there's a passenger launch from the *muellecito* (little dock) in Golfito, which normally leaves daily at around noon. Because the schedule sometimes changes, be sure to ask in town about current departure times. The trip lasts 40 minutes; the fare is $5. The *muellecito* is next to the town's principal gas station, "La Bomba."

If you plan ahead, you can call **Zancudo Boat Tours (☎2776-0012; www.loscocos.com)** and arrange for pickup in Golfito or Puerto Jiménez.

The trip costs $20 per person each way from Golfito or Puerto Jiménez, with a $50 minimum from Golfito and $60 minimum from Puerto Jiménez. Zancudo Boat Tours also includes land transportation to your hotel in Playa Zancudo—a very nice perk because there are so few taxis in town.

By Car: If you've got a four-wheel-drive vehicle, you can make it out to Zancudo even in the rainy season. To get here, follow the directions for driving to Golfito, but don't go all the way into town. The turnoff for playas Zancudo and Pavones is at

Fishing vessel at Playa Zancudo.

El Rodeo, about 4km (2½ miles) outside of Golfito, on the road in from the Interamerican Highway. About 20 minutes past the turnoff, you'll have to wait and take a small diesel-operated crank ferry. The fare is $1 per vehicle. The ferry generally operates from around 5am until 8pm; however, the hours can be erratic. Moreover, at very low tides the ferry can't run, so sometimes you must wait a couple of hours. After the ferry, you should follow the few signs and the flow of traffic (if there is any) or stick to the most worn route when in doubt.

When the ferry's not running, or waiting for the tide to come in, there's an alternative route from Paso Canoas (at the border), via the towns of La Cuesta and Laurel. This route meets the route mentioned above at the small village of Conte.

A four-wheel-drive **taxi** costs around $45 from Golfito. It takes about 1 hour when the road is in good condition, and about 2 hours when it's not. For info on getting here from San José, see p. 60.

By Bus: It's possible to get to Zancudo by bus, but I highly recommend coming by boat from Golfito, or your own car. If you insist, you can catch one of the Pavones buses in front of the gas station "La Bomba" in downtown Golfito and get off in the village of Conte. In theory, a Zancudo-bound bus should be waiting. However, this is not always the case, and you may have to wait, hitchhike, or spring for a cab, if any can be found. The entire trip takes about 3 hours; the fare is $3.

DEPARTING The public launch to Golfito leaves daily at 7am from the dock near the school, in the center of Zancudo. You can also arrange a water taxi back to Golfito, but it's best to work with your hotel owner and make a reservation at least 1 day in advance. **Zancudo Boat Tours** will take you for $20 per person, with a $50 minimum. Zancudo will also take you to **Pavones** or the **Osa Peninsula.** It costs the same $20 per person, but there's a minimum charge of $60. The bus to Golfito leaves Zancudo each morning at 5:30am. You can catch the bus anywhere along the main road.

ORIENTATION Zancudo is a long, narrow peninsula (sometimes only 90m/295 ft. or so wide) at the mouth of the Río Colorado. On one side is the beach; on the other is a mangrove swamp. There is only one road that runs the length of the beach, and along this road, spread out over several kilometers of long, flat beach, you'll find the hotels I mention here. It's about a 20-minute walk from the public dock near the school to the popular Cabinas Sol y Mar.

What to See & Do
(Or How Not to Do Anything)

The main activity at Zancudo is relaxing, and people take it seriously. There are hammocks at almost every lodge, and if you bring a few good books, you can spend quite a number of hours swinging slowly in the tropical breezes. The beach along Zancudo is great for swimming. It's generally a little calmer on the northern end and gets rougher (good for bodysurfing) as you head south. There are a couple of bars and even a disco, but visitors are most likely to spend their time just hanging out at their hotel or in restaurants meeting like-minded folks, reading a

Blue-crowned motmot.

good book, or playing board games. If you want to take a horseback ride on the beach, ask at your hotel; they should be able to arrange it for you.

Susan and Andrew Robertson, who run Cabinas Los Cocos, also operate **Zancudo Boat Tours** (℡2776-0012; www.loscocos.com), which offers snorkeling trips, kayaking tours, trips to the Casa Orquídeas Botanical Garden, hikes on the Osa peninsula, a trip up the Río Coto to watch birds and wildlife, and more. Tour prices are $50 to $75 per person per tour, with discounts available for larger groups.

For fishing, ask at your hotel, or contact the **Zancudo Lodge** (see below). A full day of fishing with lunch and beer should cost between $500 and $1,600 per boat.

Because there's a mangrove swamp directly behind the beach, mosquitoes and sand flies can be a problem when the winds die down, so be sure to bring insect repellent.

Where to Stay

If you're planning on an extended stay, there are quite a few fully equipped beach houses for rent. Once again, Susan and Andrew at **Los Cocos** (℡2776-0012; www.loscocos.com) are your best bet for lining up one of these houses.

VERY EXPENSIVE

The Zancudo Lodge ★★ Primarily a fishing lodge, this hotel is located at the north end of Zancudo, and is, by far, the most luxurious option around. All of the rooms look out onto a bright green lawn of soft grass and the small swimming pool and Jacuzzi; the beach is just a few steps beyond. Most of the rooms are in a long two-story building and feature tile floors, clean, modern bathrooms, and small verandas. There are four suites that have separate sitting rooms, hardwood floors, and more space. The lodge offers many different types of fishing excursions and packages, and boasts more than 50 world-record catches. This place is still sometimes called Roy's Zancudo Lodge, although Roy sold the place back in 2006.

Playa Zancudo (A.P. 41, Golfito). ℡800/854-8791 in the U.S., or 2776-0008 in Costa Rica. Fax 2776-0011. www.thezancudolodge.com. 26 units. $185 per person nonfishing; $400–$500 including full-day fishing. Rates are per person double occupancy and include all meals, drinks (alcoholic and carbonated), and taxes. Multiday packages available. V. **Amenities:** Restaurant; bar; Jacuzzi; pool. *In room:* A/C, TV, hair dryer, minibar.

MODERATE

Cabinas Los Cocos ★ If you've ever pondered throwing it all away, downsizing, and moving to the beach, these cabins are a good choice for a trial run. Four individual cabins are set beneath palm trees just a few meters from the beach. Two of them served as banana-plantation housing in a former life, until they were salvaged and moved here. These wood houses have big verandas and

> ### Park It
>
> If you drive down to Golfito, you can leave your car at Samoa del Sur (see "Where to Stay," above) and take one of the waterborne routes mentioned above. They charge around $10 per day, and the lot is very secure.

bedrooms, and large eat-in kitchens. Bathrooms are down a few steps in back and have hot water. The newer cabins also offer plenty of space, small kitchenettes, and a private veranda, as well as comfortable sleeping lofts. The owners, Susan and Andrew Robertson, run Zancudo Boat Tours, so if you want to do some exploring or need a ride into Golfito or Puerto Jiménez, they're the folks to see. Finally, these folks also rent out several wonderful beach houses around Zancudo.

Playa Zancudo (A.P. 88, Golfito). ☎/fax **2776-0012.** www.loscocos.com. 4 units. $60 double. Weekly discounts available. No credit cards. *In room:* Kitchenette, no phone.

INEXPENSIVE

Cabinas Sol y Mar ★ 🏖 This friendly owner-run establishment is one of the most popular lodgings in Zancudo. There are two individual bungalows and two rooms in a duplex building with a shared veranda. I prefer the individual rooms for their privacy. The bathrooms in these have unusual showers that feature a tiled platform set amid smooth river rocks. There's also a small budget cabin that is quite a good deal, as well as a fully equipped house for longer stays. You can even camp here for a few bucks per night. All of the options are just steps away from the sand. The hotel's open-air restaurant is one of the best and most popular places to eat in Zancudo.

Playa Zancudo (A.P. 87-8201, Golfito). ☎**2776-0014.** www.zancudo.com. 6 units. $25–$45 double. MC, V. **Amenities:** Restaurant; bar. *In room:* No phone, free Wi-Fi.

Where to Dine

In addition to the place listed below, you might try the tasty Italian meals at **Restaurante Macondo** (☎2776-0157) or **Alberto's Puerta Negra** (☎2776-0181). And if you want basic Tico fare and some local company, head to **Soda Sussy** (☎2776-0107) or **Soda Katherine** (☎2776-0124).

Finally, for a good breakfast, lunch, or dinner, or perhaps just a midday ice-cream treat, check out the little open-air cafe at **Oceanos Cabinas ★** (☎2776-0921; www.oceanocabinas.com).

Sol y Mar ★★ 🏖 INTERNATIONAL/SEAFOOD This is the best and most popular restaurant in Playa Zancudo. The reasonably priced menu is heavy on seafood, but features some items you won't find at most places in town, including thick-cut pork chops in a teriyaki sauce. The fresh seared tuna is always excellent, as are the twice-weekly barbecues on Monday and Friday. This is also my top choice for breakfast—the breakfast burrito should get you through most of the day. A regular horseshoe tournament takes place on Sundays throughout the high season, and there's free Wi-Fi available at the bar and restaurant.

At Cabinas Sol y Mar. ☎**2776-0014.** Main courses $3.50–$15. MC, V. Daily 7am–9pm.

PLAYA PAVONES: A SURFER'S MECCA ★

40km (25 miles) S of Golfito

Hailed as the world's longest rideable left point break, Pavones is a legendary destination for surfing. It takes around 1.8m (6 ft.) of swell to get this wave cranking, but when the surf's up, you're in for a long, long ride—so long, in fact, that it's much easier to walk back through town to where the wave is breaking than to paddle back. The swells are most consistent during the rainy season, but you're likely to find surfers here year-round. Locals tend to be pretty possessive around here (both the waves and local properties have engendered bitter disputes), so don't be surprised if you receive a cool welcome.

Other than surfing, nothing much goes on here; however, the surrounding rainforests are quite nice, and the beaches feature some rocky coves and points that give Pavones a bit more visual appeal than Zancudo. If you're feeling energetic, you can go for a horseback ride or hike into the rainforests that back up this beach town, or stroll south on the beaches that stretch toward Punta Banco and beyond, all the way to the Panamanian border. This is a forgotten and isolated destination catering almost exclusively to backpackers. So be prepared, Pavones is a tiny village with few amenities, and most of the accommodations are quite basic.

Essentials

GETTING THERE & DEPARTING By Plane: The nearest airport with regularly scheduled flights is in Golfito (p. 422). See "By Car" and "By Bus," below, for how to get to Pavones from the Golfito airport. There is a private strip at Tiskita Jungle Lodge (see below). Depending on space, you might be able to arrange transportation to Pavones on one of its charter flights even if you are not staying there.

Watching the surf in Pavones.

By Car: If you've got a four-wheel-drive vehicle, you can make it out to Pavones even in the rainy season. To get here, follow the directions for driving to Golfito, but don't go all the way into town. The turnoff for playas Zancudo and Pavones is at El Rodeo, about 4km (2½ miles) outside of Golfito, on the road in from the Interamerican Highway. About 20 minutes past the turnoff, you'll have to wait and take a small diesel-operated crank ferry. The fare is $1 per vehicle. The ferry generally operates from around 5am until 8pm; however, the hours can be erratic. Moreover, at very low tides the ferry can't run, so sometimes you must wait a couple of hours. A four-wheel-drive taxi from Golfito to Pavones will cost between $50 and $60. It takes around 2 hours.

When the ferry's not running, or waiting for the tide to come in, there's an alternative route from Paso Canoas (at the border), via the towns of La Cuesta and Laurel. This route meets the route mentioned above at the small village of Conte.

By Bus: There are two daily buses (☎2775-0365) to Pavones from Golfito at 10am and 3pm. Trip duration is 2½ hours; the fare is $3. Buses to Golfito depart Pavones daily at 5:30am and 12:30pm. This is a very remote destination, and the bus schedule is subject to change, so it always pays to check in advance.

ORIENTATION You can now find an Internet connection at **Esquina del Mar** in the heart of the village. If there are no waves, or you want some other form of exercise, check in with the folks at **Shooting Star Yoga** (☎8393-6982; www.yogapavones.com).

Where to Stay & Dine

Right in Pavones, several very basic lodges cater to itinerant surfers by renting rooms for between $10 and $20 per night for a double room; most take walk-in reservations since they don't have phones. There are also a couple of *sodas* where you can get Tico meals. The most popular spot for both cheap meals and cheap rooms is **Esquina del Mar** (☎2776-2023), which is right on the beach's edge, in front of the fattest part of the surf break. However, for in-town lodgings, I prefer **Mira Olas** (☎8393-7742; www.miraolas.com), about 2 blocks uphill from the soccer field.

For better and more healthy meals, I recommend **Café de la Suerte** ★ (☎8879-0302 or 2776-2388; www.cafedelasuerte.com), a lively little joint located across from Esquina del Mar that serves breakfasts and lunches and specializes in vegetarian items, freshly baked goods, and fresh-fruit smoothies. These folks also serve dinner during the high season, and rent out a cozy A/C-equipped cabin.

You can also check out the pizzas and Italian cuisine at **Pizzeria Valeri** (no phone) or the falafel and Mediterranean cuisine at **La Manta Club** (www.la-manta.com), where the day's surf action or a first-run movie is usually broadcast on a large screen. For a splurge, head up the hill to the **Blue Morpho Lounge** ★ (☎8396-6409), a trendy new spot serving fresh fish, pastas, pizzas, and other contemporary fare, in a stunning fourth-floor open-air space, with 360-degree views of the ocean and surrounding forests.

MODERATE

In addition to the places below, the **Riviera Riverside Villas** (☎2776-2396; www.pavonesriviera.com) offers modern, plush individual cabins, as well as several fully equipped house rentals, located a block or so inland from the water, right alongside the Río Claro (Clear River). **Cabinas La Ponderosa** (☎8824-4145; www.cabinaslaponderosa.com) is a small, beachfront collection of cabins and private, rustic villas, a little bit out of town, on the way to Punta Banco.

Casa Siempre Domingo This small hillside inn offers up the best accommodations right in Pavones. The rooms all feature high ceilings, tile floors, and two double beds (one room has two doubles and a twin). The high beds are custom-made constructions, and they're uncommonly high off the ground. The owner says the design helps capture the breeze from the picture windows, but if there's not enough, you can always crank up the air-conditioning. Meals are served on picnic tables in the large interior common space, and there is also a separate sitting room with satellite TV. The nicest feature is the huge deck, with its ocean view.

Pavones (A.P. 91, Golfito), several hundred meters south of downtown Pavones. ☎8820-4709. www.casa-domingo.com. 4 units. $100 double. Rate includes breakfast and taxes. No credit cards. *In room:* A/C, no phone.

Tiskita Jungle Lodge ★ ★ 📷 This ecolodge is nearly on the Panamanian border. The lodge itself is set on a hill a few hundred meters from the beach and commands a superb view of the ocean. There's a dark-sand beach, tide pools, jungle waterfalls, a farm and forest to explore, and great bird-watching. Most of the land here is primary rainforest; the rest is a mix of secondary forest, reforestation projects, orchards, and pastures. Accommodations are in cozy rustic cabins with screen walls and verandas. Constructed of local hardwoods, the cabins have a very tropical feel. My favorite cabin is no. 6, which has a great view and ample deck space. Some cabins have two or three rooms, perfect for families but less private for couples. Most of the bathrooms are actually outdoors, although they are private and protected, allowing you to take in the sights and sounds as you shower and shave.

Pavones (A.P. 13411-1000, San José), 6km (3¾ miles) down the road from Pavones. ☎2296-8125. Fax 2296-8133. www.tiskita-lodge.co.cr. 17 units. $272 double. Rates include 3 meals and 1 guided walk daily, and all taxes. Packages with transportation to and from Golfito or Puerto Jiménez are available. AE, MC, V. **Amenities:** Restaurant; bar; small pool; limited watersports equipment. *In room:* No phone.

12

THE CARIBBEAN COAST

Costa Rica's Caribbean coast is a world apart from the rest of the country. The pace is slower, the food is spicier, the tropical heat is more palpable, and the rhythmic lilt of patois and reggae music fills the air.

This remains one of Costa Rica's least discovered and explored regions. More than half of the coastline here is still inaccessible except by boat or small plane.

This inaccessibility has helped preserve large tracts of virgin lowland rainforest, which are now set aside as **Tortuguero National Park ★★** and **Barra del Colorado National Wildlife Refuge ★**. These two parks, on the northern reaches of this coast, are among Costa Rica's most popular destinations for adventurers and ecotravelers. Of particular interest are the sea turtles that nest here. Farther south, **Cahuita National Park ★** is another popular national park in this area, located just off its namesake beach village. It was set up to preserve 200 hectares (494 acres) of coral reef, but its palm tree–lined beaches and gentle trails are stunning.

So remote was the Caribbean coast from Costa Rica's population centers in the Central Valley that it developed a culture all its own. The original inhabitants of the area included people of the Bribri, Cabécar, and Kéköldi tribes, and these groups maintain their cultures on indigenous reserves in the Talamanca Mountains. In fact, until the 1870s, there were few non-Indians in this area. However, when Minor Keith built the railroad to San José and began planting bananas, he brought in black laborers from Jamaica and other Caribbean islands to lay the track and work the plantations. These workers and their descendants established fishing and farming communities up and down the coast. Today dreadlocked Rastafarians, reggae music, Creole cooking, and the English-based patois of this Afro-Caribbean culture give this region a quasi-Jamaican flavor. Many visitors find this striking contrast with the Spanish-derived Costa Rican culture fascinating.

Today, the Caribbean coast's main city of **Limón** is a major commercial port and budding cruise ship port of call.

Over the years, the Caribbean coast has garnered a reputation as being a dangerous, drug-infested zone, rife with crime and danger. Although there have been several high-profile crimes in the area, overall this reputation is exaggerated. The same crime and drug problems found here exist in San José and most of the more popular beach destinations on the Pacific coast. Use common sense and take normal precautions and you should have no problems on the Caribbean coast.

FACING PAGE: Limón carnival celebrant.

BARRA DEL COLORADO ★

115km (71 miles) NE of San José

Most visitors to Barra del Colorado come for the fishing. Tarpon and snook fishing are world-class, or you can head farther offshore for some deep-sea action. Barra del Colorado is part of the same ecosystem as Tortuguero National Park (see below); as in Tortuguero, there's an abundance of wildlife and rainforest fauna in the rivers and canals, which are accessible only by boat.

Named for its location at the mouth of the Río Colorado up near the Costa Rica–Nicaragua border, Barra del Colorado can be reached only by boat or small plane. There are no roads in or out of Barra del Colorado. The town itself is a small, ramshackle collection of raised stilt houses, and it supports a diverse population of Afro-Caribbean and Miskito Indian residents, Nicaraguan emigrants, and transient commercial fishermen.

It's hot and humid here most of the year, and it rains a lot, so although some of the lodges have at times risked offering a "tarpon guarantee," they're generally hesitant to promise anything in terms of the weather.

Essentials

GETTING THERE & DEPARTING By Plane: Most folks come here on multiday fishing packages, and most of the lodges in this area either operate charter flights as part of their package trips or will book you a flight.

Sansa (☎877/767-2672 in the U.S. and Canada, or 2290-4100 in Costa Rica; www.flysansa.com) has a flight that departs at 5:44am Monday, Friday, and Saturday for Barra del Colorado from San José's Juan Santamaría International Airport. The return flight to San José leaves Barra del Colorado daily at 6:38am. Flight duration is 45 minutes; the fare is $98 each way.

By Boat: It is also possible to travel to Barra del Colorado by boat from **Puerto Viejo de Sarapiquí** (see chapter 9). Expect to pay $200 to $300 each way for a boat that holds up to 10 people. Check at the public dock in Puerto Viejo de Sarapiquí or call **Oasis Nature Tours** (☎2766-6108; www.oasisnaturetours.com).

Río Colorado Lodge (☎800/243-9777 in the U.S. and Canada, or 2232-4063) runs its own launch between Barra del Colorado and Puerto Viejo de Sarapiquí (and sometimes btw. Barra and Limón), including land transportation between Puerto Viejo de Sarapiquí and San José. If you're staying at the Río Colorado Lodge, be sure to ask about this option (for at least one leg of your trip) when booking; the hotel doesn't discriminate—you can arrange transportation even if you aren't staying there. For $198 per person, you can arrange a pickup in San José, a minibus to the boat, a trip down the river to Barra, overnight accommodations at Río Colorado Lodge, and a return trip the next day, with all meals and taxes included.

ORIENTATION The Río Colorado neatly divides the town of Barra del Colorado. The airstrip is in the southern half of town, as are most of the lodgings. The lodges that are farther up the canals will meet you at the airstrip with a small boat.

The Caribbean Coast

NICARAGUA

Boca del Río Colorado
Barra del Colorado

Barra del
Colorado
Wildlife Refuge

Trinidad

NICARAGUA

SAN JOSÉ ★

The
Caribbean
Coast

PACIFIC
OCEAN

PANAMA

Boca del Río Tortuguero
Tortuguero

Tortuguero
Nat'l Park

Cariari

Parismina

CARIBBEAN
SEA

Guapiles   Guacimo   Carmen

Braulio
Carrillo
Nat'l Park

Vol. Turrialba
Nat'l Park   Siquirres

Boca del Río Pacuare

Volcán Turrialba

Matina

Central Range

Volcán
Irazú

Guayabo Nat'l Monument

Moin   Playa Bonita
Limón

Vol. Irazú
Nat'l Park   Turrialba

Cartago   Juan Vinas

Westfalia

Moravia

Tapanti (Orosi)
Nat'l Park

Cahuita   Playa Cahuita

Cahuita
Nat'l Park

Puerto
Viejo

Cerro de la Muerte

Uatsi

Manzanillo

Ojo de
Agua

Chirripó
Nat'l Park

Talamanca
Ind. Res.

Hitoy-Cerere
Biological Res.

Gandoca-
Manzanillo
NWR

Talamanca Range

Bratsi

San Gerardo

Cerro
Chirripó

BriBri
Ind. Res.

Sixaola

0   15 mi

0   15 km

La Amistad
Int'l Park

PANAMA

Fishing, Fishing & More Fishing

Almost all the lodges here specialize in fishing packages. If you don't fish, you may wonder just what in the world you're doing here. Even though there are excellent opportunities for bird-watching and touring jungle waterways, most lodges still merely pay lip service to ecotourists and would rather see you with a rod and reel.

Fishing takes place year-round. You can do it in the rivers and canals, in the very active river mouth, or offshore. Most anglers come in search of the tarpon, or silver king. **Tarpon** can be caught year-round, both in the river mouth and, to a lesser extent, in the canals; however, they are much harder to land in July

Angler pulling in fish in Barra del Colorado.

and August—the two rainiest months—probably because the river runs so high and is so full of runoff and debris. **Snook,** an aggressive river fish, peak in April, May, October, and November; fat snook, or *calba,* run heavy November through January. Depending on how far out to sea you venture, you might hook up with **barracuda, jack, mackerel** (Spanish and king), **wahoo, tuna, dorado, marlin,** or **sailfish.** In the rivers and canals, fishermen regularly bring in *mojarra, machaca,* and *guapote* (rainbow bass).

Following current trends in sportfishing, more and more anglers have been using fly rods, in addition to traditional rod-and-reel setups, to land just about all the fish mentioned above. To fish here, you'll need both salt- ($25) and freshwater ($30) fishing licenses. The lodges here either include these in your packages or can readily provide the licenses for you.

Nonfishers should see whether their lodge has a good naturalist guide or canoes or kayaks for rent or use.

Where to Stay & Dine

Almost all of the hotels here specialize in package tours, including all your meals, fishing and tackle, taxes, and usually your transportation and liquor too, so rates are high. There are no dependable budget hotels, and Barra remains a remote and difficult destination for independent and budget travelers. In addition to the places listed below, **Casa Mar Lodge** (☎800/543-0282 in the U.S. and Canada, or 2710-8093 in Costa Rica; www.casamarlodge.com) is a long-standing fishing lodge that is popular with hard-core anglers.

Río Colorado Lodge ★ This rustic lodge is one of the country's oldest and best-known fishing lodges. It was founded and built more than 30 years ago by local legend Archie Fields. The rooms are comfortable but decidedly rustic, with many showing the wear and tear of the years. The "honeymoon suite" is basically a standard room with a small mirror hung by ropes over the bed. Two of the rooms are wheelchair accessible. The nicest feature here is the large covered deck out by the river, where breakfast is served. There's also a large bar (where lunch is served) with satellite TV, a pool table, and a dartboard. The lodge runs a small "zoo" and participates in a macaw breeding project, as well as local education efforts. While their hearts may be in the right place, I find the zoo and cage conditions here rather desultory.

Barra del Colorado (A.P. 5094-1000, San José). ☏800/243-9777 in the U.S. and Canada, or 2232-4063 in Costa Rica. Fax 2231-5987. www.riocolorodolodge.com. 18 units. $2,373–$2,721 per person double occupancy for 7 days/6 nights with 4 full days of fishing, including 2 nights lodging in San José, all meals and drinks at the lodge, boat, guide, fuel, licenses, and taxes. Nonfishing guests $120–$170 per person per day. AE, MC, V. **Amenities:** Restaurant; bar; Jacuzzi. *In room:* A/C, TV (in some), no phone.

Silver King Lodge ★★ ![icon] This is the most upscale lodge in Barra del Colorado. They take their fishing seriously here—there's a large selection of modern boats and equipment, as well as a full tackle shop—but Silver King also emphasizes comfort. The rooms are immense, with two double beds, a desk and chair, luggage racks, fishing racks, air-conditioning, an overhead fan, and a roomy closet. The floors and walls are all varnished hardwood, and the ceilings are finished in bamboo. The entire complex is built on raised stilts and connected by covered walkways. The meals here feature some of the best buffet-style lodge cooking I've ever had. Each all-you-can-eat meal is anchored with at least two main dishes and a wide variety of appetizers, salads, side dishes, and desserts.

Barra del Colorado (mailing address: Interlink 399, P.O. Box 02-5635, Miami, FL 33102). ☏800/847-3474 in the U.S., or 2794-0139 in Costa Rica. www.silverkinglodge.net. 10 units. $2,220–$2,365 per person double occupancy for 3 full days of fishing, air transportation to and from Barra del Colorado from San José, all meals at the lodge, liquor, and taxes; $360–$385 per person per extra day, including all fishing, meals, liquor, and taxes; $145–$175 per person for nonfishers, with no ground transportation. AE, MC, V. Closed throughout the months of July, Aug, and Dec. **Amenities:** Restaurant; bar; Jacuzzi; small pool; sauna. *In room:* A/C, TV, no phone, free Wi-Fi.

TORTUGUERO NATIONAL PARK ★★

250km (155 miles) NE of San José; 79km (49 miles) N of Limón

Sometimes dubbed "the Venice of Costa Rica," Tortuguero is connected to Limón, and the rest of mainland Costa Rica, by a series of rivers and canals. This aquatic highway is lined almost entirely with a dense tropical rainforest that is home to howler and spider monkeys, three-toed sloths, toucans, and great green macaws. A trip through the canals is nothing like touring around Venice in a gondola, but it is a lot like cruising the Amazon basin—on a much smaller scale.

"Tortuguero" comes from the Spanish name for the giant sea turtles (*tortugas*) that nest on the beaches of this region every year from early March to mid-October (prime season is July–Oct, and peak months are Aug and Sept). The chance to see this nesting attracts many people to this remote region, but just as many come to explore the intricate network of jungle canals that serve as the region's main transportation arteries.

Very important: More than 200 inches of rain fall here annually, so you can expect a downpour at any time of the year. Most of the lodges will provide you with rain gear (including ponchos and rubber boots), but it can't hurt to carry your own.

Independent travel is not the norm here, although it's possible. Most travelers rely on their lodge for boat transportation through the canals and into town. At

Tortuguero National Park boat tour.

most of the lodges around Tortuguero, almost everything (bus rides to and from, boat trips through the canals, and even family-style meals) is done in groups. This group feeling can be intimate and rewarding, or overwhelming and impersonal.

Essentials

GETTING THERE & DEPARTING By Plane: Nature Air (☎800/235-9272 in the U.S. and Canada, or 2299-6000; www.natureair.com) has one flight that departs daily at 6am for Tortuguero from Tobías Bolaños International Airport in Pavas. The flight takes approximately 55 minutes; the fare is $107 each way. The return flight leaves Tortuguero daily at around 7am for San José.

Sansa (☎877/767-2672 in the U.S. and Canada, or 2290-4100 in Costa Rica; www.flysansa.com) has a daily flight for Tortuguero from San José's Juan Santamaría International Airport. The flight departs at 5:45am. The flight is direct and 45 minutes long. The fare is $98 each way. The return flight leaves Tortuguero daily at 7:04am for San José.

It always pays to check with both Sansa and Nature Air. Additional flights are often added during the high season, and departure times can vary according to weather or the whim of the airline. In addition, many lodges in this area operate charter flights as part of their package trips. Flights often touch down in nearby Barra del Colorado, adding on an additional 10 to 15 minutes.

Be sure to arrange with your hotel to pick you up at the airstrip. Otherwise you'll have to plead with one of the other hotel's boat captains to give you a lift, which they will usually do, either for free or for a few dollars.

By Car: It's not possible to drive to Tortuguero. If you have a car, your best bet is either to leave it in San José and take an organized tour; or drive it to Limón or Moín, find a secure hotel or public parking lot, and then follow the directions for arriving by boat below. There is also secure parking in La

Pavona, which is useful for those meeting the boats plying the Cariari and La Pavona route outlined below.

By Boat: Flying to Tortuguero is convenient if you don't have much time, but a boat trip through the canals and rivers of this region is often the highlight of any visit to Tortuguero. However, be forewarned: Although this trip can be stunning and exciting, it can also be long, tiring, and uncomfortable. You'll first have to ride by bus or minivan from San José to Moín, Caño Blanco, or one of the other embarkation points; then it's 2 to 3 hours on a boat, usually with hard wooden benches or plastic seats. All of the more expensive lodges listed offer their own bus and boat transportation packages, which include the boat ride through the canals. However, if you're coming here on the cheap and plan to stay at one of the less expensive lodges or at a budget cabina in Tortuguero, you will have to arrange your own transportation. In this case, you have a few options.

The most traditional option is to get yourself first to Limón and then to the public docks in **Moín,** just north of Limón, and try to find a boat on your own. You can reach Limón easily by public bus from San José (see "Getting There & Departing" under "Limón: Gateway to Tortuguero National Park & Southern Coastal Beaches," later in this chapter). If you're coming by car, make sure you drive all the way to Limón or Moín, unless you have arrangements out of Cariari or Caño Blanco Marina.

If you arrive in Limón by bus, you might be able to catch one of the periodic local buses to Moín right there at the main bus terminal; it costs around 50¢. Otherwise, you can take a taxi for around $6, for up to four people. At the docks, you should be able to negotiate a fare of between $40 and $70 per person round-trip. These boats tend to depart between 8 and 10am every morning. You can stay as many days as you like in Tortuguero, but be sure to arrange with the captain to be there to pick you up when you're ready to leave. The trip from Moín to Tortuguero takes between 3 and 4 hours.

As I mentioned above, it is possible to get to Tortuguero by bus and boat from Cariari. For backpackers and budget travelers, this is the cheapest and most reliable means of reaching Tortuguero from San José. To take this route, begin by catching the 9 or 10:30am direct bus to Cariari from the **Gran Terminal del Caribe,** on Calle Central, 1 block north of Avenida 11 (☎2222-0610). The fare is $2.50. This bus will actually drop you off at the main bus terminal in Cariari, from which you'll have to walk 5 blocks north to a separate small bus station. Look for a booth marked **COOPETRACA** or **Clic Clic ★**. At these booths you can buy your bus ticket for La Pavona. The bus fare is around $2. Buy a ticket for the noon bus (a later bus leaves at 3pm).

A boat or two will be waiting to meet the bus at the dock at the edge of the river at around 1:30pm (and again at 4:30pm). Check out the boats heading to Tortuguero, and pick the one that looks most comfortable and safe, then pay on board. The boat fare to Tortuguero is not regulated, and the price sometimes varies for foreigners. It can be as low as $3 each way, which is what locals pay. However, the boat captains often try to gouge tourists. Stand firm; you should not have to pay more than $5. Return boats leave Tortuguero for La Pavona every morning at 6 and 11:30am, and 3pm, making return bus connections to Cariari.

Warning: Be careful if you decide to take this route. I've received reports of unscrupulous operators providing misinformation to tourists. ***Note:*** Folks from a company called **Bananera** have set up shop at the Gran Terminal del Caribe and in Cariari, offering to sell you "packaged transportation" to Tortuguero. However, all they are doing is charging you extra to buy the individual tickets described above. Be especially careful if the folks selling you boat transportation aggressively steer you to a specific hotel option, claim that your first choice is full, or insist that you must buy a package with them that includes the transportation, lodging, and guide services. If you have doubts or want to check on the current state of this route, check out the site www.tortugerovillage.com, which has detailed directions about how to get to Tortuguero by a variety of routes.

Finally, it's also possible, albeit expensive, to travel to Tortuguero by boat from **Puerto Viejo de Sarapiquí** (see chapter 9). Expect to pay $250 to $375 each way for a boat that holds up to 10 people. Check at the public dock in Puerto Viejo de Sarapiquí if you're interested. The ride usually takes about 3 to 4 hours, and the boats tend to leave in the morning.

ORIENTATION Tortuguero is one of the most remote locations in Costa Rica. There are no roads into this area and no cars in the village, so all transportation is by boat or foot. Most of the lodges are spread out over several kilometers to the north of the village of Tortuguero on either side of the main canal; the small airstrip is at the north end of the beachside spit of land. At the far northern end of the main canal, you'll see the **Cerro de Tortuguero (Turtle Hill),** which, at some 119m (390 ft.), towers over the area. The hike to the top of this hill is a popular half-day tour and offers some good views of the Tortuguero canals and village, as well as the Caribbean Sea.

Tortuguero Village is a tiny collection of houses connected by footpaths. The village is spread out on a thin spit of land, bordered on one side

Tortuguero stilt house.

Turtle heading to sea.

> ## Turtle Tips
>
> - Visitors to the beach at night must be accompanied by a licensed guide. Tours generally last between 2 and 4 hours.
>
> - Sometimes you must walk quite a bit to encounter a nesting turtle. Wear sneakers or walking shoes rather than sandals. The beach is very dark at night, and it's easy to trip or step on driftwood or other detritus.
>
> - Wear dark clothes. White T-shirts are not permitted.
>
> - Flashlights, flash cameras, and lighted video cameras are prohibited on turtle tours.
>
> - Smoking is prohibited on the beach at night.

by the Caribbean Sea and on the other by the main canal. At most points, it's less than 300m (984 ft.) wide. In the center of the village, you'll find a small children's playground and a soccer field, as well as a kiosk that has information on the cultural and natural history of this area.

If you stay at a hotel on the ocean side of the canal, you'll be able to walk into and explore the village at your leisure; if you're across the canal, you'll be dependent on the lodge's boat transportation. However, some of the lodges across the canal have their own network of jungle trails that might appeal to naturalists.

FAST FACTS There are no banks, ATMs, or currency-exchange houses in Tortuguero, so be sure to bring sufficient cash in colones to cover any expenses and incidental charges. The local hotels and shops generally charge a hefty commission to exchange dollars. There is an **information center** (☎8833-0827) in town in front of the Catholic church. This is a good place for independent travelers looking to arrange local tours and onward travel. There's an Internet cafe (no phone) right across from the main dock in town, although I prefer the one found at **La Casona** (☎2709-8092), a small restaurant and budget hotel in the heart of the village.

Exploring the National Park

According to existing records, sea turtles have frequented Tortuguero National Park since at least 1592, largely due to its extreme isolation. Over the years, turtles were captured and their eggs were harvested by local settlers; by the 1950s this practice became so widespread that turtles faced extinction. Regulations controlling this mini-industry were passed in 1963, and in 1970 Tortuguero National Park was established.

Today four different species of sea turtles nest here: the green turtle, the hawksbill, the loggerhead, and the giant leatherback. The prime nesting period is from **July to mid-October** (Aug–Sept are peak months). The park's beaches are excellent places to watch sea turtles nest, especially at night. As appealingly long and deserted as they are, however, the beaches are not appropriate for swimming. The surf is usually very rough, and the river mouths have a nasty habit of attracting sharks that feed on the turtle hatchlings and many fish that live here.

Green turtles are perhaps the most common turtle found in Tortuguero, so you're more likely to see one of them than any other species if you visit during the prime nesting season. **Loggerheads** are very rare, so don't be disappointed if you don't see one. The **giant leatherback** is perhaps the most spectacular sea turtle to watch laying eggs. The largest of all turtle species, the leatherback can grow to 2m (6½ ft.) long and weigh well over 1,000 pounds. It nests from early March to mid-April, predominantly in the southern part of the park.

You can explore the park's rainforest, either by foot or by boat, and look for some of the incredible varieties of wildlife that live here: jaguars, anteaters, howler monkeys, collared and white-lipped peccaries, some 350 species of birds, and countless butterflies, among others. Boat tours are far and away the most popular way to visit this park, although one frequently very muddy trail starts at the park entrance and runs for about 2km (1¼ miles) through the coastal rainforest and along the beach.

ENTRY POINT, FEES & REGULATIONS The Tortuguero National Park entrance and ranger station are at the south end of Tortuguero Village. Admission to the park is $10. However, most people visit Tortuguero as part of a package tour. Be sure to confirm whether the park entrance is included in the price. Moreover, only certain canals and trails leaving from the park station are actually within the park. Many hotels and private guides take their tours to a series of canals that border the park and are very similar in terms of flora and fauna but don't require a park entrance. When the turtles are nesting, you will have to arrange a night tour in advance with either your hotel or one of the private guides working in town. These guided tours generally run between $10 and $15. Flashlights and flash cameras are not permitted on the beach at night because the lights discourage the turtles from nesting.

ORGANIZED TOURS Most visitors come to Tortuguero on an organized tour. All of the lodges listed below, with the exception of the most inexpensive accommodations in Tortuguero Village, offer package tours that include various hikes and river tours; this is generally the best way to visit the area.

In addition, several San José–based tour companies offer budget 2-day/1-night excursions to Tortuguero, including transportation, all meals, and limited tours around the region. Prices for these trips range between $90 and $200 per person, and—depending on price—guests are lodged either in one of the basic hotels in Tortuguero Village or one of the nicer lodges listed below. Reputable companies offering these excursions include the **Learning Trips** (☎800/723-2674 in the U.S. and Canada, or 2258-2293 in Costa Rica; www.costa-rica.us) and **Caño Blanco Marina** (☎2256-9444). There are even 1-day trips that spend almost all their time coming and going but that do allow for a quick tour of the canals and lunch in Tortuguero. These trips are good for travelers who like to be able to say, "Been there, done that," and they generally run between $80 and $100 per person. However, these trips spend most of their time traveling to and from Tortuguero. If you really want to experience Tortuguero, I recommend staying for at least 2 nights.

Alternately, you could go with **Fran and Modesto Watson** ★ (☎2226-0986; www.tortuguerocanals.com), who are pioneering guides in this region and operate their own boat. The couple offers a range of overnight and multiday packages to Tortuguero, with lodging options at most of the major lodges here.

BOAT CANAL TOURS Aside from watching the turtles nest, the unique thing to do in Tortuguero is tour the canals by boat, keeping your eye out for tropical birds and native wildlife. Most lodges can arrange a canal tour for you, but you can also arrange a tour through one of the operators in Tortuguero Village. I recommend **Daryl Loth** (☎ **8833-0827**; safari@racsa.co.cr), who runs the Casa Marbella (see below) in the center of the village. I also recommend **Ernesto Castillo,** who can be reached through Cabinas Sabina or by asking around the village. If neither of these guides is available, ask for a recommendation at the **Jungle Shop** (☎ **2709-8072**) or at the **Caribbean Conservation Corporation's Museum** (☎ **2709-8091**). Most guides charge between $15 to $25 per person for a tour of the canals. If you travel through the park, you'll also have to pay the park entrance fee of $10 per person.

Exploring the Village

The most popular attraction in town is the small **Caribbean Conservation Corporation's Visitors' Center and Museum ★** (☎ **2709-8091**; www.ccc turtle.org). The museum has information and exhibits on a whole range of native flora and fauna, but its primary focus is on the life and natural history of the sea turtles. Most visits to the museum include a short, informative video on the turtles. There's a small gift shop here, and all the proceeds go toward conservation and turtle protection. The museum is open Monday through Saturday from 10am to noon and 2 to 5:30pm, and Sunday from 2 to 5pm. There's a $1 admission charge, but more generous donations are encouraged.

In the village you can also rent dugout canoes, known in Costa Rica as *cayucos* or *pangas*. Be careful before renting and taking off in one of these; they tend to be heavy, slow, and hard to maneuver, and you might be getting more than you bargained for. **Miss Junie** (☎ **2709-8102**) rents lighter and more modern fiberglass canoes for around $5 for 3 hours.

You'll find a couple of souvenir shops on the main footpath near the center of the village. About 182m (597 ft.) of this path is paved with concrete. The **Paraíso Tropical Gift Shop** has the largest selection of gifts and souvenirs, by far. But I prefer the **Jungle Shop,** which has a higher-end selection of wares and donates 10% of its profits to local schools.

Where to Stay & Dine

Although the room rates below may appear high, keep in mind that they usually include round-trip transportation from San José (which amounts to approx. $100–$150 per person), plus all meals, taxes, and usually some tours. When broken down into nightly room rates, most of the lodges are really charging only between $60 and $120 for a double room. **Note:** When I list package rates below, I have always listed the least expensive travel option, which is a bus and boat combination both in and out. All of the lodges also offer packages with the option of a plane flight either one or both ways.

Most visitors take all their meals, as part of a package, at their hotel. There are a couple of simple *sodas* (diners) and local restaurants in town. The best of these are **La Casona** (☎ **2709-8092**) and the **Buddha Café** (☎ **2709-8084**). For a light meal or a sweet treat, check out **Dorling's Bakery, Coffee Shop**

Tortuguero village.

& Restaurant (☎2709-8132). This place opens very early, and stays open late during turtle nesting season, making it a good option if you've got an early departure or late-night tour.

VERY EXPENSIVE

Manatus Hotel ★★ This intimate hotel offers the most luxurious accommodations in Tortuguero. The large rooms are plush and well-equipped, with two queen-size beds, high ceilings, wood floors, tasteful local furnishings, and a host of amenities you won't find anywhere else in the area. Meals and service are top-notch here, and they have the best little spa of any local hotel, as well as an on-site art gallery. The amoeba-shaped pool is set just off the dark waters of the Tortuguero canal, with a broad deck and plenty of inviting chaise longues surrounding it. Only children over 10 years of age are allowed.

Tortuguero. ☎2239-4854 reservations in San José, or 2709-8197 at the hotel. Fax 2239-4854. www.manatushotel.com. 12 units. $390 per person for 2 days/1 night; $495 per person for 3 days/2 nights. Rates are double occupancy, and include round-trip transportation from San José, 3 meals daily, taxes, and daily tours. AE, MC, V. No children 10 and under allowed. **Amenities:** Restaurant; bar; small spa and exercise room; free-form pool; room service. *In room:* A/C, TV, minibar.

Tortuga Lodge ★★ ☺ This is one of the oldest lodges in Tortuguero, and still one of the best. My favorite feature here is the long multilevel deck off the main dining room, where you can sit and dine, sip a cool drink, or just take in the view as the water laps against the docks at your feet. There's also a lovely pool built by the water's edge that's designed to look like it blends into Tortuguero's main canal. All the rooms feature contemporary furniture, Caribbean-influenced decor, and loads of freshly varnished hardwood. If possible, I'd opt for the second-floor rooms, which come with a small, covered veranda. A two-bedroom, two-bathroom second-floor penthouse suite is available for families or those wanting more space. There are several acres of forest behind the lodge, and a few kilometers of trails wind their way through the trees. This is a great place to look for howler monkeys and colorful poison-arrow frogs. The hotel is run by Costa Rica Expeditions, one of the pioneers in the field of sustainable travel.

Tortuguero (mailing address: SJO 235, P.O. Box 025216, Miami, FL 33102-5216). **800/886-2609** in the U.S. and Canada, or 2257-0766 reservations in San José or 2709-8034 at the lodge. Fax 2257-1665. www.tortugalodge.com. 27 units. $248 double; $338 penthouse. Rates include full meal plan. Package rates with transportation, meals, and tours are available. AE, MC, V. **Amenities:** Restaurant; bar; small pool. *In room:* No phone.

EXPENSIVE

Laguna Lodge ★ This popular lodge is 2km (1¼ miles) north of Tortuguero Village, on the ocean side of the main canal (which allows you to walk along the beach and into town at your leisure). Most of the spacious rooms have wood walls, waxed hardwood floors, and tiled bathrooms with screened upper walls to let in air and light. Each room also has a little shared veranda overlooking flowering gardens. The large dining area is on a free-form deck that extends out over the Tortuguero Canal. Another covered deck, also over the water, is strung with hammocks for lazing away the afternoons. Several covered palapa huts, also strung with hammocks, have been built among the flowering ginger and hibiscus. There's a large landscaped pool, with a poolside bar and grill, as well as a butterfly garden and botanical garden.

Tortuguero (A.P. 173-2015, San José). **2272-4943** for reservations, or 2709-8082 at the lodge. Fax 2272-4927. www.lagunatortuguero.com. 80 units. $263 per person for 2 days/1 night; $330 per person for 3 days/2 nights. Rates are double occupancy and include round-trip transportation from San José, tours, taxes, and 3 meals daily. Children 5–11 pay half-price. Children 4 and under, free. AE, DC, MC, V. **Amenities:** Restaurant; 2 bars; large free-form pool. *In room:* No phone.

Mawamba Lodge ★ Located just north of Tortuguero Village on the ocean side of the canal, Mawamba is quite similar to Laguna Lodge—perhaps because the two lodges are owned by brothers. Rooms have varnished wood floors, twin beds, hot-water showers, ceiling fans, and verandas with rocking chairs. All rooms are painted in bright Caribbean colors. In 2008, a few "superior rooms" were added, with king-size beds and a few extra amenities, like hair dryers and a bathtub. The gardens are lush and overgrown with flowering ginger, heliconia, and hibiscus. There are plenty of hammocks around for anyone who wants to kick back and a beach volleyball court for those who don't. These folks also offer an extensive menu of kayaking tours and excursions, including one package in which you actually kayak part of the way into Tortuguero. On the premises are a small gift shop, a small butterfly garden, a game room, and nightly lectures and slide shows that focus on the natural history of this area.

Tortuguero (A.P. 10980-1000, San José). **2293-8181** or 2709-8100. Fax 2239-7657. www.grupo mawamba.com. 54 units. $263 per person for 2 days/1 night; $330 per person for 3 days/2 nights. Rates are double occupancy, and include round-trip transportation from San José, 3 meals daily, taxes, and some tours. Children 5–11 pay half-price. Children 4 and under, free. AE, MC, V. **Amenities:** Restaurant; bar; free-form pool. *In room:* No phone, hair dryer (in superior rooms).

Pachira Lodge The rooms in this lodge are found in a series of four-plex buildings perched on stilts and connected by covered concrete walkways in a dense section of secondary forest set in a little bit from the main canal. Each room is spacious and clean, with varnished wood floors, painted wood walls, two double beds, ceiling fans, and plenty of cross ventilation. Standard buffet meals are served in a large, screened-in dining room. There's a large, cool pool in the shape of a turtle, with children's wading pools built into the flippers. Bilingual guides and all the major tour options are available.

Tortuguero (A.P. 1818-1002, San José). ☎2223-1682 or 2256-7080. Fax 2223-1119. www.pachira lodge.com. 88 units. $259 per person for 2 days/1 night; $289 per person for 3 days/2 nights. Rates are double occupancy, and include round-trip transportation from San José, 3 meals daily, taxes, and tours. AE, MC, V. **Amenities:** Restaurant; bar; pool; small spa. *In room:* No phone.

Turtle Beach Lodge ★ This isolated ecolodge is 8km (5 miles) north of the village of Tortuguero, about 20 minutes away by boat. The grounds are set on a narrow strip of land between the Caribbean Sea and the Caño Palma canal. The accommodations are somewhat more spartan than those at the lodges listed above, but they are still clean and comfortable. The rooms are housed in a series of long buildings. Most feature exterior walls that are solid on the bottom half and pure screening above. The best rooms are the corner units, which get the most airflow and circulation. All have some form of shared or private verandas. Given its location, this is one of the more convenient lodges for viewing the turtle nestings. There's a small, turtle-shaped pool in the center of the grounds, and they have a stable of horses available for riding tours.

Caño Palma, Tortuguero. ☎2248-0707 in San José, or 8837-6969 at the lodge. Fax 2257-4409. www.turtlebeachlodge.com. 47 units. $210 per person for 2 days/1 night; $288 per person for 3 days/2 nights. Rates double occupancy, and include round-trip transportation from San José, 3 meals daily, taxes, and tours. AE, MC, V. **Amenities:** Restaurant; bar; lounge w/satellite TV; Internet; pool. *In room:* No phone.

INEXPENSIVE

Several basic cabinas in the village of Tortuguero offer budget lodgings for between $15 and $25 per person. **Cabinas Miss Junie** (☎2709-8102) and **Cabinas Miss Miriam** (☎2709-8107) are the traditional favorites, although in my opinion, the best of the batch are the **Cabinas Icaco** (☎2709-8044), **Cabinas La Casona** (☎2709-8092), and **Cabinas Tortuguero** (☎2709-8114).

Casa Marbella ★ 🌿 Right in the village of Tortuguero, this converted house is an excellent option for budget travelers looking for a bit more comfort and care than that offered at most of the other inexpensive in-town options. It's also a good alternative for those wishing to avoid the large groups and cattle-car-like operations of most big lodges here. The rooms all have high ceilings, tile floors, firm mattresses, and white walls with varnished wood trim. Part-owner Daryl Loth is a longtime resident and well-respected naturalist guide. He and his wife are dedicated environmentalists and actively involved in local community development and environmental conservation efforts. Breakfast is served on a little patio facing the main Tortuguero canal in back of the house. A library and lounge area complement the facilities, and a wide range of tours can be arranged. The newest additions here are two "superior" rooms, with direct views of the canal.

Tortuguero, Limón. ☎/fax 2709-8011 or ☎8833-0827. http://casamarbella.tripod.com. 8 units. $40 double; $50–$60 superior. Rates include breakfast. No credit cards. *In room:* No phone, free Wi-Fi.

LIMON: GATEWAY TO TORTUGUERO NATIONAL PARK & SOUTHERN COASTAL BEACHES

160km (99 miles) E of San José; 55km (34 miles) N of Puerto Viejo

It was just offshore from present-day Limón, in the lee of Isla Uvita, that Christopher Columbus is said to have anchored in 1502, on his fourth and final voyage to the New World. Believing that this was potentially a very rich land, he christened it Costa Rica ("Rich Coast"). While never supplying the Spanish crown with much in the way of gold or jewels, the spot where he anchored has proved over the centuries to be the best port on Costa Rica's Caribbean coast—so his judgment wasn't all bad. From here the first bananas were shipped to North America in the late 19th century. Today Limón is primarily a rough-and-tumble port city that ships millions of pounds of bananas northward every year. It also receives a fair share of the country's ocean-borne imports and a modest number of cruise ship callings. On days when a cruise ship is in port, you'll find the city bustling far beyond the norm.

Limón is not generally considered a tourist destination, and few tourists take the time to tour the city, except those stopping here on cruise ships. Very few choose to stay here, and I don't recommend it except during Carnaval—and even then you're better off in Cahuita or Puerto Viejo. Most travelers use it primarily as a gateway to Tortuguero to the north or the beaches of Cahuita and Puerto Viejo to the south.

If you want to get in some beach time while you're in Limón, hop in a taxi or a local bus and head north a few kilometers to **Playa Bonita,** a small public beach. Although the water isn't very clean and is usually too rough for swimming, the setting is much more attractive than downtown. This beach is popular with surfers.

Essentials

GETTING THERE & DEPARTING By Plane: Nature Air (☎800/235-9272 in the U.S. and Canada, or 2299-6000; www.natureair.com) has one flight that departs Monday, Wednesday, Saturday, and Sunday at 1pm for **Limón**

A Fall Festival

The biggest event of the year in Limón, and one of the liveliest festivals in Costa Rica, is the annual **Carnaval,** which is held around Columbus Day (Oct 12). For a week, languid Limón shifts into high gear for a nonstop bacchanal orchestrated to the beat of reggae, soca, and calypso music. During the revelries, residents don costumes and take to the streets in a dazzling parade of color. If you want to experience Carnaval, make your reservations early because hotels fill up fast. (This advice goes for the entire coast.)

Cruise ships at dock in Limón.

airport (LIO; no phone) from the Tobías Bolaños International Airport in Pavas (p. 118). The flight takes 45 minutes. This flight continues on to Bocas del Toro, Panama. The return flight leaves Limón for San José at 3:30pm. The fare is $107 one-way. Cabs wait outside for arriving flights, and the fare to downtown Limón is $6.

By Car: The Guápiles Highway heads north out of San José on Calle 3 before turning east and passing close to Barva Volcano and through the rainforests of Braulio Carrillo National Park en route to Limón. The drive takes about 2½ hours and is spectacularly beautiful, especially when it's not raining or misty. Alternately, you can take the old highway, which is also scenic but much slower. This highway heads east out of San José on Avenida Central and passes through San Pedro before reaching Cartago. From Cartago on, the road is narrow and winding and passes through Paraíso and Turrialba before descending out of the mountains to Siquirres, where the old highway meets the new. This route takes around 4 hours, more or less, to get to Limón.

By Bus: Transportes Caribeños buses (☎ 2233-8933 in San José, or 2758-2575 in Limón) leave San José every half-hour daily between 5am and 7pm from the Caribbean bus terminal (Gran Terminal del Caribe) on Calle Central, 1 block north of Avenida 11. Friday through Sunday, the last bus leaves an hour later at 8pm. The trip duration is 2½ to 3 hours. The buses are either direct or local *(corriente)*, and they don't alternate in any particularly predictable fashion. The local buses are generally older and less comfortable and stop en route to pick up passengers from the roadside. I highly recommend taking a direct bus, if possible. The fare is $4.70 one-way.

Buses leave Limón for San José every half-hour between 6am and 7:30pm, and similarly alternate between local and direct, with the last bus leaving 1 hour later Friday through Sunday. The Limón bus terminal is on the main road into town, several blocks west of the downtown area and Parque Vargas. Buses (☎ 2758-1572 for the terminal) to **Cahuita** and **Puerto Viejo** leave from here roughly every hour from 5am to 6pm daily.

Buses to **Punta Uva** and **Manzanillo,** both of which are south of Puerto Viejo, leave Limón daily at 6 and 10:30am and 3 and 6pm, from the same station.

ORIENTATION Nearly all addresses in Limón are measured from the central market, which is aptly located smack-dab in the center of town, or from Parque Vargas, which is at the east end of town fronting the sea. The cruise ship dock is just south of Parque Vargas. A pedestrian mall runs from Parque Vargas to the west for several blocks.

FAST FACTS A host of private and national banks are located in the small downtown area. You can reach the **local police** at ☎ **2758-1148** and the **Red Cross** at ☎ **2758-0125.** The **Tony Facio Hospital** (☎ **2758-0580**) is just outside of the downtown area on the road to Playa Bonita.

What to See & Do

There's really not much for tourists to do or see in Limón. The closest true attraction, **Veragua Rainforest Park** (see below), is about a 40-minute drive from the city.

If you end up spending any time in Limón, be sure to take a seat in **Parque Vargas** along the seawall and watch the city's citizens go about their business. You may even spot some sloths living in the trees here. If you want to shop for souvenirs, head to the cruise ship terminal whenever there's a ship in port, and you'll find more than your fare share of vendors. Finally, if you're interested in architecture, take a walk around town. When banana shipments built this port, local merchants erected elaborately decorated buildings, several of which have survived the city's many earthquakes, humid weather, and salty sea air. There's a certain charm in the town's fallen grace, drooping balconies, rotting woodwork, and chipped paint. Just be careful: Limón has earned a reputation for frequent muggings and robberies. Do not walk around after dark, or stray far from the city center.

A ONE-STOP SHOP RAINFOREST TOURISM SPOT

Located outside of Limón in a patch of thick rainforest south of the banana town of Liverpool, **Veragua Rainforest Park** ★ (☎ **2296-5056;** www.veraguarainforest.com) is primarily a destination for cruise ship excursions. However, this extensive complex is a worthy stop for anyone visiting the area. Attractions include a serpentarium, butterfly garden and breeding exhibit, hummingbird garden, extensive insect exhibit, free-range rainforest frog room, zip-line canopy tour, and a short tram ride that takes you to their rainforest trail system. Along the trails, you'll find a beautiful little waterfall. A half-day tour runs $65 per adult and $45 per child, and a full-day tour runs $99 per adult and $70 per child; these tour prices don't include transportation, but do include lunch. The park is open Tuesday through Sunday from 8am to 4pm.

Where to Stay & Dine

In addition to the hotel listed below, if you want to be right on the beach at Playa Bonita, check out the **Beach Hotel Cocori** (☎ **2795-1670;** fax 2795-2930), a simple hotel with a great location; the neighboring beach bar and disco can be loud, though.

Park Hotel ★ This is easily, and perennially, the best option in Limón proper—although there really isn't much competition. The hotel has an excellent location fronting the ocean, across the street from the fire station. Unlike much of Limón, which seems to be in a state of prolonged and steady decay, the Park Hotel receives regular and fairly competent upkeep year in and year out. Ask for a room on the ocean side of the hotel because these are brighter, quieter, and cooler than those that face the fire station, although they're also slightly more expensive. The suites have private oceanview balconies and larger bathrooms with tubs. The large, sunny dining room off the lobby serves standard Tico fare at very reasonable prices.

Av. 3, btw. calles 1 and 3 (A.P. 35-7300), Limón. ☎2758-3476 or 2798-0555. Fax 2758-4364. 32 units. $54–$65 double. AE, MC, V. **Amenities:** Restaurant. *In room:* A/C, TV.

En Route South

Staying at the place listed below is a great way to combine some quiet beach time on the Caribbean coast with a more active ecolodge and bird-watching experience into one compact itinerary.

Selva Bananito Lodge ★★ 🏠 The spacious individual raised-stilt cabins here feature an abundance of varnished woodwork, large private bathrooms, and a wraparound veranda with a hammock and some chairs. Half the cabins have views of the Bananito River and a small valley; the other half have views of the Matama Mountains (part of the Talamanca mountain range). There are no electric lights at Selva Bananito, but each evening as you dine by candlelight, your cabin's oil lamps are lit for you. Hot water is provided by solar panels. There's a wide range of tours and activities, including rainforest hikes and horseback rides in the jungle, tree climbing, self-guided trail hikes, and even the opportunity to rappel down the face of a jungle waterfall. The owners are very involved in conservation efforts in this area, and approximately two-thirds of the 840 hectares (2,100 acres) here are primary forest managed as a private reserve.

Bananito (A.P. 2333-2050, San Pedro). ☎2253-8118. Fax 2280-0820. www.selvabananito.com. 11 units. $260–$280 double. Rates include 3 meals daily and all taxes. No credit cards. **Amenities:** Restaurant. *In room:* No phone. You'll need a four-wheel-drive vehicle to reach the lodge itself, although most leave their rental cars in Bananito and let the lodge drive them the final bit. You can also arrange to be picked up in San José.

CAHUITA ★

200km (124 miles) E of San José; 42km (26 miles) S of Limón; 13km (8 miles) N of Puerto Viejo

Cahuita is a small Caribbean beach village and the first "major" tourist destination heading south out of Limón. Nevertheless, the boom going on in Puerto Viejo and the beaches south of Puerto Viejo have in many ways passed Cahuita by. Depending on your point of view, that can be a reason to stay or to decide to head farther south. Any way you slice it, Cahuita is one of the most laid-back villages in Costa Rica. The few dirt and gravel streets here are host to a languid parade of pedestrian traffic, parted occasionally by a bicycle, car, or bus. After a short time, you'll find yourself slipping into the heat-induced torpor that affects anyone who ends up here.

The village traces its roots to Afro-Caribbean fishermen and laborers who settled in this region in the mid-1800s, and today the population is still primarily English-speaking blacks whose culture and language set them apart from other Costa Ricans.

People come to Cahuita for its miles of pristine beaches, which stretch both north and south from town. The southern beaches, the forest behind them, and the coral reef offshore (one of just a handful in Costa Rica) are all part of **Cahuita National Park.** Silt and pesticides washing down from nearby banana plantations have taken a heavy toll on the coral reefs, so don't expect the snorkeling to be world-class. But on a calm day, it can be pretty good, and the beaches are idyllic every day. It can rain almost any time of year here, but the most dependably dry months are September and October.

Essentials

GETTING THERE & DEPARTING By Plane: The closest airport to Cahuita is found in Limón (see above). A taxi from the airport to Cahuita should cost around $15 to $20. You can also just walk the long block from the airport terminal to the main road south and flag down any of the frequent buses that pass by.

By Car: Follow the directions above for getting to Limón. As you enter Limón, about 5 blocks before the busiest section of downtown, watch for a paved road to the right, just before the railroad tracks. Take this road south to Cahuita, passing the airstrip and the beach on your left as you leave Limón. Alternatively, there's a turnoff with signs for Sixaola and La Bomba several miles before Limón. This winding shortcut skirts the city and puts you on the coastal road several miles south of town.

By Bus: Mepe express buses (☎ 2257-8129) leave San José daily at 6 and 10am, noon, and 2 and 4pm from the Caribbean bus terminal (Gran Terminal del Caribe) on Calle Central, 1 block north of Avenida 11. The trip's duration is 4 hours; the fare is $7. During peak periods, extra buses are often added. However, it's wise to check because this bus line (Mepe) is one of the most fickle.

Alternatively, you can catch a bus to **Limón** (see above) and then transfer to a Cahuita- or Puerto Viejo–bound bus (☎ 2758-1572) in Limón. These latter buses leave roughly every hour between 5am and 6pm from in front of Radio Casino, which is 1 block north of the municipal market. Buses from Limón to Manzanillo also stop in Cahuita and leave from the same spot daily every hour from 6am to 7pm. The trip takes 1 hour; the fare is $1.25.

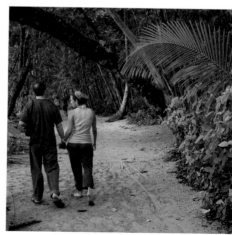
Cahuita National Park trail.

Gray Line (☎2220-2126; www.graylinecostarica.com) has a daily bus that leaves San José for Cahuita at 9:30am. The fare is $35. The return bus leaves Cahuita at 7:20am. **Interbus** (☎2283-5573; www.interbus online.com) has a daily bus that leaves San José for Cahuita at 7:50am. The fare is $39. Interbus buses leave Cahuita daily at both 7:20am and 3:15pm. Both companies will pick you up at most area hotels in both San José and Cahuita, and both offer connections to various other destinations around Costa Rica.

Buses departing **Puerto Viejo** and Sixaola (on the Panama border) stop in Cahuita at approximately 7, 8, 9:30, and 11:30am, and 4:30pm en route to San José. However, this schedule is far from precise, so it's always best to check with your hotel. Moreover, these buses are often full, particularly on weekends and throughout the high season. To avoid standing in the aisle all the way to San José, it is sometimes better to take a bus first to Limón and then catch one of the frequent Limón–San José buses. Buses to Limón pass through Cahuita regularly throughout the day. Another tactic I've used is to take a morning bus to Puerto Viejo, spend the day down there, and board a direct bus to San José at its point of origin, thereby snagging a seat.

ORIENTATION There are only about eight dirt streets in Cahuita. The highway runs parallel to the coast, with three main roads running perpendicular. The northernmost of these roads bypasses town and brings you to the northern end of Playa Negra. It's marked with signs for the Magellan Inn and other hotels up on this end. The second road in brings you to the southern end of Playa Negra, a half-mile closer to town. The third road is the principal entrance into town. The village's main street in town, which runs parallel to the highway, dead-ends at the entrance to the national park (a footbridge over a small stream).

Buses drop their passengers off at a new bus terminal that is at the back of a new minimall on the main entrance road into town. If you come in on the bus and are staying at a lodge on Playa Negra, there will be cabs waiting. Alternately, you can head out walking north on the street that runs between Coco's Bar and the small park. This road curves to the left and continues a mile or so out to Playa Negra.

FAST FACTS The **police station** (☎2755-0217) is located where the road from Playa Negra turns into town. The **post office** is next door to the police station. You can wash your clothes at the self-service **laundromat** (no phone) in front of Cabinas Vaz, or have them done for you at **Smokey's Laundry** (no phone), which is located a little bit behind Turistica Cahuita Information Center.

There are several Internet cafes around the central downtown area of the village.

If you can't find a **cab** in town, ask your hotel to call you one, or try **Alejandro** (☎8875-3209), **Wayne** (☎2755-0078), or **Dino** (☎2755-0012).

Exploring Cahuita National Park ★

On arrival, you'll immediately feel the call of the long scimitar of beach that stretches south from the edge of town. This beach can be glimpsed through

Howler monkeys.

the trees from Cahuita's sun-baked main street and extends a promise of relief from the heat. Although the lush coastal forest and picture-perfect palm lines are a tremendous draw, the park was actually created to preserve the 240-hectare (787-acre) **coral reef** that surrounds it. The reef contains 35 species of coral and provides a haven for hundreds of brightly colored tropical fish. You can walk on the beach itself or follow the trail that runs through the forest just behind the beach to check out the reef.

The best place to swim is just before or beyond the **Río Perezoso (Lazy River),** several hundred meters inside Cahuita National Park. The trail behind the beach is great for bird-watching, and if you're lucky, you might see some monkeys or a sloth. The loud grunting sounds you'll hear off in the distance are the calls of howler monkeys, which can be heard from more than a kilometer away. Nearer at hand, you're likely to hear crabs scuttling amid the dry leaves on the forest floor—a half-dozen or so species of land crabs live in this region—my favorites are the bright orange-and-purple ones.

The trail behind the beach stretches a little more than 6.4km (4 miles) to the southern end of the park at **Puerto Vargas,** where you'll find a beauti-ful white-sand beach, the park headquarters, and a primitive campground with showers and outhouses. It's a nice, flat walk, but a rewarding one because there's good wildlife viewing and access to the beach. The reef is off the point just north of Puerto Vargas, and you can snorkel here. If you don't dawdle, the hike to Puerto Vargas should take no more than 2 hours each way. Bring plenty of mos-quito repellent because this area can be buggy.

Although there's snorkeling at Puerto Vargas, the nicest coral heads are sev-eral hundred meters offshore, and it's best to have a boat take you out. A 3-hour **snorkel trip** costs between $15 and $30 per person with equipment. You can arrange one with any of the local tour companies listed below. **Note:** These trips are best taken when the seas are calm—for safety's sake, visibility, and comfort.

ENTRY POINTS, FEES & REGULATIONS The **in-town park entrance** is just over a footbridge at the end of the village's main street. It has bathroom fa-cilities, changing rooms, and storage lockers. This is the best place to enter if you just want to spend the day on the beach and maybe take a little hike in the bordering forest.

Cahuita National Park beach.

The alternate park entrance is at the southern end of the park in **Puerto Vargas.** This is where you should come if you plan to camp at the park or if you don't feel up to hiking a couple of hours to reach the good snorkeling spots. The road to Puerto Vargas is approximately 5km (3 miles) south of Cahuita on the left.

Officially, **admission** is $10 per person per day, but this is collected only at the Puerto Vargas entrance. You can enter the park from the town of Cahuita for free or with a voluntary contribution. The park is open from dawn to dusk for day visitors.

Camping is an extra $2 per person. Fifty campsites at Puerto Vargas stretch along for several kilometers and are either right on or just a few steps from the beach. My favorite are those farthest from the entrance. A small ranger station has basic shower and bathroom facilities, but they're a bit far from some of the better campsites.

GETTING THERE By Car: The turnoff for the Puerto Vargas entrance is clearly marked 7km (4⅓ miles) south of Cahuita.

By Bus: Your best bet is to get off a Puerto Viejo– or Sixaola-bound bus at the turnoff for the Puerto Vargas entrance (well marked, but tell the bus driver in advance). The guard station/entrance is only about 500m (1,640 ft.) down this road. However, the campsites are several kilometers farther, so it's a long hike with a heavy pack.

Beaches & Activities Outside the Park

Outside the park the best place for swimming is **Playa Negra.** The stretch right in front of the Atlantida Lodge is my favorite spot here.

There are plenty of options for organized adventure trips or tours while in Cahuita. I recommend **Cahuita Tours and Adventure Center** (☎2755-0000), on the village's main street heading out toward Playa Negra. They offer a wide range of tour and activity options, including glass-bottom-boat and snorkeling trips ($35 per person), jungle hikes ($35–$45), and jeep tours to a nearby Bribri Reservation ($60).

Turística Cahuita Information Center (☎/fax 2755-0071), also on the main road heading toward Playa Negra, and **Roberto Tours** (☎2755-0117), 50m (164 ft.) south of the bus stop, offer similar tours at similar prices. Most of the companies offer multiday trips to Tortuguero, as well as to Bocas del Toro, Panama.

Brigitte (☎2755-0053; www.brigittecahuita.com) rents horses for $20 per hour (you must have experience riding) and offers guided horseback tours for $35 to $55. She also rents mountain bikes for $8 per day, and even has a few rooms available.

On the main highway, just north of the main entrance to Cahuita, is the **Mariposario Cahuita** (☎2755-0361), a large, informative butterfly-farm attraction that charges $8 and is open daily from 8:30am to 3:30pm. It's best to come in the early morning on a sunny day, when the butterflies are most active.

Bird-watchers and sloth lovers should head north 9km (5½ miles) to **Aviarios del Caribe and the Buttercup Sloth Rescue Center ★★** (☎/fax 2750-0775; www.slothrescue.org). These folks run a sloth rehabilitation project and also offer guided canoe tours through the surrounding estuary and river system. More than 330 species of birds have been spotted here. The 3½-hour canoe tour costs $30 per person and leaves at 6am. There's also a 1½-hour canoe tour combination that includes a visit to the sloth rehabilitation center and a self-guided hike on its trails for $15 per person. This option is available between 8am and 2:30pm. It's best to make reservations in advance.

If you're looking to study Spanish while enjoying the beaches here, check in with **Icari The Spanish School** (☎8358-6667; www.icari-spanishschool.com). A variety of group and individual class options are available.

Shopping

For a wide selection of beachwear, local crafts, cheesy souvenirs, and batik clothing, try **Boutique Coco,** which has moved to the new mall near the bus terminal, or **Boutique Bambata,** which is on the main road near the entrance to the park. The latter is also a good place to have your hair wrapped in colorful threads

Sloth at Aviarios del Caribe and the Buttercup Sloth Rescue Center.

and strung with beads. Right in the center of town, **Bodhi's Books & Gifts** is a good new option for souvenirs. While heading north out of town, similar wares are offered at the **Cahuita Tours** gift shop. For something less formal, hand-made jewelry and crafts are sold by local and itinerant artisans in makeshift stands near the park entrance.

Cahuita locals.

If you're interested in the region, pick up a copy of Paula Palmer's *What Happen: A Folk-History of Costa Rica's Talamanca Coast*. The book is a history of Costa Rica's Caribbean coast based on interviews with many of the area's oldest residents. Much of it is in the traditional Creole language, from which the title is taken. It makes for a fun and interesting read, and you just might meet someone mentioned in the book.

If you are interested in the local music scene, pick up a disc by Walter "Gavitt" Ferguson. The local 87-year-old calypso singer and songwriter is a living legend and has two CDs of original songs, *Babylon* and *Dr. Bombodee*. Ask around town and you should be able to find a copy. If you're lucky, you might even bump into Gavitt.

Where to Stay

In addition to the places listed below, **Bungalow Malu** (☎2755-0114) is a pretty collection of individual bungalows located just across the dirt road from a long stretch of Black Beach, while its new neighbor, **Playa Negra Guesthouse** ★ (☎2755-0127; www.playanegra.cr), offers up fully equipped Caribbean-style cottages and rooms, with a shared pool.

MODERATE

El Encanto Bed and Breakfast ★★ 🍃 The individual bungalows at this little bed-and-breakfast are set in from the road on spacious and well-kept grounds. The bungalows themselves are also spacious and have attractive touches that include wooden bed frames, arched windows, Mexican-tile floors, Guatemalan bedspreads, and framed Panamanian *molas* hanging on the walls. There is a separate two-story, three-bedroom, two-bathroom house with a full kitchen at the rear of the grounds, as well as a deluxe room. Hearty breakfasts are served in the small open dining room surrounded by lush gardens. The hotel also has a small kidney-shaped pool, a wood-floored meditation and yoga hall, a covered garden gazebo, and an open-air massage room.

Cahuita (A.P. 7302-7), Limón (just outside of town on the road to Playa Negra). ☎2755-0113. Fax 2755-0432. www.elencantobedandbreakfast.com. 7 units. $70–$185 double. Rates include full breakfast. Rates slightly lower in off season; higher during peak weeks. MC, V. **Amenities:** Small pool; yoga and meditation hall; massage room. *In room:* No phone.

Hotel La Diosa ★ Close to the sea north of Playa Negra, this hotel has some of the coziest and most inviting rooms around, with excellent facilities, great grounds, and friendly hosts. The best rooms here have air-conditioning and private Jacuzzis. All have cool tile floors, rattan furnishings, and plenty of ventilation. While breakfast is served daily, there's no restaurant. The hotel is just steps from the sea, but the coast here is rugged and made up mostly of sharp coral, and not very suitable for swimming. Still, there's a pretty pool, the gardens are lush and beautiful, and a relaxed and welcoming vibe pervades this place.

Cahuita, Limón (north of town, inland from the Playa Negra road). ☎**877/632-3198** in the U.S. and Canada, or 2755-0055 in Costa Rica. Fax 2755-0321. www.hotelladiosa.net. 18 units. $70–$105 double. Rates include full breakfast. Rates slightly lower in off season; higher during peak weeks. MC, V. **Amenities:** Midsize pool; yoga and meditation room. *In room:* A/C (in some), no phone.

Magellan Inn ★ With an understated sense of tropical sophistication, this small inn has thrived over the years. The carpeted rooms have French doors, vertical blinds, tiled bathrooms with hardwood counters, and two joined single beds. Each room has its own tiled veranda with a Persian rug and bamboo sitting chairs. About half of the rooms have air-conditioning. Although there's a ceiling fan over each bed, the non-air-conditioned rooms could use a bit more ventilation. The combination bar/lounge and dining room features even more Persian-style rugs and wicker furniture. Most memorable of all are the hotel's sunken pool and lush gardens, both of which are built into a crevice in the ancient coral reef that underlies this entire region—which leads to good bird-watching.

At the far end of Playa Negra (about 2km/1¼ miles north of Cahuita), Cahuita (A.P. 1132), Limón. ☎/fax **2755-0035.** www.magellaninn.com. 6 units. $79 double; $99 double with A/C. Rates include continental breakfast. Rates slightly lower in off season; higher during peak weeks. AE, MC, V. **Amenities:** Bar; lounge; small pool. *In room:* A/C (in some), no phone, free Wi-Fi.

INEXPENSIVE

In addition to the places listed below, **Spencer's Seaside Cabinas** (☎**2755-0027**) and its somewhat funky collection of budget rooms is worth considering; its rooms are set just a few feet from the water in the heart of town. Another option is **Hotel Belle Fleur** (☎**2755-0283;** hotelbellefleur@hotmail.com), which has neat and cheery rooms set just a few feet back from the main road, close to the national park entrance.

Alby Lodge ★ 🍃 With the feel of a small village, Alby Lodge is a fascinating little place hand-built by its German owners. Although the four small cabins are close to the center of the village, they're surrounded by a large lawn and feel secluded. The cabins are quintessentially tropical, with thatch roofs, mosquito nets, hardwood floors and beams, big shuttered windows, tile bathrooms, and a hammock slung on the front porch. There's no restaurant here, but you may cook your own meals in a communal kitchen area if you wish. The turnoff for the lodge is on your right just before you reach the national park entrance; the hotel is about 136m (446 ft.) down a narrow, winding lane from here.

Cahuita (A.P. 840), Limón. ☎/fax **2755-0031.** www.albylodge.com. 4 units. $40 double. Children 11 and under stay free in parent's room. No credit cards. *In room:* No phone, free Wi-Fi.

Cabinas Arrecife Located near the water, next to Restaurant Edith (p. 462), this row of basic rooms is an excellent budget choice in Cahuita. Each room comes with a double and a single bed, a table fan, and tile floors. There's not a lot of room to move around, but things are pretty clean and well kept for this price range. A shared veranda boasts some chairs for sitting, where you can catch a glimpse of the sea through a dense stand of coconut palms. There's also a tiny pool fronting the ocean. If you want to be closer to the sea, grab one of the hammocks strung on the palms or sit in the small, open restaurant, which serves breakfast every day and dinners on demand.

Cahuita (about 100m/328 ft. east of the post office), Limón. ☎/fax **2755-0081.** www.cabina sarrecife.com. 12 units. $30 double. AE, MC, V. **Amenities:** Restaurant; pool. *In room:* No phone.

Where to Dine

Coconut meat and milk figure into a lot of the regional cuisine here. Most nights, local women cook up pots of various local specialties and sell them from the front porches of the two discos or from streetside stands around town; a full meal will cost you around $2 to $5.

In addition to the places listed below, **Choco Latte** (☎8330-0277) is a great spot for breakfast, a light bite, or gourmet coffee concoction, while **Corleone** (☎2775-0341) is the place to go for pizza, pastas, and Italian specialties. Right at the main crossroads in town, **Coral Reef** (no phone) is a good local restaurant, with a cozy open-air second-floor dining space that's great for people-watching. Another local favorite is **Relax** (☎2755-0322), which serves a mix of local, Italian, and Mexican food in a large open-air space on the road between Cahuita and Puerto Viejo.

Cha Cha Cha ★★ SEAFOOD/INTERNATIONAL Fresh seafood and grilled meats, simply and expertly prepared—what more could you ask for from a casual, open-air restaurant in a funky beach town? In addition to the fresh catch of the day and filet mignon, the eclectic menu here includes everything from jerk chicken and Thai shrimp salad to pasta primavera and fajitas. The grilled squid salad with a citrus dressing is one of the house specialties and a great light bite. The restaurant occupies the ground floor of an old wooden building. Everything is painted pure white, with some blue trim and accents. The restaurant has only a half-dozen or so tables that fill up fast.

On the main road in town, 3 blocks north of Coco's Bar. ☎8368-1725. Reservations recommended during the high season. Main courses $6–$22. MC, V. Tues–Sun 2–10pm.

Restaurant Edith ★ 🍴 CREOLE/SEAFOOD This place is a local institution, and deservedly so. Miss Edith's daughters do most of the cooking and serving today, but you will often find her on hand. The menu is long, with lots of local seafood dishes and Creole combinations such as yuca in coconut milk with meat or vegetables. The sauces have spice and zest and are a welcome change from the typically bland fare served up elsewhere in Costa Rica. It's often crowded, so don't be bashful about sitting down with total strangers at any of the big tables. Hours can be erratic; it sometimes closes without warning, and service can be slow and gruff at times. After you've ordered, it's usually no more than 45 minutes until your meal arrives.

By the police station, Cahuita. ☎2755-0248. Reservations not accepted. Main courses $3.50–$25. No credit cards. Mon–Sat 11:30am–10pm.

Sobre Las Olas ★ SEAFOOD/ITALIAN Set on a slight rise of rocks above a coral cove and breaking waves, this place has by far the best location in Cahuita. The Italian owners dish up a mix of local and Italian fare. They serve excellent fresh squid or shrimp in a tangy local coconut milk sauce, as well as a host of pasta dishes. The fresh grilled snapper is always a good way to go. I especially like this place for lunch, since you can really enjoy the view of the clear blue Caribbean Sea then. If weather permits, grab one of the outdoor tables set in the shade of coconut palms. After you finish eating, slide over and into one of the hammocks strung between those palms.

Just north of town on the road to Playa Negra. ☎**2755-0109.** Main courses $5–$30. MC, V. Wed–Mon noon–10pm.

Cahuita After Dark

Coco's Bar ★, a classic Caribbean watering hole at the main crossroads in town, has traditionally been the place to spend your nights (or days, for that matter) if you like cold beer and very loud reggae and soca music. Toward the park entrance, the **National Park Restaurant** has a popular bar and disco on most nights during the high season and on weekends during the off season.

PUERTO VIEJO ★★

200km (124 miles) E of San José; 55km (34 miles) S of Limón

Puerto Viejo is the hottest spot on Costa Rica's Caribbean coast. And I'm not talking about the sometimes stifling heat. Even though Puerto Viejo is farther down the road from Cahuita, it's much more popular, with a livelier vibe and more ongoing development. Much of this is due to the many surfers who come here to ride the town's famous and fearsome Salsa Brava wave, and only slightly mellower Playa Cocles beach break. Nonsurfers will appreciate the abundance of excellent swimming beaches, plenty of active adventure options, nearby rainforest trails, and some great local and international restaurants.

As you head still farther south, you will come to the most beautiful beaches on this coast, with white sand and turquoise seas. When it's calm (Aug–Oct), the waters down here are some of the clearest anywhere in the country, with good snorkeling among the nearby coral reefs.

This is the end of the line along Costa Rica's Caribbean coast. After the tiny town of Manzanillo, some 15km (9⅓ miles) south of Puerto Viejo, a national wildlife reserve stretches a few final kilometers to the Panamanian border.

This area gets plenty of rain, just like the rest of the coast (Sept–Oct are your best bets for sun, although it's not guaranteed even in those months).

Essentials

GETTING THERE & DEPARTING By Plane: The closest airport to Puerto Viejo is in Limón (see "Limón: Gateway to Tortuguero National Park & Southern Coastal Beaches," earlier in this chapter). A taxi from the airport to Puerto Viejo should cost around $20 to $25. Alternately, you can just walk the long block from the airport terminal to the main road south and flag down any of the frequent buses that pass by.

By Car: To reach Puerto Viejo, continue south from Cahuita for another 16km (10 miles). Watch for a prominent fork in the highway. The right-hand fork continues on to Bribri and Sixaola. The left-hand fork (it actually appears to be a straight shot) takes you into Puerto Viejo on 5km (3 miles) of sporadically paved road.

By Bus: Mepe express buses (☎2257-8129 in San José, or 2750-0023 in Puerto Viejo) to Puerto Viejo leave San José daily at 6 and 10am, noon, and 2 and 4pm from the Caribbean terminal (Gran Terminal del Caribe) on Calle Central, 1 block north of Avenida 11. The trip's duration is 4½ to 5 hours; the fare is $8. During peak periods extra buses are sometimes added. Always ask if the bus is going into Puerto Viejo (you do not want to get dropped off at the turnoff for Sixaola) and if it's continuing on to **Manzanillo** (especially helpful if you're staying in a hotel south of town). Regardless, don't be surprised if it doesn't do exactly what you were told.

Gray Line (☎2220-2126; www.graylinecostarica.com) has a daily bus that leaves San José for Puerto Viejo at 9:30am. The fare is $35. The return bus leaves Puerto Viejo at 7am. **Interbus** (☎2283-5573; www.interbusonline.com) has a daily bus that leaves San José for Puerto Viejo at 7:50am. The fare is $39. Interbus buses leave Puerto Viejo daily at both 7am and 2:50pm. Both companies will pick you up at most area hotels in both San José and Puerto Viejo, and both offer connections to various other destinations around Costa Rica.

Alternatively, you can catch a bus to **Limón** (see earlier in this chapter for details) and then transfer to a Puerto Viejo–bound bus in Limón. These latter buses (☎2758-1572) leave roughly every hour between 5am

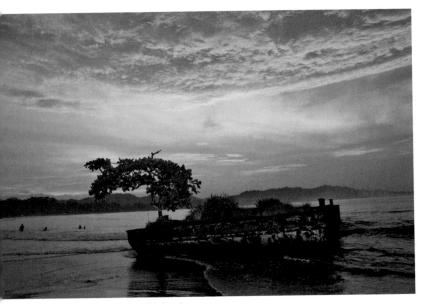

Beached barge at Puerto Viejo beach.

Puerto Viejo

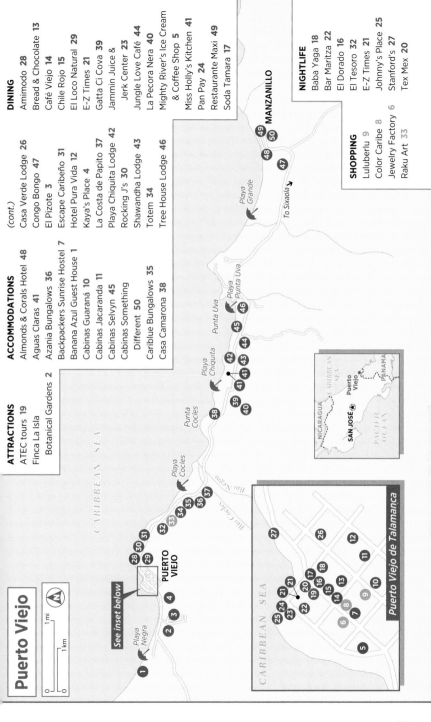

ATTRACTIONS
ATEC tours 19
Finca La Isla
Botanical Gardens 2

ACCOMMODATIONS
Almonds & Corals Hotel 48
Aguas Claras 41
Azania Bungalows 36
Backpackers Sunrise Hostel 7
Banana Azul Guest House 1
Cabinas Guaraná 10
Cabinas Jacaranda 11
Cabinas Selvyn 45
Cabinas Something
  Different 50
Cariblue Bungalows 35
Casa Camarona 38

(cont.)
Casa Verde Lodge 26
Congo Bongo 47
El Pizote 3
Escape Caribeño 31
Hotel Pura Vida 12
Kaya's Place 4
La Costa de Papito 37
Playa Chiquita Lodge 42
Rocking J's 30
Shawandha Lodge 43
Totem 34
Tree House Lodge 46

DINING
Amimodo 28
Bread & Chocolate 13
Café Viejo 14
Chile Rojo 15
El Loco Natural 29
E-Z Times 21
Gatta Ci Cova 39
Jammin Juice &
  Jerk Center 23
Jungle Love Café 44
La Pecora Nera 40
Mighty River's Ice Cream
  & Coffee Shop 5
Miss Holly's Kitchen 41
Pan Pay 24
Restaurante Maxi 49
Soda Tamara 17

SHOPPING
Luluberlu 9
Color Caribe 8
Jewelry Factory 6
Raku Art 33

NIGHTLIFE
Baba Yaga 18
Bar Maritza 22
El Dorado 16
El Tesoro 32
E-Z Times 21
Johnny's Place 25
Stanford's 27
Tex Mex 20

MANZANILLO

To Sixaola

Playa Grande

Playa Punta Uva

Punta Uva

Playa Chiquita

Punta Cocles

Playa Cocles

Río Negro

Río Cocles

CARIBBEAN SEA

Playa Negra

PUERTO VIEJO

See inset below

NICARAGUA
CARIBBEAN SEA
Puerto Viejo
SAN JOSÉ ★
PANAMA
PACIFIC OCEAN

CARIBBEAN SEA

Puerto Viejo de Talamanca

0   1 mi
0   1 km

and 6pm from in front of Radio Casino, which is 1 block north of the municipal market. Buses from Limón to Manzanillo also stop in Puerto Viejo and leave daily at 5 and 10:30am and 3 and 6pm. The trip takes 1½ hours; the fare is $2.70.

If you arrive in Puerto Viejo by bus, be leery of hucksters and touts offering you hotel rooms. In most cases, they work on a small commission from whatever hotel or cabina is hiring, and, in some cases, they'll steer you away from one of my recommended hotels or falsely claim that it is full.

Express buses leave Puerto Viejo for San José daily at 7:30, 9, and 11am, and 4pm. Buses for Limón leave daily at 6 and 9am, and 1, 4, and 5pm. Buses to **Punta Uva** and **Manzanillo** leave Puerto Viejo daily around 7:30am, noon, and 4:30 and 7:30pm. These buses return from Manzanillo at 5 and 8:15am and 12:45 and 5pm.

ORIENTATION The road in from the highway runs parallel to Playa Negra, or Black Sand Beach (this is not the same one I talked about in Cahuita), for a couple hundred meters before entering the village of Puerto Viejo, which has all of about 10 dirt streets. The sea is on your left and forested hills on your right as you come into town. It's another 15km (9⅓ miles) south to Manzanillo. This road is paved all the way to Manzanillo, although many sections are nonetheless in fairly rough shape.

FAST FACTS **Public phones** are located around town and at several hotels. Those looking to change money should head to the **Banco de Costa Rica** branch on the main road in town. There's also a **Banco Nacional** branch in **Bribri,** about 10km (6 miles) away. Both of these banks have ATMs. You'll find the **post office** in the tiny strip mall behind Café Viejo. There is a **Guardia Rural police office** (☎ 2750-0230) on the beach, near Johnny's Place (see later in this chapter).

There are several little Internet cafes around town. There are also a couple of self- and full-service laundromats—the one at **Café Rico** (☎ 2750-0510) will give you a free cup of coffee, cappuccino, or espresso while you wait.

There are a handful of taxi drivers in town. You'll either find them hanging around the *parquecito* (little park), or you can try calling **Bull** (☎ 2750-0112 or 8836-8219) or **Delroy** (☎ 2750-0132). You can rent scooters and bicycles from several operators in town. I like **Red Eye Scooter Rentals** (☎ 8395-6211), which is on the south side of town, across from Stanfords.

What to See & Do

CULTURAL & ADVENTURE TOURS The **Asociación Talamanqueña de Ecoturismo y Conservación ★★ (ATEC;** Talamancan Association of Ecotourism and Conservation; ☎ 2750-0398 or ☎/fax 2750-0191; www.ateccr.org), across the street from the Soda Tamara, is concerned with preserving the environment and cultural heritage of this area and promoting ecologically sound development. (If you plan to stay in Puerto Viejo for an extended period of time and would like to contribute to the community, ask about volunteering.) In addition to functioning as the local information center, Internet cafe, and traveler's hub, ATEC runs a little shop that sells T-shirts, maps, posters, and books.

ATEC also offers quite a few tours, including **half-day walks** that focus on nature and either the local Afro-Caribbean culture or the indigenous Bribri culture. These walks pass through farms and forests, and along the way you'll learn about local history, customs, medicinal plants, and Indian mythology, and have an opportunity to see sloths, monkeys, iguanas, keel-billed toucans, and other wildlife. There is a range of different walks through the nearby Bribri Indians' Kéköldi Reserve, as well as more strenuous hikes through the primary rainforest. **Bird walks** and **night walks** will help you spot more of the area wildlife; there are even overnight treks. The local guides have a wealth of information and make a hike through the forest a truly educational experience. Half-day walks (and night walks) are $20 to $35, and a full-day tour costs between $30 and $65. ATEC can arrange snorkeling trips to the nearby coral reefs, as well as snorkeling and fishing trips in dugout canoes. A half-day of snorkeling or fishing costs around $35 per person.

ATEC can also help you arrange overnight and multiday **camping trips** into the Talamanca Mountains and through neighboring indigenous reserves, as well as trips to Tortuguero and even a 7- to 10-day transcontinental trek to the Pacific coast. Some tours require minimum groups of 5 or 10 people and several days' advance notice. The ATEC office is open daily from 8am to 9pm.

Local tour operators **Exploradores Outdoors** ★ (☎2750-0641; www.exploradoresoutdoors.com), **Puerto Viejo Tours & Rentals** (☎2750-0411), and **Terraventuras** ★ (☎2750-0750; www.terraventuras.com) all offer a whole host of half- and full-day adventure tours into the jungle or sea for between $25 and $100 per person. One popular tour is Terraventuras' zip-line canopy tour, which features 23 treetop platforms, a large harnessed swing, and a rappel.

FROM LEFT: **Bare-throated tiger heron; Cacao tree.**

Spa treatment at Pure Jungle Spa.

Cacao beans drying in the sun.

For horseback riding, check in with **Seahorse Stables** (☎2750-0468; www.horsebackridingincostarica.com), which offers a range of tour and riding options.

One of the more educational tours is the 2-hour **Chocolate Tour** (☎2750-0075) through a working organic cacao plantation and chocolate production facility. The tour shows you the whole process of growing, harvesting, and processing cacao, and of course there's a tasting at the end. The tour is run by reservation only, and costs $18 per person, with a four-person minimum.

Scuba divers can check in with **Reef Runners Dive Shop** (☎2750-0480). The operator frequents a variety of dive sites between Punta Uva and Manzanillo, and if you're lucky the seas will be calm and visibility good—although throughout most of the year it can be a bit rough and murky here. Reef Runners has an office in downtown Puerto Viejo. Rates run between $75 and $110 for a two-tank boat dive.

A LITTLE MIND & BODY REVITALIZATION If you're looking for some day-spa pampering, check out **Pure Jungle Spa** ★★ (☎2750-0536; www.purejunglespa.com). Located at La Costa de Papito (see below), these folks have a wide range of massage and treatment options at reasonable rates. They make many of their own oils, masks, wraps, and exfoliants.

Bliss Massage Center (☎2756-8224; www.blisscostarica.com) offers up a similar menu of treatment options in the minimall in the center of downtown.

Better suited to a longer stay, **Samasati** (☎800/563-9643 in the U.S., or 2756-8015 in Costa Rica; www.samasati.com) is a lovely jungle yoga retreat and spa, with spectacular hillside views of the Caribbean Sea and surrounding forests. Rates here run between $85 and $135 per person per day, depending on occupancy and room type, and include three vegetarian meals per day and taxes. A wide range of tour, massage, and yoga packages are available. If you're staying elsewhere in Puerto Viejo or Cahuita, you can come up for yoga classes ($15), meditations ($5), or private massages ($75–$110) with advance notice. Samasati is located a couple of kilometers before Puerto Viejo (near the turnoff for Bribri) and roughly 1.6km (1 mile) up into the jungle.

NOT YOUR EVERYDAY GARDENS One of the nicest ways to spend a day in Puerto Viejo is to visit the **Finca La Isla Botanical Gardens ★★** (📞2750-0046 or 8886-8530; crgarden@mac.com), a couple hundred meters inland from the Black Sand Beach on a side road just north of El Pizote lodge. Peter Kring and his late wife Lindy have poured time and love into the creation of this meandering collection of native and imported tropical flora. You'll see medicinal, commercial, and just plain wild flowering plants, fruits, herbs, trees, and bushes. Visitors get to gorge on whatever is ripe at the moment. There's also a rigorous rainforest loop trail leaving from the grounds. The gardens are generally open Friday through Monday from 10am to 4pm, but visits at other times can sometimes be arranged in advance. Entrance to the garden or loop trail is $5 per person, or $10 with the guided tour.

Cacao Trails ★ (📞2756-8186; www.cacaotrails.com) is a one-stop attraction featuring botanical gardens, a small serpentarium, an open-air museum demonstrating the tools and techniques of cacao cultivation and processing, and a series of trails. There's also a large open-air restaurant, and a swimming pool for cooling off. You can take canoe rides on the bordering Carbon River, and even watch sea turtles lay their eggs during the nesting season. Admission to the attraction is $25, including a guided tour. A full-day tour, including lunch and a canoe trip, as well as the guided tour, costs $47. During turtle nesting season, they do night tours to watch sea turtles lay their eggs.

Finally, down around Playa Chiquita, at the Tree House Lodge (see below), there's the **Green Iguana Conservation Tour** (📞2750-0706; www.iguanaverde.com). This educational tour focuses on the life cycle, habits, and current situation of this endangered reptile. The tour features a walk around a massive natural enclosure, as well as a video presentation. The cost is $15. Regular tours are offered Tuesday, Thursday, and Saturday at 10am. Additional tours may be arranged by appointment.

SUNNING & SURFING Surfing has historically been the main draw here, but increasing numbers of folks are coming for the miles of beautiful and uncrowded **beaches ★★**, acres of lush rainforests, and laid-back atmosphere. If you aren't a surfer, the same activities that prevail in any quiet beach town are the norm here—sunbathe, go for a walk on the beach, read a book, or take a nap. If you have more energy, there's a host of tours and hiking options, or you can rent a bicycle or a horse. For swimming and sunbathing, locals like to hang out on the small patches of sand in front of Stanford's

Green iguana.

Disco and Johnny's Place. There are small, protected tide pools in front of each of these bars for cooling off.

If you want a more open patch of sand and sea, head north out to **Playa Negra,** along the road into town, or, better yet, to the beaches south of town around Punta Uva and all the way down to Manzanillo, where the coral reefs keep the surf much more manageable (see "Manzanillo & the Manzanillo-Gandoca Wildlife Refuge," below).

Just offshore from the tiny village park is a shallow reef where powerful storm-generated waves sometimes reach 6m (20 ft.). **Salsa Brava,** as it's known, is the prime surf break on the Caribbean coast. Even when the waves are small, this spot is recommended only for very experienced surfers because of the danger of the reef. Other popular beach breaks are south of town on Playa Cocles. If you're interested in surf lessons or want to rent a board, check in with **Aventuras Bravas** (☏8849-7600). They charge $10 for a half-day board rental, and $15 for a full-day rental.

Several operators and makeshift roadside stands offer bicycles, scooters, boogie boards, surfboards, and snorkel gear for rent. Shop around to compare prices and the quality of the equipment before settling on any one.

ANOTHER WAY TO GET WET & WILD Exploradores Outdoors ★ (☏2222-6262 in San José, or 2750-2020 in Puerto Viejo; www.exploradoresoutdoors.com) runs daily white-water rafting trips on the Pacuare and Reventazón rivers. The full-day trip, including transportation, breakfast, and lunch, is $99. If you want to combine white-water rafting with your transportation to or from the Caribbean coast, they can pick you up at your hotel in San José with all your luggage, take you for a day of white-water rafting, and drop you off at day's end at your hotel anywhere on the Caribbean coast from Cahuita to Manzanillo. You can also choose to use the option in the other direction.

Punta Uva shoreline.

Manzanillo offshore rock.

Green turtle.

Pineapple in garden.

Manzanillo & the Manzanillo-Gandoca Wildlife Refuge ★★

If you continue south on the coastal road from Puerto Viejo, you'll come to a couple of even smaller villages. **Punta Uva ★★** is 8km (5 miles) away, and **Manzanillo ★★** is about 15km (9⅓ miles) away. For a good day trip, you can catch the 7:15am bus from Puerto Viejo down to Manzanillo and then catch the 5:15pm bus back. There are several other buses running this route throughout the day, although it's always wise to check with ATEC (p. 466) about current local bus schedules. You could also hire a cab for around $7 to Punta Uva or $12 to Manzanillo. Alternatively, it's about 1½ hours each way by bicycle, with only two relatively small hills to contend with. Although the road is ostensibly paved all the way to Manzanillo, between the near-constant potholes and washed-out sections, it's almost like riding an off-road trail. It's also possible to walk along the beach all the way from Puerto Viejo to Manzanillo, with just a couple of short and well-worn detours inland around rocky points. However, I recommend you catch a ride down to Manzanillo and save your walking energies for the trails and beaches inside the refuge.

Manzanillo is a tiny village with only a few basic cabinas and funky *sodas,* although this has been changing in recent years. The most popular place to eat and hang out is **Restaurant Maxi ★ (☎2759-9086),** an open-air joint on the second floor of an old wooden building facing the sea. This place gets packed on weekends, especially for lunch.

The **Manzanillo-Gandoca Wildlife Refuge ★★** encompasses the small village and extends all the way to the Panamanian border. Manatees, crocodiles, and more than 350 species of birds live within the boundaries of the reserve. The reserve also includes the coral reef offshore—when the seas are calm, this is the best **snorkeling** and **diving** spot on this entire coast. Four species of **sea turtles** nest on one 8.9km (5½-mile) stretch of beach within the reserve between March and July. Three species of dolphins also inhabit and frolic in the waters just off Manzanillo. Many local tour guides and operators offer boat trips out to spot them.

If you want to explore the refuge, you can easily find the single, well-maintained trail by walking along the beach just south of town until you have to wade across a small river. On the other side, you'll pick up the trail head. Otherwise, you can ask around the village for local guides.

Sportfishers should check in with **Bacalao Tours** (☎2759-9116).

(ORGANIC) PEAS & LOVE ★ Inside the Manzanillo-Gandoca refuge is the **Punta Mona Center For Sustainable Living & Education ★** (☎2222-4568; www.puntamona.org). With organic permaculture gardens and a distinctly alternative vibe, this place is open for day visits, overnight stays, and work-exchange and educational programs. A day trip to visit the center, its garden, and facilities, including a vegetarian organic lunch, costs $45; overnight stays cost $40, including three meals.

Shopping

Puerto Viejo attracts a lot of local and international bohemians, who seem to survive solely on the sale of handmade jewelry, painted ceramic trinkets (mainly pipes and cigarette-lighter holders), and imported Indonesian textiles. You'll find them at makeshift stands set up by the town's *parquecito* (little park), which comprises a few wooden benches in front of the sea between Soda Tamara and Stanford's.

In addition to the makeshift outdoor stands, a host of well-stocked gift and crafts shops are in town. The **Jewelry Factory** and **Color Caribe,** both on the main road into town, sell a wide range of jewelry, crafts, and gift items, as well as Costa Rican hammocks. **Luluberlu ★,** located inland across from Cabinas Guaraná, features locally produced craftwork, including shell mobiles and mirrors with mosaic-inlaid frames, as well as imports from Thailand and India. For ceramics, head south to Playa Chiquita and check out the traditional Japanese-style works at **Raku Art.**

Tip: My favorite local purchase is locally produced chocolate, which comes wrapped in wax paper the size and shape of a roll of quarters. They come plain or flavored with coconut, peanuts, mint, ginger, or raisins, and can be found for sale at many gift shops and restaurants around town.

Finally, if you need a book to read on the beach, head just south of town to **Echo Books,** which has a good supply of new and used books, as well as a small cafe and gift shop. The owner also specializes in making homemade truffles and other chocolate treats from local cacao.

Where to Stay in Puerto Viejo

For a longer stay, close to town, you might want to check out **Cashew Hill Jungle Cottages** (☎2750-0256; www.cashewhilllodge.co.cr). On a hill just on the outskirts of town, these are simple but immaculate individual one- and two-bedroom bungalows, with kitchenettes.

MODERATE

In addition to the hotels listed below, **Escape Caribeño** (☎2750-0103; www.escapecaribeno.com) is another good option in this price range, located on the outskirts of town, just south of Salsa Brava.

Banana Azul Guest House ★ 🛏 At the northern end of Playa Negra, on the north end of town, this hotel has earned fast friends and hearty praise. Rooms abound in varnished hardwoods. Inside they are quite simple, with minimal furnishings and amenities, and an overhead or floor fan. Most are on the second floor of the main lodge building, and open onto a broad veranda with ocean views. The end-unit Howler Monkey suite is my favorite room here. The garden bath suites are larger units, with satellite TVs and a large open-air bathtub in their private gardens—hence, the name. Filling breakfasts are served in the common lounge area, and drinks are available throughout the day. An almost private section of beach sits just in front of the hotel, and stretches on for miles north, all the way to Cahuita National Park. No children under 16 are permitted.

Playa Negra Puerto Viejo, Limón. ☏**2750-2035** or 8351-4582. www.bananaazul.com. 12 units. $69–$84 double; $139 suite. Rates include full breakfast. Weekly and monthly rates available. Discounts offered for cash payments. MC, V. No children 15 and under allowed. **Amenities:** Bike rental; watersports equipment rental. *In room:* TV (in some), no phone, free Wi-Fi.

El Pizote This hotel is located across from a long, quiet stretch of Playa Negra, about 400m (1,312 ft.) before you reach downtown proper. The four deluxe bungalows are modern concrete-block affairs, with a small kitchenette, two separate bedrooms, one small bathroom, air-conditioning, and a private porch. Although older and somewhat funkier, the standard bungalows have much more character. These raised wooden buildings have wood walls; steeply pitched roofs; ceiling fans; private porches; and larger bathrooms. The standard rooms are housed in a U-shaped building near the large, free-form pool. These rooms are cool, and come with a ceiling fan, and a shared wraparound veranda. Everything is set amid extensive, lush gardens, assorted tropical fruit trees, and towering rainforest trees. There are hiking trails in the adjacent forest, and good bird-watching here, too. **Be forewarned:** Most of the beds here feature rock-hard foam mattresses, which may be too firm for some.

Just off the main road, about 275m (902 ft.) before you enter downtown, Puerto Viejo, Limón. ☏**2750-0088.** Fax 2750-0226. www.pizotelodge.com. 22 units. $63 double; $79 double bungalow; $109 double deluxe. AE, MC, V. **Amenities:** Restaurant; bar; pool and adjacent kids' pool. *In room:* A/C (in some), no phone.

INEXPENSIVE

True budget hounds will find an abundance of basic hotels and cabinas in downtown Puerto Viejo in addition to those listed below. Of these, **Hotel Pura Vida** (☏/fax **2750-0002;** www.hotel-puravida.com) and **Kaya's Place** (☏**2750-0690;** www.kayasplace.com) are both good bets; while **Backpackers Sunrise Hostel** (☏**2750-0028;** www.sunrisepuertoviejo.com) is a new option right downtown. However, the most popular spot for backpackers, surfers, and students is **Rocking J's ★** (☏**2750-0657;** www.rockingjs.com), a sprawling compound offering simple rooms, camping spaces, and a "hammock hotel."

Cabinas Guaraná This is one of the better options right in town, although it is several blocks from the water. The spacious rooms are painted in bright primary colors, with equally bright and contrasting trim. Rooms come with either two or three full-size beds, or a queen-size with one or two full beds. All come with tile floors, a ceiling fan, and mosquito netting. Guests can use the hotel's fully equipped kitchen to whip up meals, and there's an interesting little sitting area on a platform high up in a tree on the property.

1½ blocks inland from Café Viejo, Puerto Viejo, Limón. ☏/fax **2750-0244.** www.hotelguarana. com. 12 units. $31 double. Rates slightly lower in off season; higher during peak weeks. AE, DC, MC, V. **Amenities:** Lounge; bike rental. *In room:* No phone, free Wi-Fi.

Manzanillo beach.

Cabinas Jacarandá This small hotel has a few nice touches that set it apart from the others in the area. Guatemalan bedspreads add a dash of color and tropical flavor, as do tables made from sliced tree trunks. Most rooms and walkways feature intricate and colorful tile work; in addition, Japanese paper lanterns cover the lights, mosquito nets hang over the beds, and covered walkways connect the various buildings in this budding compound. Massage and yoga classes are offered on-site. If you're traveling in a group, you'll enjoy the space and atmosphere of the biggest room here. If the hotel is full, the owners also rent a few nearby bungalows.

1½ blocks inland from Café Viejo, Puerto Viejo, Limón. (/fax **2750-0069.** www.cabinasjacaranda. net. 14 units, 13 with private bathroom. $32–$45 double. MC, V. *In room:* No phone.

Casa Verde Lodge ★★ This is my favorite hotel right in Puerto Viejo, regardless of the price. A quiet sense of tropical tranquillity pervades this place. Most rooms here are large, with high ceilings, tile floors, private bathrooms, and a private veranda. Those with shared bathrooms are housed in a raised building with a wide, covered breezeway between the rooms. The front and back porches of this building are hung with hammocks and surrounded by lush gardens, where you'll find the showers and toilets. There are also two fully equipped apartments available in a neighboring duplex. Everything is very well maintained, and even the shared bathrooms are kept immaculate. The hotel also features lush gardens, a small but well-stocked gift shop, a good-size outdoor pool with a waterfall, and a separate outdoor massage hut. Even though it's an in-town choice, there's great bird-watching all around the grounds. The owners here are deeply involved in the local community and in improving the environmental and educational opportunities in the region.

A.P. 37-7304, Puerto Viejo, Limón. (**2750-0015.** Fax 2750-0047. www.cabinascasaverde.com. 17 units, 9 with private bathroom. $38–$50 double with shared bathroom; $70 double with private bathroom. Rates include taxes. Rates slightly lower in off season; higher during peak weeks. Discounts offered for cash payments. AE, MC, V. **Amenities:** Bike rental; outdoor pool; massage hut. *In room:* TV (in some), no phone.

Where to Stay Between Puerto Viejo & Manzanillo

All the hotels listed below are located along the road south of Puerto Viejo heading toward Manzanillo. This is one of the most beautiful and isolated stretches of beach in Costa Rica. The single coastal road here has been paved all the way to Manzanillo, greatly improving access to this area. I recommend that you rent a car if you plan to stay at one of these hotels because public transportation is sporadic and taxis aren't always available. If you arrive by bus, however, a rented bicycle or scooter might be all you need to get around once you are settled.

VERY EXPENSIVE

In addition to the place listed below, the former tent camp **Almonds & Corals Hotel** (☎2272-2024 reservations in San José, or 2759-9057 at the hotel; www.almondsandcorals.com) offers rustically luxurious bungalows and suites in a lush forest setting near Manzanillo. These folks have done much to conserve the forests and wildlife around the hotel, and their efforts have earned them "4 Leaves" from the CST Sustainable Tourism program.

Tree House Lodge ★★★ 🎁 The individual houses here are the most unique and stylish options on this coast. All are distinct and quite large, with fluid and fanciful architectural details and tons of brightly varnished woodwork. As the name implies, the Tree House is built into and around a large *sangrillo* tree. The Beach House is closest to the sea and actually features an ocean view from its kitchen and broad deck. However, the crowning achievement is the three-bedroom, two-bathroom Beach House Suite, with its spectacular domed bathroom, which during the day is lit by sunlight streaming through scores of colored glass skylights. All of the houses are beautiful, and you'll spend much of your time here marveling at the creative touches and one-off furniture. This property is set right off Punta Uva, one of the nicest swimming beaches on this coast.

Punta Uva, Puerto Viejo, Limón. ☎**2750-0706.** www.costaricatreehouse.com. 4 units. $250–$390 double. No credit cards. *In room:* A/C (in some), full kitchen.

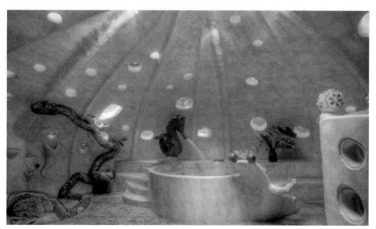

Tree House Lodge.

MODERATE

Although I find the other options listed in this section far more charming, surfers might look into **Totem** (☎**2750-0758**; www.totemsite.com), which offers comfortable rooms, set just off the road, right in front of the beach break in Playa Cocles.

Aguas Claras ★ 🏠 These brightly painted individual bungalows are built on raised stilts and feature fancy gingerbread trim. They are all of wood construction, and all come with private verandas and fully equipped kitchens—although some have just a two-burner cook-top, while others come with a full stove and oven. Inside, they are bright and airy, with either wood or tile floors. There are two one-bedroom cottages, two two-bedroom affairs, and one three-bedroom house. The compound is just a few steps away from a lovely section of Playa Chiquita, and the restaurant here, Miss Holly's Kitchen (see below), is excellent. Maid service is provided every other day. If you book 5 nights, the 6th night is free.

Playa Chiquita, Puerto Viejo, Limón. ☎**2750-0131.** Fax 2750-0368. www.aguasclaras-cr.com. 5 bungalows. $70–$220 bungalow. AE, DC, MC, V. **Amenities:** Restaurant. *In room:* Kitchenette, no phone.

Azania Bungalows ★ This collection of individual bungalows is an excellent option for those seeking a quiet, romantic tropical getaway. The spacious bungalows are set apart from each other amid the hotel's high flowering gardens, giving each a sense of seclusion. All come with one queen-size bed and one double bed downstairs and another double bed in the small loft. The thatch roofs are high-pitched and, combined with large screened windows, allow for good cross ventilation. The lounge area features a television with satellite TV, a small lending library, and a collection of board games. Some of the best features here include the refreshing free-form swimming pool and the open-air thatch-roofed poolside restaurant.

Playa Cocles, Puerto Viejo, Limón. ☎**2750-0540.** Fax 2750-0371. www.azania-costarica.com. 10 bungalows. $85 double. Rates include full breakfast. AE, DC, MC, V. **Amenities:** Restaurant; bar; bike rental; pool. *In room:* Fridge, no phone, free Wi-Fi.

Cariblue Bungalows ★★ This small resort is a wonderful choice. The rooms are spread around well-tended and lush grounds. My favorites are the older raised-stilt wood bungalows, with spacious bedrooms and a small veranda with a hammock. The nicest features here are the bathrooms, with their intricate mosaic tile designs. Deluxe rooms and bungalows come with televisions and air-conditioning. The standard rooms are in a series of concrete-block buildings with high-pitched thatch roofs. They are also spacious and comfortable, but not quite as private or charming as the bungalows. Another option is a two-bedroom house with a full kitchen, for families or for longer stays. A large free-form swimming pool has a swim-up bar, and the restaurant here serves up excellent Italian and local cuisine. Cariblue is about 90m (295 ft.) or so inland from the southern end of Playa Cocles.

Playa Cocles, Puerto Viejo (A.P. 51-7304), Limón. ☎**2750-0035** or ☎/fax 2750-0057. www.cariblue.com. 16 units, 1 house. $95–$120 double; $220 house. Rates include breakfast buffet. Rates slightly lower in off season. AE, MC, V. **Amenities:** Restaurant; bar/lounge; bike rental; Jacuzzi; pool. *In room:* A/C (in some), TV (in some), hair dryer, no phone, free Wi-Fi.

Casa Camarona Casa Camarona has the enviable distinction of being one of the very few hotels in this area right on the beach. There's no road to cross and no long path through the jungle—just a small section of shady gardens separates you from a pretty section of Playa Cocles and the Caribbean Sea. The rooms are in two separate two-story buildings. Definitely get a room on the second floor: Up there you'll find spacious rooms painted in pleasant pastels, with plenty of cross ventilation and a wide shared veranda. I don't know who designed the first-floor rooms, but several of them have such low ceilings that I feel as tall as Yao Ming—and believe me, I'm not. The hotel keeps some chaise longues on the beach under the shade of palm trees, and a beach bar is open during the day, so you barely have to move to quench your thirst.

Playa Cocles, Puerto Viejo, Limón (mailing address: A.P. 2270-1002, Paseo de los Estudiantes, San José). 2283-6711 or 2750-0151. Fax 2222-6184. www.casacamarona.co.cr. 17 units. $70–$85 double. Rates include continental breakfast and taxes. AE, MC, V. **Amenities:** Restaurant; bar. *In room:* A/C (in some), no phone.

Playa Chiquita Lodge ☺ Set amid the shade of large old trees a few kilometers south of Puerto Viejo toward Punta Uva (watch for the sign), this lodge has several wooden buildings set on stilts and connected by a garden walkway. Wide verandas offer built-in seating and rocking chairs. The spacious rooms are painted in bright colors. Throughout the day, free bananas and coffee are available. The owners have three children, ranging from a young child to a couple of teenagers. Guests are invited to join in the nightly family-style dinners, and travelers, especially those with kids, often feel like part of the family. A short trail leads down to a semiprivate little swimming beach with tide pools and beautiful turquoise water. This stretch of beach is the site of a daily 4pm volleyball game. These folks also rent out fully equipped houses for those interested in longer stays or more privacy and independence.

Puerto Viejo, Limón. 2750-0062 or /fax 2750-0408. www.playachiquitalodge.com. 12 units. $60 double. Rates include breakfast. AE, MC, V. **Amenities:** Restaurant. *In room:* No phone, free Wi-Fi.

Shawandha Lodge ★★ 🏨 Isolated and romantic, the individual bungalows here are rustically luxurious. Creative flourishes abound. The thatch-roofed, raised bungalows feature high-pitched ceilings, varnished wood floors, and either one king-size bed or a mix of queen-size and single beds. The bathrooms are works of art, each with original, intricate mosaics of hand-cut tile highlighting a large, open shower. Every bungalow has its own spacious balcony, with both a hammock and a couch, where you can lie and look out on the lush, flowering gardens. The beach is accessed by a private path, and a host of activities and tours can be arranged. There's a large open-air restaurant and lounge where meals and drinks are served. The menu is an eclectic mix, featuring fresh fish and meats in a variety of French, Caribbean, and Polynesian sauces.

Puerto Viejo, Limón. 2750-0018. Fax 2750-0037. www.shawandhalodge.com. 13 units. $115 double. Rates include full breakfast. AE, MC, V. **Amenities:** Restaurant. *In room:* No phone.

INEXPENSIVE

Down in Manzanillo, the simple **Cabinas Something Different** (2759-9014) is a good option, while **Congo Bongo** (2759-9016; www.congo-bongo.com) offers fully equipped houses in a lush forest setting.

La Costa de Papito ★ This small collection of individual and duplex cabins is just across from Playa Cocles, about 1.6km (1 mile) south of Puerto Viejo. The wooden bungalows come with one or two double beds, artfully tiled bathrooms, and an inviting private porch with a table and chairs and either a hammock or a swing chair. There's also a larger, two-bedroom unit. There's an excellent restaurant in-house, and the Pure Jungle Spa (see above) is on the grounds, as well.

Playa Cocles, Puerto Viejo, Limón. ☎2750-0704 or ☎/fax 2750-0080. www.lacostadepapito. com. 13 units. $54–$78 double. AE, DISC, MC, V. **Amenities:** Restaurant; bar; bike rental; small spa; watersports equipment rental. *In room:* No phone.

Where to Dine in Puerto Viejo

To really sample the local cuisine, you need to look up a few local women. Ask around for **Miss Dolly, Miss Sam, Miss Isma,** and **Miss Irma,** who all serve up sit-down meals in their modest little *sodas.* In addition to locally seasoned fish and chicken served with rice and beans, these joints are usually a great place to find some *pan bon* (a local sweet, dark bread), ginger cakes, *paty* (meat-filled turnovers), and *rondon* (see below). Just ask around for these women, and someone will direct you to them.

If you're looking for a light bite for breakfast, lunch, or a snack, check out **Pan Pay** (☎2750-0081), a French-run bakery and sandwich shop next to Johnny's Place (see "Puerto Viejo After Dark," below). Also, **Jammin' Juice and Jerk Center** (☎8826-4332), in the same building, specializes in jerk chicken, salads, and fresh juices. For casual fare, try **E-Z Times** (☎2750-0663), which is right in front of the water near the heart of town.

Puerto Viejo has a glut of excellent Italian restaurants; in addition to the places listed below, **Amimodo** (☎2750-0257) is a fine restaurant.

Finally, if you're just looking for something to cool you off, try **Mighty River's Ice Cream & Coffee Shop** (☎2750-2016), which has delicious homemade ice cream.

Bread & Chocolate ★ ☺ BREAKFAST/AMERICAN Perfect for breakfast or lunch, this place is almost always bustling and full. Breakfasts feature waffles, French toast, and pancakes served with some namesake fresh chocolate sauce, or egg dishes served with home-baked biscuits, bagels, or whole wheat bread. For lunch, sandwiches, which are served on the aforementioned homemade bread, include BLTs and Jerk sandwiches. Those with kids or a child within might want to sample the PB&J or PB&Chocolate, again made with homemade ingredients. Both breakfast and lunch are served all day. Don't leave without trying or buying some of their brownies and truffles.

> ## That Rundown Feeling
>
> Rundown (or *rondon*) soup is a spicy coconut milk–based soup or stew made with anything the cook can run down—it usually includes a mix of local tubers (potato, sweet potato, or yuca), other vegetables (carrots or corn), and often some seafood. Be sure to try this authentic taste of the Caribbean.

Half block south of Café Viejo. ☎2750-0723. Main courses $3.75–$6. MC, V. Wed–Sat 6:30am–6:30pm; Sun 6:30am–2:30pm.

Café Viejo ★ ITALIAN This place is set on the busiest corner of "downtown" Puerto Viejo. White gauze curtains help to slightly shield this open-air spot from the hustle and bustle just outside. Still, it's often loud and crowded inside as well, and that's part of the charm of this popular place. You can get a wide range of pastas and thin-crust wood-oven pizzas here, as well as more substantial fish, chicken, and meat entrees. The grilled whole fresh fish is an especially good option. On weekends, a late-night lounge scene sometimes erupts, with electronic music and dancing.

On the main road. ☎**2750-0817.** Main courses $8–$25. MC, V. Wed–Mon 6–11:30pm.

Chile Rojo ★ 🍴 PAN-ASIAN/MEDITERRANEAN Housed in a large, new space on the second floor of Puerto Viejo's new minimall, this long-standing restaurant continues to serve up excellent Pan-Asian, Mediterranean, and vegetarian fare at very reasonable prices. Bright tablecloths, a lively bar scene, and an open kitchen make this place inviting. If you want to people-watch, grab a seat at the long line of stools that line the street-facing, open-air wall that runs along one side of the restaurant. Standout menu options are green Thai curry served with fish, chicken, or vegetables or seared fresh tuna steak with a ginger-soy dressing. There are also daily specials, and occasional live concerts here.

2nd floor of new shopping mall downtown. ☎**2750-0025** or 8994-7636. Main courses $3.50–$11. No credit cards. Thurs–Tues noon–11pm.

El Loco Natural ★★ 🎁 INTERNATIONAL A friendly, hippie vibe pervades this open-air restaurant. Seating is at heavy wooden tables, and if the few smaller, more private tables are taken, you can take any empty seat at one of the larger communal tables. The short menu features several vegetarian items, as well as fresh fish and some chicken and meat dishes, prepared in curry, Thai, and Mexican sauces. There's often live music here, ranging from reggae to jazz to Latin American folk.

On the main road just south of downtown, about 1 block beyond Stanford's. ☎**2750-0530.** Main courses $4–$15. No credit cards. Thurs–Mon 6–10pm.

Soda Tamara 🍴 COSTA RICAN This little restaurant has long been popular with budget-conscious travelers and has an attractive setting for such an economical place. The painted picket fence in front gives the restaurant a homey feel, and the best seats can be found on the front veranda facing the street, or in the large open-air dining area. The menu features standard fish, chicken, and meat entrees, served with a hefty helping of Caribbean-style rice and beans. You can also get *patacones* (fried chips made out of plantains) and a wide selection of fresh-fruit juices. A second-floor open-air bar is open nightly from 6pm until the last straggler calls it quits.

On the main road. ☎**2750-0148.** Main courses $3.50–$30. AE, MC, V. Daily 11:30am–10pm.

Where to Dine Between Puerto Viejo & Manzanillo

As the beaches stretching south of Puerto Viejo keep getting more popular, there has been a corresponding increase in the number of places to grab a meal. In addition to the restaurants listed above and below, **Cabinas Selvyn** (no phone) at Punta Uva is an excellent option for local cuisine and fresh seafood. **Jungle Love Café** (☎2750-0162) serves up praise-worthy pizzas, pasta, and fusion cuisine, in a little space on Playa Chiquita.

Finally, if you make it as far south as Manzanillo, **Restaurant Maxi** ★ (☎2759-9086) is your best bet. This open-air spot is always packed, especially for lunch. A fresh-fish plate will cost you between $6.50 and $14; lobster, in season, will run between $15 and $35, depending upon the size. Whatever you order comes with rice and beans, *patacones* (fried plantain chips), and a small side of cabbage salad.

Gatta Ci Cova ★ ITALIAN An extension and variation on their nearby and extremely popular restaurant, La Pecora Nera (see below), this simple place serves a range of panini sandwiches and thin-crust pizzas. Located in an open, two-story building, the main dining room is on the second floor, watched over by a giant stuffed black jaguar on the stairway railing. Downstairs is a more informal bar area. Try the four-cheese pizza with fresh pear slices and pine nuts, or the fresh fish *panino* with grilled zucchini and olive paste. There's always a two-course daily plate of an antipasto and pasta dish, with a glass of wine or beer for around $12. This is a great place for lunch or a light dinner.

Just beyond the soccer field on the main road through Cocles. ☎2750-0490. Pizzas and panini $5–$10. AE, MC, V. Tues–Sun noon–10:30pm.

La Pecora Nera ★★★ ITALIAN This open-air joint on the jungle's edge has a deserved reputation as the finest Italian restaurant in the region, if not the country. Owner Ilario Giannoni is a whirlwind of enthusiasm and activity, switching hats all night long from maitre d' to chef to waiter to busboy in an entertaining

---

On to Panama

Costa Rica's southern zone, particularly Puerto Viejo, is a popular jumping-off point for trips into Panama. The nearest and most popular destination is the island retreat of Bocas del Toro. Most tour agencies and hotel desks in the area can arrange tours to Panama.

If you're doing it yourself, it's fastest and easiest to fly directly from Limón on **Nature Air** (☎800/235-9272 in the U.S. and Canada, or 2299-6000; www.natureair.com), which has a flight that departs the Tobías Bolaños International Airport in Pavas at 1pm, Monday, Wednesday, Saturday, and Sunday, stopping in Limón en route to pick up and discharge

passengers. The one-way fare from Limón is $107.

Alternately, you can sign up for the daily **Boca's Shuttle** (☎2750-0626; www.bocasshuttle.com), which will take you via land and boat for $34 each way; check the website or call for departure times. Or, you can take the local buses to the border at Sixaola. All the border formalities can be handled easily at the border, and onward connections wait on the Panamanian side to take you by bus and boat to Bocas del Toro.

If you're planning on spending any time touring around Panama, be sure to pick up a copy of *Frommer's Panama*.

blur. Sure, he's got some help, including his grandmother, who makes gnocchi, but it sometimes seems like he's doing it single-handedly. The menu has a broad selection of pizzas and pastas, but your best bet is to just ask Ilario what's fresh and special for that day, and to trust his instincts and inventions. I've had fabulous fresh pasta dishes and top-notch appetizers every time I've visited. The various carpaccios are fabulous, and the gnocchi here is light and mouthwatering.

50m (164 ft.) inland from a well-marked turnoff on the main road south just beyond the soccer field in Cocles. ☎2750-0490. Reservations recommended. Main courses $10–$22. AE, MC, V. Tues–Sun 5:30–11pm.

Miss Holly's Kitchen ★ 🍴 INTERNATIONAL Although they only serve breakfast and lunch, this little cafe is a favorite spot for locals and visitors alike. Breakfasts feature fresh baked goods, omelets, and local favorites such as rice and beans with eggs. For lunch the menu shifts to a range of green and hearty salads, and various sandwiches. I like grabbing one of the tables on the small wooden cottage's wraparound veranda. But you can also just order at the deli counter inside and have a picnic on the beach. If you're traveling with a laptop, this is a great place to take advantage of some free Wi-Fi.

At Aguas Clara, Playa Chiquita. ☎2750-0131. Breakfast $7–$8; sandwiches and salads $7–$8. MC, V. Wed–Mon 8am–4pm.

Puerto Viejo After Dark

There are two main disco/bars in town. **Johnny's Place** ★★ is near the Rural Guard station, about 100m (328 ft.) or so north of the ATEC office. You'll find **Stanford's** overlooking the water out near Salsa Brava just as the main road heads south of town. Both have small dance floors with ground-shaking reggae, dub, and rap rhythms blaring. The action usually spills out from the dance floor at both joints on most nights. I prefer the atmosphere at Johnny's, although both have tables, chairs, and candles set out on the sand, near the water's edge.

One of the more popular places in town is the new **Tex Mex** restaurant and bar, which is located right where the main road hits the water. Another option is the **Sunset Bar,** which is near the water, beside the bus station, and sometimes features live music. For a more sophisticated ambience try the downtown **Baba Yaga** ★, or the ocean-side **E-Z Times.** An open-air bar on the second floor of **Soda Tamara** (p. 479) is a casual and quiet place to gather after dark. **Rocking J's** (p. 473) often features live music. Finally, for a more local scene, check out **Bar Maritza's,** in the center of town, right across from the basketball court, which really seems to go off on Sunday nights.

You can also take advantage of the pool table, board games, and DirecTV (usually showing sporting events) at **El Dorado,** in front of the ATEC office (p. 466), as an alternative to the loud music and dance scenes of the other joints mentioned above.

Heading just south out of town, the **Cut Back** is a popular spot with backpackers and bohemians, with a solid after-hours scene. Farther south of town, at the start of Playa Cocles, **Café Mango** at **Cabinas El Tesoro** shows large-screen movies or has live music just about every night.

FAST FACTS: COSTA RICA

Area Codes There are no area codes in Costa Rica. All local phone numbers are eight-digit numbers.

Business Hours Banks are usually open Monday through Friday from 9am to 4pm, although many have begun to offer extended hours. Post offices are generally open Monday through Friday from 8am to 5:30pm, and Saturday from 7:30am to noon. (In small towns, post offices often close on Sat.) Stores are generally open Monday through Saturday from 9am to 6pm (many close for 1 hr. at lunch) but stores in modern malls generally stay open until 8 or 9pm and don't close for lunch. Most bars are open until 1 or 2am, although some go later.

Drinking Laws Alcoholic beverages are sold every day of the week throughout the year, with the exception of the 2 days before Easter and the 2 days before and after a presidential election. The legal drinking age is 18, although it's only sporadically enforced. Liquor—everything from beer to hard spirits—is sold in specific liquor stores, as well as at most supermarkets and even convenience stores.

Driving Rules See "Getting There & Getting Around," p. 54.

Electricity The standard in Costa Rica is the same as in the United States: 110 volts AC (60 cycles). However, three-pronged outlets can be scarce, so it's helpful to bring along an adapter.

Wherever you go, bring a **connection kit** of the right power and phone adapters, a spare phone cord, and a spare Ethernet network cable—or find out whether your hotel supplies them to guests.

Embassies & Consulates The following are located in San José: **United States Embassy,** in front of Centro Commercial, on the road to Pavas (☎2519-2000, or 2220-3127 after hours in case of emergency); **Canadian Consulate,** Oficentro Ejecutivo La Sabana, Edificio 5 (☎2242-4400); and **British Embassy,** Paseo Colón between calles 38 and 40 (☎2258-2025). There are no Australian or New Zealand embassies in San José.

Emergencies In case of any emergency, dial ☎911 (which should have an English-speaking operator); for an ambulance, call ☎128; and to report a fire, call ☎118. If 911 doesn't work, you can contact the police at ☎2222-1365 or 2221-5337, and hopefully they can find someone who speaks English.

Gasoline (Petrol) Gasoline is sold as "regular" and "super." Both are unleaded; super is just higher octane. Diesel is available at almost every gas station as well. When going off to remote places, try to leave with a full tank of gas because gas stations can be hard to find. If you need to gas up in a small town, you can sometimes get gasoline from enterprising families who sell it by the liter from their houses. Look for hand-lettered signs that say GASOLINA. At press time a liter of super cost 435 colones, or roughly $2.95 per gallon.

Holidays For information on holidays see "Calendar of Events," on p. 51.

Hospitals In San José try **Clínica Bíblica** (Avenida 14 btw. calles Central and 1), which offers emergency services to foreign visitors at reasonable prices (☎2522-1000; www.clinicabiblica.com), or the **Hospital CIMA** (☎2208-1000; www.hospitalsanjose. net), located in Escazú on the Próspero Fernández Highway, which connects San José and the western suburb of Santa Ana and has the most modern facilities in the country.

Insurance For information on traveler's insurance, trip cancellation insurance, and medical insurance while traveling please visit www.frommers.com/planning.

Internet Access Cybercafes can be found all over Costa Rica, especially in the more popular tourist destinations. Moreover, an ever increasing number of hotels, restaurants, cafes, and retailers around Costa Rica are offering high-speed Wi-Fi access, either free or for a small fee. Throughout the book, I list which hotels provide free, or for a fee, Wi-Fi and high-speed Ethernet access. For help locating cybercafes and other establishments where you can go for Internet access, please see the destination chapters throughout this book.

Language Spanish is the official language of Costa Rica. However, in most tourist areas, you'll be surprised by how well Costa Ricans speak English. *Frommer's Spanish PhraseFinder & Dictionary* is probably the best phrase book to bring with you; also see Chapter 14 for some key Spanish terms and phrases.

Laundromats Laundromats—be they full-service or self-serve—are not extremely common in Costa Rica. Outside of San José, dry cleaners are also often hard to find. Hotel laundry services, which can sometimes be expensive, are far more common. That said, most major tourist destinations have one or more laundromats catering to travelers.

Legal Aid If you need legal help, your best bet is to first contact your local embassy or consulate. See "Embassies & Consulates," above, for contact details. Alternatively, you can pick up a copy of the *Tico Times,* which usually carries advertisements from local English-speaking lawyers.

Mail At press time, it cost 170 colones (30¢) to mail a letter to the United States, and 190 colones (34¢) to Europe. You can get stamps at post offices and at some gift shops in large hotels. Given the Costa Rican postal service's track record, I recommend paying an extra 500 colones (89¢) to have anything of any value certified. Better yet, use an international courier service or wait until you get home to post it. **DHL,** on Paseo Colón between calles 30 and 32 (☎2209-0000; www.dhl.com); **EMS Courier,** with desks at most post offices nationwide (☎800/900-2000 in Costa Rica; www. correos.go.cr); **FedEx,** which is based in Heredia but will arrange pickup anywhere in the metropolitan area (☎800/463-3339; www.fedex.com); and **United Parcel Service,** in Pavas (☎2290-2828; www.ups.com), all operate in Costa Rica.

If you're sending mail *to* Costa Rica, it generally takes between 10 and 14 days to reach San José, although it can take as much as a month to get to the more remote corners of the country. Plan ahead. Also note that many hotels and ecolodges have mailing addresses in the United States. Always use these addresses when writing from North America or Europe. Never send cash, checks, or valuables through the Costa Rican mail system.

Newspapers & Magazines There are six Spanish-language dailies in Costa Rica and one English-language weekly, the *Tico Times.* In addition, you can get *Time, Newsweek,* and several U.S. newspapers at some hotel gift shops and a few of the bookstores in San José. If you understand Spanish, *La Nación* is the paper you'll want. Its "Viva" and "Tiempo Libre" sections list what's going on in the world of music, theater, dance, and more.

Passports See www.frommers.com/planning for information on how to obtain a passport.

For Residents of Australia Contact the **Australian Passport Information Service** at ☎131-232, or visit the government website at www.passports.gov.au.

For Residents of Canada Contact the central **Passport Office,** Department of Foreign Affairs and International Trade, Ottawa, ON K1A 0G3 (☎800/567-6868; www.ppt. gc.ca).

For Residents of Ireland Contact the **Passport Office,** Setanta Centre, Molesworth Street, Dublin 2 (☎01/671-1633; www.irlgov.ie/iveagh).

For Residents of New Zealand Contact the **Passports Office** at ☎0800/225-050 in New Zealand or 04/474-8100, or log on to www.passports.govt.nz.

For Residents of the United Kingdom Visit your nearest passport office, major post office, or travel agency or contact the **United Kingdom Passport Service** at ☎0870/521-0410 or search its website at www.ukpa.gov.uk.

For Residents of the United States To find your regional passport office, either check the U.S. State Department website or call the **National Passport Information Center** toll-free number (☎877/487-2778) for automated information.

Police In most cases, dial ☎911 for the police, and you should be able to get someone who speaks English on the line. Other numbers for the **Judicial Police** are ☎2222-1365 and 2221-5337. The numbers for the **Traffic Police (Policía de Tránsito)** are ☎800/8726-7486 toll-free nationwide, or 2222-9330.

Smoking While not as high a percentage as most Europeans, a large number of Costa Ricans smoke, and public smoking regulations and smoke-free zones have yet to take hold. Restaurants are required by law to have nonsmoking areas, but enforcement is often lax, air-circulation poor, and the separating almost nonexistent. Bars, as a whole, are often very smoke-filled in Costa Rica.

Most higher-end hotels have at least some nonsmoking rooms. However, many midrange hotels and most budget options are pretty laissez-faire when it comes to smoking. Whenever possible, the presence of nonsmoking rooms is noted in hotel listing description information.

Taxes There is a national 13% value added tax (often written as i.v.i. in Costa Rica) added to all goods and services. This includes hotel and restaurant bills. Restaurants also add on a 10% service charge, for a total of 23% more on your bill.

There is an airport departure tax of $26. This tax must be purchased prior to check-in. There are desks at the main terminal of all international airports where you can pay this tax. Some local travel agencies and hotels offer to purchase the departure tax in advance, as a convenience for tourists. You must give them authorization, as well as your passport number, and pay a small service fee.

Although you can pay the airport exit tax with a credit card, it is charged as a cash advance. Most credit card companies hit this kind of transaction with a fee and begin charging interest on it immediately. It is best to pay the airport tax in cash, either dollars or colones.

Telephones See "Staying Connected," on p. 71, for tips on calling to and from Costa Rica.

Throughout the book, I haven't listed phone numbers for bars or clubs in small towns and villages. Reservations are never necessary, and in most cases you're never more than a few blocks away if you need to find out if it's open. The same is true for most shops and souvenir stands in these smaller destinations, towns, and villages. If for any reason you need to contact one of these places, ask at your hotel desk, and they'll certainly have the number if there is one.

Time Costa Rica is on Central Standard Time (same as Chicago and St. Louis), 6 hours behind Greenwich Mean Time. Costa Rica does not use daylight saving time, so the time difference is an additional hour April through October.

Tipping Tipping is not necessary in restaurants, where a 10% service charge is always added to your bill (along with a 13% tax). If service was particularly good, you can leave a little at your own discretion, but it's not mandatory. Porters and bellhops get around 75¢ per bag. You don't need to tip a taxi driver unless the service has been superior; a tip is not usually expected.

Toilets These are known as *sanitarios, servicios sanitarios,* or *baños.* They are marked *damas* (women) and *hombres* or *caballeros* (men). Public restrooms are hard to come by. You will almost never find a public restroom in a city park or downtown area. There are usually public restrooms at most national-park entrances, and much less frequently inside the national park. In the towns and cities, it gets much trickier. One must count on the generosity of some hotel or restaurant. Same goes for most beaches. However, most restaurants, and, to a lesser degree, hotels, will let you use their facilities, especially if you buy a soft drink or something. Bus and gas stations often have restrooms, but many of these are pretty grim.

Visitor Information In the United States or Canada, you can get basic information on Costa Rica by contacting the **Costa Rican Tourist Board** (**ICT,** or Instituto Costarricense de Turismo; ☏**866/COSTA RICA;** www.visitcostarica.com). Travelers from the United Kingdom, Australia, and New Zealand will have to rely primarily on this website because the ICT does not have toll-free access in these countries.

In addition to this official site, you'll be able to find a wealth of Web-based information on Costa Rica with a few clicks of your mouse. In fact you'll be better off surfing, as the ICT site is rather limited and clunky. See "The Best Websites About Costa Rica," on p. 27, for some helpful suggestions about where to begin your online search.

You can pick up a map when you arrive at the ICT's information desk at the airport, or at their downtown San José offices (although the map included with this book is generally better). Other sources in San José for detailed maps include **Seventh Street Books,** Calle 7 between avenidas Central and 1 (☏**2256-8251**); **Librería Lehmann,** Avenida Central between calles 1 and 3 (☏**2223-1212**); and **Librería Universal,** Avenida Central between calles Central and 1 (☏**2222-2222**).

Perhaps the best map to have is the waterproof country map of Costa Rica put out by **International Travel Maps** (www.itmb.com), which can be ordered directly from their website, or any major online bookseller, like Amazon.com.

Water Although the water in San José is generally safe to drink, water quality varies outside the city. Because many travelers have tender digestive tracts, I recommend playing it safe and sticking to bottled drinks as much as possible. Also avoid ice. See p. 64 in "Planning Your Trip to Costa Rica" for more advice.

AIRLINE, HOTEL & CAR-RENTAL WEBSITES

MAJOR AIRLINES

Aeroméxico
www.aeromexico.com

Air France
www.airfrance.com

Air New Zealand
www.airnewzealand.com

Alitalia
www.alitalia.com

American Airlines
www.aa.com

British Airways
www.british-airways.com

Caribbean Airlines (formerly BWIA)
www.caribbean-airlines.com

Continental Airlines
www.continental.com

Cubana
www.cubana.cu

Delta Air Lines
www.delta.com

Frontier Airlines
www.frontierairlines.com

Iberia Airlines
www.iberia.com

Japan Airlines
www.jal.co.jp

JetBlue Airways
www.jetblue.com

Korean Air
www.koreanair.com

Lan Airlines
www.lanchile.com

Lufthansa
www.lufthansa.com

Northwest Airlines
www.nwa.com

Quantas Airways
www.quantas.com

TACA
www.taca.com

United Airlines
www.united.com

US Airways
www.usairways.com

DOMESTIC AIRLINES

Nature Air
www.natureair.com

Sansa
www.flysansa.com

MAJOR HOTEL & MOTEL CHAINS

Best Western International
www.bestwestern.com

Clarion Hotels
www.choicehotels.com

Comfort Inns
www.ComfortInn.com

Courtyard by Marriott
www.marriott.com/courtyard

Crowne Plaza Hotels
www.ichotelsgroup.com/
crowneplaza

Days Inn
www.daysinn.com

Doubletree Hotels
www.doubletree.com

Four Seasons
www.fourseasons.com

Hampton Inn
www.hamptoninn1.hilton.com

Hilton Hotels
www.hilton.com

Holiday Inn
www.holidayinn.com

Hyatt
www.hyatt.com

InterContinental Hotels & Resorts
www.ichotelsgroup.com

Marriott
www.marriott.com

Quality
www.QualityInn.ChoiceHotels.com

Radisson Hotels & Resorts
www.radisson.com

Ramada Worldwide
www.ramada.com

Residence Inn by Marriott
www.marriott.com/residenceinn

CAR-RENTAL AGENCIES

Adobe
www.adobecar.com

Alamo
www.alamo.com

Avis
www.avis.com

Budget
www.budget.com

Dollar
www.dollar.com

Hertz
www.hertz.com

National
www.nationalcar.com

Payless
www.paylesscarrental.com

Thrifty
www.thrifty.com

14

SPANISH TERMS & PHRASES

Costa Rican Spanish is neither the easiest nor the most difficult dialect to understand. Ticos speak at a relatively relaxed speed and enunciate clearly, without dropping too many final consonants. The *y* and *ll* sounds are subtly, almost inaudibly, pronounced. Perhaps the most defining idiosyncrasy of Costa Rican Spanish is the way Ticos overemphasize, and almost chew, their *r*'s.

If you're looking for a more comprehensive dictionary and language resource, pick up a copy of *Frommer's Spanish PhraseFinder & Dictionary*, or *Frommer's Spanish Phrasebook and Culture Guide*. Both are excellent pocket books with a wealth of information to make your travel interactions more rewarding.

BASIC WORDS & PHRASES

English	Spanish	Pronunciation
Hello	Buenos días	*bweh*-nohss *dee*-ahss
How are you?	¿Cómo está usted?	*koh*-moh ehss-*tah* oo-stehd
Very well	Muy bien	mwee byehn
Thank you	Gracias	*grah*-syahss
Goodbye	Adiós	ad-*dyohss*
Please	Por favor	pohr fah-*vohr*
Yes	Sí	see
No	No	noh
Excuse me (to get by someone)	Perdóneme	pehr-*doh*-neh-meh
Excuse me (to begin a question)	Disculpe	dees-*kool*-peh
Give me	Deme	*deh*-meh
Where is . . . ?	¿Dónde está . . . ?	*dohn*-deh ehss-*tah*
the station	la estación	la ehss-*tah*-syohn
the bus stop	la parada	la pah-*rah*-dah
a hotel	un hotel	oon oh-*tehl*
a restaurant	un restaurante	oon res-tow-*rahn*-teh
the toilet	el servicio	el ser-*vee*-syoh
To the right	A la derecha	ah lah deh-*reh*-chah
To the left	A la izquierda	ah lah ees-*kyehr*-dah
Straight ahead	Adelante	ah-deh-*lahn*-teh
I would like . . .	Quiero . . .	*kyeh*-roh
to eat	comer	ko-*mehr*
a room	una habitación	oo-nah ah-bee-tah-*syohn*
How much is it?	¿Cuánto?	*kwahn*-toh
When?	¿Cuándo?	*kwan*-doh
What?	¿Qué?	keh
Yesterday	Ayer	ah-*yehr*
Today	Hoy	oy
Tomorrow	Mañana	mah-*nyah*-nah
Breakfast	Desayuno	deh-sah-*yoo*-noh
Lunch	Almuerzo	ahl-*mwehr*-soh
Dinner	Cena	*seh*-nah
Do you speak English?	¿Habla usted inglés?	*ah*-blah oo-*stehd* een-*glehss*
I don't understand Spanish very well.	No entiendo muy bien el español.	noh ehn-*tyehn*-do mwee byehn el ehss-pah-*nyohl*

NUMBERS

English	Spanish	Pronunciation
0	cero	*ser*-oh
1	uno	*oo*-noh
2	dos	dohss
3	tres	trehss
4	cuatro	*kwah*-troh
5	cinco	*seen*-koh
6	seis	sayss
7	siete	*syeh*-teh
8	ocho	*oh*-choh
9	nueve	*nweh*-beh
10	diez	dyehss
11	once	*ohn*-seh
12	doce	*doh*-seh
13	trece	*treh*-seh
14	catorce	kah-*tohr*-seh
15	quince	*keen*-seh
16	dieciséis	dyeh-see-*sayss*
17	diecisiete	dyeh-see-*syeh*-teh
18	dieciocho	dyeh-see-*oh*-choh
19	diecinueve	dyeh-see-*nweh*-beh
20	veinte	*bayn*-teh
30	treinta	*trayn*-tah
40	cuarenta	kwah-*rehn*-tah
50	cincuenta	seen-*kwehn*-tah
60	sesenta	seh-*sehn*-tah
70	setenta	seh-*tehn*-tah
80	ochenta	oh-*chehn*-tah

DAYS OF THE WEEK

English	Spanish	Pronunciation
Monday	lunes	*loo*-nehss
Tuesday	martes	*mahr*-tehss
Wednesday	miércoles	*myehr*-koh-lehss
Thursday	jueves	*wheh*-behss
Friday	viernes	*byehr*-nehss
Saturday	sábado	*sah*-bah-doh
Sunday	domingo	doh-*meen*-goh

SOME TYPICAL TICO WORDS & PHRASES

Birra Slang for beer.

Boca Literally means "mouth," but also a term to describe a small appetizer served alongside a drink at many bars.

Bomba Translates literally as "pump" but is used in Costa Rica for "gas station."

Brete Work, or job.

Buena nota To be good, or have a good vibe.

Casado Literally means "married," but is the local term for a popular restaurant offering that features a main dish and various side dishes.

Chapa Derogatory way to call someone stupid or clumsy.

Chepe Slang term for the capital city, San José.

Choza Slang for house or home. Also called *chante*.

Chunche Knickknack; thing, as in "whatchamacallit."

Con mucho gusto With pleasure.

De hoy en ocho In 1 week's time.

Diay An untranslatable but common linguistic punctuation, often used to begin a sentence.

Estar de chicha To be angry.

Fria Literally "cold," but used to mean a cold beer—*una fria, por favor.*

Fut Short for *futbol,* or soccer.

Goma Hangover.

Harina Literally "flour," but used to mean money.

La sele Short for *la selección,* the Costa Rican national soccer team.

Limpio Literally means "clean," but is the local term for being broke, or having no money.

Macha or **machita** A blond woman.

Mae Translates like "man"; used by many Costa Ricans, particularly teenagers, as frequent verbal punctuation.

Maje A lot like *mae,* above, but with a slightly derogatory connotation.

Mala nota Bad vibe, or bad situation.

Mala pata Bad luck.

Mejenga An informal, or pickup, soccer game.

Pachanga or **pelón** Both terms are used to signify a big party or gathering.

Ponga la maría, por favor This is how you ask taxi drivers to turn on the meter.

Pulpería The Costa Rican version of the "corner store" or small market.

Pura paja Pure nonsense or BS.

Pura vida Literally, "pure life"; translates as "everything's great."

Qué torta What a mess; what a screw-up.

Si Dios quiere God willing; you'll hear Ticos say this all the time.

Soda A casual diner-style restaurant serving cheap Tico meals.

Tico Costa Rican.

Tiquicia Costa Rica.

Tuanis Means the same as *pura vida,* above, but is used by a younger crowd.

Una teja 100 colones.

Un rojo 1,000 colones.

Un tucán 5,000 colones.

Upe! Common shout to find out if anyone is home; used frequently since doorbells are so scarce.

Zarpe Last drink of the night, or "one more for the road."

MENU TERMS

FISH

Almejas Clams

Atún Tuna

Bacalao Cod

Calamares Squid

Camarones Shrimp

Cangrejo Crab

Ceviche Marinated seafood salad

Dorado Dolphin or mahimahi

Langosta Lobster

Lenguado Sole

Mejillones Mussels

Ostras Oysters

Pargo Snapper

Pulpo Octopus

Trucha Trout

MEATS

Albóndigas Meatballs

Bistec Beefsteak

Cerdo Pork

Chicharrones Fried pork rinds

Chorizo Sausage

Chuleta literally chop, usually pork chop

Cordero Lamb

Costillas Ribs

Delmonico Rib-eye

Jamón Ham

Lengua Tongue

Lomo Sirloin

Lomito Tenderloin

Pato Duck

Pavo Turkey

Pollo Chicken

Salchichas Hot dogs, but sometimes refers to any sausage

VEGETABLES

Aceitunas Olives

Alcachofa Artichoke

Berenjena Eggplant

Cebolla Onion

Elote Corn on the cob

Ensalada Salad

Espinacas Spinach

Frijoles Beans

Lechuga Lettuce

Maíz Corn

Palmito Heart of palm

Papa Potato

Pepino Cucumber

Tomate Tomato

Yuca Yucca, cassava, or manioc

Zanahoria Carrot

FRUITS

Aguacate Avocado

Banano Banana

Carambola Star fruit

Cereza Cherry

Ciruela Plum

Durazno Peach

Frambuesa Raspberry

Fresa Strawberry

Granadilla Sweet passion fruit

Limón Lemon or lime

Mango Mango

Manzana Apple

Maracuya Tart passion fruit

Melón Melon

Mora Blackberry

Naranja Orange

Papaya Papaya

Piña Pineapple

Plátano Plantain

Sandía Watermelon

Toronja Grapefruit

BASICS

Aceite Oil

Ajo Garlic

Arreglado Small meat sandwich

Azúcar Sugar

Casado Plate of the day

Gallo Corn tortilla topped with meat or chicken

Gallo pinto Rice and beans

Hielo Ice

Mantequilla Butter

Miel Honey

Mostaza Mustard

Natilla Sour cream

Olla de carne Meat and vegetable soup

Pan Bread

Patacones Fried plantain chips

Picadillo Chopped vegetable side dish

Pimienta Pepper

Queso Cheese

Sal Salt

Tamal Filled cornmeal pastry

Tortilla Flat corn pancake

DRINKS

Agua purificada Purified water

Agua con gas Sparkling water

Agua sin gas Plain water

Bebida Drink

Café Coffee

Café con leche Coffee with milk

Cerveza Beer

Chocolate caliente Hot chocolate

Jugo Juice

Leche Milk

Natural Fruit juice

Natural con leche Milkshake

Refresco Soft drink

Ron Rum

Té Tea

Trago Alcoholic drink

OTHER RESTAURANT TERMS

Al grill Grilled

Al horno Oven-baked

Al vapor Steamed

Asado Roasted

Caliente Hot

Cambio or vuelto Change

Cocido Cooked

Comida Food

Congelado Frozen

Crudo Raw

El baño Toilet

Frío Cold

Frito Fried

Grande Big or large

La cuenta The check

Medio Medium

Medio rojo Medium rare

Muy cocido Well-done

Pequeño Small

Poco cocido or **rojo** Rare

Tres cuartos Medium-well-done

OTHER USEFUL TERMS

HOTEL TERMS

Aire acondicionado Air-conditioning

Almohada Pillow

Baño Bathroom

Baño privado Private bathroom

Calefacción Heating

Caja de seguridad Safe

Cama Bed

Cobija Blanket

Colchón Mattress

Cuarto or Habitación Room

Escritorio Desk

Habitación simple/sencilla Single room

Habitación doble Double room

Habitación triple Triple room

Llave Key

Mosquitero Mosquito net

Sábanas Sheets

Seguro de puerta Door lock

Silla Chair

Telecable Cable TV

Ventilador Fan

TRAVEL TERMS

Aduana Customs

Aeropuerto Airport

Avenida Avenue

Avión Airplane

Aviso Warning

Bus Bus

Cajero ATM, also called *cajero automatico*

Calle Street

Cheques viajeros Traveler's checks

Correo Mail, or post office

Cuadra City block

Dinero or plata Money

Embajada Embassy

Embarque Boarding

Entrada Entrance

Equipaje Luggage

Este East

Frontera Border

Lancha or bote Boat

Norte North

Oeste West

Occidente West

Oriente East

Pasaporte Passport

Puerta de salida or **puerta de embarque** Boarding gate

Salida Exit

Tarjeta de embarque Boarding pass

Vuelo Flight

EMERGENCY TERMS

¡Auxilio! Help!

Ambulancia Ambulance

Bomberos Fire brigade

Clínica Clinic or hospital

Doctor or **médico** Doctor

Emergencia Emergency

Enfermo/enferma Sick

Enfermera Nurse

Farmacia Pharmacy

Fuego or **incendio** Fire

Hospital Hospital

Ladrón Thief

Peligroso Dangerous

Policía Police

¡Váyase! Go away!

COSTA RICAN WILDLIFE

or such a small country, Costa Rica is incredibly rich in biodiversity. With just .01% of the earth's landmass, the country is home to some 5% of its biodiversity. Whether you come to Costa Rica to check 100 or so species off your lifetime list, or just to check out of the rat race for a week or so, you'll be surrounded by a rich and varied collection of flora and fauna. The information below is meant to be a selective introduction to some of what you might see.

In many instances, the prime viewing recommendations should be understood within the reality of actual wildlife viewing. Most casual visitors and even many dedicated naturalists will never see a wild cat or kinkajou. However, anyone working with a good guide should be able to see a broad selection of Costa Rica's impressive flora and fauna.

There are scores of good field guides out there; two of the best general guides are **The Field Guide to the Wildlife of Costa Rica,** by Carrol Henderson, and **Costa Rica: Traveller's Wildlife Guides,** by Les Beletsky. Bird-watchers will want to pick up one or both of the following two books: **A Guide to the Birds of Costa Rica,** by F. Gary Stiles and Alexander Skutch and **Birds of Costa Rica,** by Richard Garrigues and Robert Dean. Other specialized guides to mammals, reptiles, insects, flora, and more are also available. In Costa Rica, **Seventh Street Books,** on Calle 7 between avenidas 1 and Central in San José (☎2256-8251) always has a great selection, including many of the specialized guides which they produce under their own publishing house imprint Zona Tropical (www.zonatropical.net).

See "The Lay of the Land" in chapter 2 for more information, as well as "Tips on Health, Safety & Etiquette in the Wilderness" in chapter 5.

FAUNA
Mammals

Costa Rica has more than 230 species of mammals. Roughly half of these are bats. While it is very unlikely that you will spot a wildcat, you have good odds of catching a glimpse of a monkey, coatimundi, peccary, or sloth, or more likely any number of bats.

Jaguar *(Panthera onca)* This cat measures from 1 to 1.8m (3½–6 ft.) plus tail and is distinguished by its tan/yellowish fur with black spots. Often called simply *tigre* (tiger) in Costa Rica. **Prime Viewing:** Jaguars exist in all major tracts of primary and secondary forest in Costa Rica, as well as some open savannas. However, jaguars are endangered and extremely hard to see in the wild. The largest concentrations of jaguars can be found in Corcovado National Park on the Osa Peninsula.

Jaguar

Ocelot *(Leopardus pardalis)* Known as *manigordo,* or "fat paws," in Costa Rica, the tail of this small cat is longer than its rear leg, which makes for easy identification. Ocelots are mostly nocturnal, and they sleep in trees. **Prime Viewing:** Forests in all regions of Costa Rica, with the greatest concentration found on the Osa Peninsula.

Ocelot

Jaguarundi *(Herpailurus yaguarondi)* This smallish to midsize cat, with a solid black, brown, or reddish coat, can occasionally be spotted in a clearing or climbing trees. The jaguarundi has a unique look for a wild cat, with a face often compared to that of a weasel or otter. Jaguarundi are diurnal hunters. **Prime Viewing:** Most frequently spotted in middle elevation moist forests. Sometimes mistaken for a tayra.

Jaguarundi

Paca *(Agouti paca)* The paca, a nocturnal rodent, inhabits the forest floor, feeding on fallen fruit, leaves, and some tubers dug from the ground. **Prime Viewing:** Known as *tepezquintle* in Costa Rica, these are most often found near water throughout many habitats of Costa Rica, from river valleys to swamps to dense tropical forest. However, since they're nocturnal, you're much more likely to see their smaller cousin, the diurnal agouti or guatusa.

Paca

Tayra *(Eira Barbara)* This midsize rodent is in the weasel family. Tayras run from dark brown to black, with a brown to tan head and neck. Long and low to the ground, they have a long bushy tail. **Prime Viewing:** Known as *tolumuco* or *gato de monte* in Costa Rica, tayras are found across the country, in forests as well as plain areas, and in trees, as well as on the ground.

Tayra

Baird's Tapir *(Tapirus bairdii)* Known as the *danta* or *macho de monte,* Baird's tapir is the largest land mammal in Costa Rica. Tapirs are active both day and night, foraging along riverbanks, streams, and forest clearings. **Prime Viewing:** An endangered species, tapirs can be found in wet forested areas, particularly on the Caribbean and south Pacific slopes.

Baird's Tapir

Coatimundi *(Nasua narica)* Known as *pizote* in Costa Rica, the raccoonlike coatimundi can adapt to habitat disturbances and is often spotted near hotels and nature lodges. Active both day and night, it is equally comfortable on the ground and in trees. **Prime Viewing:** Found in a variety of habitats across Costa Rica, from dry scrub to dense forests, on the mainland as well as the coastal islands. Social animals, they are often found in groups of 10 to 20.

Coatimundi

Collared Peccary *(Tayassu tajacu)* Called *saino* or *chancho de monte* in Costa Rica, the collared peccary is a black or brown piglike animal that travels in small groups (larger where populations are still numerous) and has a strong musk odor. **Prime Viewing:** Low- and middle-elevation forests in most of Costa Rica.

Collared Peccary

15

Northern Tamandua *(Tamandua Mexicana)* Also known as the collared anteater (*oso hormiguero* in Spanish), the northern Tamandua grows up to 77 centimeters (30 in.) long, not counting its thick tail, which can be as long its body. It is active diurnally and nocturnally. **Prime Viewing:** Low- and middle-elevation forests in most of Costa Rica.

Northern Tamandua

Three-Toed Sloth *(Bradypus variegates)* The larger and more commonly sighted of Costa Rica's two sloth species, the three-toed sloth has long, coarse brown-to-gray fur and a distinctive eye band. They have three long and sharp claws on each foreleg. Except for brief periods used for defecation, these slow-moving creatures are entirely arboreal. **Prime Viewing:** Low- and middle-elevation forests in most of Costa Rica. While sloths can be found in a wide variety of trees, they are most commonly spotted in the relatively sparsely leaved Cecropia (see later in this appendix).

Three-Toed Sloth

Mantled Howler Monkey *(Alouatta palliate)* Known locally as *mono congo,* the highly social mantled howler monkey grows to 56 centimeters (22 in.) in size and often travels in groups of 10 to 30. The loud roar of the male can be heard as far as 1.6km (1 mile) away. **Prime Viewing:** Wet and dry forests across Costa Rica. Almost entirely arboreal, they tend to favor the higher reaches of the canopy.

Mantled Howler Monkey

White-Faced Monkey *(Cibus capucinus)* Known as both *mono carablanca* and *mono capuchin* in Costa Rica, the white-faced or capuchin monkey is a midsize species (46cm/18 in.) with distinct white fur around its face, head, and forearms. It can be found in forests all around the country and often travels in large troops or family groups. **Prime Viewing:** Wet and dry forests across Costa Rica.

White-Faced Monkey

Red-Backed Squirrel Monkey *(Saimiri oerstedii)* The smallest and friskiest of Costa Rica's monkeys, the red-backed squirrel monkey, or *mono tití,* is also its most endangered. Active in the daytime, these monkeys travel in small to midsize groups. Squirrel monkeys do not have a prehensile tail. **Prime Viewing:** Manuel Antonio National Park and Corcovado National Park.

Red-Backed Squirrel Monkey

Central American Spider Monkey *(Ateles geoffroyi)* Known as both *mono araña* and *mono colorado* in Costa Rica, the spider monkey is one of the more acrobatic monkey species. A large monkey (64cm/25 in.) with brown or silvery fur, it has long thin limbs and a long prehensile tail. It is active both day and night, and travels in small to midsize bands or family groups. **Prime Viewing:** Wet and dry forests across Costa Rica.

Central American Spider Monkey

Nine-Banded Armadillo *(Dasypus novemcinctus)* This is the most common armadillo species. Armadillo is Spanish for "little armored one," and that's an accurate description of this hard-carapace carrying mammal. The nine-banded armadillo can reach 65cm (26 in.) in length and weigh up to 4.5kg (9.9 lb.). The female gives birth to identical quadruplets from one single egg. **Prime Viewing:** Low- and middle-elevation forests, as well as farm lands, in most of Costa Rica. These prehistoric-looking animals are nocturnal and terrestrial.

Nine-Banded Armadillo

Birds

Costa Rica has more than 880 identified species of resident and migrant birds. The variety of habitats and compact nature of the country make it a major bird-watching destination.

Jabiru Stork *(Jabiru mycteria)* One of the largest birds in the world, the jabiru stork stands 1.5m (5 ft.) tall, with a wingspan of 2.4m (8 ft.) and a .3m (1 ft.) bill. An endangered species, the jabiru is very rare, with only a dozen or so nesting pairs in Costa Rica. **Prime Viewing:** The wetlands of Palo Verde National Park and Caño Negro Wildlife Reserve are the best places to try to spot the jabiru stork. The birds arrive in Costa Rica from Mexico in November and fly north with the rains in May or June.

Jabiru Stork

Keel-Billed Toucan *(Ramphastos sulfuratus)* The rainbow-colored canoe-shape bill and brightly colored feathers make the keel-billed toucan a favorite of bird-watching tours. The toucan can grow to about 51 centimeters (20 in.) in length. It's similar in size and shape to the chestnut mandibled toucan. Costa Rica also is home to several smaller toucanet and aracari species. **Prime Viewing:** Lowland forests on the Caribbean and north Pacific slopes.

Keel-Billed Toucan

Scarlet Macaw *(Ara macao)* Known as *guacamaya* or *lapa* in Costa Rica, the scarlet macaw is a long-tailed member of the parrot family. It can reach 89 centimeters (35 in.) in length. The bird is endangered over most of its range, particularly because it is so coveted as a pet. Its loud squawk and rainbow-colored feathers are quite distinctive. **Prime Viewing:** Carara National Park, Corcovado National Park, and Piedras Blancas National Park.

Scarlet Macaw

Resplendent Quetzal *(Pharomchrus mocinno)* Perhaps the most distinctive and spectacular bird in Central America, the resplendent quetzal, of the trogon family, can grow to 37cm (15 in.). The males are distinctive, with bright red chests, iridescent blue-green coats, yellow bills, and tail feathers that can reach another 76cm (30 in.) in length. The females lack the long tail feathers and have a duller beak and less pronounced red chest. **Prime Viewing:** High-elevation wet and cloud forests, particularly in the Monteverde Cloud Forest Preserve and along the Cerro de la Muerte.

Resplendent Quetzal

Magnificent Frigate Bird *(Fregata magnificens)* The magnificent frigate bird is a naturally agile flier, and it swoops (unlike other seabirds, it doesn't dive or swim) to pluck food from the water's surface—or more commonly, it steals catch from the mouths of other birds. **Prime Viewing:** Along the shores and coastal islands of both coasts. Often seen soaring high overhead.

Magnificent Frigate Bird

Montezuma's Oropendola *(Psarocolius Montezuma)* Montezuma's oropendola has a black head, brown body, a yellow-edged tail, a large black bill with an orange tip, and a blue patch under the eye. These birds build long, teardrop-shape hanging nests, often found in large groups. They have several distinct loud calls, including one that they make while briefly hanging upside down. **Prime Viewing:** Low and middle elevations along the Caribbean slope, and some sections of eastern Guanacaste.

Montezuma's Oropendola

Roseate Spoonbill *(Ajaia ajaja)* The roseate spoonbill is a large water bird, pink or light red in color and with a large spoon-shape bill. Also known as *garza rosada* (pink heron). They were almost made extinct in the United States because their pink wings were sought for feather fans. **Prime Viewing:** Low-lying wetlands, both fresh and salt water, along both coasts.

Roseate Spoonbill

Cattle Egret (Bubulcus ibis) The cattle egret changes color during breeding: A yellowish buff color appears on the head, chest, and back, and a reddish hue emerges on the bill and legs. They are usually seen anywhere there are cattle, hence the name, but are also often found following behind tractors. **Prime Viewing:** Throughout the country.

Cattle Egret

Boat-Billed Heron (Cochlearius cochlearius) The midsize boat-billed heron (about 51cm/20 in.) has a large black head, a large broad bill, and a rusty brown color. **Prime Viewing:** Throughout the country, near marshes, swamps, rivers, and mangroves.

Boat-Billed Heron

Laughing Falcon (Herpetotheres cachinnans) The laughing falcon is also known as the *guaco* in Costa Rica. It gets its name from its loud, piercing call. This largish (56cm/22-in.) bird of prey's wingspan reaches an impressive 94 centimeters (37 in.). It specializes in eating both venomous and nonvenomous snakes but will also hunt lizards and small rodents. **Prime Viewing:** Throughout the country, most commonly in lowland areas, near forest edges, grasslands, and farmlands.

Laughing Falcon

Mealy Parrot (Amazona farinose) Called *loro* or *loro verde* this large, vocal parrot is common in lowland tropical rainforests on both coasts. Almost entirely green, it has a touch of blue on the top of its head, and small red and blue accents on its wings. *Loro* means parrot, and *verde* means green, so you and locals alike may confuse this parrot with any number of other local species. **Prime Viewing:** Lowland rainforests on the Caribbean and Pacific coasts.

Mealy Parrot

Scarlet Rumped Tanager (Ramphocelus costaricensis) With a striking scarlet red patch on its backside, this is one of the most commonly sighted tanagers in Costa Rica. It is known locally as *sargento* or *sangre de toro*. For true ornithologists, a recent reclassification has divided the Costa Rican scarlet rumped tanagers into two distinct species, Passerini's Tanager, which is found on the Caribbean slope and lowlands, and Cherrie's Tanager, which is found along the Pacific slope and lowlands. **Prime Viewing:** Throughout the country, in lowland and mid-elevation areas.

Scarlet Rumped Tanager

Osprey (Pandion haliatus) These large (.6m/2 ft., with a 1.8m/6-ft. wingspan) brownish birds with white heads are also known as *gavilan pescador* or "fishing eagle." In flight, the osprey's wings "bend" backward. **Prime Viewing:** Lowland coastal areas and wetlands across Costa Rica; they can be seen flying or perched in trees near water.

Osprey

Pygmy Owl (Glaucidium brasilianum) Unlike most owls, this small (about 38cm/15 in.) grayish brown or reddish brown owl is most active during the day. **Prime Viewing:** Low and middle elevations along the north Pacific slope, in both wooded areas, as well as forest edges and farmlands.

Pygmy Owl

Violet Sabrewing (*Campylopterus hemileucurus*) The largest hummingbird found in Costa Rica, the violet sabrewing shines a deep purple when the sun strikes it right. Its beak is long, thick, and gently curving. **Prime Viewing:** Mid- and higher-elevation rain and cloud forests countrywide.

Violet Sabrewing

Clay-Colored Robin (*Turdus grayi*) In a country with such a rich variety of spectacularly plumed bird species, this plain brown robin is an unlikely choice to be Costa Rica's national bird. However, it is extremely widespread and common, especially in the central valley urban areas, and has a wide range of pleasant calls and songs. Known locally as the *yiguirro,* it has a uniform brown coat, with a lighter brown belly and yellow bill. **Prime Viewing:** Low and middle elevations nationwide, especially in clearings, secondary forests, and amid human settlements.

Clay-Colored Robin

Amphibians

Frogs, toads, and salamanders are actually some of the most beguiling, beautiful, and easy-to-spot residents of tropical forests.

Marine Toad (*Bufo marinus*) The largest toad in the Americas, the 20-centimeter (8-in.) wart-covered marine toad is also known as *sapo grande* (giant toad). The females are mottled in color, while the males are uniformly brown. These voracious toads have been known to eat small mammals, along with other toads, lizards, and just about any insect within range. They also have a very strong toxic chemical defense mechanism. **Prime Viewing:** In forests and open areas throughout Costa Rica.

Marine Toad

Mexican Burrowing Toad (*Rhinophrynus dorsalis*) The bloblike, 7.6-centimeter (3-in.) Mexican burrowing toad will inflate like a blowfish when frightened. It often has a single red, orange, or yellow line down the center of its brown or black back. **Prime Viewing:** Pacific lower-elevation forests and moist grasslands and farmlands.

Mexican Burrowing Toad

Red-Eyed Tree Frog (*Agalychnis callidryas*) The colorful 7.6-centimeter (3-in.) red-eyed tree frog usually has a pale or dark green back, sometimes with white or yellow spots, with blue-purple patches and vertical bars on the body, orange hands and feet, and deep red eyes. This nocturnal amphibian is also known as the gaudy leaf frog or red-eyed tree frog. **Prime Viewing:** Low- and middle-elevation wet forests throughout Costa Rica. This is a very beautiful and distinctive-looking frog that you will certainly see on T-shirts and postcards if not in the wild.

Red-Eyed Tree Frog

Green and Black Poison Arrow Frog (*Dendrobates auratus*) Also called the harlequin poison-arrow frog, the small green and black poison arrow frog ranges between 2.5 and 4 centimeters (1–1½ in.) in length. It has distinctive markings of iridescent green mixed with deep black. **Prime Viewing:** On the ground, around tree roots, and under fallen logs, in low- and middle-elevation wet forests on the Caribbean and southern Pacific slopes.

Green and Black Poison Arrow Frog

Ring-Tailed Salamander *(Bolitoglossa robusta)* This midsize black salamander can grow to 13cm (5 in.), and is distinguished by its namesake yellow to orange ring near the upper portion of its tail. **Prime Viewing:** Middle and higher elevation wet forests across Costa Rica.

Ring-Tailed Salamander

Reptiles

Costa Rica's reptile species range from the frightening and justly feared fer-de-lance pit viper and massive American crocodile to a wide variety of turtles and lizards. **Note:** Sea turtles are included in the "Sea Life" section below.

Boa Constrictor *(Boa constrictor)* Adult boa constrictors (*bécquer* in Costa Rica) average about 1.8 to 3m (6–10 ft.) in length and weigh over 27 kilograms (60 lb.). Their coloration camouflages them, but look for patterns of cream, brown, gray, and black ovals and diamonds. **Prime Viewing:** Low- and middle-elevation wet and dry forests, countrywide. They often live in rafters and eaves of homes in rural areas.

Boa Constrictor

Fer-de-Lance *(Bothrops atrox)* Known as *terciopelo* in Costa Rica, the aggressive fer-de-lance can grow to 2.4m (8 ft.) in length. Beige, brown, or black triangles flank either side of the head, while the area under the head is a vivid yellow. These snakes begin life as arboreal but become increasingly terrestrial as they grow older and larger. **Prime Viewing:** All regions.

Fer-de-Lance

Mussurana *(Clelia clelia)* This bluish black, brown, or grayish snake grows to 2.4m (8 ft.) in length. While slightly venomous, this snake has rear-fangs and is of little danger to humans. In fact, it is prized and protected by locals, since its primary prey happens to be much more venomous pit vipers, like the fer-de-lance. **Prime Viewing:** Open forests, pastures, and farmlands across Costa Rica.

Mussurana

Tropical Rattlesnake *(Crotalus durissus)* Known as *cascabel* in Costa Rica, this pit viper has a triangular head, a pronounced ridge running along the middle of its back, and (of course) a rattling tail. It can reach 1.8m (6 ft.) in length. **Prime Viewing:** Mostly found in low elevation dry forests and open areas of Guanacaste.

Tropical Rattlesnake

Leaf-Toed Gecko *(Phyllodactylus xanti)* Spotting the 6.8-centimeter (2½-in.) leaf-toed gecko is easy—it loves to be around buildings and other areas of human activity. **Prime Viewing:** Common on the ground and in the leaf litter of low- and middle-elevation forests throughout the country.

Leaf-Toed Gecko

Smooth Gecko *(Thecadactylus rapicauda)* The smooth gecko's autonomous tail detaches from its body and acts as a diversion to a potential predator; it grows back later in a lighter shade. **Prime Viewing:** Low-elevation wet forests on the Caribbean and southern Pacific slopes, as well as in urban and rural residential environments.

Smooth Gecko

Green Iguana *(Iguana iguana)* Green iguanas can vary in shades ranging from bright green to a dull grayish-green, with quite a bit of orange mixed in. The iguana will often perch on a branch overhanging a river and plunge into the water when threatened. **Prime Viewing:** All lowland regions of the country, living near rivers and streams, along both coasts.

Green Iguana

Basilisk *(Basiliscus vittatus)* The basilisk can run across the surface of water for short distances by using its hind legs and holding its body almost upright; thus, the reptile is also known as "the Jesus Christ lizard." **Prime Viewing:** In trees and on rocks located near water in wet forests throughout the country.

Basilisk

American Crocodile *(Crocodylus acutus)* Although an endangered species, environmental awareness and protection policies have allowed the massive American crocodile to mount an impressive comeback in recent years. While these reptiles can reach lengths of 6.4m (21 ft.), most are much smaller, usually less than 4m (13 ft.). **Prime Viewing:** Near swamps, estuaries, large rivers, and coastal lowlands, countrywide. Guaranteed viewing from the bridge over the Tarcoles River, on the coastal highway to Jacó and Manuel Antonio.

American Crocodile

Litter Skink *(Sphenomorphus cherriei)* This small, brown lizard has a proportionally large head and neck, and short legs. A black stripe extends off the back of its eyes and down its sides, with a yellowish area below. **Prime Viewing:** Common on the ground and in leaf litter of low- and middle-elevation forests throughout the country.

Litter Skink

Slender Anole *(Anolis [norops] limifrons)* This thin, olive-colored lizard can reach 5.1cm (2 in.) in length. There are some 25 related species of *anolis* or *norops* lizards. **Prime Viewing:** Lowland rainforests nationwide.

Slender Anole

Sea Life

Boasting over 1,290km (780 miles) of shoreline on both the Pacific and Caribbean coasts, Costa Rica has a rich diversity of underwater flora and fauna.

Whale Shark *(Rhincodon typus)* Although the whale shark grows to lengths of 14m (45 ft.) or more, its gentle nature makes swimming with them a special treat for divers and snorkelers. **Prime Viewing:** Can occasionally be spotted off Isla del Caño, and more frequently off Isla del Coco.

Whale Shark

Leatherback Sea Turtle *(Dermochelys coriacea)* The world's largest sea turtle (reaching nearly 2.4m/8 ft. in length and weighing more than 544kg/1,200 lb.), the

Leatherback Sea Turtle

leatherback sea turtle is now an endangered species. **Prime Viewing:** While these large reptiles do nest off Tortuguero, their prime nesting site in Costa Rica is Playa Grande, near Tamarindo.

Olive Ridley Sea Turtle *(Lepidochelys olivacea)* Also known as *tortuga lora,* the olive ridley sea turtle is the most common and popular of Costa Rica's sea turtles, famous for its massive group nestings, or *arribadas*. **Prime Viewing:** Large *arribadas* occur from July through December, and to a lesser extent from January through June. Playa Nancite in Santa Rosa National Park and Playa Ostional are the prime nesting sites.

Olive Ridley Sea Turtle

Moray Eel *(Gymnothorax mordax)* Distinguished by a swaying serpent-head and teeth-filled jaw that continually opens and closes, the moray eel is most commonly seen with only its head appearing from behind rocks. At night, however, it leaves its home along the reef to hunt for small fish, crustaceans, shrimp, and octopus. **Prime Viewing:** Rocky areas and reefs off both coasts.

Moray Eel

Humpbacked Whale *(Megaptera novaeangliae)* The migratory humpbacked whale spends the winters in warm southern waters and has been increasingly spotted close to the shores of Costa Rica's southern Pacific coast. These mammals have black backs and whitish throat and chest areas. Females have been known to calve here. **Prime Viewing:** Most common in the waters off of Drake Bay and Isla del Caño, from December through April.

Humpbacked Whale

Bottle-Nosed Dolphin *(Tursiops truncates)* A wide tail fin, dark gray back, and light gray sides identify bottle-nosed dolphins. Dolphins grow to lengths of 3.7m (12 ft.) and weigh up to 635 kilograms (1,400 lb.). **Prime Viewing:** Along both coasts and inside the Golfo Dulce.

Bottle-Nosed Dolphin

Manta Ray *(Manta birostris)* Manta rays are the largest type of rays, with a wingspan that can reach 6m (20 ft.) and a body weight known to exceed 1,361kg (3,000 lb.). Despite their daunting appearance, manta rays are quite gentle. If you are snorkeling or diving, watch for one of these extraordinary and graceful creatures. **Prime Viewing:** All along the Pacific coast.

Manta Ray

Brain Coral *(Diploria strigosa)* The distinctive brain coral is named for its striking physical similarity to a human brain. **Prime Viewing:** Reefs off both coasts.

Brain Coral

Invertebrates

Creepy-crawlies, biting bugs, spiders, and the like give most folks chills. But this group, which includes moths, butterflies, ants, beetles, bees, and even crabs, includes some of the most abundant, fascinating, and easily viewed fauna in Costa Rica. In fact, there are nearly 500,000 recorded species of invertebrates in Costa Rica, with more than 9,000 species of butterflies and moths alone.

Blue Morpho *(Morpho peleides)* The large blue morpho butterfly, with a wingspan of up to 15 centimeters (6 in.), has brilliantly iridescent blue wings when opened. Fast and erratic fliers, they are often glimpsed flitting across your peripheral vision in dense forest. **Prime Viewing:** Countrywide, particularly in moist environments.

Blue Morpho

Leafcutter Ants *(Atta cephalotes)* You can't miss the miniature rainforest highways formed by these industrious little red leafcutter ants carrying their freshly cut payload. The ants do not actually eat the leaves, but instead feed off a fungus that grows on the decomposing leaves in their massive underground nests. **Prime Viewing:** Can be found in most forests countrywide.

Leafcutter Ants

Golden Silk Spider *(Nephila clavipes)* The common Neotropical golden silk spider weaves meticulous webs that can be as much as .5m (2 ft.) across. The adult female of this species can reach 7.6 centimeters (3 in.) in length, including the legs, although the males are tiny. The silk of this spider is extremely strong and is being studied for industrial purposes. **Prime Viewing:** Lowland forests on both coasts.

Golden Silk Spider

Mouthless Crab *(Gecarcinus quadratus)* The nocturnal mouthless crab is a distinctively colored land crab with bright orange legs, purple claws, and a deep black shell or carapace. **Prime Viewing:** All along the Pacific coast.

Mouthless Crab

Sally Lightfoot Crab *(Grapsus grapsus)* Known simply as *cangrejo* or "crab," this is the most common crab spotted in Costa Rica. It is a midsize crab with a colorful carapace that can range from dark brown to deep red to bright yellow, with a wide variation in striations and spotting. **Prime Viewing:** On rocky outcroppings near the water's edge all along both coasts.

Sally Lightfoot Crab

FLORA
Trees

Despite the cliche to the contrary, it's often a good thing to be able to identify specific trees within a forest. I've included illustrations of leaves, flowers, seeds, and fruit to get you started.

Ceiba *(Ceiba pentandra)* Also known as the kapok tree, ceiba trees are typically emergent (their large umbrella-shape canopies emerge above the forest canopy), making the species among the tallest trees in the tropical forest. Reaching as high as 60m (197 ft.), their thick columnar trunks often have large buttresses. Ceiba trees may flower as little as once every 5 years, especially in wetter forests. **Prime Viewing:** Countrywide.

Ceiba

Guanacaste *(Enterolobium cyclocarpum)* The guanacaste tree is one of the largest trees found in Central America, and gives its name to Costa Rica's northwestern-most province. It can reach a total elevation of over 39m (130 ft.); its straight trunk composes 9 to 12m (30–40 ft.) of the height (the trunk's diameter measures more than 1.8m/6 ft.). **Prime Viewing:** Countrywide.

Guanacaste

Strangler Fig *(Ficus aurea)* This parasitic tree gets its name from the fact that it envelops and eventually strangles its host tree. The *matapalo* or strangler fig begins as an epiphyte, whose seeds are deposited high in a tree's canopy by bats, birds, or monkeys. The young strangler then sends long roots down to the earth. The sap is used to relieve burns. **Prime Viewing:** Primary and secondary forests countrywide.

Strangler Fig

Cecropia *(Cecropia obtusifolia)* Several Cecropia (trumpet tree) species are found in Costa Rica. Most are characterized by large, handlike clusters of broad leaves, and a hollow, bamboolike trunk. They are "gap specialists," fast-growing opportunists that can fill in a gap caused by a tree fall or landslide. Their trunks are usually home to Aztec ants. **Prime Viewing:** Primary and secondary forests, rivers, and roadsides, countrywide.

Cecropia

Gumbo Limbo *(Bursera simaruba)* The bark of the gumbo limbo is its most distinguishing feature: A paper-thin red outer layer, when peeled off the tree, reveals a bright green bark. In Costa Rica the tree is called *indio desnudo* (naked Indian). In other countries it is the "tourist tree." Both names refer to reddish skin. The bark is used as a remedy for gum disease; gumbo limbo–bark tea allegedly alleviates hypertension. Another remarkable property is the tree's ability to root from its cut branches, which when planted right end up, develop roots and leaves, forming a new tree within a few years. **Prime Viewing:** Primary and secondary forests, countrywide.

Gumbo Limbo

Flowers & Other Plants

Costa Rica has an amazing wealth of tropical flora, including some 1,200 orchid species, and over 2,000 bromeliad species.

Guaria Morada *(Cattleya skinneri)* The guaria morada orchid is the national flower of Costa Rica. Sporting a purple and white flower, this plant is also called the "Easter orchid" as it tends to flower between March and April each year. **Prime Viewing:** Countrywide from sea level to 1,220m (4,000 ft.).

Guaria Morada

Heliconia *(Heliconia collinsiana)* There are more than 250 species of tropical heliconia, of which more than 40 are found in Costa Rica. The flowers of this species are darkish pink in color, and the underside of the plant's large leaves are coated in white wax. **Prime Viewing:** Low to middle elevations countrywide, particularly in moist environments.

Helicona

Hotlips *(Psychotria poeppigiana)* Related to coffee, hotlips is a forest flower that boasts thick red "lips" that resemble the Rolling Stones logo. The small white flowers (found inside the red "lips") attract a variety of butterflies and hummingbirds. **Prime Viewing:** In the undergrowth of dense forests countrywide.

Hotlips

Red Torch Ginger *(Nicolaia elatior)* Called *bastón del emperador* (the Emperor's cane) in Costa Rica, the tall red torch ginger plant has an impressive bulbous red bract, often mistaken for the flower. The numerous, small white flowers actually emerge out of this bract. Originally a native to Indonesia, it is now quite common in Costa Rica. **Prime Viewing:** Countrywide, particularly in moist environments and gardens.

Red Torch Ginger

15

Poor Man's Umbrella *(Gunnera insignis)* The poor man's umbrella, a broad-leaved rainforest ground plant, is a member of the rhubarb family. The massive leaves are often used, as the colloquial name suggests, for protection during rainstorms. **Prime Viewing:** Low- to middle-elevation moist forests countrywide. Commonly seen in Poás National Park and Braulio Carrillo National Park.

Poor Man's Umbrella

INDEX

See also Accommodations index, below.

General Index

A

Abercrombie & Kent, 94–95
Abya Yala (San José), 172
Accommodations, 15–22, 68, 73–74. See also Accommodations Index
Active vacations and adventure trips, 93–115. See also specific activities
best, 8–11
suggested itinerary, 88–89
ACTUAR, 71
Adventure Education Center (AEC) Spanish Institute, 112
Aerial trams, 178, 180
Africa Mia (near Liberia), 200
Aggressor Fleet Limited, 101, 255
Air travel, 54, 55
All Souls' Day/Día de los Muertos, 52
Alma Ata Archaeological Park, 292
Ama Tierra Retreat & Wellness Center (near Jacó), 344
American Express, San José, 126
Annexation of Guanacaste Day (Liberia), 51
APREFLOFAS (Association for the Preservation of the Wild Flora and Fauna), 114
Aqua Sport (Playa Hermosa), 211
Architecture, 34–35
Arenal, Lake, 315–321
Arenal National Park, 109, 300
Arenal Volcano, 296, 299–300
accommodations, 308–311
Ark Herb Farm (Heredia), 189
Art, 35–36
Arte Latino (San José), 168
Art galleries, 168–169, 317
Aserri, 150
Asociación de Voluntarios para el Servicio en las Areas Protegidas (ASVO), 114
ATMs (automated teller machines), 62
ATV tours. See Four-wheeling and ATV tours
Auditorio Nacional (San José), 172, 173
Avellana Waterfall & Trails, 424
Aventuras Naturales, 106, 184
Aviarios del Caribe (Cahuita), 459

B

Bahía Culebra, 209
Bahía Salinas, 205–209
Bajo del Tigre Trail, 328
Baldi Hot Springs (La Fortuna), 303

Ballena Marine National Park, 381–382
Ballena National Park, 384
Ballooning, 103
Bananas, 291
Barra del Colorado, 438–441
Barra Honda National Park, 108, 276
Basílica de Nuestra Señora de los Angeles (Cartago), 185
Bat Jungle (Monteverde), 330
Beaches. See also specific beaches and entries starting with "Playa"
Bahía Salinas, 207
best, 7–8
Corcovado National Park, 414
Bed & breakfasts (B&Bs), 21–22. See also Accommodations Index
Beverages, 45–47
Bijagual, 346
Bike Arenal, 96, 305
Biking and mountain biking, 95–96
Arenal area, 304–305
Jacó area, 346
Lake Arenal, 318
near San José, 181, 184
Puerto Jiménez, 416–417
Quepos area, 368
Tamarindo, 234
Birding Club of Costa Rica, 97, 164
Birds and bird-watching, 13–15, 96–97
Cahuita, 459
Caño Negro, 305–306
Carara National Park, 345
Golfito area, 425
Monteverde, 326–327
Playa Nosara, 282
Puerto Viejo (Limón), 467
San José, 163–164
Zoo Ave (Alajuela), 162
Blue Lake, 199
Boat excursions, cruises and charters. See also Fishing
Guanacaste, 211
near San José, 181
Palo Verde, 200
Playa del Coco, 218–219
Puerto Viejo, 290
Quepos, 366
Tamarindo, 235
Tortuguero, 447
Books, recommended, 39–40
Bosque Eterno de Los Niños, 328
Braulio Carrillo National Park, 109
Britt Expresivo (San José), 172
Bugs and bites, 64–65
Bullfights, 164

Bungee jumping, 98, 178, 302–303
Business hours, 482
Bus travel, 58, 60
Buttercup Sloth Rescue Center (Cahuita), 459
Butterfield & Robinson, 95
Butterfly Farm (near Alajuela), 159–160
Butterfly Garden (Monteverde), 330
Butterfly gardens and farms, 159–160, 262, 330, 368, 459

C

Cabo Blanco Absolute Nature Reserve, 263
Cabo Blanco Nature Reserve, 263, 270
Cabo Matapalo, 409
Cabuya, 263
Cacao Trails (Puerto Viejo), 469
Café Britt, 167
Café Britt Farm (near Heredia), 160
Café Expresivo (San José), 175
Café Milagro (San José), 167
Café Monteverde (San José), 167
Café Trébol (San José), 167
Cahuita, 454–463
Cahuita National Park, 111, 455, 456–458
Calendar of events, 51–52
Calypso Tours, 181, 252
Camping, 98
Cahuita, 458
Jacó area, 351–352
Playa Junquillal, 247
Puerto Viejo (Limón), 467
Rincón de la Vieja National Park, 198
Tamarindo, 241
Canoe Costa Rica, 106
Canoeing, 106, 305
Caño Island Biological Reserve, 405
Caño Negro National Wildlife Refuge, 109–110, 305–306
Canopy tours (zip-lines), 9, 99–100, 301
Guanacaste, 212
Jacó area, 346–347
Malpaís, 270
Monteverde area, 328–329
Montezuma, 262–263
Puerto Viejo, 290–291
Quepos/Manuel Antonio area, 368
Sámara, 275–276
San José area, 178
Tamarindo, 236
Canyoning, 9, 301–302, 328–329
Carara National Park, 343, 345–346

Car breakdowns, 57
Caribbean coast, 77, 80, 437–481
Caribbean Conservation
    Corporation, 114
Carnaval, Limón, 451
Car-rental agencies, 55–57
Carrera Campo Traviesa Al Cerro
    Chirripó, 393
Carrera de San Juan, 51
Cartago, 184–185
Car travel, 54–58
Casa Delagua, 317
Casa del Soñador (near Cachí),
    186
Casa Orquídeas (near Golfito),
    425
CASEM (Monteverde), 332
Casinos, San José, 177
Castro's (San José), 173
Cathedral, San José, 155
Cellphones, 72
Center for Agronomy Research
    and Development (CATIE;
    near Turrialba), 187
Central Pacific Coast, 79,
    339–396
    national parks, 110
Central Valley, 77–78
    national parks, 108
    restaurants, 150
Centro Lingüístico Conversa, 112
Centro Nacional de Arte y
    Cultura (San José), 156
Centro Panamericano de
    Idiomas, 112
Cerro de la Muerte, 390
Cerro de Tortuguero, 444
Chelles (San José), 175
Children's Museum (San José),
    157
Chirripó, Mount, 391–393
Chirripó National Park, 110,
    391–393
Chocolate Tour, 468
Climate, 50
Coast to Coast Adventures, 8,
    94, 96, 98, 103, 184
Cocalito Beach, 407
Coco Gym (Playa del Coco), 218
Coconut, 42
Cocos Island, 254–255
Coffee, 136, 167, 331
Complejo Ecológico La Catarata
    (Bijagual), 346
Copacabana (San José), 174
Copa del Café (San José), 51
Corcovado National Park, 110,
    400, 409, 412–415
Costa Rica Biking Adventures,
    96, 181
Costa Rica Expeditions, 71, 94,
    97, 178, 182
Costa Rica Experts, 95
Costa Rica Golf Adventures, 103

Costa Rican Language Academy,
    112
Costa Rica Outdoors, 9, 101
Costa Rica Rainforest Outward
    Bound School, 114
Costa Rica Spanish Institute, 112
Costa Rica Sun Tours, 71, 94, 97,
    178, 182
Coter, Lake, 318
Credit cards, 62
Crime, 65–66
Crocodiles, 343
Cruise lines and ships, 54
Cruise ships and lines, 100
Cultural tours, Puerto Viejo,
    466–467
Currency, 61–62
Curú Wildlife Refuge (near
    Tambor), 258
Customs regulations, 53

D

Day hikes and nature walks,
    best, 11–13
Dengue fever, 63–64
Desafío Expeditions, 9, 89, 99,
    298, 301, 304, 305, 324
Día de la Pólvora, 52
Día del Boyero (Escazú), 51
Día de San Ramón, 52
Diamante Waterfalls, 383
Dietary red flags, 64
Disabilities, travelers with, 66
Diving Mania, 101
Diving Safaris de Costa Rica,
    101, 211
Dolphin-watching, 366
Dominical, 379–390
Dominicalito, 382
Drake Bay, 398–408
Drinking laws, 482
Driving rules, 57
Dry season, 50

E

Eating and drinking, 42–46
Ecolodges and wilderness
    resorts, 20–21. See also
    Accommodations Index
Ecological Sanctuary
    (Monteverde), 328
Ecoscapes Highlights Tour,
    184, 291
Eco Teach, 114–115
Eco Termales (near La Fortuna),
    303
Ecotourism, 68–71
El Chorro (Montezuma), 262
El Cuartel de la Boca del Monte
    (San José), 175
Electricity, 482
El Observatorio (San José), 175
El Pueblo (San José), 173

Else Kientzler Botanical Garden
    (Alajuela), 160–161
El Tobogán (San José), 174
El Tope and Carnival (San
    José), 52
El Trapiche Tour (Monteverde),
    331
Embassies and consulates, 483
Emergencies, 483
Entry requirements, 52–53
Escazú, restaurants, 153–154
Escondido Trex, 106, 415
Escuela D'Amore, 114
Etiquette and customs, 41
    in the wilderness, 111–112
ExperiencePlus! Specialty
    Tours, 96
Exploradores Outdoors, 106,
    184, 467, 470

F

Families with children, 15–17, 67
Ferries, 60
Field Guides, 97
Fiesta de la Yeguita (Nicoya), 52
Fiesta del Maíz (Upala), 52
Fiesta de los Negritos (Boruca),
    52
Fiesta of Palmares, 51
Fiesta of Santa cruz, 51
Fiesta of the Diablitos (Rey
    Curré), 51, 391
Fiesta of the Virgin of Los
    Angeles (Cartago), 51
Fiesta of the Virgin of the Sea
    (Puntarenas), 51, 250
Films, 40
Finca Modelo Canyoning Tour,
    329
Fincas Naturales/The Nature
    Farm Reserve (Quepos),
    368
Fishing and sailboat charters,
    101–102, 472
    Arenal area, 303
    Barra del Colorado, 439–440
    Golfito, 424–425
    Jacó area, 347–348
    Lake Arenal, 317–318
    Manuel Antonio, 366
    Playa del Coco, 219
    Playa Flamingo area, 226
    Playa Junquillal, 247
    Playa Nosara, 282
    Puerto Jiménez, 416
    Quepos, 367
    Tamarindo, 236
Fishing lodges, 102. See also
    Accommodations Index
Forester Instituto Internacional,
    112, 114

Four Seasons Resort (Papagayo Peninsula)
golf course at, 103
spa and yoga classes, 104
Four-wheeling and ATV tours, 9
Arenal area, 301
Jacó area, 346
Manuel Antonio, 367–368
Tamarindo, 234–235
Frog Pond of Monteverde, 330

G

Galería Amón (San José), 168
Galería Jacobo Karpio (San José), 169
Galería Kandinsky (San José), 169
Galería 11'12 (San José), 168
Garra de León golf course (Guanacaste), 102
Gasoline, 56, 483
Gays and lesbians, 66
San José, 177
Global Volunteers, 115
Gold Museum (San José), 158
Golf, 102–103
Jacó area, 347
Playa Conchal, 225
Playa del Coco, 218
San José, 164
Tamarindo, 235
Golfito, 421–428
Gray Line Tours (San José), 155
Grecia, 190
Grecia Regional Museum, 190
Green Iguana Conservation Tour (Playa Chiquita), 469
Guaitíl, 237
Guanacaste, 78, 192–247
national parks, 108–109
Guayabo National Monument, 108, 181, 187

H

Habitat for Humanity International, 115
Hacienda Barú (Dominical), 383
Hacienda Guachipelin, 201
Hacienda Pinilla (near Tamarindo), 236
golf course at, 102, 235
Hacienda Pozo Azul (Puerto Viejo), 290
Hang gliding, 103
Health concerns, 63–65
in the wilderness, 111–112
Heredia, 188–190
Herradura Hot Springs, 396
Herrera Botanical Gardens, 416
Hiking and trekking, 10, 181
Arenal area, 304
Corcovado National Park, 414
Dominical, 383
Lake Arenal, 318

Manuel Antonio, 365–366
Monteverde area, 327–328
Mount Chirripó, 391–392
Puerto Viejo, 291
Rincón de la Vieja National Park, 199
San Isidro, 394
History of Costa Rica, 29–34
Hitchhiking, 60
Holidays, 50, 483
Holy Week, 51
Horizontes, 71, 94, 155, 178, 182
Horseback riding, 103
Arenal area, 304
Jacó area, 347
Lake Arenal, 318
Monteverde area, 329
Montezuma, 262
near San José, 181
Playa Flamingo area, 225
Playa Nosara, 282–283
Puerto Viejo (Limón), 468
Quepos/Manuel Antonio area, 368–369
Tamarindo, 235
Hospitals, 483
Hot springs, 201, 302–303, 396
Howler monkeys, 113
Hummingbird Gallery (Monteverde), 332

I

Iglesia de Cañas, 196
INBio Park (Heredia), 161, 189
Independence Day, 52
Institute for Central American Development Studies (ICADS), 114, 115
Instituto Costarricense de Turismo (San José), 120
International Beach Clean-Up Day, 52
International House Costa Rica, 114
Internet and e-mail access, 72–73, 483
Irazú Volcano, 182
Irazú Volcano National Park, 108
Isla del Caño, 367, 405
Isla del Coco, 254–255
Itineraries, suggested, 80–91

J

Jacó and environs, 339–359
accommodations, 348–352
beaches and outdoor activities, 344–348
beaches around, 344–345
getting around, 342–343
nightlife, 356–357
restaurants, 353–356
shopping, 348
traveling to, 340, 342

Jade Museum (San José), 156
Jardín de Serpientes (Puerto Viejo), 292
Jazz Café (San José), 176
Jogging, San José, 165
Juan Santamaría Day, 51
Juan Santamaría International Airport (San José), 117–118, 120

K

Kayaking, 10, 106
Jacó area, 347
Manuel Antonio, 366
Playa Flamingo area, 226
Playa Nosara, 283
Puerto Jiménez, 415
Puerto Viejo, 292
Key Largo (San José), 175–176
Kiteboarding (kitesurfing), 10, 107, 208, 318

L

La Cangrejo Waterfall, 199
La Casona (Santa Rosa National Park), 207
La Cruz, 205–209
La Fortuna, 296–307
accommodations, 306–311
getting around, 299
nightlife, 312
restaurants, 311–312
shopping, 306
traveling to, 296–299
La Isla Botanical Gardens (Puerto Viejo), 469
La Negrita (Cartago), 185
Lankester Gardens (Cartago), 162, 185
La Paz Waterfall Gardens (near Varablanca), 162
Las Corridas a la Tica (San José), 164
Las Posadas, 52
Las Quebradas Biological Center (near San Isidro), 394
Lava Tours, 96
Lay of the land, 36–38
Legal aid, 483
Leptospirosis, 64
Liberia, 194–205
Limón, 52, 451–454
Little Theater Group (San José), 172
Llano de Cortes Waterfall, 199
Lodges. See Accommodations
Los Sueños Marriott Ocean & Golf Resort (Playa Herradura), golf course at, 102
Luna Lodge (Playa Carate), yoga and wellness programs, 104

M

Mahogany Park (near San José), 181
Mail, 484
Malaria, 63
Malpaís, 268–273
Manuel Antonio National Park, 110, 347, 359–379
  accommodations, 370–375
  exploring, 364–366
  getting around, 363–364
  nightlife, 378–379
  restaurants, 376–378
  traveling to and from, 361–363
Manzanillo, 471–472
Manzanillo-Gandoca Wildlife Refuge, 471–472
Mariposario Cahuita (Cahuita), 459
Mariposario Montezuma Gardens, 262
Marriages in Costa Rica, 59
Marriott Costa Rica, golf course at, 102
Meals and dining, 43
Medical requirements for entry, 53
Money and costs, 61–62
Monkeys, 113
Monteverde and environs, 321–339
  accommodations, 332–335
  getting around, 325
  nightlife, 337
  restaurants, 335–337
  sights and activities, 327–331
  traveling to, 322, 324–325
Monteverde Biological Cloud Forest Reserve, 110, 322, 326–327, 335
Monteverde Institute, 115
Monteverde Serpentarium, 330
Mosaikos (San José), 176
Motorcycling, 103–104
Mud baths, Liberia, 201
Multispa (San José), 165
Mundo Aventura, 104
Museo de Arte Costarricense (San José), 156
Museo de Cultura Popular (Heredia), 189
Museo de Jade Marco Fidel Tristán (San José), 156
Museo de los Niños (San José), 157
Museo Histórico Cultural Juan Santamaría (near San José), 159
Museo Histórico Marino (Puntarenas), 251–252
Museo Nacional de Costa Rica (San José), 157–158
Museos del Banco Central de Costa Rica (San José), 158
Music, 41–42

N

National Museum (San José), 157–158
National Orchid Show, 51
National parks and bioreserves, 107–111
National Parks Foundation office, 107
National Symphony Orchestra (San José), 172
National Theater Company (San José), 172
Nature Air, 71
Nature Expeditions International, 95
Nature Lodge Finca Los Caballos (Montezuma), 103, 266
Newspapers and magazines, 484
Nicoya Peninsula, 78–79
Nightlife, best, 25–27
Northern zone, 79, 109–110, 288–337

O

Ojo de Agua (near San José), 166
Ollie's Point, 211, 216
Orchid Garden (Santa Elena), 331
Organization for Tropical Studies, 115
Original Canopy Tours, 99, 181, 329
Orosi Valley, 185–186
Osa Peninsula, 400
Overseas Adventure Travel, 95

P

Pacific coast, 76–77
Pacuare River Tours, 106
Palo Verde National Park, 108–109, 200
Panama, 480
Papagayo Peninsula, 209–215
Paragliding, 103
Parque del Este (near San José), 163
Parque La Sabana (San José), 163–165
Parque Marino del Pacífico (Puntarenas), 252
Parque Reptilandia (near Dominical), 384
Parque Valle del Sol, 102, 164
Parque Vargas (Limón), 453
Parque Zoológico Simón Bolívar (San José), 158–159
Paseo de los Turistas (Puntarenas), 251
Passports, 52–53, 484
Petrol, 483
Piedra Colorado, 263

Piedras Blancas National Park, 422
Pineapple plantation, 292
Pirujas (sand fleas), 64
Planning your trip, 49–74
Playa Avellanas, 244–245
Playa Barrigona, 275
Playa Bejuco, 344
Playa Blanca, 207, 208, 345
Playa Bonita, 451
Playa Brasilito, 223, 225
Playa Buena Vista, 275
Playa Cacao, 424
Playa Carrillo, 275
Playa Conchal, 222–223, 225
Playa de Jacó, 339–359. See also Jacó
Playa del Coco, 216–222
Playa Doña Aña, 252
Playa Espadilla, 364–366
Playa Espadilla Sur, 365
Playa Esterillos, 344, 357–358
Playa Flamingo, 223, 224–225
Playa Grande, 231–245
  accommodations, 241–242
Playa Guiones, 282
Playa Hermosa (Guanacaste), 209–215
Playa Hermosa (near Dominical), 382
Playa Hermosa de Jacó, 340, 344, 357–359
Playa Herradura, 340, 344, 352–353
Playa Junquillal, 208, 245–247
Playa La Penca, 223, 225
Playa Manta, 345
Playa Manuel Antonio, 365
Playa Matapalo, 379
Playa Montezuma, 260–267
Playa Nacascolo, 209
Playa Nancite, 207, 208
Playa Naranjo, 207
Playa Negra (Cahuita), 458
Playa Negra (Guanacaste), 244–245
Playa Negra (Puerto Viejo), 470
Playa Nosara, 280, 282
Playa Ocotal, 216
Playa Ostional, 282, 286
Playa Panamá, 209–215
Playa Pan de Azúcar, 223, 225
Playa Pavones, 433–435
Playa Pelada, 282
Playa Plantanares, 415, 418
Playa Potrero, 223, 225
Playa Sámara, 273–280
Playa Santa Teresa, 268–273
Playa Tamarindo, 231–245
Playa Tambor, 256–259
Playa Tivives, 252
Playa Uvita, 382
Playa Zancudo, 429–432
Poás Volcano, 183

Poás Volcano National Park, 108
Police, 484
Psycho Tours, 9, 100, 416
Puerto Jiménez, 409–421
Puerto Vargas, 457
Puerto Viejo (Limón), 463–479
Puerto Viejo de Sarapiquí,
 288–296
Punta Catedral, 365
Punta Coral, 181, 252
Punta Leona, 344–345
Punta Mona Center For
 Sustainable Living &
 Education (Manzanillo), 472
Puntarenas, 78, 249–256
Punta Uva, 471
Pura Vida Botanical Gardens
 (Bijagual), 346
Pure Trek Canyoning, 9, 99, 301

Q
Quepos, 360–364, 369
Quetzals, 98, 326–327, 392, 395

R
Railbike Tour, 184
Rain Forest Aerial Tram, 100,
 178, 292–293, 346
Rainforests, 414, 453
Rainy season, 50
Regions in brief, 76–80
Reserva Sendero Tranquilo
 (Monteverde), 328
Restaurants, best, 22–24
Rey Curré, 391
Rincón de la Vieja National Park,
 109, 198–199, 203–204
Rincón de los Monos, 261
Río Fortuna Waterfall, 304
Rio Locos, 106
Río Perezoso, 457
Ríos Tropicales, 107, 184
Riptides, 65
Road conditions, 56–57
Rock climbing, 104
Ruta de los Conquistadores, 96

S
Safaris Corobicí, 13, 200, 201
Safety concerns, 65–66, 111–112
Salsa Brava, 470
Samasati (Puerto Viejo), yoga
 retreat, 104
San Isidro de El General,
 390–395
San José, 77–78, 117–191
 accommodations, 129–146
 arriving in, 117–119
 doctors and dentists, 126
 drugstores, 126
 emergencies, 127
 express mail services, 127
 eyeglasses, 127
 faxes, 127

finding an address in, 120
fruit vendors, 147
getting around, 123–126
hospitals, 127
Internet access, 127
laundry and dry cleaning, 127
layout of, 121
maps, 127
national parks near, 108
neighborhoods in brief, 121–123
nightlife, 171–177
outdoor activities and spectator
 sports, 163–166
photographic needs, 127–128
police, 128
post office, 128
restaurants, 147–155
safety, 128
shopping, 166–171
side trips from, 177–191
sights and attractions, 155–162
taxis, 124
time zone, 128
tours, 155
visitor information, 120
weather, 128
Santa Elena, 324, 326
Santa Elena Cloud Forest
 Reserve, 327
Santa Juana Mountain Tour
 (Quepos), 369
Santa Rosa National Park, 109,
 206–208
Santa Teresa, 268–273
Sarapiquí River, 184
Sarapiquís Rainforest Lodge,
 292
Sarchí, 190–191
Scuba diving, 10, 100–101
 Caño Island, 405
 Dominical area, 384
 Isla del Coco, 254
 Jacó area, 348
 Playa del Coco, 219
 Playa Flamingo area, 226
 Puerto Viejo (Caribbean coast),
 468
 Quepos, 367
 Tamarindo, 236
Seasons, 49–50
Sea turtles, 105
 Playa Grande, 236–237
 Tortuguero, 445–446
Selvatura Park, 328–329
Senior travelers, 67
Serendipity Adventures, 94, 96,
 98–99, 103
Serenity Spa (Jacó), 104
Shakespeare Bar (San José), 176
Shopping, 46–47
Sierra Club, 95
Simbiosis Spa (Liberia), 201
Sirena, 414, 415
Sky Trek (Monteverde), 327–329

Sky Walk (Monteverde), 327–328
Smithsonian Institute, 95
Smoking, 485
Snakes, 64, 292, 330
Snorkeling, 100, 367, 457
Soccer (fútbol), 165–166
Southern zone, 79, 398–435
Spanish language classes,
 112, 114
 Cahuita, 459
 Dominical, 384
 Manuel Antonio area, 369
 Monteverde, 331
 Nosara, 285
 Playa Flamingo, 225–226
 Sámara, 276
 Tamarindo, 232
Spas and yoga retreats, 104–105
 Jacó, 347
 Manuel Antonio area, 369
 Playa Nosara, 283
 Puerto Viejo (Limón), 468
 San José, 164–165
 Tamarindo, 237
Spider monkeys, 113
Spirogyra Butterfly Garden (San
 José), 159
Squirrel monkeys, 113
Stone spheres, 404, 405
Student travelers, 67
Sueño Azul Resort (Las
 Horquetas), 104
Sun exposure, 65
Surfing, 105–106
 best places for, 9, 11
 Dominical, 382
 Guanacaste coast, 211
 Jacó area, 348
 Manuel Antonio, 366
 Playa del Coco, 219
 Playa Flamingo area, 226
 Playa Junquillal, 246
 Playa Nosara, 282
 Puerto Jiménez, 416
 Puerto Viejo area, 469–470
Sustainable tourism, 68–71
Sustainable volunteer projects,
 114–115
Swimming, San José, 166
Swiss Travel Service, 13, 71, 155,
 178, 182, 200, 211

T
Tabacón Grand Spa Thermal
 Resort (Arenal Volcano),
 104, 302–303
T'ai Chi in Paradise, 102
Talamanca Mountains, 467
Tamarindo, 231–245
Tapantí National Park, 186
Taxes, 485
Taxis, 60
Teatro Melico Salazar (San
 José), 173

Teatro Nacional (San José),
172, 173
Telephones, 71–72, 485
Temperatures, average daytime
high, in San José, 50
Tennis, 164, 236
Teoretica (San José), 169
Terciopelo Cave, 276
Terra U (San José), 177
Tico Travel, 95, 106
Time zone, 485
Tipping, 485
Tirimbina Rainforest Center, 292
Tobías Bolaños International
Airport (San José), 118–119
Toilets, 485–486
Tortuga Island, 100, 252
Tortuguero National Park, 111,
184, 441–450
Tortuguero Village, 444–445,
447–450
Tour agencies, 93–95
Transportation within Costa
Rica, 55–58, 60
Traveling to Costa Rica, 54–55
Tropical Birding, 97
Tropical Bungee, 98, 104, 178
Tropical illnesses, 63–64
Turrialba, 186–188
Turtles. See Sea turtles
Turu BaRi Tropical Park, 99,
180, 347

U

Ultralight flights, Dominical
area, 384
Ultralight tour, 369
Undersea Hunter, 101
Urban Canopy Tour, 178
Utopia (San José), 174

V

Venado Caverns, 306
Veragua Rainforest Park, 453
Vértigo (San José), 174
Victor Emanuel Nature Tours, 97
Vida, 115
Views, best, 24–25
Visitor information, 486
Volcanoes, 182–183
Volunteer and study programs,
112, 114–115

W

Wakeboarding, Lake Arenal, 318
Water, drinking, 486
Waterfall Canopy Tour
(Montezuma), 262–263
Waterfalls
Bijagual, 346
Dominical area, 383
La Cangrejo, 199
La Fortuna, 304
Montezuma, 261–262
Wayra Instituto de Español, 114
Wayra Instituto de Español
(Tamarindo), 232

Websites, best, 27
Weddings, 59
Wellness centers, 237, 344
Whale-watching, 406
Wheelchair accessibility, 66
White-water rafting, 9, 106–107,
184, 200–201, 292
Wi-Fi access, 73
Wildlife, 38, 495–505
Wilson Botanical Gardens (San
Vito), 425
Windsurfing, 10, 107, 318
WINGS, 97
Witch's Rock, 208, 211
Women travelers, 67
World of Insects (Monteverde),
330
World of Snakes (Grecia), 190

Y

Yoga retreats and spas, 104–105.
See also Wellness centers
Jacó, 347
Manuel Antonio area, 369
Playa Nosara, 283
Puerto Viejo (Caribbean coast),
468–469
San José, 164–165
Tamarindo, 237

Z

Zarcero, 191
Zoo Ave (Alajuela), 162

Accommodations Index

A

Agua Luna (Puerto Jiménez), 418
Aguas Claras (Puerto Viejo), 476
Aguila de Osa Inn, 406–407
Albergue Mirador de Quetzales, 396
Alby Lodge (Cahuita), 461
Alta Hotel (near Santa Ana), 140
Amor de Mar (Montezuma), 264
Apartotel Flamboyant (Jacó), 350
Arco Iris Lodge (Monteverde), 333
Arenal Kioro, 308
Arenal Observatory Lodge, 310
Arenal Pacífico (Jacó), 350
Arenas del Mar (Manuel Antonio), 370, 372
Aurola Holiday Inn (San José), 129–130
Azania Bungalows (Puerto Viejo), 476

B

The Backyard (Playa Hermosa), 358
Bahía del Sol (Playa Potrero), 227
Banana Azul Guest House (Puerto Viejo), 472–473
Barceló Playa Tambor Beach Resort, 259
Best Western El Sitio Hotel & Casino (Liberia), 202
Best Western Jacó Beach Resort, 350–351
Best Western Tamarindo Vista Villas, 240
Bosque del Cabo Rainforest Lodge (Osa Peninsula), 420
Buena Vista Lodge, 203

C

Cabinas Arrecife (Cahuita), 461–462
Cabinas Guaraná (Puerto Viejo), 473
Cabinas Jacarandá (Puerto Viejo), 474
Cabinas Jiménez (Puerto Jiménez), 418
Cabinas Las Olas (Playa Avellanas), 244–245
Cabinas Las Olas (Playa Hermosa), 359
Cabinas Los Cocos (Zancudo), 431–432
Cabinas Mary (Tilarán), 320
Cabinas San Clemente (Dominical), 386

Cabinas Sol y Mar (Zancudo), 432
Café de Paris (Playa Nosara), 284
Cala Luna, 238
Camping Brasilito (Playa Brasilito), 229
Caño Negro Natural Lodge, 313
Cariblue Bungalows (Puerto Viejo), 476
Casa Camarona (Puerto Viejo), 477
Casa Corcovado Jungle Lodge (Osa Peninsula), 407
Casa de las Tías (Escazú), 141
Casa del Mar (Sámara), 278
Casa Marbella (Tortuguero), 450
Casa Roland Marina Resort (Golfito), 426
Casa Siempre Domingo (Pavones), 435
Casa Turire (Turrialba), 187–188
Casa Valeria (Sámara), 279
Casa Verde Lodge (Puerto Viejo), 474
Celeste Mountain Lodge (near Bijagua), 203
Centro Turístico Samoa del Sur (Golfito), 426
Chalet Nicholas (Tilarán), 320
Clarion Amón Plaza (San José), 131–132
Club del Mar Condominiums & Resort (Jacó), 349
Coco Bay Hotel & Casino (Playa del Coco), 220
Corteza Amarilla Art Lodge & Spa (near Santa Ana), 140–141
Costa Coral (Playa Tambor), 259
Costa Paraiso Lodge (near Dominical), 389
Costa Rica Backpackers (San José), 135
Courtyard San José, 141
Crocodile Bay Resort (Puerto Jiménez), 417
Crowne Plaza Corobicí (San José), 137
Cuna del Angel (near Dominical), 388

D

Domilocos (Dominical), 386
Doubletree Cariari by Hilton (San José), 144
Double Tree Resort Puntarenas, 253
Drake Bay Wilderness Resort, 408

E

Ecoplaya Beach Resort (near La Cruz), 208–209
El Diriá (Tamarindo), 238
El Encanto Bed and Breakfast (Cahuita), 460
El Establo Mountain Hotel (Monteverde), 332–333
El Gran Ceibo (Golfito), 426–427
El Jardin (Montezuma), 264–265
El Mono Azul Hotel (Manuel Antonio), 374
El Ocotal Beach Resort (Playa del Coco), 220
El Pizote, 473
El Punto Bed & Breakfast (Liberia), 202
El Remanso (Osa Peninsula), 420–421
El Rodeo Country Inn (San Antonio de Belén), 145–146
El Silencio Lodge & Spa (near Sarchi), 191, 314
El Velero Hotel (Playa Hermosa), 214

F

Fenix Hotel (Sámara), 277
Finca Rosa Blanca Coffee Plantation & Inn (Heredia), 142
Finca Valverde (Monteverde), 333–334
Flamingo Beach Resort (Playa Flamingo), 227–228
Flamingo Marina Resort Hotel and Club, 228
Florblanca Resort (Santa Teresa), 270
Four Seasons Resort Costa Rica (Papagayo Peninsula), 212
Frank's Place (Malpaís), 271–272

G

Gaia Hotel & Reserve (Manuel Antonio), 372
Gavilán Sarapiquí River Lodge (Puerto Viejo), 295
The Gilded Iguana (Playa Guiones), 285
Golfo Dulce Lodge, 427
Grand Papagayo (Guanacaste), 212–213
Gran Hotel Costa Rica (San José), 132

H

Hacienda Guachipelin (near Liberia), 203–204
Hampton Inn & Suites (San José), 145
Harbor Reef Lodge (Playa Nosara), 284

The Harmony Hotel & Spa (Playa Nosara), 283–284
Hilton Garden Inn Liberia Airport, 202
Hilton Papagayo Resort (Playa Panamá), 213
Holiday Inn Express (San José), 145
Hostal La Botella de Leche (Tamarindo), 241
Hotel Alamar (Puntarenas), 253
Hotel Aranjuez (San José), 135
Hotel Arco Iris (Tamarindo), 240
Hotel Bella Vista (La Cruz), 205
Hotel Belvedere (Sámara), 277–278
Hotel Borinquen Mountain Resort (near Liberia), 204
Hotel Bougainvillea (San José), 146
Hotel Boutique Jade (San José), 138
Hotel Boyeros (Liberia), 202
Hotel Brasilito, 229
Hotel Britannia (San José), 132–133
Hotel Bula Bula (Playa Grande), 241
Hotel Cacts (San José), 138
Hotel Capitán Suizo (Tamarindo), 238–239
Hotel Casa Alegre (Santa Ana), 141
Hotel Colonial (San José), 135
Hotel Costa Verde (Manuel Antonio), 373–374
Hotel Del Rey (San José), 133
Hotel Diamante Real (San Isidro), 394
Hotel Diuwak (Dominical), 384–385
Hotel Doña Inés (San José), 132
Hotel Don Carlos (San José), 133
Hotel Don Fadrique (San José), 138–139
Hotel El Jardín del Edén (Tamarindo), 239
Hotel El Sapo Dorado (Monteverde), 333
Hotel Finisterra, 214–215
Hotel Fonda Vela (Monteverde), 334
Hotel Fuego del Sol (Playa Hermosa), 358
Hotel Giada (Sámara), 278
Hotel Grano de Oro (San José), 137
Hotel Guanacaste (Liberia), 203
Hotel Guanamar (Puerto Carillo), 277
Hotel Heliconia (Monteverde), 333
Hotel Hibiscus (Playa Junquillal), 247

Hotel Iguazú (San Isidro), 394
Hotel 1492 Jade y Oro, 139
Hotel Jinetes de Osa (Drake Bay), 408
Hotel La Aurora (Montezuma), 266
Hotel La Diosa (Cahuita), 461
Hotel La Fortuna, 307
Hotel La Mariposa (Manuel Antonio), 372–373
Hotel La Mirada Inn (La Cruz), 205
Hotel La Punta (Puntarenas), 254
Hotel Las Brisas (Puntarenas), 253
Hotel Las Colinas (La Fortuna), 307
Hotel Las Tortugas (Playa Grande), 241
Hôtel Le Bergerac (San José), 139
Hotel Los Crestones (San Isidro), 395
Hotel Los Mangos (Montezuma), 265
Hotel Lucy (Montezuma), 266
Hotel Luna Azul (Playa Ostional), 286
Hotel Magic Mountain (La Fortuna), 306
Hotel Malinche (Manuel Antonio), 375
Hotel Mar de Luz (Jacó), 351
Hotel Milvia (San José), 139
Hotel Mirador Pico Blanco (near Escazú), 141
Hotel Naralit (Tilarán), 320
Hotel Nine (Jacó), 349–350
Hotel Parque del Lago (San José), 137–138
Hotel Pasatiempo (Tamarindo), 240
Hotel Playa Bejuco, 358
Hotel Playa Hermosa Bosque del Mar, 214
Hotel Playa Negra, 245
Hotel Plinio (Manuel Antonio), 374–375
Hotel Poco a Poco (Monteverde), 334
Hotel Posada del Museo (San José), 135
Hotel Presidente (San José), 133–134
Hotel Pueblo Dorado (Tamarindo), 240
Hotel Punta Islita, 279
Hotel Rincón de San José (San José), 132
Hotel Roca Verde (Dominical), 385
Hotel Rosa del Paseo (San José), 138
Hotel San Bosco (La Fortuna), 307

Hotel Santo Tomás (San José), 134
Hotel Sí Como No (Manuel Antonio), 373
Hotel Sierra (Golfito), 426
Hotel Sugar Beach, 228
Hotel Tilawa (near Tilarán), 319
Hotel Tioga (Puntarenas), 253
Hotel Verde Mar (Manuel Antonio), 375
Hotel Villa Casa Blanca (Playa Ocotal), 220–221
Hotel Villas Gaia (Playa Tortuga), 389
Hotel Zabamar (Jacó), 352

I

Iguana Lodge (Playa Plantanares), 418
Iguanazul Hotel (Playa Junquillal), 247

J

JW Marriott Guanacaste Resort & Spa (Hacienda Pinilla), 244

K

Kap's Place (San José), 135
Karahé (Manuel Antonio), 375

L

La Carolina Lodge (near San Miguel), 203
La Costa de Papito (Puerto Viejo), 478
L'Acqua Viva (Playa Guiones), 284
La Cusinga Lodge (Bahía Ballena), 389
Lagarta Lodge (Playa Nosara), 285
Laguna Lodge (Tortuguero), 449
La Laguna del Lagarto Lodge (Boca Tapada), 314–315
La Paloma Lodge (Drake Bay), 407–408
Lapa Ríos (Osa Peninsula), 421
La Quinta de Sarapiquí Country Inn (Chilamate), 296
La Selva Biological Station (Puerto Viejo), 293
Las Gaviotas Hotel (Golfito), 427
Los Altos de Eros (near Playa Negra), 244
Los Sueños Marriott Ocean & Golf Resort (Playa Herradura), 352
Lost Iguana Resort, 309–310
15 Love Bed & Breakfast (Tamarindo), 238
Lucky Bug Bed & Breakfast (Nuevo Arenal), 319

M

Magellan Inn (Cahuita), 461
Maiyra's (Playa Potrero), 229
Makanda By the Sea (Manuel
    Antonio), 373
Malpaís Surf Camp & Resort, 272
Manatus Hotel (Tortuguero), 448
Marriott Costa Rica Hotel (San
    José), 143
Mawamba Lodge (Tortuguero),
    449
Milarepa (Santa Teresa), 270–271
Moana Lodge (Malpaís), 271
Mono Congo Lodge (Playa
    Negra), 244
Montaña de Fuego Inn (La
    Fortuna), 310
Monteverde Lodge & Gardens,
    334
Mystica (near Tilarán), 319

N

Nosara Beach Hotel, 283

O

Orquídeas Inn (Alajuela), 146

P

Pachira Lodge (Tortuguero),
    449–450
Pacific Edge (Dominical),
    385–386
Paradisus Playa Conchal, 227
Park Hotel (Limón), 454
Parrot Bay Village (Puerto
    Jiménez), 417
Peace Lodge (near San José),
    143–144
Pensión de la Cuesta (San José),
    135, 137
Playa Chiquita Lodge (Puerto
    Viejo), 477
Playa Grande Surf Camp (Playa
    Grande), 241
Playa Nicuesa Rainforest Lodge
    (Golfo Dulce), 428
Pochote Grande (Jacó), 351
Posada del Tope (Liberia), 203
Pura Vida Hotel (Alajuela), 145

Q

Quality Hotel Santa Ana, 141

R

Radisson Europa Hotel (San
    José), 132
Rara Avis (near Las Horquetas),
    294
Raya Vida Villa (San José), 134
Real InterContinental San José
    (Escazú), 140
Rincón de la Vieja Mountain
    Lodge, 204
Río Colorado Lodge, 440–441
Ripjack Inn (Tamarindo), 242

S

Samara Tree House Inn
    (Sámara), 278
Sarapiquí Rainforest Lodge,
    294–295
Savegre Mountain Hotel, 396
Selva Bananito Lodge, 454
Selva Verde Lodge (Chilamate),
    294
Shawandha Lodge (Puerto
    Viejo), 477
Silver King Lodge (Pavones), 441
Sleep Inn (San José), 132
The Springs Resort & Spa (near
    La Fortuna), 308
Sueño Azul Resort (Las
    Horquetas), 295
Sueño del Mar (Tamarindo), 239
The Suites at Café de Playa
    (Playa del Coco), 220

T

Tabacón Grand Spa Thermal
    Resort, 308–309
Talari Mountain Lodge (San
    Isidro), 395
Tambor Tropical, 259
Tango Mar Resort (Playa
    Tambor), 259
Taylor's Inn (San José), 134
Termales del Bosque (San
    Carlos), 312–313
Terraza del Pacífico (Playa
    Hermosa), 358–359
Tilajari Resort Hotel (San
    Carlos), 313
Tiskita Jungle Lodge (Pavones),
    435

Tortilla Flats (Dominical), 386
Tortuga Lodge (Tortuguero),
    448–449
Tranquilo Backpackers (San
    José), 135
Tranquilo Backpackers (Santa
    Teresa), 271
Tree House Lodge (Puerto
    Viejo), 475
Trogon Lodge, 396
Trópico Latino Lodge (Santa
    Teresa), 271
Tsunami Backpackers
    (Tamarindo), 241
Turtle Beach Lodge
    (Tortuguero), 450

V

Villa Alegre (Playa Langosta),
    239–240
Villa Blanca Cloud Forest & Spa
    (San Ramón), 314
Villa Caletas, 353
Villa Decary (Nuevo Arenal),
    319–320
Villa del Sol B&B (Playa del
    Coco), 221
Villa del Sueño Hotel (Playa
    Hermosa), 215
Villa Lapas (Tárcoles), 353
Villas Nicolás (Manuel Antonio),
    374
Villas Sol Hotel & Beach Resort
    (Playa Hermosa), 213–214
Viña Romantica (Alajuela), 145
Vista del Valle Plantation Inn
    (Alajuela), 145
Volcano Lodge (La Fortuna), 311

X

Xandari by the Pacific (Playa
    Esterillos), 357
Xandari Resort & Spa (Alajuela),
    144

Y

Ylang Ylang Beach Resort
    (Montezuma), 263–264

Z

The Zancudo Lodge, 431

PHOTO CREDITS

p. i: © Thornton Cohen; p. iii: © ImageSync Ltd/Alamy; p. viii: © Fernando Carcamo; p. 1: © kevinschafer.com; p. 3, top: © Ken Cedeno; p. 3, bottom: © Thornton Cohen; p. 6: © Zach Holmes/Alamy; p. 8, top left: © Jason Kremkau; p. 8, top right: © Jason Kremkau; p. 9: © Thornton Cohen; p. 10, top left: © Thornton Cohen; p. 10, top right: © Brandon Cole; p. 11: © Adrian Hepworth; p. 12: © Jason Kremkau; p. 13: © kevinschafer.com; p. 14: © kevinschafer.com; p. 15: © Ken Cedeno; p. 16: © Ron Niebrugge/wildnatureimages.com; p. 18: © Thornton Cohen; p. 21: Courtesy Tortuga Lodge; p. 23: © Thornton Cohen; p. 25: © Adrian Hepworth; p. 26, top: © Ken Cedeno; p. 26, bottom: © Thornton Cohen; p. 28: © Adrian Hepworth; p. 30: © Adrian Hepworth; p. 32: © Adrian Hepworth; p. 35, top: © Steve Bly/Alamy; p. 35, bottom: © Thornton Cohen; p. 37, top left: © Adrian Hepworth; p. 37, top right: © Jason Kremkau; p. 38: © Adrian Hepworth; p. 43: © Adrian Hepworth; p. 44: © Ken Cedeno; p. 45, top left: © Thornton Cohen; p. 45, top right: © Thornton Cohen; p. 47: © Adrian Hepworth; p. 48: © Thornton Cohen; p. 75: © Jason Kremkau; p. 78: © Thornton Cohen; p. 79: © Adrian Hepworth; p. 80: Courtesy Tabacon Grand Thermal Spa; p. 82: © Thornton Cohen; p. 84, top left: © Thornton Cohen; p. 84, top right: © Thornton Cohen; p. 86: © Thornton Cohen; p. 87: © Thornton Cohen; p. 88, top left: © Jason Kremkau; p. 88, top right: © Thornton Cohen; p. 90: © Ken Cedeno; p. 91: © Ken Cedeno; p. 92: © Thornton Cohen; p. 116: © R1/Alamy; p. 119: © Ken Cedeno; p. 122, top: © Ken Cedeno; p. 122, bottom: © Ken Cedeno; p. 123: © Ken Cedeno; p. 124: © Ken Cedeno; p. 136: © Ken Cedeno; p. 142: © frankduffyphoto.com; p. 143: Courtesy Marriott; p. 147: © Ken Cedeno; p. 155: © Ken Cedeno; p. 157: © Ken Cedeno; p. 158, top: © Ken Cedeno; p. 158, bottom: © Ken Cedeno; p. 159: © Ken Cedeno; p. 160: © Jason Kremkau; p. 161: © Jason Kremkau; p. 163: © Ken Cedeno; p. 164: © Juan Carlos Ulate/Reuters/Corbis; p. 165: © Oliver Berg/epa/Corbis; p. 167: © Jason Kremkau; p. 168: © Ken Cedeno; p. 170: © Ken Cedeno; p. 171: © Ken Cedeno; p. 172: © Ken Cedeno; p. 174: © Ken Cedeno; p. 180: © Jason Kremkau; p. 182: © Adrian Hepworth; p. 183: © Ken Cedeno; p. 184: © Adrian Hepworth; p. 185: © Adrian Hepworth; p. 186: © Adrian Hepworth; p. 187: © Adrian Hepworth; p. 188: © Raymond Pauly; p. 189: © Adrian Hepworth; p. 190: © Adrian Hepworth; p. 191: © Jason Kremkau; p. 192: © Thornton Cohen; p. 194: © Thornton Cohen; p. 196: © Thornton Cohen; p. 197: © Thornton Cohen; p. 198: © Adrian Hepworth; p. 199: © Thornton Cohen; p. 200, bottom left: © Thornton Cohen; p. 200, bottom right: © kevinschafer.com; p. 201: © Thornton Cohen; p. 206: © Thornton Cohen; p. 208: © Thornton Cohen; p. 211: © Atlantide Phototravel/Corbis; p. 213: Courtesy Four Seasons; p. 217: © Thornton Cohen; p. 218: © Thornton Cohen; p. 219: © Brandon Cole Marine Photography; p. 223: © Ken Welsh/age fotostock; p. 225: © Thornton Cohen; p. 226: Courtesy flamingobeachcr.com; p. 230: © Thornton Cohen; p. 231: © Thornton Cohen; p. 235: © Thornton Cohen; p. 237: © Gary Braasch/CORBIS; p. 246: © rowanpix.com; p. 248: © Jason Kremkau; p. 252: © Richard Cummins/Alamy; p. 254: © Brandon Cole Marine Photography; p. 255: © kevinschafer.com; p. 257: © Martin Rogers/CORBIS; p. 258: © Adrian Hepworth; p. 261: © Martin Rogers/CORBIS; p. 263: © Kevin Schafer/CORBIS; p. 268: © Jason Kremkau; p. 269: © Jason Kremkau; p. 270: © Brownie Harris Photography, Wilmington, NC; p. 274: © ImageSync Ltd/Alamy; p. 275: © Jason Kremkau; p. 277: © Jason Kremkau; p. 281: © Adrian Hepworth; p. 283: © Jason Kremkau; p. 287: © Thornton Cohen; p. 291, bottom left: © Ron Niebrugge/wildnatureimages.com; p. 291, bottom right: © Randall Hyman; p. 293, top left: © Adrian Hepworth; p. 293, top right: © Jason Kremkau; p. 297: © kevinschafer.com; p. 300, bottom left: © Thornton Cohen; p. 300, bottom right: © Thornton Cohen; p. 301, top left: © Thornton Cohen; p. 301, top right: © Thornton Cohen; p. 302: © Thornton Cohen; p. 303: © Thornton Cohen; p. 304: © Thornton Cohen; p. 305: © Thornton Cohen; p. 306: © kevinschafer.com; p. 309: © Thornton Cohen; p. 313: © Thornton Cohen; p. 315: © Thornton Cohen; p. 317: © Captain Ron Saunders Lake Arenal/www.arenalfishing.com; p. 318: © Thornton Cohen; p. 322: © ImageSync Ltd/Alamy; p. 325: © Thornton Cohen; p. 328: © Adrian Hepworth; p. 330: © Thornton Cohen; p. 331: © Thornton Cohen; p. 332: © Thornton Cohen; p. 336: © Thornton Cohen; p. 338: © kevinschafer.com; p. 340: © Thornton Cohen; p. 343: © Thornton Cohen; p. 344: © Thornton Cohen; p. 345: © Adrian Hepworth; p. 348: © Thornton Cohen; p. 360, top left: © Jason Kremkau; p. 360, top right: © Ken Cedeno; p. 365, top left: © Ken Cedeno; p. 365, top right: © Ronald Reyes; p. 367, top left: © Thornton Cohen; p. 367, top right: © Ryan Candee; p. 368: © Thornton Cohen; p. 370: © Robert Harding Produc/age fotostock; p. 380: © Oliver Gerhard/Alamy; p. 382: © Thornton Cohen; p. 383: © Thornton Cohen; p. 384: © Ron Niebrugge/wildnatureimages.

com; p. 385: © Thornton Cohen; p. 391: © Ken Cedeno; p. 392: © kevinschafer.com; p. 397: © Thornton Cohen; p. 400: © Brandon Cole Marine Photography; p. 402: © Adrian Hepworth; p. 403: © Adrian Hepworth; p. 404: © Thornton Cohen; p. 405: © Ken Cedeno; p. 406: © Brandon Cole Marine Photography; p. 409: © Ken Cedeno; p. 412: © Ken Cedeno; p. 414: © Adrian Hepworth; p. 415: © Thornton Cohen; p. 416: © Thornton Cohen; p. 419: © Thornton Cohen; p. 422: © Thornton Cohen; p. 424: © Thornton Cohen; p. 425: © Thornton Cohen; p. 429: © Thornton Cohen; p. 431: © kevinschafer.com; p. 433: © Thornton Cohen; p. 436: © Ian Cumming/AXIOM/age fotostock; p. 440: Courtesy Jim Kaufman; p. 442: © Adrian Hepworth; p. 444, bottom left: © Adrian Hepworth; p. 444, bottom right: © Profolio Editions/age fotostock; p. 448: © Adrian Hepworth; p. 452: © Danita Delimont/Alamy; p. 455: © Adrian Hepworth; p. 457: © kevinschafer.com; p. 458: © Adrian Hepworth; p. 459: © Adrian Hepworth; p. 460: © Adrian Hepworth; p. 464: © Adrian Hepworth; p. 467, bottom left: © kevinschafer.com; p. 467, bottom right: © Adrian Hepworth; p. 468, top left: © Adrian Hepworth; p. 468, top right: © Adrian Hepworth; p. 469: © Jason Kremkau; p. 470, bottom left: © Jason Kremkau; p. 470, bottom right: © Adrian Hepworth; p. 471, top left: © Mark Conlin/Larry Ulrich Stock; p. 471, top right: © Adrian Hepworth; p. 474: © Adrian Hepworth; p. 475: © Adrian Hepworth